Praise for *Rewrites* and *The Play Goes On*

"Neil Simon has created that rare thing: an autobiographical page-turner. It's a funny and moving work. I cried till I laughed."
—Steve Martin

"Funny, intelligent, bittersweet. . . . Ought to be required reading for everyone who aspires to a career in playwriting, fiction, or poetry."
—Jonathan Yardley, *The Washington Post*

"Exhilarating. . . . Simon is a superb and introspective raconteur."
—*Publishers Weekly*

"Neil, while telling the absolute truth, makes things both funnier and more positive. And then I realize with a pang that this is truly how it was."
—Mike Nichols

"Warm, open, and highly readable. . . . Simon is a born wordsmith, and his rich, rare, wise memoir is as enjoyable as a good novel."
—*Booklist*

"Fascinating."
—*Chicago Tribune*

"Very funny."
—*New York Post*

"A compelling page-turner."
—*The Denver Post*

"One wonderful read."
—Larry King, *USA Today*

"Courageously honest and revealing."
—Gwen Verdon

"A knockout autobiography."
—*The Hollywood Reporter*

"A brilliant and honest look at what makes Simon tick."
—*Milwaukee Journal Sentinel*

"Only the hardest heart will get through the final chapter . . . unmoved."
—*The New York Times*

Neil Simon's Memoirs

Rewrites and *The Play Goes On*

Neil Simon

Simon & Schuster Paperbacks

NEW YORK   LONDON   TORONTO   SYDNEY   NEW DELHI

Simon & Schuster Paperbacks
An Imprint of Simon & Schuster, Inc.
1230 Avenue of the Americas
New York, NY 10020

First Simon & Schuster trade paperback edition December 2017

SIMON & SCHUSTER PAPERBACKS and colophon are registered trademarks
of Simon & Schuster, Inc.

For information about special discounts for bulk purchases, please contact
Simon & Schuster Special Sales at 1-866-506-1949
or business@simonandschuster.com

The Simon & Schuster Speakers Bureau can bring authors to your
live event. For more information or to book an event, contact the
Simon & Schuster Speakers Bureau at 1-866-248-3049
or visit our website at www.simonspeakers.com.

Manufactured in the United States of America

1   3   5   7   9   10   8   6   4   2

Library of Congress Cataloging-in-Publication Data has been applied for.

ISBN 978-1-5011-5500-0
ISBN 978-1-5011-5503-1 (pbk)
ISBN 978-1-5011-5501-7 (ebook)

Contents

Introduction

My dear friend and colleague Matthew Broderick, the original Eugene Morris Jerome, alter ego of Neil Simon in *Brighton Beach Memoirs* and *Biloxi Blues*, once said that when he was very young, he actually thought that Neil Simon was not a person but the name of some factory in Newark that manufactured all these hilarious and touching comedies that were then shipped out and presented on Broadway to great acclaim. Considering Neil's extraordinary output and level of success, that was an understandable theory for a youngster. Yet all that remarkable work really did come from the mind of one shy boy from the Bronx, Marvin Neil Simon.

I myself first encountered Neil Simon when, at the age of eleven, I joined a play-of-the-month club called The Fireside Theatre. One of the first plays I ordered was a new comedy from the celebrated author of *Barefoot in the Park* called *The Odd Couple*. I was so excited when it arrived; it felt like Christmas morning. It was a beautiful hardcover copy with many black-and-white Martha Swope photographs of the production and its two stars, Art Carney and Walter Matthau. I couldn't wait to start reading it and wound up taking it to school with me. It was a strict Catholic school run by an elite force of deadly Dominican nuns. During a world geography class, I had hidden my precious copy of the play inside my textbook. I was reading the scene where Felix has cleaned up Oscar's apartment and made sandwiches for the poker game. Two of the players were discussing how beautifully made the sandwiches were and a third player says, "Are you listening to this? Martha and Gertrude at the automat." I burst out laughing and the nun in charge, Sister Liam Neeson, said, "What's so funny, Mr. Lane?" And I said, "The International Date Line is imaginary? Hilarious!" And she beat me senseless.

Let's get this out of the way: When it comes to Neil Simon, I am not objective. I am an unabashed fan. He was and remains one of my theatrical heroes. Far too many years ago, I almost went to college and found myself at an admissions interview for the NYU School of the Arts. At a certain point, the interviewer asked me to name my three favorite playwrights. I said Eugene

O'Neill, Samuel Beckett, and Neil Simon. The interviewer looked slightly aghast and I said, "He writes about people in pain too. It just comes out differently." I didn't get in, but I didn't want to go to college anyway. I wanted to work in the theater. And eventually I got to work with Neil Simon.

In 1987, I auditioned for the national tour of *Broadway Bound*, and later that day was offered the role of the older brother, Stanley. Neil was there, but I didn't get to meet him. In fact, that didn't happen until several months later at opening night in Los Angeles, at the Ahmanson Theatre. After the show, there was a knock at the door and I opened it and there he was: taller than I imagined, with the famous horn-rimmed glasses and that mysterious Mona Lisa smile that seemed to say, "I know something you don't know, and I'm probably going to write a play about it." I was terrified to meet one of my heroes, and I think he sensed that and immediately put me at ease. He was very kind and complimentary about my performance, and when he left I was walking on air. I felt I had pleased the master and it felt great.

To be honest, that's really been the basis of our relationship. I never wanted to let him down or disappoint him. And when I did well by him it was incredibly gratifying. Several years later, Jerry Zaks asked me to do a new play by Neil about his time writing for Sid Caesar, called *Laughter on the 23rd Floor*. Jerry said Neil wanted me to play the role of Milt, one of the comedy writers. I said I would be happy to play anything in it and especially to get the opportunity to originate a role in a new Neil Simon play. They were going to have a reading of the play, and at the last minute Jerry asked me to read Max Prince, the character based on Sid Caesar. He said they were looking for a big, burly actor to eventually play the six-foot-two, two-hundred-and-fifty-pound Caesar, but for the purpose of the reading, he felt I would bring the right energy to it. When we did the show I would still play Milt, but for now I was to render unto Caesar the things that are Caesar's. I suddenly realized that in a sense I would be auditioning for what was the lead in the show, but put that aside and tried to find my inner Sid. The reading went exceptionally well, and afterward Neil and Jerry decided that I should play Max, that now they couldn't see anybody else doing it, which was surprising but very exciting.

Someday, when I decide to write my memoirs, I'll tell you more about that experience, but I did have the joy of going out of town with a new Neil Simon play and watching the great man in action. One day during a rehearsal, I saw him scribbling on his yellow legal pad and I got up the nerve to say, "What are you writing?"

He said, "A speech for you, actually. We'll put it in a few days from now when you've had time to learn it."

He showed it to me and I said, "Why wait? Let's put it in tonight!"

He loved my enthusiasm and my fortunate facility for learning material quickly. From then on, he felt comfortable giving me new lines, even at the last minute, and I was thrilled at the chance to try them out for him. One day, we were discussing a scene in my dressing room and I noticed Neil kept looking over at the large humidifier sitting on the dressing table as we chatted. It was a big blue tank from which steam would slowly and steadily rise. Finally we finished talking, he went to the door, and with perfect timing he turned back, pointed to the tank, and said solemnly, "By the way, Nathan, I think your fish is dead."

In 1995, I had the pleasure of performing a tribute to Neil at the Kennedy Center Honors. It was a sequence in which Christine Baranski and I would read monologues from Neil's plays, and then the legendary Sid Caesar would speak in double-talk foreign gibberish. You had to be there, but Sid was nothing short of brilliant and brought down the house. And I got a few laughs myself reading Oscar Madison's famous tirade about all of Felix's annoying habits.

About eight years later, Neil wrote me a beautiful note saying he was remembering my performance of that speech and wanted to see me do the whole thing. He said he had been holding on to the rights to *The Odd Couple* for a long time in the hope that I would one day play Oscar Madison in a Broadway revival. Talk about a delayed reaction. I almost fainted. What an honor. My eleven-year-old self cried, and I leaped at the chance to do what I think is a classic twentieth-century American comedy by one of the theater's greatest writers. And coming full circle, I used the very same copy of the play that I had hidden in a textbook when I was a kid, and sheepishly asked Neil to sign it. A long way to go to get an autograph.

Well, enough of my stroll down memory lane with Mr. Simon. It's time for you to start yours. What you are about to read is a very intimate look at a very private person. At first, he tells the wonderful Moss Hart *Act One* part of the story: his attempts to break into the theater after writing for television with his first play, *Come Blow Your Horn*, which survived by the skin of its teeth thanks to, of all people, Noël Coward and Groucho Marx. Why didn't they ever do *The Odd Couple*? It also contains two great love stories: Neil and his first wife, Joan, and Neil and his best director, Mike Nichols. Neil very touchingly and winningly brings both of these fascinating people to life again. Not surprisingly, he also beautifully captures the painstaking process of writing and putting on a Broadway play. It is not for the faint of heart. And this was a pleasant surprise: Neil is just as insecure and neurotic as the rest of us. What a relief. He just tends to put all those hidden feelings into his characters and stories.

Anyway, with success comes failure and with great happiness comes great sadness. Such is life, and Neil's is no exception, but he shares it all with tremendous candor and intelligence and wit. And as his life becomes richer and deeper and more complicated, so does his work. I'll let him tell you how and why. It's a great and unique story in the American theater, with a track record rivaled only by Shakespeare.

What I hope will happen after you finish this is that you will want to read the plays. Building on the work of his idols, George S. Kaufman and Moss Hart, Neil forged his own style of comedy, creating indelible characters with whom we can all identify, laughing with them one minute and crying for them the next. It is a formidable body of work that culminated in his great autobiographical trilogy and the Pulitzer Prize–winning *Lost in Yonkers*. And yet in spite of all his countless awards, as the critic Clive Barnes once wrote, "Like Noël Coward, Neil Simon is destined to spend most of his career underestimated but very popular." Comedy has always been the poor cousin to drama, but I think it's time for a reassessment and a fresh look at some of those wonderful plays. In the meantime, I know you will enjoy this funny and heartfelt remembrance of a life brilliantly spent in the theater.

—*Nathan Lane*

REWRITES

REWRITES

Acknowledgments

For their encouragement and care in guiding me through the dangerous shoals of writing prose, I wish to thank Michael Korda, Charles (Chuck) Adams, Gypsy da Silva, and Virginia Clark. Also to Morton Janklow for pointing me there.

For Diane

Introduction

There's a small piece of property I own. Quite small. It's about three feet wide and twenty-eight feet long. It's carpeted, usually in a somber red or sullen blue, sometimes with a nondescript pattern made indiscernible from the hordes of feet that have trampled upon it in shoes, boots, high heels, low heels, black formals, and brown loafers, wet from rain and slush or dusty from the accumulation of a thousand miles of travel. It has indentations made from canes, crutches, and wheelchairs. It is vacuumed daily, cleaned perhaps once a year, but no amount of janitorial attention can remove the grime of chocolate mints, Cokes, wine, spritzers, or that indefatigable nemesis, gum.

I did not buy this tiny piece of real estate. It was not given to me. No money, no contracts, no negotiated deals are in banks or in lawyers' files putting claim and title to my rights. I own it because I took it. I made it my own, as a bear would stake out a cave and make it his. I would fight to keep this space and by sheer tenacity have warded off all pretenders to this tiny dot, this isle between aisles, this rug-covered haven, this fortress, this wee Kingdom of Carpeteria.

True, there may be late arrivals who intrude or dawdle upon it, but they move quickly away as I come headlong with head down across my twenty-eight feet of no man's land.

As darkness falls quickly over my domain, I tense up, withdraw into myself, and become oblivious to family or friends who call out their "Hello," "I hear it's great," or "Break a leg." I begin to traverse my nine-plus yards from one end to the other, my intense concentration broken only by the sound of a cough, the rustle of a Bloomingdale's shopping bag, or the loud, screeching siren of an ambulance three blocks away rushing some poor soul to intensive care, who never for a moment gives a thought that his misfortune might be causing my own.

This is the back of the house, where I pace on opening nights. On preview nights. On theater party nights. On the matinees and evenings when the critics now appear days before what used to be called "the opening." My private path is located in the Shubert Theatre in New York. And the Imperial, the Plymouth, the Eugene O'Neill, the Brooks Atkinson, the Broadhurst, the Marriott Marquis, the Richard Rodgers, even one bearing my own name. One usually has to die before a theater is named after him, posthumously. I had the good fortune to have the Nederlanders, who owned it, call it the Neil Simon, prehumously.

My space is not restricted to New York theaters. You will also find it in New Haven, Philadelphia, Boston, Detroit, Chicago, Los Angeles, San Diego, Winston-Salem, Duke University, London, Bristol, Bournemouth, and Brighton. Anywhere I have a play about to open, I hang my shoes.

This book is about the eighty-nine-odd thousand miles that I have paced, fretted, smiled, frowned, sulked, sworn, beamed, gleamed, and moaned. In my space I walk alone. I am not, however, the only one who has a space. The director has a space, the producer has a space; and the backers, and our wives, good sports all, choose a quiet spot against the back wall, watching us all carefully like doctors and nurses awaiting the possible onslaught of a hurricane. I do, occasionally, pass the director and producer, who walk at different tempos and in opposite directions. At some point, we pass like ships in the night, shaking our heads bleakly at the ice floes which seem to lie ahead, or giving each other an encouraging raise of an eyebrow, a nod that the fog seems to be lifting in the second act.

This journey is currently nearing the end of its fourth decade. We won't make the entire trip this time out. I'll explain.

I've never tried to plot out my plays through to the end, since I've found it as much an exercise in futility as trying to predict what would happen in my own life a month hence. They both invariably unfold and reveal themselves when the appropriate time comes. Therefore, I've never really worried how the play would end. Or where. As I would approach the last thirty or forty pages, I would begin to get an inkling, a glimpse of the last scene, the final curtain. Suddenly, five or three or even two pages before my now expected conclusion, much to my surprise, I would stop writing. Things would appear crystal clear on the paper. The play was done. There was no need to go any further. Everything I wanted to say had just been said. It was finished. All that remained to do was type in the word "Curtain," and turn off the IBM and the lamp over my desk.

This is not unique to playwrights. Some years ago I had seen a television documentary on the great abstract artist Willem de Kooning at work on a canvas. Three days of intensive painting were condensed by montages and time-lapse photography into one hour of PBS airtime. De Kooning never slowed the feverish pace at which he worked. Not even when it seemed the canvas could no longer carry the weight of a single drop more of cobalt blue or a speck of crimson. The form and character of the painting kept changing before my eyes, and I had no idea what it was that would ultimately make de Kooning satisfied. Again and again he found some shade or space that benefited from his quick dabs at the canvas. Once more his delicate brush moved toward the exquisite explosion of colors that stood on the easel before him, but this time he hesitated, his brush poised a millimeter away from making contact, hovering over his work, held in momentary suspension as his eyes darted everywhere. Suddenly, with the artist's infallible instincts, he pulled the brush away, stepped back, and said quite simply, "No. It's done." He never looked back.

So it was with me as the pages of my life unfolded in this, my intended autobiography. For anyone who was interested, I'd lay out before them my life and my work and how one fed off the other. No worrying what the end would be. Obviously it would not be the very last day of my life, because I had no intention of meeting *that* deadline just to get a published book in the stores. Being dead limits the amount of promotional tours you can make. No, I was quite happy to write about my life up until the present day and present time, now when I'm in my late sixties.

Yet somehow as I wrote, touching on a period in my life when I was forty-six, something told me to stop. I did not want to go past the last sentence that now appears in the last chapter, because the events that transpired then were a conclusion of another kind. My life had reached both a zenith and at the same time, come to a crashing halt. That story was the one I wanted to tell. The aftermath and what came in the ensuing years can wait their turn.

Rewrites reflects the formative and possibly the most exciting stages of my life (as well as the most terrifying), and I have a passion for beginnings. Beginnings always hold out the allure of wondrous and adventurous things to come. Retracing those early steps helped me to understand why I ever took the road and direction in my life that I did—although, quite frankly, I don't think I ever really had a choice. Nor did I ever regret it.

At any rate, one day I decided to write a play . . .

N.S.

THE HORN BLOWS

1

IN THE SPRING OF 1957, I was unhappily in California working on a television special. I was thirty years old and knew that if I didn't start writing that first Broadway play soon, I would inevitably become a permanent part of the topography of the West Coast. The very thought of it jump-started me to my desk.

I sat at the typewriter and typed out "O N E   S H O E   O F F," all in caps and putting a space after each letter and a double space after each word, trying to picture what it would look like up on a theater marquee. Four spaces down, in regular type, came "A New Comedy." I sat back and studied it. Not a bad start for a first play. Then I suddenly wondered: when they wrote together, did George S. Kaufman type this out or did Moss Hart? No, it must have been Hart. He was the eager young writer poised behind the trusty old Royal machine while Kaufman, the seasoned old pro, would be lying across a sofa in his stockinged feet munching on his handmade fudge, bored by such prosaic labors as manual typing. Kaufman had probably put in enough time punching the keys back in the old days when he was drama critic for *The New York Times*. How I envied young Moss Hart being in the same room with the great Kaufman, knowing he would be guided through the pitfalls of playwriting much as any cub reporter would feel the security of marching behind Henry M. Stanley as he guided his pack-bearers across the African plain in search of the great missionary, and then, upon finding him, having the coolness and gift of a great journalist to put quite simply and memorably, "Dr. Livingstone, I presume?" . . . But, I had no Henry M. Stanley to teach me the impact of brevity in great moments. As a matter of fact, I had no George S. Kaufman, no fudge, no nobody. I had me. Not only had I not written a play before, I had never written anything longer than twelve pages, which was all that was required for a TV variety sketch back in the mid-1950s. Even that was a major step up from the one-liners I used to write with my brother,

Danny, when we were earning our daily bagels working for stand-up comics and sit-down columnists.

Now I was faced with 120 pages to feed, complete with characters, plots, subplots, unexpected twists and turns, boffo first-act curtain lines, rip-roaring second-act curtain lines, and a third act that brought it all to a satisfying, hilarious, and totally unexpected finish, sending audiences to their feet and critics to their waiting cabs, scribbling on their notepads in the darkness, "A Comic Genius Hit New York Last Night." . . . At least Lindbergh had the stars to guide him. I didn't even know how to change the typewriter ribbon. Nevertheless, I pushed on.

I was about to jump four spaces down to write the simple word "by," no caps, this to be followed by my name a little farther down the page, when it suddenly occurred to me that of the only two lines I had written so far, one of them was inordinately stupid. "A New Comedy" . . . I had seen this printed in the theater section of the *Times* for eons, seen it on billboards and marquees all over New York, and it never hit me until just now . . . "A New Comedy"? Was this to make it clear to the audiences they should not confuse this with "An Old Comedy"? Shouldn't it just be "A Comedy"? And even that was a matter of opinion. A century ago, Chekhov had written "A Comedy" before such plays as *The Seagull* and *The Cherry Orchard*. According to his biographers, however, neither of those plays was ever staged as a comedy during his lifetime, much to his beleaguered protests. So much for interpretation. Novels never made any such pronouncements. My copy of *War and Peace* never said, "A New Epic Drama by Leo Tolstoy." Never once in any movie theater did I see the screen titles come up and read, "*Some Like It Hot*, A New Farce by Billy Wilder and I. A. L. Diamond." If novelists trusted their readers to discover what their books were about and filmmakers didn't feel it necessary to spell it out, why do playwrights or their producers hold their audiences in such low esteem? Would I be brave enough to break with tradition? Since I had not yet typed in "by" and "Neil Simon," I didn't feel I had enough experience.

I plunged back into intensive work and finished typing in "by" and "Neil Simon." I sat back and studied my work so far. It was good but something was missing. It did not occur to me to type in the lower right-hand corner of the page "1st Draft, Oct. 15, 1957." I never assumed there would be a second draft or, God forbid, a third draft. Wasn't writing a hundred and twenty pages accomplishment enough? Surely I would change a few words here and there, possibly cut a few lines or add some last-moment inspirations of wit, but new drafts? It was unimaginable. Did Shakespeare do rewrites? How? He obviously wrote in longhand on cheap parchment with a scratchy quill. His plays ran four hours and he wrote thirty-seven of them, not to mention the sonnets, letters to actors and producers, love notes to Anne Hathaway, and excuses for delayed payments to roof thatchers and the local dung heating suppliers. The quills needed for this enormous output alone must have taxed the poultry growers of the region to their capacity. The acting roles in each of the plays numbered in the thirties, which meant at least that number of additional scripts, not to mention those for stage managers and understudies. Even if he had friends and apprentices quill-copy each play to make up the additional scripts, it must have meant thousands upon thousands of naked fowl running around central England. The time, the labor, the costs, and the wear and tear of stress on Bill Shakespeare would certainly inhibit and pro-hibit the luxury of rewrites. He was certainly in the top three of the world's greatest geniuses and if he had to do without rewrites, why should I worry about them? But I did. I typed in "1st Draft, Oct. 15, 1957," took it out of the typewriter, put it on my desk face down, inserted the next blank piece of paper in the machine, and said to myself, "Now . . . how do you begin a play?"

All I had was the subject. Not a story, not a plot, not a theme, just a sub-ject. Actually, the subject was my third priority. Number two on my list was a desire to write for Broadway. Number one—and this was my dominating motivation, far and above all the others—was a desperate and abiding need to get out of television. In the mid-1950s, when some great electronic genius picked up the coaxial cable that would interconnect all television stations from coast to coast, plugged it into a wall socket, and saw that it worked, my days in New York were numbered. Television, like the film industry some forty years prior, was going west with all the young men. California had the largest studio space, the sun for shooting outdoor scenes, and the smog for shooting London scenes. It all seemed to make sense. Not to me, and cer-tainly not to my wife, Joan. We loved New York. Life without New York was inconceivable. I grew up on the streets of Washington Heights in upper Man-hattan; Joan was raised a horse's canter away from Prospect Park in Brooklyn and about a home run's length away from Ebbets Field. I was a Giants fan; she, of course, was a Dodgers fanatic. We were the Montagues and Capulets of baseball, who found true love despite this insurmountable barrier. When the Polo Grounds was finally toppled into dust and Ebbets Field was dismantled brick by brick, downing a vial of poison each was not totally out of the question. Moving from New York to California was. If possible, Joan was even more adamant than I was. To her, New York was the center of the universe. It was the ballet, the theater, the museums, *The New York Times,* the Seventy-second Street Marina, steamed clams in Montauk, fall drives through Vermont, the U.S. Open in Forest Hills, sailing in Long Island Sound, old bookstores, Greenwich Village pubs where you could see Franz Kline paintings and Maxwell Bodenheim poems tacked to the walls in lieu of their paying their bar bills. And yes, even walking barefoot in Washington Square Park with a feisty dog named Chips, on a cool October night, sitting on a park bench till three o'clock in the morning facing the great Arch and the elegant brownstones and mews where Henry James's heroines once looked longingly through a candlelit window for a lover who never returned. Leave all this for what? Houses built on stilts in a place where Lorenz Hart said the nights were cold and damp and the ladies were mostly tramps? "We're just not going to California for the rest of our lives," Joan said in that tone that never beat around the bush, and would certainly never beat around a giant redwood.

There was, unfortunately, little to keep me in New York. All the television shows I had worked for in the past—*Your Show of Shows* with Sid Caesar, Phil Silvers in *Sgt. Bilko, The Red Buttons Show,* and many more—were either defunct or had moved to California. Worse still, my friends, the writers, had all gone where the work was. I couldn't believe that the brightest and wittiest of them all, the staff of the Caesar show—Carl Reiner, Larry Gelbart, Mel Brooks, and Sid Caesar himself—were now living in the place we had been satirizing for so many years. The L.A. networks pounced on them all with golden offers, as well they should. But it was still beyond my understanding how you could look out a window, see a palm tree in the sun, and think funny. If that were possible, surely there would be great Hawaiian comedy writers by now. I was one of the few who remained in New York, devoid of work and three-fourths of my closest friends. Even my older brother, Danny—my mentor, my spokesman, the Kaufman to my Hart—moved west to a place called the Valley. From his letters and picture postcards, the Valley looked like America's Shangri-la, a place where your life span could increase by a hundred and fifty years. The catch was that when you eventually did die, it surely wouldn't be from laughing.

Money never mattered much to Joan. She could and did live contentedly in our first apartment, a one-room, five-story walk-up in the Village. It had a small dressing room which she converted to an even smaller bedroom. It had a low doorway and I couldn't see how she could get a bed in. It would, I thought, have to be born in there. Never underestimate the wiles and ingenuity of a newlywed decorating her first apartment. I came home that first night we moved in, having put in a full day on the Caesar show, and found the bed in the room. "How?" I asked, expecting some reasonable answer. "I don't know," she replied. "I just did it." With the bed now in the room, reaching and touching all of the four walls, I stood amazed. Perhaps she had rented the apartment next door, broken down the adjoining wall, shoved the bed in, quickly replastered the wall, and broken the lease on the adjoining apartment—all in one afternoon. She was capable of things like that.

One could open the window by standing on the bed, but opening the small closet on the opposite wall was another matter. What we did was walk across the bed, pull the closet door open about three inches, a major feat in itself, then you would squeeze your arm through, reach in, feel around, and whatever you pulled out was what you wore that day. No one noticed, because people in the Village dressed strangely anyway. When I came home at night the bed was neatly made. A shoehorn was her only possibility. The apartment was on Tenth Street between Fifth Avenue and University Place, three blocks from New York University. Walking our dog past NYU at night was the closest I came to a college education.

The kitchen was comprised of a "sinkette," and an antique two-burner stove which was powerful enough to warm water but not actually boil it. The apartment's main attraction was a red brick fireplace that could fill the room with smoke in three minutes flat. Some of this, fortunately, could escape through the large hole in the glass skylight fourteen feet above. Unfortunately, this also permitted rain, sleet, and snow to fall gently and otherwise on the sofa, the only good piece of furniture we had. This meant that Joan redecorated the room every time the weather changed. It had the advantage of making it seem as though we lived in a six-room apartment. As for amenities, there was a vertical bathroom. No tub, just a shower big enough for you to make a phone call but not large enough for you to bend over and wash the lower half of your body. This may have been the reason Joan liked to walk barefoot in the park so much.

We moved there on the day we were married, September 30, 1953, after a rather austere ceremony that took place in the Criminal Courts Building in lower Manhattan. We were married by a judge whose new false teeth had not yet properly settled in his mouth, so that when he tried to pronounce our names, we sounded vaguely Armenian. In attendance were Joan's mother and father, a sweet, happily married couple, and my mother and father, who were separated and did not speak to each other. At least not in the first person, anyway. At the end of the ceremony, the best my father could manage to my mother was "Congratulations to her." My mother nodded back, looking in the opposite direction. From moments like this, the seeds of comedy are born. Joan was gloriously happy up in our tree house on Tenth Street. I was gloriously happy with Joan, although not quite as stoic. I would announce with a touch of sarcasm as we squirmed into our miniature bed, "We'll be sleeping from left to right tonight."

On April 25, 1957, Ellen Marie Simon was born. She was six and a half pounds and Joan was in labor for eighteen hours. By the time Ellen entered the world at 7:28 that morning, the long struggle of labor and birth had taken its toll on the baby. Her head was as pointy as a dart. With the twisted mind of a comedy writer, I looked at her in panic, thinking, will she sleep in a crib, or do we just throw her into a dartboard at night? It was with great trepidation that I asked the obstetrician, "That er . . . pointy head . . . that does go away, doesn't it?" He assured me that by nightfall her head would settle nicely.

The jobs were getting scarcer in New York, our savings were dwindling, and with Ellen now in our lives, we had no choice but to move to a larger, but more expensive apartment. Larger was no problem because every apartment in New York was larger. We moved down a few hundred feet on Tenth Street to a more prosaic and adult building. This one had an elevator, ten floors, a doorman, two bedrooms with reachable closets, a stove that made hot food, a full bathroom with a tub, and a living room that was protected from the elements, which meant that our furniture placement could remain stable. A week after we had moved in, we realized we had suddenly grown up. Our bohemian life, such as it was, was behind us. We missed the hole in our skylight, the light snowfalls in the living room, and the bedroomless bedroom where we were forced to sleep tightly in each other's arms, knowing that being an inch apart was not only physically impossible, but was also gloriously wonderful. The compensation was that now we had Ellen. Within a month it was clear she was going to be as beautiful as her mother, especially now that her head no longer looked like a sharpened pencil.

Suddenly, a call came from my agents at the William Morris office. Would I like to work for Jerry Lewis again? I had previously written one television special for him with Mel Tolkin, who was formerly the head writer on *Your Show of Shows*, where we worked together. Mel was not available for this second show, and Jerry asked if I would do it alone. There were two drawbacks to this. One was that it would be in California; the other was that it would be for Jerry Lewis. Admittedly, I was once caught up in the Dean Martin/Jerry Lewis craze that had swept the country a few years before. Jerry was that wild, uninhibited lunatic who was half child, half cheetah, and he surprised us all with the anarchy of his behavior. He made me laugh in spite of myself, because I saw something in him that was missing in me and perhaps in most of us—the freedom from being so fearful of how people judged us. Elvis Presley soon proved you could do the same thing with music. Jerry had his fans, no doubt of that, but it was pushed to ludicrous excess when France practically made him their patron saint. Since then, however, he had split with Dean Martin, and the half-mad child without his keeper and protector was now simply behaving like a demented adolescent that someone had deserted in the streets. One minute he was the goonlike simian, walking like a flamingo, who has just been hit by a bus, speaking like a human adenoid, then suddenly, as the audience's laughter hit its peak, he would become a hip, articulate, cool performer with a Sinatra-like grip on a cigarette. We all felt as if we'd been had. He turned comedy on and off like a lightbulb. It was as though he were showing homemade films of himself as the funny, incorrigible kid, then quickly turning the lights back on, revealing the suave, sophisticated performer he had matured into so "brilliantly." We longed for Jack Benny who was always Jack Benny, the eternal thirty-nine-year-old lousy violinist tightwad we could always depend on.

All this aside, I took the job. Okay, so I wouldn't be writing for the facile, sharp-tongued wit of Phil Silvers, or for the almost classic and timeless humor that Sid Caesar spoke in English, French, Italian, German, and Japanese. A buck was a buck and you do what you have to do, I thought in Sam Spade–ese, a language I spoke fluently to myself as I walked down shadowy streets. When somebody kills your partner, you have to do something about it. That's the way things are . . . Why couldn't the Morris office get me a Bogart picture? I would love to have words like that spitting out of my typewriter. Instead, I was going west to write for a spastic, aging bellhop.

A separation did not appeal to either Joan or me, so we reached into our well-lit closet, picked out clothes of our choosing, wrapped Ellen, now four months old, in her Gandhi-like cottons, and headed west on a pre-jet flight that lasted fifteen hours. As the plane touched ground at the L.A. airport, Joan turned to me in her seat and shouted above the roar of the engines, "Don't you just hate this place?" Actually, it wasn't all that bad. We rented a charming little Tudor house off Coldwater Canyon, owned by an English actor of little renown, who made his living by playing barristers or members of Parliament, all of whom, alas, got murdered twelve minutes into the Sherlock Holmes films that were his specialty. Living in a little bit of England was a treat we didn't expect to find in the City of Angels. Unfortunately, the houses that surrounded us were a little bit of Spain, a little bit of France, a little bit of Switzerland, a little bit of Gingerbread, and a little bit of Halloween. I don't remember the name of our street, but I imagine it was something like Potpourri Lane.

On our very first day there, we were busy unpacking and not speaking to each other, because thirty-eight seconds had gone by where we couldn't find Ellen. Joan had actually had me outside the house looking for wolves carrying off small bundles, when suddenly there came a knock on the door. Only in Hollywood would I write a phrase like, "when suddenly there came a knock on the door" . . . I opened it and saw a tall, heavyset man who looked somewhat familiar to me. When I realized who it was, my mouth dropped open with a thud. It was Ward Bond. Now you have to be at least over fifty and a film aficionado to know about Ward Bond, but he was part of my childhood spent in neighborhood movie theaters, a world of memories. Ward Bond, of a hundred films made at Warner Bros. Ward Bond, who appeared with Cagney, Edward G. Robinson, and John Wayne. Ward Bond, the friendly California cop in *The Grapes of Wrath*, who told Henry Fonda and the Joad family, "You're best be goin' back where you come from. There weren't no work out here." But mostly it was Ward Bond from *The Maltese Falcon*, playing the police sergeant Tom Polhaus, who first told Bogart/Spade of the murder of his partner, Miles Archer. Was Ward Bond Sergeant Polhaus or was that Barton MacLane? Either way, there he was at my kitchen door, about as big as he looked up on the giant screen.

"Excuse me, sir. My name is Ward Bond."

The fact that he felt the need to tell me his name was as incredible as his calling me sir. He had a slight smile on his face, the kind a cop makes when he tries to make you feel it's nothing personal about his having to arrest you. Maybe word had already spread through these hills that Joan and I had been bad-mouthing L.A. ever since we picked up our rented car, and he wasn't about to take any of that smart-ass New York wise-guy talk from two punk kids. When Joan and the thirty-eight-seconds-lost baby appeared next to me, he smiled and tipped his hat to the womenfolk.

"Nice to meet you, ma'am. Boy or girl?"

"Girl," Joan said, touched by the big man's cordiality.

He reached out and wiggled Ellen's tiny toes with his big, warm hands. "Hi, little lady. Now aren't you pretty?" Joan was completely won over despite the fact she wouldn't know Ward Bond from Montgomery Ward. "I'm the neighborhood representative for fire control," said Ward, who was now apparently my neighbor. "Just want to make sure you don't leave those exposed dry leaves and brush around the house. Once the Santa Anas start blowing, this place could go up like a tinderbox." Never before in my city-bred life did I have to worry about dry leaves, dry brush, or tinderboxes. And who was Santa Ana? Was he the philosopher or the Mexican general who slaughtered every last man at the Alamo?

"Don't worry. My husband and I will take care of it as soon as we put the baby to sleep."

It was the first time in our three-year marriage she had ever referred to me as her "husband." "It makes us sound so old," she would say. Chances are, if Ward Bond had stayed five more minutes, Joan and I would have become "Maw and Paw." He smiled, tipped his hat, wiggled Ellen's toesies, and then shook my hand. His grip was so tight, his fingerprints suddenly and permanently became mine. He then turned and rode off into the sunset in his Chevy pickup, probably to join a poker game over at the Duke's house with John Ford, John Huston, Victor McLaglen, and a couple of cousins from Dublin, in case they felt like brawlin' afterward.

So ended our first day in California.

I GOT SOME INKLING of who Jerry Lewis, the man, was when he showed me around his Pacific Palisades home, and opened the double double-doored clothes closet in his immense private dressing room. It was mirrored from wall to wall, and from the size of it, I thought I may have taken a wrong turn in his house and wandered into the Royal Quarters in Versailles. In the closet there hung about twenty-five identical black tuxedos, an equal number of identical black suits, and at least that number of sports jackets in various shades, but no less than five each in the exact same pattern and color. Pleated white shirts were lined up on hangers, looking like a hundred maître d's parading for inspection. He kept pulling open drawer after drawer—which slid out speedily and noiselessly—to show me his endless array of sport shirts, casual shirts, pool shirts, pajamas, handkerchiefs, and boxer shorts, like a child might show off for you his lifetime collection of marbles. More to be admired than adorned. His socks and his sweaters, mostly cashmere, were all red. Not some. All. The red socks were lined up in rows, side by side, enough to be hung on fireplaces for a thousand Christmases. There were enough shoes in the shoe closets to last out the combined careers of Fred Astaire, Gene Kelly, and Secretariat. As we left the thickly carpeted room to continue our tour of his house in the Pacific Palisades, he tossed me a red cashmere sweater with matching socks, the first of a plethora of gifts I was to receive.

Generosity was not one of Jerry's shortcomings. As we went from room to room seeing his kitchen, his screening room (where one could play back a Jerry Lewis appearance anywhere in the world with the flick of a switch), his office, his electronic system (which could not only hear his children's breathing at night but could probably take their temperature as well)—the presents in my arms kept mounting. The tour plus lunch took about an hour and a half. The discussion of what I was to write for the show took about three minutes.

"You know what I do, kid. I trust you. If you screw something up, don't worry. I'll make it funny." He immediately made a face and a rabbit sound and I laughed, I admit it. "When you're through writing, call me." He opened the front door. "We'll have fun, you'll see. I didn't get this house for being stupid. And I never read a book in my life. Here, take this." He threw me a silver cigarette case with a caricature of him engraved on top, smiled warmly at me, and as I started for my car, he yelled out for all to hear, "Thief! Thief! Stop him!" Then he closed the door and went back in. I opened the door of my car, my arms filled with, among other things, red socks, a red sweater, a green Jerry Lewis baseball cap, and a yellow umbrella, making me look like a burglar with bad taste.

I had two sketches to write in six weeks. On the Caesar show, we used to write two sketches in two days, but then, of course, there were eight of us. Now, for the first time in my life, I was flying solo.

Writing becomes easier for me when I know who I'm writing for. When Danny and I were writing monologues for comics in the early days, we never just wrote a routine then looked to sell it to someone. We tailored it for specific comics. The bad comics just did jokes and we weren't interested in just jokes. The really funny men, like Buddy Hackett or Phil Silvers, had their own unique style, their own particular vision of life. We wrote our routines specifically for them, and we had the ability to capture their rhythms and their personalities. This is contrary to writing for the theater or films. You write a play, then cast your actors. And I never wrote a film for a specific actor, because the chances of getting that actor—especially a star—were somewhere between slim and anorexic. I'll amend that. I wrote two films which actors had already agreed to do, based on the premise alone: Richard Dreyfuss and Marsha Mason in *The Goodbye Girl* and Jack Lemmon in *The Out-of-Towners*. Once they agreed to sign on, I tailor-made the parts to fit their specific and unique gifts. It is, I imagine, easier to paint a portrait when someone is sitting for it.

Writing for Jerry Lewis didn't present any real problems for me. As a matter of fact, I had the feeling that if I just gave him a premise and twenty props, he would be just as funny as with anything I could write for him. But I wasn't being paid to think of twenty props. Knowing his loony, bombastic style, I was not likely to go astray and dash off some witty Noël Coward–type drawing-room comedy. Unless, of course, there were two baboons sitting at the piano. With Jerry you go for the jugular. I finished both sketches in five days, writing full days and most nights. One sketch had Jerry as the inspector from the Department of Safety, looking over a factory for danger areas. Once he walked in wearing his ill-fitting suit and that Jewish Inspector Clouseau look on his face, the die was cast. Within seconds, he was twisted, mangled, pressed, stomped, and stretched in every machine and moving part he came in touch with. The other sketch, though vague in my mind now (I have not saved one single line of anything I ever wrote in my ten years in television, nor any of the comedy monologues Danny and I wrote in those developing years), was equally physical in its humor. I presented the sketches to Jerry in his offices on the Paramount lot. He sat and read them in stony silence. Not a sound, not a peep, not a smile, not a chuckle. He breezed through the pages, tossed them on the coffee table—just missing the coffee mugs shaped in his own image—leaned back with his hands behind his head, and said, "I love 'em. Hysterical! We're finished. Wasn't that easy?"

"But you never laughed once," I said.

"I'll laugh when we do it. I'm not funny when I read."

"So what about rewrites?" I asked.

"We'll fix it in rehearsal. You're such a worrier. Go home. I'll see you in five weeks."

"That's it?" I said in amazement. "No meetings? No conferences? No nothing?"

The telephone rang. He was immediately on to other business. Another film, club dates in Vegas, interviews. He kept talking as he threw me something in cashmere, a red scarf with his signature in gold. As he talked, he put up his hand to me, spreading out his fingers, meaning, "I'll see you in five weeks," waved, threw me a kiss and a walnut, and swiveled his chair around as he gave an interview completely as Melvin, the thirty-six-year-old man with the fourteen-year-old brain. I was out the door, looking for my car, wondering what in the world I would do in Hollywood with five weeks and a red scarf on my hands.

"WHY DON'T YOU start that play you're always talking about?" Joan offered as she tried to get the clothes washer to work, this being the eighth time it had broken down in the week we'd been there. She knew better than to ask me to help, since my skills with all things mechanical and electrical were limited to turning on a light switch or turning it off, but not necessarily both. My way of dealing with being alone in a house where the toilet won't stop running and overflowing is to pretend to be writing, not even noticing that the water is up to my ankles, and then acting out surprise when Joan comes in and screams, "Are you going to wait until the house floats away before you call a plumber?" Actually, I probably would.

"I don't have a play that I'm always talking about," I answered, handing her a wrench she had totally no use for. "I just want to *write* one."

"So think of one," she said, looking at a valve whose purpose must have been a mystery even to the company who made it.

"Think of a play? A whole play? With a beginning, middle, and end? Do you have any idea how hard that is? It would take me two or three years at least. And what if it wasn't any good? What would we do for money?"

"We'll get by. Just write the play," she said as she clicked on a switch that started the washing machine working better than it did even when it was new, which I doubt it ever was. I was convinced it was made by the Dr. Frankenstein Company, with abnormal parts taken from the deceased bodies found in some washing-machine graveyard.

Two days later I typed out the title page.

ONE SHOE OFF

A New Comedy

by

NEIL SIMON

1st Draft

Oct. 15, 1957

THE GAME'S AFOOT

2

I SUPPOSE I KNEW all along that I was going to write about my family. It's not that they were particularly funny or oddball. This was no *You Can't Take It with You* family, with a mother who wrote plays and a daughter who practiced her ballet steps in the living room and an eccentric father who made fireworks in the cellar. Nor were there any *Arsenic and Old Lace* inhabitants, with charming elderly aunts who served elderberry wine spiced with arsenic, sending aging male guests to their final resting place in the Panama Canal, again in a cellar, which was being dug by their dotty brother who thought he was Teddy Roosevelt.

In the first place, we had no cellar. We lived in a two-bedroom apartment on 185th Street and Fort Washington Avenue in upper Manhattan. My father, Irving Simon, was a piece-goods salesman. I was twelve years old before I found out that piece goods were the swatches of material that would be ordered in bulk by the dress manufacturers located in the garment center on New York's Seventh Avenue. I always wondered what magic my father performed to sell his swatches to the buyers, who were seeing other salesmen all day long. Did he spin wondrous words describing the fine and delicate feel of the fabrics, pointing out the lustrous tones and shades of the colors, running his manicured finger along the intricately detailed designs and patterns, likening them to the great tapestries of France or the incomparable subtlety found in Japanese watercolors? . . . Hardly. Mostly he told jokes. Dirty jokes. Moron jokes. Jokes about card players in Miami who cheated on their wives. Anything that would get a laugh and would make the swatch buyers smile when Irving Simon walked into their showrooms. Arthur Miller knew and chronicled that territory better than any man that lived. Not that my father was a funny man. He never said a witty or humorous thing in his life.

A joke is something someone else tells you, which is then passed on to someone else who hasn't heard it as yet. No one knows where those jokes come from. *No one.* They are as difficult to trace as the day the universe was born. It is inconceivable to me that there is a man who does nothing else but sit in a dark office all day long waiting for an inspiration from God, when suddenly, he grabs his pen and writes swiftly, "A Jew, a Catholic, a Protestant, and an atheist are playing golf in Palm Beach. Suddenly a naked woman comes running out of the bushes with a basketball in her arms . . ." I must stop here because I don't know the ending to the joke. The joke, in fact, doesn't exist. I invented the beginning because most jokes start with such beginnings. The truth is, there isn't a single joke I ever heard in my life that I can remember. This, coming from the man most critics have dubbed "The King of the One-Liners." My not being able to remember a single joke must seem as totally bizarre and unlikely as your walking into Brooks Brothers and not finding one button-down white Oxford shirt.

But it's true. In the first place, I hate jokes. I cringe when someone in the tennis club sits down at my table and says, "Hey, Neil. You'll like this one. A man walks into his bedroom and finds his wife in bed with two men, a horse, and a midget in a Santa Claus outfit . . ." Immediately, my eyes glaze over, a smile freezes on my face, I stop listening but I keep nodding, watching his lips to see when they stop, so I'll know the joke is over, which is my signal to fake laughter and say, "That's funny, Ben. Really funny. I have to remember that." Then they usually add, "You can use that in one of your plays," as they get up and leave, happy that they may have made a contribution to the literature of the theater. I suppose they think that in the middle of *Lost in Yonkers*, when Bella, the retarded daughter who is begging her aged, repressive, coldly distant mother to let her have her own babies, sees that she is getting nowhere with the old lady and suddenly takes another tack: "All right, Momma. What about this? . . . A man walks into his bedroom and finds his wife in bed with two men, a horse, and a midget dressed in a Santa Claus outfit."

MY MOTHER was born Mamie Levy in the Harlem section of New York around 1900. I have no exact date of her birth because she herself never knew. She told us she knew she was born on the second night of Rosh Hashanah, a holiday marking the beginning of the Jewish New Year. The second night of Rosh Hashanah would give you no clearer date of your birth than if you said you were born six days after the World Series usually begins. Her parents emigrated from Russia to America some twenty years earlier—leaving, I'd guess, a week and a half after Labor Day. I don't know what inspired my grandparents to give all their progeny Irish first names—Mamie, Kate, Francie, and

Mike—which my parents continued with their children, Danny and Neil, but it prompts me to think they must have come from the County Cork section of Russia. The one exception was my uncle Sol, who, I imagine, must have changed his name from Sean. Actually, I was born Marvin Neil but dropped the Marvin when I found it impossible to think that Marvin Simon would ever be announced on the public address system at Yankee Stadium as playing center field for the injured Joe DiMaggio. My point was proven years later when a hapless first baseman for the New York Mets showed us you couldn't make it in the bigs with a moniker like Marvin Throneberry. Perhaps it wasn't just his name. He also couldn't run, hit, or catch.

I view the marriage between Mamie and Irving Simon through a child's memory, a recollection distorted by the pain and ugliness and fury of their clashes and the sudden idyllic joy and happiness I often saw them share together. The truth, I'm certain, lies somewhere between the two images.

I think it's fairly well documented that our characters are shaped in those first four or five formative years of our life. I think mine was carved in granite in the first eight months. Tied with a rope to my high chair for fear I'd fall out, I took to claustrophobia like a duck to water. I have stopped 747 jets on the tarmac taxiing out to their flight positions in order to get out and breathe. Obviously a major airline is not going to fall twenty minutes behind their schedule because you're having an anxiety attack. You need a much stronger excuse, something along the lines of holding your side in pain and exclaiming, "Excuse me. I'm a doctor and my appendix has just burst!" I have panicked in the back of a New York City taxi so small that I couldn't get my hand out of my pocket, because the zipper on my winter parka wouldn't open. You can't quite scream out to a driver named Abdul Kashfir, "My zipper won't open! Help me! Help me!" What you do is simply say to the driver, "Oh, I forgot something important. Let me out here, please." He does, even though you might be on the George Washington Bridge midway between New York and New Jersey. You pay him, get out, rip open the zipper with your Swiss Army knife (you must always carry one), take a deep breath of fresh air, and then pray that there is another cab driver idiotic enough to be crossing the bridge without a passenger.

My personality would best be described as anal-retentive simply because my mother refused to allow me to become anal-unretentive. I'll spare you the graphic details.

Self-reliance was taught to me the hard way. Since my father left and separated from my mother at least eight times during my childhood, being away anywhere from a month to a year at a time, with my brother almost eight and a half years older than I and either at school or working part-time after school, I was left solely in the care of my mother. She was a good woman and as hard-working as any mother could possibly be. Through the normal childhood illnesses, she was always there for me, caring and healing and loving. On the hot city summer nights in an airless bedroom, she would come in every hour and cool my forehead with a damp cloth or wrap me in blankets to ward off the winter chill that fought its way easily through the rickety radiators that did more clunking than heating. It was when she felt helpless, as when my fever rose to a hundred and five, that I felt my own helplessness. She would curse my father for his absence and run out to the hallway, banging on the doors of neighbors to help her find a remedy, screaming up to a God who had once again abandoned her. This behavior most certainly would have to be linked to when, as a young girl, her dress caught fire and burned her across the chest from her throat to just above the breastline. It scarred her and indelibly changed her life forever. As I lay in bed listening to her wailing public pleas for someone to come to aid her ailing child, it frightened me more than my own illness. I thought it was my fault, my weakness and frailty that caused her such visible anguish, and I vowed, even at that early age, that if I could take care of myself, heal myself, I would spare her such painful remorse. From that point on I would, in such cases where I could, refuse all aid, help, assistance, advice, and comforting. To this day it's even hard for me to ask my wife for a cup of tea. It's difficult for me to call a friend and ask for a favor. I have driven myself to a hospital rather than put someone out. I do not in any way look upon these traits as attributes or strengths. They have, instead, cut me off from my own feelings, never nurturing the inner child in me, nor letting me be able to ask for what I wanted or needed. "Do it yourself, Neil," was my bravura stance, while, "Why do I feel so alone?" was my silent cry for understanding. The voices of a dozen analysts are clearly apparent when I repeat the words, "You grew up too soon. Your parents may not have given you what you needed but it's obvious you also never took what was offered." It's far easier for me to give a present than to receive one. Far easier for me to love someone than to let myself be loved. I resisted for years the value of teachers. I learned from my brother about writing or driving a car or hitting a baseball more by osmosis than by listening. I heard what he was saying, but I was quickly computing how I could do it my own way instead of his. Once, driving back from Bucks County, Pennsylvania, to New York in the first car we bought and shared together, it was my turn to drive. At the very first intersection we came to, he suddenly yelled, "You took the wrong turn. Go back." I refused. I said, "I want to try this way." He said, "You're going in the opposite direction." I went my way. I wasn't adventurous or out to prove others wrong. I was obstinate. The hour-and-a-half trip back to New York took three and a half hours . . . my way.

If character is fate, as the Greeks tell us, then it was my fate to become a playwright, not my destiny. Destiny seems to be preordained by the gods. Fate comes to those who continue on the path they started on when all other possible roads were closed to them. Fate is both your liability and your hope. For a man who wants to be his own master, to depend on no one else, to make life conform to his own visions rather than to follow the blueprints of others, playwriting is the perfect occupation. To sit in a room alone for six or seven or ten hours, sharing the time with characters that you created, is sheer heaven. And if not heaven, it's at least escape from hell. After ten years of writing with my brother or with other staff writers, together in one room, screaming for my own voice to be heard, or whispering it to another writer with a voice more commanding than my own, the day I typed the title page of that first play in the unlikely environs of Coldwater Canyon I knew I had found not only the one thing I was certain would make me happy, but I also knew I was about to enter the only world in which I could possibly exist.

DESPITE THIS sudden elation that I had chosen not just to be a writer but a playwright, a new sense of gloom descended on me. It was possible that I might one day get a play of mine on Broadway, but it was also a dead certainty that I would be at the mercy of the most feared men in my life. The critics. These were the ogres, the taste- and opinion-makers who reviewed the likes of Arthur Miller, Tennessee Williams, William Inge, Lillian Hellman, Samuel Beckett, John Osborne, Clifford Odets, Jean Genet, and Jean Anouilh. These playwrights were all, at one time, hailed and cheered by the critics, and then, just as quickly, excoriated by them. There was no safety or refuge in prominence. The same fate awaited all those masters of comedy—Noël Coward, Garson Kanin, Lindsay and Crouse, and my all-time idols, Kaufman and Hart. These were all giants, all members of the royal family of the theater, who fared well more often than not but who all had the experience, the talent, and the stamina to face up to reviews that started with "Not up to his usual standard, in fact, far below it, last night at the Music Box Theater . . ." The irony was, I'd settle for that. I'd take "not up to his usual standard" any day. At least they would have thought I had a standard. How could I even get into that illustrious crowd when I had just finished writing a sketch where Jerry Lewis falls into a vat of hot oatmeal? And here I was, sitting at the kitchen table in my underwear, typing at two in the morning, "A New Comedy by . . ." They would just be waiting for a kid like me, coming out of TV no less, ready with their deadly one-liner reviews: "A young writer named Neil Simon thought he could make it on Broadway last night. He should have stayed Marvin." I already had two friends from television, both highly regarded by their peers, who had tried their hand at plays. Both made it to Broadway with great expectations. They were immediately shot down—crashed, burned, and closed after three performances. I knew I was about to put a year and a half of my life on the line. One rarely, if ever, has a big hit the first time out. The very best I could hope for was a play that would have a modest run, was dismissed but not killed by the critics, and might encourage me to spend another year or two writing a better play. All this, mind you, without the slightest guarantee of a nickel for your efforts. This was the positive side. The downside was, as Lillian Hellman put it, "there is nothing worse than the public humiliation of a failed play." An out-and-out failure would mean the end of a dream, the beginning of poverty, and the awful prospect of moving permanently to California and writing episodes of *Gilligan's Island* for the rest of my life. The irony was that *Gilligan's Island*, though only in production three years, proved to be one of the longest rerun shows ever on television; it continues to run in syndication to this day and has made its creators more money than the combined royalties of all the playwrights I mentioned above. I know I was better than *Gilligan's Island*—who wouldn't be?—but its enormous success puzzled me to distraction. It was the work of the Cowards, Kaufmans, and Harts that I aspired to, and if just writing the title page of a new play meant anything, I was closing in.

Joan had the confidence in me that I needed and depended upon. Above all others, she was the one person in the world that I respected most. As I said before, riches never held any allure for her. She was in for the long haul and was ready to make any and all sacrifices for me to at least take a shot at it. When we first became engaged, I wanted to take her to a jewelry store and buy her a ring. Instead, she led me to a pet shop, looked around, and spotted a scruffy silver-gray miniature poodle sitting on the floor tied to a table leg.

She pointed to him and said, "There's my engagement ring." She clamped a leash on his collar and bounded out the front door with him while I stayed behind, paying for an engagement dog. Chips, which she immediately named him, was so excited by his newfound freedom that he pulled Joan four blocks down Madison Avenue, and I thought I'd need a cab to catch up with them. I was twenty-six years old and this was the first dog I'd ever had in my life. I had never dared ask for one when I was a child because no animal, unless he lived in a plastic bubble, could be clean enough to live in my mother's house or survive her cooking.

To actually sit down and write that first play, I had to indulge myself in a mind game. If I put Broadway out of my head, if I didn't have to face critics; if *The New York Times* couldn't splatter my name across its pages and then place it in the Obituary section, my fear dissipated. The writing of the play was simply going to be an exercise, not to be shown to anyone save Joan and Chips, if he was so inclined. All I had to do was write a hundred and twenty pages that were coherent, interesting, and hopefully, funny. I had nothing to prove to anyone except myself. Singing *Rigoletto* alone in the shower is a lot less stressful than auditioning onstage at the Metropolitan Opera House. With nothing at stake now, I was suddenly liberated and the pages began to flow. *One Shoe Off*, a title that was soon to be changed twice, was centered around the relationship of two parents and their two sons, one son being eight and a half years older than his brother. Alan, the older son, was fashioned after Danny, who was dedicated to the indefatigable and successful pursuit of women. The younger one was named Buddy, a nickname given to him by his brother, just as it was Danny who was the first one ever to call me "Doc." I was called Doc by all my writer friends and all the comics we started to write for. Even Joan called me Doc throughout our entire marriage.

The assumption by most was that since I had helped a few friends with troubled plays in tryouts, I was considered a play doctor. Hence, Doc. Wrong. I did very little play-doctoring, being almost always too busy trying to save one of my own. The simple truth was that when I was a child of three, someone gave me a toy doctor's kit, which included a bottle of sugar pills, two tongue depressors, and a plastic stethoscope. Danny put the stethoscope into my ears and I pretended to listen to his chest. I nodded my head and said, "You sick," and the only remedy for his illness was for me to eat two sugar pills. I loved this game and played it until all the sugar pills were gone, thus retiring from the medical profession. Since Danny had gotten used to calling

me Doc, the name stuck. I was Doc Simon for the next twenty-four years, because Danny felt that the team of Danny and Doc Simon would be more easily remembered in the business. It stopped when Max Liebman, the producer,
hired us to write for *Your Show of Shows*. Max, having the style and class of a
Viennese gentleman, would not sully his writing credits with such a déclassé
name as Doc. Our names appeared on separate lines as Danny Simon and
Neil Simon, and Doc disappeared forever—except for among a few diehards
on the West Coast who still think I prefer it. I don't.

By the end of the first week I had written eighteen pages. Proud of myself,
I took Sunday off and on Monday morning reread what I had written. Eighteen pages suddenly got distilled into three pages. Over the years I have found
that putting a play, or even one act, into a drawer and not looking at it for at
least a few weeks makes wondrous things happen. Its faults suddenly become
very clear. When I take it out and reread it, it has disconnected from my daily
thoughts, that stream of consciousness that pours out so confidently on a
minute-to-minute basis, and goes quickly from the subjective to the objective. At that point the words no longer seem to come from me but rather it's
as though some unknown person has sent it to me through the mail, asking
my opinion of it. As I read it, what's good remains good, but what's bad jumps
off the page and smacks me right across my ego. My thick black indelible pen
puts a line through every inferior word and sentence, blocking it out forever
for any theater historian who might find it one day and say, "My God! How
could he write such crap?" I can. We all can. We all do. In painting, as in composing or any art form, what you take out is as important as what you leave in.
There is a story of an art teacher in a third-grade class who obtained wonderful results from her students. The parents, amazed, wanted to know how this
art teacher could make their eight- and nine-year-olds better painters than
previous teachers had. The woman explained, "I just know when to take it
away from them." Sid Caesar once gave me the best advice about cutting: "If
they don't hear it, they never know you wrote it."

In the second week I wrote another twenty pages and took Sunday off at
the beach, and what I read on Monday I reduced from twenty to four pages.
In two weeks I had a total of only seven pages. I began to think, "God created
the universe in six days and on the seventh day He rested. And on Monday
morning He had a lot of rewriting to do."

My five weeks of freelancing were quickly up. It was time to do *The Jerry
Lewis Show*. I put the work into my suitcase, sixty-seven original pages now

pruned down to twenty-four, with the title changed from *One Shoe Off* to *The Mating Game* to *Come Blow Your Horn.* Knowing the end of our California stay was coming soon, Joan was already packed, anxious to get back to any concrete street she could walk on. Ellen was now able to climb out of her play-pen, making a valiant effort to try to climb up to the famous HOLLYWOOD sign on the hill above. We put her on a short leash with a bell on it. Poodles are amazingly intelligent dogs and Chips knew something was afoot. For the entire last week, he sat quietly inside an open suitcase, lest we forget him.

We had six days to rehearse the Lewis variety show and on the seventh day, it went on the air. Just as God had done before me.

All went well with rehearsals. Jerry was warm, friendly, confident, and funny. There was no joke that couldn't be saved by him suddenly turning his head, looking straight into the camera, and making that chimpanzee pout that we all seemed to recognize in a distant relative. Another gift awaited me as we began to work. The script I wrote was on the desk in bound leather with my name embossed in gold and the all-too-familiar caricature of Jerry's face on the cover. I was almost ready to open my own Jerry Lewis franchise store. The show was being produced and directed by Ernest Glucksman, an old friend, whom I can honestly say gave Danny and me our first break.

When Danny was twenty-three years old, he had a job as assistant man-ager of the boys clothing department at Abraham & Straus, a prominent department store in Brooklyn. Ernie Glucksman was a freelance director/producer, mostly of industrial shows, and produced the summer seasons of plays and revues for Green Mansions, a resort in New Hampshire. Green Mansions was very much like Tamiment, in the Pocono Mountains of Penn-sylvania, where Danny and I later served our apprenticeship writing our first "professional" sketches, and where we met our wives. Ernie was hired by Abraham & Straus to put on their annual employees show with original sketches and songs, mostly dealing with the life and strife of working in a department store. Since the actors were all employees, it was only fitting that the entire audience was made up of employees, so aiming most of the jokes at the executives and floor managers was sure to bring down the house, but also ran the risk of bringing down the ire of some humorless higher-up. Ernie was an old hand at this and knew the problems of finding adequate actors, comics, dancers, and singers from a pool of shoe salesmen, lingerie sales-women, wrappers, packers, and elevator boys. This was not exactly MGM. Danny introduced himself to Ernie and read him a few monologues he had written with his fifteen-year-old brother with the curious name of Doc. Ernie was not only impressed with the material, he was taken with Danny's comic acting ability. He asked Danny to costar in the show and commissioned the Brothers Simon to write the comedy sketches.

We spent two months writing three sketches, with Danny pushing me to work nights and weekends. During the days I slept through my classes at De-Witt Clinton High School in the Bronx, failing an English Lit class while I was honing my Comedy Lit future. When the big night finally arrived, I sat in the audience with my mother and opened the program. It was only one folded sheet, but on the inside page there was Danny's name in large, bold letters alongside the all-employee cast. Down below, in much smaller letters, it read,

Comedy Sketches
by
Danny and Doc Simon

I stared at it. I closed the page, opened it, and stared at it again. Throughout the entire show, I kept opening the page, looking at our names. Then I looked in my mother's program to see if they left it out of hers. Did the stout woman in the bright red dress who looked as though she worked in the Confectionery Department know that she was actually sitting next to the fifteen-year-old coauthor of the Comedy Sketches? I said to my mother in a voice loud enough to hear in both directions, "Gee, I hope the sketches we wrote tonight really work." My mother said, "Stop worrying. You're always worrying." The stout woman said nothing. She was busy looking in the program to see if her sister in Ladies Hose was going to be in the big finale. I think the only time I looked up on the stage was when Danny was on. He had such guts, unbelievable nerve. He talked a little too loud and a little too fast but he knew how to make the audience laugh and showed some irritation at his coactors' inability to read the lines the way Danny expected. Danny was a born director and teacher.

Finally, they did our sketches. I lowered my head and held my breath. If they were awful, the stout woman in the red dress would turn to her friend and say, "What do you expect from a fifteen-year-old?" But the audience laughed. A lot. Even the lady in the red dress. With just a minimum of skill and a dash of talent, it's not too hard to get laughs from a thousand employees watching a sketch where two derelicts named Mr. Abraham and Mr. Straus meet on the street:

ABRAHAM: Hey! What do you do for a living?
STRAUS: Me? Nothing. What do you do?
ABRAHAM: I don't do anything either.
STRAUS: Perfect. Why don't we open a department store in Brooklyn?

The house roared and applauded. I was stunned. I didn't think it was *that* funny. I began to think, maybe we should only write for Abraham & Straus and forget about Broadway. Money wasn't everything. Laughs were. The show got a standing ovation. I went home on the subway with my mother, opening and closing the program a dozen times. I looked at it sideways, and then upside down on my lap, hoping the man holding the strap above me would glance down, see it, and go home and tell his family who he stood over in the subway. The Grand Illusions of youth. At home, I put the program on the night table, opened it up, left the light on, and redreamt every word of ours on the stage. There was no stopping me now. I was bitten.

NOW, ELEVEN YEARS later, I was working with Ernie Glucksman again, this time on my own and for considerably more than just my shared name on the program—fifteen hundred dollars a week, plus expenses, for a six-week stint, plus a large portion of my fall wardrobe, albeit red cashmere. At the first full-cast reading of the script, Jerry, Ernie, and I listened and watched for the cast's and our own reactions. Laughter in all the right places is a good sign. Laughter in the right places *and* the wrong places is a sign of nervousness and a need to please those whose ego needs pleasing in *all* places. Mine never did. I took what came, disappointment and all. I don't know where or when I learned it, but in listening to a script read for the first time, I was its toughest audience. No matter what the vocal reaction was around the table, I could almost always tell what wouldn't work in front of an audience. This is not to say that I could tell what *would* work, because it's harder to discern what is good than what is *not* good. Good feels like "maybe"; not good feels like "not a chance in hell." Since this was my first time out as a one-man writing staff, I reserved my judgment until I saw the sketch rehearsed by the actors.

Jerry seemed pleased at the reading and the rehearsals went extremely well, because Jerry never rehearsed the sketch exactly as written or without breaking into it with asides—to the crew, to me, the cast, and to himself. Jerry made the rehearsal hilarious but I wasn't quite sure if what I wrote was the main reason it was so funny. I had my doubts.

Saturday, the day of the live broadcast, came, with an expected viewing audience of about 25 million people. Two reasonably intelligent people sitting alone in the theater scares me. Twenty-five million unseen viewers spread out across America is an abstraction and never fazed me. If you can't hear the tree in the forest falling, you can't hear someone in Indiana not laughing. At two o'clock in the afternoon we did a full-dress rehearsal before a capacity audience who would serve as our "testers." But you learn very soon that you can't depend on the reactions of a tourist audience, because not only did they get in free, but they felt that their own enthusiastic laughter might actually go over the airwaves, making them an important and essential part of the show. Their first Hollywood break. To encourage all this, the network sends out a "warm-up" man to woo the audience into a receptive state of mind. He is usually not an actor or a comic but a staff announcer with the wit and humor of a tree trunk and the personality of someone running a Bingo game. "Today Jerry and the gang have got a show that's going to pop the buttons off your pants, folks, so men, loosen those belts and suspenders, ladies, do the best you can." Gales of laughter. Could this possibly be what was preparing me for Kaufman and Hart? What else did I expect from six hundred people who had nothing else to do on a Saturday afternoon in Burbank, California?

In the two previous days of rehearsal, each section of the show was precision-timed down to the quarter of a second for music, commercial breaks, the sketches, Jerry's opening monologue, and final credits. There were a genius and a genius assistant who sat with stopwatches (computerized in today's world) and could time a show—despite all its stops, missed lines, slow set changes, and an impromptu imitation of a gorilla making love to a truck that Jerry dropped in to lighten the atmosphere—without missing a beat. No matter what was added or left out, the time geniuses would click their watches and say "54:32," or "54:33.50." Not much variance. You had the feeling that in Greenwich, England, they checked in with the NBC stopwatchers for the correct time. After the final dress rehearsal, before the button poppers and the suspender looseners, the show got huge laughs and tumultuous applause. There was, however, something amiss. I could hear a buzz from backstage and the pitter-patter of frantic executives running around in their loafers. I looked around, puzzled, when suddenly Ernie Glucksman grabbed me by the arm and pulled me toward Jerry's dressing room. "Dockie, baby, we got what they call in Spanish, one big fucking problem."

"What's wrong?" I asked. "Didn't they like it?"

"Too much. The show is long, kid," Ernie said as we crawled over cables, wires, and caterers. We pushed toward his room through the rack that carried the three new tuxedos for Jerry's perusal. "We're almost eight minutes over, booby. *Oy veys mir*," he said in reassuring Yiddish. Thank God Ernie hadn't lost total touch with his roots.

In his dressing room, Jerry, in a terry-cloth robe and red jockey shorts (cotton, for a change), was going over his script with a pencil, munching on jumbo shrimps hung over a silver serving tray, which looked like a seafood tiara. We had exactly an hour before we did the show live, time to be used for Jerry to nap, shower, shave, and select the all-important tuxedo. He didn't look happy. "All right, guys. What the hell do we do?" Jerry said in the first serious tone of voice since I met him. It was refreshing to hear there was a professional side to Jerry and it took me by surprise. I said, I suppose to ease the tension, "Why don't we do it the way it is and you can be eight minutes short on your next show?" Jerry glared at me and said, "I want my fucking sweaters back, you putz." It was said affectionately. He handed me the tiara, tilting a shrimp toward me, and we momentarily bonded. As Ernie and Jerry started to make some hurried suggestions, I took out my pen and started to make big Xs through my script. Jerry looked up at me. "What are you doing, Neilman?" he said, crowning me with a new nickname signifying friendship. "I think I have some cuts, Jerry. If we just try to cut some words or sentences, it's going to be hard for the cast to memorize. We'd have to rehearse it for an hour, which we don't have. There are some half pages we can lose and never miss." With my pen I just kept X'ing out half- and three-quarter pages. "Let's go from the middle of page eight straight to the top of page ten. Then we can cut the big speech on page eleven and pick up again in the middle of page twelve. That's four minutes just there alone and we'd never miss it." Ernie looked over his script to see how it would affect the continuity of the sketch, but Jerry just looked at me, straight at my face and into my eyes. It was a look I had yet to see cross between us and I was somewhat apprehensive.

"No good?" I asked nervously. "It's just a suggestion."

Jerry shook his head either in consternation or admiration. "That's the first time since I've been in this business that I've ever seen a writer who was eager to cut his own material. It doesn't bother you?"

"No. Why should it? We don't have time for it. We have to cut something. Why lose the really good stuff? I think we should just drop it."

Jerry tossed me his script and pencil and said, "You cut it. Any way you want. I trust you. I have to shower." He got up and went into his bathroom.

Ernie looked at me with a smile. "You did good, booby."

I was stunned by Jerry's pragmatic acceptance without any loss of ego or need to control. It was an important moment for me, and one that I held onto throughout my entire career. I had found the voice that had been stifled in a room with other writers. Maybe I hadn't learned to write well yet, but I sure knew when to cut.

Joan, Ellen, Chips, and I flew back to New York the following Monday. The only thing awaiting me now was to finish the three acts of *Come Blow Your Horn*, and to find a way to feed my family through the three years I needed to write it.

ACTUALLY, *COME BLOW YOUR HORN* took a year to write and two and a half years to rewrite. I did twenty-two complete versions, starting on page 1 and finishing on page 125 every time, and almost never did I repeat myself. There was barely any similarity between the first draft and the twenty-second. And barely any similarity between the twenty-second draft and the one that first appeared on the stage on opening night in New York. The play was so primitive in its earliest versions, it bordered on Neanderthal. Reginald Rose, author of the teleplay and subsequent film *12 Angry Men* and the hit TV series *The Defenders*, was one of the first of many friends who read an early draft and offered advice. After admitting he had laughed on almost every page, he then got down to the nitty-gritty.

"When Buddy makes an exit in the first act, where does he go to?" he asked quite simply.

I looked at him quizzically. What was he getting at? Was it important? I shrugged and answered helplessly: "I don't know. He just goes out. To a movie. For a walk. A soda. A magazine. What difference does it make?"

"It makes all the difference in the world. You don't make characters exit to clear the stage. They have to have a life of their own *offstage*. When they come back, we want to know where they've been, and why they came back when they did and not some other time."

I stared at him, trying not to look foolish. "Oh. Wait a minute. You're talking about *good* plays. I'm not up to *good* plays yet. I just want to write a *play*."

But his point was made. I started from page one again and made sure everyone had a reason to come and go, that the audience knew where they

had been and what happened to them while they were gone. I was starting to put flesh on their bones and hair on their heads. To give them minds
and decision-making capabilities independent of the ones I gratuitously gave
them was still five drafts in the future.

All these drafts were done at night and on weekends. I devoted the normal
working hours to making a living by writing for television. *Come Blow Your
Horn* took the equivalent of the combined hours, months, and years I put in
writing *The Red Buttons Show*, the *Sgt. Bilko Show*, *Caesar's Hour*, and finally
The Garry Moore Show, a weekly variety program on CBS which featured a
bright new and dazzlingly funny comedienne, Carol Burnett. I would come
in at eight o'clock in the morning and work on my play for two hours, typing
on Garry Moore's stationery, before tackling the Carol Burnett sketches at ten
o'clock. Not only was Garry unknowingly subsidizing me while I worked for
him, but he eventually became one of the first investors in *Come Blow Your
Horn*, so he eventually got his money back for the typing paper I "borrowed"
from him, and then some.

During my days on the *Sgt. Bilko Show*, starring the inimitable Phil Silvers, I met a man who became a second brother to me, since my first one,
Danny, had moved to Shangri-la in the sun and was making a name and a tan
for himself in Hollywood. Billy Friedberg, a wonderful writer and editor, was
twelve years my senior but about forty years my superior in his knowledge
and experience in the ways and back alleys of Broadway. He was a cousin
to Lorenz (Larry) Hart, the brilliant lyricist who, with Richard Rodgers, co-
authored some of the brightest and most sophisticated songs and scores in
theatrical history. Billy and I spent two years writing Max Liebman's "spectac-
ulars" for NBC, along with writer Will Glickman, a funny, mustached dandy
who looked like a Jewish French colonel in the Foreign Legion, if you want
to get into oxymorons. We did two shows a month. One was a star-studded
revue with impeccably and lavishly staged musical numbers and comedy
sketches written by us for the likes of Ray Bolger, Maurice Chevalier, Nancy
Walker, Tyrone Power, a young Tony Randall, and Bert Lahr, one of the funniest men who ever lived. Bert was a compulsive worrier who never thought
his performance was good enough. After convulsing the entire crew, cleaning
ladies, and makeup people during a run-through of one of his sketches, he
would turn out to the house and ask poignantly, "Wuz that funny? I don't
tink that wuz funny. We got to make it funnier." If he made it any funnier, he
would have committed genocide. The second show of the month, done just

two weeks later, featured adaptations of old Broadway musicals, which we refined, edited, updated, and goosed-up laugh-wise. We did *Knickerbocker Holiday, Dearest Enemy, Best Foot Forward*, and others too distant to remember.

You can add another year to my newly acquired college education on this enterprise. By retracing the steps of the former great book writers of Broadway musicals, I was learning form, construction, motivation, and character—that is, as much as was permitted by the constraints of musicals written in the twenties, thirties, and forties. Since this was such a heavy workload for the three of us, my hours working on my play were reduced to two twenty-minute bus rides back and forth between our apartment on Tenth Street to the show's offices on Fifty-fifth Street. I was writing more slowly now and more illegibly, thanks to the potholes that New York bus drivers took great pains in never missing.

I showed Billy Friedberg draft number seven. He too laughed on every page and then got down to his own special and sage advice: "Some of your characters never meet. They all must have a scene with each other so that their characters and lives connect. Draw their names in a circle and then draw a straight line from each character to the other, so that they all eventually criss-cross in the play. It doesn't hold true for *all* plays, but you'll find it pretty much true in most *good* plays."

Draft number eight now required my mastery of the higher forms of mathematics, a subject I was so inept in that I once took a math test in high school and my paper was returned with a graded score of "five." My teacher further humiliated me by saying "A five is worse than a zero. A zero would mean you simply gave up, didn't answer all the questions, and just handed in your paper. But when you get a five, that means you tried and that's all you were capable of." She further advised me not to go into a career that required the use of any numbers whatsoever.

IN LATE 1959, I finished draft number eighteen and decided to send the play out into the world with a quarter taped to its first page in case it got hungry and needed subway fare back to the care and safety of my desk drawer. Joan was no longer an objective voice, since she had read all eighteen complete versions and was beginning to think *War and Peace* was a short story. The first outsider to read the play was Helen Harvey, my agent at the William Morris Agency. I dropped it off in person at her office, fearing larcenous postmen or delivery boys with aspirations of becoming playwrights, and left her office feeling as guilty as a parent leaving his five-year-old at the dentist's because the sound of pain emanating from his child was too much to bear. In my case it was worse because I was leaving a three-and-a-half-year-old. I arrived home on Tenth Street twenty minutes later and took it as a complete rejection to find out that Helen had not called yet. My God, the woman had twenty minutes to read the play, what *else* did she have to do? Joan was playing on the living room floor with Ellen, both of them rolling around, having a wonderful time.

"Look, Ellen. It's Daddy . . . Daddy, you want to play with us?"

I stared at both of them with contempt. How could I ever trust this woman again? Was Ellen so ungrateful to a father who had fed and nurtured her for all of her two years on earth not even to *ask* if Daddy's agent liked Daddy's play?

The phone rang. Joan picked it up. It was her mother. They began to talk while I stood there shocked and hurt that she would actually talk to her mother at a time like this. It was possible that Helen Harvey was trying to get through, kept getting a busy signal, hung up, and tossed my play onto a pile of new plays she was no longer interested in. "If he doesn't care enough to keep his line open, this man isn't really interested in writing for the theater. Too bad. The kid had promise." I drank a double scotch, plopped down on the sofa, and watched my wife and daughter resume playing, while my head and heart pounded so loudly, I expected outraged complaints from the neighbors.

Helen Harvey called the next day. I never really heard what she said. It was something like, "[garble garble garble] liked it [garble garble garble] funny and touching [garble garble] needs work [garble garble] Wednesday at three o'clock [garble garble garble]."

I went in the kitchen and tried to tell Joan what Helen had to say, repeating her conversation as best I could. Joan, who was feeding Ellen, looked confused, but Ellen liked the "garble garble" part and clapped and said "More, Daddy, more."

Indeed, as I sat before her desk in her office on Wednesday at three, Helen Harvey, ungarbled, said she liked the play. She more than liked it. She offered me no more constructive criticism than to correct my spelling, which was noteorriosslee bad.

"What you need now is a director to guide you through the rewrites and to help mold and reshape the play."

Was Helen seriously suggesting that some living, human professional might actually be interested in directing this? I suppose I had never given any thought that this play would actually be rehearsed, acted, directed, and put on a stage. I thought it was just for writing. "Still working on my play," I could say years from now at some literary party, giving the impression I was at labor on some monumental theatrical achievement. "He's working on a play," some young admirer would say from the corner of the room, glancing at me but never actually up to looking straight into my eyes.

"I was thinking of Herman Shumlin," offered Helen Harvey. Thinking she was changing the subject, I said, "Really? Why would you be thinking of him now?"

"To direct your play."

Herman Shumlin? *The Herman Shumlin??* He was—and had been for the past twenty-five years—one of the most important and respected directors in the theater. He had directed Lillian Hellman's *The Little Foxes, Watch on the Rhine*, and countless other outstanding dramas. He was major league. I was a batboy for the Tuscaloosa Tomcats.

"Don't send it to him. He'll laugh at you," I pleaded.

"No. He'll laugh at the *play*. He's been looking for a comedy for years."

How did she know this? Did she actually know him? I was suddenly in awe of Helen Harvey.

"I'll send it to him today," she went on. "All he can do is say no."

I was petrified. Not so much at having him direct the play; I was petrified at the thought of just meeting him. He'd probably say things like, "Why do you want to be a playwright, son? I remember once talking to Eugene O'Neill up at Provincetown. Gene was a stubborn Irish kid, you know, and hell, it took me weeks to get him to rethink *Mourning Becomes Electra* . . . What'd you think of that play, boy?" . . . I would try to look as if I was thinking deeply but would end up saying, "May I use your bathroom, please?"

Two days later Herman Shumlin had my play. It was early July, and Joan, Ellen, and I took up summer residence in a rented cottage on Fire Island. We were in the Fair Harbor section, which was pretty much an artists colony—mostly writers, journalists, and neophyte politicos. Theodore H. White, the foremost chronicler of presidential elections, was our next-door neighbor. Teddy was on a first-name basis with senators, congressmen, the cabinet, and everyone straight up to the White House. I wasn't even on a first-name basis with Teddy. He eliminated that problem when he introduced himself and I suddenly found myself in the company of a warm, funny, generous, and extremely intelligent man.

He was Boston, Harvard, and class. Looking every bit the quintessential writer, Teddy often smoked a pipe. I loved the way he kept packing the
bowl with fresh tobacco while the embers on the bottom still glowed and
burned. His pipe never went out, like some homage or tribute at the Tomb
of the Unknown Writer. The first chance I had, I stopped in at Dunhill's on
Fifth Avenue and tried on fifteen or twenty pipes, looking at myself in the
mirror, the pipe bit held near my mouth but not in it, lest they charge me
eighteen dollars for a pipe that was now considered "used." I then noticed
that Teddy was also a cigarette smoker, the kind who was never bothered by
smoke wafting up into his eyes; those who were bothered, he regarded with
disdain, much as Bogart did when handing Mary Astor over to Ward Bond at
the end of *The Maltese Falcon*, saying, "I'm not going to play the fool for you
or anyone, sweetheart."

I tried my first cigarette, sitting at my typewriter, gazing at a blank wall,
looking for inspiration as I inhaled the burning tobacco, which only got as
far as a quick glance at my lungs, then turned around in panic and raced back
out of my mouth, causing an eruption of coughing that rattled the fragile
wooden shingles of our rented cottage. It was clear I was never going to be
the writer Teddy White was.

A week went by and then the phone rang.

I assumed it was Helen Harvey calling to tell me that Herman Shumlin
thought she had taken leave of her senses. He wanted to say the play was one
step below amateur, but he had not as yet come across the word in his lexicon.
I picked up the phone.

"Mr. Simon?"

"Yes?"

"Herman Shumlin."

"Oh. Oh. Yes. Oh . . . Hello."

"I read your play."

"Yes, I know. I mean I know that it was sent to me. To you . . . So you read it?"

"Yes. I just said that."

"Yes, I know. I'm sorry. The dog was barking . . . So you read it."

"I liked it. Wonderful dialogue."

"Really?"

"You have a very keen ear for comedy. Very fresh. Very original. I laughed
a great deal."

"I'm glad. That's really terrific."

"Of course it's not a play yet."

"Oh, I know. I know that. It's still got a lot of holes in it. Lots of gaps. But I think the overall construction is pretty good, don't you?"

"No."

"No?"

"It has no construction. It's just very funny dialogue broken up by scene changes."

"Ah. Yes. I see what you mean. That's a good point. I hadn't thought of that."

"Can we get together? I'd like to talk to you about my ideas."

"You have ideas already? Wow. Yes. Absolutely. Whenever you want."

"How's tomorrow?"

"Tomorrow? Oh. Well, we have some guests coming tomorrow. I'm not sure I could get into New York and back in time."

"What time are they coming?"

"About noon, one o'clock."

"Well, we have all morning. I could take the first ferry over. Say about eight, eight-thirty."

"You mean you'd come out *here*?"

"I have the schedule in front of me. There's an eight-twenty-seven ferry. Meet me at the dock. I'll be wearing a white suit. Nice speaking to you. Goodbye."

There are some moments that come only once in a lifetime. They're not so much the ones that are expected, like pulling yourself up the slats of a crib and standing for the first time. It's not that memorable morning you went riding for two whole city blocks for the first time without falling off your two-wheeler bike, which until now seemed unconquerable. I am talking about a millimeter of time when the impossible suddenly falls into the realm of possibility. That moment when you feel that those impenetrable walls forever closing you off from a world that will never be open to you actually have a door, and that door, for one instant, one fleeting moment, has cracked ajar ever so slightly, and a tiny sliver of light and opportunity has presented itself to you just enough to say, "There *is* hope." Herman Shumlin saying "I liked your play" was that moment for me.

He arrived on Fire Island, in white suit, promptly on the 8:27. There was an awful stench at the dock that morning since the local mainland sanitation workers had gone on strike and were picking up no garbage that day. Instead, the summer residents who were going back to the city that morning carried their garbage with them in any bag, receptacle, or old suitcase they could find. I can still remember the incongruous sight of Charles Collingwood, the noted CBS commentator—who dressed and spoke with all the dignity and aplomb of the American Ambassador to the Court of St. James—carrying two large grocery bags, slightly damp, and filled with the bones, skin, wings, and remains of the weekend's barbecue in his arms, kissing his wife good-bye, and sailing off into the smelly sunrise.

Herman Shumlin was probably about sixty, quite dignified, affable, and charming, if not entirely accessible. He wore his experience and success on his person as a notable would unostentatiously wear his little red Legion of Honor badge almost indiscernibly in his lapel. In other words, I trembled at his every word. The more he spoke about my play the more he seemed to depart from my play, and the conversation drifted into the play he would like me to write instead of the play I had already written. The crack in the door was getting narrower and narrower. One specific he pointed out was that he didn't quite like the character of the older brother. The older brother was, in a sense, fashioned after my brother, Danny, who, as it turned out, would appear again and again in at least five future plays of mine, all in varied and unexpected incarnations.

At the time I was doing those early drafts of *Come Blow Your Horn*, Danny and I were at the apex of sibling rivalry. In fact, I think I out-sibled him by ten to one. After an entire childhood of idolizing him, learning from him, fearing him, respecting him, and loving him, I was also beginning to feel dominated by him and I had an urgent need to separate from him, to become, in a term not yet then in fashion, my own person. Paradoxically, I wanted both to overshadow him and to please him with my work. One can imagine a rising young basketball star wanting to stuff a basket "in the face" of his brother and still wanting the praise and encouragement of his "opponent" who had just been faked out of his shoes by a flashy move. This is something that plagued me play after play, because what I wanted more than anything, beyond critical praise, was to get the acclaim and acknowledgment from Danny. Danny never denied it to me, but in the beginning it wasn't wholehearted. The fact is, I probably never would have been a writer if it were not for Danny. Once, when I was fifteen years old, he said to me, "You're going to be the best comedy writer in America." Why? Based on what? How funny could I be at fifteen? It's as if Columbus's brother said to him when he was twelve, "Chris, one day you're going to sail across the sea and discover a new world, probably landing at San Salvador first." Danny's overwhelming belief in me must have settled quietly in some corner of my mind because I worked without fear, knowing I had the ability to get it down on paper and get it right. I wasn't very good at group meetings, but put me alone in a room with a pen and a piece of blank paper, it wouldn't stay blank very long.

No one has yet determined, to my satisfaction, what elements of nature, genetics, and environment have to combine to form a man or woman with a keen sense of humor. Poverty? Perhaps. It's there in the backgrounds of Chaplin and Noël Coward. And certainly in Dickens, whose ironic and satirical comedy belie the hardships of a ten-year-old boy who spent fourteen hours a day working in a factory. Bigotry? Quite possibly. The Jews, according to comic writer Mel Brooks, have been funny for two thousand years, since the pharaoh expelled the Hebrews from Egypt. Mel would probably say, as a two-thousand-year-old Jew in Egypt, "We were glad to get out. It was hot, it was buggy, building the pyramids was a lousy job, and we couldn't stand the Egyptian kids begging from us in the front of our hotels."

Poverty and bigotry, plus at least a half-dozen factors more, might start to explain where the comic spirit is born. In my case you would certainly have to add "encouragement." Whether it was Danny's self-sacrifice by putting his own aspirations on hold for the sake of nurturing mine, I can't tell. Danny certainly wanted success for himself as much as he did for me. But at some point along the way, he must have said to himself, "If I can't be the best hitter on this team, then I'll be the best manager in this league." This is attested to not only by me, but also by Woody Allen, who has been quoted as saying, "Everything I learned about comedy, I learned from Danny Simon."

I believe my writing those first drafts of *Come Blow Your Horn* was a signal that the prodigal son was about to say good-bye to his brother/father, and strike out on his own. As I grew older, I never doubted Danny's opinions or talent. But they were always *his*, and it soon became clear that his point of view was not necessarily mine. I sometimes felt that he took the position of "older brother" rather than "senior writer," and I soon found I rejected his ideas as I might have rejected a suit of clothes he picked out for me, preferring instead the one that I thought fit my style. You need not be writers to be subjected to being sibling rivals. Brothers or sisters eventually resent each other, otherwise why would those Greeks have written all those tragedies?

Eventually we went our separate ways, but not without hurt and pain. I'm happy to say our mutual respect and love eventually returned. But even now, in our later years, with Danny retired from writing, he can tell me what he honestly thinks after reading a new play of mine, and my first reaction will always be, "He's teaching me again."

Director Herman Shumlin was no slouch when it came to drama, and he quickly sensed the rivalry between the two young brothers when he read *Come Blow Your Horn*. When he pointed out to me that the older brother was not a likable character, I had the temerity and chutzpah to say to this knowledgeable man, "What's wrong with that? Do you have to like every character in a play?"

"No. Just in comedy."

"Why?"

"Because if we don't like him, we don't root for him. This is a family comedy, not a political diatribe. Save your anger for a deeper play, but let's have the audience like this family and take them to their hearts."

This was advice from a man who knew enough about villains from the Hellman plays alone, and I understood what he was getting at. But I was frustrated in having to conform to theatrical tradition. Eventually I'd get to my villains, but in the ugly face of pragmatism, I chose to lose the battle and win a production. But it didn't quite happen that way. During the ensuing months of rewriting the older brother into a funny and likable person, I was reshaping the play into a more acceptable comedy that fitted the fashions of the early sixties. I didn't exactly consider it a compromise. I considered it a valuable learning lesson. Herman Shumlin eventually dropped the play in favor of what suited his own considerable talents best, a political drama. When he finally moved on, he left me with a much improved play desperately in search of a director/producer. Enter Max Gordon.

Max Gordon was a producer from the old school, whose very name was bandied about in plays and films of that era as the archetypal cigar-smoking Broadway producer. He had presented Garson Kanin's smash hit play *Born Yesterday*, and was the heir to the mold of Sam H. Harris, the producer of many of the Kaufman-and-Hart classic comedies. Max had an office high above a theater just off Broadway, either the Belasco or the Morosco, in the same manner that David Merrick once had offices above the St. James Theatre or Alexander H. Cohen had them above the Shubert Theatre, which was soon dubbed the Cohenesco. To get to Max Gordon's office, you went through a side door in the lobby of the theater and took a two- or three-pas-senger elevator, depending on the girth of the passengers, up to the top floor. You were let out, or squeezed out, into what appeared to be the Museum of the American Theater, if you just went by the red-velvet wall covering, the countless posters of shows that were presented at that theater, and the age of Mr. Gordon's secretary. Max Gordon knew theater and he knew plays, not only because he had produced quite a number of successful ones, but also by virtue of never missing an opening night on Broadway of *anyone's* play.

I had received my phone call from Helen Harvey two days before. "Max Gordon read your play. He wants to see you in his office on Tuesday."

"Did he like it?"

"Well, I don't think he'd be asking to see you if he *hated* the play."

"Did he have anything nice to say about it?"

"I didn't speak to him. I spoke to his secretary."

"Did *she* have anything nice to say about it?"

"I didn't speak to her when she made the appointment. She spoke to my assistant, Ronnie."

"Did *Ronnie* have anything nice to say about it?"

"Ronnie loves your play."

"Well, *that's* a good sign, isn't it? What did Ronnie say?"

"Nothing. She hasn't read the second act yet."

In this business you look for bread crumbs and settle for what the pigeons couldn't get to that day. The meeting with Max Gordon in his office was brief and to the point.

"I read your script, kid. Good dialogue. Funny. Someday you're going to write a great play. This isn't it."

I nodded, waiting for more. None was forthcoming so I pushed my luck. "Can you tell me what's wrong with it?"

He looked up, surprised to see I was still there. Out of some sense of benevolence, he shared his wisdom with me. "A play is like a house. It has to be built on a solid foundation. You don't have a solid foundation here. What you've got is a house built on sand. Once the curtain goes up, your play is going to sink right into the sand. You understand what I'm saying?"

"Yes. Too much sand."

"Right. One last thing before you go."

I hadn't even made a move toward the door.

"Characters."

"Characters?"

"There's no play without characters. First you get your characters, then you get your story, then you get your dialogue. If you got a story and dialogue but no characters, what have you got?"

"A sand castle."

"Now you understand. Okay. Nice meeting you, kid. If you ever write a great play, let me read it first. Close the door."

As if I would even *know* when I wrote a great play.

This was getting hard. Not only did I have sand at the bottom of my play, but as I looked down, I noticed my feet were showing signs of becoming clay. I was thirty-one years old, the age that most ball players were considered middle-aged, and budding playwrights had already sprouted little playlets. Yet the only progress I had made was that I wrote funny dialogue for people who were not really characters, were occasionally unlikable, and were all sitting in a house with no foundation.

More phone calls from the indefatigable Helen Harvey, more appointments with the unending lists of producers who were all looking for that one-set, small-cast, hilarious comedy but preferably from a name writer with a great track record. The fact that I met so many top producers and directors that year who laughed at my play, encouraged me to write more, but weren't really interested in producing it actually made me feel as if I were doing well. After all, I met David Merrick, Garson Kanin, Jule Styne, Cyril Ritchard, and George Abbott's secretary (no one actually *met* Mr. Abbott, but that was close enough). After another dozen complimentary turn-downs, Helen sent the play to Arthur Cantor. Mr. Cantor, who still maintained his press-agent card and business, had recently produced Paddy Chayefsky's brilliant comedy *The Tenth Man*, directed by Tyrone Guthrie and coproduced with someone with the unlikely name of Saint Subber. Arthur was probably the most enthusiastic of all the producers I met, and after reading my play a third time, he called me and said he had a wild but possibly brilliant idea for someone to direct the play: Preston Sturges, possibly the most innovative and idiosyncratic film director in Hollywood, and in my mind second only to the greatest, Billy Wilder. "What do you think of that idea?" Arthur said on the phone. Mr. Sturges's career had pretty much bottomed out in California, and he was now back east trying to resurrect his golden days in the theater where he had first made his name with a sparkling comedy, *Strictly Dishonorable*.

As awestruck as I was at the prospect of working with Preston Sturges, I wasn't quite convinced he would like my kind of comedy or would even understand it. I was writing about a Jewish family in Manhattan, with a father who was in the wax fruit business; all he wanted was for his older son to get married and carry on his name in the great tradition of wax fruit entrepreneurs. Sturges wrote comedies about millionaires and women who ran off to Palm Beach, and a film director named Sullivan who wanted to travel and find out why he had lost his audience. Sturges was a social commentator and I was a meat-and-cabbage-soup kid. Arthur said Sturges was very interested, but I'm not sure that meant he read the play because Mr. Sturges was very difficult to get on the phone. I never did find out nor did Mr. Cantor. Preston Sturges never did manage to resurrect his career, either in New York or Hollywood; he died of a heart attack in August 1959.

I was getting closer to the geniuses but farther away from a production. As for Arthur Cantor, he came very close to saying yes, but made a right turn somewhere and stopped on the word "no." He did, however, send the play to Mr. Subber, whom everyone called Saint. I always thought Saint Subber should have produced *Saint Joan* in St. Louis, just to read the *Variety* headline, especially if it failed: "THREE SAINTS DON'T MAKE A NICKEL."

Okay, set out the champagne glasses. Saint Subber liked the play. He *loved* the play. He was going to *do* the play. All he needed now were the backers to put up the money. Call *Variety*: "SAINT LOOKING FOR ANGELS." Let me set the record straight here. Saint Subber was no neophyte producer scrounging around agents' offices for any play that was neatly typed to put on Broadway. Talk about track records, he had already produced the plays of William Inge, Carson McCullers, and Hugh Wheeler, and was negotiating with Tennessee Williams and Truman Capote. Not only had I met a Saint, I was about to enter the gates of Playwrights Heaven.

I spent the next four months doing all the rewriting the knowledgeable Mr. Subber suggested. He lived in a minuscule townhouse not much more than ten feet wide on Sixty-fourth Street off Park Avenue. He had an elevator that made Max Gordon's seem like a 747. When I delivered new pages to him each day, I insisted on staying in his house while he read them, so that we could quickly discuss his impressions afterward. But that was not really my motive. Saint was a notorious giggler, and I desperately needed to hear someone actually laugh aloud at what I wrote. I sat in the tiny room next to his study, and his laughter wafting through the door was a balm to my bruised and diminishing confidence. After four months of my intensive rewriting,

Saint called me to his house. He reluctantly decided to pass on the play. He felt the play could make a damn good sprint but couldn't go the full distance. The door with a crack of hope was finally slammed shut and locked. It was doubly disappointing, because Saint made more sense to me than any producer I had met till then, but despite the fact that he insisted we would work again on something someday, I felt my play sinking swiftly into the sands of my inexperience, with no one in sight to throw me a rope. There was to be no play in my future and I wondered if I had a future at all. I came home wondering how I could break the crushing news to Joan, who greeted me at the door with a smile, a hug and a kiss before I could say a word.

"I'm pregnant," she said, exuding such extreme joy that it quickly negated any possibility of my telling her that if I was going to support this new child, it would never be with the royalties from a play. In the next few days, when the phone calls to and from Saint Subber ceased, Joan didn't have to ask what happened. Instead she took the positive approach that this could all be a blessing in disguise. She suggested we leave New York and move up to Vermont, where we could buy an old barn and twelve acres of land for ten thousand dollars, rebuild the house ourselves, and bring up our children with dogs and horses. I could write articles for magazines, because we really didn't need much money to live on in Vermont. But she never dealt with the realities of it. The first week there I would try my hand at rebuilding, and without fail, I would nail my thumb to a wall, step on a rake and lose all five toes, and get kicked in the groin by a horse, leaving me impotent and a contralto. As the old saying goes, "You can take the boy out of the city, but you'll probably bury him on the farm."

Three and a half months later, I was picking up television work here and there, and the pickings were scant since the exodus of television to the Promised Land in L.A. was at full speed. One day while I was in the middle of work, Joan called me to come home quickly. She was having terrible stomach cramps. I rushed her to New York Hospital and in the cab we both knew what it was. A miscarriage. When they wheeled her out of the O.R., she reached up, took my hand, squeezed it, and with tears on her face she said, "It was a boy. It was the sweetest little boy . . ." Plays and farmhouses soon vanished from our immediate cares and concerns, and life intruded, as life has a way of doing.

BUCKS COUNTY

3

IT WAS A BLEAK, cold March, with the wind blowing in from the East and an offer coming in from the West. NBC wanted me to join the writing staff of a new variety show they were putting on in the fall, in Los Angeles, of course. The money was more than I had ever made before, and Joan and I looked at each other ruefully. "Well, maybe it's more interesting out there now," she said philosophically and half-heartedly. The phone rang. It was Helen Harvey, and from the tentative sound in her voice, I did not have great expectations.

"Can we have lunch tomorrow?" she offered.

I told her about the NBC offer for the fall.

"That's wonderful," she said with some enthusiasm, "but there's something I think we should talk about. And it won't interfere with your going to California."

We met for lunch. I ordered a roast beef sandwich and a Coke, she had a brisket on rye and a cup of coffee.

"Do you realize," I said between bites, "four months from now I'll be eating salads and herbal teas for lunch?"

I'm not quite sure why we diehard New Yorkers looked down our noses at Los Angeles, even knocking their health-food style as something to be avoided at all costs, while we gorged ourselves on sandwiches piled high with fats and named after comedians like Henny Youngman or Milton Berle. I once coined a New Yorker's description of L.A., which has been repeated often, but just for the record, let's call it a summer rerun:

"In New York when it's 16 degrees in the winter, it's 78 in Los Angeles. And in New York, when it's 102 in the summer, it's 78 in Los Angeles. However, in New York there are 4 million interesting people and only 78 in Los Angeles."

Los Angeles magazine promptly listed their seventy-eight most interesting people. It was an easy joke on my part and probably unfair to L.A., although I think I shortchanged them by about twenty people.

"Is this a good-bye lunch?" I asked Helen, this being my time to garble, with a half a pound of roast beef heading for my mouth.

"I just hate to see you go without ever having a chance to see your play on a stage somewhere. If you saw it performed, I'm sure you'd see the weaknesses and the strengths and maybe then you'd know how to fix it. The play has so much promise and so do you, and I'd feel awful if both of you passed up what could be your last opportunity."

"And where would that be, pray tell?"

"Summer stock."

The roast beef hit the bottom of my stomach, unchewed and untasted. Summer stock was where old plays go to expire in the heat of a country night. Suddenly 78 in Los Angeles seemed a lot more comfortable than 102 on a stage somewhere in the mosquitoed woods of New Jersey. In 1960, there was very little of what we now call regional theater. Regional theater today is a most prestigious, experimental, and groundbreaking way of presenting plays, from Shakespeare, Ibsen, and Chekhov to new, young, and untried authors. But in 1960, summer stock was known as the straw hat circuit. The only new plays tried there were ones that might have a part that attracted a name Hollywood or Broadway actor; the play itself was more than likely not going to have a life once the autumn leaves began to fall. Not only was summer stock a last ditch for my play, but that ditch would inevitably be its burial ground.

The one theater that seemed interested was the Bucks County Playhouse in New Hope, Pennsylvania. It did, in fact, have one of the more reputable summer theaters, and Bucks County itself was dotted with the summer homes of such theater luminaries as Moss Hart, Oscar Hammerstein II, and S. J. Perelman. There was a good chance that George S. Kaufman or Harpo Marx might drop in for croquet or tennis, or with an idea for a new show. At the very least, it would be a nice place for Joan, Ellen, and me to spend a summer before we moved to our cozy little cottage near the La Brea Tar Pits.

The Bucks County Playhouse was then run by a congenial man named Michael Ellis, and he intended to produce *Come Blow Your Horn* with William (Billy) Hammerstein, son of Oscar. They both liked the play and promised that if it was well received in Bucks County, they would make their best efforts to move the play to New York. I had heard *that* before and took it with a grain of salt, which I added to my last bite ever of a New York deli sandwich.

I was to be paid a minimum royalty for the three weeks the play would be performed there, plus room and board in a local citizen's house. If I had seen it first, I would have asked for the board to be in the bed in the room of the house.

The exciting news was that we finally had a director. I was not deterred by the fact that he had never directed a play before, and since we were both virgins, we had fear as a common bond. His name was Stanley Prager, a former actor, who for years had played second bananas in B pictures and had moved up to play the best friend of second bananas in A pictures. He was called "Stosh" by all who knew him, and everyone I ever met who knew him liked him. Somewhat squat and chubby, he had an effervescent personality and the warmest smile. He was quick to laugh at anything that approached humor, including his own tasty contributions. He told me he had once appeared in a Broadway revue with Bert Lahr. Bert Lahr, as I already mentioned, valued a laugh onstage as much as a collector valued a Renoir in his study, and anyone who came close to stealing it would pay the direst penalty. Lahr would call Stosh into his dressing room every night and say, "Don't ever move onstage while I'm talking. If I see you move, kid, you're fired. Understand?" Stosh nodded obediently. That night, during a scene, Stosh had an urgent need to scratch his nose and was stoically waiting for Lahr to finish his speech. But the itch was not to be denied, and Stosh raised his hand quickly, scratched his nose in a flash, and quickly lowered his hand. But Bert grabbed his wrist in midair, held it tightly, and yelled for all in the theater to hear, "I told you not to move!" It got a huge laugh from the audience because there was nothing that Bert Lahr said that wasn't funny. And Stosh didn't lose his job.

Since *Come Blow Your Horn* was ostensibly about my family, the four main parts to cast were my brother and me, my mother, and my father. I pictured a young Jimmy Stewart for the older brother. What we got was Gene Rayburn, a television game-show host, and although a very likable and cheerful man, he was not much of an actor and talked to the other characters in the play as if he were asking them a question worth nine hundred dollars with only ten seconds to answer. The younger brother was Warren Berlinger, a nephew of Milton Berle, and a very funny, talented young actor who had recently appeared on Broadway in James Leo Herlihy and William Noble's *Blue Denim*. The mother of this obviously Jewish family was Pert Kelton, who was as Irish as Pat O'Brien on St. Patrick's Day. But what she lost in authenticity she more than made up in her skill and hilarious way with a line. The father was played by David Burns, who never went a season without being on Broadway and who had appeared in the original production of Kaufman and Hart's *The*

Man Who Came to Dinner. Davey Burns had the funniest foul mouth I ever heard but because he couched everything he said in such a dignified and innocent manner, hardly anyone blinked when he came into rehearsal ten minutes late and apologized in a mock British accent, "I beg your pardon everyone. Please forgive me. I was in the lavatory having my cock sucked by the most charming cleaning lady." Pert Kelton would throw up her arms and say, "Oh, Davey, you are disgusting." To which he replied indignantly, "Some cleaning woman I never met is sucking my cock and you call *me* disgusting?"

The three weeks of rehearsals in Bucks County went well despite the fact that it was 102 degrees both day and night, since country heat cannot distinguish between the sun and the moon. We rehearsed on the second floor of a garage, where old tires were stored, and that summer we scientifically proved that the stench of burned rubber cannot be removed from clothing or hair. In no way, however, did this discomfort diminish my exhilaration of being in rehearsal.

I couldn't tell whether the play was really funny or not, because Stanley Prager laughed on every line and his laughter was so infectious, we all joined in—while I fervently hoped that Stanley's responses were based on a genuine reaction and not some weird facial tic.

The Bucks County Playhouse was built on the banks of the Delaware River, and there is a mark carved in the wood about six inches above the box office window to denote where the river flooded New Hope and the theater some years past. Another thing for me to worry about. I could picture the play going along beautifully, when suddenly a summer storm hit and soon the river banks succumbed to the onrushing water and the entire audience was being paddled in rowboats to higher ground, while the actors, true to their craft, remained onstage saying their lines until the waterline reached their lower lips, and I clung to a weather vane atop the theater beseeching the cast to "Try to finish the first act, then save yourselves." Playwrights have no mercy.

Opening night in Bucks County, the summer of 1960. Even now as I reread that sentence, it looks to me like a date to be remembered in the Civil War. Bull Run, Bucks County, they all blend together in the mind of someone about to face battle for the first time. As I remember it, it was a hot night and yet I shivered with cold. Or, it was a very chilly night but I sweated profusely. It was one of those. Joan and I were the first ones in the theater and we sat on the aisle in the very last row. If the going got tough, we could always get to our car quickly and hie up to Vermont and see if that ten-thousand-dollar farm was still available. The audience filed in, chatting among themselves, discussing mostly what they had for dinner. I don't know what else I expected. Maybe something like, "We hear this is wonderful. Some friends of ours passed the garage where they were rehearsing the other day and heard gales of laughter coming from the second floor, despite the stench of the old tires."

Helen Harvey came in, waved to me, and gave me the thumbs-up sign. Or perhaps it was a signal that she needed a lift back to New York after the show. Alexander Cohen, the producer, came in with his wife, followed by the actors' agents, friends, and relatives, a few critics for the local New Hope newspaper, and a few second-string critics from Philadelphia, while the majority of the seats were taken up by Real People—a group I had entirely forgotten about. Real People are the fairest audience you can get, because they have no emotional interest in the event they are about to witness. They just want to be entertained. I'll buy that.

Like most people in the theater that night, I expected the house lights to dim, the curtain to rise, and the play to begin. No such luck. Michael Ellis appeared onstage in front of the house curtain, a spotlight picking up the dour look on his face. I was sure he was going to announce that the entire cast had all suddenly been attacked backstage by a swarm of bees, had gone into respiratory shock, and were all being driven to the hospital in New Hope's only ambulance. Fortunately it wasn't that bad. But close. When the Real Person next to me saw the dismayed look on my face, he informed me that Mike Ellis *always* came out to talk to the audience before each new production, revivals and all. Mike Ellis just liked being onstage and possibly took the job as managing director just to make these appearances. But tonight he had something else to say. His speech went something like this:

"Good evening. As our regular subscribers already know, I am Michael Ellis, incumbent managing director of the Bucks County Playhouse. For those of you who are here for the first time, I am still Michael Ellis, managing director of the Bucks County Playhouse." (Oh my God. Another stand-up comic. I sank lower in my seat as he went on.) "Tonight we are presenting a new play, *Come Blow Your Horn*, by a new playwright, Neil Simon. Whether the play or the playwright are ever heard from again remains to be seen." (Joan sank two inches lower than me.) "My partner, William Hammerstein, and I are hoping to bring the play to Broadway. After tonight, you may think we're crazy." (If he asked me, I could have told him right then.) "We think it's a very funny play. We saw the dress rehearsal yesterday and loved it. Of course, we've been wrong before." (If I had a gun, I could have picked him off easily from my aisle seat. The worst I could have gotten was "understandable manslaughter.") "Naturally we're going to have to raise money for this play to go to Broadway. Our budget calls for seventy-five thousand dollars. In your programs you will find forms for you to indicate whether you liked the play and if so, are you willing to invest in it, and if so, how much." (Why didn't he just play a banjo and have a monkey go around with a tin cup?) "We'll take *any* investment, from seventy-five thousand to ten or twenty dollars. It might make a nice graduation or bar mitzvah gift for your kid." (Three and a half years of work for *this*? I worked with Herman Shumlin, Max Gordon, Garson Kanin, and almost heard from Preston Sturges. Maybe I should have passed a note up to Mike Ellis saying I was going blind and if the play were a success, I would be able to have that eye-saving operation. Mike Ellis went on. He was already on longer than our first act.) "So I hope you like this play. If not, don't tell your friends. We still have three weeks to play here."

He bowed to a smattering of applause and a prayer from me that the flood would hit before he got off the stage. The houselights dimmed and the curtain went up on a play that the audience had just been warned about, like a new strain of flu. The first fifteen minutes of act 1 went like a case of double pneumonia, please notify the immediate family. It was mostly my fault. Gene Rayburn had three consecutive telephone calls to make, giving all the exposition of the play in two pages of single-spaced dialogue that made Mike Ellis's speech seem like entertainment. I sat there in a state of doom and despair, as if someone onstage had just fired a gun at me, and I could see the bullet moving slowly and inexorably toward my brain, and I was either unable to move or didn't wish to, hoping to get my wretched existence over with. I know Joan saw my head shaking slowly from side to side with my eyes closed, a sign that I was eagerly awaiting my soul to leave my body and let the paramedics deal with the zipper bag. She was annoyed with my attitude and tried to point out something I was missing.

"They like it. They're paying attention. They're listening."

"They're not supposed to be listening. They're supposed to be laughing." And suddenly it came. With Pert Kelton's entrance, followed by a scene with David Burns, the laughs started to come. I had a notebook and a pen in my lap, ready to write down every line and moment that didn't work. I never touched them once during the entire performance. I found afterward, as I did for my entire career in the theater, that I could reread a script later that night and tell exactly how, where, and to what degree the audience responded, as well as what worked and what needed rewriting. My experience on *The Jerry Lewis Show* was now paying off.

The evening was a roller coaster of ups and downs. The highs sent me soaring, the lows made me want to dash back to my room and board and rewrite the scene instantly, hoping to get the new words back to the actors before the final curtain fell. It was clear at the small party afterward that we had neither a hit nor a flop. What we had was a play that needed a great deal of work but certainly had promise. Mike Ellis and Bill Hammerstein were noncommittal but polite. They wanted to think about it.

"Come to my office tomorrow morning at ten and we'll talk about it," said Mike, in the shortest speech he made that evening. In parting I asked, "What about the forms in the programs? Did anyone want to invest?" He said, "Well, we have about three hundred dollars in definite commitments." Sometimes I shouldn't ask questions.

The next morning I was awake at six. Considering I didn't fall asleep until four, it was little more than a nap. I have found it almost impossible to sleep the night after an opening. Good or bad. If the play was a hit, you couldn't wait for the sun to come up and read all the reviews. If it was a flop, you knew you could sleep as late as you wanted because your phone would not be ringing. And the absence of a phone ringing can keep you awake like no other sound in the world.

At ten o'clock I presented myself before Mike and Billy. It was obvious they had met earlier and discussed their situation. This time Billy did the talking. He had a quiet presence about him. He chose his words carefully and looked just enough like his father, Oscar, to intimidate me:

"We're concerned but not disillusioned. It's really up to you now. There's the makings of a funny, entertaining play here. The people liked it last night. Not loved it, but liked it. So the question is not so much do we have faith in the play but do we have faith in you. Here's our proposition. We'll take an option on the play for six months and pay you the Dramatists Guild minimum. You have six months to rewrite the play. If we read it and like it, we shoot for Broadway. If we don't like it, well, maybe you'll write another one someday."

"I accept," I said, way before he finished saying "another one someday."

The Dramatists Guild minimum on an option couldn't have been more than three hundred dollars in 1960. It would mean giving up the well-paying job in California and betting everything we had that I could fix the play up in this one last assault to conquer Mount Everest.

When I got back to our room, I started to explain their proposition to Joan. She said, "Yes," before I could finish saying "conquer Mount Everest." We stayed in Bucks County for a few more performances of my play, making mental notes, and drove back to Fire Island. I awoke the next morning at 5:30 to do the thing I liked best about writing. Rewriting. I have often explained in interviews that a playwright has one advantage over screenwriters. An audience will tell you immediately what's wrong, and you can go home and fix it. With a screenwriter, once they've shot your scene, it's history. Or blasphemy. The more live performances of my play I see, the more chances I get at improving it. It's as if you were in school taking a test, and initially walking away with a grade score of 65. But the next day you get to take the exact same test, with the same questions, but now with new answers that you've thought about overnight. You're bound to improve into the 70s, 80s, and upward. Never, however, will you ever get 100. That's saved for Shakespeare. The catch is, you not only must be willing to rewrite, but you must be *able* to rewrite. Some writers freeze at the mention of a new sentence, word, or comma. They feel they have worked on a play or even a scene so often, there's nothing more they can say about it. This happened to me once in a play I was doing with Mike Nichols. I was stuck and stuck badly. Mike said, calmly, as usual, "Stop trying to fix what you have. Throw it out of your mind. It doesn't exist anymore. Now go back and write it." When I did, I felt liberated from the obligation to fix something that wasn't working. Now I could create something that didn't have a negative history.

In attacking *Come Blow Your Horn* again for what now seemed to be the zillionth rewrite, I felt fresh, renewed, and invigorated. The pages that didn't work in New Hope were now retired to a wastebasket on Long Island and replaced with entirely new words and ideas. Gone were the interminable expository phone calls, now replaced with scenes that dramatized events instead of declaring them. The play started to come to life for me for the first time. I must remind you and myself that as I look back on it today, *Come Blow Your Horn* still remains a very primitive play. But for me at the time it was like climbing out of the primeval slime onto the shore, and carefully heading for firmer ground that would bypass the sands that Max Gordon had warned me about.

I FINISHED the rewrites in six weeks, not months. I delayed sending it to Mike and Billy for fear they'd have less respect for something done so quickly. For me it wasn't quickly. It was written in the time it took me to write it originally.

I spent another month doodling with words here and there and discovered that you can, if you want, rewrite forever. I remember the first model airplane I made when I was a boy. It was balsa wood, and it was all completed and perfect and maybe just needed a shade of sandpapering. In an effort to make it the smoothest model plane in existence, I sandpapered it into smithereens. There *is* a time to stop, and that applies to most things in life.

I sent two copies of the rewritten play to the Messrs. Ellis and Hammerstein with less trepidation than I thought I would have. It felt good to me and I reasoned that if they rejected it, I might still get a producer to put it on, since our production in Bucks County had caused, if not a buzz, at least a flutter. When Mike and Billy read the new script, I got my buzz. They loved it and started to draw up the contracts for the new production. I wanted to add the stipulation that under no circumstances could Mike Ellis get up on the stage opening night and make a speech. Stanley Prager was rehired to direct, and Pert Kelton and Warren Berlinger were asked to repeat their roles. Gene Rayburn was replaced by Hal March, another game-show host. Was there some strain of virus that attracted game-show hosts to this part? Hal March, however, was a first-rate comedian and had been featured in quite a few films and television shows before he was catapulted to prominence as host of *The $64,000 Question*. David Burns was offered something more stable than we could guarantee. He took the lead opposite Carol Channing in *Hello, Dolly!* and was gainfully employed for as long as he wanted. In his place we found Lou Jacobi, whom I remembered as being hilarious when I first saw him in *The Tenth Man*.

Not only did we have a cast, we had the Walnut Theater booked in Philadelphia and the Brooks Atkinson Theatre in New York, albeit tentatively, depending on how it went in Philly according to the Brooks Atkinson's owner, Michael Myerberg. Mr. Myerberg was the original producer of Thornton Wilder's *The Skin of Our Teeth*, and if he was looking for another abstract work of genius from our little comedy, I was worried. Our cast and director, however, were undaunted and pressed on. After four weeks of rehearsal in New York, the cast and I boarded the train for Philadelphia. If my boyhood dream of replacing Joe DiMaggio in center field was not fulfilled, the dream was surpassed by the reality of heading out of town on a train with my first play. I thought of Moss Hart, and his wonderful autobiography, *Act One*, where he described his great thrill of doing exactly what I was doing now. I even wondered if I was sitting in the same seat on the same train heading for the same city he did with his first hit play with Kaufman, *Once in a Lifetime*. I was awakened by the conductor, who told me if I didn't get off I'd be heading for Baltimore. Stosh Prager was standing on the station platform with the rest of the cast, laughing as I stepped off the moving train.

"You weren't going to tell me?" I asked.

"Well, we figured after two or three weeks alone in Baltimore, you'd figure something was wrong and come looking for us."

Later that day, we went through our first technical rehearsal on the set we were seeing for the first time.

"I didn't know there was a window there."

"I thought the door was supposed to open *out* instead of in."

"Steps? We didn't rehearse with steps."

"I can't get through the door with my bundles. We either need a bigger door or smaller bundles."

"Can somebody get the stink out of my bathroom? I think someone left a dead actor from the last show in there."

No doors, no lights, no props worked correctly. The cushions on the chairs were either too soft or too hard, leaving the actors sitting together on the stage all at different heights, looking like a pipe organ. Why did I think everything was supposed to go right as it did in movies made about the theater, like when mammoth curtains parted and there were Fred Astaire and Ginger Rogers on a stage big enough to fit the entire population of Brazil during Carnaval? In real theater it never happens that way. At six o'clock we took a dinner break and went to a local restaurant usually inhabited by a dozen other actors from six different shows all simultaneously trying out in Philadelphia. Television and videocassettes had not yet made their inroads on an audience's desire to see live theater. Suddenly Stosh yelled out to someone at the corner table.

"*Bert!* Bert, it's Stosh!"

There was Bert Lahr sitting with the cast of his latest vehicle. Bert looked at Stosh and said, "I was talking. I told you not to move" . . . then Bert broke up laughing, knowing full well it was at his expense. Stosh introduced me, saying, "This is Doc Simon. The kid's written a funny play, Bert." Bert looked at me and said quite earnestly, but still in that Cowardly Lion's voice, "Is it about anything? If it's not about anything, they won't like it. Make sure it's about something, kid," then wished me good luck and turned back to his party.

When we got back to our table, I asked Stanley worriedly, "*Is* our play about anything?"

"Sure. It's about laughing your fucking head off for two hours. Try the braised beef with horseradish, you'll love it."

AS JOAN AND I were getting dressed in the hotel for the big night, I was reading opening-night telegrams from friends and family. Some of the twenty-odd producers who had taken an interest but passed on the play sent warm best wishes. I thought that was very decent of them. I noticed that Joan was edgy and restrained and barely talking to me, and before we knew it, we were in the middle of an argument. Why and about what, I can't remember, except that it was about something minor and insignificant. It wasn't until later on I realized that Joan was afraid—not of failure, but of success. What would it do to me? What would it do to us? Until now, our seven years together had been the happiest period of our lives, because we had lived it freely, unencumbered, and much the way we wanted. If the play, and indeed I myself, were suddenly thrust into the spotlight, how would that impact on our privacy and our lives? Many years later Dustin Hoffman told me the story of the day he found out he got the part in *The Graduate*. He had auditioned many, many times for director Mike Nichols and finally was summoned to Hollywood to make a screen test. Allegedly, one of the electricians on the soundstage watched Dustin's seemingly unimpressive behavior in front of the camera and said to Dustin after a few takes, "Save your money, kid." Dustin went back to New York, where he was making a meager living in off- and off-off-Broadway plays, although no one disputed his enormous talent. He was living with his wife in a West Side apartment and was expecting a call at three o'clock telling him whether he had landed the role in *The Graduate*. He paced nervously in his bedroom. His wife was in another room far down the hallway when the phone rang. Dustin peeked out of the bedroom and looked at his wife standing near the phone. He looked at her, too nervous himself to pick it up. She did. She murmured a few "yeses" and "I sees" and "Yes, I'll tell him. Thank you," and then quietly hung up the phone. She looked up, and she and Dustin looked at each other for a moment before she spoke, their eyes meeting over the long stretch of hallway. Then she said softly, "You got the part." And Dustin realized at that moment that his marriage was over. It was the most honest and revealing confession anyone had ever made to me, and yet it was so human. The marriage did in time end, and whether it was due to Dustin's enormous success in *The Graduate* and the major triumphs that soon came to him, only his wife and he can say. Yet, in retrospect, I think Joan must have feared something like that as we argued pointlessly before leaving for the theater. It soon passed, however, and we sat in our usual back row aisle seats, her hand on top of mine, squeezing love and encouragement into me as the curtain went up, revealing what the rest of our lives would be like.

HOW ABOUT an opening night when a man in the balcony dies in the first act? Twenty minutes into the play, we heard a woman scream from upstairs, *"Harry!! Harry!! Oh, my God, help me someone!!"* Then came the hustle and bustle of feet running up stairs and down stairs, ushers scattering everywhere. Most people, not knowing the seriousness of the screams, looked up at the balcony annoyed, thinking it was a family squabble or the misbehavior of an out-of-control drunk. Poor Harry died of a heart attack in the upstairs lounge, despite the efforts of the paramedics, who soon whisked Harry and his bereaved wife into a waiting ambulance. Somehow the play carried on, missing only a few beats before laughter soon replaced tragedy. The play was hitting on all cylinders, the actors gaining momentum and confidence as they glided effortlessly from act to act. The final curtain came down to thunderous applause and a partial standing audience. Mike Ellis grabbed me in the back of the theater and hugged me. "What did I tell you?" he beamed. Tally the scorecard. One career started, one life ended. Theater, like life itself, follows the ritual of evolution. Birth, life, death, birth.

It's one thing to get a standing ovation on opening night. It's quite another to read the reviews the morning after. Since the theater is such a unique business, one must view it in a light far different than most entertainment industries. A film opens in anywhere from four hundred to fifteen hundred theaters on a single day. That film will have anywhere from three to five screenings a day in each theater. One single television show can be viewed by millions on any given night. And while a newly published book, granted, is read by only one person in one chair, there may be three hundred thousand people sitting in three hundred thousand chairs all over the country reading that book that day. The total number of critics, in all the cities and towns where those films, television shows, and books are being experienced on that single day, is enormous.

Lo, the poor theater. A play opens in *one* theater, is viewed by not more than twelve hundred people and reviewed by, let's say, thirty critics, and of those thirty, only about five or six have some real clout. If those five or six critics look unfavorably on your work, those other twenty-five won't help save you from a quick demise, unless, as rarely happens, all twenty-five form a united front in highly praising what they saw that night. In other words, success in the theater depends on a *mano a mano* encounter. And the bulls have sharp horns. The audience happens to sit on the horns of that dilemma. They need to be told *officially* by the clout critics that this play is worth coughing up the money for a ticket, sixty dollars in today's world, about six dollars in the world of 1961, which was worth more than today's sixty.

What about word of mouth? Well, that helps a great deal, providing that enough mouths have used enough words by having enough bodies in the seats seeing the show before the producer runs out of money to cover his early losses. If I seem negative about this system, I've misled you. I like it. It's a fair system. Hard, but fair, and maybe only fair because it's the only one we have. So we live with it. The plain fact is, you have to be good. Or popular, which doesn't rule out being good, just as being good doesn't rule out actually being bad. If you're neither good nor popular, you have no legitimate squawk. Just pack up your typewriter, go stare at the clouds somewhere, and try to think of another play. But I digress. Let's move back to Philadelphia.

The phone in our hotel room rang at 7:45 A.M. They had no fear I would be sleeping. Even Joan opened both eyes, watching me reach for the phone.

"Hello?"

"We have the reviews. We're sending them up."

"Tell me. Good or bad?"

"Read them yourself. We'll call you later."

Click.

I looked at Joan. "It doesn't sound good to me."

"Did they say that?"

"They didn't say anything. They just said, 'Read them yourself.'"

"So why do you assume it's negative?"

"Because I'll save time being disappointed. If they're bad, I'll be halfway over my grief."

It took an hour, our time, for the bellboy to deliver them; five minutes his time. We spread the papers out on the bed and turned the pages slowly. When we got to the theater section, I squinted, fearing the sight of blood. We picked the *Philadelphia Bulletin* first because their critic, Ernie Schier, had the most clout. He started his review with, "The theater season has bounced to its feet with *Come Blow Your Horn*, a laugh-happy, bell-ringing farce which opened last night at the Walnut."

I quickly closed the page before I could read any more. Joan said, "Oh my God," as quietly as exuberance could be expressed. Her hands were on both of her cheeks, feeling the warmth that had just flushed into them. My mouth was dry. I was afraid to be jubilant, for fear that his next paragraph would start off with "However . . ."

I opened the page again. Mr. Schier went on: "*Come Blow Your Horn* contains some of the funniest writing and situations since Moss Hart and George S. Kaufman were pounding out their Broadway hits."

I dropped the paper and fell to the floor on my back, arms outstretched beyond my head and my feet spread apart, eyes closed. I looked like a dead gingerbread man. Joan let out a cowboy whoop of joy as she leaped from the bed, landing on top of me. We lay there, looking into each other's eyes, nose to nose, and we kissed and we hugged and somebody had tears in their eyes. Probably me.

In the three and a half weeks we played Philadelphia, we were a virtual sellout. We had a hit. A huge hit. In Philadelphia, that is. If we'd had Mary Martin or Ethel Merman in our cast, the news of our triumph would have sent skyrockets bursting over New York. With a new playwright, however, and a game-show host as our star, the news of our success slipped into New York as unnoticed as an out-of-towner looking for a waiter in Lindy's. Despite a favorable review in *Variety*, the clarion that had awakened the ticket brokers in New York, we arrived in town with an advance sale of a little over two hundred dollars. With six dollars as the top price of a ticket in the orchestra, we were guaranteed to fill at least thirty-three seats for one performance. Since there were a little over a thousand seats at the Brooks Atkinson Theatre, we had as much chance of surviving as a parachutist jumping out of a plane with only a frayed lace handkerchief to hold above his head. We played two previews to adjust to the new acoustics in the theater, and the show ran twelve minutes shorter than in Philadelphia—based on the Newtonian theory that empty seats do not laugh. Nor do they applaud, which made curtain calls both unnecessary and ostentatious.

Opening night, however, was a different story. Every seat was filled and bodies were crammed into the standing room section in the rear. Everyone connected with the show invited every friend and relative they could muster, and if need be, they would have dug up the remains of their grandparents, dressing them and propping them up in their seats with programs glued to their hands and smiles pushed into their faces.

Joan and I dressed quietly at home, mumbling prayers under our breath like bullfighters murmuring novenas at five minutes to four on a Sunday afternoon in Seville. We opened a bottle of little-known champagne and spread grocery-bought caviar on saltine crackers, a ritual which we were to follow for the next twelve years, and toasted our luck to keep the wolf from our door and our suitcases from going to California.

We arrived by cab at the theater a half hour before curtain time. The lobby was jammed with faceless people who spoke a language never before heard by me. I soon realized I was in a state of terror with butterflies in my stomach that had turned into bats driven mad by cheap champagne and reprocessed caviar. The only face I recognized was Max Gordon's. I smiled and waved to him and he looked at me blankly, then turned away to his very attractive companion. Well, I guess he'll have a good time *after* the show. The lights blinked, signaling the play was about to start, much in the same manner the electricians try out their voltage prior to executions at Sing Sing Prison. The witnesses filed into the theater.

Joan and I chose to stand in the rear to keep the pounding of my heart from annoying anyone and causing them to miss a single word of dialogue. The houselights dimmed and the curtain went up. I could not believe my eyes. Somebody must have gotten into the theater in the afternoon and moved the stage back about a quarter of a mile. No, maybe closer to a half a mile. The actors looked to be about three inches tall and their voices sounded like Tinker Bell trapped inside a bottle. My knees buckled under me and I looked aghast at Joan and said, "What happened? I can't see it. I can't hear it. What are we going to do?" She barely looked at me but kept her eyes glued to the stage, a smile on her face, apparently enjoying the proceedings . . . What proceedings? I didn't see any proceedings . . . Suddenly, I heard laughter from the audience. I couldn't imagine what had happened. Maybe someone in the fifth row had said something derisively funny to his friend in the next seat and it soon got passed around the theater, causing gales of laughter from everyone. Joan must have heard it too because now she was also laughing. Was I the only one left out of the joke? Was I the joke? The laughter started to come more rapidly, this time from the balcony as well. Could it possibly be the play that was amusing them so? But how? The actors on stage, now about two miles away, looked and sounded like Lilliputians begging in their tiny voices for the giant Gulliver not to step on them. The first-act curtain came down. Was that possible? It was only up for five minutes. It was supposed to run almost an hour. The houselights went up and people rose from their seats, smiles on their faces as they mingled happily in the aisles. I grabbed Joan's hand and pulled her quickly out into the street, then through the stage door and down into a dark corner in the basement. I grabbed her by the shoulders and looked at her with panic in my eyes.

"What happened? I didn't see it."

"You didn't see what?"

"The play. I didn't see the play. How'd it go?"

"Didn't you hear the audience?"

"How could I hear them? They were all laughing at something."

"I think you need a drink."

"I'm never doing this again. I don't care if it's a hit or a flop, I can't stand the pressure. This is a stupid way to spend your life. Let's move to California. We could be happy there. We could make friends with Ward Bond; he seemed to like us."

Fortunately, Joan didn't hear any of this because she had gone to get me a drink. I continued ranting to myself until she returned. She handed me a half-filled bottle of cheap brandy and I started guzzling it in the dark, looking like Ray Milland on the Monday through Friday prior to *The Lost Weekend*. She carefully led me back upstairs to our places just as the houselights were dimming.

"The lights are out. Something happened to the lights."

"They're supposed to go out. The second act is starting."

"Did any people come back?"

"I think they all did. Get ahold of yourself."

"Me? I'm fine. Maybe I'll wait outside."

She grabbed my hand and squeezed it so hard it practically bent my wedding ring. She held me to my spot and escape was impossible. How did this beautiful, five-foot-three girl get so strong? Acts 2 and 3 seemed to go a little better. I actually heard some of it, and fortunately, a few of the stagehands found time out from their card game to move the stage about two football fields closer to the audience. The curtain came down. The audience was on their feet, applauding. Well, not all, but some. Certainly not the deceased grandparents who had to remain until the theater had emptied and relatives could reclaim their inert, smiling corpses. The critics had left en masse as soon as their intuition told them an ending was approaching. I wanted to rush out on the street as they all jumped into their waiting cabs and yell to them, "They're applauding inside. Don't you want to hear them applauding?" Apparently, they didn't.

We went backstage to give praise to the actors and director for their wonderful job, mostly conjecture on my part. Special thanks went to Lou Jacobi, who played the father; he had received huge applause at one inspired piece of business. As he berated his playboy older son for neglecting his duty in the family business and his obligation as a son by failing to get married, his harangue fell on deaf ears, so he turned to an empty chair, leaned over, and pleaded his case to a four-legged upholstered friend: "Do you hear how a son talks to a father? What are you going to do with a boy like that? Heh?" I loved the "Heh," because he was actually asking the chair for a response. We all seemed to recognize that father.

As I made my way unnoticed by the backstage well-wishers—like most anonymous first-time playwrights—I suddenly realized that Joan was not behind me nor anywhere in sight. I fought my way from dressing room to dressing room, exchanged hugs and kisses and congratulations for a play whose future was still undetermined, and went back to look for Joan. I found her near the stage door, sitting on a chair next to the doorman, quietly smoking a cigarette.

"Where were you? I thought you were behind me."

"No. I was here."

"Why didn't you come with me?"

"It's not my world. It's yours."

She said it without rancor or vindictiveness or any feeling I understood. She had stood by me from the beginning to the end of the three years we had waited to get here, but she wanted no part of my life backstage. This pattern continued for most of our married life, and it was a cause of great consternation to me. I felt guilty about something, but what? It was a part of her I never understood, or worse still, should have but never could.

The opening night party was another matter. Our mutual friends and relatives were there and Joan was now her beaming, ebullient self, smiling and making sure everyone had a place to sit and something to eat. But getting there took some doing. We arrived at Sardi's on a cold, blustery night, waited in line to check our coats next to the windy front door, and stood behind a host of first-nighters I neither knew nor recognized. A large man stood on the steps leading up to the second-floor festivities, collecting the printed invitations and barring crashers from hoisting a free meal. I nodded and smiled at him and started up the stairs with Joan, when a stiff arm shot out and blocked my way.

"Invitations, please."

"It's okay. I'm the author."

"Sorry. Invitations only," as he kept us at bay with one arm and lowered the other to permit a couple to go upstairs who had been invited by the wardrobe lady's cousin.

"I don't need an invitation," I said. "I wrote the play."

"That's your job," he said without looking at me. "Mine is to let in only people with invitations."

I looked at Joan, feeling that every ounce of respect she ever had or would have for me was draining away before my eyes. I was about to jump in and risk life and limb to rescue my dignity when Hal March, our star, walked in with his wife, Candy, and stepped quickly into the main room to take the customary standing ovation for any star who opens in any play. He then turned back, saw me, and said, "Hey, babe, what are you standing *here* for?" I looked at him and answered, "Waiting for you, of course." The four of us were admitted quickly and graciously, without invitations. I may not have guts but I am quick with a desperate, snappy answer.

IN THE MIDST of lasagna, creamed chicken, tiny roast beef sandwiches, chianti, vodka, kisses, hugs, and congratulations, a murmur went through the second-floor dining-room crowd: "The reviews are in." The room went silent with anticipation, not much different than when people are listening for those first early returns on election night. Suddenly someone rushed to the telephone booth—a young man with glasses whom I had never seen before, but I assumed was part of our entourage. Why else would he be the one in the phone booth getting the reports from our press agent at our advertising agency? It was so crowded around the booth that I couldn't get closer than twenty feet away. I had to stand on a chair and raise myself on my toes to get a view of what was happening. As I craned my neck, I could see the head of the young man. He had something of a smile on his face and was nodding into the phone more than speaking into it. Nodding seemed promising. Joan, standing miles down on the floor beside me, tugged on my pants leg like a child wanting to hear what the Macy's Thanksgiving Day Parade looked like. There was more nodding from the foreign correspondent at the front, then he quickly hung up and opened the folding door, a broad smile on his face.

He held up his right hand in the air for all to see, clenched his fist, and gave us a thumbs-down.

A thumbs-down?? Then why was he smiling? Why was he nodding? What was he so happy about, and who was this little shit that no one seemed to know when I asked them? It was, obviously, a bad review. I never found out who the review was from or who the young man was who took such delight in telling the opening-night crowd that so far our show stunk. The bad review suddenly took a distant second place to my concerns about the manner in which some people were so happy and eager to inform you that you didn't do well. In that moment, I realized I was in a cold and uncaring business, not at its core, but at least in the ruthlessly competitive areas, and I learned from that night on to keep my guard up. Conversely, I also knew that if the kid in glasses heard a rave review on the other end, he would have given us a cheering thumbs-up, cashing in as the bearer of good news, jumping out of the phone booth, hugging and kissing everyone as if he had written, directed, starred in, and put up most of the money for Broadway's newest hit. If ever I seemed distrustful and distant on opening nights in the ensuing years, you can lay the blame on that phone call on the second floor of Sardi's.

By morning I had read most of the reviews.

The New York Times: "In *Come Blow Your Horn*, Neil Simon has put together an old-fashioned Broadway product that seemed to have gone out of fashion—a slick, lively, funny comedy. Its subject matter is thin, but it is smoothly plotted and deftly written. Best of all, he has provided some explosively hilarious moments rooted in character."

Thank you, Howard Taubman.

The *Journal-American*: "The audience at the opening of *Come Blow Your Horn* whistled, screamed, and all but tore up the seats in approval of this new comedy by Neil Simon last night. And indeed, it is funny—but it *isn't that funny.*"

So said John McClain. At least he was fair enough to report that the audience liked it, even if he himself wasn't all agog. I put that down on the list of good reviews, but it *wasn't that good.*

The *New York Mirror*: "*Come Blow Your Horn* isn't much of a play but it shoots off laughs with the rapidity of a machine gun. That's thanks to an excellent cast of farceurs who really know how to explode gags."

Thus spake Robert Coleman. It was the first but certainly not the last time

I was accused of shooting off "machine gun" laughs. I was fast becoming "Rat-a-tat-tat Simon," the laugh mobster of New York.

The *New York Post*: "With a certain amount of reluctance, I must concede that much of *Come Blow Your Horn* is entertaining. The play, which is always a trifle ramshackle, does keep growing in effectiveness and the third act is quite delightful. Nor can Mr. Simon's ability to write a good amusing line be dismissed from attention."

Richard Watts, as far as I was concerned, always told it like it was. Over the years, I found him to be a compassionate reviewer though not easy; he was not quick to maim or bury aspiring playwrights, unlike some of our latter-day critics, who follow the pattern of today's society—use a gun if necessary. Mr. Watts didn't throw his hat in the air for our play, but he did tip it slightly in our direction, just enough to offer encouragement that I could have a career in the theater, if I was able to elevate my aspirations.

As for the other reviews, there were a few out-and-out pans, conveniently lost by me, and an occasional rave—but nothing to compare to Ernest Schier's line, "the funniest writing and situations since Moss Hart and George S. Kaufman." All in all, I thought I was treated fairly, since there was some consistency to the critics' opinions. Our little ship was still afloat, if not exactly sailing high into New York Harbor with steam horns blasting from all three stacks. The next day would be the crucial test, when the box office would or would not respond to the critics' scorecard. The box office opened at 10 A.M. If it was a hit, a line would be forming outside the theater by 9 A.M. I arrived at 10:30, hoping to see a policeman on horseback trying to herd back the hungry ticket buyers. What I saw upon my arrival was an empty lobby. The only man near the box office was the doorman, prepared to keep the hordes of scalpers from grabbing up all the best seats. Instead, he and the lonely man sitting inside the box-office window, with stacks of unsold tickets behind him in the racks, chatted together while they drank coffee from cardboard cups.

I went backstage and saw a glum trio sitting in the second row, still with their hats and coats on and their feet up on the empty row in front of them. They were Mike Ellis, Billy Hammerstein, and Wally Fried, our company manager. Even in the confines of the darkened theater, I could clearly see the cloud of gloom that hung ominously over their unhappy faces.

"I guess we're in a little trouble," I said, half mockingly and half suicidally.

Billy Hammerstein's eyebrows raised a half inch, then came down slowly in a death shrug, showing the virtuosity of his other facial muscles. Mike

Ellis came right to the point. "We put up the closing notice. The show's over Saturday night."

I wasn't shocked or stunned. The empty lobby outside had already taken care of those two reactions. Possibly what I was hoping for was a last-minute rousing pep talk from a football coach from Notre Dame. "What's wrong with you boys? Sure we may be down at halftime, but we're not dead by a long shot. Now let's get out there and fight, fight, fight!" There was no Notre Dame in Mike Ellis and Billy Hammerstein, but out of nowhere came a Brooklyn College version of a Knute Rockne speech. It was from Wally Fried, whom I hardly knew up till this point. But he was clearly more experienced in the "getting to the public" business than all three of us put together.

"I wish you guys would listen to me," Wally pleaded. "This is not a critic's show. It's an audience's show. You saw that in Philadelphia. Sold out for three weeks and not a single walkout, except for the guy who died in the balcony—and even he didn't want to go."

Billy peered up from under the brim of his hat. "Okay, so it's an audience's show. So where's the audience?"

"Out there on the streets," said Wally, working up a steam of optimism. "Only they don't know the show is that funny yet. We have to show them. Let's paper the house. Give the tickets away on street corners. Send them to nurses in hospitals, to soldiers at the USO. Put a kid in front of Sardi's at lunch- and dinnertime and hand them out. Get the bodies in here and watch the word of mouth."

I chimed in. "But if we give the tickets away for free, won't the word spread to other people who want to get in for free?"

"Of course," said Wally. "We just do it for a week, maybe ten days, then we stop. We act like it's a hard ticket to get. If we don't start selling some tickets by then, we close. But this way, you've got a fighting chance."

Wally was inspiring. I suddenly saw a bluebird flying over the stage. Okay, so it was a large moth, but hope usually distorts the truth in an effort to overcome reality. Billy Hammerstein tipped his hat back so that we could finally see his eyes. He looked at Mike Ellis and said, "Let's give it a shot." He suddenly sounded like Captain John Paul Jones. Everyone to battle stations, men.

That afternoon we had five kids out on the street and in front of Sardi's handing out tickets for a brand-new show, which had received some really-good-to-fair reviews, for absolutely no charge at all. The passersby were skeptical. After all, these were jaded New Yorkers. They could understand discount tickets, but free tickets must mean it's a real clinker. Most took them, some handed them back, others threw them in wastebaskets, and some put them in their pockets without much interest. But somehow, through Wally's magic, about three hundred people showed up at the theater that night. They were a little disappointed that the Cokes and chocolate-covered mints weren't free as well, but their response to the show was enormous. The next night we sold about a hundred tickets and had about four hundred on the cuff. It was a slow, arduous, and costly process, but we all cut our royalties and the theater owner chipped back some of his take as well. It was a community sacrifice. Although we were making some progress, if the numbers didn't reverse to more tickets bought than those given away for free we'd be gone in a few days. That Friday night we sold about three hundred tickets and packed the rest of the house, with almost eight hundred tickets given to every off-duty nurse, bored soldier or sailor, or out-of-town visitor, all of whom thought New York was truly a wonderland and never knew theater tickets usually weren't free. Mike Ellis, ever the pragmatist, said we'd give it till Wednesday but if some major turnaround didn't happen by then, we were throwing in the towel. "Why don't we give away free towels?" I offered in jest. Jests were not in fashion that week at the Brooks Atkinson Theatre. The next three days didn't improve much in the dollar department. We still had packed houses, but at those prices, why not? What we needed now was a miracle. That Monday night, the miracle happened.

Irving "Swifty" Lazar, the diminutive, dynamic agent, was a powerhouse who stood five foot nothing and represented half the great literary figures on both continents and was fast closing in on Asia. He spent half his life on the phone with the likes of Ernest Hemingway and Irwin Shaw and James Jones and Noël Coward and the other half with the heads of every major New York publishing house and Hollywood film studio. In between, he managed to take three to four showers a day. Irving had an "out, damned spot" complex but it didn't stop him from traveling to every dingy corner of the world, defying disease and decay from Calcutta to Khartoum, packing an extra-large suitcase with Lysol disinfectant. He didn't look strong enough to get his first serve over in Ping-Pong, but he would ski down every Alp, ride an Arabian horse like a sheikh, and handle a rifle at the foot of Kilimanjaro if it meant getting a shot at signing Norman Mailer or William Styron.

Since I was soon to become a failed playwright, or as George Axelrod, author of *The Seven Year Itch*, named someone who only did it once, "a play-wrote," it was highly unlikely that Irving Lazar would soon be crossing paths with the likes of me. Even in a shower. Three nights before the final curtain was to fall, closing the first and last chapter on my playwroting career, Irving Lazar was in New York, as was Noël Coward, as was Fate, who fortunately decided not to go to Cincinnati that night. Noël Coward, not surprisingly, was an avid theatergoer, and having seen everything in New York with one night to spare, went on Swifty's hunch that they might have a few chuckles at this *Come Blow Your Horn* thing. I was not at the theater that night. If I were and knew that Noël Coward was in the audience, it would have taken a Saint Bernard with a keg of brandy around his collar to get me through the evening.

Leonard Lyons, the noted columnist for the *New York Post*, was head and shoulders above his peers. He never dawdled with cheap gossip. He was a raconteur in ink. His column, which ran from top to bottom on the page, was filled with anecdotes and generally amusing stories of the rich, the famous, the talented, and the notorious. He met them all on his nightly rounds of every club, restaurant, party, opening, opera, or ball game. He didn't drop names. He placed them carefully and artfully at the head of every paragraph like a diamond in Tiffany's window. You couldn't pass by without looking. Items like:

"The Aga Khan was eating a steak at '21' last night, adding calories to his already great fortune."

"As I entered Toots Shor's beanery, Joe DiMaggio in his usual corner table was telling the young Mickey Mantle how to look out for the sprinkler holes while chasing down fly balls in center field."

And then one day, out of the blue, unbelievably, like a gift from heaven, this:

"Noël Coward looked up from his chili con carne while Irving 'Swifty' Lazar noticed that his eggs benedict looked like a Picasso. 'I've just seen the funniest play in New York,' said Noël. 'Swifty, dear boy, what was the name of it?' '*Come Blow Your Horn*,' Lazar said as he cut into his priceless Picasso."

You couldn't buy, rent, or steal that kind of publicity. The next morning there were twenty-five people on line at the box office. By that weekend, the Brooks Atkinson Theatre was two-thirds filled and every seat was bought and paid for. We dipped again on the usually hard-to-sell Monday and Tuesday performances. On Wednesday, Leonard Lyons rode to the rescue again and who was leading the charge? Irving Lazar. This time he brought Groucho Marx to the play. In Lyons' column the next day, Groucho was reported saying, "I laughed my head off at *Come Blow Your Horn*. And for me that's an improvement." There was a line again that night in the lobby. All the good reviews, all the good word of mouth couldn't add up to just two quotes from Noël Coward and Groucho Marx. Billy Hammerstein and Mike Ellis took down the closing notice. The play ran for close to two years, never much more than at half capacity, but it paid off and then some. Paramount made a film offer, which included my writing the screenplay if I chose to. Now, thirty-five years later, I still receive royalties on the stock and amateur productions that continue to play all over the world.

The joy, the exaltation, the euphoria lasted about a month. Then one night, about two in the morning, Joan turned on the light and saw me sitting up in bed, staring into space.

"What's wrong?" she asked.

"What do I do now?" I said.

THE GIRL FROM BLACK MOUNTAIN

4

I TURNED DOWN the option to write the screenplay for Paramount. There went seventy-five thousand dollars, but I had about two inches of my foot in the door of the theater and was not about to give up my toehold to the beckoning finger of Hollywood. They went on without me to make the film of *Come Blow Your Horn*, starring Frank Sinatra, and I was anything but pleased with the results. Whatever charm the play might have had was lost in a ring-a-ding-ding pseudo-hip Hollywood comedy that had more glitz than wit. It was a profitable picture for Paramount, opening at the Radio City Music Hall, and although I walked by it twenty times to see a title of mine on the marquee, I was up to more important things. I cut the umbilical cord that had tied me and fed me through the television tubes and set up shop as a full-time playwright. I went in search of an office, my very own, a room with a view of my future, cut off from the security of a weekly paycheck but freed from the bondage of having to satisfy someone else's demands of what they wanted me to write.

I found my refuge atop a four-story walk-up in a brownstone right next door to the Paris Theater, an art-film house on Fifty-eighth Street just off Fifth Avenue, facing the Plaza Hotel. It was a large, single room with dark oak-paneled walls left over from the Age of Innocence, when it was once the sole domain of one of New York's wealthy families. It had a fireplace, not usable, and a view, not visible because of the clinging vines outside the window that must have started clinging before the house was built. But to me it was heaven. I furnished it sparsely with a small sofa, a desk, a typewriter, a chair, and a lamp. I put up the final touch, a dartboard, just to get my mind limbered up in the mornings before I started to attack the dozens of unformed ideas I had for new plays. Not satisfied with just trying to hit the bull's-eye, I devised a dart baseball game. Outs were anything in the outer perimeter of the board, singles were in the first inner circle, doubles and triples were in the third inner circle, and a home run was a bull's-eye. What started out as a minor diversion soon became a one-hundred-game season, culminating in the Yankees playing the St. Louis Cardinals in the World Series.

I spent the first two months in that room entirely engrossed by the outcome of that championship season. Not only did I not put down a single word on paper, I rarely answered the telephone. Soon I began to send out for lunch, especially when my beloved Yankees were getting triples and homers in clusters. When batting for the Cardinals, I kept my integrity by aiming really hard for the bull's-eye, but if the dart missed its mark, I exclaimed audibly and sportingly, "Too bad, kid. Nice try." For two months I lied to Joan. I told her the new play I was feverishly working on was coming along nicely, but it was too soon to talk about it. I began to leave for my office earlier each morning, sometimes skipping breakfast because I was coming up to the last few crucial games of the series. Autumn madness came to an abrupt halt when I reluctantly took a call from my business manager. Did I neglect to say I had acquired a business manager? I didn't have that much business to manage, but I had been advised by friends that I was now in the business-manager bracket. I didn't know that one play made a bracket. Admittedly I was a novice at business and, quite frankly, had very little interest in it. Investing money to me was a gamble, and the only thing I was willing to gamble on was my time and what I could write in that time. Still, I might be foolish in not taking advantage of all the golden opportunities that were now being set before my eyes.

As I was led into the impressive offices of the duly recommended business manager, intimidation took over. I was taken in by anyone who had plaques on his wall and photographs of celebrities with their arms around him. It didn't occur to me that it didn't necessarily mean they were clients. At any wedding, communion, or bar mitzvah, it's not hard to get your picture taken with a notable friend of the friend who invited you. Six degrees of separation from the high and mighty can sometimes be only two degrees. I sat in the chair opposite the Great Investor feeling that my feet didn't quite touch the floor. I should have come with a grown-up. I nodded at everything the Great Man said to me in his fast-talking financial mumbo-jumbo, pretending I understood everything about debentures, tax shelters, depreciation on investments, and appreciation of capital. My mind kept wandering to other things as his lips kept moving rapidly and seemingly silently, and I felt as if my life had just jumped into an Ingmar Bergman film without the English subtitles. I thought if I said "yah, yah" a few times, I might make an impression on him. Finally I was told that because of my now prominent status in the entertainment business (apparently he hadn't heard that I couldn't get into my own opening-night party at Sardi's), I was being allowed to invest with an otherwise exclusive financial group who had the inside track on all the best deals now being made on Wall Street. I wondered if our "group" would meet once a month at the "club" and have brandy and cigars and talk about fortunes made and suicides committed. I tried hard not to let the Great Man see how my opportunistic glands were salivating.

I came home that night and told Joan the great news. I had just invested twenty-five thousand dollars in a tax shelter whereby we owned cattle in Wyoming. Joan was thrilled because of her natural love of animals. She even planned on going out west that summer so the family could give names to all of our cattle. I didn't have the heart to tell her our cattle was for eating, not cuddling. As it happened, it turned out to be for neither. The telephone call that caught me with dart poised in hand as the Yankees were coming to bat was from my business manager. There was solemnity in his voice. A winter blizzard had come up in Wyoming and froze my investment to death. Twenty-five thousand dollars were lying stiff in the tundra, hooves pointing up at the sky. If they were a tax shelter, why the hell didn't they take cover under the shelter? When I told Joan, her tears were shed in mourning over the cattle, not at my fiscal wipe-out. This was the first of many financial disasters in my career, none of which I had the foresight to avert, even after changing business managers after each carnage that reduced my life's savings. The World Series came to an abrupt and incomplete finish. I went quickly back to work while I still had enough to ward off destitution, and wondered why I didn't have the sense to have invested in lamb chops, baked potatoes, and sour cream.

HEEDING THE ADVICE of Max Gordon, I kept thinking of characters, not stories or plots. Who did I know that I found interesting, unusual, intelligent, and complex, someone I thought the audience would care about? I was about to ask Joan for a suggestion when I stopped. Who else but Joan herself? If I could put all the charm, the warmth, the humor, the passion, and the uniqueness of Joan on the stage, I felt the audience would fall in love with her as quickly as I did.

From the first moment I met her in 1952 at Camp Tamiment, the summer resort in the Pocono Mountains in Pennsylvania, I was taken not only by the intense beauty of her face, the lissomeness and athleticism of her body, but by the unpredictability of her nature, the open abundant smile that gave a glimpse into her joyful, sunny, and warm disposition, and then suddenly that stern look that could cross her face as quickly as a summer squall, giving a hint into a darker and angrier side.

There was in her a complexity and intelligence I had never met in a woman before. She had gone to school at Black Mountain College in North Carolina, an experiment in higher education that attracted the most esoteric and groundbreaking group of students and faculty that wisdom and intellectual curiosity could bring together. Black Mountain caused quite a stir in academia in the late forties and early fifties. It was more of a farm than it was a campus, but it wasn't agriculture it had on its mind. She may have been on a tractor in the mornings but in the afternoons she studied poetry with William Carlos Williams. I didn't actually meet her in 1952. I saw her. She was a counselor at the children's camp that was adjacent to Tamiment. My brother and I were on the entertainment staff, writing comedy sketches for the hour-and-a-half variety shows presented each weekend of the ten-week summer. I would see her briefly on the tennis courts whacking the ball across the net with power that belied her size, or riding a horse, or leading a group of happy kids on a hike through the woods. I envied every one of those eight-year-olds. I never met her then because she was engaged to a Harvard Law student, a bright young man and the son of a prominent figure in the New York labor unions. They were to be married that winter. It took Ira Gershwin to encapsulate my thoughts: "They're writing songs of love but not for me."

In 1953 Danny and I went back to Tamiment. We were still making only twenty dollars a week for the ten-week summer, but the opportunity to hone our craft by writing for live audiences was a great allure to us, not to mention the opportunity we had to meet pretty young girls who came up in buses, trains, and family cars, staying for a week, to be replaced by the next entourage the following Monday morning. Since most of the resort guests were single, those of us who worked on the entertainment staff held some mystic allure to the new guests who came in from New York, Philadelphia, and New Jersey. True, we were mere novices ourselves, but any actor, actress, dancer, or writer appeared to be worldly and exotic to those who spent their lives as salespeople, dental assistants, or accountants. Marriage was on the minds of many, romance for the most idealistic, and sex for more than I even imagined.

Speaking for myself and Danny, we would have *paid* twenty dollars a week for this opportunity. We roamed the social hall nightly where the big band on the stand did their part in setting the scene, with their Glenn Miller– and Tommy Dorsey–style renditions of irresistible love songs wafting over the lake on moonlit nights; it was even better when rain pelted the windows and the soft overhead lighting made even the plainest look like the fairest. Danny chose to circle, I chose to stand in the doorway, arms folded, one leg crossed over the other as I leaned against the wall and looked disdainfully bored, waiting for the opportunity to mention I was a writer. I was so cool, when two pretty girls walked by and smiled "Hi," I barely mumbled a reply and continued gazing into my boredom. The truth was I was still painfully shy and woefully inexperienced in the art of wooing a woman into anything that resembled a car, a blanket on the lawn, my room, her room, a canoe, or a bench on the darkened tennis courts. I was too naive to notice they had already said yes to me while I went on just trying to lure them out of the social hall. Even after we were together, alone in the shadows of her cabin, I was still maneuvering while she watched me from the bed, half dressed and bewildered that I was still talking instead of unbuttoning.

It couldn't be this easy, I thought. I was a late bloomer, and even in the era of late bloomers, I began to think I'd never make it into the florist's shop. It didn't happen until I was twenty-one and that was even after a year and a half in the Air Force, stationed in Biloxi, Mississippi, and Denver, Colorado. Did I meet girls? Oh, yes. Dozens and dozens. Did they like me? It seemed that way. I thought, however, my charm was because I never made a move on them. Kissing, petting, and talking were my specialties. If talking counts as a score, I had more women than you can imagine. As for the act itself, I needed a hint from the girl, like throwing me down on the bed and scream-ing, "You're not getting out of here until you do it to me." This didn't come up too frequently. On occasion, my hands, now thoroughly disgusted with my lack of initiative, would start to roam on their own, fed up with waiting for *me* to make a decision. I sometimes followed their lead but if the girl would show the slightest timidity in my going all the way, I backed off, never noticing the look of disappointment or boredom in her face. Some thought it was because I didn't like them, others because I was shy, and still others thought I was just being cool even before cool got to be cool.

But coolness got me no further than shyness. At twenty-one, I was a hor-monal fault in the earth just waiting for the girl, the time, and the place to shift my plates. My brother, Danny, on the other hand, never met a woman he didn't want to bed and never even waited for the bed to accomplish his desires. To him, sex was a shooting gallery, and every duck that popped up was more desirable than the last one. He rarely missed. He was so outrageously aggressive, he could tell within five minutes of meeting a girl whether she would or wouldn't. He was so quick, even if the girl thought she wouldn't, she soon found out she did. If I was a late bloomer, he was the Botanical Gardens. If he even sensed a turn-down, he moved on quickly. He had no time to waste and it was rare that Danny ever wasted his time. The contrast in our behavior and attempted seductions was enormous. This was all, of course, in a pre-AIDS world. He was a man of his time, the last of the great gunfighters. If I thought he was crass, I was wrong. Women loved Danny, long after their affairs were history. They wanted to mother him, take care of him, or just spend time with him. Who else, then, would I turn to in my time of need?

Soon after my twenty-first birthday, Danny said, "Enough is enough." He took me, willingly but shakingly, to a grim hotel in the Grim section of Manhattan. I sat on a chair in the lobby trying to look like a war veteran just released from a hospital where my wounds recently healed, while Danny stood behind a limp palmlike tree talking to a cigarette held up by a woman's face. She nodded, stomped the cigarette out in the potted plant, and walked toward the elevator with nary a look in my direction. This was not going to be a lasting and devoted relationship, I thought, quickly assessing the situation. Danny signaled for me to walk toward the elevator. I tried my best to appear as though the young virgin who was originally scheduled to be there had suddenly taken ill, and I, a professional dancer at the Latin Casino nightclub, was going to fill in so as not to make the young woman's evening a waste of time and income.

As I got closer, I noticed the young woman was not actually young, but she was attractive in that sort of "hanging around the docks" way. Danny mumbled her name to me but it didn't really register since I thought there was little chance of it coming up in the ensuing hour. Or more likely, five to ten minutes. The elevator opened and Danny gave me a wink and headed out of the hotel. I was flabbergasted. For some insane reason, I thought Danny would be coming up with us. I'm not sure what I expected Danny to do up there for me. Perhaps act as my second, help me undress, give me some last-minute instructions, maybe even give me a foot up as I began to ascend the bed.

The elevator door slammed shut and the elderly operator never even asked for a floor number. Aha! This has happened before, I quickly surmised. In the ride up, the woman never said a word. She never even looked at me. Well, what was I expecting? That we'd hold hands? We were let off on the fifth floor and I followed her wordlessly down a hallway which made the word "dingy" seem hopelessly inadequate. She opened the door to the room, leaving the splendor of the hallway far behind us. There was a bed, a chair, a bureau, a bathroom, and a window. I felt I had three options. To sit on the chair, take a bath, or jump out the window. She walked over to the bureau, opened her purse, took out a small notebook, and jotted something in it. The book was well worn and she was writing in the back of it, giving me a clear idea of how many others had preceded me into this boudoir from hell. She took off her coat, hung it up in a closet that no self-respecting moth would visit, and started to remove her costume jewelry, carefully placing each piece on top of the bureau. No doubt some ingrate had run off with all her jewelry in a previous encounter and she had to make up the lost nine dollars' worth herself.

It was at this point I noticed something very interesting. She didn't seem to know I was in the room. She still hadn't looked at me or addressed me by name or gender. I decided to make a definitive choice. I sat on the chair, still with all my clothes on, including my raincoat, clasped my hands together, hung my head down, and gazed at the floor. I was not going to do a thing until I was given explicit instructions.

"You all right, honey?" I suddenly heard from across the room.

I looked up.

"Me? Oh, yeah, I'm fine. Just didn't want to rush you."

I heard concern but no instructions, so I held my ground. This time, however, I didn't look down. She was undressing, not slowly, not teasingly, not tauntingly, just undressing, as if readying herself for a physical examination. It suddenly became clear to me why she made a living at this. She was in very good shape. Terrific shape, if you really want to know. The dress came off, the shoes came off, the stockings and garters came off, and she was now up to the bra and panties. Surely she would remove those in the bathroom or under the bedsheets. No chance. The bra came off, then the panties, and the only thing left to take off was her wristwatch.

She walked to the bed, sat down on the edge, crossed her legs, smiled at me with her eyebrows, and took the watch off. She placed it face up on the nightstand next to the bed. Obviously this adventure had a time limit.

She needn't have bothered. I was willing to pay for what I had just seen and thank her for a wonderful and rewarding evening. The truth was that at that moment, I didn't like her all that much but I was hopelessly in love with her. I wondered if marriage was out of the question but with that watch ticking away through our senior years, it would cost me a bloody fortune. She sat up in the bed and lit a cigarette and I knew it was my time to undress. Amazingly, without any previous experience, I managed to take off all my clothes without for a moment revealing any private part of my body. She was not impressed. I hopped on to the other side of the bed, pulling the sheet over my waist, and propped my head up with my hand and my elbow pressed against the bed looking at her as if we were going to discuss the latest French film we had just seen, probably *Les Enfants du Paradis*. She took another drag on her cigarette and I knew I had about two more puffs before I would be called to action. I tried to look rueful and pensive, as if I were still dealing with a great loss in my recent past, hoping to evoke a sign of compassion from her. She took another drag and looked at her watch.

"I'm here, honey. You got something else you want to do?"

"No, no. No. Just waiting for you to get through with your cigarette."

She mangled it in the ashtray, slid downward, and I knew that conversation was no longer my ally. She took my hand and put it on her breast like a gas station attendant pointing to a map and telling me how to get to Route 405. If I knew what happened in the ensuing minutes, I would describe them in great detail. What I remember, however, was not much different than slipping into that timeless zone after a shot of liquid Demerol just prior to having disc surgery. I could hear voices, one possibly my own, but had no sense of place, feeling, understanding, or reality. The only word I clearly remember was her saying, "Relax." "Relax" was usually followed by "honey," "sweetie," "babe," or "kid." What amazed me was that there were actually men before my time who had achieved the state of "relaxed," and at that moment, they were the faceless superheroes of my life. I faintly remember the sounds of my own grunts and groans, none of them emanating from a source of pleasure but rather from the futile effort of what seemed like trying to squeeze my entire body into a tube of toothpaste. And still the incessant and humiliating attempts to ease my struggle with "Relax, sugar. I'm on your side."

I would have paid her double the money if she would have let me get up and go home, running and dressing in the hallway if need be, and I would have doubled *that* money if she never entered my name in her worn little book, for fear some Masters and Johnson research group would buy it from her and reveal all to the world. Then, by some miracle, a sudden explosion gave relief to my tortured body, and as I lay limply on my side in a profusion of sweat, I thought I might not be suited for sex but I might be very good at giving birth to babies.

In the next few minutes, as she lit another cigarette, we actually made a small dent in the conversation. I asked questions, she gave vague answers.

"Where are you from?"

"Upstate."

"Upstate New York?"

"No. Just Upstate."

"Do you get many . . . you know . . . guys like me?"

"No, honey. You were the best. The absolute best."

"You're kidding, right?"

She looked at her watch. "I've got twenty minutes to get uptown."

"You mean you've got another . . . you know . . . appointment?"

"You know any doctors who only have one patient?"

She slipped her watch on and crossed the room, putting her stockings on first. I looked at her voluptuous body and wanted to sing, "Bess, You Is My Woman Now." I tried one last time at conversation. I asked her who was the best lover she ever had. I suddenly realized it was an adolescent and impertinent question, even given our cash-and-carry situation, but she took no offense. She stared out the window for a moment, not lost in thought but in memory.

"A man I knew a few years ago. He was older."

"How old?"

"Fifty-four."

She continued getting dressed and I could tell she didn't want to go any further with that one. I had touched a nerve I never would have expected to have existed in her mind or body. Once there was a good time in her life, and from the look in her eyes, it would never come back again. I dressed quickly and placed the twenty dollars on the nightstand as Danny had instructed me. I felt better about not having to bring up the subject of money at all. She was half dressed and redoing her makeup in the mirror as I opened the door, wondering how to end the evening.

"It was er . . . nice meeting you."

She said, "Yeah," and waved to me with her back still toward me.

I rode down the elevator wondering if the elderly operator could sense the enormous change that had come over me. He never took his eyes off the *Daily News* sports section.

By the time I got back to the apartment Danny and I were now sharing on the Upper West Side, he was in bed, about to turn off the light.

"How'd it go?" he asked as he yawned.

"It was good," I answered, hoping that understatement would be a sign of my newfound maturity.

His light went off, and as I pulled my shoes off in the dark, he asked, "Did you leave the money like I said?"

"Yeah. I left the twenty on the nightstand and left."

His light went back on.

"Twenty? . . . I said fifteen. It took me a half hour to talk her out of twenty. When are you going to learn?"

I thought I just did.

I NO LONGER NEEDED Danny to give me a leg up, but I could have used some expert advice in spotting dangerous choices in the matter of bed partners. I was as gullible in that area as I was naive in business matters. When I was twenty-three, I met a very attractive woman at a friend's party. She was a dark-haired, olive-skinned beauty of about twenty-eight. After being introduced by our host, we immediately fell into easy conversation and, as happens in quick, mutual attraction, felt as though we had known each other for years. I felt a relationship about to blossom. The party seemed to be drawing to a close as more and more coats kept disappearing from the bed inside. I asked if I could take her home. She thanked me but said she had to meet her cousin a few blocks away. I asked for her phone number but she said it would be better if I gave her mine. It wasn't hesitancy I sensed from her but rather her own way of controlling the situation. If I had any doubts of her interest in me, they were quickly erased by the intensity of our good-night kiss at the elevator. Even in that kiss I felt that she was in charge and I was the recipient of her strong feelings.

A week went by and when the phone rang, I was relieved to hear her voice. She was warm and seductive in the way she told me she had been thinking of me and wanted to call but couldn't because she had been out of town. I asked when we could meet and she said tomorrow night at seven. Though this was not said in a whisper, the volume of her voice was down a few decibels. The seven o'clock time wasn't even negotiable.

"Shall I pick you up?" I asked.

"No. I'll come to your place. Give me your address."

"What about dinner?"

"Whatever you want."

I gave her my address and heard the click on the other end just as I was saying, "Well, I look forward to see—"

There were only two possibilities. She was either married or a member of the CIA. It could also be that an over-protective parent or a very demanding employer monitored her every move. Or possibly she was crazy as hell. In the meantime, what should I do about dinner? Book a restaurant, order in some Chinese, or stock up on canned goods and crackers? This suddenly made my first-time experience in the grim midtown hotel seem as innocent as my high school prom.

Our apartment was on the ground floor, what they laughingly call a garden apartment. About three potted plants could barely squeeze into the outside "garden," and the plants would have to give up any thought of ever growing. At seven o'clock on the dot, the doorbell rang. I pressed the buzzer to the outside door and opened my own door. She looked gorgeous even though most of her face was covered with a large, expensive Italian silk scarf. I opened my arms to greet her but she pushed me back into the apartment and locked the door behind her. She gave me the kind of kiss that would be banned in late thirties movies. As my lungs searched hard to find where my breath was, she was moving quickly around the apartment pulling down shades, drawing curtains, and locking the door to my miniature garden. All this without saying a word to me. The possibilities quickly narrowed. She was married or she was totally out of her mind, or very possibly both. But God, was she beautiful.

The question of food never came up in the next hour. Make that an hour and a half. At one point in the proceedings, I could have sworn she let in her two identical sisters, because one woman could not possibly cover all that territory by herself. Finally, she went into the bathroom, stayed about twenty minutes, and came out with a towel turbaned perfectly over her wet hair and another draped around her body. She sat on a chair at the far side of the room, her legs tucked neatly under her, and asked if I had any Amaretto. Amaretto? It sounded like a drink but for all I knew it could have been an after-shave lotion. She settled for the beer I kept in the refrigerator and waved off my offer of a glass. She finally took a deep breath, the first since she had arrived, as she leaned her head back and gazed at the ceiling.

"God, we must be crazy," she said.

The words "we" and "crazy" in the same sentence got my attention very quickly. I suddenly felt like a coconspirator to a crime I had no idea we had committed.

"Are you married?" I asked, deciding to get right to the felony.

"Christ, no," she answered. "You think I'd marry *him*?"

Two things now became frighteningly apparent. There was a "him" and there was something so awful about "him" that she'd never consider "marrying" him.

I smiled, trying to appear as if I had these conversations regularly. "Who's 'him'? Your boyfriend?"

She laughed. "Boyfriend? . . . Listen, he's not a boy and he's not a friend. You don't want to know."

No, I didn't, but I asked anyway. "So what is he?"

She took a long time in answering, mostly because she kept thinking she heard sounds in the apartment above. "Who lives just above you?"

I looked up at the ceiling. "No one. A woman. About eighty, eighty-five. Why?"

She didn't waste time answering. "He's someone I see. Actually, he's a good guy. But if he walked in here right now, you know what would happen to us? . . . By the time the police found our bodies, they wouldn't be able to tell which one was which."

I suddenly felt the need of a large Amaretto. I stopped asking questions. I realize now that if this had happened four years later, my frozen feet would have been sticking up out of the snow right next to my frozen cattle.

Why didn't Danny warn me about times like this? He was still sore because I paid twenty dollars instead of fifteen.

I didn't hear from her for quite some time. I hoped, no, "prayed," that "him" asked "her" to become "his." Then twice while I was out, she rang and told Danny to say she had called. No forwarding number. Fine with me. I was not about to dial my own death sentence. One night six months later, I was walking past the theater on Broadway that now houses the *Late Show with David Letterman*. It was a crisp night, and I had my hands in my coat pockets and my head down to avoid the chilling wind. I suddenly looked up and there she was, five feet in front of me, walking toward me with a man a good three inches shorter than she was and a good fifteen years older. He had her arm wrapped tightly in his. My eyes opened in recognition and a fatal "Hi" was about to fall from my lips when her eyes signaled in a split second, "Make a sound and we're both dead. Right here on Broadway." My open mouth quickly turned into an innocent cough, giving my hand a chance to conceal my mouth and my identity. I kept on walking, breathing, and living.

Two nights later my phone rang. It was her. No hello. No how are you. No whispering. She was obviously in a safe place . . . probably the vault of the Chase Manhattan Bank.

"God, we almost bought it, didn't we?" she said.

"Yeah," I answered, hoping to make the conversation as brief as possible.

"You know what he was saying to me as we walked up the street?" she asked.

"No. What?"

"He said, 'If you ever cheated on me with some two-bit flashy greaseball, I'd kill you with my own hands. I just hope it would be with a nice, clean-cut-looking kid like that' . . . Isn't that something?" she added.

I said, "Yes. I'm enormously flattered."

She continued. "And then I said, 'What would you do if I *did* cheat with a kid like that?' And he said, 'I'd find out where he lived and bury him right next to you.'"

I paused, trying to think of how to change the subject. "So, how's it going with you two?" was all I could muster.

"Pretty good," she said. "We're getting married next month . . . Don't worry. I'm not inviting you."

I thanked her for her kindness and wished her much happiness. As soon as I hung up, I changed my phone to an unlisted number. From then on, every time I read about some young hood killed in gangland fashion, the parts of his body spread out over New Jersey, I wondered if he had met a dark-haired girl at a party who said to him as they kissed at the elevator, "It's better if you give me your number."

SECOND CHANCES

5

IN 1953, in the second week of that second summer at Tamiment, there was a softball game between the entertainment staff and the hotel staff. Our outfield consisted of three dancers, all ballet trained, with the agility and grace to make sure bets they'd end up with Balanchine. When a ball was hit to the outfield, they first counted as dancers do—"and three and two and one and"—then they soared into the air, pirouetted, stretched their athletic limbs to full extension, reached for the ball, and smiled with gleaming teeth as the ball soared twenty feet over their heads. They did, however, all land on their feet in perfect unison, arms all stretched out as one to their audience. It was easier for them to catch a ninety-four-pound ballerina than a ten-ounce softball. Halfway through the first inning, we were behind six to nothing, despite constant "bravos" from the ballet aficionados in the crowd.

We came in from the field to take our first at bats. I was hitting fifth and stood behind the batting cage to see what kind of stuff their pitcher had. Their pitcher had the kind of stuff dreams are made of. It was Joan Baim, looking even more beautiful than she had the summer before. She was wearing a black T-shirt, white tennis shorts, and scruffy white sneakers; her hair was in a ponytail. She also had a humdinger of a right arm. She threw as hard as she could, and she was all business out on the mound.

My roommate, Larry Holofcener, our lyricist who worked with Jerry Bock, the composer who went on to write *Mr. Wonderful* starring Sammy Davis, Jr., was standing next to me watching Joan as intently as I was. "God, she's incredible, isn't she?" Larry said to me.

"She would be if she wasn't so married," I answered.

"Oh, she's not married. She broke off with that guy last winter . . . You're up at bat."

Yes, I was. In more ways than one. I wanted to meet her but not like this. A line drive hit into the pit of her stomach was not going to get me off on the right foot. We had two men on base and two out. I had been playing ball since I was seven years old, from daybreak to dusk, in every schoolyard and park in Washington Heights, every summer of my life. Danny, again my mentor, had taught me how to hit and field. When he wasn't being my George S. Kaufman, he was being my Casey Stengel. I got to be a pretty fair ball player. When I was nineteen and in the service, I played shortstop on the Air Force team that featured three ex–New York Yankees and two former St. Louis Cardinals. Facing a big leaguer was a lot less nerve-racking than facing this beautiful little package of dynamite who was now on the mound. She smiled at me as she went into her windup, and all I could think of was "She's not married."

Strike one as the ball whizzed by me across the plate. She smiled again as she toed the mound, and as she prepared to throw I said to myself, "Is that smile meant for me?"

Strike two as the ball cut across the outside corner of the plate. This had gone far enough. I can't let this happen, I thought. Don't let her show you up. Go for the fences, kid, she doesn't have a thing—except that smile, and that figure, and that wonderful quality of being singularly available.

She paused on the mound, turned her back on me, rubbed the ball in her hands, then turned and faced me. Now she had a look of determination as if I were the one man on this team she wanted to get out. Well, at least being an adversary was a start. She threw the ball with her same motion but took a little speed off it, throwing my timing off as I swung.

I did something worse than striking out. I hit a piddling little bouncer to the mound. She fielded it easily, catching it with her bare hand to further my humiliation, and then held the ball as she watched me racing toward first base. Then at the last possible moment, she fired the ball to the first baseman and I was out by a foot and a half.

I trudged out to my position in the field thinking this must have been what broke off their engagement. No marriage could last if you kept hitting piddling little grounders to the pitcher. He got off lucky, if you asked me.

As I passed her coming off the mound, I looked at her and said, "I'll get you next time."

She smiled and said, "Fine. I'll be at the dance hall tonight."

I shaved, showered, shampooed, and shaved again. I tried on every possible combination of shirt, pants, and shoes I had in my tiny closet. I Old Spiced myself until I smelled like that seaman coming back from Singapore with his bag on his shoulder. Señoritas would wave to me from their haciendas but they didn't have a chance. I had a date with a pitcher who got me out four times, leaving nine men on base.

I arrived at the dance hall and leaned against my private post, listening to Gershwin, and Rodgers and Hart, waiting for her to appear. It didn't take long. Although the dance floor was fairly crowded, there she came in the arms of Larry Holofcener, floating, sailing, flying, twirling around the floor, people making way for this, the greatest dance team since Fred Astaire first met his sister, Adele. It looked like the scene from *Gone With the Wind* when Scarlett and Rhett stopped the Civil War for twenty minutes. Although Larry looked more like Leslie Howard than Clark Gable, he had charm, humor, and was so light on his feet I'd want to dance all night with him too. Finally, after three numbers, they danced their way over to me and Larry introduced us.

"Want to dance?" she asked.

"Aren't you tired?" I asked hopefully.

"Oh, no. I love dancing. Come on."

She pulled me out on the floor and started to twirl as she did with Larry. I wasn't quite twirlable. I was from the "walk this way, walk that way" school of dancing. No one got out of the way for us. Not only was Larry a better dancer than I was, but he had gotten three base hits off her that afternoon.

"You're right," she said. "I am a little tired. Let's take a walk."

We walked down to the lake and didn't say very much at first. It didn't seem necessary. There are those rare times in life, if you are fortunate enough, that you have a relationship begin long before you consciously start it yourself. Something takes over on its own that moves and guides you toward each other, making every sound that's uttered and every look that passes between you seem inevitable and safe and wonderful. When it's wrong, nothing helps. When it's right, nothing is needed. We talked for nearly two hours, and everything said was both silly and profound. Even if we tried, we couldn't get out of the way of what was coming at us.

I walked her home through the dark, wooded paths that led to the cabin her family rented every summer. We never really reached for each other but at some point our hands joined and words seemed even less important than before. Her parents were asleep and we went in to share a Coke. There was a small oil painting on the wall, unfinished but interesting. I asked who the artist was. She said she wasn't sure it was an artist but that she had painted it. I asked to see some others. They were mostly all portraits that revealed more about her feelings than those of her subjects. All except for one that I couldn't take my eyes off. It was a picture of two women standing together, but a million miles apart. Possibly a mother and daughter. They were both beautiful and distorted at the same time. The distortion seemed to come from an inner anger that neither one could speak aloud to the other. They were interchangeable, as if the younger woman was what the older woman once was, and the older was what the younger woman would one day be. It was frightening and dark but enormously revealing and vulnerable in its truthfulness. Before I could ask her about it, she quickly put it away, afraid I might possibly read into it more than she was willing or able to come to terms with herself. She walked me down to the beginning of the path that led back to the camp. We kissed. I looked at her and said, "When did this start?" She looked at me and said, "Just before you asked that question."

I looked for her the next day but couldn't find her. I called several times but she was never in. That night I decided to go back to her cabin to see what was happening. Her father told me she was down at the lake fishing. I got lost three times trying to find the lake. It was now pitch dark and I feared I'd never find my way back. Finally, at the edge of the lake, I heard something moving slowly in the water. I called out her name a few times before she answered. She was alone in the blackness of the night, rowing slowly through the water. I asked if she had caught anything. She said she wasn't trying to. Just thinking . . . I told her I had been looking for her all day, and asked was anything the matter. She didn't answer for a few moments, then called out, "Would you like to stay over tonight?" We slept on the porch of the cabin, huddled together on the tiny cot she used to sleep in as a child. This was early July. By the end of September, we were married.

LITTLE CAESAR

6

BAREFOOT IN THE PARK was the title of the play I started writing about Joan. I learned early on, from all the plays I had seen or read, that every play must be about an event. Like the first time that "something" has ever happened. The first time the ghost of his father appears to Hamlet. The first time that Blanche DuBois comes to New Orleans to live with her sister, Stella; the first time Blanche meets Stanley Kowalski. The event doesn't always have to be major as far as the audience is concerned, but it has to be a major event in the lives of the leading characters. In the case of *Barefoot*, it was the very first day of the newlywed couple, Paul and Corie Bratter, in their new Greenwich Village apartment. I have always tried to put up stumbling blocks for my characters, something they're not prepared for, something that will interfere with their plans: obstacles, hurdles, conflicts that not only make their lives more difficult, but which afford me the opportunity to put them in a humorous situation.

In the case of *Barefoot*, I made it an empty apartment. The furniture had not yet arrived, the telephone had not been installed. Granted not the problems Medea faced, but comedy is another ball game. I didn't have to search too far to find the obstacles I needed, because they had already existed in our real lives: the apartment was five flights up, not counting the stoop, the water had not been turned on as yet, there was a hole in the skylight, there was no tub, just a shower, and on a cold day in February, the heat didn't work. Corie wanted it all to be perfect when Paul arrived home from work, but Paul was in another frame of mind. He had just got his first case in the new law firm where he was working and had to prepare a very complex brief that night. Nothing was working out for either of them, and despite the fact that it was clear they were deeply in love, that love was going to be sorely tested in the very first scene of the play. In truth, the only times Paul and Corie were nice to each other were in the first few minutes of the first scene and not again until the last few minutes of the play. The play having established their love, the audience never worried that they would part but seemed to enjoy and identify with the insecurity newlyweds go through in that first baptismal week of marriage.

The writing, however, did not come all that easily to me, given the fact that it had taken me three years to write my first play, that it was a minor hit, and that it owed its existence to a smart company manager and the praise of two world-famous performers. In other words, I didn't have all that much confidence in myself, and a writer without confidence is like a metaphor without something to compare itself to.

It took four months to finish the first act and then I stopped to take a vacation with Joan and Ellen. We decided to go to Switzerland. It was our third trip to Europe, the first being in 1954 soon after we were married. In the summer of 1954 I had less than three thousand dollars in the bank, but I did have the security of a job in the fall working with Danny on *Your Show of Shows* with Sid Caesar. Joan and I booked passage on the French liner the *Liberté*, economy class. We had double-decker bunks, not very conducive to a honeymoon, in a tiny windowless cabin made smaller by the seemingly endless miles of pipes coiling around the walls like a large family of frozen boa constrictors. Our room also sat two decks above the ship's huge engines, and hitting an iceberg was our only hope of stopping that infernal noise. Joan, normally a good sailor and fisherman, was seasick for five days and rarely came down from her bunk, even during fire drills. "If it goes down, it goes down. Leave me alone."

Conversely, I, who got seasick driving over the Triborough Bridge, suffered no ill effects at all. I ate, jogged around the decks, and read happily while sunning myself in a deck chair. Until the night I went down to see a movie in their large and beautiful art deco theater. The houselights dimmed, the large velvet curtains parted, and the picture began. Ten minutes into the film, all I could see was the swaying curtains, gliding slowly back and forth, right to left, left to right, endlessly. I broke the record for the hundred-yard dash on a passenger steamer from the movie theater to the rail of B Deck, losing a lot more than my dignity. Joan smiled briefly as she heard me climb into my bunk moaning. I ate lightly until we reached Le Havre.

We took the boat train from the dock to Paris. Although the war had been over for nine years, from our train window you could still see the scars and devastation of the carnage that was left in the countryside. Bombed-out houses, farms, and churches stood there in the open like giant broken flower pots, lending a trace of macabre beauty with the weeds and flowers and small trees that grew out of them. Bicycles were everywhere and the clothing people wore were more remnants than fashion. France was still digging out.

But Paris was Paris, and as we walked out of the train station and saw it before our eyes, it was impossible to think that this city was once occupied by the German army. We stayed in a small room in a small pension that looked out over a wild but prospering garden. It was airless and stiflingly hot that July, but when you don't know that one day most rooms like this would have air-conditioning and CNN, who could complain? Innocence is such a virtue.

The one area where I had trouble with Joan was that she was a smoker and I was not. It wasn't her smoking that bothered me as much as her obsessive reliance on it. She was certainly in the right city for smokers, because not to smoke in Paris was like not loving wine and cheese and bread. With nothing hanging from my lips, I was the one who stood out as a foreigner. If she woke at dawn and there was not a cigarette in her purse, she would throw anything on and rush down the street in a panic looking for a sign that said TABAC. She spoke French rather fluently and I felt a bit of a toad as Joan ordered every meal in every restaurant and had humorous exchanges with waiters while I glumly sat there feeling like one of the Beverly Hillbillies.

Tension was mounting between the lovebirds as we sat silently at a sidewalk café. I felt my Jewish-American New York conformity made her wish I were more Continental. I wished she would stop blowing smoke in my face. We had words and then louder words, and she got up and left me sitting there like her abandoned half-eaten croissant. I watched her disappear around the corner, my only consolation being I knew she didn't have a sou in her pocket. I was suddenly alone in a strange city where hardly anyone could or wanted to speak English, without a clue of where our pension was or how to pronounce the name of it. I wandered the streets thinking that if I could keep walking in a westerly direction, I would soon reach a port where a freighter could take me home even if I had to swab decks. Who wanted to be married to a Francophile smoker anyway? French men and women probably never kissed because their lips were always burnt and blistered.

An hour later I wandered into a part of the city that no one had seen since Toulouse-Lautrec took tiny steps through the narrow streets. I turned the corner and I could see Joan standing alone, on the opposite corner, as lost as I was. Our eyes met and without a word, we ran, rushing into each other's arms while a thousand violins played the theme of Now, Voyager. We found a taxi and sped back to our pension, making love in a 110-degree room. We left for the Gare de Lyon to take a train to our next city. We arrived as the gates were closing and the train was just starting to move away from the platform. Joan stopped in her tracks, devastated. But I picked up our bags and ran like all hell, calling out to Joan to run as well. Someone in the last carriage saw our plight and opened up the door as the train picked up speed. Joan was now trailing closer to me as I hurled our two bags into the car, jumped in, then, with one hand outstretched, pulled Joan on to the train after me. We fell into seats on opposite sides of each other, and Joan looked at me as she never had before. Although James Bond hadn't been invented yet, Joan's amazed and admiring eyes seemed to conjure him up in the person of the young Jewish-American sitting opposite her. It was not the kind of thing I did often, but sometimes once is enough.

In Europe we covered seven countries in six weeks, traveling from France to Belgium, Switzerland, Italy, Spain, England, and Ireland. The entire trip, meals included, cost $3,000, and on our last day in Italy we bought our first painting for $150. We landed in New York with $120 in our bank account. Joan, as I mentioned, never minded living on the edge.

We went back again in 1956, this time on the *Île de France*, again in economy but on this voyage with the luxury of a pipeless room. Our room, however, was about twenty feet away from the ship's kitchen, and I can tell you that French cooking tastes a lot better on the plate than it smells in your bedroom. This time we covered the northern countries, from Holland to Norway, Sweden, Denmark, and Finland, stopping in Paris and London on the way back. In two summers I had made up for all the culture I had missed in the preceding thirty years. The world of art and music and ballet opened up to me for the first time and I was soon addicted to it, searching out museums, galleries, and concerts everywhere we went. Growing up in a house where there was not a *single book* on a shelf leaves you amazingly unprepared for the civilizations that had been going on for thousands of years but which had miraculously managed to skip over our little apartment in Washington Heights.

Now for our third European visit, the trip to Switzerland was wonderful. We arrived in the small village of Arosa in the middle of the night, sinking into beds so deep you actually fell asleep before your body came close to where the mattress began. We woke early in the morning, amazed to find ourselves high in the middle of the Alps, feeling as if we had wandered into Shangri-la. We played golf in a cow pasture eight thousand feet high, where a ball sailed farther and higher than any pro ever hit one in Augusta, and the traps were not sand but what the cows deposited on their feeding ground. After three weeks of being as close to heaven as the lack of oxygen would allow, I was ready to go home and attack the second act of *Barefoot*.

My heart sank as I reread the first fifty-two pages I had left on my desk three weeks before. It didn't seem funny this time. Who rewrote it while I was gone? And what Broadway audience would find the petty problems of a couple of newlyweds worth taking an evening out of their lives? I called Saint Subber, the producer I felt was the most knowledgeable of all those I had met in my first foray into the theater, and asked him to read it. I sat in the little alcove outside his office as he read. No giggles this time, but roars of laughter emanated from his always frail body. He came out sooner than I expected with a broad grin on his face. "I love it. It's wonderful. This one I want to do. This one I can't *wait* to do."

I was buoyed by his enthusiasm but not convinced he was right, nor was I sure I had the stamina or the talent to finish it. He begged me to just go on with it, do a first draft, and then make a decision about doing the play. I agreed, went home, put it back in the typewriter, but just couldn't get out of the gate with it. It seemed to be staring back at me saying, "I dare you to write me. You're not good enough. You're not ready. The first one was a fluke." I prayed that the voice I heard belonged to me and not to someone who had wandered into the room just to set me straight. I was so dismayed, so disheartened, and so terribly frightened. Was this the end of the road for me? I didn't have the strength to throw a dart into the board. Let the Yankees fend for themselves this year, I declared. I'm in trouble. Deep trouble. If only the phone would ring, offering me a way out.

The phone rang. There was a God, even if his name was Ernest Martin, who coproduced with his partner, Cy Feuer, such hits as *Where's Charley?*, *Guys and Dolls*, *How to Succeed in Business Without Really Trying*, and go on from there.

"I saw your *Come Blow Your Horn*," he said. "You write funny, you know that?"

Not this week, I wanted to say, but settled for a simple "Thank you."

"Cy and I just bought a book called *Little Me*. We wanted to do it as a musical. We think you can write it, if you're interested."

Of course I was interested. I thought it unwise to tell him I couldn't get past the first act of my second play, but there was always the possibility that he and Cy could lead me by the hand through the intricate maze of writing a musical.

"Can I read the book first?" I asked. As if he were going to say, "No, you can't. You have to write the musical first and then maybe we'll let you read the book afterwards." Pull yourself together, Neil.

"I'll get it to you today. You get back to us after you finish it." This sounded promising. At least I didn't have to pick him up at the ferry at eight in the morning.

Little Me was a pastiche, written by Patrick Dennis, the story of a starry-eyed girl who came from the wrong side of the tracks in a small midwestern town and proceeded to marry seven men, each one richer than the preceding one, who coincidentally and/or conveniently all die one after the other, leaving Belle Poitrine occasionally pregnant and consistently wealthier after each passing. I needed my Berlitz French/English book to translate Belle Poitrine into Large Breasts. That will give you some idea of Belle's attractions and the tone of Mr. Dennis's book.

It was funny but it was book funny, not stage funny. It would take more than an adaptation. It would require an entirely new script, trying as faithfully as possible to follow Mr. Dennis's story line but allowing me a free hand. I'm sure Mr. Dennis thought my hand was given too much freedom for his taste, but such are the sacrifices you make when you turn your work over to another author. From the moment I put the book down, I had one very clear idea in my head. I called Ernie Martin.

"I like the book and I'd like to try writing it. But you can't use seven men to play her seven husbands. Let's get one man to play them all and make it a star turn."

"Who should that be?"

"I can only think of one person. Sid Caesar."

I had worked for three years with Sid Caesar on television and knew his talents as well as anyone. They were prodigious. I felt also that Sid would be comfortable with me.

The other attraction for me was that Bob Fosse was going to choreograph and codirect with Cy Feuer. I knew Bob socially but would have given anything to work with him. Bob had a wonderful but dark sense of humor that showed up in his work as well as his life. With the exception of Jerome Robbins, for my money Fosse was the best choreographer who ever worked in the theater.

From the day rehearsals began, Fosse was the one I looked to for guidance and inspiration. At 10 A.M. that first morning, the actors read the script and the composers sang the songs. Huge applause from everyone at the end. Actors, dancers, producers, scenic and costume designers, all in attendance, proclaimed the script was absolutely hilarious and the score was the freshest heard on Broadway in years. Yet all the while, I kept my eyes glued to Fosse's reactions. For me, his approval or disapproval was all that mattered.

Bob Fosse worked out the dance numbers weeks before the show went into rehearsal, alone in a mirrored room, with a pianist and his wife, Gwen Verdon, to help him flesh out the numbers. Bob and Gwen did everyone's part, whether it was sixteen dancers or twenty. No one was allowed in but I would often stand outside the room just listening to the rhythms and to Bob and Gwen counting steps. Once Bob allowed me to watch for a few minutes. I was mesmerized, as anyone would be when those two were moving together in a mirrored room.

Sid Caesar signed on, with one small caveat. Once we opened in New York, he wanted to do a weekly half-hour television show, shooting it on his off day in the theater. This worried me, as it would any cardiologist in the world. And why would people pay to see Sid Caesar when they could get him free on Saturday night? Already the problems had started. On the second day of rehearsals, the choral director took the singing chorus of twelve into a separate room to go over one particularly difficult but rousing number. He stopped them every eight bars or so to go over corrections and then continued on. When he got to the end of thirty-two bars, he clapped his hands for the chorus to stop, but one soprano kept belting away, her eyes closed in rapture, caught in the gaiety and spirit of the number. The director clapped his hands again and then called her name. She wouldn't or couldn't stop singing. Worriedly, he went to her, shook her arms, and called to her. The singing, now almost at a hysterical pitch, went on and on until the others in the group silently left the room in embarrassment and for fear of her and their well-being. Nothing stopped her. Finally, an ambulance was summoned and she was taken away for observation, still singing as she crossed town, and for all we know, she may still be at it as I write this some thirty-odd years later. I hope she's well.

After endless day-after-day rewrites, we were ready for our first run-through. I was actually pretty proud of what I had done, and the constant laughter by the cast reassured me that maybe we had something pretty funny.

The first run-through brought our first audience, small as it was. It included the spouses of the producers and creative staff, and just a few friends, maybe a dozen in all. I sat in the third row with Joan as the stage manager called, "Curtain!" There was no curtain to go up just as there was no orchestra as he called out, "Overture!" One piano and a few chairs will do for a run-through. It was amazing how much laughter came from those dozen viewers.

The show breezed by, each number going well, each scene hilariously played by Caesar and Company. God, how I loved the theater. How lucky I was to be a part of it. What a joy to look forward to spending my life in this glorious business . . . And then, quite suddenly, the sound of silence. Not from the stage, but from the twelve viewers, who now sat in unpredictably stony silence. We had hit a dry patch so arid you could lay a beach blanket on it.

I quickly got out of my seat, walked to the back of the theater, sat on the steps to the balcony, and stopped listening to what was being said onstage. There was no point in listening to what I knew would never be in the show *on* and *if* there was an opening night. This was not like the cloud of fear that came over me during the first preview of *Come Blow Your Horn*. This was a clear recognition that we had just lost the audience, and we lost them because of what I had written. I didn't know how to face Cy and Ernie and Bob and Joan. This was trouble, and I was too inexperienced to know that trouble was the norm for most musicals. No one said anything during the intermission and I didn't give them much chance, as I sat alone back in the shadows of the steps, only now about ten steps higher.

The second act picked up momentum, thanks to a brilliant dance number that Fosse had created, and although we didn't have the laughs we had in the first act, the mini-audience came to life again and there was hope and promise in Mudville that day.

I sat up the whole night trying to examine how, where, and why I had gone wrong. And as the morning light filtered into the room, despair suddenly turned into optimism, not because I knew how to fix it, but because I was now determined that I *would* fix it. Believe me, that's a very large barrier to get over, and you save the time you would use in being terrified and stuck, and put it to work in dealing with the various possibilities you could try in *making* it work. The first realization is that the concept of the scene is wrong and then, after many attempts, a promising concept appears, and once you've discovered that, the dialogue comes more easily and begins to pump life into what was once inert, inept, and in trouble.

What I rewrote seemed to be a vast improvement, and we had our final run-through before leaving for Philadelphia.

"Is anyone coming to watch today?" I asked Cy Feuer.

"Yes," he said. "A friend of mine."

"*One* friend? That's all?"

He looked at me with a Cheshire Cat smile on his face. "He'll be enough."

Five minutes before the run-through started, a man walked in leaning on a cane despite his robust physique. It was John Steinbeck. In 1962 he had been awarded the Nobel Prize for Literature; this was the closest I had come to meeting a great American writer. Steinbeck was a good friend of Cy and Ernie's, and I sensed he enjoyed the company and gaiety of those who worked in the theater, especially musicals. Steinbeck had a voice that seemed to come from the bowels of the earth, with a persistent cough that made the journey along with it. The run-through began, with everyone playing for this one man, who sat on a metal folding chair, leaning on his cane, occasionally laughing or coughing. It was hard to tell which. When it was over, Cy and Ernie crossed to him and said, "What do you think, John?" Steinbeck smiled and squinted at Cy and Ernie, knowing full well about their nonstop string of hits, and said, "It'll do. But remember, you can still only eat two eggs a day." It sounded like the philosophy of someone out of *The Grapes of Wrath*. He saw everything in life in terms of the common man, success included.

We opened in Philadelphia to great critical reviews but somehow we all knew better. A couple of numbers didn't work well, and although the audience laughed more than we had anticipated, there was still a feeling of emptiness at the end of the evening. As I walked along the street with Cy Feuer the next morning, he suddenly broke into laughter. He said, "I've never been in this position before. We have a smash hit and I'm thinking maybe we should close it." I knew what he meant. A theater audience is a unique audience. All their laughter and all their applause doesn't always coincide with how they feel when the curtain goes down. All their cheers and bravos do not always turn into good word of mouth. They may be happy in the moment but uninvolved on the way home. Something Cy said to me during this time has stayed with me forever: "Don't think about the good things in a show. The good things take care of themselves. It's the bad parts that'll do you in."

Cy Coleman wrote the music and Carolyn Leigh wrote the lyrics. It's been my experience in working on musicals that if a number isn't working, the composer can willingly sit down and come up with a dozen new melodies, whereas the lyricist will fight for every word or rhyme to his or her dying breath. This, of course, is a generality and only applies to those it only applies to. There was one number in *Little Me* that, try as they might, just wouldn't work and never did at any performance. It was about a group of female dancers who went to the front lines in World War I to entertain the troops. It was called "The Girls of Seventeen." Bob Fosse restaged and re-choreographed the number six times, giving it his best shot every time out. It refused to budge. Cy Feuer came to the theater that night and reluctantly told Cy Coleman and Carolyn that he was cutting the number from the show. Coleman shrugged but understood. Carolyn held her ground. She said, "Fosse didn't stage it well." I never saw anyone work harder than Bob Fosse, and if he couldn't budge a number, it was an unmovable mountain. Cy Feuer dismissed her complaint and said the number was out of the show as of that night. Carolyn screamed that he was violating her rights as a member of the Dramatists Guild. A producer could not cut or change an author's material without "said author's permission." She may have been right about that, but an audience is not terribly interested in backstage squabbles. They were bored with it and didn't feel like paying good money for being bored. I tried to reason with Carolyn, as did Coleman and Fosse, but she was adamant.

The curtain went up that night and when it came time for "The Girls of Seventeen," it had mercifully disappeared from the show. Carolyn ran out of the theater and returned minutes later with a uniformed Philadelphia policeman. Standing behind the cop, she pointed to Cy Feuer and shouted, "That's the man. I'm making a citizen's arrest." When she tried to explain why, the befuddled officer looked at the stage to see what grounds she had. He stayed until the final curtain, then turned to all of us and said, "Pretty damn good show," and left. The next day Carolyn and Cy wrote a new number. Carolyn could be a major pest at times, but she was a wonderful lyricist and then some.

Sid Caesar, as brilliant a comedian as I've ever met, had trouble learning his lines. He never stuck to them on our television shows but always covered them with something just as funny. The stage was another matter. There discipline reigns king. One of the seven characters Sid played in *Little Me* was Noble Eggleston, the richest, most talented, most brilliant, most liked and handsomest boy in town. So brilliant that he went simultaneously to Harvard and Yale, where he studied medicine and law, hoping one day to become a "legal doctor." Forbidden by his society mother to marry Belle, who was from the wrong side of the tracks, he married a girl his mother picked out for him. As Noble said, "She and my mother are very happy." Meanwhile Belle married a wealthy businessman.

She and Noble meet years later aboard the *Titanic* while both are strolling the deck. Noble is now a surgeon and a judge. It's a foggy night and the big horns keep blasting through the scene. Belle says to Noble, "Do you think there's any danger?"

Noble says, "No, no. It's nothing. Just a huge iceberg just ahead."

Then Belle, still in love with Noble, bursts out pleadingly: "Oh, Noble. Isn't there some way we can keep on seeing each other?"

Noble answers, "What do you want to do? Sneak around back alleys, checking into cheap hotels, lying to our family and friends?"

She says, "No. Of course not."

He answers, "Well, it was just a suggestion."

It was one of the biggest laughs of the night.

At one performance in Philadelphia, after Belle said, "Of course not," Sid replied, "Well, it was just a situation."

No laugh. Obviously.

When I went backstage to see Sid, he asked me why that line didn't get a laugh tonight. I told him. "You didn't say 'It was just a suggestion.' You said 'It was just a situation.'"

Sid looked at me bewildered and said, "What's the difference?" It didn't seem to be wise to correct Sid because he looked as though he was about to get one of his Wolf Man headaches. I always followed the dictum, "Let sleeping large angry comedians lie."

As I left, Cy Feuer entered the dressing room and I heard him say, "Sid, I just have a couple of notes for you. Nothing big." Cy didn't know how big "Nothing big" could be. "I thought it was a good show tonight, Sid," Cy began diplomatically. "Just a little slow."

Sid looked up at him through his dressing mirror. The red flag had just been waved in front of his horns. Sid rarely attacks with anger. Sid just sarcastics you to death. I could hear him through the door. He was very polite.

"A little slow? Really? You mean a little *slow* slow or like turtle slow? Or was it *really* slow like a glacier slow? If you want, I could speed it up a little. I could make it so fast, the audience doesn't even have to come in. They could just go to the box office, buy their tickets, and go home. Show me how slow it was, Cy. I'm young. I could sit here till I'm sixty, seventy, I'm in no hurry."

Cy knew his head was in the noose and he slipped out carefully, laughing good-naturedly at Sid, and said, "Forget it. Not important. See you tomorrow. Get a good night's sleep."

Sid said, "A slow sleep or a fast sleep? I got all kinds of sleep. You come up, watch me, and pick out one you like."

Cy was gone before he could yell "Taxi." Sid walked back to the hotel with his personal manager, who was always at his side. Sid kept murmuring to himself, "Too slow, heh?" He did it in ten different languages and twenty different dialects. When they got to Sid's suite, Sid went calmly into the bathroom, put his huge, strong hands on both sides of the sink, yanked it and part of the wall out, and threw the sink into the bathtub, then turned to his manager and said, "Ask Cy if that's fast enough." Sid had a certain kind of logic but you didn't always want to be in the same room when he expressed it.

The show played seven weeks in Philadelphia, then went on to New York. Unlike *Come Blow Your Horn*, we arrived to a huge fanfare, thanks to the good press in Philly and the power of the Feuer and Martin name above the title. We had a double-page cover on *Life* magazine, with seven photos of Sid Caesar as the seven characters he was playing in the show. We had a good advance sale, opening at the Lunt-Fontanne Theatre, not really one of my favorites. By now, Joan and Gwen Verdon were both pregnant, and the two of them stood at the back of the theater during our last technical rehearsals. Joan was a few months ahead of Gwen and both looked radiantly beautiful and happy. Fosse and I had grown to be close friends by now, enhanced by our moving into the same building where they lived in the penthouse at Sixty-ninth Street and Central Park West. Bob was exactly one week older than I was and it became a running joke with us. I always kidded him about how much I looked up to him and hoped I looked as well as he did when I became his age.

The reactions of the New York preview audiences were a mixed bag. One night, as I stood at the rear of the theater, the curtain went down at intermission and two couples came up from opposite aisles, apparently friends. The first couple said, "Isn't this the funniest thing you've ever seen? We think it's brilliant." The second couple said, "We hate it. We're leaving. Call you tomorrow." In a sense, I thought they were both right. With a play or musical, a comedy or drama, you lay down the ground rules to the audience in the first ten minutes. Consistency is the keynote. The play can have twists and turns, surprises and jolts, but it can never deviate from the tone you establish in the beginning. It's as inviolable to mix styles in a play as it would be if the great French mime Marcel Marceau spoke just one single word in the entire evening. Just so, although we don't truly believe that Harpo Marx can't speak, we just accept his muteness because they made that a rule from the moment we first saw him. The audience makes a silent pact with you to dispel their belief for two hours plus, as long as you uphold your part of the bargain to tell your story with wit and style and truth and imagination. We know that the actor playing Peter Pan can't fly, but we accept that Peter Pan himself can fly. After all, didn't Tinker Bell tell us "We must believe." Children and adults did what she asked. *Little Me*, however, had style trouble. We were both farcical and satirical at the same time. We told the audience that Noble and Belle really loved each other, but neither the writers nor actors nor directors really believed it. We were asking the audience to accept what we ourselves were making fun of. It was a good joke, but still a joke, and it's hard to maintain a joke for two and a quarter hours, no matter how well it's told. We did have our admirers because they were willing to accept us on our own terms, but those who like to believe in and care for the characters they were watching felt cheated. I've always found audiences greedy, and they have a right to be. They don't demand perfection but they do have to care, to be involved, to be moved, to be part of the experience.

You can very often tell by the way an audience is dressed what kind of a reception to expect. Tuxedos and evening gowns are like a torpedo coming at you midship. Those people would obviously be part of a big charity event, having paid a small fortune for their tickets and the lavish chicken dinner that has preceded it. If there was dinner, it follows that there were drinks. If there were drinks, it also follows that there will be drunks and latecomers, the worst being a drunken latecomer. This was the crowd that faced us at our crucial last preview in New York. The house was half filled as the overture started, two-thirds filled as the curtain went up, and the final three hundred stragglers filed in feeling for their seats in the half-darkened theater all during the first scenes. Fosse, Cy Coleman, and I stood at the rear of the theater knowing it was going to be a long quiet night. Fifteen minutes into the first act, a tuxedoed man got up from his aisle seat in the second row and bobbed, weaved, and staggered his drunken way up the aisle, stopping to say hello to people he never met in his life. Fosse took one look at him and said, "If he doesn't throw up on anyone in the audience, I'd say we got off lucky." As he passed the three of us in search of the men's room, he screamed at the top of his voice, "This is the worst piece of crap I've seen since *My Fair Lady.*" Since it made no sense at all, we were rather flattered.

Little Me opened on Saturday night, November 17, 1962. John Chapman of the New York *Daily News* said, *"Little Me* is inventive, funny, attractive and expertly staged but has little if any sentimental worth." There it was, exactly as I feared. Laughs will only get you just so far. Walter Kerr in the *Herald-Tribune* wrote, "The enterprise breathes an atmosphere peculiarly located between mockery that means it, with malice, and mockery that it couldn't care less so long as it succeeds in figuring out the next blackout." All in all, Mr. Kerr enjoyed the show but slyly pointed out that those looking to take these shenanigans seriously, beware. We did have many out-and-out champions. *Time* magazine said, "The results may be frivolous, but synthetic frivolity on the rampagingly funny order of *Little Me* appears too rarely on Broadway." John McClain of the *Journal-American* said, "If the press agents of *Little Me* were looking for a quote from me they can help themselves to any of the following: 'Smash Musical,' 'Sumptuous Success' or maybe just 'Hail Caesar.'"

Sid Caesar did, in fact, conquer Broadway, and our reviews, all in all, were of the kind that hits are made of. We had a decent run but not what we might have expected after such plaudits. My feeling was that once we got past the sophisticates of New York, the audiences from across the bridges and tunnels were looking for a little more heart mixed with their hilarity. We did the show in London a year later with surprisingly better results. I rewrote it and placed the locale in England. The business of Belle being from the wrong side of the tracks was much more relevant there, since those who weren't of the upper class were *all* from the wrong side of anywhere. Harold Hobson, the respected English critic, wrote, "It is a true work of art, in that it maintains a personal attitude towards life and society without once losing it. It is an attitude of amused mockery of English social institutions and class consciousness with a properly distanced accuracy astonishing in an American show." It was shortly after that I decided to become an Anglophile. I started wearing English tweeds and a Burberry raincoat.

ABOUT THIS TIME my father's health began to fail. He was sixty-seven years old and suffered from heart disease. Not available to him in those days were pills that could reduce his blood pressure, and knowledge that exercise could have held off his condition from worsening, or that a proper diet could have put it off for years. I always had mixed feelings about my father. It was hard to get a permanent fix on a man who so often left my mother, and in so doing, left me and my brother as well, often with hardly enough money to feed us. His own father had died when my dad was quite young, and I never recall him ever mentioning anything about his father.

My dad worked hard and I knew that he loved me, but he fought constantly with Danny, who I felt was taking the brunt of my father's misplaced anger. My father was an uneducated, unworldly man, but when the bitter quarrels with my mother were not dominating our lives, he was warm and caring. Not the kind of caring where he could take me in his arms and hug me but rather he'd give me a painful pinch on my knee to show his affection, which left me with a loving, red welt on my leg. In *Brighton Beach Memoirs* I put my own experience into the words of my girl cousin, but what I wrote was my own deep feelings about my father. I talked about how he came home on a cold winter's night and hung his large blue overcoat in the hall closet and then said to me, "I have a package of gum for you. It's in my coat pocket." He'd turn to read his newspaper while I went to the closet. I put my hand into forbidden territory, his deep, warm pocket, reaching for the package of gum, but what I really felt was a sense of secrecy and intimacy I could share with my father, something he was unable to give me in a more open and vulnerable way. I could feel the cellophane worn off a pack of cigarettes, a match book, a pencil, a single Life Saver, a paper clip, bits of tobacco, all giving me a hint and smell of what his day was really like. I was able to get close to him without his knowing; he was inviting me to share a moment of his life despite his inability to give it through a touch or a caress. I think even giving me the gum from his own hand was too much affection for him to show, or maybe he just wanted to play out the game of hide-and-seek, knowing how it could titillate a young boy.

To give him the benefit of the doubt, how could he be a father without ever knowing what it was like to have had one? He never read my report cards. He never asked about them. The business of my education was put in the hands of Danny. My father was often cruel to my mother, not in a physical way but in some immature, petulant way that would embarrass her, frighten her, or humiliate her. He could sleep next to her for a month without uttering a single word to her.

One night my mother had four or five women over to play cards in the kitchen. My father, in his pajamas, came out of his bedroom, walked wordlessly into the kitchen, got himself a glass of water, drank it, and then left wordlessly, turning off the lights as he went, leaving the card game in complete darkness. The women were so frightened, one of them said "Should we light a candle or what?"

Another time, he had the flu but turned down all offers from my mother or Danny or me to get him medicine or food. He remained stoically stubborn in his bed, coughing loudly enough for us to hear on the other side of the apartment. He was shooting little pellets of guilt at us all. My mother finally made dinner and the three of us sat down to eat. No sooner did we begin than the doorbell rang. My mother got up and answered it. It was a delivery boy from the local deli. He said, somewhat confused as he saw the hot meal on the table before us, "I have a tuna sandwich and a coffee for Mr. Simon." My mother pointed and said, "In the bedroom." He delivered his package to my father, then walked out, looking at us as if to say, "What kind of family is this?" I would have answered if the word "dysfunctional" was in use at the time.

One night my mother came home about 11 P.M., after visiting her sister. The lights were out in the house as she opened the door. Knowing my father was home, she thought this very curious. She turned on the hall light and screamed in terror as she saw the body of a man lying on the floor before her. As she looked closer she realized it was not a body at all but rather my father's suit, jacket and trousers, laid out in full length, shoes at the bottom and a hat where the head should be. What my father intended I dare not even guess, but to my mother's credit, instead of getting angry, she burst out laughing and continued to laugh as she got into bed next to my silent father. This was not exactly music to his ears. She left the clothes where they were so that my father would have to bear the humiliation of picking them up in the morning.

My father never wore casual clothes. I saw him playing in a softball game wearing his gray suit pants, black, pointy, shined shoes, and his white-on-white dress shirt, no tie, but sleeves rolled up to his elbow. If he got a hit, he would run the bases but never slide. Better to be tagged out than ruin a good pair of pants. He wore this exact outfit on the beach. His body, except for his face, was as white as the day he was born. He once decided to take driving lessons and was doing fairly well behind the wheel as long as they were on flat streets. The one time he had to drive uphill, he panicked halfway up and leaped from the moving car, leaving the instructor to reach over and grab the wheel as he jammed on the brakes. That was the end of his driving. Though he made many flights to Florida, he never quite got over his fear of flying and never once looked out the window. He said to me, "You can ask any-one. No one ever saw me looking out the window." Where would I begin in finding people to ask if they ever saw my father looking out a plane window? Then there were the times he was loving and affectionate with my mother. He would sit in the kitchen playing gin rummy with someone who always looked like a tough adversary. We all knew that if my father won, our weekly financial problems would ease a little. A loss was like a tiny crash in our fam-ily stock market. He would call out to my mother as the hands became more crucial, "Come in here, honey. Let me rub you for luck." Then he would rub my mother's arms and her back, and as I heard their words from my bed, I breathed a sigh of relief and welled up with tears. For a while, anyway, there would be peace in the house.

His sense of logic often baffled me. On the high Jewish holidays, the only times in the year that we would attend synagogue, I sat with my father in a suit and tie during those stiflingly hot early autumn days. The Jewish prayer books were written in Hebrew on one side of the page and in English on the other side. Although I could read Hebrew, it only meant I could pronounce the words without knowing what they meant. As the congregation would stand and chant the prayers in Hebrew, I would say mine in English so that I would know what I was saying. My father would look down at me with annoyance and say, "In Hebrew. Read in Hebrew." I would say, "I don't know what the Hebrew means." He answered, "Do what I say. God doesn't under-stand English." Go fight that one.

On my birthday, the Fourth of July, my father would come home with a large box of fireworks—Roman candles, skyrockets, the whole works. He would then take me to the back of the park, with a group of other kids I didn't know following him like the pied piper. I was very excited about his doing this for me. Then he handed out all the fireworks to the other kids but I didn't get any. I looked at him, surprised and crushed. "Don't I get any?" He said, "I don't want you getting hurt," as he handed out the last Roman candle. I got hurt without ever touching one.

If he wasn't a terrific father, he was a wonderful grandfather. He adored Ellen. He would come over to our apartment on a Sunday morning, refus-ing breakfast of course, because he made a steadfast rule: "I never eat in my children's house." He thought he would bankrupt me by having a bagel and cream cheese and a cup of coffee. He had the strangest ideas of what a father did to make his children happy. Once there, however, he couldn't wait to take Ellen across to Central Park and push her on the swing to her heart's content. When she saw her grandpa, she always drew a picture for him. He treated it and cherished it as though it were a Renoir, not that he ever heard of Renoir. When Ellen and I went to visit him in his apartment on Central Park South, I was amazed and delighted to see that every picture she ever drew or painted was taped to the walls, a miniature gallery of Ellen's output. There was a weekly ritual. After Ellen presented him with her latest work—she was now in her crayon period—he took her down to the toy store and told her she could buy only one toy, but it could be any toy she wanted. It took her a minimum of forty-five minutes and eight times around the store to make her selection. I kept whispering in her ear, "Take something already," but he urged me not to rush her. She knew what she wanted. He had more patience than I did, which is very often a trait of grandparents.

My father did not live alone. He soon introduced me to the woman he now called his wife. Alone in the bedroom with him, I said, "How could she be your wife? You're not even divorced from Mom."

He said, "Yes, I am. I did it last week."

"Where?" I asked.

"In New Jersey," he answered.

In those days no one could get divorced in New Jersey. You could get fireworks there but not a divorce. "Mom would have to sign the divorce papers," I argued.

"No," he answered. "I went to a judge who doesn't need any." That was the end of the discussion.

My mother soon found out and wanted to sue him for bigamy. Danny and I prevailed upon her not to press it. She had no intentions of remarrying and we knew my father didn't have a long life ahead of him. Reluctantly, my mother yielded.

The woman my father declared to be his wife was nothing like what I expected. She was a very nice, decent woman and seemed to care for my father a great deal. This was something I could never tell my mother and I avoided talking about it as best I could.

Since my father never encouraged Danny or me about "this writing business," it was very hard to impress him with whatever small ascents we made toward our aspirations. He did, however, introduce us to two men who booked most of the acts into the big and small hotels that covered the Catskill Mountains, a two-hour drive from New York. Their names were Beckman and Pransky. Through them we met all the young comics of the time and it led to our writing stand-up material for them, earning our first monies as writers, which we then contributed to our parents to pay our share of the household expenses. We met not only the young but the old comics, former stars who were now on their way down, hoping to find renewed life with the fresh new jokes supplied by us two young kids. One of them was a former vaudeville great named Willie Howard. He was a pint-sized man with a huge head of hair. We were invited to meet him in his suite at the Astor Hotel on Broadway. Mr. Howard greeted us at the door, not of his suite but rather his small, single, drab room with a bath. He was wearing a faded bathrobe over pajama tops, dark blue pants with suspenders, argyle socks, and a pair of slippers. I remembered seeing him when I was a young boy and how the tears ran down my cheeks at his preposterously funny routines. After a short talk, it appeared that Mr. Howard didn't really want new material, but someone to punch up the old routine he'd been doing since his heyday in the twenties. It also seemed pretty clear from his surroundings and our conversation that he'd be hard put to pay us much, if anything. We said our good-byes and left; for me it had been a very touching experience. The look and dress of Willie Howard, the seediness and sadness of his room, and the improbability that he would ever work much again stayed with me for years and finally became the model in my mind for what later would be *The Sunshine Boys*.

Knowing my mother would be there, my father did not come to the opening night of *Come Blow Your Horn*. He did come a few nights later. It was clearly our family up there on the stage and I was worried, to say the least, how my father would react to seeing himself in full view, to be judged by the press and the public. For me it was a whimsical portrait, blustering and funny, and adored by most audiences. I dared not look at him during the performance even though I chose to sit up in a box where he was in my direct line of view. I hoped for the best. I waited for him in the lobby as the curtain came down. He saw me, nodded to me, and took me aside. Not even *The New York Times* review was as important as this. "It was very nice," he said. "The audience liked it a lot. You wrote all of it or the actors wrote some?"

"No, Dad. It doesn't work that way. I wrote the whole play."

"Very good. Very nice," he continued.

I gathered my strength and asked him what he thought of the father. "He was the best one," he answered. "I know so many men just like him."

He never saw that it was him. He didn't even consider the possibility. Not only was I off the hook, but my father went to work the next day, extolling the virtues of his son's wonderful play to everyone he met.

"Wait'll you see the father," he would say. "He's hilarious." I had finally crawled out of my father's coat pocket and into his heart. He would call me each day to tell me how many tickets he was selling in the garment district. As far as my father was concerned, it wasn't Noël Coward or Groucho Marx who had saved my play. It was Irving Simon.

Soon after *Little Me* opened, he called and asked if I could meet him in Central Park. I said I would and that I'd bring Ellen with me. "No," he said. "Just you."

I sat on the bench where we always met, and as I saw him approaching, I could see he walked gingerly, not with the usual sprightly gait I was accustomed to. He looked pounds thinner and when he reached me, he sat and looked away, tears in his eyes. I sat quietly, waiting for him to gather himself. He asked me how Joan and Ellen were and was I feeling well, all questions meant to delay what he really had to say. His lips were trembling as he started to speak, and the stifled sob was even more distressing than if he had just let the tears flow. "What is it, Dad? Tell me. Are you all right?"

Every time he tried to speak, he fumbled; he took out a handkerchief to blow his nose and hide his face when anyone passed within earshot. "I don't know how to say this. I've never taken anything from you or Danny. You know that. Am I lying?"

"No, Dad. You never let us give you anything. What is it? Money? Just tell me, I'll give you whatever you need."

He covered his eyes with his hands and this time the sobs came uncontrollably. He told me what he needed and swore it was only a loan. He would pay me back one day, "As God is my judge." I told him I would send him a check in the morning. I knew he was never a strong man, never a fighter, or even a self-sufficient man, despite the fact he always worked hard. He depended on the love and sympathy of his sisters, his nieces, and his nephews, who I think knew his faults but all loved him. I knew and saw both sides.

We hugged as he got up to leave; he was hardly able to look at me as he went. For a man who wouldn't even share a Sunday breakfast with me, this had to be the hardest day of his life. I never told my mother what happened but I think somehow she knew. I grew up seeing the torment of broken families, broken lives, and broken hearts, and although I always found the absurdity of how we live our lives, I always looked for the pain when I wrote about it. Writing about it in a play or on this page doesn't lessen the pain, but it allows you to look at it from a distance, objectively instead of subjectively, and you begin to see a common truth that connects us all.

THE CHRISTMAS CHILD

7

I NOW HAD two shows running on Broadway, neither one a disaster, neither one a triumph. They were stepping stones leading in no particular direction, rather just waiting to see which fork in the road I would follow. Neither one made me rich, all for the better since my luck with investments no doubt would have wiped out the entire cattle population of the plains, making them disappear from the West faster than the buffalo. What money I did hold on to served to subsidize me through the next year or so without my having to turn to television. Joan and I spent every possible night at the theater, seeing everything, good, bad, or indifferent. One tends to learn infinitely more from the bad than the good, and one learns nothing from the brilliant. The brilliant is born out of a writer's pain, some divine inspiration, and a slight bit of madness. You can aspire to it but you can't plan on it, especially if you know your limitations. Your horizons can expand, however, if you allow yourself the possibility of failure. You must, in fact, court failure. Let her be your temptress. There must be danger in the attempt and no net strung across the abyss to break your fall. And then there are the lucky few who have the innocent ignorance of not even realizing that danger exists.

You can't use the brilliant as a guideline to follow because there are no signposts to point the way. You simply jump off the cliff of your imagination and tackle the great Devil of Despair, as Van Gogh often did, because he had the temerity to compete with God. I wasn't quite ready to take on God just yet. Not even an angel. I was, at the most, willing to follow a young rabbinical student from a local synagogue.

You could learn a lot, though, from the mediocre and the bad. It's easy to spot, not only during a heavy night at the theater, but because you come across it in your own work, and if you do it often enough, you begin to recognize the signals. Stop! Go back to start! Pay five dollars to Community Hospital! You can never say to yourself, "I think there's a problem here but maybe I'm wrong. Maybe they'll like it." They won't. They barely like it when you think it's wonderful, so what chance do you have when you try to slip something by that even you have doubts about? Your best bet, I've always found, is to show your work to just two people. One is the most honest person you know, the other is the smartest person you know. Joan was the most honest. I was soon to meet the smartest.

On Christmas Eve, 1962, the mound in the bed sleeping next to me was Joan, profoundly pregnant and due any day now. My mother slept over that night in the event that Ellen, now five, had to be alone while Joan and I went to the hospital to pick up her sibling. At about 11:15, as Santa was delivering his toys to Sweden and Denmark and heading west, Joan nudged me gently and whispered in a calm voice, "I think it's time to go." She moved slowly, I moved like a whippet. I waited impatiently for her, afraid she would miss one of the great experiences of her life. As we got out on the street, light snow was falling. The lights of Central Park shimmering through the trees put Macy's windows to shame. It was a perfect night and all was still in the city. I hailed a lone cab coming slowly and quietly down the street, and as he stopped, my impulse was to say, "Take me to a manger." As I carefully helped Joan into the back, I said to the driver, "New York Hospital. Drive carefully, my wife's having a baby." The cabbie barely looked at me and said, "It'll cost you double." I said, "For driving carefully or am I paying for the baby?" He said, "Christmas Eve. Double fare." I wanted to say I could have gotten Dancer and Blitzen for double fare but let it go.

At 10:14 on Christmas morning, Nancy Elizabeth Simon, at seven pounds, six ounces, was born. Joan's labor was easier this time, and Nancy came into the world with an unpointed head. I don't know if there's a correlation between an easy birth and a blissful child, but in this case, it worked out that way. Early in the afternoon I went home to get my mother and Ellen to take them to the hospital. I realized that no one had taken Chips out to walk since ten the previous night and the poor dog was bursting at the seams. He emitted little whimpers of "Hurry, hurry," in the elevator. I rushed him or vice versa across the street to the park. The temperature had dropped about fifteen degrees and the night's snowfall had turned the park to a giant sheet of ice. Once outside, Chips strained at the leash and I unsnapped his collar as he slid twenty yards to the nearest tree. He stood with his leg up so long, I could have read the entire *New York Times*. Once relieved from a night and half a day of bondage, he ran wildly through the park when suddenly I heard the most awful and chilling screech, the kind that only a wounded animal could make, followed by pitiful whimpers of pain and helplessness. I found Chips lying on his side in the snow, unable to move. I picked him up in my arms and rushed as fast as I could to the nearest vet, about ten blocks away. It was Christmas Day, with little chance I'd find anyone there. I rang. The door opened. It was the good doctor himself, who had come in to look after another dog, one in even worse shape than Chips.

The doctor examined Chips and told me he had torn tendons and cartilage in his right hind leg. The damage was so bad, he said, he would have to amputate. Joan adored Chips, as we all did, and I trembled at the thought of telling her the news on this, the day she had just given birth. I would not, however, take it upon myself to make this decision without her knowledge. I ran outside to a public phone and explained things to her. She screamed at me. "No one is going to amputate his leg! Take him to Dr. Krause. He's the only one I trust." I got Dr. Krause on his home phone number and he promised to meet me in his office in half an hour. I sometimes think veterinarians have more compassion for their animal patients than people doctors. As Dr. Krause examined Chips on his table, he repeated the prognosis. Amputation was probably the right choice, but if Joan and I wanted to devote a great deal of time and effort, we might be able to save his leg. It was put in a splint, he was given a shot to ease the pain, and I took Chips back home in a cab.

After three weeks, I returned with Chips to Dr. Krause's office. He examined the leg and said that Chips' leg would have to be gently massaged four times a day without fail, for three to five months. And even then the doctor couldn't be sure if he would heal. For the next few weeks, Chips lay in the back of my closet, somewhere behind my shoes and tennis racket. He barely ate or drank. I had to carry him out once a day to the park because, champion that he was, he would not relieve himself on paper. Once in the park, I placed him next to his favorite tree; he lifted his leg and promptly fell over on his side. From then on, I had to prop him up with one hand and hold his body up with my other hand as he did his business. I was suddenly getting strange looks from nannies in the park, as if I were a new kind of pervert that threatened their neighborhood.

It pretty much fell to me to become his masseur while Joan was busy nursing Nancy. Day after day, week after week, month after month, I massaged his hind leg. Joan and Ellen pitched in as well but I seemed to be his masseur of preference. I did it in front of football games, basketball games, and all through *The Perry Como Show*. After a while, I thought I was being had. Chips was walking well around the house but when he saw me, he started to limp. With gritted teeth, I put him up on the bed, rolled him over on his side, and saw him gaze out the window as if to say, "How lucky can a dog get?" Nancy was six months old by now, and I played less with her than I did with Chips' hind leg. The doctor finally pronounced him well and fully healed, thanks to Joan's last-minute reprieve, but whenever I came home, he leaped on the bed, rolled over on his side, raised his right leg, and looked at me as if to say, "Where were you? You're ten minutes late today."

ONCE OUT OF THE masseur business, I turned again to my former profession, playwriting. I reread the fifty pages of *Barefoot* that lay neglected these many months. This time I liked it. It wasn't a farce and it wasn't a satire. It was a romantic comedy, with people you could know and care about. I sat down and finished it in three months, then brought the completed play to Saint Subber, sat again in his tiny alcove, and listened hopefully for his giggles. This time he was laughing loudly and tried unsuccessfully to muffle his sounds of pleasure. Saint was always afraid to praise me too much for fear it would go to my head. All the praise in the world wouldn't go any higher than my knees, not because I was modest but because I still had good reason to be modest. He opened the door to his office, holding the script in his hand, never raising his head. I had no idea what to expect. Finally he looked up.

"I think I have a brilliant idea for a director."

"A director? To direct *this*? Are you telling me you like it?"

"The play? The play is wonderful. It can't miss."

Not a word about what was wrong with the play or what should be rewritten. How could I have gone from twenty drafts of *Come Blow Your Horn* and twenty turn-downs from twenty other producers to not only praise for *Barefoot* on the very first reading by just *one* producer but a quick decision to get the play headed for Broadway as soon as possible? One could say that the success of *Come Blow Your Horn* had lessened Saint Subber's fear of going with an unproven playwright. There was, however, another factor, something more important that truly good producers have. Great instincts. *Barefoot*'s premise was sound. The humor and dialogue jumped off the page. Saint knew in his heart that it would go through rewrites, restructuring, but he also knew on instinct that I had the ability and desire to do it. When you read something good, it's too soon to quibble about details. That's a given as part of the process. What Saint wanted now was a director to lead me through that process. He continued:

"Don't you want to hear my idea for the director?"

"Yes. Of course."

"Mike Nichols."

"Mike Nichols? He's not a director. He's a comic."

Mike Nichols and Elaine May had taken America by storm with their high-style wit, and their sophisticated but hilarious routines. They were in a class by themselves, already having had their two-person show on Broadway play to adoring reviews. Unlike most comedians, however, they were brilliant actors. I wasn't so much skeptical at Saint's proposal as I was surprised.

"Has he ever directed?"

"No. But he wants to."

The idea suddenly seemed inspired. Without knowing him, I instinctively felt he would elevate my humor, bringing a sophistication to it I lacked. Saint called Mike's agent and found out that Mike was now striking out on his own as an actor and was presently in Seattle playing the Dauphin in one of those plays that have Dauphins in them. A week later Mike called Saint, told him he had read the play, loved it, and wanted to meet with us as soon as he was through Dauphining. Mike would talk like that. If he thought it was time for lunch, he would say "Eatage?" At the end of the day, he would ask "Stoppage?" This is not an illustration of his wit, but just an example of how Mike avoided putting anything in a mundane way; inventing words was his way of never being boring. Ever. From the moment I met him in Saint's office, I knew I was meeting someone special.

He was an incredible audience and no one I knew laughed as fully and as appreciatively as Mike. But his broad, winning smile could also mean two things. If you made a suggestion, his smile could mean "That's pure genius," or, "Surely you're not serious about that." He could be warm and giving but then in the same tone put someone down without them ever knowing it. Once during a tryout in Boston, two women in the last row were chatting nonstop throughout the play. Mike, in that same warm way, leaned over and said, "Excuse me. Are the actors speaking too loudly for you?" Never getting it, they answered, "Oh, no. They're fine, thank you." His eyes were penetrating and expressive, and he could say more with a glance than most of us could with a paragraph. I remember once making a suggestion for a piece of business and Mike didn't say a word. He just looked at me poutingly like a child, as if to say, "Poor baby. Came up with a dumb dumb idea." It was never insulting. It was always helpful. If you came up with something he liked, his eyes would just open wide and he'd nod ever so generously. To this day, a telephone call from Mike would immediately make me raise my IQ by forty points and speed up my thought processes by seconds, otherwise I'd be trailing far behind. Joan would sometimes walk into my room, listen, and say, "That's Mike you're talking to, isn't it?" The only thing common about Mike, at least in the early sixties, was his taste in foods. He lived on bologna sandwiches and doughnuts. He could walk into rehearsal, look around, and say, "Is it possible there're no doughnuts? There's no point in rehearsing if there're no doughnuts." Success and high cholesterol changed all that eventually, but I gathered it's what Mike survived on as a student in Chicago. Being an immigrant, he didn't know there were other kinds of food.

Now we started to cast. We had all seen a terrific actor—handsome, intelligent, fresh, and funny without ever trying to be—in a light comedy called *Sunday in New York*. His name was Robert Redford. Another young actress was appearing in the play *Take Her, She's Mine*. Her name was Elizabeth Ashley. She was a beautiful young girl, feisty and funny, with a southern accent and the best stage voice I'd heard since Margaret Sullavan, leaning toward one day becoming in the deep range of Tallulah Bankhead. The mother was going to be played by the wonderful Mildred Natwick, who was presently doing *Waltz of the Toreadors*. The reading of the play was just going to be for ourselves, no one else invited, and would take place in Saint Subber's tiny townhouse. It never occurred to me the actors might be nervous. What I did notice was that no one laughed during the play. No one. Mike just stared at the actors, observing them, listening, occasionally smiling and consistently smoking. No more of those encouraging reactions from Saint. Once again, my old friend Panic visited me. He whispered in my ear, "Get out! Dump it! You were right the first time you quit on it. It's about nothing . . . nothing . . . nothing."

I barely remember the actors leaving. There were polite handshakes, "Good seeing you, Mike," "Thanks for asking me to read," and they were gone. Saint, Mike, and I were alone. The first voice heard was that of Mr. Panic. "Can we still get out of the Bucks County booking?"

Saint looked at me expressionlessly. Mike looked at me as if I were insane.

"Didn't it occur to you that the actors were nervous? They didn't even hear the comedy. They were worried about themselves."

One year old and already at my desk. When you write plays, you have to start early.

My Mafioso period. I was sixteen or so. The bag contains either my laundry or rewrites.

At Fort Dix, New Jersey, 1940.
My mother on the left in her
General Custer hat, then my
brother Danny, next my father
Irving, and me with more hair
than I'll ever have again.

In the Air Force, Denver, Co., 1945. Out of this came *Biloxi Blues*.

Our first paying jobs as writers, getting $25.00 a week at Camp Tamiment. That's me, Phil Leeds, and my brother Danny. It looks like we're posing for our first postage stamp.

Me at 19 with Danny, dressed in identical suits and glasses. We had just gotten our first job, writing for CBS television.

Writing the NBC specials, in the writer's room. The dapper Will Glickman is on the left, Billy Friedberg in the middle, and me.

Joan before I met her, probably about a year old and already growling at the camera. With her mother Helen Baim.

Our engagement party at Tamiment—Helen, me, and Joan.

The wedding picture. I'm on the left.

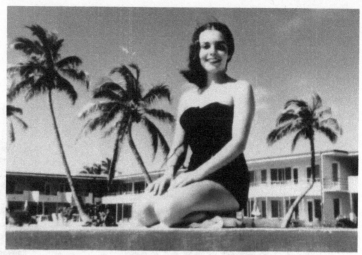

The first honeymoon, in Miami Beach.

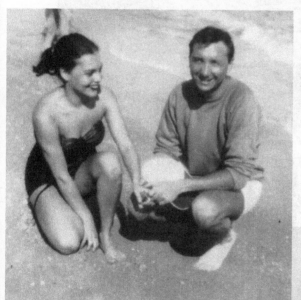

Still on the honeymoon. I love the way Joan's looking at me here.

A second honeymoon; our first trip to Europe. Here I am in Rome.

The thrill of a lifetime: the morning after the opening night of *Barefoot in the Park*, with Mike Nichols.

Me at home and at work, on Sixty-second Street.

Back in Florida with Ellen; she was about two years old. (*Mort Kaye Studios, Inc., Palm Beach, Florida*)

A break in the action in making *After the Fox*, with Peter Sellers.

On the set of *Sweet Charity,* with Bob Fosse and Gwen Verdon.

In Chinatown with Bob Fosse—and his ever-present cigarette—Paddy Chayevsky, Joan, and Buddy Hackett.

That meal, me with my favorite author, Paddy Chayevsky.

My mother, Mae Simon, the woman who turned down Harry Truman.

The Man of the Year Award from *Cue* magazine with New York Mayor John Lindsay and Jerry Orbach.

While making *The Out-of-Towners* with Jack Lemmon.

The house we rented in Pollensa, where we were not permitted to leave the island.

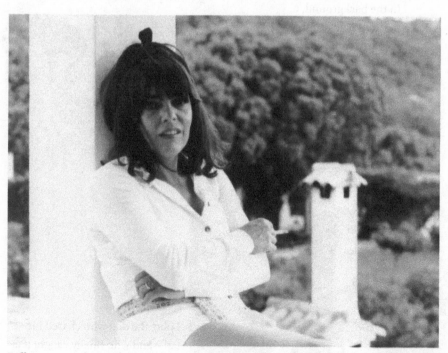

Pollensa was a beautiful place, and despite her lack of a smile, Joan was really happy here. It was the first time we had been truly alone.

What Joan loved to do most—preparing a meal. In Pollensa, with Nancy.

In the background, a Roman aqueduct. In the foreground, Nancy.

Lobo, the dog who chased his tail—and who finally caught it at the end of the summer.

Opening night in the dressing room of *Last of the Red Hot Lovers*. Here is the star, Jimmy Coco, visited by my favorite actress, Maureen Stapleton.

Opening night of *The Sunshine Boys*. Sam Levine on the left and Jack Albertson on the right.

Dad reading his reviews to Ellen and Nancy.

Summer at Amagansett. Joan, Ellen, Nancy, and Chips, who I massaged for six months.

Our house in East Hampton. I wrote five plays here, working in the room off to the left.

I love this picture of Joan, taken in East Hampton. The house was rented and has since been torn down and replaced by Steven Spielberg's new house.

This is the house I bought in Bedford Village without telling Joan.

The last picture I took of Joan; with Ellen and Nancy.

"No, no. They were fine. The play stinks. Let's not do it."

"Calm down," Mike said. "I was very happy. Once they're relaxed in rehearsal you'll change your mind. I'm not *positive* it's good but I *think* it is. Anyway, it'll be fun trying." He put an Oreo cookie in his mouth and one in his pocket and left. I went out a few minutes later, got into a cab, and forgot my address.

It was the only rehearsal of a play of mine that I almost never went in to watch. I wandered up and down the hallway, peeked in once in a while, heard my words, heard Mike talking, heard them asking him questions, but never heard any laughter. Perhaps I had written a new socially conscious drama. Maybe I was the new Arthur Miller. Maybe I was going out of my mind. I paced the hallway again and dropped into another rehearsal that sounded a lot better than mine. They were doing a revival of *Room Service*. No wonder they were all having a good time. I stayed in the building all day and Mike would occasionally come out to ask for a few changes. I was glad to have something to do. I did them rapidly and wanted to slide them under the door, but instead braved it, came in, watched a few minutes of rehearsal, and had totally no opinion of what I was watching. I was no longer panicked. I was now a tall statue of dry ice, leaving trails of vapor behind me as I went back to anonymity in the hallway. Once I heard a huge laugh coming from the rehearsal room. I couldn't resist. I ran in to hear what part of the play they were doing. They weren't. They had taken a break and Mike was regaling them with hysterical stories about his life. It was not beyond me to ask Mike to tell his stories on the stage at Bucks County and let *Barefoot in the Park* tiptoe away in the silence and darkness of the night. They resumed rehearsing and I went back to being dry ice in the hallway.

After three weeks in a rehearsal hall, we moved to an empty theater, our last week before going to Bucks County. I watched bits and pieces from the darkened corners at the rear of the theater and began to see what Mike had done. He had turned the play from artifice to believability. Whatever the actors did seemed natural. Whatever they said seemed like words they themselves had thought of. In the middle of the second act, Paul and Corie (Redford and Ashley) get into a terrific fight. So vehement are their emotions and feelings and hurts that Corie asks Paul for a divorce, just one week after they have gotten married. We were able to see the love and laughter through their pain but they were unaware of it, unaware that there might one day be an audience viewing this. They were living it. I watched them doing their big "first marriage fight" scene from the back of the theater with Mike and then whispered quite earnestly:

"I don't think we should be watching this."

He looked at me puzzled. "Why not?"

"Because it's too private. Too intimate. I feel like I'm eavesdropping, watching something that's none of my business."

Mike smiled at me. "Good. Then it's working," he said.

No wonder there were very few laughs during rehearsals. Everyone was too busy being involved with the characters they now inhabited. We were ready for an audience.

My second time working at the Bucks County Playhouse I didn't have as many butterflies in my stomach. Mike had a net that caught them all for me. Although he was seven years younger than I was, it wasn't surprising that Mike was fully in charge. He didn't have to take it. You just gave it to him. Whenever the play started to veer toward getting laughs, Mike warned the actors. "Who told you this is a comedy? We're doing *King Lear* here." And doing it with the intensity of *Lear* is exactly what made it so funny.

I had never met anyone like Redford before. Certainly not in New York City. He may have looked like the Marlboro Man but he had a keen and deceptive intelligence. He didn't always open up to who he was, because to tell the truth, I think that at twenty-six he was still forming his personality, and being an actor was possibly in conflict with the man he was trying to be. He had, at the time, just completed building his own A-frame house in the mountains of Utah, and for all I knew, he planted, grew, and chopped down the trees and fashioned the logs himself, and melted down iron into nails at night. I knew little about his background or education but he seemed to have all the solid, patriotic values of James Stewart in *Mr. Smith Goes to Washington*. This didn't stop Bob from racing across America for our first day of rehearsal in his beat-up old car, finding roads where they didn't exist, and breaking speeding records while accumulating enough tickets to subsidize most U.S. highways. But he got there on time. He started out as a commercial artist and was a brilliant caricaturist. He did sketches of the entire company but no one ever posed for them. He sat quietly in a semi-lit corner of the theater during rehearsals, presumably studying his lines, but instead stealing our physical and personal foibles and committing them to pages in his sketchbook. They were deft, clever, and certainly humorous. Humor, however, was something that Redford tried very hard to avoid in his stage performance.

At least *obvious* humor. He knew, of course, that he was in a comedy, but he never wanted the laughs to come from *him*. They had to emanate from the character. When he did say or do something we thought was funny, he would stop and say, "Why are you laughing?"

"Because it's funny," Nichols explained.

"All right," Bob allowed. "But if you see me doing it again, I'm taking it out. If it's not real, I'm not doing it."

Elizabeth Ashley was living proof that Scarlett O'Hara existed. She was a vixen but you couldn't help falling in love with her. She was a stunning-looking girl from the South, with a charismatic personality and a deep, rich voice perfectly suited for the stage. She also had a vocabulary so foul there wasn't a word she could utter that wasn't first used in every branch of our armed forces. Once a reporter came to me and asked if it were true that Elizabeth Ashley cursed like a pirate's parrot. I tried to protect her and said, "No. Not at all. Where did you hear that?" He said, "Elizabeth told me."

Mildred Natwick, who played her mother, seemed like the head nun at the Sacred Heart Church. It was that very quality which made her humor as an actress and a person so surprising and delightful.

From the moment the curtain went up on the first performance at Bucks County until it fell at the end of the play, there was nonstop laughter. This was not a satire that divided the audiences of *Little Me*. This was close to real life and closer still to the lives of the New Yorkers who climbed those five flights themselves. (For the French version, I had to make it seven flights. In Paris, five flights would be a luxury apartment.) Even before the local reviews came out, word had buzzed back to New York, and the city folk started to make the trek down to New Hope nightly. A lot of the stir had to do with the coterie of friends that Mike had, from a young Stephen Sondheim to Susan Sontag to poet Robert Graves. I thought if these were his friends now, who would he know when he became really famous? Goethe? Molière? Leonardo da Vinci?

Following our success in Bucks County, we moved to New Haven. I had never met Richard Rodgers before but he came up to me, grabbed my arm, and said immediately after seeing the play, "It's irresistible. Absolutely irresistible." I thought he was quoting me a song he wrote with Larry Hart.

We *finally* moved on to New York, opening at the Biltmore Theatre on October 23, 1963. Fifteen minutes after the curtain went up, critic Robert Sylvester got up from his seat and marched up the aisle, heading for the men's room. My heart sank. He looked at me standing next to Mike and whispered,

"Don't worry. It's a smash." It was the earliest review I ever got. There was a party later at Tavern on the Green, and when more people arrive than you've invited, you know you've got a success, because everyone wants to be in on the celebration. And a huge celebration it was. The reviews were almost anti-climactical to the word that spread around the rooms.

Walter Kerr of the New York *Herald-Tribune* said, "The curtain goes up on an empty apartment and Mr. Simon proceeds to fill it up with a play. By improvising as freely as he does, Mr. Simon arrives at exactly what's meant by entertainment." John McClain of the *Journal-American* summed it all up succinctly: "*Barefoot in the Park* is the funniest comedy I can remember—it's as simple as that." One reviewer amused me. Although highly complimentary, he thought we milked the joke too much of everyone breathing so hard every time they came up the five flights. Think of it. What should we have done? In the second act no one gets out of breath anymore because we've seen it? Have they all gone to gyms and gotten themselves into top shape, including Corie's sixty-ish mother? In the actual apartment I lived in with Joan, I often couldn't get our dog, Chips, to climb the five flights. He stopped on the third floor and waited for me to carry him. And then I had to spoil him more with all that massaging later on.

So there I sat at the party drinking anything they put before me. I was completely stunned, not from liquor, but from emotion. I never dreamed anything like this would happen to me. I didn't know quite what to feel, how to react to it, how to accept it. Joan was thrilled and showed no signs that sudden acclaim would affect our lives in a negative way. I talked to reporters for the first time in my life. I fumbled over my thoughts, tripped over my feelings. "Mr. Simon" (I was asked twenty times), "what does it feel like to have a smash hit?" I knew how it felt to be drunk but I didn't know how to feel success. Mike, on the other hand, was articulate and witty. I could be that way with him but I couldn't do it in front of a camera. What it felt like, I suppose, was that it wasn't happening to me. It might have been happening to a *part* of me, the part that sits alone in a room, blocks out all other thoughts from his mind, thinks, and types . . . but it hadn't yet affected the part that lives outside the writing. The one who has a wife and children and leads a fairly humdrum daily life. I had never been surrounded by reporters before or had my picture taken forty times with a smiling celebrity, who suddenly became my best friend without ever having met me before.

What had really changed? My career was not now automatically guaranteed to be a success in the theater forevermore. It was just one hit. The critics are very quick and happy to discover a new talent, which you eventually pay for as the years go by. After all, you can only be discovered once. Was there something inside of me which allowed me to enjoy my moment but not be elated or overcome with it? I had been taught somewhere in my background that Jews did not gather around a campfire talking about the possessions they had with them, for they would surely be gone in the morning. You did not boast about your good fortune because God would certainly punish a boaster. I was not overly religious, in fact hardly religious at all, but your culture, by osmosis, or what you hear around the dinner table as a boy, brands fears and superstitions into your mind forever. I had no trouble in keeping things in perspective that night. You don't change, but what happens is that *other* people's perspective of you changes. The feeling of happiness you feel inside doesn't compare to the enormous degree of elation they *assume* is happening to you. And you feel you're letting them down if you don't act in a manner that coincides with their assumption. I was now being treated differently. No guard asked for my invitation to the party. People waiting on line for their buffet dinner called out, "Hey, Neil. You don't wait on line tonight. Grab a plate and get yourself something." Since I couldn't feel me, I decided to feel nobody by downing two vodkas and three glasses of champagne. Ah, now that feels more like success.

The real enjoyment, the true happiness, the essence of the joy came later that night, as Joan and I lay in bed, looked at each other, and laughed, knowing that in the morning I would still have to take Chips out for his walk and Joan would have to make breakfast and take Ellen to school. And John Steinbeck was right. You could still only eat two eggs for breakfast.

ONE QUESTION that has invariably been asked of me in almost every interview I've ever done is "Which of your plays is your favorite?"

I find the question, in its literal sense, impossible to answer. Does the question mean: "Which was the most successful?" "Which did I write better than any of the others?" "Which do most *other* people like the best?" "Which did the critics seem most pleased with?" Etc. . . .

For me the answer can be more closely found when I ask myself the following: "In what stage of my own development as a writer was I when I wrote the play?" "Was I a happy person at the time, and did this play make me happier?" "Did this play break new ground for me, enabling me to move to a farther-reaching place?" "Did I like the company of actors, the director, the new friendships I made, and the city where we tried it out?" "Did it achieve what I was aiming at?" "Was the opening-night party a blast?" "Why am I even thinking about this question?"

Well, you can't shove all those questions through your mind as the reporter patiently sits there waiting for an answer. The true answer is, there's about eight or nine I could say yes to in that little mind quiz I often play. And in all of those, I was unhappy with parts of the plays. The reporters are disappointed with that answer. It's not much fun for them. As in a lot of things in life, they want you to name names, and you usually get in trouble when doing that. I'll tell you this though. Doing *Barefoot in the Park* was about as much fun as a playwright like me could have.

IF ANYONE ENJOYED the success of *Barefoot*, there was no one more elated than my mother. I could barely get her on the phone the next day. She called every one of her relatives and every friend's relatives. She was taking ticket orders in her house and relaying them to the box office. My father, in kind, was the hit of the garment industry. He didn't have to tell jokes now to get attention. All he had to do was to get the out-of-town buyers tickets to his son's new play.

I WAS ALSO NOW HANDLING my business in a different way. After *Come Blow Your Horn* opened, I had come to a realization. Despite the fact that Helen Harvey played a big part in getting me to try *Come Blow Your Horn* in Bucks County, I never felt that the William Morris Agency had much belief in my future. Nor could I count on Helen being employed there in the years to come. I saw no reason for paying an agency 10 percent of every penny I made for every play I wrote for the rest of my life. The most I could count on was their asking for opening-night tickets. It seemed to me that the more successful I could become, the more money *they* would make. If I fell flat on my face, were they going to help write new plays for me? If they were getting work for me, then I would be happy to share the profits with them. In this case, however, a playwright creates his *own* work. I divested myself of agents and decided to look for a lawyer, who, for a fee, would represent me in my dealings. However, before this happened, Irving Lazar once more entered the picture.

I picked up the ringing phone and Irving got right down to business, as usual. "If I can get you three hundred thousand dollars for the film rights to *Barefoot*, will you sell it?" I still didn't want an agent but I was willing to work with Irving on a deal-to-deal basis, because if nothing else, he did his work. I said I would accept it. "Swifty" was aptly named. He called back later that day. "You got it, kid. Three hundred grand. Congratulations." What I didn't know was that Irving had sold it to Paramount for *four* hundred thousand and pocketed the extra hundred thousand for himself. What he did was not ethical but not illegal. He was not actually my agent, just a dealer. He told me afterward exactly what he did. "I asked you if you would accept three hundred thousand. You accepted and got it. What's the difference what I got? No one else would probably have gotten you that much." He could be right. I had no complaints but got a glimpse of how this business works. I didn't have an agent for the next thirty years. I didn't see any reason for paying an agent's commission for work he didn't get me. I had to sit down and write the play myself. It was a smart move, except for on one occasion where I paid dearly.

For his part in the play's success, Mike Nichols won the Tony Award as Best Director. I agreed to write the screenplay. Robert Redford went on to become one of Hollywood's biggest stars. The play ran on Broadway for close to four years. I had Joan, Ellen, and now Nancy . . . The joy of it all was beginning to seep in.

Shortly after the play was deemed a smash hit, Bob Fosse threw a party for me in his apartment and there was a large gathering of our mutual friends. Bob could be very cutting and very loving at the same time. He stood on a table, made sure everyone had a drink, then raised his glass.

"Okay, a toast to Neil. Tonight is the last night he'll have any friends."

We laughed at the truth of it. The truth is, unfortunately, that success breeds jealousy and jealousy breeds contempt. I only thought of it as I lay in my bed later that night. Surely the world couldn't be that cold, that petty, that cynical. Or was that Bob's own cynical attitude? Or was I making too much of a friendly joke? Everyone loves a winner until the winner keeps winning too much and too often. I wasn't even remotely in that situation, so at least I consoled myself by thinking my friends would always be my friends.

A few weeks after the play opened, I was being interviewed by two reporters from *The New York Times* for a special piece on me. The interview took place in my apartment. "Who are you?" they asked. "Where did you suddenly pop up from?" I told them I already had two shows on Broadway, but they brushed that aside. *Barefoot* was major league and the story sounded better if they made it sound as if I just walked on the scene. In the middle of the conversation, the phone rang. I excused myself and answered it. It was my cousin, who informed me that my father had just died from heart failure. I hung up the phone solemnly and told the reporters, who respectfully offered their sympathy and left quickly. I walked to the window and looked out at Central Park where I could see the bench on which my father and I had our last conversation together. I thanked God that I had made my peace with my father before he died . . . and was hoping that by now he finally thought I had chosen the right profession.

A COUPLE OF SWELLS

8

IN 1952, the first of our two summers working at Camp Tamiment, when I first saw Joan from afar, and when she was still engaged to a lawyer, Danny was knee-deep in his own romance. He met a beautiful young girl named Arlene Friedman, a philosophy wizard who would rather sing than go to Harvard. That winter they were married, and the following summer Arlene returned to Tamiment as part of the entertainment staff. They soon had two children, Michael and Valerie, and when Danny and I went our separate professional ways, he bought a house in Encino, California, and was making a very comfortable living as head writer on many of our top television shows. The marriage, unfortunately, lasted only nine years. It was a hard breakup for Danny, and my personal feeling was that he carried a torch for her that eventually dimmed, but it was years before it ever burned out. He never remarried, nor did she, and I never quite understood why not. He had plenty of opportunities since he eventually dated half the female population of Southern California.

Danny was always careful about his money. He was generous with other people but he treated himself as Scrooge would treat his clerks. Danny once bought six pairs of socks, then drove back four miles to the store because after he arrived home he found there were only five pairs in the bag. Economically he may have been right, but I could never understand losing an hour of your life to get back $1.20. Danny adored his two children and I think from the time of his divorce, he considered every penny he made as security for the future of Michael and Valerie. Danny and I had a good friend named Roy Gerber, a theatrical agent and one of the most congenial and fun-loving men I ever met. At about the same time Danny broke up with Arlene, Roy broke up with his wife, Connie. Their breakups led to a new union, more famous and longer-lasting than their two marriages combined.

The two men had alimony and child support to pay. Money was going out and the drain weighed heavily on Danny. He proposed, in a manner of speaking, that he and Roy move in together to cut down on their rent, utilities, and all other expenses. This union didn't prosper any better than either of their first marriages.

I was in California on business, and Danny and Roy invited me to dinner. I asked where the restaurant was in case I was late. The restaurant was their apartment. Danny was the cook and Roy was the husband who usually came home late for dinner. Your average American couple. They generally ate at home together even on double dates with women. The money saved on restaurants and tips could eventually put Danny's children through college . . . and put Roy in an asylum. When Danny made his pot roast for four (he was an excellent cook) and the girls showed up an hour late because Roy never told them exactly when to arrive, Danny almost killed Roy with his spatula.

To me and to anyone else seeing it, the situation was hilarious. I told Danny it was the premise of a brilliant comedy, whether as a film or a play. He agreed and told me he intended to sit down and write it. Danny rarely ever wrote alone, starting with his collaboration with me, through all his years working with other writers on TV. Danny liked to talk when he wrote. He liked to pace. He liked to eat. He even liked to play. When we were together, he would say, "Do you want to play golf today?" I was *always* ready to play golf. "On one condition," he warned. "We work while we play." As I stood on the first tee, eyeing the fairway that spread out some four hundred yards in front of me, I would be about to swing when Danny would say, "How about a sketch about a couple buying a house?" I liked the idea of the sketch and I also liked the idea of hitting Danny in the head with my driver. Maybe a two-iron would have been better. You can imagine what Roy Gerber went through.

For months Danny tried to put the play on paper. He rarely got past page fifteen. I kept calling him from New York, urging him to continue. I thought the idea couldn't miss. Try as he might, he gave up on it. "You know how to write plays. I don't. You write it instead." I told him I would but made it clear my concept would certainly be different from what Danny may have had in mind. I couldn't write with him looking over my shoulder. I said I would see the characters in a different way, in a more objective light. Danny himself later admitted to me that he would probably never have seen Felix in the way I perceived him. I had to do it in my own style, in the rhythms of speech I was now working in. He gave me carte blanche and I gave him a percentage of my earnings from the play in perpetuity. For the past thirty-some years we've both been making money from it.

That summer Joan and I rented a house in Amagansett, Long Island. Our circle of friends continued to grow enormously, and since the Hamptons were at the time primarily an artists' and writers' colony, we tended to drift into theatrical circles. The Fosses, Bob and Gwen, were there, with their new daughter, Nicole, born a few months after Nancy; the girls' mutual friendship and closeness grew and remains intact to this day, when they are both now new parents themselves. We met Hal Prince, and Betty Comden and Adolph Green, and composers like Frank Loesser and Burton Lane, and directors like Sidney Lumet and Gene Saks, and actors galore.

The summers, however, were not pure vacations for me. Although there were lots of parties, lots of golf and tennis and fishing, I still worked five days a week. I worked each day in a small, hot room upstairs in nothing but shorts, trying to figure out how to do the Danny and Roy play. The title came to me very quickly. I liked *The Odd Couple* not only because they certainly were one, but because I favored titles that were already part of the language, which automatically made them sound familiar and easy to remember. So it was with *Come Blow Your Horn; The Star Spangled Girl; Plaza Suite; Promises, Promises; Last of the Red Hot Lovers*, and *The Gingerbread Lady*. It's hard even today to pick up a newspaper and not see someone like Bill Clinton talking to Bob Dole without the caption reading, "The Odd Couple." I think now when people see those words strung together in a newspaper or a book, they tend to think of the play or the film or more likely the television series more than they would think of the phrase that was in use far before I ever thought of using it.

I had already fleshed out the characters of Danny and Roy, making them opposites in many more ways than they were in life. I made Danny a finicky and compulsive demander of neatness and order, which Danny was not, and I made Roy sloppy, disorganized, and grouchy, none of those characteristics really fitting Roy Gerber's true nature. Roy and Danny actually liked each other very much, and aside from Danny's need to have Roy and friends come to dinner on time, they got on pretty well. As a result of my changes, however, the play's characters now found it was not only difficult to live with each other on a day-to-day basis—as it is for almost all of us—but that they were complete opposites, unable to be together under *any* circumstances. For Roy's character, I picked the name Oscar Madison, with the hard *K* sound, because it made me visualize a stronger person, more dominating, and I knew that Madison was really a pen name used by the writer of a daily sports column instead of the name he was born with, which I assumed to be something like

Oscar Morrowitz. I wanted a prissy name for Danny's counterpart and chose Felix because he sounded like a cartoon character, a shy and finicky person. I made him Felix Ungar without realizing that I had already used that name in *Come Blow Your Horn*, to identify an unseen character who was an acting coach. I was enamored of the name, however, and when its earlier use was pointed out, I decided to use it here anyway. I have rarely heard from people who knew or cared that I'd used the name twice. I imagine they think I have some mysterious and important attachment to the name and used it for personal reasons. Nope. Just liked it.

What I needed in the beginning of the play was exposition, a way to show and explain Oscar's sloppiness and Felix's neatness and childlike behavior in dealing with problems in his marriage and daily life. If both men were going to be divorced, I had to show why the wives had left them, which turned out to be the same reasons that Oscar and Felix could not get along with each other any more than their spouses could. I also knew I would never show the wives in the play. If I had, they might have come out as shrews, berating their husbands for their behavior, and the audience would feel the men were well out of it. On the other hand if I made the women quite sympathetic, we might have lost some empathetic feelings for Oscar and Felix. It's better for the audience to picture the wives in their own minds.

Who then would be the other people in the play, the ones who detailed the characteristics of Felix and Oscar, a Greek chorus so to speak, without actually making them just that, a Greek chorus? One day sitting on the beach with Joan and the girls, I said I was going to take a walk along the shore, hoping I'd come back with a form for the play. Since we were still in the days of three-act plays, I thought in terms of triangles. Connect point A to point B at the top, down to point C, and C connects back across to point A again. The final connection is not the end but rather the beginning of a new triangle, one that we never see but know that it's there in the future. The future is what the rest of our characters' lives are going to be, which we can imagine but not necessarily predetermine. At least it gave me an image to work on as I walked along the hot sand, hoping the ocean water that cooled my feet would do the same for my sweaty, furrowed brow. As my feet sank into the wet sand, I kept thinking of what Max Gordon said: "Characters. Structure. What you got here is a house that's going to sink in the sand."

Two and a half hours later and sunburned to a crisp, I returned, and sat on Joan's blanket with a smile on my face big enough to make you think I was Michelangelo walking back into his studio and saying, "I got it. A big tall naked guy and I'll call him David."

"I have the form for the play."

"Really? What is it?"

"The first act begins with a poker game, the second act begins with a poker game and the third act *ends* with the poker game."

She smiled, knowing I was happy, but it didn't hide the puzzled look on her face.

"No, no," I pleaded to her raised eyebrows. "It's okay. I know it doesn't sound like anything but I have a place now, a setting to root it in. I know what the apartment looks like, what it smells like. There're toys and crayoned pictures and dying goldfish left behind by Oscar's small son for his dad to take care of. I know where the doors are, where the kitchen is, I know how they dress. I know who the other poker players are, what they do for a living, and how much this game means to them."

"That's wonderful," she said encouragingly. "Want a tuna salad sandwich?"

I sat on the blanket, watched the girls fearlessly playing games with waves that chased them back to shore, but all the while I was just aching to get back to that hot room upstairs, strip down to my shorts, and begin writing. Back home, late that afternoon came a phone call from Irving Lazar in California.

"Paramount wants to know when you're going to deliver that screenplay for *Barefoot*, kid. You got anything yet?"

I knew they couldn't release the film until the end of the play's run on Broadway, and we were still in our first year. I had plenty of time. I told Irving I wasn't ready for it yet, that I wanted to work on a new idea for a play I was just starting.

"What's the idea for the play?"

"It takes too long to tell."

"Tell me in two sentences. Noël Coward could tell me in one."

"Well, it's about two men who are divorced, move in together to save money to pay their alimony, and have the same fights with each other as they did with their wives."

There was a pause for a moment before Irving spoke.

"How soon can you get out to California?"

"California? What for?"

"I want you to tell the head of Paramount exactly what you just told me. I'll sell the picture rights for more than we got for *Barefoot*."

"Irving, you don't understand. There's nothing written yet. Not a line. Not a word. Aren't they going to want to read the play before they buy the film rights?"

"Listen to me, kid. If there's one thing I can do, it's sell a good idea. This isn't good. It's terrific. I can get Billy Wilder to direct. I want you out here as fast as you can. Congratulations."

He probably was already on the phone to Billy Wilder. Suddenly the train was traveling too fast for me. I have never liked getting paid for something *before* I wrote it. The pressure on me to deliver the goods becomes too great. I'd be trying to create something they already owned. I'd feel as though I'd sold a part of myself rather than something I've written. The gamble is what I love about the theater. The game is simple. You write it, they put it on; if they like it, you make money. If they don't, *you* don't. I was also afraid that once Paramount bought an unwritten idea, they might want to have input into what I wrote in the play version, to share in my creation and push me in a direction they thought would make a good movie and possibly alter what *I* thought would make a good play. The reason I had turned down doing the screenplay of *Come Blow Your Horn* was that I didn't want to get sucked up into the Hollywood system. The money was their lure but once they have something you want, you're in their power. I didn't want to be in the power of *anyone*. I was perfectly happy if I could write plays for the rest of my life. I called Irving back a few minutes later and explained my feelings to him.

"Listen to me, young man," he said in a condescending tone—but he probably talked to Noël Coward the same way, probably saying, "Now listen to me, old boy . . ." He continued: "Paramount trusts you. I trust you. You gave them a hit with *Come Blow Your Horn*, and they know they bought a winner with *Barefoot*. Don't be a schmuck. You're a better writer right now than all the high-priced old farts they have sitting on their asses in Hollywood. I promise you they won't touch the play. Now meet me out here as fast as you can. I gotta go, John Huston's on the other line."

When I told Joan about our conversation, I realized what thrilled me most was not so much that Paramount might buy the rights to something I hadn't written yet, but that I had caused John Huston to be kept waiting. It's moments like this you remember most. I pictured myself in Hollywood one day, walking into Romanoff's, crossing over to Huston's table, and saying, "Hello. My name is Neil Simon. I believe I once kept you waiting on 'Swifty' Lazar's line." Then Huston would throw his bourbon in my face, punch me out with one short clip to the jaw, pick me up, buy me a drink, and say, "You've got guts, kid. I like that." And we'd become pals and we'd go marlin fishing in Mexico and ride to the hounds in Ireland. Katie Hepburn would come up for the weekend with Spencer Tracy and we'd get in a little croquet after lunch while I—but there it was. Getting sucked into the Hollywood dream. Careful, Neil. Stick to Forty-seventh Street and Broadway.

A week later Joan and I flew out to Los Angeles, and as we descended, I said, "Look. It's not so smoggy today." She said, "Because nobody's driving. They're all dead in their houses." God, I liked her. Our first night there, Irving threw a "Welcome to Hollywood" party for me upstairs at the Bistro. Present at the well-dressed shindig were Rosalind Russell, Billy and Audrey Wilder, Jack Lemmon, Natalie Wood, Fred Astaire, and Gregory Peck, among many others, with their spouses and guests. When I was introduced by Irving, Rosalind Russell gave me a big smile, said "Hi," just like in *Auntie Mame*, and turned quickly back to her conversation with Tony Curtis. Jack Lemmon walked by, smiled, and said, "How you doin', sport?" on his way to the men's room. They weren't being rude. I don't think they knew who I was or what I was doing there. If Irving Lazar had called his friends and said, "I'm giving a little dinner party at the Bistro for this wonderful spoons player from Guatemala," they would all have come. Irving threw great parties. I did see Natalie Wood once look at Joan very carefully because that night, Joan looked remarkably like Natalie Wood. Joan soon appeared out of the dark and took me aside. "I want to go home. If you want to stay, stay. I'll get a cab."

What did I do now?

"Why? What's wrong?"

"I was in the ladies' room. You don't know how they talk out here. They're making millions of dollars a year and they're complaining their maids are stealing cornflakes from them. Can we please go?"

"We can't just walk out. I'm the guest of honor."

"What honor? No one's talked to you yet. Two women took me aside and said, 'Watch it, honey. These women will pounce on your husband like wolves at a campfire.' I want to leave."

We finally did but not before Fred Astaire accidentally brushed past my shoulder. I didn't think I could accurately say to people, "I once danced with Fred Astaire," but I did come awfully close.

Two days later, Irving came to pick me up at the Beverly Hills Hotel for the meeting with the Paramount executives. I was concerned that I didn't have more to tell them than the brief description I had given him.

He sneered. "I wouldn't let you tell them even if you knew. That's all they get. You tell them the idea and they get twenty-four hours to make up their minds, otherwise I go to Warner Brothers."

He was serious. It worked for Irving, because he rarely made idle threats. Twenty-four hours is why they called him "Swifty."

"Don't give them a chance to think about it, kid. If we wait, then they know you're hungry. Let them be the ones who are hungry." It was all a game, like playing baccarat at Monte Carlo. Who knew from Monte Carlo?

As we waited out front for the valet to bring Irving's car up, another car pulled into the hotel's driveway first. The woman at the wheel jammed on her brakes and screamed, "He's dead! Kennedy's dead! They killed the president!" For a moment I thought it was phony. That they were shooting a scene for some film with the camera hidden in a second-floor window. It took seconds to know this was the real thing. The doorman and others rushed to her car, to calm her down and listen to the news report on her blaring radio. Walter Cronkite's somber voice was announcing the astonishing news. We all stood there numb, unable to comprehend what was happening. It couldn't be true. It wasn't possible. Irving turned white and said, "Jesus Christ." There were tears in his eyes and he didn't know which way to move. People kept turning to each other as if maybe we could do something about it. It was like Pearl Harbor Day only this war was over in ten seconds. Irving finally looked at me and said, "Not a good day to talk to Paramount."

The irony and unwitting black humor of what he just said sounded like something out of Nathanael West.

"I'll call you in a few days, Neil." Calling me Neil instead of "kid" showed at least some deference to the seriousness of the situation. He got into his car and drove off, and I rushed up to our room where a devastated Joan was glued to the television. She burst into tears, wondering what kind of a world did we bring our children into. That was my "Where were you when Kennedy was shot?" story.

We stayed in our room, watching it all on TV: the flight of Air Force One, with Lyndon Johnson and Mrs. Kennedy in her blood-stained dress; the bizarre swearing-in ceremony; the murder of Lee Harvey Oswald. We were there a week when we decided to go home. Irving called. He was still shaken by the events but said, "I know it's a difficult time to do this, but Paramount wants to see you tomorrow."

"Irving, how can I talk about a funny idea to anyone at a time like this? I don't have the stomach for it and how receptive could they be?"

"This is Hollywood, kid. They can do anything."

The next morning as we drove out to the Paramount lot on Melrose Avenue, I wondered if I could even think of a first sentence to say. Irving took care of all that. There was some talk about the horror of the assassination, then Irving switched the mood and miraculously got things back to business as usual. "Neil didn't want to come today and we can all understand that. But life moves on. Tell them the idea, kid."

The executives all leaned back in their seats and listened. I told them exactly what I had told Irving, with no embellishments or attempts to try to make it sound funny. They smiled, some nodded, but they didn't comment any further than "cute idea." Irving said to them, "That's all Neil is going to tell you now but he's got the entire story laid out in his head. He showed me some pages and they're hilarious." He even laughed out loud at some imaginary jokes that I was supposed to have already written. The man was a marvel. Then he rose and said, "I hope we can do business, boys. You know my usual deal. I promised Warners I'd give you twenty-four hours before we go over and talk to them." His "usual deal" offer sounded as meaningless as Claude Rains saying in *Casablanca*, "Round up the usual suspects," but they knew better. Irving didn't play games and they were aware they really only had twenty-four hours.

He drove me back to the Beverly Hills Hotel. "My hunch? They'll snap it up in a minute. They'd be fools not to. I'll call you tomorrow." And he was off to another studio, probably to give Harry Cohn and Columbia twenty-four hours on another writer's script.

We had an early flight back to New York the next morning and I didn't expect to hear from Irving until we arrived home later that night. We were just out of the door with our bags when the phone rang.

"We're in business, kid. And I bettered the *Barefoot* deal. What did I tell you? Have a nice flight, say hello to your delicious Joanie, and call me whenever you have something on paper." I didn't ask what his cut was but since it didn't affect mine, I was happy with the deal. I had the freedom to write the play as I wanted to.

As the plane took off, Joan looked out the window and said, "I'm not coming back here. Ever." I wasn't listening. I had a spiral notebook on my lap and was writing, "*The Odd Couple.* Act 1. Scene 1. A sloppy apartment on the West Side of New York on a hot, humid summer night."

SOME PLAYS COME EASILY, some take time, and some feel as though you're pushing Noah's Ark, after the flood, up Mount Ararat, animals included. This time the first act came easily. I knew the atmosphere, the talk, the drinks, the smoke, and the food from the occasional poker games I attended with friends, writers, agents, and actors. Occasionally a psychiatrist slipped in but I suspected he was there on the same mission as I was: observing behavior. I am not now nor ever was a good poker player. I went because I loved the banter, the jokes, and the sandwiches from the Carnegie Deli. It was my night for male bonding, which came less frequently for me once I was married and had children. I played carefully but not because I was afraid to lose money. I just didn't want to look like an idiot. Little did they know that before every game I reread *The Education of a Poker Player.* I might as well have read the Gutenberg Bible. I'm not very good when it comes to following directions. Rarely did I stay in a pot long unless I had three of a kind or better, like a Royal Flush. Anything less and I would throw in my hand. Since these were not dummies I was playing with, they knew I only bet when I had something. That's tantamount to having them deal you with your cards exposed to the table.

Luckily, it was not a serious poker game. It was fun, laughs, beer, and great sandwiches. The only night it felt like big-time poker was the night that Sidney Poitier blew into the room like a tornado. Sidney was not a regular, just an occasional drop-in. Sidney is a congenial, warm, friendly man but when you play tennis with him, you'd best wear a suit of armor. And when you play poker with him, you'd best go to the movies. He sat down and started betting and raising and reraising his raises, winning every hand and soon making his piles of chips look like the skyline of Manhattan. In an hour we were glad to get out with our shoes and socks. I don't know if Sidney had better cards than we did but his confidence level was so high, we assumed that the five cards he had facing down were all aces. Rarely did he ever have to reveal his hole card since rarely did we ever stay in the game long enough to see it. My hunch was that he bluffed half the time. The man was simply a better actor than we were—and most other actors I knew for that matter.

The stage was now set for me to write the opening scene. The set decoration and grimy atmosphere drew a clear portrait of Oscar, the slob, even before he made his entrance into the poker game. It was a smoke-filled room ("Blow toward New Jersey, willya?"), magazines and old newspapers everywhere, a rotting Christmas tree drooping in the corner since his wife and child left him the previous December. Either Oscar never hired a cleaning lady or else they took one look at the apartment and ran for their lives. In the midst of the players' constant bickering and complaining about Oscar's slovenly way of life, from overflowing ashtrays to a broken refrigerator ("He's got milk in there that's not even in the bottle"), Oscar makes his entrance with beer cans and sandwiches tucked under both arms. The food consists of "brown sandwiches and green sandwiches," which were either "very old cheese or very new meat." Oscar was now established.

Felix Ungar was an hour late for the game, a rare occurrence for him. He could usually tell time better than his watch. During the game, one of the players' wives calls with the news that Felix Ungar has just been thrown out of his house and marriage. Knowing Felix as they do, they fear the worst. Once locked in the john in his office after everyone had gone home, Felix panicked that he would be trapped in the stall and wrote out his entire will on a roll of toilet paper. In short, he's an over-reactor. Felix finally arrives at the game and it's not long before he threatens to commit suicide, an idle threat because he makes certain that no one is more than half a step behind him before he heads toward anything dangerous like a window. The game ends because of Felix's histrionics, and the first act concludes with Oscar generously taking Felix in as his roommate, despite every indication that this union would lead to more trouble than Jimmy Hoffa ever had with his.

The second act begins with a major change in the poker game. Everything in the room has been sanitized, waxed, and polished, including the playing cards. When Felix demands that the players use the little coasters under their wet drinks, the end of an era has truly come. If they're going to be nagged to death, they may as well stay home with their wives and save money. For me, the play was off and running, especially with a scene where sex-starved Oscar fixes up Felix on a double date with a pair of attractive and obviously willing English émigrés who live upstairs, Cecily and Gwendolyn, the Pigeon Sisters. I made them English rather than American because I knew I would do a scene where Felix had to be left alone with his two sweet but tipsy guests. With Felix, a very faithful and traditional husband, he would have neither a common culture or a single word of conversation that would come easily, ensuring that he would bungle the evening and drive Oscar to apoplexy and beyond. The second act was safely home, I thought complacently.

I finished the third act happily and sent the play off to Mike Nichols and Saint Subber. Their reactions were jubilant. Saint booked the theaters for the fall, and Mike and I went about casting the play. I had first seen Walter Matthau playing Nathan Detroit in a revival of *Guys and Dolls* at the New York City Center. It was love at first laugh. I knew this was a man heading for stardom, and I prayed my play would be the vehicle that would catapult him there. We sent the script to Walter in California. We met with and cast Art Carney as Felix. Art was a vastly underrated actor/comedian who was generally overshadowed by the mammoth Jackie Gleason. Not in my book. I preferred Carney's nuances and deftly understated characters to Gleason's "Watch out, pal, I'm taking the stage" brand of comedy. After Matthau finished the script, he told his wife, Carol, "I've just read something that's going to run on Broadway for ten years." He then called Saint Subber and said he would do the play on two conditions. One, that he could invest ten thousand dollars and two, that he wanted to play the role of Felix. It would have been the blunder heard 'round Shubert Alley. I called Matthau and asked why he wanted to play Felix when he would not only be perfect as Oscar, but that he *was* Oscar. Walter replied, "I know. It's too easy. I could phone Oscar in. But to play Felix, that would be acting." I said, "Walter, do me a favor. Act in someone else's play. Do Oscar in mine." He eventually saw the light and the possibility of multiplying his investment and accepted the role of Oscar.

All the other parts were cast except the Pigeon Sisters. Mike and I both knew we needed the sound of authenticity in these roles and decided to cast them in England. The only problem was that Mike was now involved in doing a new play, Murray Schisgal's *Luv*, with Alan Arkin, Eli Wallach, and Anne Jackson. It became Mike's second smash hit in a row. Since Mike couldn't go, he delegated me to go to London and cast the ladies myself. I considered myself a fairly good judge of picking actors for my plays but would feel naked without the triumvirate of director, writer, and producer making the final choice. As I left for England, Mike put a heavier weight on my shoulders by saying, "I trust you."

I auditioned well over a hundred girls and had about thirty return for second readings. Years later, Marsha Mason sat in the darkened theater for the first time as we auditioned actors for a new play of mine; never being in the position of picking actors, but only of being picked or not picked herself, she made an observation. She watched everyone's readings and made notes of the ones she liked, then compared them with the ones we picked. Her list was almost exactly the same list of actors that we had chosen. "I see how it goes now," she said. "You don't pick them. They pick themselves." She was absolutely right. Somehow an actor comes out on the stage with the confidence, the knowledge, the instinct, or just the plain chutzpah of saying to themselves, "This part is mine. It belongs to me." So it was when Carole Shelley and Monica Evans came on the stage to read in London. I hardly had to make a choice. I knew nothing of their background or training. I merely said to both of them, "Would you like to come to New York and do this play for Mike Nichols and me?" A week later they were in New York.

When I returned, Mike and I resumed putting the final touches on the script. The night before rehearsals began, Saint Subber threw a small party for the cast. The first reading of the play and rehearsals were to begin at ten the next morning. Mike and I were standing in a corner, drinks in hand, when I said to him, "Do you feel confident about the play?"

"Of course. I love it. Why do you ask?"

"Well, I think we're both professionals and I think we both know what we're doing. Yet at twelve-thirty tomorrow, after the reading, we're going to find out we have some big trouble spots in the play and neither one of us knows where they are now. Why is that?"

"Good question. Let's wait till twelve-thirty tomorrow and see."

Nothing seemed to break Mike's confidence or his cheerful demeanor. Then again, Mike was a wonderful actor and could probably hide anything.

At ten the next morning, the actors all greeted each other and sat down at the table with their scripts, pencils, and coffee, ready to read. The anticipation was high. The laughter from the cast and those of us listening came on the second line of the play, and the fourth line and the sixth and seventh lines; it never seemed to stop. By the end of the first act, we were all exhausted from laughing. Walter Matthau leaned over to Saint Subber and whispered, "Can I up my investment to twenty thousand?" Mike closed his eyes and gave me an angelic smile. We took a very quick coffee break, as anxious as a pleased audience to get back to the play.

The second act topped the first act. Walter and Art Carney were marvelous, and Carole Shelley and Monica Evans were the surprise of the day. No one knew them and didn't know what to expect. It was like discovering a gold mine. Mike, who had not had a chance to hear them before, since his time was taken up with the opening of *Luv*, looked at me across the table as the ladies read and he smiled from ear to ear. The second act came to a smashing conclusion. We stopped and Walter Matthau said, "You know what the trouble with this play is? We don't give the audience a chance to stop laughing. Maybe we should make the intermissions longer."

Saint Subber, wiping his eyes, said, "You don't need me here. I'm going out to start selling tickets," and he promptly left. My fears from the night before today seemed like nothing more than nerves. What could possibly go wrong now? Even if the third act wasn't up to the first two, I still felt we had a hit. Two minutes into reading the third act, I realized how wrong I was. It was unimaginably bad. A pall fell over the room. Perhaps Saint Subber already knew it, which was the reason he didn't hang around to listen to it. I glanced at Mike as the actors droned on, and raised my eyebrows at him, meaning this was what I meant last night. Now we knew where the trouble was. We got through it somehow and the room grew strangely quiet. Matthau suddenly had second thoughts about doing the play. He thought the third act was god-awful and complained it was not the original third act we had first sent him. He was right about that. Mike and I always knew the original third act went awry, and I had rewritten it to Mike's satisfaction since the original play had been sent out to the actors.

I unhappily have almost never saved first versions of my plays. Especially in those early days. I saved only what I kept in. Otherwise I would need a warehouse to store all that material. You see, I never expected to be a successful playwright nor thought anyone would want the various drafts one day. Therefore I haven't the slightest idea what was in the original third act or why it went wrong. And to fix it, I did dozens of rewrites, some improving, some not. I think no reader would know or understand why the third act went wrong. Laymen rarely do. Professionals rarely do. Unlike a book, a dramatic or comic scene may read well but not *play* well, which is a mystery to us all.

Mike behaved with the cast as though nothing was really wrong. It just needed a little tinkering, Mike told them in a very convincing manner. I wasn't so convinced. He then said to the cast, which was the tip-off, "I don't think we need to read through the play again. Why don't we take a lunch break and just start staging the play from page one?"

I watched them all leave the theater but I never got up from my chair. Mike rose slowly, putting on his jacket, lost in thought. I looked at him. "What do we do?"

"Well, I'm going out to lunch. Then I'm going to start directing the first two acts. You go home and write a new third act."

A *new* third act? It had taken me months to write the original third act, not including the changes to get what we had now. I knew I would have no more than five or six days to write a whole new third act and for Mike to read it, approve it, and have another reading of it before we started rehearsing it. We had, in effect, three and a half weeks before we left for our first tryout in Wilmington, Delaware. The pressure on my shoulders was so great, I couldn't move from my chair.

"You want to talk about it at lunch?" Mike offered.

I looked at him. "Lunch? Who's going to swallow for me?"

I needed to get home quickly, to my room, to my typewriter, or to a building contractor who might be able to get out the cement that had just formed and hardened inside my head.

I walked home from the theater in dazed silence, trying to get some idea started in my head before I got home. I didn't want to walk into my room facing a typewriter that was going to say to me, "Got yourself in it *this* time, didn't you, big shot? Well, I'm waiting for you to be brilliant. Anytime you're ready."

I walked from Broadway and Forty-fourth Street to Fifth Avenue and then turned uptown. At Fiftieth Street I paused in front of St. Patrick's Cathedral. In all my thirty-six years in New York, I had never gone into St. Patrick's Cathedral. I suddenly found myself walking up the steps and entering the most imposing building in all of New York. Inside I sat down in an empty pew to gather my thoughts. Being a Jew, I knew this was the wrong time and the wrong place to start praying for help. But after a few minutes, I heard an inner voice speak to me, perhaps God Himself. He said, "If you have wandered into this cathedral, it's with good reason. If this is the place where you will find peace of mind to do your work, so be it . . . But don't make a habit of it."

As I stepped outside, I realized that I had walked all the way there in a pouring rain and perhaps that's why I stepped into St. Patrick's. Of course. That was it. My brief moment of Catholicism had been tempered by my inherent Talmudic reasoning. There's always an answer for every question. Including the answers you make up for the sake of expedience.

I went home and started to work. The paper kept flying in and out of the typewriter like a montage in the remake of *The Front Page*. I worked ten to twelve hours a day and smoke was coming out of my fingers. I rewrote the entire third act from beginning to end in less than four days. I read it and thought it was damned good. Better than damned good—but I didn't think cockiness was in order just yet. I rushed down to the Plymouth Theatre where Mike was somewhere deep in the second act, making wonderful progress. I waved the pages over my head, a victorious smile on my face. He called a break in the rehearsal and sat in the front of the orchestra, smoking a cigarette as he read silently. Every once in a while his wonderful high-pitched laugh came gushing out up to the very rafters of the theater. He finished it, looked at me with hope, and said promisingly, "Could be."

He called the actors back to the table again to read the new third act. I sat there, head down, not looking at anyone, just waiting for the big laughs that were soon to come . . . and I waited . . . and waited. It was, if possible, worse than the previous third act that everybody hated. I was amazed at how wrong I could be, how blind I was during those four enormously prolific days. It was as though my inner compass had gone wrong. I was following a star that was nothing more than a reflection of the light over my typewriter. Would playwriting ever come easy?

Mike and I secluded ourselves in the stage manager's office. "Don't tell me to go home and write another third act, because there *are* no other third acts. I've used them all up. I'm running on empty. Why don't we just do the first two acts and reduce the ticket prices by a third?"

Mike looked worried for the first time, and I sensed two doughnuts being sent for posthaste. "Well, here's what we'll do," he said. "You go home and keep trying. Try anything. Try something bad, who knows, it might be good. Something will come. I'll rehearse the original third act. We still have some time before the first preview, and I can't just keep rehearsing the first two acts. And then we have those three and a half hours on the train to Wilmington to talk. That's not so bad, is it?" I began to wonder what he was smoking.

There's a point that comes in which you think there's nothing you can put down that's any good, and your own judgment isn't worth the paper you're not writing on. Some people misinterpret what writer's block is. They assume you can't think of a single thing. Not true. You can think of hundreds of things. You just don't like any of them. And what you like, you don't trust. I stayed at home and worked for eight days. I didn't pull out the bad pages, roll them into a ball, and toss them into a wastebasket, the room slowly filling up to my neck as though I were drowning in bad writing. I just stared out the window, and after a few days I could tell the exact number of leaves on the tree outside my room. In the fall and winter, it's not as difficult as in the spring and summer. If a good idea seems to come along, you look away from the tree and look at a wall. A wall is not so distracting. The wall tells you not so much whether the idea is good or not, but how far down the road it can take you. Where does it go? Usually noplace. So you go back to the window and notice a new bud on the far branch. On the ninth day I gave up and went to watch rehearsals, hoping something there might spark me. Mike was working on the second-act poker scene and I sat down behind him. "It looks good," I whispered to him.

He smiled a little smile, knowing well enough that if I had something to show him, he would have heard from me by now. As he watched the actors, he said aloud to the cast, "Something looks wrong. Hold it, guys." He turned to me. "Wouldn't these guys have a television set on? Watching a ball game or a fight?"

"Well, they might," I said, which was not really the truth. I had never played in a poker game where the TV was on. There was too much at stake on the table. Secondly, even if we took that liberty, I thought a TV set on the stage during a scene would be enormously distracting to an audience. But I was hesitant in stopping Mike from trying things, inasmuch as I hadn't been contributing all that much for over a week myself. Mike told the stage manager to bring on a television set, put it next to the card table, and turn it on. I began to get nervous. The TV was turned with its back to the audience, but we could hear the voices of some soap opera. It was competing with the dialogue, and I liked my dialogue better. I still said nothing. Then Mike said to the stage manager, "That's no good. The audience will think we're faking it. Turn it around so the audience can see it." They turned it around. Mike didn't like the soap opera so they turned the dial past cartoons, the news, a game show, and then a documentary. "Leave it there," said Mike. "We'll get a tape of a baseball game later. Go on, guys."

They continued playing the poker game as the set showed us some archaeological findings in Tibet. I was about to go insane. Surely Mike could see how distracting it was, how unbearably annoying. But he said nothing and just stared at the stage. The actors kept saying their lines amid the ringing of ancient Tibetan bells.

I couldn't contain myself any longer. I leaned over Mike's shoulder and said, "Don't you find that distracting?"

He didn't answer me. The scene went on. "Mike, the audience is going to watch the television, not the play."

Still no answer. I was petrified he was going to leave it in. I finally said, "Mike, please take it out. I hate it."

He still didn't answer, then suddenly turned around and said, "I'm sorry. I didn't hear you. I was watching the television." Then he called out to the stage manager, "Kill the television. I hate it," then looked at me. "What were you saying?"

I shrugged innocently. "Nothing. It was a good try."

As the scene continued, Mike suddenly turned around to me and said, "Can we talk for a minute?" It sounded ominous. I nodded and we walked to the back of the theater. He paused a moment before he spoke.

"I've been thinking. Why don't we take out the poker game?"

I looked at him and smiled. Why would he take me all the way to the back for some stupid joke? His face remained serious. He wasn't joking.

"You're not serious, are you? Why would we take it out?"

"Don't you find it boring?"

"The *poker game*? It's the best thing we have in the show. And we have it in each act. There'd be nothing left in the play."

"Can't I just try it?"

"Mike, you've been watching it every day, six days a week. *I'm* not bored with it. I just watched it. It's hilarious. The audience hasn't even seen it yet."

He thought about it for a second. "Maybe you're right."

Then he turned and went back to his seat, continuing the rehearsal. Directors get blocks too. Only they don't look at a tree. They just keep watching the same scene over and over again.

Finally it was time to leave for Wilmington, and our cast boarded the train in good spirits, despite the fact that we had a well-rehearsed play with a third act that didn't work. Amazingly what *did* help was the three and a half hours Mike and I had on the train. It was the longest period we'd been able to spend together since we began rehearsals. It was wonderful to be able to exchange ideas again. The first thing we did was to clear away all the debris in the third act and see if there was anything worth saving. There wasn't, unless I decided to type on the other side of the paper. It had to go sooner or later. We talked incessantly, sparking each other as only people on the same wavelength could. Some of the ideas we came up with were terrible, but that was to our advantage because we knew we didn't have to go down those same misleading paths again. It narrowed our choices. Together we thought of some promising possibilities, but Mike knew they'd only be as good as I wrote it.

When I was finally able to say to him with a shred of hope, "I like that. I think I can do that," an excitement started to rumble in my head. I was about to move to another car on the train so I could start to make notes. Just then the conductor announced, "Wilmington next."

We checked into our hotel rooms and I never saw Mike or the cast for almost two days. I worked all that day, had dinner sent up, and continued to work as the maid came in to turn down the bed and leave a mint on my pillow. Sometimes I really look forward to that chocolate mint on the pillow. Little things like that make playwriting on the road worth putting up with. At two in the morning, my eyes were drooping and I knew I needed a few hours' sleep. I removed my shoes and socks and fell on the bed. Then I heard it. Music coming through the wall behind my bed. I tried putting a pillow over my head but to no avail. Who could be playing music at two o'clock in the morning and how could I silence it? Finally I called the front desk and spoke to the night clerk. "Excuse me. This is Neil Simon in 506. I'm the writer who's working on the play that's opening next door this week, and there's someone playing their radio in the next room. I don't want to be a bother but I can't sleep and I can't work."

"I'm sorry, sir. What would you like me to do about it?"

"Couldn't you call him and tell him to turn it off?"

"He could have fallen asleep with the radio on. I wouldn't like to wake him."

"I understand. But this is an emergency. I wouldn't ask if it wasn't."

The clerk reluctantly agreed to call the room. I waited. The music continued playing. Then my phone rang.

"I woke the gentleman in the room next to yours. He said his radio wasn't on, he was fast asleep, and he didn't want to be annoyed again. I'm sorry, sir. Goodnight."

He hung up the phone and the music continued. My only choice was to sleep on the sofa in the other room. It was a small sofa and the only thing that would fall asleep would be my feet. I lay on the bed, twisting and turning, and still that incessant music. . . . I decided to call down and see if there was another room I could move into. I turned on the light next to my bed to see what time it was. The clock now said 2:45. Behind the lamp I saw a box. My eyes were still blurry but I soon noticed that the box was a radio. It was on. It was *my* radio that was driving me insane, turned on by the maid when she made up my bed. I hated myself, I hated the radio, I hated the maid, and

I hated the little chocolate mint she left on my pillow. Wise men say that it is during these dark ominous hours of the night that our true souls awake and tell us what we are. Mine told me that I was a neurotic, nervous, panicky schmuck. I slept till nine the next morning.

I wrote all the next day and night. The next morning I called Mike in his room. "I'm sorry if I woke you but I think I have something. You want to read it?"

"Why not? Meet me for breakfast in twenty minutes."

It was a large dining room filled with businessmen getting their deals started early in the day. We found a corner table and I sat next to Mike, too nervous to eat the eggs I ordered. He, however, did well with a mushroom omelette, never missing a page or a bite. Intermittently some small laughs came, then some big enough to turn the heads of all the gray-suited men in the room. When he finished, he drank his coffee then looked at me. "I like it. It's not there yet but it's on the right track. Still, with all its faults, it's better than we have now. Much better."

I breathed a sigh of relief. "So what do we do? What if I just kept working on it, and we can put it in in Boston?"

I heard his answer as he gathered the entire cast and crew together in the hotel ballroom where we were rehearsing while they put the set up in the theater.

"Doc has written a new third act. [I was still known as Doc in those days.] I like it. It still needs work but I want to put it in. Why don't we read it first, then we'll talk about it."

Generally speaking, when large pieces of new material go into a play, the actors have the difficult task of rehearsing the new material in the daytime and playing the old version at the evening performances. A demanding but necessary practice. They finished reading the act and all looked up and agreed it was better than what we had now. All were excited about putting it in in Boston after our week's run in Wilmington.

"We're not waiting for Boston," Mike said, which shocked the group. "We have two and a half days to learn it and put it in here. I want to open with this. Here's my reasoning. Why do a bad third act well when we can do a good third act badly? It'll get better each night we do it."

The actors were stunned at the proposal of learning an entirely new third act, more than forty pages, *and* staging it, *and* rehearsing it in two and a half days. Still no one said a word, because Mike was our Commander-in-Chief.

Then the only one who dissented, and vehemently, was Walter Matthau. "It's ridiculous," he said. "I'm not going out in front of an audience and humiliate myself. I've never been unprepared in my life and I'm not going to start now. No way. We'll do it in Boston."

I have rarely, if ever, seen Mike take someone on face-to-face. He didn't need to. He was always cool enough, reasonable enough, and funny enough to persuade them to at least try it his way. He made it a challenge for them. "Relax. It's only a play. It's Wilmington, the audience knows it's a tryout. If we botch it up, do you think thousands of people will be waiting at the stage door with torches and big sticks ready to kill us? Let's rehearse today. If it goes well, we'll continue. If not, we'll put it in in Boston." Matthau found that reasoning hard to argue with, and begrudgingly agreed.

Art Carney was more reasonable. Art said, "Hey, I'm having trouble learning the first and second acts, so not knowing the third act is the least of my troubles." Carney would never really be in trouble. The audience adored him from *The Honeymooners* show, and he was at that time a bigger star than Walter. Art's only problem was that he was going through some domestic problems of his own and playing Felix was like playing himself, a man trying to revive his life after a failing marriage. In many ways, his offstage troubles made the onstage Felix even more believable.

The first day of rehearsing the new third act went well enough to continue it into the next day, but it was anything but smooth. Matthau walked in in the morning, dark circles under his bloodshot eyes, and he practically broke down in tears. "I can't do it. I got ten minutes' sleep all night. I even put the script under my pillow hoping the words would seep through. I'm not doing it. I'll quit first, I swear to God."

It was quiet in the room. Mike waited for the right moment and then said, "All right, Walter, I've got it solved. The rest of the company will do the new third act and you can still do the old third act."

There was silence before Matthau smiled then laughed in spite of himself. "All right, you bastard. I'll go out there and make a fool of myself. But at the curtain calls, I'm going to say to the audience, 'Ladies and gentlemen, I did my best. Blame this shit on Nichols and Simon.'"

Mike agreed it was a fair trade. The tension was broken but it didn't make the rehearsals less painful. Watching this new third act being rehearsed was like watching a group of mental patients trying to do a play as part of their rehabilitation. A bit like *Marat/Sade*. Whole speeches and sometimes entire pages were jumped; no one quite knew where to move, when to exit, or when to come on. Matthau kept yelling at each actor, "Don't look to me for help. I don't know what the hell the next line is either." Sometimes I thought this room full of bumper cars crashing into each other was funnier than anything I could write. There was no turning back now, and on the night of the third day, we were to do the first actual performance of *The Odd Couple* in front of a live audience. As the actors put on their makeup in their dressing rooms, you could hear them mumbling bits of the third act to themselves. When the stage manager finally knocked on Matthau's door and said, "Five minutes, Walter," Walter screamed back, "Come back in an hour. I'm not ready yet."

The curtain, at long last, went up. As we hoped for, the first two acts were wonderful. The laughs came as loud and as quickly as they did the first time we read it around the table. As the audience filed out for a smoke after the second act, you could hear a buzz, a sense of excitement, the smell of a hit. They were back in their seats quickly, always a good sign, in anticipation of how the play will resolve itself in the third act. Since they were already in a good mood, you got a residual favorable response hung over from the first two acts. They were ready to laugh at almost anything now. Almost. Almost lasted about five minutes and then we were on our own. Suddenly mistakes were being made onstage, whole speeches were dropped, and the actors' timing was way off. Some lines were forgotten then ad-libbed by a quick-thinking or panicky actor, with words that made no sense at all but at least sounded as if they belonged in *The Odd Couple*, and not *Antony and Cleopatra*. Despite the chaos and confusion that went on onstage, the third act actually showed some promise. Audiences rarely know when speeches are left out or whole pages omitted. They assume what's put on the stage is exactly what the author and director intended. Audiences may be more sophisticated today, but when I wrote the *Sgt. Bilko Show* my father once asked me, "Do you just write Phil Silvers' lines or do you write lines for the other actors too?"

As the curtain came down on a somewhat wobbly third act, we got a rousing reaction from that gracious and forgiving first preview audience. With two more additional performances under our belt, we improved the third act somewhat and finally opened for the critics. They were amused and loved the cast, admitted it was very funny, but were not carried away with praises. One reviewer liked the third act better than the first, but we paid little attention to such erratic judgment. We had come a long way since that first reading in New York and were now on our way to Boston, where a much more demanding and experienced set of reviewers would be waiting for us. We never stopped puttering with the third act, and the actors were now learning new pages of old rewrites and new rewrites of old pages.

Mike, Walter, Art, Saint Subber, and I checked into the Ritz-Carlton Hotel, across the street from the Boston Common. Cambridge was just across the river, and I went immediately to the Harvard bookstore and bought half a dozen spiral notebooks with narrow lined pages. I have filled notebooks with my plays from every college and university I ever visited, from Harvard to Yale, Duke, UCLA, Stanford, Loyola, Georgetown all the way to Oxford in England and Trinity in Dublin. In a sense, I think this made me feel I had finally earned a college degree, majoring in Drama and Hotel Rooms. After we settled into our rooms, Saint invited Mike and me to come to his suite to assess our problems and to discuss how to fix them. Saint and I were still talking about our troubled third act but Mike was strangely silent. He just kept looking around the room. Saint told us of his plans to advertise the show in New York, and while I listened, Mike got up and walked into Saint's bedroom. When he came back, he said to Saint in a very straightforward way, "You have a better suite than I do."

Saint laughed. He said, "No, Mike. You're on the floor above me. It's the exact same suite."

Mike shook his head. "No. Yours is decorated nicer than mine. I have this ugly wallpaper in my bedroom."

Saint didn't know whether he was serious or not, but said, "Would you rather have my suite?"

Mike answered, "Would you mind?"

"If it's important to you, sure. Take it."

Ultimately, Mike decided not to, but there was that about Mike. It's only my perspective but I always thought Mike needed the best not just to make himself more comfortable, but so that everyone should know that Mike was the number-one man. Not that anyone thought he was anything else, but still Mike sometimes needed something material, a gesture, a sign other than just a compliment to either reassure him of his worth or to remind us. It wasn't ego or a greediness but something that I felt went back to his childhood. He needed to prove to himself—either because of a childhood illness or fleeing from a world about to explode in Europe to a new life in America, with a new language and a new culture—that he not only survived but had the strength and intelligence to become someone special. Only on a few rare occasions did his need to make us reward him for his work ever conflict with me personally. That aside, I would work with him still on any occasion and under any circumstances.

My suite was the smallest of all but still it was the biggest suite I'd ever had. Space wasn't all that important to me. My mother hammered it into my head to never leave my clothes lying around. If you finished reading the newspaper, put it in the trash can. One of the most meaningful awards I ever won came after I had done four or five plays in Boston and the maids in the Ritz-Carlton voted me the Neatest Play-wright ever to work at the hotel. Sometimes an anal personality has its rewards.

The tryout in Boston was the first time I found that critics can be very helpful, especially when you had a seasoned and knowledgeable man like Elliot Norton. When you open in New York a critic can only tell you if you did it well or if you failed. A critic out of town has the opportunity, if they don't abuse it, to tell you where you can fix it. The out-of-town critic is the pediatrician who can help you make and keep your baby healthy. The New York critic either gives your creation his college degree or his death sentence. The playwright also has the obligation to discern which out-of-town critic to respect. He's not always the one who gives you good reviews. He's the one who, if he sees the slightest bit of talent in the work, wants to urge the writer in the direction of improvement.

Elliot Norton's first-night review of *The Odd Couple* was a bonanza of accolades, despite his disappointment with a faltering third act. Unfortunately, the headline of his review read, "Oh, For A Third Act." What happened to "Funniest First Two Acts Ever Seen"? Despite his carping, we became an immediate hit in Boston, the hottest ticket in town short of the Boston Celtics or Red Sox games. Two days later, Mike, Walter Matthau, Art Carney, and I appeared on Elliot Norton's local TV show in which he chatted with the creators and stars of Boston's latest tryouts. Walter and Mike were very funny, Art looked like he'd rather be somewhere else, and my mind literally *was* somewhere else. I barely heard what the others were talking about because I was still trying to figure out how to get over that stop-and-go third act. Suddenly Elliot Norton was talking to me, asking what changes I had in mind. I lied, naturally, saying I was very deep into some new things I was going to put in soon.

"You know what I missed in the third act?" Norton offered.

I didn't really want to know what he missed in the third act, but I feigned rapt attention. He told me eagerly: "I missed the Pigeon Sisters. They were so darned funny and I wondered why you didn't bring them back."

A lightbulb did not go on above my head. It was a two-mile-long neon sign. Why hadn't I thought of that before? The Pigeon Sisters, of course! I was out of the studio before Mr. Norton could say, "Thank you, boys, and good luck with the play." I missed the next two performances while I put the Pigeon Sisters into the third act. I was so excited about what I was writing, the Philharmonic Orchestra playing Beethoven in my bathroom would not have distracted me.

There followed another breakfast with Mike in his suite. He laughed more than I ever saw him laugh before. "You can't put this on the stage," he said. "People will die in their seats." In this business we are all prone to excesses, but what good is an ego if you can't take it and air it out once in a while? As we rehearsed the new scene the next day, we could barely breathe from our own laughter. The actors giggled nonstop, and they had to repeat some lines five times before they could gather themselves and move on. The next night the new scene went into the play, and Mike and I stood in the back of the theater as the play rollicked along in the first two acts. The third act started off strong and then came the Pigeon Sisters. If the audience thought what they had seen so far was funny, they were about to explode. The Pigeon Sisters came on and did their new scene to perfection. There was not a laugh. Not one. None. Zero. Zip. Zilch. Mike and I quickly pushed the exit doors open and walked a death march out into the lobby.

"What happened?" I said. "Are we *all* crazy? You, me, the entire cast? Didn't we think that was hysterical?"

Mike, like Hercule Poirot, solved the mystery of the missing laughs in seconds. "The jokes *are* great. But it doesn't matter. The audience doesn't like what's happening."

"What do you mean?"

"They don't like the turn in the story. The characters are going in a direction that seems wrong to them. They're unhappy, that's all."

"The *whole* audience?"

"They're more objective than we are. We're too close to it. But I feel the Pigeon Sisters are right to be in the third act. We just have to find another reason for them to come in."

"This is my last play, Mike."

"I know. But after you fix it, you'll change your mind."

Two more days and nights at the typewriter. I had now switched from chocolate mints on the pillow to candy bars, boxes of cookies, and peanuts. The maids noted the change. When I came back to Boston a few plays later, the management of the hotel, being very considerate, sent up a basket with candy bars, cookies, and peanuts. I never touched them. I only needed them to get me through the Pigeon Sisters rewrites. As if I didn't have enough on my mind, Walter kept badgering me about a line he didn't like. It was, in fact, not even his line but a comment Felix made, after turning down another date with the Pigeon Sisters and suggesting that Oscar take them both out himself. He said, "What's wrong, Oscar? You don't like doubleheaders?" I knew the line was bad and always intended to take it out, but that meant I'd have to replace it with something else and at that moment I had bigger worries than changing a single line.

Nevertheless, Walter kept pestering me about the line. "The audience doesn't like it. Can't you hear that?" Of course I heard it, but I kept telling Walter to wait until I finished rewriting the Pigeon Sisters' new scene. The next morning I got a letter from a professor at Harvard who told me he saw the play last night and absolutely loved it. If he had any objection, it was to the "doubleheader" line that Mr. Carney uttered in the second act. He wished us well, and signed the letter, "Morton Cantrow, Ph.D., English Dept., Harvard University." Perhaps the line was more offensive than I thought, so I sat down, took it out, and wrote a new line. I handed it to the cast that afternoon and I saw a smile on Walter's face. I looked at him and said, "You bastard. You wrote the letter, didn't you?" He said, "It worked, didn't it?"

Two days later I got a phone call at six o'clock in the morning. It had to be an emergency. It was a Dr. Baumgarten from Detroit calling me. At first I thought it was Walter but soon realized it wasn't.

"What is it?" I asked, completely in the dark.

"Well, my wife and I saw the play last night and thought it was wonderful. I just had some ideas I thought I might share with you, about things I didn't think worked."

"And you're calling from Detroit?"

"No. From the airport here in Boston. We're catching a seven o'clock plane and I wanted to speak to you before I left."

"And you call me at six o'clock in the morning? What kind of a doctor are you?" I asked.

"I'm a dentist."

"May I have your number in Detroit, Dr. Baumgarten?" He gave it to me, adding, "I usually get home by five o'clock if you want to call me in Detroit."

"No. I intend to call you at three in the morning to give you some advice about how to pull teeth." I slammed down the phone and never got back to sleep. Nice way to start the day.

As I worked, Elliot Norton called me to see how things were going. I was touched and amazed by his avid and earnest interest in helping me out. He even offered to have lunch with me if I felt a conversation with him might help. Nothing like that ever happened in my playwriting life again. In time, I brought in the new scene. None of us laughed in rehearsal, no tears of joy from Mike. It's not that we didn't like it. We were just afraid to be wrong again. Because I had to rush it in, the dialogue I was writing was not as sharp as in my first try, but I found out that no matter how funny lines are, they're nothing more than funny lines if they do not push the play forward. It's what happens to characters in the story that interests an audience more than anything. The new dialogue went in that night. The audience lit up. They laughed even on lines I didn't think were terribly funny. The characters were now believable in a manner that pleased and amused the audience, that made them empathetic to the foibles of these people we had just spent an evening with. In the ensuing weeks, I was able to replace the weaker lines with better ones, but it was the characters and the story's development that pleased the audience so much. We were home at last and the journey of doing it together, as a team, as a family, as a life experience was as meaningful to me as having a success. It was what made me want to come back, to keep writing plays, hoping to repeat that incredible odyssey we had just gone through. They don't all have such happy endings. Elliot Norton came again to see the play shortly before we left Boston for New York. He took no self-serving credit for having said, "Why don't you bring back those Pigeon Sisters?" He just wrote a final review extolling the virtues of the newly polished comedy and predicted it would be an enormous hit on Broadway. It never occurred to me that would be an understatement.

THE AFTERMATH

9

AS I WALKED CHIPS on his once-again four healthy legs on Central Park West at three o'clock in the morning following the opening-night party for *The Odd Couple* in New York, March 10, 1965, I stopped to look up at the sky. The stars were bright and shining and the moon cast a soft glow on the fashionable buildings along Fifth Avenue. My heart was no longer thumping with excitement. My head was slowly clearing of the effects of four glasses of champagne. My ego was not bursting with pride as it had been a few hours before, when review after review poured in, each outdoing their praise for New York's latest and biggest hit. All those feelings were now subdued to the quiet happiness I was enjoying, walking along with my dog, who would not personally prosper from this giant windfall. As John Steinbeck's dog, Charley, would probably say to Chips, "You can still only eat two bowls of Purina Dog Chow a day."

What I was thinking about was how did all this happen to me? I had the most wonderful wife a man could want, two incredible children, the perfect dog, my health, and a sonic boom of a hit that would eventually reverberate around the world. As I looked up to the heavens, I whispered to a nameless God whose existence I still had trouble accepting, "If this is all the good and happiness I ever receive for the rest of my life, it will have been enough."

Then I turned, walked back to the apartment house, and opened the front door. Before entering, though, I looked at the sky again and whispered, "I'm not saying you should stop giving it to me. I just want you to know I appreciate it."

SCALPERS WERE NOW GETTING hundreds of dollars for a pair of tickets for *The Odd Couple*. Requests for foreign productions came pouring in from all around the globe. I was being inundated with requests for interviews from the press, magazines, and television. I still had no secretary because there was no place to put her in my tiny office, and I didn't want her to invade the privacy of our home. I had no wish to expand my life, to set up a production office with people busily handling what I knew I could handle myself. As far as I could tell, nothing had changed in my life except that I had two plays on Broadway. We had a Dominican maid named Soila who couldn't clean the apartment because the phones rang incessantly. We only had one line so that if I were busy with something, Soila would pick up the phone for me, then say to me in her rich, heavily Spanish accent, "Meeser Simone, you dentist call, say he needs two seats." I'd answer, "Fine. Tell him it's okay." Then she'd say to me, "What seats should I geeve him? The ones from the kitchen?"

In the midst of this glorious madness, Joan turned to me in bed one night and said, "Let's move to England. Let's live there for a while."

"Yeah, that would be great, wouldn't it? Someday it'll happen."

"No. I mean now. Let's go now."

"Now? How can I go now? You mean give up my work?"

"You can still write in London, can't you? All you need is a desk and a typewriter. I'm sure they have them in London."

"Well, yes, I suppose so . . . but what about the girls? Ellen's still in school."

"She can go to school in England. Wouldn't it be wonderful to live in London for a year or even six months? No phone calls. No visitors. Why wait till we grow old to do those things? This is the time to enjoy our lives. Tell me one good reason why we shouldn't do it."

I stared at the ceiling and thought . . . and thought . . . then looked at her. "I can't. When do you want to leave?"

"This summer. Okay?"

"Okay."

She smiled and turned into my arms. "You'll never regret it. I promise."

SHORTLY BEFORE WE LEFT, my new business manager came to me with a proposition. I don't remember if it was Paramount who offered it or my manager who dreamed up this deal. I had recently formed my own corporation called Ellen Enterprises. Its only holdings were two properties, *The Odd Couple* and *Barefoot in the Park*. The offer was for Paramount to buy Ellen Enterprises from me for a $125,000 capital-gains deal. It was a great deal of money but I didn't understand the benefit of the deal. When I was a teenager, I'd walk by a clothing store and say to my friend Herb Levinson, "You see that suit in the window? It's no good."

"Why not?"

"If it was any good, why would they be selling it?"

It was a joke, of course, but I was afraid to get into business dealings I didn't understand. I already had one bad experience with cattle bones scattered across the plains of Wyoming. "Why would I want to do that?" I asked my manager.

"I'll tell you why. You still keep the stage rights to *The Odd Couple*. You still get your money for writing the movie. You still get your money for the *Barefoot* movie. And on top of that, you get a hundred and twenty-five thousand dollars. Look, you've had two small hits and two gigantic hits. Do you know what the possibilities of your writing more hits are? Even *one* more. A thousand to one. No, *ten* thousand to one. There're maybe three or four writers in the history of the American theater, playwrights I'm talking about, that have done that. You could have two, three, five more flops before you wrote another hit. It could take you seven, eight years, *if* you even wrote another hit. I think you're nuts if you pass this up."

My lawyer shrugged and I got the feeling he was agreeing with my manager. The final decision, obviously, was left to me. No one was telling me what the downside was. Maybe there *was* no downside. Maybe I never *would* write another hit again. I didn't even have an idea for another play yet. And even *The Odd Couple* had come close to not making it. What if I couldn't get Mike Nichols to direct again? My lawyer and my business manager certainly knew more about business than I did. I talked it over with Joan that night. She knew less about business or money than I did. Once she had come home and said, "Look at this beautiful table I bought. And it was only five thousand dollars." I looked at the table. It was an antique but very small. I looked at the receipt in her hand, then said to her, "No, Joan. It's not five thousand. It's five *hundred*." "Oh," she replied. "That's better, isn't it?" This was a girl who got a scholarship in poetry from the Sorbonne. My mind was on London, on our lives, on the two movies I still had to write. I had no way to know what the right thing to do was aside from the prodding of my manager. I accepted the deal.

In total, this is what I got: $125,000. Although it didn't become clear to me for some time, this is what I lost. Paramount made a TV series of *The Odd Couple* starring Tony Randall and Jack Klugman. Those were one of the ancillary rights Paramount got in buying Ellen Enterprises. I never received *one* cent from the series. I had my name on every episode but I never saw a dime, a nickel, or a penny. It ran for years and will run in syndication for years and years to come. Not just in America but all over the world. The value of what I had given up for *The Odd Couple* series was in the millions. Probably a great deal of millions. It gets worse. I also gave up *all* the stage rights to *Barefoot in the Park*. It's one of the most performed plays of all the plays I've written. They're still doing it today in Japan and Russia and Germany and India. From the day I signed that agreement, I never received a penny in royalties. And I never will. Add another million or two to my losses on *The Odd Couple*. My children will never see that money nor will my grandchildren. There's no point in talking about hindsight because there was no way to tell what the future was going to hold. If only the man who made the deal for Paramount's side could have been *my* business manager. No one stole the money from me. No one forced me to make the deal. It was a judgment call, and I let the wrong person sway me in making that judgment. I tried to rationalize it. Okay, I have no instincts about money, no expertise. I don't know how to perform brain surgery either, although there's one man I would like to have performed it on. I also couldn't make a pair of pants, fix a broken stove, or bake a Girl Scout cookie. I can, on the other hand, write plays. I still had my future ahead of me. There was no use in crying over a spilt fortune. I swore from that moment on I would never make a blunder like that again. Did I? I hope you'll stay with this book long enough to find out.

In June, Joan, Ellen, Nancy, and I, and a young nanny named Pam, flew to London to find a place to live. I was now on my guard, watching every penny. If some real estate agent standing at Heathrow Airport told me he could get me Buckingham Palace for a six-month rental, I'd make certain to see the plumbing worked before I'd sign any papers.

IN LONDON TOWN

10

IN 1965, the dollar was worth something in London. You could buy a Sea Island cotton shirt for less than it costs to have it laundered in a good hotel today. You could see Laurence Olivier playing *Othello* for less than it costs to buy a soft drink in any theater in New York today. The Soho section of London behind Theater Row on Shaftesbury was filled with wonderful Jewish restaurants where the waiters spoke in a Cockney Yiddish accent that not even Professor Higgins could decipher.

We arrived in England in late June, when Wimbledon was about to start, and the Beatles had exploded. We checked into a hotel and left Nancy and Ellen under the charge of Pam, an English girl who had come to New York in search of a job as a nanny and found it with us, not realizing she was going to end up back in England, not too far from where she grew up.

Joan and I went to an estate agent to help us find a flat. From that last sentence alone, you can see how quickly we picked up the English vernacular. Mrs. Quixton, our agent, spoke quickly and softly, with a permanent smile on her face that made all consonants sound like vowels and all vowels sound like the chirping of birds. I was soon up to eighteen "beg pardons" a minute, and Joan kept pretending to understand by giving Mrs. Quixton an "aha" after every unfathomable sentence. This was still before American TV shows had invaded England's homes and made an impact on much of their culture. They had not, before that, been Americanized, or even McDonalded, and English was still their own language. Therefore the English still spoke as the English did, and as beautiful as it was, it was still a little difficult for Americans to pick up at first hearing. We decided to just keep following Mrs. Quixton around London until we saw what we liked, and then we'd shout "This one!"

We followed the bird chirpings for two days until we arrived in Brompton Square in the Knightsbridge section of London, a few blocks away from Harrods, the Bloomingdale's of England. It was a horseshoe bend of identical houses, all with white front doors, and in its center a park with a small gated playground and sitting area. It seemed that at any moment, a production number from *Oliver!* would burst through every door and window with flower girls singing, "Who will buy this wonderful morning?" Joan and I said in unison, "This one."

It was an old, narrow, five-story townhouse with a rather austere and cold kitchen in the basement and another kitchenette on the fifth floor. We had never seen a kitchenette on the fifth floor before, but then we never had to climb down five flights of stairs and then up if we chose to have a midnight snack. It came completely furnished, well kept, although they appeared to be the original furnishings from when the house was built around 1860. You felt as though there should be a red velvet rope protecting each room from the daily tours that would surely be coming, led by elderly Mr. Quixton, a guide in his spare time, giving an example of how people lived in the last century— which was apparently not much different than how they lived in this century. In other words, we loved it.

This was England, the way we pictured it from seeing all those early Alexander Korda and Sydney Box films. The rooms were small, as were the people in 1860, but off the mini-living room there was a mini-library. It had no books except those used to find telephone numbers, but there was a large oak desk with a worn leather top and a big squeaky leather chair behind it. I was in heaven. My very own place to write, possibly on the same desk where the original owner had opened his morning London *Times* and read the latest installment of *Great Expectations.* Had I been raised in this house, my first play would have been *Come Blow Thy Horn.* We moved in the next morning.

I had never seen Joan so happy. She loved the isolation found in being away from a world that intruded on our family. Ellen and Nancy were a bit bewildered at first but loved the excitement and the adventure of it. Nancy went to sleep at nights thinking that Peter Pan would fly in her window and whisk her away to places where you never had to grow up. On our very first day there, we met Sybil Burton, then apart from husband Richard. She was now living with her daughter, Kate, on the other side of the crescent in Brompton Square, just opposite our house. Kate and Ellen were just about the same age and they met in the little gated park between our houses. They got to know and like each other in their first meeting, and Ellen, like most children who are suddenly transported to a new home, wanted to integrate into her new environment quickly. Only an hour had passed when Ellen burst into our house with pretty, red-haired Kate just behind her. In an Oxfordian accent that Ellen didn't have an hour before, she asked politely, "Mummy, mummy, may I have a penny for some sweets," sounding slightly more British than Kate. Who could foretell that some thirty-odd years later, Kate Burton would be starring on Broadway in my play *Jake's Women*, playing the part of Joan, with her friend Ellen in the audience?

There was a large contingent of temporarily expatriated Americans in London, mostly actors, writers, directors, and producers, all working or waiting for work on films or in plays. They all gathered in Hyde Park every Sunday morning on a realigned soccer field to play softball. The English passersby watched with puzzled curiosity as we played a game that slightly resembled their cricket in that they both used a bat and a ball. I saw a young, agile John Cassavetes hit a double to the outfield, where Ernest Borgnine fumbled it, and as Cassavetes rounded second, Ben Gazzara stood on third base with a half-smoked cigar in his mouth, screaming "Throw the fucking ball, you stupid bastard!" The English bystanders moved their children away from the scene in haste.

I started writing an original screenplay called *After the Fox*, a comedy caper that took place in Cairo and in Rome. If I could get it made, we could spend another year abroad. In the meantime, we put Ellen in an English school, which soon made her aware that she hadn't been speaking English at all. After the first week, she began to skip the school lunches, passing up the gruel-like food and waiting till she got home at three, when she would devour a tuna fish sandwich, or tunny, as they call it. After she saw *My Fair Lady* she made up her own lyric called "Why Can't the English Learn to Eat?" Nancy, just about two years old, wanted to get the bottled milk they left outside our basement door and carry it up to the fifth floor by herself. With the two large, freezing bottles in her hands, putting them on the step in front of her for each step she took herself, she made it to the top floor exhausted and older. After three days of this, she switched to toast and jam for breakfast.

While I worked, Joan explored London with the girls, devouring as much of historical England as she could, and trying to convince me that we should move permanently to some rural thatched-roof house in a forest in any place that ended with -ussex, -essex, or -issex. This search for the perfect little part of the world that would isolate us from television, newspapers, relatives, or the threat of an atomic bomb dominated her thoughts. During the Cuban missile crisis, when it seemed the powers of the world were getting ready to blow us to kingdom come, with each country landing in the former country of the other for no sensible reason, Joan had looked for a haven. When I was in Philadelphia with *Little Me*, she had begged me to come home in the middle of the production, so that if we died, we'd all die together. Not an uncommon fear for wives and mothers, and fathers for that matter, to have in a world that seemed to be heading for quick oblivion. Her point must have made a deep impression on our children, since Ellen and Nancy, both raising young children today, do not live in large metropolitan areas.

In the seven months we lived in London, we saw two days of sun. To be more accurate, we saw two days of sun briefly peeking through the gray clouds and disappearing quickly down to Spain. The damp weather continued throughout most of the summer, such as it was, and the chilling damp cold started in mid-October. The world had not yet heard of global warming or of holes in the ozone. In all the old houses, as ours was, all the plumbing was placed outside the houses, clinging tenaciously to the outer back walls, as if trying to keep warm themselves. The inside rooms were heated . . . no, strike that . . . they were warmed . . . no, strike that as well. Let's just say that the biting chill was minutely lessened by electric heaters that were placed in various positions around the house and only warmed you if you were standing not more than a few inches away from them. There were none placed in the bathrooms, so by the time November came howling in, a 7 A.M. trip to the bathroom made it an adventure in ice sitting. The English, however, never paid much attention to the weather. They were, on the whole, a much hardier people than Americans, who in the winter complain when the heat in their apartments doesn't match the average temperature in Miami.

Among the people I soon met in London, one of the most colorful was an ex–New Yorker named Harvey Orkin. Harvey was working for Creative Management Agency as an artist's representative. In the early sixties, the CMA office was one of the most important theatrical agencies in the entertainment world. Harvey dressed like a dandy in his Savile Row suits and wide Windsor collars and muted ties. He had a quick, biting sense of humor reminiscent of S. J. Perelman's. Once when I was riding with him in a crowded elevator, Harvey looked down at his shaking hands and said aloud for everyone to hear, "Christ, I have a hangover the size of India and I've got a twelve o'clock surgery call. Well, I can only do my best." The English adored Harvey because of his outrageous New York Jewish humor, and he soon became a frequent guest on British talk shows, so frequent, in fact, that he seemed to be hosting his own.

Harvey became my English connection, and Joan and I were soon being invited to dinners and parties where we began to meet the inner circle of London's theatrical elite, from the brilliant critic Kenneth Tynan to James Mason and Maggie Smith and Peter Sellers, and then coincidentally enough, to Kate's father, Richard Burton, and Elizabeth Taylor. English cocktail parties looked very much as they did in plays by Noël Coward and Terence Rattigan. At least they still did in the sixties. The conversations were witty and intelligent, sometimes silly, often scandalous, occasionally funny, and predominantly baffling to us two young Americans. The talk dealt mostly with British politics, British finance, British sex mores, and the British theater, with names of actors, writers, and manager/directors we often had never heard of. We were back again to saying "beg pardons" and "ahas" to get us through the evening. There were beautiful young women married to older men who were CEOs of businesses that ended with Ltd., and older jewel-bedecked women with younger men they introduced as their nephews. They seemed to have known each other for centuries, and only on rare occasions spoke to Joan or me and asked what we did.

On hearing that I was an American playwright, one dowager said to me, "I adore American plays. We saw *Long Day's Journey into Night* at Wyndham's last week. It was great fun." I'm sure Eugene O'Neill would have been pleased.

Despite their regal dress and manners, many of the people we met had nicknames like Binky, Toady, Birdy, and Dodo. Binky Beaumont was the foremost producer of plays and musicals in London. He talked as if he were the Chancellor of the House of Lords and gave you the impression that he was third in line in ascension to the throne. Nothing could shake his English equilibrium. Mike Nichols met Binky a few times when we were preparing to do *Barefoot in the Park* in London starring Marlo Thomas and Daniel Massey. One day Binky invited Mike to have lunch with him at the Savoy Grill. The Savoy Grill, at that time, was so toney you not only had to wear a tie, but it was their option to *approve* of the tie you were wearing. Mike knew that nothing could crack Binky's composure but that day he was going to make a concerted effort. At a novelty shop Mike bought a fake beard that was so obviously false, you could almost see the price tag on it. He put it on just before he entered the Savoy and was ushered to Binky's table, as Binky rose and shook Mike's hand, greeting him with "So good to see you again. You're looking wonderful," as Mike sat, with Binky either not noticing or caring to notice that Mike was wearing this frizzy fur thing on his face. The beard was about ten inches long and was so badly made that you could see the space between Mike's chin and the beard itself. Mike kept reattaching the cardboard hooks that hung around his ears. Binky never mentioned the beard to Mike throughout the lunch and continued his conversation as Mike felt for the space in the beard where he could slip bites of his smoked salmon. At the end of a productive meeting, Mike left, throwing his beard away in the nearest trash bin on the street. When Binky met Mike in his office the next day, Mike was now beardless but again Binky made no mention of his having worn one the day before, or his missing one today. You must admit that was composure of the highest order.

I finally finished the first draft of *After the Fox* and asked Harvey Orkin to read it and let me know his opinion. He agreed and called me as soon as he was finished.

"I love it. You know who would be great in this? Peter Sellers. Do you mind if I send it to him today?" Peter Sellers was then at the height of his career. Following all of his notable successes in British films from *The Lady-killers* to *I'm All Right Jack*, he had gone on to work brilliantly in the Stanley Kubrick films *Lolita* and *Dr. Strangelove*. He then moved on to *The Pink Panther*, which, together with its sequels, would prove to be of great commercial success. He had recently gone to America to make a film with Billy Wilder called *Kiss Me, Stupid*. During the filming, Sellers had had a heart attack and withdrew from the film. Peter had a terrible reputation for being trouble on the set or not even showing up till late afternoon. He was quite moody, being difficult one moment, and just as suddenly, totally charming and funny the next. Sometime later when Billy Wilder was asked about Peter's heart attack, he responded, "Heart attack? You have to have a heart before you can have an attack." As yet, I was not privy to all this information.

All I knew was that Sellers loved my script and wanted Harvey Orkin to drive me out for a meeting at Peter's new house in the country he had bought for his new bride, a beautiful young Swedish actress named Britt Ekland. Actually, it was an ancient house, at least two hundred years old, recently refurbished by one of the Beatles and sold to Peter. When we arrived at the picturesque cottage, Peter was on a bicycle doing laps around the house as part of his rehabilitation. Harvey and I spent the better part of an hour walking or trotting to keep up with Peter as we talked to him about the script. Next to Mike Nichols, Peter Sellers was the most appreciative audience for comedy I ever met. When there was a line in the script he liked, he laughed uproariously, then repeated the line aloud to himself as if he had never heard it before, and laughed twice as hard.

To be quite honest, I would never have picked Peter for the role in my picture. To my mind, it needed an authentic Italian like Marcello Mastroianni or Vittorio Gassman. I didn't want the main character burlesqued in any way and wasn't sure Peter would be as believable as an Italian as he would be as a Frenchman. His Clouseau was perfect because the character tried to have great dignity, much as an Englishman would have, whereas the Italian was a common man, a thief, highly emotional and temperamental. Still, it was hard to turn down Peter Sellers. He was immediately on the phone to Italy, asking Vittorio De Sica to direct it. Fat chance, I thought. De Sica was the director of such classic Italian films as *Shoeshine, The Bicycle Thief*, and *Miracle in Milan*, and a leader in the neorealism movement. I was sure he would be polite to Peter but eventually turn him down. To my great surprise, De Sica liked the script and told Peter he would do it. We next went to David Picker, then the head of United Artists, who bought the whole package at once; we were in business. Joan was beside herself when she found out we would be spending four or five months in Italy. And Ellen was happy, because she was now learning Italian in school.

A few weeks later, Peter invited Harvey and me and our wives to a small dinner at his country house. It would be a two-hour drive to get there, but it was also an invitation I could hardly refuse. Harvey rented a chauffeur-driven Bentley, an expense I'm sure that CMA would gladly pay, since Peter was a client and they were anxious for him to do another film. I still had no agent, just a lawyer, Albert DaSiva, to negotiate for me. It was a bone-chilling night, and when we arrived from the long drive, we were given hot toddies to warm us up, spiced with enough liquor to make them lethal. Little did I know how badly I would need them that night. Peter and Britt were the only ones present when we arrived, and I thought the six of us would have a relaxing evening. Soon after, we heard horns tooting in the driveway. There were to be other guests at this dinner. Peter had once starred on a highly successful radio show in England, which eventually was transformed to television, called *The Goon Show*. The title alone explained the tooting horns.

I had not really seen the group perform before but knew they were enormously popular in the low-comedy vein, tossing out puns and outrageous jokes that never failed to land. This group were not anywhere in the high-style comedy of the Monty Python players or Dudley Moore and Peter Cook or the cerebral comedy of the *Beyond the Fringe* alumni. Sellers was the budding genius of the Goon Gang, together with Spike Milligan, a hysterically unpredictable madman, who reminded me of an even more extreme Jonathan Winters. There were two more in the Gang, Harry Secombe, a large, heavy-laughing, good-natured soul, and Eric Sykes. Spike did not show up for the dinner but Harry and Eric were there with their wives. It was all very friendly, and we were made to feel welcome and at home with the Goon Gang. Harvey Orkin was dipping into the hot toddy bowl and was slowly getting blotto. Harry and Peter then began to teach me how to bow and Joan to curtsy. Apparently neither Harvey nor Peter had remembered to tell us that the last guests still to arrive were Princess Margaret and Lord Snowdon. When the royal couple finally made their royal entrance close to 10 P.M., a butler opened the door and all of us bowed or curtsied (Harvey did both), as Joan and I looked at each other, heads bowed to the floor, holding back an enormous urge to giggle.

The Snowdons were placed at the other end of the table with Peter and Mrs. Secombe, much to my relief, since "What's new at the palace?" was about as far as I would get with them, conversation-wise. Dinner finished about eleven-thirty, with Peter laughing at everything Princess Margaret said, more from politeness than from her overwhelming sense of humor, one would presume. I knew we still had a two-hour drive back to London and was hoping the Princess would soon be finished sending Peter into gales of laughter, and through with her trifle and coffee. Neither would be the case. It seemed Princess Margaret was a great fan of the Goon Gang and came especially for a private performance of half their entire repertoire of hilarious skits.

We gathered in the living room. No one could sit or stand before the Princess did, but otherwise she was treated as just plain folk. Lord Snowdon was actually charming and easy to talk to, a trait very often found in people not born to the crown. It was rumored that the Princess was very taken with Peter before Lord Snowdon entered the picture, but Joan and I were too naive to believe such hearsay. On the other hand, Joan never would believe that John F. Kennedy had an affair with Marilyn Monroe. I think some women cling to those beliefs for fear that one day they may have to believe it about their husbands.

Princess Margaret roared, or came as close as a Princess can come to roaring, at every joke she must have heard the Goon Gang do a hundred times before. Harvey Orkin was now completely sotted, and although he did his best to maintain his composure, his eyes had completely vanished from his face so that all that remained were his eyebrows and a few lashes protruding from a crease where his eyes used to be. It seemed finally that the evening was drawing close to an end. Not yet, I'm afraid.

Apparently Sellers had told Princess Margaret that I was the foremost comedy writer in America and that Harvey was the wittiest and drollest American he knew. The Princess said, "Well, then, now it's the American's turn. Please do something for us, won't you?"

We were cheered on by Peter and Britt, applauding loudly for us to get up and do a routine. Harry Secombe kept yelling, "Let's hear it from the Yanks."

To protest would have been a slight to the Princess, and I looked to Harvey for help. By now Harvey couldn't see at all but he did hear my voice. "What'll we do?" I asked Harvey in despair. "I don't know any routines. I'm not a comic."

"Let's ad-lib something and get the fucking thing over with," Harvey mumbled. The guests all sat there surrounding the Princess, smiles beaming in anticipation of what was to come from the "Funniest Yanks in America."

Finally Harvey said in desperation, "Okay. I'm a hooker on Waterloo Bridge. Neil is a senator from Georgia looking for a little action at government cost." Princess Margaret's blank stare was only outdone by my own. Our hosts' smiles changed swiftly to bewilderment.

Harvey didn't make things any easier for me by saying, "You first, Neil." If I'd had a sword, I would have plunged it down from his heart to his shoes. Having no choice but to perform, the two of us started ad-libbing, exactly about what has been erased from my memory for the sake of my sanity. Joan and Harvey's wife, Gisella, started to laugh, not at our witty remarks but at our predicament. Peter laughed because he knew we were dying and he was enjoying the spectacle.

About three minutes into our fiasco, the Princess silently stood up and walked into the other room, followed by Lord Snowdon, Peter, Britt, and Harry Secombe, who, on his way out of the room, turned back and said, "Keep it up, boys. It's always hard getting started in this business." We not only lost our audience but I thought we were also in danger of losing our passports. Joan and Gisella were half laughing and crying, showing both compassion and a much darker side of their natures at the same time.

Harvey kept babbling on, doing his impression of an English hooker, until I said, "No, Harvey. It's over. I know you can't see but they've all gone." It was now two-thirty in the morning. Harvey, having taken another drink, looked as if the rest of his features were about to vanish as well; he bore a remarkable resemblance to a Dick Tracy character called "No Face." Back in the other room, I whispered to Peter that it was very late and that I thought we should be heading back to London now. Peter said that wasn't possible. No one is allowed to leave before the Princess. It would be very bad form.

I suddenly saw the four of us being thrown into the Tower of London, where we found the remains in our cell of the two young princes who had been done in by Richard III. Fortunately, the Princess and Lord Snowdon left at about three, and we were gone right on the heels of their royal wheels. In the Bentley going back to London, Harvey fell into a deep sleep, more along the lines of a coma, while Joan and Gisella talked about the problems of American children adjusting to being in English schools. I sat there glumly, knowing I had blown every chance I ever had of becoming the first American to be knighted by the Queen. Since the roads were empty, our driver was doing a swift eighty-five to ninety miles an hour. At one point, he saw a truck ahead and quickly slowed to fifty. The jolt awakened Harvey, who sat upright and said, "Are we here?" and opened the door of the speeding car. All three of us grabbed Harvey before he bounced out onto the highway, but the force of the wind blew the entire door off its hinges, and it flew back on the highway behind us. The driver's only exclamation was "Oh, dear." He stopped the car, walked back about fifty yards, retrieved the heavy door, and put it into the trunk—which now wouldn't close—and drove slowly back to the city. It was still freezing cold and the wind howled inside the rear of the car as we all bundled together. When the CMA office received a bill for an entire door being ripped off a new Bentley, Harvey Orkin had to do some pretty fancy transatlantic explaining about something he had no memory of ever happening.

A month later, De Sica came to London to confer with Peter and me. De Sica was an inveterate gambler and probably came to London not only for our conference, but to hit all of London's best gambling casinos along Curzon Street, where you wouldn't be too surprised to find yourself at the baccarat table sitting next to Goldfinger. De Sica, in his early sixties, was still a very elegant and handsome man. He was well known and treated everywhere in Europe as royalty. In Italy he was respectfully called Commendatore. To me it seemed improbable that he would want to do this film for artistic reasons; rather, it was a way to pick up more gambling money from an American film that paid him far more than any of his Italian classics. Yet, as we talked about my screenplay, he said he saw overtones of a social statement to be made, of how the pursuit of money corrupts not only those in business but those in the arts as well.

The story of *After the Fox*, briefly, for the few who saw it and don't remember it, was about a small-time thief and safecracker named Aldo Vanucci who has been caught and sent to jail. When his cohorts tell him about a huge job coming up, one that can result in millions, he tells them he is through with crime. Yet once he hears that his sister, Gina, has become a streetwalker in Rome, he decides to break out of jail and take on the deal that's come up in order to save his beloved sister. He doesn't realize his sister is *not* a streetwalker but is only playing one in a low-budget picture being filmed on the streets of Rome. The deal that is presented to Vanucci (Peter Sellers) is that thieves have stolen an enormous amount of gold bullion in Cairo but have not figured out a way to smuggle it into Italy. Vanucci then comes up with a brilliant scheme. He will pose as a great new avant-garde filmmaker, cast his cohorts as photographers and actors, and film a picture about smugglers that takes place at a beach in a small town. What the smugglers in the film are doing is bringing large amounts of gold bullion into Italy. The eager townspeople are so excited at the prospect of being in a film, they agree to play small parts, as do the real police, who play the dupes who let the smuggled gold into the country. It is, then, a film within a film within a film, with plenty of room to take potshots at the over-praised new directors in the Italian film industry. I think that's what interested De Sica. Not to make fun of himself as much as of those new upstarts that now were mimicking him and Rossellini and Fellini. Quite honestly I saw it just as a farce, but if De Sica knew a way to give it some importance, it was in my best interest. I was there to learn, not to quibble.

It would be seven or eight months before production would start, but De Sica insisted that I collaborate with his own writer, Cesare Zavattini. Zavattini was a brilliant writer, having done most of De Sica's best films. A date was set up for Zavattini and me to meet in London to start our collaboration. I was already intimidated by his credits and reputation. It did not help any to learn that he also spoke not a word of English, while I spoke even less Italian. It was arranged that we would have an interpreter with us at all times. I immediately pictured a scene from *Duck Soup*, the Marx Brothers film where Chico was trying to talk to the ambassador from Sylvania, played by Louis Calhern, with

Harpo interpreting each speech with his eye gestures, his whistle, and the honking of his horn. I wasn't very far from wrong.

On the prearranged date, I arrived at the Savoy Hotel and knocked tremulously on the door. It was opened by a rotund, short, bald man near sixty, with a very serious demeanor that made him look more like a scientist than a screenplay writer. He smiled at me, extending his hand. *"Buon giorno,"* he said slowly, knowing that I was not facile in his own language.

"Buon giorno, grazie," I said, trying to improve his impression of me with my addition of the phrase "Thank you." I had now used up most of my known Italian vocabulary, aside from the names of foods I knew fairly well, but I didn't think that *vitello* and *osso buco* would come up much in our meetings. He showed me into his suite, which seemed a little too luxurious for his taste, and started to talk to me rapidly in Italian. I tried my best to explain, *"No comprendo-pas Italienno,"* which was a bad mixture of French and Italian, to say nothing of butchered syntax. He shrugged his shoulders, which made everything else on his body shrug as well, realizing that nothing could happen until the interpreter showed up. He offered me some coffee.

"Caffè?" he asked. I nodded to tell him that I understood but didn't care for any. He took my nod for a yes and I got coffee. It was getting very awkward in there, and I would have settled for Harpo Marx at any price. We sat in opposite chairs, facing each other. There were long silences. Then he picked up my script, riffled through the pages, and said slowly so that I might understand, *"Buono.* Good. I like."

That cheered me up immensely. I answered, "Oh, *grazie. Io amore* your films. *Comprendo?"*

"Si. Si. Grazie mille." Then still holding up my script, he said, "Much . . . er . . . much . . ." He couldn't find the words, then pantomimed writing on the script. I thought I got it. "Much rewriting? Fix? Some no good?"

"Si, much no good," he retorted. *"Molto* no good."

We were beginning to understand each other but it forewarned a lot of problems. I countered with, "Yes. *Comprendez.* It's just my first draft . . . first draft . . . *Primo attempto."*

He didn't get that but nodded anyway.

A half hour passed, and the interpreter still hadn't shown up. Zavattini and I gave up on communication and finally each picked up a magazine, thumbing through them like two patients waiting for a multilingual dentist. Finally the interpreter arrived—a short Italian, with close-cropped hair and a bushy mustache, about forty-five. There was something about him I didn't like. Perhaps it was because he took five minutes to explain to Zavattini why he was late, and then in English, said to me, "Sorry. The traffic was bad."

I began to see I was going to get short shrift in this interpreting business. One could see in a second that he, Mario, I believe his name was, idolized Zavattini. I, on the other hand, was a nobody. Once we started to work, Zavattini spoke to Mario for minutes on end, giving him an entire synopsis of what he felt was wrong with the script.

Mario then explained to me in English, "Zavattini feels the core of the spirit of the problems you have presented lacks a justification for denying the morality of the causes of the postwar generations which we must try to scrape from the soul of the human heart."

I suddenly wondered if I was in the right suite. Either Zavattini was running for political office, or the interpreter was late because he had just come from a class that was trying to teach him English. Zavattini looked at me, waiting for my comments. My comments on what? I said, quite frankly, "I don't think I understand what Mr. Zavattini is saying." This one sentence took five minutes to translate to Zavattini.

This exchange went on for about three hours. Zavattini was losing patience with me and started screaming at the interpreter. Finally a second interpreter was brought in to see if he could clarify matters. This was a more patient man. After he heard Zavattini's remarks, then translated them in a clear and simple way to me, I began to see what Zavattini wanted. He had very clear, concise, and intelligent comments that I could readily understand and agree with. The second interpreter took me into the other room and explained to me that Mario was a writer himself—not very successful—but a writer. He might have, in an innocent way, been trying to insert his own ideas into the script with no harm intended to me. He then went back and told Mario to give a simple, clear, word-for-word interpretation of what Zavattini and I had to say to each other. Mario agreed, shrugging his shoulders. From that moment on, Cesare and I got along famously and I made the changes within three days.

Despite our warm and mutual collaboration, however, I felt the comedy I had originally intended would clash violently with Zavattini's serious philosophy of life, and his well-intentioned social statements would be lost in what was primarily a farce. Or the farce would soon disappear. I hoped and depended on what director De Sica would do to pull all of this together.

The picture was to be shot the following summer in Rome and on the island of Ischia, near Naples. Whether the film would come out right or not, it still looked as if Joan and I and the girls were in for a wonderful summer. After spending Christmas in London, we returned to New York. Our seven months in England was a memorable time for us, but Ellen yearned to get back to her school friends, and I was anxious to get back in time to see the National Football League championship game. The one thing I deeply missed in living abroad was watching American sports. Reading baseball or football scores in the Paris edition of the *Herald-Tribune* three days after the actual game was played left a lot to be desired.

Once back home, I began to work on the screenplay of *Barefoot in the Park*. Arguably, I think I wrote about seven good screenplays among the twenty or so I did over the years; I even managed to get four Academy Award nominations. Still, I never considered myself a first-rate screenwriter. For one thing, I only did well when I had a really good director, which overall was not the case. The theater was and is my first love, and many of my early screen works were really more photographed stage plays than films. Perhaps I was a little too stubborn in trying to retain most of the dialogue of the plays. Composers who wrote the scores for my films found it a difficult job, because I rarely left space where people were not talking. I don't underplay the value of good, sharp dialogue on the screen, as for example in Howard Hawks' *His Girl Friday* with Cary Grant and Rosalind Russell, a remake of the great stage comedy *The Front Page*. The skillful acting by these two well-cast stars and the brilliantly fast-paced directing of Hawks made the dialogue seem to *be* the actions, and each word and sentence was a visual image in itself. Where I had trouble with the screenplay of *Barefoot* was my inability to let go of the stage play. Actually, I didn't think I was *having* trouble with the screenplay. No one told me. Not Paramount Pictures, nor director Gene Saks, nor the actors, nor producer Hal Wallis. They liked it, they rehearsed it, they shot it, they released it, and it was a huge hit. What then am I complaining about? I suppose that when I see it now, I know it could be better.

Another reason I was uneasy and unsure of myself in films was that I missed the collaboration between the writer and the director that you have in the theater. Very few writers are even on the set when a film is made, but I couldn't see myself missing a day of rehearsal in the theater. To add to all this, neither Joan nor I had any desire to move to California. That did not, however, stop us from moving in New York. After experiencing the joys of a townhouse in London, we bought a very small one on Sixty-second Street between Third and Lexington avenues. It was twelve feet wide, and the girls' bedrooms on the fourth floor were like horizontal telephone booths. Perhaps in some ways, we were reliving our early days in that fifth-floor walk-up in *Barefoot*. Maybe it was just that we were always comfortable in small quarters. We were moving up in the world but we weren't getting any wider.

The insecurity of the writer is an ever-constant battle, and even though *The Odd Couple* was the breakthrough play I had been hoping for, I still felt that I hadn't proven myself to myself. Woody Allen once remarked that to write comedy is like eating at the children's table. I wonder what Charlie Chaplin would have thought of that overstatement, yet I know what Woody meant. In many quarters, to write comedy brings you popularity and success. To write drama brings you respect. That argument has and will go on for years with no resolution. But I knew that eventually I wanted to write darker plays, although not dramas. I wanted to write comedies the way that dramatists wrote dramas. The line between the two sometimes is no wider than a strand of hair, but it must be as strong as a tightrope if you're going to try to balance yourself as you cross from one end to the other. It was not something I could just leap into. I would have to grow into it. When the time was ready, I would feel it within myself. I bided my time by writing the *Barefoot* screenplay and *After the Fox*. At Paramount, Hal Wallis, the producer of *Casablanca* and at least fifty other first-rate films, was given *Barefoot* to add to his collection. It looked like my play was in good hands. Then the following summer we'd be off to Rome.

If life was so absolutely perfect for me now, why did I suddenly find myself in need of an analyst? One very obvious answer would be because life was so absolutely perfect for me. Nothing seemed to go wrong. I was being offered films from every major studio, and Saint Subber kept urging me to write that next play since there was now an audience out there waiting for a new Neil Simon work. I was thirty-three years old before my first play reached Broadway, fairly old by most standards. Nothing spectacular had ever happened to me as a child. Then why all of this now? Why so suddenly? When I was twelve years old, during the Depression, I would have made a pact with the devil to sell my soul for a guaranteed income of a hundred dollars a week for my lifetime. I had friends but I was not the most popular boy in my neighborhood, nor was I the best athlete, and I was far from the best scholar.

I did, however, have a fantasy when I was about ten. It wasn't a dream that crawled into my sleep but a day-to-day fantasy that persisted during my waking hours. I thought I was born a king. Not of America, not of any country, but a king of some vast domain that existed in my mind. In the fantasy, the entire world knew of my noble birth, but they were sworn to secrecy not to reveal to me the truth of my majestic lineage for fear of spoiling me.

Actually, there was no lineage. My parents and Danny weren't of royal blood. I came into the world as a Virgin King, so to speak, the first of my line. At ten, you're permitted to make allowances. Even my friends in school knew I was destined to one day be their king, as secretly told to them by their parents, but all kept silent or pretended that I was no different than they were. It amazed me how wonderfully everyone played out their parts. My school teacher knew. The barber who cut my hair knew, even though he often failed to brush away the small cut hairs from my neck that irritated me so. Done, no doubt, to throw me off any track that may have hinted as to my true identity. My Hebrew school teacher often berated me for not studying, and for being lazy, and said I would amount to nothing. What a great performance he put on, I thought to myself. Even Carl Kreissman, the class bully, who punched me twice and almost broke my nose, took his life in his hands with this effrontery. Such was the devotion to his future king that he would gladly sacrifice my wrath to keep the secret as he had sworn to do since he was a child.

Then I began to feel impatient. I thought I was ready to know. How long were they going to play this game? Even my best friend, Herb Levinson, kept his silence. One day I finally tested it. We were walking along the park, Herb tossing his football in the air. I looked around, making certain I would not be heard, then whispered, "It's all right, Herb. I know the truth. I know who I am. It's all right for you to tell me that you know as well. You will not be punished, this I swear." Perhaps the bus that went by as I spoke prevented him from hearing me, or maybe it was out of fear that he paid no attention. He gripped the ball and said, "Go out for a long pass." I did, and dropped the ball, showing I was just as human as he was.

By the time I was twelve, I was beginning to have my doubts. No one, ever, showed a sign of cracking. I still held out hope that I would yet become their once and future king, but by the time I was thirteen, my voice was changing, I was growing taller, but I was not yet very regal. As thirteen went to fourteen, royalty became less important than girls. In fact, if Betty Tarr, sitting in the third row of my history class, would let me have my way with her, I would abdicate my throne. Dreams of all I surveyed went out just as puberty was coming in.

This fantasy of power was not much different than the one I had when I was six and seven. In those days, I was invisible. "The Shadow" of my time. When I went on the long trolley car trip to visit relatives in the East Bronx, I would arrive and then sit in a chair in the living room, willing myself to be unseen. Only when they offered a cookie or some ice cream did I allow myself to remove the spell over them. But once having finished my just deserts, I disappeared from sight once again. I don't for a minute think that these trips of fantasy were peculiar to me. I was probably running into invisible kings in every neighborhood I ever went to. Still, in the back of my youthfully imaginative mind, I was wondering if my fantasies would ever become a reality in some other form. It didn't occur to me all these years later that all this sudden success I was having was the prophecy come true.

One review of The Odd Couple following on the heels of Barefoot led one decidedly biased reviewer to call me "The New King of Comedy." A little part of my mind said, "Uh-oh. Is it coming true after all?"

The fact that I was becoming a public figure in the press didn't prevent me from being a private figure in my work. As the actors performed on the stage, I stood in the darkness at the rear of the theater. I was, for the most part, invisible. Prophecies were piling up.

When I was graduating from my grade school, the teachers asked all the students to dress in white. This placed a financial hardship on my parents. We couldn't afford a white suit, such as a few of my classmates planned to wear, but my mother sacrificed some of the money she kept in a jar, unknown even to my father, and bought me a nice white shirt, a pair of white pants, and white shoes—which I knew, even if she didn't, that I'd never wear again. White shoes on a kid living in a tough neighborhood is like wearing a sign—"Punch me for free."

The day before graduation, which was to be held in the open schoolyard, I read in the paper they were predicting rain for the next day. My mother's hard-saved money would literally be washed away in a downpour. I stayed up most of the night praying over and over again, repeating one simple sentence: "Please don't let it rain tomorrow . . . Please don't let it rain tomorrow . . ." I even fought off sleep to get in a few more entreaties to God. I woke up the next morning and the sun was shining brightly. It continued to shine all day, and I stayed as white as a new pillowcase.

This caused me to think that I possibly had still one more power: if I prayed hard enough, God would grant me my wish. I told no one about this new relationship I had with the Almighty. I knew He wouldn't betray me, and I swore to keep my half of the bargain. I didn't want to test this new power since it was my belief that it was not unlimited. Only those most-needed wishes would be granted. I wanted the Yankees to win the pennant that year, but I did not go to God for this. Let some other Yankee fan use up one of his wishes for that one. I saved my wishes for only the most important events in my life. Or in the lives of the members of my family.

This was not just a child's game, but one I adhered to into my adulthood. There was one constant wish I made even though I knew it couldn't be delivered at my will. The wish was to meet the perfect girl. When Joan came into my life, I was glad I hadn't wasted my wishes on frivolous things. This sounds so banal as I write it, but I never prayed to God for a play of mine to be a hit. The plays were in my domain and I didn't want God to interfere, thus robbing me of my own satisfaction of doing my work well. Also, I was wise enough to know I couldn't write a hit every time out, thereby erasing the possibility that God was no longer interested in granting my wishes. Obviously they have not all been granted. I still save up for only the ones that are of major importance. Although these are all childish fantasies, I feel they are very important and healthy ones. You have to believe in something. Yourself or God. Since I am still skeptical about the existence of a God—except when I need Him badly—I tend to trust myself the most. If you think you have no power over your life, you dismiss any worth to your existence. You are at the mercy or whim of life itself, and I find that to be the most hopeless and helpless position to be in.

So there I was in the analyst's office, happily married, successful in my work, with the possible attributes of still becoming a king, making myself invisible, and having a very good relationship with God. I was there, I suppose, to reconcile myself with all that had been given to me. Fifteen minutes into the first session, the word "guilt" appeared. To say that I was happy and successful did not mean that all was divine. I still had a few demons to deal with. When I married Joan, I ended my relationship with Danny as a writing partner. I had always suffered, to some degree, from claustrophobia as a child. Nothing, however, compared to what happened to me when I broke up with Danny in 1954. On that first trip to Europe with Joan after breaking with Danny, everything closed in on me. On the *Liberté*, I tried our cabin door ten times before I went to bed to make sure it would open again. I did the same in every lavatory on every plane I took at that period. I woke up in the middle of the night in our hotel room in Paris in sheer terror, and one night I ran stark naked out into the hallway, running to escape from myself, before Joan threw a bathrobe around me and coaxed me back into the room.

When we climbed to the top of Notre Dame, up a circular staircase with ever-diminishing slits of daylight coming through what passed for windows in the eleventh century, and with the crowds filling the stairway behind me blocking any chance to retreat down the same staircase, I thought the only way to get down was to jump from the gargoyle-protected open tower. Joan was suddenly seeing a part of me she had had no access to before and it frightened her. I tore bits of paper into even smaller pieces and threw them from the top of the cathedral, watching them float downward, symbolizing some kind of freedom I wish I had. When we went to Switzerland, I breathed easier at the open spaces and the green valleys, yet woke up in the middle of the night, actually visualizing the Alpine mountains all around us closing in on me and imprisoning me in a snow-capped jail.

In Rome I finally received a letter from Danny in California saying he was set up on a top TV show paying him a very good salary. My anxiety let up and I breathed a sigh of relief. Danny was alive and well, living among the orange blossoms. Sixty pounds of guilt were lifted from my psyche. I got through the rest of the trip in much better shape. After we returned from Europe, Joan and I went back to Tamiment, staying out the last days of August with her parents, Moe and Helen, in their cabin in the woods, and sleeping in the same bed we had made love in for the first time. All was well again. Then, quite suddenly in the middle of the night, I jumped out of bed, running into the dark woods, heading for the lake with Joan chasing me in her pajamas. I stopped at the edge of the lake, sobbing my shameless tears in front of her. When would I resolve this guilt and what was I so guilty of?

The success that soon came to me only worsened my symptoms. In writing a play for Broadway, you have taken the first step in setting yourself up for failure. I expected it as part of the game. Yet I worked on each play feverishly, with a drive and energy that knew no bounds in my effort to make them a success. And each success put me more in the spotlight, despite the fact that my appearing in news interviews and TV talk shows was the very opposite of my true nature. I was shy, introverted, nervous, and frightened. I was beginning to wonder who I really was. In the introduction to the first published version of my collected plays, I likened myself to a mythical Gothic character, a Frankenstein or Werewolf by night, a quiet, unassuming fellow in the light of day. I felt I had stopped relating to people as friends, relatives, acquaintances. Instead they turned into my victims, as I ripped their private souls from their being, feeding my hunger, my insatiable desire to use them in my writings, in my plays, in my thoughts. Then in an instant, a casual comment was made and suddenly the monster disappeared. I would awaken, as if from a brief trance, and see them as they really were. People I cared about. People I loved.

This may seem a bit melodramatic, I admit, but still somewhere in the back of my mind I thought I was the robber of phrases caught, characteristics trapped in a butterfly net, defenseless personalities brazenly stolen and stored away in my larder for the times it would be hard to find fresh game. I had a fanciful mind, to say the least; I was someone who had seen too many Universal black-and-white horror films as a boy and who always went back for more. This, however, was all in my favor in my quest to become a better writer. Where it left me a little short was in my effort to mature as a healthy, well-rounded responsible adult. The first year of analysis was, in a sense, an attempt to introduce me to myself. To try to meld the two beings that dwelled simultaneously in my mind and have them become friends.

"Neil, this is the writer."

"Neil, this is the person who doesn't write. Mostly, he lives."

"Nice to meet you."

"Likewise."

I slowly began to understand Neil the person, but Neil the writer baffled me. He was infinitely smarter than I was, cleverer, more imaginative, and far more outgoing. I could talk with ease to Neil the person. We discussed baseball, movies, books, children, and we occasionally played tennis with other real people. Neil the writer had time for only one thing: he wrote. That was all he wanted or could do. I had no idea how he structured plays, created characters, plotted stories, gave flesh to boneless figures, and very often did this quite humorously. However he did that, I knew I couldn't. As a matter of fact, I don't think the writer really liked me. He felt I wasted time. He would keep pulling me back to the typewriter like a jealous lover. More and more he would take over Neil the person's time. Joan saw what was happening and acted as a go-between. Some nights after dinner, Neil, the husband and father, would walk upstairs to his desk, putter around, look at some pages the other fellow had written during the day, then suddenly change from one to the other, sit down, and continue to add more pages.

"Stop it," Joan would say from the doorway. "That's enough for today. Now is *our* time."

She was the anchor in Neil's life, the only one that both Neil the person and Neil the writer trusted. They were always secure knowing she was there for them.

LA DOLCE VITA

11

IN MAY 1965, I left for Italy to start production on *After the Fox*. Joan was going to join me in early June as soon as the girls finished school. I was put up at the Hilton on top of one of the Seven Hills of Rome. It was temporary until United Artists found more permanent quarters for me, Peter Sellers, and John Bryan, our producer. Bryan was at one time one of the foremost film set designers in England; his memorable set for David Lean's production of *Great Expectations* still lingers in my mind. The scene in the dreary, foggy graveyard, when a young, frightened Pip is suddenly grabbed by an escaped prisoner who comes out of nowhere, is second in terrorizing me only to the horrific killing of Martin Balsam by a screaming old woman on the stairs of the Bates house in *Psycho*. Now, coincidentally, John Bryan was our producer and Martin Balsam, an old friend of mine, was playing an American theatrical agent in our film.

The "fake film" that was to be made in the small seaside village where the gold was to be smuggled also needed a bona fide movie star to convince the local police that this was indeed a first-rate film. For the film star, we hired the perfect man: Victor Mature. Mature, still looking quite good, was in semi-retirement in Rancho Mirage, California. He decided to come out of his comfortable residence to play our star, a man whose career was supposed to be on the skids, but hopefully would be resurrected by the convincing conniver played by Sellers. Two other main parts were still to be cast, Aldo Vanucci's (Sellers') beautiful young sister and his mother.

The decision as to who would play his sister was a fait accompli. Peter suggested his new wife, Britt Ekland. It was more of an ultimatum stated in the style of a suggestion. De Sica, wanting a happy star, succumbed quickly and hired her. It was not a problem for him. In the making of his classic *The Bicycle Thief*, he had found a man on the streets who had never acted before. In De Sica's hands, the man gave a brilliant performance and immediately became a major star in Italy, wanted by every film company. After two more films, it became evident the man had not a shred of acting ability without De Sica to guide him. A few years later, he took his own life. Britt was a beautiful, personable young woman with little or no acting experience, but De Sica would take care of that. What was of more concern was that she was blond and blue-eyed, with the upturned nose, fair skin, and brilliant white teeth of a Scandinavian. That was fine except she had to play a poor urchin of the streets of Rome. The black wig they gave her made her look like an expensive mannequin—but Gina Lollobrigida had an upturned nose too, so maybe the purists would forgive us.

The main problem was to get Britt's Swedish accent to sound Neapolitan. Not only was it Swedish, but it also had a decidedly English accent. She looked and sounded like a tourist on her first visit to Italy. Still, she was eager to work hard, which she did; her beauty lit up the screen and Peter was very happy. You win some, you lose some.

The last part to be cast was that of the Italian mother. In our minds, we all had a clear vision of that person. After auditioning dozens of older women, De Sica was still not happy. He wanted the real thing here. One night we all went out to dinner in a wonderful restaurant near the Grand Hotel. It was small but frequented by the rich and the celebrated. When you walked into a restaurant in Italy with Vittorio De Sica, they rolled out a Linguini with Red Sauce carpet for you. I could get used to this kind of living. I never had to look at a menu or a check. De Sica didn't order. They just brought out everything. United Artists, who paid, unfortunately never got to taste any of this. As we ate, we saw a couple at a table in the adjoining room, also being treated like royalty. It was Rossano Brazzi, an Italian film star who had also made it big in America; he was memorable as Katharine Hepburn's lover in David Lean's *Summertime*, and also in the film version of Rodgers and Hammerstein's *South Pacific*. Brazzi, an astonishingly handsome man, was sitting with a rather portly woman, quite a few years older than he. De Sica stood up and announced, "There's our mother. That's the face I'm looking for." He crossed to Brazzi's table, they hugged as two stars would, and he bowed to the woman. Apparently he asked the woman if she would like to test for the role of Peter Sellers' mother in his new film. The woman said, somewhat huffily, "I'm not an actress." That was not a problem for De Sica. When he returned to the table he told us she had agreed to test for the role. When we asked who she was, De Sica said, "It's Rossano's wife, Lydia." Someone else would have gotten his eye blackened for that incident. Instead, De Sica got his actress.

THE FOLLOWING WEEKEND, De Sica, John Bryan, and I drove out on a Saturday morning to the Dino De Laurentiis Studios, about an hour outside of Rome. John Bryan decided to drive to learn his way around the countryside. De Laurentiis wanted to show us the wonderful facilities he had available there, since we hadn't chosen where to shoot the interior scenes as yet. I use the word "we" loosely, since I had no idea why they asked me to come along. De Sica certainly knew what he wanted, and John was there to make the deal. I think John asked me out of politeness, to assure me he was going to include me as part of the team. I still felt lucky they were producing it at all.

De Laurentiis opened the studio with his own key. I didn't see a watchman about anywhere. In Italy, many things are done in peculiar ways—at least peculiar compared to the way we do them in America. Italy has national train strikes that last an hour and ten minutes. It's not that the strike was settled. It was just a protest strike, and an hour and ten minutes seemed time enough for them. I was once in Venice at the Hotel Danieli. It was during a very festive holiday, and the Danieli was the place to be because the guests could sit on the outside patio, where they served lunch and dinner, and watch the magnificent procession of colorfully decorated boats going through the Grand Canal. It was also the perfect spot to see the great fireworks lighting up the sky to end the holiday. As Joan and I took our seats on the patio with the other guests, feeling lucky to have gotten a table, we all kept looking around for the waiter. No waiters were in sight. They had all gone on strike. No food, the manager said, shrugging his shoulders helplessly. We were starving and went down the narrow streets to find a restaurant. They were all on strike. After an hour, we found one restaurant open. It was quite a large place, with everyone sitting at candlelit tables, and there was one table left. They were candlelit because the electric company had gone on strike as well. For the eighty customers sitting there, there was only one waiter. He owned the restaurant and his wife cooked in the back. The other fourteen waiters were on strike, no doubt sitting on the patio of the Danieli with their own sandwiches, watching the fireworks. The waiter told us no hot food. Only cold dishes. We would have settled for potato chips and an Amaretto. Suddenly, the lights went back on. A cheer from the hungry crowd. The owner smiled, said the electricity was back on, and started taking orders for hot dishes. As soon as he got to the kitchen door, the electric company went back out on strike. The waiter/owner shouted out, "Sorry. No more hot dishes." This all happened to me years after the time we arrived at Dino's studios, so I was not yet accustomed to the Italian ways of doing things.

After De Laurentiis showed us through the huge, very modern sound-stages, he then wanted to show us the offices above the stages. We got into a small self-service elevator, and I had an impulse to say, "I'll wait down here." John Bryan, however, took my arm and we all got in. "Tight squeeze, wouldn't you say?" said John in his understated way. Halfway up, the elevator stopped dead between floors. My heart did the same thing. I must have been running on batteries.

"Ah," said De Laurentiis calmly, "this happens sometimes. Nothing to worry." John Bryan pressed the alarm button. No sound except that of heavy breathing in tight quarters. De Laurentiis said it wouldn't help even if the alarm worked, since the studio was closed and no one came in on Saturdays.

I'm not quite sure how they understood what I said because my voice came out between chattering teeth and heavy panting: "You mean we're in here until Monday morning?"

"No, no," De Laurentiis said, laughing. "My wife is expecting me for dinner. If I'm not home by eight and do not call, she'll come here to look for me. This has happened before."

This was 10 A.M., in May, an hour away from Rome, and we might be in this oven until eight at night, unless Mrs. De Laurentiis decided to eat out with some friends that night.

De Sica looked nervous and started to talk to De Laurentiis in Italian, very rapidly, not about the elevator, but about the picture business. I could pick up a word here and there. John Bryan suddenly got a case of the giggles. I don't know if he found it amusing or if he was terrified, but on and on he giggled. I started to unbutton my shirt and I knew I was about three minutes away from taking off all my clothes, as most claustrophobics are prone to do. Fortunately, I realized the act of humiliating myself in front of De Sica and De Laurentiis would probably be the talk of all Rome the next morning, or Monday morning as the case might be, so I kept my shirt on. But I literally thought I would go out of my mind.

In one last mad act of desperation, I pressed the button that all of us had already pressed twenty times each. Miraculously, the elevator started to move and we all got off on the third floor, as if nothing had happened. In fact, nothing *did* happen, since we weren't in there for more than two minutes. Whether it was the elevator or something even more frightening, De Sica decided against the studio, and John Bryan was so happy, he couldn't stop giggling. Eventually we signed with Cinecittà, a government-owned studio on the Appia Antica. As we drove back to Rome, I thought to myself that none of them knew we had less than a thousand-to-one shot of getting out of the elevator without my help. We would have been there all day or all weekend had I not used up one of my cherished and highly valuable wishes to God.

JOAN, ELLEN, NANCY, and our nanny, Pam, arrived at the beginning of June, just as the film started shooting. We stayed on at the Hilton until the houses they rented for us were vacant. De Sica wanted some more work from Zavattini and me, and of course, the ever-present Mario was there again, interpreting and misinterpreting. The rest of the cast arrived, and aside from Victor Mature, Martin Balsam, and Akim Tamiroff, none spoke English. The members of Vanucci's gang, the police, the extras, everyone spoke only Italian. That meant all their lines would be spoken phonetically, mouthing English as best they could, and their voices would be dubbed in later in England. So if you were on the set, you would hear an actor say, "Wa tie eezd datrog cumn," which when dubbed would be, "What time is the truck coming?" It saved me a great deal of digestive problems by not coming around the set when the non-English-speaking actors were working. Since Mario, the misinterpreter, was also hired as dialogue coach to these actors, he would give them the meaning of these English words. He was never right once. De Sica had to change everything when he was on the set.

De Sica, however, was not always on the set. He would take two-hour lunches and an hour for a nap. He came back refreshed and awake, ready to work, just as the sun was going down. Each day, about four, he would make a call to a Casino in Monte Carlo and make a bet. "Ten thousand lire on number six black." Then he would wait patiently on the phone as the little ball rolled around the wheel, then stopped. He heard the result, cursed in Italian, and came back to work.

Whatever his faults, I cannot say enough about my respect for De Sica. He was a charming and brilliant man, despite his idiosyncrasies. He spoke English fairly well, but missed certain nuances and had trouble with the idioms I so often use in my scripts. One day I wrote a new piece of dialogue and brought it to Peter. His character, Vanucci, had escaped from jail and was now rounding up his band of thieves to tell them he had accepted the offer to come in on the big gold caper. He gets on the phone, calling each gang member, and using coded sentences that only they would understand. He gets in a phone booth, looks around to be sure he will not be heard, dials the number, and then speaks softly: "The Fox prowls. The moon rises. When the hawk flies, the pigeons take wing." He waits a moment, then says into the phone again, "Oh. Sorry. Is your papa home? Well, when he comes home, tell him Aldo called and said, 'The Fox prowls. The moon rises. When the hawk flies'—never mind. Go back to bed. I'll call your papa later."

When I showed the dialogue to Peter, he roared with laughter. He said, "We must show this to Vittorio. It's hysterical. Let's go." We rushed over to De Sica's office, and Peter read the dialogue as Vanucci, doing it perfectly. De Sica stared at us. He didn't get it. He shrugged, mystified. "American humor," was his only comment. When your director doesn't get the jokes in a comedy, the only word that comes to mind is "fatal." To make things worse, De Sica, as was his privilege, insisted on having his own editors, who had been with him for years. They were two middle-aged women who spoke no English at all, and this was their first English-speaking film. Therefore, when it came to the editing, they didn't listen to the dialogue. They just ran the scenes through their editing machines and when they saw a beautiful shot, they simply cut then and there. It was beginning to look like a wonderful travelogue of Italy with absolutely no humor at all. Most of these cuts were reassembled in London, retrieving much of the humor from the original takes, but some wonderful laughs are lying unlaughed at in a cutting room in Italy.

I wrote a scene to take place on the Via Veneto, the most famous and widest street in Rome, akin to Broadway and Forty-second Street or Piccadilly Circus. It was a sequence that ran only three minutes. I thought De Sica would cut it out since he said it would be impossible to shoot on the Via Veneto. The police would never close it off, unless we were lucky enough to have the police go out on strike. The huge hotels like the Excelsior would object, as would all the shop owners and outdoor cafés. It would be pandemonium on the streets.

As if it were no problem at all, De Sica decided to have the Via Veneto rebuilt on the studio lot. Not scaled down but to its true proportions. They rebuilt the entire Via Veneto, the Excelsior Hotel, the shops, the cafés, the traffic, everything, three long blocks' worth. It was a monumental job and I couldn't see how they could manage it on the film's budget, three million dollars. That sounds small today, but in 1965, three million was the average cost for a major film. Labor was cheap in Italy and the craftsmen were superb. You couldn't tell the difference on-screen or offscreen as you looked at the Via Veneto set standing on the studio lot. I was enormously impressed. Now if we could only get the actors to stop saying, "Wa tie eezd datrog cumn?"

A few days later, two things arrived from New York. One was my new business manager, David Cogan, and the other was a carton containing boxes of Mallomars, sent by one of my cousins, Honey Wolosoff, who had just been in Italy and knew of the lack of American delicacies (junk food, to be more exact) to be found there. Although there was hardly any food comparable to good Italian cooking, we were delighted to receive by air a half-dozen bagels (carefully sealed in silver foil), Hershey bars, and four boxes of Mallomars, a childhood favorite, made of marshmallows covered with dark chocolate. We parceled out the goodies and I got one box of Mallomars for myself, which I kept in our bedroom.

David Cogan came to look after my interests on the picture, although I thought my interests were being very well watched over by John Bryan, a knowledgeable and first-rate producer. One of David's attributes, or faults, depending on one's own needs, was to attend to matters that were beyond business, meaning our personal affairs—such things as matters between Joan and me, our children, what schools they should go to, our health, their health, and what we should eat in the restaurants he picked out. It was either very caring on his part or very intrusive. Take your pick.

After an hour and a half of playing tennis with David in Rome, with him telling me how to play a shot even as my racket was coming back to hit the ball, I decided to call it a day. A good choice, since I knew I had a night with him coming up. After a hot shower, I lay on my bed relaxing, when suddenly I heard a terrible sound. It was my teeth chattering. Joan brought me a brandy as she got ready for the evening, and I managed to get dressed while my body was shivering, which made it difficult to button my buttons, tie my tie, and zip my zipper. While I was still chilled and aching, we met David in the lobby, and he whooshed us away to one of Rome's better restaurants. I was not in the mood to be whooshed. The dinner was superb, despite my feverish hand that shook a perfectly good soup over my perfectly good suit. I drank a few glasses of wine, hoping the alcohol would calm the few nerves that were still functioning. The conversation was going along nicely until David looked at Joan and me and said, "So when are you two going to have another baby?"

He could turn from manager to mother-in-law on a dime.

"We haven't discussed it," Joan said. "Right now Ellen and Nancy are all we want."

"But look what beautiful children you have. Are you telling me you don't want another one like them?"

"We didn't say that, David. All Joan said was for right now it's fine. Okay?"

He looked directly at me. "What are you afraid of?"

Joan gave me one of those looks that said, "Would you please bop this man on the head with the wine bottle."

"David, we're not afraid to have more children. Why do you bring up such a thing now? Besides, that's personal. Maybe we will, maybe we won't. We don't know. Now let's drop it."

He had already thrown enough cold water on me for the day, now he was heating me up. He pursued the subject. "Why are you afraid to discuss it?"

I could feel a small sailor's knot tying itself up in my stomach. "I'm not afraid to discuss it. Why are you so adamant about pursuing it?"

"I'm not adamant. You just haven't given me a good answer as to why you won't have another child." His wine consumption had been slowly rising.

"David, I don't want to have another child because it might be a boy and grow up to be like you. Okay?"

Nothing ruffled David. He put his arm around me, gave me a grand-mother's kiss on the face, and said, "Don't you know how much I love you two? The both of you?"

"Thank you. We love you too."

Joan didn't second the motion.

David raised his glass in a toast and said, "Then have one for me. I just want to see you two kids have another child."

I suddenly thought he was one of the devil people from *Rosemary's Baby.* I heard myself screaming aloud in the restaurant: *"We're not having a baby! Even if Joan wants one. Will you please drop the subject!!"*

David picked up the check. "We'll charge it to the picture," he said.

We left the restaurant and squeezed into the back of a small Fiat taxi. The rock in my stomach now turned to pure pain. Pure and unadulterated. We said good night in the lobby and quickly went to our rooms. I fell on the bed. The pain was excruciating. I had never experienced anything quite like it in my life.

"Joan! I think you'd better call the concierge. I need a doctor. Something's really wrong."

She called down and asked the manager if they could get a doctor. They told her it was eleven-thirty on a Saturday night and they might have trouble finding one, but they'd do their best. A half hour passed and no help was forthcoming. My pain had now become so unbearable that Joan was getting very nervous. She called David and he said he'd be right up.

Ten minutes later the doctor and David showed up at the same time. The doctor spoke halting English. I told him my symptoms; he examined my back, my pelvic region, my stomach, everywhere, without coming to a conclusion. I began writhing in the bed.

The doctor told Joan he would have to give me morphine to ease the pain. David was asking me useless questions like, "What do you think it is?" I could have said, "You!" but I didn't think that would ease the situation.

They all waited in the other room for the morphine to take effect. I could hear their voices murmuring, sounding to my irrational mind like "Should we bury him here or send the body back home?" When they came back in, it was clear the morphine had no effect. The pain was as bad as ever, and this puzzled the doctor. My speech and thoughts started to slur but the pain didn't let up. I began to get frightened myself. I motioned for Joan to lean down. She put her head next to mine. I whispered almost incoherently, "I love you. If anything happens, tell the girls I love them. I'm sorry that this had to happen."

My words were becoming even more unintelligible. The room was spinning and things looked fuzzy, but I could see David by the fake fireplace, leaning against the mantelpiece. I motioned for Joan to lean over again. I mumbled to her . . . "Ma marz."

"Ma Marz? . . . You want me to call your mother?"

"No. Ma marz." I tried to point to David. She turned and looked at David. He was eating my box of Mallomars. It was all I could think of. She was too embarrassed to say to him, "How could you eat a dying man's last Mallomars?" Instead, she simply took the box off the mantelpiece and put it next to me, pretending I wanted one. One was all I could want because one was all that he had left. A few minutes later I passed out.

My eyes opened at six in the morning in a Catholic hospital where all the nurses were non-English-speaking nuns, and there was a large Christ on a Cross hung on the wall over my head. About five of the nuns were standing around me, all smiling, and I thought they were about to sing, "The hills are alive with the sound of music." The head nurse had a chart and started asking me questions in Italian. I kept saying, "No. I don't understand. I'm American.

Is there anyone here who understands English?" She acted as though I were answering her questions because every time I spoke, she wrote down something on her chart. When the doctor came in, he took the chart, read it and nodded to her, as though he understood. What did he understand? That I said, "I'm American. Does anyone here speak English?"

They took me upstairs and took X-rays. It looked to be a very old X-ray machine, probably the very first experimental model. I was no longer in a Bergman film. I was now the central character in a Kafka story. They were very warm and polite with me and fed me well, and the nuns always smiled when they came in. Two days later the pain had subsided and Joan took me back to the hotel, neither of us ever learning what caused the attack or what cured it. The only two answers I could come up with were that David Cogan went home or I passed a kidney stone the size of his head.

The filming moved on to the island of Ischia, a beautiful and tranquil spot in the Mediterranean, one not run over with tourists or sightseers. Its chief claim to fame was that it had a wonderful hotel with a spa, featuring the famous mud of Ischia. Joan and I were given a room on the top floor, and Ellen, Nancy, and Pam were sequestered down the hall. One night, about two in the morning, Joan and I were awakened by a noise that could only be described as someone on the floor directly above us moving a piano from one side of the room to the other. It came again the second night, once more at about two in the morning—a piano moving slowly above us. We asked the concierge the next morning if anyone was moving furniture in the room above us in the middle of the night. He said there was no room above us. Only the roof. It was not possible. No further explanations.

On the day following the night of the unexplained noise, I told De Sica about this weird phenomenon. He looked alarmed, then explained to the crew what I had just told him. They all grew very silent, giving each other ominous glances. De Sica said to me, "This is not a good sign. I will have your room changed." The next night Joan and I were in a new room and waited up till two in the morning. We heard no sound, no piano being moved. Somehow we missed hearing it. It had become a mystery for us to solve and now it was gone, its secret still intact. I don't know if it's true of all Italians or just Italian film crews, but they were a very superstitious people, always on the lookout for bad signs. De Sica had his bed moved so that he now slept from north to south rather than from east to west. An east-to-west bed was another bad omen. He also complained of not being able to sleep well because the island was part of an inactive volcano. It hadn't poured down lava since the Stone Age, but still he was intent on finishing our work on Ischia before hot bubbles started to appear under our doors. "Pompeii was a terrible way to die," he warned us.

Perhaps it wasn't all nonsense, because problems suddenly began to crop up for us. On Victor Mature's first day of shooting on the beach, a car and driver were sent to pick him up at 7 A.M. When he came out of the hotel, he saw a driver with a small Fiat. He looked around and said, "Where's my car?" His driver told him this *was* his car. The only road around the hills and small mountain to the beach was very narrow, and one must drive slowly and carefully to avoid mishaps. In the Fiat it would take about thirty-five minutes to reach the beach.

Mature insisted his contract clearly stated that he was to be driven to all locations in a limousine. "That is not possible," said the driver. A limousine had never gone on that road. Mature was adamant. No limousine, no Mature. He went back to his room to wait.

When De Sica heard of this, he was furious. I'm sure he considered the fault was all mine, since I had been sleeping in a room with a piano moving overhead. Valuable time was being lost and he wanted to shoot quickly and get off Ischia before the first eruptions started.

Finally a limousine was found. It was an old Cadillac limo, white. Joan and I were watching from our window, and I turned to her and said, "Uh-oh. A white limousine is a very bad omen."

Mature got in the back, satisfied he was being treated like a star at last. The driver crossed himself. As he drove off his family wept and headed for the nearest church. As they made the slow turns around the tiny road, helpers before and at the rear of the car called out warnings to stop, back up, and proceed slowly. They made the thirty-five-minute trip in close to two hours.

Peter Sellers heard of this and demanded that he too must have a limousine. He told John Bryan that he was the star of the film, not Mature, and demanded that he get a limo as well. And not just any limo. It had to be white. And no, he would not share with Mature.

He might as well have asked for a white rhino. Tiny little Ischia was not inundated with limousines. They finally found a black one, probably used for funerals, which was appropriate because it looked very likely that it would be used for one again very soon.

Peter drove off in his hearselike limo as the citizens of Ischia lined the road, crossing themselves and rubbing their rosary beads. Fortunately, we had no mishaps, but we did lose about four hours a day on transportation.

In the meantime, De Sica sat alone on the beach in his director's chair, waiting to see if any of his stars made it through alive. To keep his nerves from completely unraveling, he went to our small production office on the beach where he discovered the phones were temporarily out. He found a yacht docked in the tiny harbor and asked the English owners if it were possible for him to make an important radio call abroad. They were more than happy to oblige for the privilege of watching the film being made. De Sica stood by as the radio operator called the Casino in Monte Carlo, where he bet ten thousand lire each on numbers twelve and twenty-three. The operator stayed on the line; he heard the bad news and nervously reported it to Vittorio. Clearly we were getting off to a bad start.

Two days later, Mature arrived on the beach on time but in a fury. In order to make up the lost limo time, they had woken him at five in the morning. Mature, who was usually very easy to work with, and who seemed to be enjoying the role he was playing, suddenly got into a fit over having to redo a take five times as he stood in the water up to his knees. He walked out of the water, picked up his script from his canvas chair, yelled, "The hell with this goddamned picture!" and threw the script into the ocean. Everyone stood still. I mean *everyone*. In Italy, throwing a script into the sea was like giving the pope a five-dollar tip after an audience with his eminence. It's simply not done. Now they were all sure to die for this breach of respect. They all wanted to walk off the picture. De Sica finally calmed them down, and the sacred script was fished from the waters and set out in the sun to dry. The local priest made a blessing over it.

Minor and major mishaps continued to happen. A camera was knocked over by a large wave and the expensive lens was ruined. The crew started having accidents, including cuts, deep and small, broken bones, a couple of concussions, and a collision in which a truck hit a car and the car went through a store window. It got to the point that doctors paid daily visits to the set without even being sent for.

Occasionally a minor dignitary would visit the set—the mayor of Ischia, a few Italian film stars who sailed over in boats to have lunch with De Sica and Peter. One Italian government official on holiday visited the set, accompanied by his wife, who was wearing a purple dress. The visual impact of a heavy-set woman in a purple dress in broad daylight was difficult enough to contend with, but wearing purple on the set was the cardinal sin in Italian filmmaking. Even if a cardinal himself wore it.

The entire crew walked off the set. De Sica dismissed everyone else, expecting the worst calamity. The crew went back to their rooms and immediately showered down with the most powerful astringent they could find to wash away this newest curse that had befallen them. The next day an order was issued, no more visitors on the set. Princess Margaret, however, came down for a day, and for her they made an exception. Had she shown up wearing purple, however, she would have found an empty beach.

Joan, Ellen, and Nancy were not considered visitors. They were family and were treated by the crew with affection and respect. A chair was always set up for Joan a few feet away from the camera. Between takes, De Sica would have Ellen and Nancy on his knee, and would charm them with his smile and warmth. Victor Mature often gave the girls a ride home in his white limo, now much safer since De Sica had had the road widened at great expense to United Artists. At the end of each day, we would all return to our hotel, and as the sun would slowly diminish, we all gathered in a small courtyard to have a drink, each one of the principals picking up the tab as his turn came. But Victor Mature always stayed in his room, and when the drinks were served, he would stick his head out of his third-floor window, hold up a glass of red wine, and call out *"Salute!"* to the rest of the company, thus avoiding ever having to pick up a check for a round of drinks.

One night I was called inside for a telephone call from the States. I couldn't imagine who it was or what it could be about. It was Saint Subber.

"Congratulations," he said.

"For what?"

"You won."

"Won what?"

"The Tony Award."

"I did?"

I was shocked and delirious. Mike Nichols had also won, his third straight Tony. I won as Best Author for *The Odd Couple*, while Frank Gilroy won for Best Play for *The Subject Was Roses*. It actually didn't make much sense. Either the winner as Best Author of a play wrote the Best Play, or the winner of Best Play was actually the Best Author. It was the last year they ever split that into two categories, but at least I got my Silver Medallion. It was on this happy note that we soon sailed back to the Italian mainland to finish shooting at Cinecittà.

We moved into our rented houses on the Appia Antica, the oldest road leading into Rome. It was actually a compound of three houses, one large main house and two smaller guest houses, set far enough apart to give us all some privacy. Peter and Britt took the large house while John Bryan and his family, and Joan and I and the girls, took the two smaller guest houses.

A few days later I got a phone call from New York. It was Bob Fosse. He had just finished writing a new musical for Gwen Verdon, an adaptation of Federico Fellini's film *Nights of Cabiria*, all about a street-walker and her dreams of being rescued from her sordid life by a man of great respectability. The title of Bob's show was *Sweet Charity*, Charity being the leading lady's name. The title seemed a little cloying to me, almost announcing what a golden heart our heroine possessed. It didn't have Bob's usual gritty point of view.

He asked if he could send me the script because he felt it was lacking in humor. I said I'd be glad to read it, but I couldn't work on it since I was already dividing my time between shooting *After the Fox* and writing the screenplay of *Barefoot*. Bob doesn't take no easily. His script arrived in Italy about eight days later despite its package marked "Urgent," "Special Delivery," "Via Air," "Post Haste," etc. You can't rush the Italians if they don't wish to be, and the wonders of Federal Express were still twenty years in the future.

I read the script as soon as I received it. Fosse was wrong. It didn't need humor. It *desperately* needed humor. And it needed it fast because he was going into rehearsal in August and this was the beginning of July. I sat down and spent one long night removing the lines that didn't work and inserting new and what I hoped were funnier ones. I sent it back to Bob through the United Artists parcel, which was flown back to New York every day.

Three days later, another phone call from New York. Fosse again.

"I love the new lines. You can't stop now."

"Bob, I just don't have the time. I can barely get *Barefoot* done."

"I'm not letting you off the hook. You owe me one."

"For what?"

"I'll think of something."

"Bob, you know if I could—"

"I'll find a way to convince you."

A week later, another phone call, but not from New York. It was Bob at the airport in Rome. "I'm here. I brought a tape of the score. You have to listen to it. Pick me up at TWA." And he hung up.

I found him sitting alone on the bench, his arms stretched over the back, with a cigarette dangling from his lips, probably from his third pack of the day. He was wearing black pants, a black shirt, white socks, and black shoes. He looked ready to go on and do his famous "Steam Heat" number from *The Pajama Game*. He carried one small suitcase, signifying he wasn't staying long, and one large, heavy tape recorder, signifying he had only one purpose to his visit.

Joan and I sat on the sofa in our living room as Bob applied the electrical adapter to his tape machine. He wound and rewound the tape quickly so he could start the number exactly on cue. He pushed all the furniture back against the walls so he could freely demonstrate the songs.

"This number takes place the first time we see these sleazy dance-hall girls that Charity works with. When the lights come up, it's all dark blues and reds and a black background, and lots of smoke in the foreground. We see seven or eight girls, some with legs wrapped around a brass bar, two girls leaning against each other, a few of them smoking, all in cheap wigs, tight short skirts, beauty marks, and tons of makeup. They're the pits, got it?" We got it. He put on the tape. We heard the first beats of the rhythm section and the girls began to sing and talk to the unseen customers: "So you want to have fun, fun, fun . . . , So you want to have laughs, laughs, laughs. . . ."

Joan and I were pulled into the number immediately. You knew this was something special, something we hadn't heard in musical comedy before. Bob positioned himself as each new girl sang with all her seediness, lust, and hopeless sadness, yet there was remarkable humor to it. The minute they blared out, *"Hey, big spender, spend . . . a little time with me,"* I was sold.

It was Cy Coleman's music at its best, and with it were Dorothy Fields' great lyrics—tough, funny, and Brechtian. Before I could say a word to Bob, he motioned for me to be quiet. The tape started again. The next number was Latin, angry, filled with emotion, and strong, earthy determination as three forlorn dance-hall girls began to sing "There's Gotta Be Something Better Than This." This was a number for Gwen and someone like Chita Rivera and another girl.

At the end, Joan and I burst into applause. Then she turned to me and said, "If you don't do this show, you and I are through."

Bob said, "You want to hear more?"

I said "No. Who wants to sit here and listen to the best score I have ever heard? Turn it off."

Next came a march. A happy march. A happy love song march. A happy love song dancing march. "This is for Gwen," he continued. "She's just been proposed to. All her dreams have come true. A big brass band comes out, and Gwen, in a sexy uniform, is the leader."

We heard Gwen singing, "I'm a brass band, I'm a clarinet . . . I'm a bass trombone," and Bob started to dance as Gwen would do in the number. Joan and I sat there, our breath taken away, and just stared at Bob.

Bob was a paradox because he had an enormous ego, yet he never believed what he did was good enough. He looked at us tentatively and asked, much like a child would ask a parent if he or she liked his drawing of a cat, "What do you think? I think it's kind of good, don't you?"

"No. I hate it, Bob," I said. "But I'll pay you to let me be part of this show. My only problem is, I don't think I can finish the rewrites before you go into rehearsal."

"You'll finish it," said Joan. "I know you. You'll write it in your sleep."

The three of us stayed up till the early hours as Bob explained how he saw the show—the sets, the costumes, every little detail was in his mind. Yet the book, as written by Bob, would need extensive revisions if the humor and the story of Charity's plight were to come up to the level of the score. What felt good to me was that this time just Bob and I would be collaborating, since he was directing as well. There was no doubt we could work well together. He left in the morning and Carlo, our houseman, was cleaning up cigarette butts and ashtrays until late that afternoon.

I knew there was no way I could be on the set of *After the Fox* every day and still complete the rewrites of *Charity* and *Barefoot*. Then again, in an eight- or ten-hour shooting day on a film, only about an hour and a half is the actual time it takes to shoot. The rest of the time is devoted to the crew readying and lighting the sets, while the actors nap, read, or play cards. I brought my writing pads with me and started to work on *Barefoot*.

When people see a writer on the set with a pad and pencil, they usually stay clear of him, not wanting to interrupt the creative process. I soon realized that nothing distracted me. I could write while they talked or banged nails into wood or yelled at each other during a poker game. It's not that I didn't hear it, but I was so focused on what I was writing that it just didn't intrude. I did this over the next twenty-five years, on every film I ever wrote. While the cast and crew thought I was slaving away on the script we were shooting (forgetting that since they were shooting it, it was already written), I was actually working on the next project. With all that noise I couldn't read a book or do a crossword puzzle, but I could write a script. How, I don't know. Tunnel vision might be an appropriate explanation. Each night after dinner, I worked on *Charity*. Although Joan knew I was giving up time with her and the girls, she made allowances with this one. She loved the project, she loved Bob and Gwen, and their daughters and ours were best friends. It was a family affair.

As *After the Fox* was coming close to finishing, I still watched every take, listening to endless variations of "I tin we gun puldese us, buz" ("I think we're going to pull this off, Boss"). We finished principal photography on the same day I finished the screenplay to *Barefoot* and sent it off to Paramount. It would take about seven months before the picture went into production, so that now I could turn all my attention to *Sweet Charity*. As I worked on the musical, I realized it was not the kind of book I would have done, had I started from scratch. There was something artificial about this story and I didn't think I could write it with a sense of reality, as I normally could with a play. I couldn't create a real life for Charity—imagining where she came from and how she ended up in a dance hall.

In a musical, the lines are short and basically lead up to the song, which gives us the emotion and character, so working in a musical is generally a thankless job for the bookwriter. But Gwen and Bob were too brilliant a team for me to walk away from. Actually, I wanted to see the show more than I wanted to write it, but once committed, I threw myself into the project with abandon.

Joan and the girls flew back to a roasting August in New York while I had to fly to London with Peter and Britt to see a first cut of the film. We landed in London at night, and Peter, Britt, and I were picked up together in one car. It was good to see London again, and as the car turned through the theater district, we saw a large marquee on the Globe Theater where *The Odd Couple* was playing with Jack Klugman and Victor Spinetti. The play was a huge success there; someone had told me that Harold Pinter had said, after seeing the show, "Now this is what the theater should be about." I hoped it wasn't an apocryphal story.

As the car passed the marquee, Britt shouted, "Oh, look, Peter. There's Neil's play. We must go and see it."

Peter looked at her, his nostrils flaring in anger; then he looked at me and said, "What the hell's going on between you two?" Peter's rages and jealousies knew no boundaries.

The car stopped at my hotel and I was very glad to get out. If Britt had shouted, "Oh, look, Peter. There's Chekhov's *The Seagull*. Let's go see it," Peter would very likely have said, "What the hell's going on with you and that dead Russian?"

GETTING TO KNOW ME

12

IT FELT GOOD to be back in New York. Back to our own friends, to our own bed, to seeing the new shows, back to Joan finishing the house on Sixty-second Street and me catching up with the Giants and the Yankees. *Barefoot* and *Odd Couple* were holding up fine on Broadway, and I was about to start a musical that looked more than promising.

The first cut of *After the Fox* I had seen in London looked like a mishmash, and they brought in new editors who were wise enough to know that when there's a joke, it's best not to cut out the punch line.

As for me, I felt a change in myself—more confidence, more energy, a greater sense of direction. The problem was that the division between the boy who was born Marvin and the man who was now called Neil was growing wider and farther apart. Instead of one maturing, and merging gradually into the other, the first one stayed hidden, silently nagging to be heard by the one who was becoming more public, more distant from his longtime friends, his cousins, his origins. It amazes me that one remembers so little of those first two years of life but how enormously they mold and shape the adult to be, leaving permanent, indelible, yet invisible scars that never reveal when and why and how they were put there. Only the reactions and behavior that follow in maturity offer evidence that somewhere in that infant and childlike mind are recorded and filed away pain and fear that is destined to reoccur for all the days to come. I started analysis again, and while talking about my daily routine, the joys of family, friends, work, and their rich rewards, a single word or phrase uttered could suddenly send tears to my eyes, or arouse anger and rage at something I didn't know was repressed, but was struggling now to resurface and to show its face and form to me. I was writing plays that made people laugh; I wanted a response from the audience that would make up for whatever it was that was missing from those formative years of mine.

When an audience laughed, I felt fulfilled. It was a sign of approval, of being accepted. Coming as I did from a childhood where laughter in the house meant security, but was seldom heard as often as a door slamming every time my father took another year's absence from us, the laughter that came my way in the theater was nourishment. The more I heard, the more I needed. There was never enough. True, Joan and the girls filled our house with their own laughter—but I was never threatened by their leaving. They filled up all my todays and tomorrows, but there was a hurt coming from my yesterdays that made me feel frightened and abandoned. Analysis is an arduous and frustrating process. There is no magical button to press that pushes life forward. The process makes you go further back than you care to go, to the very spot that you're running away from. Even my making the analyst laugh was to relieve the pressure she was putting on me, and maybe divert her constant efforts to force memory. It's a day-to-day repetition that reveals occasional droplets of truth that dry up before you can catch them in your hand. And there's always that goddamn time limit. If we applied *any* time limit to making love—nothing so generous as the fifty minutes we get with our analyst, but a shorter period where just before climax is reached, you hear a voice say, "Well, I'm afraid that's it for today. Let's pick up again on Wednesday"—there'd be even more frustrated people in the world than we have now, if that's possible. So come next Wednesday you try to recapture where you were in that deep, dark tunnel, hoping to see a pattern being formed by the tiny threads of information our psyche allows us to glimpse from time to time.

For me, at least, the pleasant memories are never as clear or as prominent as the ones that left some damage. Like that of a little boy standing holding his mother's hand on a hot summer's day, beads of perspiration dropping from the mother's hand to the boy's fingers. He is afraid to let go for fear she will feel rejected. Her life is filled with rejection. They stand there on a shadeless street, eyes glued to a wooden frame house. The mother watches diligently, hoping to catch the boy's father coming out the door of a strange woman's house. The mother reminds him that if they see the father, the boy will confront him and will swear in court that he witnessed the father's infidelity. The boy can hardly catch his breath for fear the father will appear, forcing him to betray his father, and if fear stops the words from being said, he will betray his mother. The boy has no free choice, and no one is there to tell him the right thing to do. On one side is his mother, on the other, his father, yet he is desperately alone. Fortunately the father does not appear that day, and the mother and son walk home, knowing another day will soon come when this will be repeated and repeated. All the boy wants is to be free, to run as fast and as far as he can. To hide in the darkness of a movie theater, where Charlie Chaplin will give him ninety minutes of respite, and laughter is the only escape.

The father leaves home, another break in the semi-continuity of security in the boy's life. He learns never to depend on what will happen from day to day and that the only one he can count on being there for him is himself. The father leaves the mother almost penniless. The meager amount of subsistence he sends from time to time would barely feed a mother and two sons for a week. She has no occupation, no skills, no visible means of support. She is forced to take in boarders to keep Danny from leaving school to become their sole support. The boarders are two brothers, owners of a small neighborhood butcher shop. They are coarse, distant, lacking in warmth or friendliness. The mother moves out of her bedroom so they can have it and she sleeps on the small sofa in the living room. The butchers pay half their rent in cash and half in produce, the meat they didn't sell that day. Lamb, chicken, liver, and ground chuck appear on our table, bartered for our dignity and privacy. They keep to themselves and are poor substitutes for a father who was a poor substitute for one himself.

The two boys feel their home has become diminished in size, leaving them less room in a house that was small enough to begin with. The younger boy tries not to come home as much, because it's lonelier there than anywhere else. He spends his afternoons in the public library, doing his homework and reading books of adventure and travel, anything that will transport him to distant places. His body is trapped but his mind finds freedom in his flights of fantasies, and he takes refuge there—in his imagination. His father calls to see him. The boy walks alongside him on the street as the father asks about what's going on in the house, how do the men behave with their mother. The implication is clear even to a seven-year-old. Has the mother rented out herself as well as her apartment? The boy is again asked to betray a parent. The mother sometimes has card games in her kitchen at night, and the friends and neighbors who play put a quarter into a glass before each game for the use of the hall. The mother doesn't play. She can't afford to lose the six or seven dollars she earns as proprietor of the game. The boy is happy that the mother has friends to be with, but he feels there's something tawdry about renting out the kitchen table where you eat for people to gamble.

The boy visits his aunts and uncles, his father's side of the family. They have apartments where cool breezes flow through their rooms in the summertime. They eat better and dress better and send their sons and daughters to colleges. The boy feels embarrassed for his shabby clothes and one pair of shoes. The mother threatens to take the father to court for nonsupport of his family. The father's brother-in-law, a burly, strong man, comes to the mother's house and threatens to beat her if she doesn't leave her husband in peace. The mother screams loudly as he raises a hand as if to strike her. A neighbor calls the police. Suddenly there are crowds in front of the building as two policemen climb the steps to deflect the trouble on the third floor. The mother is hysterical.

The boy watches from across the street with his friends, too frightened and too ashamed to admit to them that this is the family to which he belongs. He buries the scene in the back of his mind. If he doesn't think of it, perhaps it will go away. Or better still, he can pretend it never happened at all. And so he does. Until one day he believes the lie. When you start believing the lie, what is the truth? And if you don't know the truth, then who are you? Well, you can always be someone else, someone who is not connected to your past. But who? Perhaps the part of you that loves to sit in darkened movie theaters or in a corner of the public library on rainy afternoons, immersed in a fictional and imaginative world that is as real as your own fantasies will make it. Just because the movie is over or the library closes at six doesn't mean you have to leave it behind. You can take it home in your head and believe that's where you really live. Slowly, determinedly, the young boy moves out of the squalid world of his unhappiness and straight uptown, where bright music plays in his head at the touch of a thought. He burrows himself deeper and deeper and is gradually lost behind the facade of the new friend he has just created. The new boy loves his sudden emergence into this world, with a clean slate where he can create a whole new set of memories, fashioned to fit whatever pleases him most, much like the movies he's seen or the books he's read. It's a delusion but it's freedom.

But the irony is, the "new boy" knows he's a creation, that whatever he does is a charade, that he's a fake, a fraud. But who's to expose him? No one really. Certainly not his former self, because he needs the new one now. Why miss this golden opportunity to escape the pain of growing up in a world where he was always frightened and unnoticed? The "new boy" chooses to keep playing out the game and gradually he loses touch with the other boy, forgets who he really was and why he always looked for places to hide. Life, however, doesn't let you off that easily. "New boy" can't keep "younger boy" in the closet forever. The "younger boy" is still the true soul, the owner of his own identity. He is just putting a mask on his newfound friend, to do his work, to play his games, to create his stories, to take his bows and collect his rewards. The result is that neither one of them are very happy, because the "young boy" regrets giving away what should be his, and "new boy" doesn't really know who it is that people are reacting to. He never trusts their responses, the praise, the good things that come his way. He feels they belong to "young boy," who in turn rejects them because he knows he had to reinvent himself in order to be worthy of the gifts that are being left on his doorstep.

But there's no turning back now. "Young boy" eventually fades away, then cuts off entirely from the new young man who eventually emerges, leaving only a shadow that appears occasionally to trouble his dreams. The new boy now gives himself up to play out all his games, to give life to the multitude of stories that pour into his mind, to commit them to paper. People seem to like them. They laugh. They recognize the characters. It's usually themselves they recognize, or it's the person sitting next to them that they came with. "New boy" gets pats on the head. "Young boy" is sitting alone way up in the last row watching all this, wondering why the characters onstage seem familiar to him. But sadly, he's sitting alone.

After a while I stopped analysis because the present was a much pleasanter place to be than the past. Life is good again, until those times when your behavior reminds you you've not really made peace with the old pain, but merely covered it with layers of rationalities. Intellect is sometimes the great denier and time is the great arbiter.

IT WAS THE BEST OF TIMES

13

NINETEEN SIXTY-SIX was a very good year. With Bob Fosse in charge, we rehearsed *Sweet Charity* and avoided almost all of the problems of musicals in trouble. I did all my rewrites at home at night and early in the morning, because I never wanted to miss a moment of watching Bob and Gwen work. True, much of their work was prepared in advance, but at least half was created on their feet in a rehearsal hall. Cy Coleman often sat at the piano improvising variations on the themes of the score to fit Bob's need in creating a dance. Gwen's and Bob's minds and feet worked as one, and as he was showing her a move or a step, she already knew it before he finished.

Bob loved props. Hats especially, all kinds of hats. And canes and white gloves and anything else he saw on the set or even something that someone wore or carried into rehearsal. If someone ordered pizza, the pizza box stood a good chance of ending up in the number. He would use chairs, benches, pillows, lamps, baseball bats, scarves—every inanimate object he found would immediately become part of the character and would enhance it.

Bob became less self-conscious about having me around and I was allowed to watch all the musical rehearsals. He would still mutter his insecurities to me, the same old "Is this any good?" or "You hate it, right?" The greatest thrills I'd have came when he would ask if I saw anything that could help the number. I rarely did, but once I suggested that a girl stick her head out of the side of the curtain about twelve feet in the air (standing on an unseen ladder, of course). Bob tried it, liked it, and left it in. I felt as if Monet had handed me a brush and said, "Put another water lily in where you think it needs one."

Gwen was a dream to watch and a joy to work with. Bob pushed her hard, wanting her to shine, but not many people would have the strength, the fortitude, or the talent to meet his demands. Fighters come out at the bell. Gwen came out on the downbeat. She did everything he asked, including the impossible. She was a beautiful woman but never used her sex onstage except in a humorous way, which only made her more sexy. She wasn't a great singer but her husky voice and personality were unique; I would rather hear her sing onstage than Ethel Merman or Mary Martin. She played her scenes so well, you would have hired her even if she couldn't dance. She had a smile and a laugh that were irresistible. Joan gave me complete permission to be in love with her, an emotion I shared with every other man who ever watched her perform.

We opened out of town, in Detroit, and were there over Christmas and New Year's. The Fisher Theatre was a cavernous auditorium, housed in the huge office building also owned by the Nederlander family. Working with lyricist Dorothy Fields was a major joy and surprise for me. When I met her, she was in her sixties and reminded me a little of Lillian Hellman. She was tough, all business, and could meet a crisis with the best of them. She was the exception to the rule I mentioned before about lyricists. It was easier for her to rewrite a song than to fight for one. And took less time. What I didn't know about her was that she was fond of a drink at dinner. She was even fonder of two or three drinks even without dinner. When she appeared at the theater every night for the evening performance, she was dressed in her Park Avenue best, always looking elegant. She didn't stand too well, however, as a result of a martini or two, and often leaned on a friendly arm or a bannister to give her balance, although she never lost her dignity. Be that as it may, at nine o'clock in the morning she was fresh, alert, and had already written a new set of lyrics that would knock your socks off. Whether it was a ballad or a comedy song, she always delivered overnight and first-class. I'm sorry I only had one opportunity to work with her.

When the curtain came down on opening night in Detroit, it was to thunderous applause. It didn't hurt that the first five rows were completely filled with Jimmy Nederlander's friends, many of whom were investors in the show. They liked it so much, they all came again and again during the run, and although their laughter began to diminish after they heard the jokes for the third time, it never stopped the audience from loving every minute of it. My gut feeling was that when we got to New York, we'd be a hit because of Bob, Gwen, and the score. I knew I'd take plenty of potshots for a book that wasn't up to the rest of it, but I felt that I did the best I could with material that didn't really suit me. I would probably ride in to a hit on the coattails of Fosse and Gwen's work, but the experience was worth it.

The next morning the local Detroit reviews came out. They glorified

Gwen, praised the score, and gave Bob his due. What shocked me was that they thought the book was superb. "Maybe Neil Simon's best," one even said. It was a curious feeling as I sat in my hotel room reading these notices and thinking, They're wrong. Not to say we didn't get enormous laughs, but Bob's choreography, as danced by Gwen and the chorus, and Cy Coleman and Dorothy Fields' score were far more original and daring than anything I could contribute.

I was not foolish enough to look a gift rave in the mouth, however, and I walked over to the theater to see if everyone was jubilant. I walked in the stage door and down past the empty seats in the theater. The chorus was onstage brushing up on a few numbers while Bob sat atop a ladder putting them through their paces. The cigarette didn't hang from his mouth this morning. It drooped. I suddenly felt something was wrong. As I appeared at the foot of the stage, Bob turned and looked at me. He smiled with a scowl. "Hey," he shouted with mock enthusiasm. "Let's give a big hand to the star of the show, Neil Simon." It was like a dagger made of pure ice, aimed straight at the surprised look on my face. The rest of the company applauded and I couldn't tell if they were happy for my praise or afraid not to back Bob up in his black mood. They were all, man and woman, devoted to him.

I suddenly felt like a villain, a cheat. Like the woman who won the Boston Marathon by dropping out of the pack and taking the subway almost to the finish line. I didn't think this was the place for a silly confrontation with Bob, so I left the theater and went out for a bitter breakfast. Months before, he had practically pleaded with me to do the show, flown out on his own to Rome to convince me, and was delighted with what I did. And now he was angry that my reviews over-shadowed his. The irony was that he was right to be angry. Perhaps I was running on a high with some of the critics, after back-to-back hits with *Barefoot* and *Odd Couple*.

As I sat in the restaurant, I thought to myself, What do I do now? Not fix up the parts of the script that still needed some brightening for fear it would anger Bob even more? Or maybe I should just go back home, since I thought they had a hit without any more additions from me. Obviously I was being as petty as I thought Bob was being in his greeting to me.

Later on, during a break, I talked with Bob and apologized good-naturedly for my less-than-deserving reviews. He laughed and smiled a real smile, the warm generous smile that so often crossed his face. "I swear I'm not upset," he said. "You deserved it. It's terrific work."

"It's not," I said. "It won't happen this way in New York." Suddenly we were in another stupid argument, each one taking the other's side this time around. "Fuck 'em," he said. "I think we all did a great job."

We walked back to the stage, friends once more, and I said, "I'll tell you what. I'll take out the scene in the closet [which had the funniest lines in the show] if you take out 'Big Spender' and 'Brass Band.'" (Naturally, they were both show-stopping numbers.) We both laughed knowing what an insane business we were in. Even if you're out of town with a show that wasn't in trouble, you can always manage to create some.

All our families came out for Christmas and New Year's. We spent Christmas morning opening gifts, with Nancy getting twice as much because Christmas was her birthday as well. I always felt she got cheated because she never had a special birthday of her own but had to share it with someone who was far more well known than she was.

In the afternoon we all went to the movies. What was special about it was that it was Nancy's first time in a movie theater. The film was *101 Dalmatians* and she was very excited. We sat down behind another family with their children. Nancy was quite small, so we asked if she could see all right. Since there was nothing on the screen as yet, she quietly nodded yes to us. The movie was wonderful and Ellen lapped it up. Nancy sat quietly eating her popcorn and every once in a while she'd look at Joan or look at me and smile. She was having a wonderful time. I did notice, however, that she didn't react as vocally as Ellen at the funny parts or look as frightened in the scarier parts. After a while, I put my head down and kissed her cheek and as I did, I turned and looked at the screen. I couldn't see the screen. All I could see was the large back of the father sitting in front of her. She had seen nothing of the movie. I picked her up in my lap for the rest of the film. When we left the theater I said to her, "Nancy, if you couldn't see the movie, why didn't you say something?" She shrugged and said, "I liked it anyway." That's how she was—never complaining. I don't know if she ever saw it again but if she hasn't, I think her all-time favorite movie was the one she saw that day, *28 Dalmatians.*

During the last few previews, Stanley Donen came out to see the show at Fosse's request. Stanley Donen directed the classic film *Singin' in the Rain* and at least half a dozen more of the best musicals MGM ever made. If he didn't know about musicals, no one did. After the show that night, Donen and Fosse went out by themselves. I had no idea about what Donen thought, but I think I guessed the next morning when Bob asked me to have breakfast alone with him.

"Okay, what did Stanley think of the show?" I asked.

"He loved it," Bob said. "He thinks it could be brilliant."

Could be always means not yet. "What part didn't he like?"

"The ending."

What Bob had taken from Fellini's original film, he had tried to put into the first draft of his musical. Charity gets turned down on her wedding day, and pushed off a bridge in Central Park; she crawls out soaking wet, gets her purse stolen again, but walks off hopeful that life will get better. I thought it was a wonderful ending and asked what Donen didn't like about it.

"It's not tough enough," Bob said. "It should be grittier, darker. Charity should be devastated and the audience should feel her pain. Now it's just funny and kind of sweet."

I looked at Bob and was bewildered. He was the one who had called it *Sweet Charity*. As it was, John McMartin, a warm and likable actor, walks out on Charity at the end, and despite his sincere, befuddled, and funny performance, he got boos from many women at the curtain calls. He smiled good-naturedly at it as he bowed, knowing it was the character they were booing and not the actor. What did bother him was when he walked out the stage door after each performance, women would say with a smile, "You rat. Why didn't you marry that girl?" He would usually shrug and say, "I do in the sequel."

I said to Bob, "This is not *Stella Dallas* we're doing here. I don't think we're trying to rip people's hearts out. Once you turned it into a musical, the tone automatically changed. The audience is having a good time. I think we're fortunate the audience cares so much about Charity. To suddenly pull the rug from under the show and make it darker and grimmer would be awkward and really pretentious."

He looked at me determinedly. "Why not? Who says you can't? Who made that rule?"

"I didn't. But I think if the show grows darker at the end, you have to prepare the audience for it somewhere in the play. Tell about her real life and why she became a dance-hall hostess." (In the film, she was a streetwalker, but Bob already had taken the grit out when he turned her into a dance-hall girl, a change which I thought right for a musical.)

"I want it darker," he repeated.

This could go on all night, I realized. "Bob, I always said from the beginning, this is your show, not mine. Mine are the plays I write. I told you I would do whatever I could to help. I didn't write it. I rewrote it. If you want it darker, here's my black pen. You write it. I hope it works. I'll be in New York and you can always call me and I'll come back to fix anything you want. Except the ending." I left and went back to my hotel to pack my bags.

In the morning Bob called me. He said, "I still think I'm right . . . but I'm not positive. I need time to think about it. In the meantime, I hope you'll stay with the show."

I did. It's impossible to tell, even in hindsight, who was right. It was Bob's choice to make. I felt, even with the plays that I wrote, that a show has a mind of its own, and it's wrong to push it in a direction it doesn't want to go. We left the ending as is and Bob never brought it up again. He eventually *did* move toward the darker material that attracted him so, and he became a brilliant film director and writer, with *Cabaret*, starring Liza Minnelli, *Lenny*, with Dustin Hoffman as Lenny Bruce, and his achingly honest autobiographical musical film, *All That Jazz*. Bob is still the only director who won the Oscar, the Tony, and the Emmy all in the same year, 1973. His determination paid off in the end.

SWEET CHARITY was to be the renaissance of the Palace Theater, once the mecca of the greatest acts in vaudeville. When vaudeville slipped into oblivion, the theater slipped into darkness and eventually was ignominiously transformed into a movie house, and not a very prestigious one at that.

In the mid-sixties, the Nederlander family took over the Palace and gutted and refurbished it to its former grandeur. *Sweet Charity* was to be the first legitimate show to play there in almost twenty-five years. When we returned from Detroit, I took Ellen with me to see how the refurbishing was going. Workers were furiously hammering, sawing, and painting, trying to make our first preview three days away, but I was skeptical at what I saw. Only half the orchestra seats were set up, a third of the carpeting had been laid, and workmen on scaffolding everywhere were pounding, painting, and panting. I stood at the rear of the orchestra on the aisle, where two metal circular holders had been put in place awaiting the red velvet rope that would be clipped in and lifted by the ushers and closed by them to keep latecomers from rushing down the aisle in mid-performance.

Ellen stood quietly next to me watching the frantic activity as I chatted with owner/producer Jimmy Nederlander, who wondered himself whether we'd meet the deadline. As we talked, Ellen kept interrupting by saying quietly, "Daddy?" and I kept saying, "Not now, honey. I'm talking to Mr. Nederlander." Jimmy and I kept chatting and Ellen kept saying quietly, "Daddy?" Finally I turned to her and said brusquely, "What is it?" She said, "I can't get my finger out." Somehow she had wedged her thumb into the circular metal holder and it had gotten stuck.

At first I tried carefully and patiently to remove it, but somehow her thumb had enlarged since she had put it in. I asked stupid father questions like, "Why did you put your thumb in there?" as if magically those words would make the thumb slip out. It wouldn't budge, and I could see panic creeping into Ellen's nine-year-old face.

Now I started to worry. Especially when she tearfully asked me if they would have to cut off her thumb. I said, "Of course not," although the panic in my mind kept telling me that they would either have to remove the entire back row or Ellen would be standing there a week later on opening night with her thumb in the hole as the first-nighters smiled at the little nine-year-old usherette. I added more wonderful fatherly advice like, "You should never put your thumb in places like that," not only scaring Ellen more but making her think it would be all right to put *other* fingers in similar holes if the opportunity arose again.

Jimmy called one of the workmen over. He had hammers and pliers protruding out of his overall pockets, and the expression on Ellen's face was saying, "Oh my God. They're going to pull my thumb out with pliers." At least little Jack Horner had the sense to put his thumb in a pie.

At that moment all I could think of was how much I hated Bob Fosse for calling me in Rome to work on this show and disfiguring my daughter for life. The workman pulled out a little jar, rubbed some grease on Ellen's finger and it slipped out smoothly, quickly, and quietly. Which was exactly how we left the theater. And I cautioned Ellen not to tell her mother about the episode for fear that Joan would never let me be alone with Ellen outside the house until she was twenty-one.

DESPITE OUR FEARS, the theater was finished in time, and Sweet Charity opened on January 29, 1966. I've often thought it was a weird phenomenon that when I heard a huge laugh from the audience I never saw who it was laughing. Certainly not the two people sitting on the aisle in the last row or the two couples sitting in the fifth row on the other side of the orchestra. Yet there were the laughs—long, loud, and coming from everywhere. Strangely enough, people who buy standing room are more apt to be laughing aloud than those sitting in front of them. Why? They wanted to see this show so badly, they were willing to stand for it, just as the groundlings who stood in all sorts of weather for hours on end at Shakespeare's Globe Theatre in London, where there was no roof or heat to protect them from the elements, always appreciated and responded more openly than the dukes, earls, and lords who sat in their private boxes protected in an enclosure.

Where else does the laughter come from? The mezzanine and the balcony and even from the second balcony, if there is one. Does anyone cheer in a ball game more than the kids out in the sun-drenched bleacher seats? The greater the sacrifice, the more appreciative the crowd.

Laughter doesn't always affect a critic's opinion of a play, but it doesn't hurt to have it. On opening night, back when the critics still came en masse, we would all try to place our friends and family sporadically in the first five rows, where their friendly laughter could cheer the actors on and the sound of that laughter would waft backward, covering the entire orchestra. But not on the opening night of *Sweet Charity*. Almost none of us had access to the seats in the first five rows. The Nederlanders gave all those seats, minus the ones reserved for the more important critics, to all their friends and investors who flew in from Detroit. Since it was the third, fourth, or fifth time many of them had seen the show, instead of laughing, they whispered the lines they knew by heart in unison with the actors on stage. The critics must have thought we had three hundred understudies sitting in the best seats in the house. Although the musical numbers were greeted with thunderous applause, the funny lines were greeted with murmuring, as if people in church were mumbling their prayers in hushed, reverent tones. If I could have found Jimmy Nederlander that night, I would have shoved his nose in the hole once filled with Ellen's thumb.

Despite the lack of friendly support from the first five rows, the critics hailed the show on opening night. Walter Kerr said, "A whoosh of choice champagne. The dances and everything else breeze by, whiz by, strut by, and fly by like a galaxy of comets on the loose." *Cue* magazine said, "*Sweet Charity* makes one very proud of the American musical comedy." Even the usually dour Edwin Newman of NBC-TV said, "By a long way, the best musical of the season."

Bobby and Gwen were the toast of the town, and Cy Coleman and Dorothy Fields's score was on everyone's approval list. Did the critics carp about anything? Of course. The book, just as I predicted in Detroit. They liked it well enough, but it was mildly dismissed as the ring necessary to show off the diamond that sparkled at its center. I expected this reaction, because I knew what I wrote wasn't coming from my own voice. It didn't matter. We had a large hit and I was glad to be part of it. The interesting thing is that of all the musicals I ever worked on, *Sweet Charity* remains the most popular by far, and almost thirty years later is performed more than any other musical I was connected with. All that is great, but actually I got all that I ever wanted or expected in having the chance to watch Bob Fosse and Gwen Verdon work together.

MEANWHILE, *After the Fox* opened to puzzled reviews. It seemed to the critics to be the work of a Chinese cook making an Italian dinner for a Jewish family. (If only it said that in the ads, I think people would have come.) No matter how clearly the dubbed voices sounded on the screen, it still looked like the actors were saying, "Wa tie dabus cumn, buz?" The reviews were half-hearted and the theaters half-filled. Naturally, I was disappointed that my first film was not a success, by a long shot, but I was not at all surprised. I could tell it wasn't headed for glory when I saw the first few days of filming back in Italy. Harvey Orkin, my drinking pal from London, flew down, at the bequest of his client Peter Sellers, to see a rough cut of the picture. Harvey proclaimed it a film masterpiece. Whether he really meant it or was still not recovered from his hangover after the Princess Margaret dinner, I couldn't tell. Either way, this was no masterpiece. I believe, when Princess Margaret herself saw the finished film, she left more quickly than the night she took a royal powder during the Orkin/Simon performance at Peter Sellers' party. To give the picture its due, it was funny in spots, innovative in its plot, and was well-intentioned. But a hit picture? Uh-uh. I think to save money, the producers made another movie on the back of the film we just used. It only confirmed to me that I was at my best with plays, in the theater, where I was rushing to on the first plane out after the film was completed.

On the positive side, we'd had a great summer, and I loved the people I met, like Sellers, Vittorio De Sica, and Victor Mature. I have some wonderful snapshots I took during the shooting, but until that becomes a category at the Academy Awards, they'll stay in my scrapbook. There are, however, always lessons to be learned from a failure. Mine were: never collaborate with a writer who doesn't speak a word of your language; never work with a director who speaks *half* your language and is doing the picture strictly for the money; and never work on a film that can be doomed to failure because a woman in a purple dress walked on the set.

Still today, *After the Fox* remains a cult favorite. You can even rent it in some video stores, although you have to show them a card saying you're a member of a cult. They do, however, draw the line at the Ku Klux Klan.

ON THE OTHER HAND, the film of *Barefoot in the Park* was a smash. It was the first time I had worked with director Gene Saks. I knew him initially as an actor; he was brilliantly funny in Paddy Chayefsky's *The Tenth Man* and then as a neurotic TV clown in Herb Gardner's wonderful play *A Thousand Clowns*. The first time I saw Gene's work as a stage director was in *Nobody Loves an Albatross*, starring Robert Preston. It was the first time I ever saw the actors leave the stage empty for a time as they went into other rooms to converse. The audience was left in the room by themselves, and even though it was only for about thirty seconds, I thought it was a very brave choice for Gene to make. The play may have been unfulfilled, but the direction wasn't. The second time I saw Gene's stage direction was in Joe Stein's adaptation of Carl Reiner's book, *Enter Laughing*, starring Alan Arkin. I don't believe I had ever laughed that much at any play prior to that time. It was simply hilarious, and at times I literally fell out of my aisle seat, wiping the tears of laughter from my eyes.

Since Mike Nichols didn't want to repeat his direction of *Barefoot* for the screen, I told Paramount I thought Gene Saks would be the perfect choice. The only trouble with some of Gene's work on the screen was the same trouble I often have on the screen. We're both a little stage-bound. We continue to see a proscenium theater even as we are looking through the lens of a camera. True, the film may have been a little static in a cinematic sense, but Gene was brilliant with the actors, and the chemistry between Robert Redford and Jane Fonda was magical. Mildred Natwick reprised the role of the mother she played onstage and was again superb. Hal Wallis produced the film and seemed more interested in bringing the picture in under budget than spending time on interesting camera angles. At one point when they were shooting on the studio soundstage, Gene did three takes then walked away to talk to the actors. When he returned, the set had been taken down and stored, the crew ready to move on to the next location. Gene suddenly shouted, "Where's the set? I'm not finished shooting." Hal Wallis said, "Sorry, you have to speak up, kid. Otherwise we move to the next shot." Gene soon learned to speak up.

The picture opened in 1967 at the Radio City Music Hall and broke the box office record for any film that had played that illustrious theater up to that date. I thought that was rather nice.

MY FAVORITE PLAYWRIGHTS in the 1960s were Tennessee Williams, John Osborne, Peter Shaffer, and Paddy Chayefsky. Paddy was the only one I knew personally, which gave him the edge, and I not only admired his talent, I admired his outspoken convictions, his hatred of anything phony, his unending energy, his humanity, and his desire to do good work. He often said, "To be sensitive is to be in pain every day," and I rarely saw Paddy not in pain. If it wasn't always there overtly, it was there nonetheless, lying dormant, even when he was playing poker, at a football game, or laughing at a party where he was always the star attraction. When Paddy walked into a room, your attention stood at attention. I loved all his early teleplays and Broadway plays, from *Middle of the Night* to *The Tenth Man* to *Gideon*. His films were always dangerously daring, from *The Goddess* to *The Hospital* and *Network*. Paddy is still the only person to win three Academy Awards for screenwriting. It's not difficult to see why two of his closest friends were Bob Fosse and playwright Herb Gardner; together they made a trio of hysterically funny misanthropes. To see them talking on the corner of Fifty-fifth Street and Sixth Avenue, you would think they were all waiting for Godot.

There is a reason I give you this brief biographical sketch, because it leads into the next play I chose to write. As our circle of friends grew, so grew our social life, and eventually we were attending two or three dinner parties a week. Joan decided to throw a New Year's Eve party and invite only everyone we liked. Our little house on Sixty-second Street couldn't accommodate a third of them, but fortunately they all seemed to come in shifts, drifting in and out as they made the usual procession from party to party, staying longest at the one they liked most. Little Ellen and Nancy sat at the top of the wooden-banistered staircase watching the proceedings, the entrances, the exits, the desserts that were being passed around.

Our party went on into the early hours of the following year. At one point Steve Lawrence and Eydie Gormé arrived and sang about four songs. (And about two days later our front doorbell rang. It was a piano tuner. He said he was a much-needed gift from Steve and Eydie.) About one in the morning, the party was in full swing, and Paddy Chayefsky was there holding court for about twelve people crammed onto a sofa that sat four. Suddenly, Leonard Lyons, the *New York Post* columnist, walked in with an attractive couple, the man looking very familiar. He turned out to be one of the original seven astronauts, and if my faulty memory serves me well, I would say it was M. Scott Carpenter. If I'm wrong, I don't want the Carpenters to be held accountable for my story, so if I may, I'll just call them Mr. and Mrs. Astro. Mr. Astro was a trim, handsome young man (right, like an astronaut is going to be about sixty-three years old and forty pounds overweight) and he must have been tired of questions about outer space, but he was warm and generous, and he satisfied all our curiosities.

Paddy, at the other end of the room, was talking at top speed and his volume was turned up. He would have been a great debater, easily talking well for either side, but I always enjoyed his own views the most. Mrs. Astro drifted quietly over to hear Paddy taking center stage, and after a while, this very attractive and intelligent woman interjected and disagreed with Paddy's thesis. Surprised and startled, he answered her politely. "With all deference to your illustrious husband, dear lady, and your well-stated opinion, I beg to differ with you." Then on he went, ranting and raving about some injustice he saw being committed in the name of the so-called American way of life. She listened for a while, then came back and challenged him again. Her point again was well made, but it was obvious she was from a part of the country that was ideologically and geographically alien to most of us. She was a conservative, how ultra I couldn't say, and her ideas were the very antithesis of Paddy's, who was consistently against any system that put itself ahead of anyone's individual rights. It soon turned into an exciting confrontation, and half the room moved over to hear and watch this battle royal.

What made the exchange unique was that there was an added dimension. She was so regal and so likable, that no matter what she said that irritated Paddy, you could see that Paddy was attracted to her. He was actively going toe-to-toe with her, giving her no quarter, slamming down her ideas as drivel and her politics as antiquated, dangerous, and balderdash, but he did so with a glint in his eye, almost furious with himself because he knew he couldn't help liking her. When the argument went well past the point of either side making any headway, Mr. and Mrs. Astro got ready to leave with Leonard Lyons. Before they got to the door, Paddy crossed to her, bowed, graciously kissed the lady's hand, and said with a smile, "On the other hand, I may be completely wrong." She smiled, and told Joan and me that she'd had an absolutely wonderful time.

The next morning I was at my desk, making a few notes before the New Year's Day football games started. I wrote down, "A possible play about a man and woman who hate each other's politics but are still attracted to each other's intelligence and where and how could that lead to a romantic comedy." I knew it was a good idea. I didn't know what the problems would be until I had started to write it, about a week later. To capture on paper merely the political, historical, and religious knowledge of Paddy Chayefsky would take me ten years, and that would be just a start. I've always thought that a writer could not accurately portray, in words and thought, anyone who was much smarter than himself.

Paddy did tons of research on every project he wrote, including riding all night long in police cars looking for background on criminal life. No doubt by the time he finished writing *The Hospital*, he had enough credits to get a degree from Johns Hopkins. I, on the other hand, hardly ever did research. I wrote primarily about behavior, and at least I was a careful observer and student on that subject. Unfortunately, when I tried to write about the conservative woman, I found I disliked her politics so much, I made her disagreeable. So I reduced their ages, taking some of their wisdom, experience, and maturity away, thus giving myself an equal footing with them. I made him a radical student at Berkeley, while she was a former beauty queen at a southern university.

In the process, she became a cliché, someone you'd see on a bad sitcom, the kind of character who believed America, right or wrong; mothers, good or bad; apple pie, fresh or stale; and Elvis Presley, just the way he was. As a result, she and the student were no longer equals, even though I had learned from G. B. Shaw always to make your protagonist and antagonist equal adversaries, so that the audience was always in doubt as to who was right and who was wrong. The living example of the pair I was trying to create would be the two real adversaries in the 1992 presidential elections, the Democrats' James Carville and the Republicans' Mary Matalin. They married after the election, which at least gave some credence to my play's feasibility.

I set the play in San Francisco, a city I had never once visited. If I couldn't describe the apartment where they lived, or picture the stores where they bought their groceries or the restaurants they ate in, authenticity went out the window. I was writing in a vacuum. Mistake number one.

I called the play *The Star Spangled Girl*, which automatically left the Paddy character out of the title, thus making it the girl's story. Mistake number two.

Still, I never give up on a project until I've written at least thirty-five pages. This time I wrote only about thirty-two before I stopped; clearly I was losing interest. Instead of throwing it away, however, I threw it over to Saint Subber's office. I had grave doubts about what I had written and was hoping he would confirm my fears, lest I waste months of my time in continuing. His rejection would not devastate me. My ego does not extend to defending inferior work. This time I didn't sit outside his alcove waiting to hear his laughs. I sat at home waiting for a quick and abrupt phone call. When it came, his reaction floored me. He loved it. He thought it was better than *Barefoot in the Park*. He thought it was a sure Tony winner. I thought Saint needed a two-year vacation in Tahiti. I told him it would never work and that I hated writing it. My instincts kept shouting at me on every word. "Schmuck, what are you doing? Get rid of this crap and find yourself a good play. Or go to the movies. Or to Tahiti with Saint." When you write something you like, the pages fly by. When you know it's not good, each key on the typewriter weighs about ten pounds and you need to see a chiropractor every morning.

Once again Saint pleaded with me to finish it first and then make a judgment on it. It was the same advice he had given me on *Barefoot* and he was right on that one. He was also right when he walked out of the third act of *Odd Couple* at the first reading. It's hard to dismiss two smart calls in a row. So I drudged my way through the next two months and finished the play. By then, Saint had already set a rehearsal date and booked a theater to open it in New York. I felt like Oliver Hardy saying to Stan Laurel, "Another fine mess you've gotten me into." Fortunately Mike Nichols was busy doing a film, which saved him the embarrassment of turning it down.

We started casting the play without a director. First we picked Anthony Perkins, who was no Paddy Chayefsky lookalike and had never done a comedy on Broadway before. But he was a fine actor, looked like a leading man, and had the benefit of being extremely intelligent. Tony happily agreed to do the play. In the role of his best friend and chief writer for their Berkeley radical newspaper, we cast Richard Benjamin, who had done a fine job for us playing the lead in the national company of *Barefoot*, as Paul, and then in

The Odd Couple, playing Felix to Dan Dailey's Oscar. Richard was funny and extremely bright as well. All we needed now was a conservative Miss America and a director who could be very honest with me. If Saint was wrong, I wanted to hear it from someone else.

So far, Saint, Tony Perkins, and Richard Benjamin loved a play that I wasn't very fond of. Saint came up with another of his inspired ideas for director. George Axelrod was a very talented writer who had a smash hit on Broadway with *The Seven Year Itch* and was responsible for helping to make Marilyn Monroe an even bigger star when Billy Wilder directed her in the film (having her stand on Lexington Avenue over a subway grating with gusts of wind from the speeding trains lifting her skirt and career to the skies, while Joe DiMaggio, still my boyhood hero and then her husband, stood grimly by, knowing his marriage was about to blow up as well). George also wrote fine film adaptations of *Bus Stop* and *The Manchurian Candidate*. He had only one drawback as a stage director. He had never done it before.

We met him a week later at his house in Los Angeles. The meeting went very well, and George seemed to like the play very much. He decided to do it and he told his wife just as she came in with a tray of iced tea. She said, "I know. I overheard it. I just booked our favorite suite in the hotel in Philadelphia."

It almost sounds like I'm knocking her when I say I thought Connie Stevens was perfect for our all-American, conservative, baton-twirling college beauty queen. Subconsciously the character was a joke to me and I was not about to help her out any. I even named her Sophie Rauschmeyer, which was indicative of my reluctance to give this girl any dignity. Self-destructive, you might say. And you might be right.

The one good thing the play had going for it was that it was funny. Funny came naturally to me, but I missed out on a great opportunity to give the play a Hepburn-Tracy quality by not incorporating the bright, witty, and strong convictions that I saw demonstrated that night at my New Year's Eve party. I gave up a Lincoln-Douglas debate for a Bob Hope–Bing Crosby picture. I blocked out my integrity and settled for a night of fun, which in many respects, it turned out to be.

Another of the problems we encountered was that it soon became clear that no matter how gifted and talented a writer George Axelrod was, he was not cut out to be a director. He mostly amused us with some very funny anecdotes of his past experiences, but as amusing as they were, it didn't get the first act staged. Perkins and Benjamin were no dummies, and they knew they were pretty much on their own when it came to directions. They soon were directing all their questions and suggestions to me, as I sat on the opposite end of the row from George. I tried to silently indicate they should be talking to George about that, but they had made up their minds and I was the one they turned to. George was quite decent about it, and I felt he was somewhat relieved not to have all that burden laid on him.

As for Connie, she was a sweet, happy, and fun girl to work with, but I soon learned who I was dealing with when a discussion about music came up and Connie insisted we all rush out to buy the album of the best music heard in America today. It was Hawaiian singer Don Ho singing "Bubbles, Pretty Bubbles."

The play was not exactly a smash in Philadelphia, but the audiences seemed to enjoy it, mostly because Tony Perkins and Richard Benjamin found the perfect tone with which to play this light comedy, and they made it breezy and smart. Connie, unfortunately, had a very small voice and everyone beyond the fourth row had to lean forward for the entire play. Finally I decided to get someone to train her, suggesting a very good voice teacher to help her learn to project. Later she told me she had called the voice teacher. "What did he tell you?" I asked. "Nothing," she said. "He couldn't hear me on the phone." Nevertheless, the audience generally enjoyed her performance and winning personality.

We opened in New York to surprisingly favorable reviews, although they were far from unanimous. Ted Kalem of *Time* magazine pointed out that "*The Star Spangled Girl*, as another hit, joins *Barefoot in the Park*, *The Odd Couple*, and *Sweet Charity*, making Neil Simon the first playwright since 1920 to have four Broadway shows running at the same time." Richard Cooke of *The Wall Street Journal* called it "the best new comedy to come along this season." But Walter Kerr of *The New York Times* said, "Neil Simon didn't have an idea for a play this year but he wrote it anyway." I thought that was a brilliantly written line. However, I thought he was only partly right. I *did* have a good idea for a play this year, but I wasn't quite up to the one I had in mind. Still, we ran for a full season on Broadway and another season on the road.

During the Broadway run, Connie Stevens, as likable as she was, was pure Hollywood and didn't quite understand the disciplines of the theater. She was going with Eddie Fisher, the singer, at the time, and at one point he was playing in Puerto Rico while she was on our stage in New York. On her day off, Sunday, she flew down to be with him, planning to be back for our Monday-night performance. An hour before the curtain on Monday, we got a frantic call from Connie that her plane had a flat tire and she couldn't be back in time to make the performance. The understudy went on and did a perfectly fine job. Tuesday night we got another call from Connie, still in Puerto Rico. "You'll never believe this but the plane had a flat tire again and I can't make the show." She was right. We never believed it. What was she flying on, the Used Car Airlines? Out of a million possible other lame excuses, couldn't she at least come up with something else?

The third night she still didn't show and again the understudy went on. Near the end of the second act (of a three-act play) Connie rushed breathlessly through the stage door. The stage manager saw her and said, "Connie, forget it. The understudy already played the first two acts." Undaunted, she quickly got into her costume and appeared on stage for the third act, surprising the very pants off Tony Perkins and Richard Benjamin. But if they were shocked, imagine what the audience thought, as they quickly scurried through their programs to see if the author intended that two women play the part of Sophie. To make matters worse, as the final curtain dropped and then went up again, Connie called out her understudy and they took bows together. (I'm sure many people in the audience went to their eye doctor the next day to see if they had developed double vision.)

To top things off, as the curtain was about to descend for the last time, Connie stopped it, then held up her hand, inviting the audience to please stay for some wonderful news. With bated breath, they all took their seats again. I thought surely her announcement would be, at the very least, that all nations had just decided to do away with all nuclear weapons. I was close. Connie bubbled onstage like Don Ho and said, "I am very happy to announce that I just got engaged to Eddie Fisher." Then she held up her finger to show them her ring. Our stage lights were still on, and the sparkle from the huge diamond half-blinded the audience. More business for the eye doctors. Unfortunately, the marriage didn't last much longer than the play. Fortunately, there were remarkably fewer flat tires on planes flying from Puerto Rico.

THERE WAS A PARTY after the opening night of *The Star Spangled Girl*. It was far from opulent, a sign that Saint Subber didn't want to spring for any unnecessary expense for a play that looked problematic. It took place at a bar and restaurant on Third Avenue. By the time Joan and I arrived, the guests were already there, about two drinks ahead of us. The first person I saw as I walked in was Martin Balsam, my friend and one of the actors in *After the Fox*. He stood against the wall, with probably his third drink in his hand, caught my eye, shook his head "No," smiled, and gave me a thumbs-down.

I was momentarily shocked by both his audacity and his honesty. I went over and hugged him and said in his ear, "I know. I know."

He said, "Doc, baby, I love you. What am I going to do, bullshit you?"

I said, "No, but at least let me get in the door first."

His honesty was a lot easier to take than that always safe, always meaningless, "Well, you did it again." Marty took a chance of hurting me by his remark, but he knew me better than that. He knew that I knew and that I didn't bullshit myself either. Somehow I wasn't as depressed as I thought I'd be, but drinking vodkas quickly can do that to you. After your third one you actually believe you're having a good time. "Jeez, no more of those worries that I can do no wrong. Hell, this isn't so bad," as another vodka goes down, looking for another part of your brain it can render immobile.

I'm usually funniest when there's trouble, and I was hysterical that night. In fact, I was funnier than the play. I was loving with my friends, I was warm and chummy with not such good friends, and I went to the bar to order another Brain Blocker. Two attractive young actresses surrounded me and laughed at everything I said. They posed for a picture, throwing their arms around me. They were flirting with me and I did the only decent thing a man could do in a situation like that: I flirted back.

Joan looked at me from the corner of the bar and gave me a look that said in no uncertain terms, "Watch yourself, honey." I straightened up and suggested we leave, since the only ones who were still there celebrating were my not so good friends and the two giggling actresses. We got home about two-thirty in the morning, with Joan helping me up the stairs. I was even funny crawling up the steps. Before we could make it up the landing, I could feel the largest upchuck since the San Francisco earthquake about to erupt. I just made it to the bathroom, dropped on my knees, and made a sacrificial offering to the Great God of the toilet bowl. I threw up everything I had eaten since the first day I started writing *The Star Spangled Girl*. Nothing connected to that play stayed in my mind or my body.

And then I started to cry, there on the floor. It was unending, fathomless, wrenching shame and anger pouring from my body. I wasn't upset because I didn't write a big hit. I was upset because I knew from the beginning it didn't ring true, that it wasn't good enough, and yet I had let Saint Subber talk me into doing it. It wasn't his fault. I was the one who pulled the trigger. As breath and speech came back between sobs, I looked at Joan and said, "I will never, ever do that again." In the final analysis, if I don't like what I'm writing, what's the point of doing it?

I got a few hours of sleep that night, and then for the next two days and nights I stared at the wall . . . then took a piece of paper, put it in the typewriter, and wrote two words: *Plaza Suite.*

BEFORE 1966 WAS OVER, I did what I said I wouldn't do. I got myself involved in another business deal. However, since this time it was a business I knew something about, it appealed to me. David Cogan, still my business manager, suggested that I buy, along with him and some other investors, the Eugene O'Neill Theatre. I was to put up half the money, David and his investors the other half. His reason for my buying the theater was "Why pay money to landlords when you can be the landlord yourself? If you put your own plays into the Eugene O'Neill Theatre, it would be putting rent money into your own pocket." It sounded simple enough. I talked it over with Joan. She said it sounded all right, as long as I didn't wake up again in a Catholic hospital in Rome. I made the investment, and before long I found out I didn't know the first damn thing about owning a theater. And David ran me a close second.

THE SUITE LIFE
14

WRITING THE SCREENPLAY of *The Odd Couple* was the easiest job I ever had. I used virtually all the dialogue from the play in the film script, and in order to take the action outside the apartment into the streets of New York, I made minor adjustments in the dialogue, so that playing a scene on Riverside Drive near Grant's Tomb seemed perfectly natural. When Jack Lemmon did his moose calls to clear up his sinus problems, it was far funnier taking place in a luncheonette, because it provided an opportunity for all the customers to look curiously at Jack each time his horn blew again. It made Walter Matthau equally funnier because every time Jack honked, Walter half smiled and looked away, pretending he didn't really know this man he was sitting with, and why was he doing those weird duck imitations?

It was the first time I had worked with Jack Lemmon, and the first time I had seen him since he said to me, "How you doin', sport?" at Irving Lazar's party. Jack Lemmon is a director's dream, a writer's savior, and a gift to the audience from a Harvard man who decided to turn actor. I never once saw Jack argue with a writer or a director. Conversation, yes. Suggestions, yes. Fights, not that I ever saw. If some dialogue or a scene wasn't working, Jack assumed it was his fault and made it his business to make it work. He rarely failed.

During every break in the shooting, Jack didn't waste time on small talk or card games. He would sit in his chair in the corner, going over his lines. He was a perfect match for Walter because oddly enough, the so-called straight man in the piece must be even more convincing than the so-called funny one. Jack is the one we have to believe and Walter is, in a sense, the Greek chorus. Whatever Walter says about Jack's (Felix's) idiosyncrasies really mirrors what we ourselves feel about him. To hear an actor say exactly what we've just been thinking is very funny to an audience. And of course, nobody says it as funny as Walter.

Jack has one of the widest ranges of any actor I can think of. He is equally as funny in one of the greatest farces ever made, *Some Like It Hot,* as he is moving in *Days of Wine and Roses*, or as touching as he is in *Glengarry Glen Ross*. The other important quality Jack has is something an actor can neither learn, be directed to do, nor buy for all the money in the world: you can't help but like him. He is also appreciative and complimentary to the written word, and if he doesn't like it, he will play it full out anyway and let *you* pick up that it doesn't work. He once said in an interview, "Neil writes in definite rhythms and as in music, you can't skip any of the notes. If his prepositions and conjunctions, such as *but, if, and, or,* and *it* are left out, the music is wrong." When I heard this, I was taken aback for a moment. I was unaware that this was true. I never said to an actor, "You left out the *but* in that sentence. I need the *but.*" It was the actors themselves who felt they had skipped a beat. In one play I did, the leading actress came to me during previews and begged me to take out a line. It was not the first time she had brought this up, and I kept saying, "Let me think about it." Then one night she was adamant.

"Neil, please take it out. It's only a short sentence but for me it interrupts the flow of the speech and takes the emphasis away from the point the character is trying to make here."

I liked the line but I trusted her instincts and without any fuss, I finally agreed that she could drop the line. She hugged me in gratitude and went out onstage that night and did the speech. But she did not omit the line. Puzzled, I searched for her when the act was over and asked, "Did you forget to leave the line out?"

"No," she said. "Just as I got to it, I knew I needed it. There would have been a big, empty hole if I left it out. But thanks, anyway."

Years later, I worked with actor Christopher Walken in the film of *Biloxi Blues*, where he had a long, frenzied speech attacking one of the least able soldiers in the company. During the first rehearsal of the speech, Chris improvised everything, never saying a single word I wrote, but paraphrasing, adding, subtracting, and throwing in any piece of madness that came into his head. I sat there mesmerized. What I heard, I thought was brilliant. As it ended, he smiled at me and said, "I'm sorry. I got carried away."

"No, no," I said. "It was magnificent. Infinitely better than what I wrote. Please use it in the scene instead."

He shook his head, "No. Sometimes I have to do that to clarify in my own mind what exactly the speech is about. Now I know. Your words are better, believe me. I really want to say it as written." Then he added with a smile, "Besides, I'd never remember what I ad-libbed in a million years."

Hearing dialogue on the stage or screen is completely different than reading it silently from the printed page. In one, you hear what the *actor* says; in the other, you hear in your head what you imagine the *character* sounds like. Oftentimes audiences are disappointed with the film version of a book they read. The actor now playing the role doesn't sound like the character they heard in their head as they read it.

Which brings me back to Jack Lemmon. Once I knew he was going to play Felix in the film of *The Odd Couple*, I was able to fashion certain lines and mannerisms that I knew he could do better than anyone. It was a perfect marriage between writer and actor.

Howard W. Koch, formerly VP of production at Paramount and one of those responsible for buying *The Odd Couple*, was our producer. He gave Gene Saks, who was directing again, far more leeway than Hal Wallis had by not rushing the production; yet we still came in well within budget. We used the apartment house where Howard had lived as a boy on West End Avenue as the building where Oscar and Felix shared an apartment.

I was on the set almost every day, not to protect my film or to make instant changes, but for the sheer joy of watching Walter and Jack work. One day we were filming on Broadway in the Seventies. Felix was missing and his poker cronies were in a cab looking for him, worried that he may have finally carried out his threat of suicide, which he made on a daily basis. Suddenly, crossing the street on her way home just a few blocks away, Walter's mother saw her son leaning out the cab window as the cameras mounted on the hood of the taxi were shooting the scene. "Walter, what are you doing here?" she shouted. "Come up, I'll make you dinner." Without a break in the action, Walter yelled back, "Not now, Mom. We're looking for Felix," then to the boys in the cab he smiled and said, "My mother. She follows me everywhere." I guess Walter figured they could later dub in "Oscar" over the mother's saying "Walter," work it into the picture, and get his mother a day's pay for a bit part and probably screen credit. Unfortunately the mother was not a member of the Screen Actors Guild.

Walter didn't win an Oscar for playing Oscar, because he had already received one the year before for the first film in which he costarred with Jack Lemmon, *The Fortune Cookie*, but his comet rose even higher after his success in *The Odd Couple*. Walter's mother said, "Walter, you don't have to make any more movies. You're too big a star."

The stars and our ensemble company were perfect, and the picture was a huge success. It came at just the right time for Paramount. A very young Robert Evans was made executive VP of a very troubled studio, and our picture, coupled with the equally successful *Rosemary's Baby*, pushed its stock up on a par with the big boys. *The Odd Couple* opened at the Radio City Music Hall and broke the house record set the previous year by *Barefoot in the Park*.

I'd had an enormous run from 1961 through 1968, and I felt, if not quite on top of the world, at least that I was living on one of the higher floors. But the thought was always there that they could take it away as fast as it came, a symptom all too familiar to almost everyone I knew or read about in show business who rose quickly to the top. In my insecurity I wondered when I would be accepted as having "arrived," and I constantly thought maybe one more play would do it. It never happens, of course. No shadowy figure appears in the middle of the night to deliver a letter that says "You've arrived." Success is not something you can hold in your hand. Joan was something I could hold. And Ellen and Nancy—I could hold them.

For as many people out there who applaud your work, there're an equal number who dismiss it out of hand. I once met Pauline Kael, the former film critic for the *New Yorker*, who was held in very high esteem—except by anyone I ever spoke to. There was no denying she was a brilliant writer who seemed to prefer Polish or Czech films made on a budget of twelve dollars with stories somewhat on the lines of "How a Greek sailor wakes up on the beach one morning with a woman's brown shoe in his pocket. The rest of the picture traces his search for the meaning of this discovery." Fortunately the picture invariably ends before you ever find out. That was Art. I didn't write Art.

We met one evening as we were leaving Sardi's restaurant, where the New York Film Critics Awards were being handed out. I was not there to get one. I was there to hand out one. Presenting was better than being in the running, because you stood no chance of losing—unless, of course, you handed one out to a loser by mistake. Ms. Kael and I were both standing under a canopy as the rain pelted New York, and I had very little sympathy for the fact that her new shoes were getting wet, since she had stepped on my own feet every time I had something to show the public. As we both waited silently for a cab, we glanced at each other, knowing someone had to say something first. She made a halfhearted attempt at a smile, and said, "I haven't been awfully nice to you over the years, have I?" I made a full-hearted attempt *not* to smile, and said, "No, you haven't." She said, "Well, it's hard not to knock you. You keep coming around so often." Then she got in her cab and quite surprisingly flew up into the night sky, as I thought I heard a cackle in the distance. Yet I didn't dislike her. I admired the way she wrote and respected how deftly accurate she could sometimes be. Sometimes, however, was a rare occasion. If she had said to me as we waited for the taxi, "I'm sorry, but I just don't like your work," I could have dealt with it. Like grabbing the cab before she did. But her objection to me was that I was prolific, as if had I written fewer films she would have liked them.

That's about as much of a diatribe as I will unleash against critics in this book. Critics, like I do, come around so often. There are a great many critics that I like and an equal number that I *dis*like. The totality of the reviews a play or movie receives is always a fairer judge than the comments of any single reviewer. To be perfectly truthful, I've learned things about my own work from critics who sit on both sides of the fence. Walter Kerr blew hot and cold with me, yet I never thought his remarks were personal. He had no prejudice toward me. Once in his seat on opening night, he hoped for the best, then wrote the truth, as he saw it. I will always cherish his review, "Neil Simon didn't have an idea for a play this year but he wrote it anyway."

I NEVER SAW it coming, but in 1967, my fortieth birthday sneaked up behind me, slapped me on the back, and said, "Welcome to the other side of life, pal." Joan and I had been married fourteen years. Where did it go and why so quickly? My mother was now past seventy, Ellen could catch fly balls in Central Park, Nancy could throw them halfway back, and poor old Chips was having trouble getting up our four flights of steps. What was most distressing, though, was that many of our close friends were splitting up and getting divorced.

Since man's life expectancy in the mid-1960s was in the sixty-eight to sixty-nine range, I realized I was now a member of "The Middle-Aged Club." I didn't even have to sign up for it. They notify you by the candles on the cake. In Paddy Chayefsky's film *Network*, William Holden, fifty-seven and afraid to break up his marriage to start anew with a younger Faye Dunaway, sees the reality of a bleak future. "We can't start a new life now," he says to her. "I'm closer to the end than to the beginning."

I considered myself a little right of dead center, and although my mortality was not a daily nagging problem, it was now the first time I really became aware of its existence. A different tone began to creep into my writing. I don't think one just decides to write more serious plays. Life dictates where your pen will move. It starts taking on your own inner fears, your responsibilities, your new, mature awareness that life isn't just about you, about your own needs or your own self-importance. You suddenly become aware that old people you know weren't always old. It was not their occupation in life, as we supposed. They were once the way you are now, and inevitably you will eventually be like them, with others thinking you were always old. You will have to make the same journey, taking on the same pains, the same aches and anxieties, the same sorrows, the same losses. Your insight into the world becomes much larger, more objective, and unavoidably clearer. I still wanted to write comedy, but I wanted to add darker chords, where happiness can turn on a dime to anguish, as fast as a phone call can disrupt a peaceful night's sleep at two in the morning with desperate and calamitous news. I wanted to write about the unpredictable, the sudden surprises, the things we always thought happened to someone else, not to us. I wanted to write for a single person in a single seat in the theater, man or woman, young or old, and have them say quietly to themselves, "He's writing about me."

I had no troubles with my fortieth birthday. It was no big deal. It's when you become forty-one and forty-two that you say to yourself in horror, "Oh my God. This thing keeps going on. I thought you got a break after forty." In my fortyish friends I saw minor but perceptible changes taking place in their marital relations, and even though their love may have grown deeper, gnawing thoughts began to hack away at them. They tried to ignore those initial signs that the excitement that once burned so brightly was becoming dulled, and they sensed that unless they used great care in crossing that dangerous bridge they were coming to, they might well enter a new world of foolishness, selfishness, deceitfulness, blindness, and—the ultimate price one paid—loneliness. I saw friends in their forties trying to look like they were in their thirties, in order to get the attention of women in their twenties.

I was in London about this time and had scheduled lunch with an English drama critic I knew. He was a very intelligent man, but like so many Englishmen, so very conservative as well, the kind that goes to his club with no real purpose other than to go to his club. I was sitting in the restaurant when he entered. I didn't recognize him. He was wearing tight bell-bottom trousers, a ruffled shirt, and a jacket that was better suited for riding than dining. His hair was below his collar in the back, and he wore bangs. He looked like my image of the manager of the club in Liverpool where the Beatles first started. I thought it was a joke, that he was kidding me the way Mike Nichols had worn a long, fake beard to test Binky Beaumont's ability to keep a straight face. He was not kidding. He was not only serious, he looked deadly unhappy.

As we ate, he confessed to me he didn't know what was happening to him. It was as if Mr. Hyde had moved in and killed off Dr. Jekyll. He hated himself for what he had become, but he couldn't help himself. Since we were both about the same age, he wanted to talk to me to see if it had happened to me as well. "Not really," I said, "because I wouldn't buy an outfit like that."

He told me he had left his thirty-eight-year-old wife, whom he still loved, for an eighteen-year-old girl he couldn't live without. He said, "I don't want this to happen but I can't stop it." Eventually, as the years went by—or possibly because the eighteen-year-old turned twenty-eight—he came to his senses, but I don't know what trail of havoc he left behind . . . or if he still kept that Beatles outfit in his closet in the event he had a relapse.

I wanted to write a play based on this theme but not to go to such extreme styles of fashion. Americans don't usually like costume plays. I wanted to tell the story of a forty-seven-year-old woman who tries to revitalize her failing marriage by returning to the very same suite at the Plaza Hotel where she and her husband spent their honeymoon night some twenty-three years ago. Hence, *Plaza Suite*.

To set up an appropriate atmosphere, the wife orders up some caviar and champagne. Sadly, when her husband arrives, he's in a foul mood because of a business deal he hadn't settled and mentions he may even have to work that night. She tries to divert his problems and turn him toward the night at hand. Their anniversary. She points out how lucky they were to get the same suite that they had stayed in on their honeymoon night. He glances at it but has little memory of this being the suite. She persists, standing at the window pointing out the exact same view they had, except that the hotel once directly across the street has now been torn down. "If it's old and beautiful, it's gone in the morning," she says a little glumly, giving us an indication that perhaps that's what she thinks the husband is now thinking of her. He bends a little, allowing that this may have been the same view but not the same suite, since the original suite was a few floors higher. She's definitely not making any headway.

He is piqued because his wife took this time to have their house in the suburbs repainted, forcing them to stay at the Plaza. This was a ploy on her part, unstated, but one that I considered to be the truth. Sometimes it's not vital to tell the audience or to make it clear that you intended for this information to be true. I'd rather that *I* know it, the director knows it, and just possibly the actors know it. You have to leave the audience some work to do on their own, because their own discovery of the truth ultimately is more interesting to them.

As he talks, the husband seems preoccupied, dismissing the wife as if she has faded into the room's wallpaper; he is more concerned with the new cap he just had put on his tooth, and the tone of his skin. This man has just turned fifty and he doesn't like growing old, and damned if he's not going to put up a hell of a fight.

"Do you think this cap looks too white to you?" he says, baring his teeth, completely unaware of how vain he is showing himself to be. "No," she says with a sense of mockery. "Goes very nice with your blue tie."

Humor and sarcasm are her only weapons to fight this battle, even though she knows she's doomed to lose. She suspects he's seeing another woman and odds are it's his secretary. She tries to get him to sit down long enough to make an honest effort to discuss the changes that have come over their marriage. He finally sits and stares out the window. "What's wrong with us, Sam?" she asks plaintively.

He takes his time before answering: "When I was in the Navy, all I wanted when I got out was to get married, have kids, and make a decent living. Well, I got it all. The marriage, the kids, and more money than I ever dreamed of making."

"Then what more do you want?" she asks.

". . . I just want to do it all over again. Start the whole damn thing from the beginning."

She gets up from the sofa, knowing she has lost, that there is no way to hold on to this man any longer. In ironic anger she says, "Well, frankly, Sam, I don't think the Navy would take you again."

Sam gets a call from his secretary. After hanging up, he tells his wife the deal can't wait. He has to go to the office now. On his way out, the waiter enters with the champagne and caviar. The husband says, "I'll call you later. Don't wait up for me," and brushes by the befuddled waiter.

The waiter turns and looks at the wife. "Is he coming back?" he asks.

She looks at the closed door and says, "Funny you should ask that."

After this, I wrote on the page, "End of Act 1." The only problem was, I knew there was no act 2. Or act 3. Their story had already been told, because there was no inevitable answer. I wanted the audience to figure out for themselves if he comes back or not. (The women thought, as much as I could pick up from the babbling in the lobby when the play did open, that "Of course he'll come back. He'll get tired of the bimbo." Or, "I hope so. He'd be a fool not to." Or, "She doesn't need him. She can do better than him." All very good possibilities. The men were perhaps understandably more reticent about their answers, for fear of betraying not necessarily their plan of action but certainly their thoughts.)

So there I was with what I thought was a wonderful one-act play and the problem of what to do for the rest of the evening. One possibility was to play out all the alternate choices that could happen in that situation. It wasn't as intriguing though as leaving the audience to think about it on their way home, as well as the state of their own marriages. It didn't take long for me to decide to do four one-act plays about different people, all played by the same two stars, in different situations that all take place in the same suite. It took me two months to select nine possible ideas and finally to choose the best three. The idea was to vary the styles of the other plays so that the entire evening could comprise a drama, a satire, a comedy, and a farce. Before I even sent the finished first draft to Saint Subber, I first sent it to Mike Nichols. He read it that night, called back, and said, "I love it. Let's do it in the fall." When I showed it to Saint, he was just as excited as Mike.

The trick now was to find the two stars, good enough and flexible enough to play four different characters in one night and make us believe we were actually watching *eight* different actors. We each made some lists of names. Two names appeared on all three lists, among many others. They were George C. Scott and Maureen Stapleton.

Maureen was a star on Broadway by virtue of appearing in outstanding supporting roles for years, and then finally with her name above the title as everyone recognized her superb talent. She was equally at home in comedy or drama. She was also one of the funniest women offstage that I ever met. Outrageous sometimes, belying the soft-spoken, warm, and caring woman she was. She costarred in the film of *Bye Bye Birdie* with Ann-Margret, in Ann-Margret's first major screen role. Legend has it there was a large wrap party at the end of shooting and one of the executives got up and made a toast to Ann-Margret, predicting she was going to be a major star. This was followed by similar toasts by others involved with the production, all men and all mentioning Ann-Margret. Then they asked Maureen to get up and say a few words. After much appreciative applause from the crew and company, Maureen said, "Well, I guess I'm the only one here who doesn't want to fuck Ann-Margret." Obviously that was not said cold sober. Maureen was a dedicated worker and an equally dedicated drinker. The drunker she became, the funnier she was. What Maureen said under the influence was always the truth—and the truth, no matter how much it may cut into the marrow, is what ultimately makes us laugh. Onstage, there was always something magical about her performances; she was often compared to Laurette Taylor.

George Scott had already been in half a dozen plays on Broadway and God knows how many off-Broadway in which he invariably received brilliant reviews. He was talked about all over New York and Hollywood as our next great star, but he still hadn't found the vehicle that would make his name known throughout the country. On Broadway, he still hadn't had the benefit of a play that was a hit. He could be trouble, because he had a reputation as being tough. He didn't need that reputation. All you had to do was look at him, and you would back off from this man who stood with his shoulders up to his neck and had a chest that could probably frighten a bear back to its cave.

Both Maureen and George could easily be defined as classic actors, she probably more suited to the plays of Chekhov and Tennessee Williams, while George could take on Shylock and Lear and Cyrano, yet both could easily be brilliant in a farce like *Room Service*. We don't have many actors like that in America, at least not in these times. I never really wanted comics in my plays, with the rare exception of a Sid Caesar, or a Bert Lahr, if I could have gotten him on the stage. (Bert Lahr would have been incredible in *The Sunshine Boys*.) I wanted first-rate actors who could play comedy, the reason being that with people like Maureen and George, you never see the comedy coming. You're watching what you think is basically a serious play and suddenly you find yourself laughing your head off. Three of America's greatest actors are Brando, De Niro, and Pacino. However, it's very hard for them to do comedy. Fortunately, they don't have to, because we're perfectly happy to see them in what they do best.

I was keeping my fingers crossed in our attempt to get George and Maureen. Maureen wasn't a problem. Mike Nichols just asked her. Maureen is no fool. George would be trickier to land. Saint called George's agent and told her of the play. She said it was doubtful George could do it, since he had so many offers on the table. Still, as a favor to Saint, she arranged a lunch at Sardi's East for me to meet George and asked that I bring the script. I thought it odd that he didn't want to read the script before meeting me, but maybe he wanted to size me up. Next to him, I was a 32 small.

Sardi's East was a new (and short-lived) restaurant in Manhattan's East Fifties, with small offices to let in the building just above it. I went to the restaurant at the appointed hour with more than a little trepidation. I am terrible about explaining my plays. Not that I consider myself inarticulate, but I always wanted the plays to speak for themselves. If there were nuances in the dialogue or a description of a character's feelings, I just couldn't say it without losing the nuances. I also don't want to sell my plays. I'm not a salesman. I'm not my father. I don't want to have to be funny as myself, Neil, for someone to believe my play is good.

When I arrived at Sardi's East, George was sitting at the table, looking more like he was on a throne. His agent, a warm, intelligent, and pragmatic woman (she'd have to be to handle George), sat next to him. He greeted me with a cordial but very quick smile, the kind that vanishes even before it is completed. There was very little small talk. Something about the weather, something about the restaurant, and that was it.

George looked at the script in my hand and said, "Is that it?"

"It" was what I had been working on for nine months. I nodded. He reached out, took it from my hand, flipped through the pages, then said, "*Plaza Suite*, eh?" I don't think he had a clue as to what it was about.

He suddenly rose and looked at us. "You two have lunch. I'll go up and read it. I'll be down when I finish." And he was gone.

I turned to his agent. "You mean he's going to read it *now*?"

She was looking over the menu and muttered, "Why not?"

"It's a long play," I said. "I haven't cut it yet. It could take a long time."

She shrugged slightly and said, "So eat slowly. He's worth it."

We sat eating our lunch, finished in about forty-five minutes, and then filled in about another hour and a half with any story we could think of. She could see my impatience as I kept looking at my watch.

Suddenly George entered the room without a single expression on his face, except for the possible hint of disinterest. He stopped to say hello to some friends at another table, and whatever they said amused him and he laughed loudly. By the time he got back to our table, the smile had vanished from his face. He sat, threw the script on the table, looked me straight in the eye, and said, "I like it. Let's do it."

I said, "Really? Just like that?"

He answered, "I read it, I liked it, let's do it. What else is there to say?"

I got up, shook his hand, shook hers, and said, "I'm glad. I mean really, really glad." I left the restaurant, walked the twenty blocks back to my house, and said to myself, "This guy could be a lot of trouble, but by God, he sure is straightforward."

After you sign your star actors and cast the supporting roles, it doesn't mean you suddenly go into production. The actors could still have a film to do, or the director is in the midst of another production, or the theater you want won't be available for another six months. This is the difficult time for the playwright. Having done all your rewrites and editing, you have all this time to wait and worry, which is generally the time I use to start writing another play just to keep my mind off the one that's waiting to go on. Most often, these time-filler plays fizzle and disappear; other, rarer times, they become the following year's play. If I didn't work during this waiting period, I would worry that the actors would get ill, or change their minds about doing the play after they'd read it a few more times or a friend had read it and said, "What do you want to do this for?" Contracts are not always signed on the day someone agrees to appear in your work. We have often played a year on Broadway without a signed contract with the theater owner. Sometimes you just go on good faith. As mammoth as the Broadway theater appears to be, it is often run like a neighborhood store with neon lights.

With nervous time on my hands, Joan suggested this could be the perfect opportunity for the trip to Japan that we had always planned. Joan's mother, Helen, said she'd stay with the girls, and we got a new nanny to replace Pam, who got homesick for England, her England, and left. Accompanying us on the trip were a couple, Bud and Rita Satz, whom we had met some time back in Round Hill, Jamaica, where Bud, quite a good tennis player, had introduced me to the finer points of tennis on the resort's grass courts, where I played in my bare feet, having forgotten to bring any tennis shoes.

We flew from New York to Los Angeles, then on to Honolulu, where we stopped to refuel. On the trip cross-country, I had given Bud my copy of *Plaza Suite* to read, which I don't readily do with friends, but Bud and Rita were avid theatergoers and rarely missed any show on or off Broadway. I was anxious to hear what he thought of the play. I did warn him to be careful with the script, since it was the only copy I had with dozens and dozens of new, handwritten changes scratched in the margins, which, if lost, would mean weeks, if not months, to redo. Bud said he would protect it as he would the Holy Grail. I told him that wouldn't do me any good because I had no rewrites on the Holy Grail.

Sitting two rows behind us on the plane, Bud broke into continuous bursts of laughter as he read, which happily kept me from sleeping or reading a book. He had not quite finished reading when we arrived in Honolulu, where we got off the plane for a brief layover. It was unusually hot for Hawaii, this being the end of July, and we welcomed the cool air-conditioning of the plane when we reboarded.

We noticed that three-quarters of the original passengers had left and had been replaced with the same number of passengers flying on to Japan. They were all Japanese, mostly well dressed, looking not like tourists but the gathering of highly rated employees of a successful Japanese business corporation. I noticed that the Japanese men all took off their jackets and ties and put on kimonos. Their shoes and socks came off next and were replaced with very simple but attractive sandals. The women put kimonos on over their light summer dresses and replaced their shoes with the same sort of sandals. They were quiet and polite, and talked to each other in hushed tones, as if showing respect for the airplane as some sort of temporary temple that would take us across the sea to their home. I thought it was all rather charming.

We buckled our seat belts and were heading for the runway, finally on our way to Japan. Joan was looking at her guide books as I looked out the window, watching the takeoff. We picked up speed as we rolled down the runway, and the engines were roaring. Everything was fine except for the fact that the plane was not lifting off the ground. I'm no expert flyer, although I've put in my share of mileage, but it seemed to me that we were well past the point of takeoff. I slid my hand over and put it on Joan's. She looked at me, saying "What's wrong?" I said, half-kiddingly, "I don't think this thing is going to take off, unless we're on a train that's going to Japan."

She looked out the window and realized it *was* a long time in going down the runway. Our speed picked up a little but not our plane. She suddenly looked at me, terror in her eyes, and all I could see was her thinking, "Who'll take care of the girls?"

Suddenly we heard the brakes screeching as the plane was attempting to abort takeoff. Sparks were flying out of the left side of the plane, and although there was no screaming, there was instantly troubled mumbling circulating through the plane. I could see the end of the runway ahead and I knew if we didn't take off soon, we would all be in the Pacific Ocean. Then there was a loud pop, almost an explosion, and the plane shifted to the left and dipped down as the pilot tried to turn away from the end of the runway. I heard the stewardess yell to her friend, "We blew a tire."

The plane was now skidding on its side, the tip of the left wing scraping furiously along the ground, sparks and bits of fire jumping out. With all that fuel on board, my biggest fear was that the plane could explode any second. It seemed an eternity before the plane came to a stop, smoke pouring out of the left wing and tire. We couldn't have been more than a hundred yards short of the end of the strip . . . and probably our lives.

The pilot suddenly came on the speaker. "Ladies and gentlemen. Please do not panic. Everything's under control but you must listen to me carefully. Our left tire has blown, but there doesn't seem to be too much damage to the aircraft. However, for safety's sake, we must all disembark as quickly and as orderly as we can. Please take off your shoes. Without exception, do not wear your shoes. Do not carry anything. Everything will be retrieved later. Please line up in orderly fashion at the exit door closest to you. Do not try to open them. Our crew will handle that. They will release rubber tubes that will inflate as soon as they are released. Do as the crew instructs you. When you go down the chute, sit upright, your legs held together. Try to slide down the center to avoid serious injury. Again, do not wear shoes, for fear of catching them on the chute. The crew will be on the ground waiting to catch you. The moment you're on the ground, please move away from the aircraft as quickly as you can. There is no danger but we do appreciate your cooperation. Thank you."

There was silence. Somehow we were not frightened as yet. It was more like an adventure, since no one seemed to be hurt. The crewman opened the first door and almost simultaneously the rubber chute inflated and a slide appeared from the plane down to the ground about twenty feet below. We heard sirens and saw ambulances rushing toward us. Joan and I were standing nearest to the door. Suddenly we heard screaming in the back of the plane. Someone had inflated the escape chute before the door was fully opened, and it proceeded to fill up the back of the plane like a giant balloon. There were at least thirty people trapped behind it and you could hear their muffled screams. The stewardess called to us quickly. "Out, please. Do move quickly. Come on, you first." She was looking at Joan. Joan looked at me and said, "You go first." There was no time to argue. I stepped to the door in my

stockinged feet, sat down, crossed my arms over my chest and slid down. I
went like a bullet. Just as my feet touched the ground, the crewman caught
me and said, "Move on, sir. Away from the plane." I waited till Joan came
down safely, then the two of us ran about thirty yards away from the plane,
stopped, and looked around. From our vantage point, you could see everything that was happening. Firemen were hosing down the tire and the left
wing. Then the Satzes came down, Bud grinning all the way, like a child going
down the slide in the park.

Suddenly I felt a searing heat, not on my body but on the soles of my feet.
It felt like I was standing on hot, burning coals. The temperature on the field
was well over 100 and the concrete we were standing on, exposed to the tropical sun since daybreak, was at least 120. Not a place you'd want to be standing
in thin cotton socks. Joan had on little anklets and quickly felt the embers
beneath her as well. We started jumping around, trying to walk on our toes,
then on one foot at a time. Nothing helped. Then came the Satzes, who, by
the time they reached us, had started jumping around like fresh popped corn.
They joined us in looking for a shady spot. The only one in sight was the air
terminal at the far end of the field. Given the heat and the distance, there were
only half a dozen desert animals who might have made it.

Then came the sight of the three hundred Japanese in their kimonos sliding down the chute, all maintaining their calm. Wait till they hit the blistering
tarmac in their bare feet, I thought to myself. It would look like the grill at
Benihana's. When they slid down, they all smiled appreciatively to the crew
who had assisted them, some bowing, if time permitted. The bowing stopped
suddenly as something told them their feet were on fire. Suddenly there were
three hundred Japanese jumping up and down and yelling the same way as
Joan and I and the Satzes. "Oh! Oh! Wo! Ooh! Ahh!" Pain sometimes knows
no language barrier.

More fire engines came to pour water on the burning tire and wing but
there was not a drop to spare for our scalded feet. There should be a Federal
Aviation law that all landing fields must be required to have large vats of
Vaseline on the tarmacs or at the very least, five hundred pairs of slippers of
all sizes. Joan and I were now both in excruciating pain, yet hysterical at this
display of silent-movie antics that looked like it came right out of the Chaplin
Studios.

Suddenly I spotted a green patch about fifty yards away. It looked as
though it was grass, cool, green grass, and I shouted to everyone, "Over

there! There's grass!" I started to run at top speed, with Joan and the Satzes right behind me, knowing full well that there wasn't room for us and all three hundred Japanese on this little oasis. I could just see it: We'd be pushing and shoving each other off, fighting for our own spots, like the passengers who fought to get into the lifeboats when the *Titanic* was going down. I'd deal with that later, however; I just wanted to get there.

I was the first to reach the grass, only to find out that it wasn't exactly grass, but some bushy shrub filled with thousands of burrs, so sharp they no doubt could penetrate a pair of hiker's boots in seconds. Joan and the Satzes soon joined me on Burr Island and we quickly took up a new cry of pain, saying things like, *"Yowee! Christ! Oh, shit! Goddamn! Wo wo wo!"*

We quickly jumped off back onto the tarmac because *"Oh! Ah! Yow!"* was better than *"Oh, shit! Goddamn! Oh, Christ!"* We got off Burr Island just as some fifty Japanese got on, and we soon learned what cursing and swearing sounds like in Japanese.

Eventually buses appeared to get us and we all quickly piled on, sitting on seats or on the floor, but all holding our feet about three inches in the air. As we looked at the Japanese, who were also in pain, they were soon all laughing as hard as we were. But perhaps laughing means something else in Japanese.

An hour later we were all sitting in the terminal, the soles of our feet being treated by baggage handlers temporarily converted to doctors. Then the baggage carts were rolled in, dumping six hundred and forty shoes and sandals in a pile so high they looked like a small leather mountain or possibly a new piece of abstract art, the kind that would probably sell for $2 million at Sotheby's. It took us a long time to sort out our shoes, and you can imagine how long it took for the Japanese to sort out their sandals.

After another hour of signing papers, reporting our injuries and losses, we were told there would be another plane leaving for Japan in three hours. Joan and I looked at each other. Not a chance. We told the Satzes we weren't going on but would look for a nice, safe hotel in Hawaii. Bud and Rita were content to stay with us, especially since there were more tennis courts in Hawaii. Of course, we'd have to play in wheelchairs for the first two days. We booked a hotel from the airport, then took a cab as the contrite airline promised to have our luggage delivered by early evening.

As we rode to the hotel, the cool, blue waters washed up against the beaches and we knew we were in heaven. Suddenly I moaned in desperation. "My script! Where's my *Plaza Suite* script?" Bud smiled as he took the rolled-up script out of his jacket pocket and held it up. I said, "You weren't supposed to take anything going down the chute."

"What are you going to do?" he asked. "Report me?"

I hugged him and said, "What can I do for you?"

He smiled and said, "Easy. Two seats for opening night."

What a bargain.

WE STAYED a week in Hawaii, then on to California and the Beverly Hills Hotel. Joan took tennis lessons from the hotel pro, Alex Olmeda, once one of the top players in the world. He kept laughing in surprise as Joan slammed back shot after shot, hitting balls swiftly over the net. If she had put her mind to it and started at eight years of age, she might have made the circuit. As she rushed to the net, Alex hit a high lob over her head. She turned quickly to run the ball down before it was out of reach. Suddenly her ankle turned and she went down hard. It started to puff up even as we ran out to her; the ankle was broken. We flew back to New York three days later, Joan boarding the plane in a wheelchair with her foot in a cast up to her knee, and holding a cane. Between that, the aborted takeoff in Hawaii, and the sight of three hundred and twenty people doing a barefoot Irish jig on the searing tarmac, going into rehearsal with George Scott in a new play suddenly seemed like the vacation I was hoping for.

THIS BEING the third play I was doing with Mike Nichols, I decided to sit four rows behind him in the theater, watching every move he made, listening to every word he said, watching his style, his tricks, his attack on the art of directing. I did this in the realization that one day I might want to direct a play myself, and what better teacher could I find? After watching the first ten days of rehearsal, I had learned nothing. I saw nothing. He had no tricks. He had no modus operandi. No method, no style. What he had mostly was his intelligence: his knowledge outside the world of the theater; his keen, sharp eye for the manners and behavior of people. Not only did he give the actors a sense of encouragement and security, but he allowed them the freedom to try what they wanted, and if he liked it, he left it in. He was always in control but never a browbeater, never a Svengali, never a tyrant. If he did see a selfish actor, one who wanted to position himself in a better light for his own sake, he would cut him off right there. I once saw him fire an actor on the spot for that infraction, making it clear to everyone what the rules were, and that it was clearly Mike who made the rules. He didn't care what it cost if a new and difficult prop had to be made or scenery rebuilt. He would throw out costumes he had already approved of, because the next week he thought they were wrong. With the exception of *The Odd Couple*, some of the successes I had with Mike (and they all were) made somewhat less profit than other plays I did, perhaps because of his excesses. In the end it didn't matter; what we ended up with was always a better play. He often came late while everyone sat around waiting. Sometimes he gave a valid excuse, other times he offered none. If he had a cold, he had gofers to get him hot soup, nasal spray, and a surprise. He always asked for a surprise. The ten-year-old in him never completely went away.

His real test came about two weeks into rehearsal. George Scott did not show up one day. He did not call in, he didn't answer his phone, and he never returned our messages. He was missing, plain and simple. We heard this behavior was not unusual for him. He was once married to actress Colleen Dewhurst; then they divorced, but still maintained close contact with each other. Finally they married again and finally divorced a second time. George had served in the Marines during the war, although he hardly ever talked about it. He was a private man in so many ways, yet then just as suddenly he could be warm and friendly and accessible to everyone. The stories went around Broadway about George's disappearances and drinking, although I personally never saw him drink except at one opening night party. He seemed to be happy in those first weeks of rehearsal, loved working with Maureen and Mike and the cast, and usually left at night in a good mood. If Mike was working on act 1, scene 2, then stopped at night, we would pick up in the same place the next morning. George was always prepared for the next day. I had heard from a friend that from time to time George was visited by a black mood that overcame him. He could sometimes sense when it was coming and warn friends in advance, but it came nonetheless. Still, the day of his disappearance, we had not been warned by him of any problems, and we weren't quite sure what it was.

The next day rehearsals began at 10 A.M. and still no George Scott. After waiting for an hour, this anxious playwright said to Mike, "What should we do?" Mike said, "Hope," and then asked the understudy to rehearse with Maureen. Maureen hated the understudy, not necessarily personally, but who could come close to replacing George C. Scott? She swore to us she would never go on with the understudy. Maureen, who might have been as affected by George's moods as anyone, insisted on calling him "The Pussycat." When she walked in on that second day, she asked, "Is the Pussycat here?" When she heard he wasn't, she sat down in her chair, opened her purse, and said, "Well, then, it's a good day to smoke."

At 3:30 in the afternoon, George walked in, his hands deep in his overcoat pockets, looking as though he had just relived World War II. The scowl on his face was so menacing, it would have scared even him. I was certain he might smash in the face of the first person who talked to him. I looked at Mike, who was up on the stage talking to the company manager. He turned and saw George, who now stood still, seemingly frozen to the spot. He didn't seem to be looking at anyone in particular. How was Mike going to handle this? I wondered. Take George into another room and have a warm, comforting chat with him? Possibly, but not likely. Would Mike call a half-hour break, let George pull himself together, and try to rehearse? Also possible. Obviously he wasn't going to berate him in front of the company. Mike wanted to live as much as any of us.

What Mike actually did was the simplest of all things: he looked over and said, "Hi, George. We're on act one, scene two. You're on the phone calling this girl in New Jersey." There was a silent moment where no one moved or breathed, then George slowly walked to the bed, sat down, picked up the phone, dialed, thought for a second, and called out "Line." The stage manager quietly gave him his line, and George picked up his cue and proceeded with the scene as though he had never been gone. No word was ever mentioned about the incident. That's why I don't direct, and why Mike justly receives his surprise when he's not feeling well.

WE WERE BACK in Boston, at the Ritz-Carlton. Mike had his favorite suite, Saint had Mike's second favorite suite, and I had my small suite filled with a basket of peanuts and cookies that the thoughtful manager had sent to me, which I barely touched.

The first three previews went off without a hitch. George and Maureen were working in tandem as one, each knowing the other's timing, supporting each other on the stage; the audience ate it up. From all indications—the good word of mouth and the mounting box-office sales—we were heading for a big one. The play now consisted of three one-act plays instead of four. I cut the first one in rehearsal; it was virtually a monologue for George about a businessman who was headed for New York, gets his plane diverted to Boston due to a major snowstorm, and loses his luggage and his pills for his fragile stomach and fiery temper. If he's not in New York by 9 A.M., he loses a new job. It was funny, but it seemed to work against the major piece of the evening, about the fifty-year-old husband with the fading wife. We wanted to start with drama, not comedy. A few years later I turned that first piece into a film, *The Out-of-Towners*, with Jack Lemmon. Waste not, want not.

The Boston opening went as well as any I had had up till this time. In some ways it surpassed *The Odd Couple*. Elliot Norton didn't have a single quibble about this one. As the curtain fell, everyone backstage started to celebrate. George Scott knew it played like hell, and he was even hugging the electricians. He was jubilant. He invited the entire cast and crew up to his hotel suite for a party while we waited for the reviews. Joan and I walked across the Boston Common in a light snowfall. She said to me, "If you're not happy tonight, I'll kill you." No, this was a glorious night and nothing could spoil it.

We arrived at George's suite and it was jammed with happy, laughing actors and crew. Two reviews had already come in and they were both smashing. George and Maureen were drinking champagne and both were funny as hell, hugging each other and saying in the foulest language how much they loved each other. Phone calls kept coming in from Saint Subber through the press agent's office: "They're *all* good. Not a bad one in the bunch." Mike was grinning from the left side of his face all the way out into the hallway. The door was open all the time, and as other guests in the hotel passed the room, they shouted in *"We loved it! You've got a winner!"*

George fought his way through the crowd, picked up the phone in the corner, and started to dial. He yelled to us, "Hold it down a minute, kids. I got a call to make." Suddenly he was laughing and shouting into the phone, almost close to tears. He was speaking to his ex-ex-wife. "Colleen? . . . Yeah, yeah, it was a nice show . . . Nice, my ass, it's a hit. A great big fucking hit. I'm finally in a goddamn hit, can you imagine that?" He laughed loudly at whatever she said, and we finally had the sense to be quiet so he could talk. If Colleen was the first one he called, you knew there was still a strong bond between these two.

Two hours later, the stage manager and assistant stage manager helped Maureen get to her room. She still had a glass in her hand and was saying, "If I wake up alone tomorrow, someone will pay for it." They got her into her room and sat her on the bed. As they started out, she said, "Hey! Wake me at noon. Take me to the theater. And have someone remind me what play this is. It's about a hotel or something, isn't it?" She fell back on the bed laughing.

Mike, Joan, and I rode up on the elevator together. He said, "There's a matinee tomorrow so I won't call the cast, but maybe you and I could meet for an hour or two. One o'clock all right?"

I said, "Meet about what? Is there something in the play that's not working?"

He said, "Oh, I'm sure if we look hard enough, we'll find something." He kept me busy night and day.

We all retired. It was hours before Joan and I could fall asleep or even wanted to. We were cherishing moments. In the darkness of the night, an hour after we had fallen asleep, the phone rang. I turned on the light and looked at the clock. It was twenty to four in the morning. What crank dentist from Pittsburgh was calling me at this time? I picked up the phone. It was Mike. I have heard Mike unhappy. I have heard him angry. I have heard him morose. I had *never* heard his voice filled with such deep, dark despair. I wouldn't even dare guess what horror I was about to hear.

"Can you come to my room?" he said.

"Now?"

"I think you'd better."

"It's a quarter to four."

"As fast as you can."

"Is it bad?"

"Bad doesn't describe it."

Joan sat up in bed and looked at the clock. "What is it?"

"I don't know. I sense tragedy. I'll call you later."

I didn't wait for the elevator. I ran up three flights of stairs, pulling on my pants, shoes, and a shirt as I ran to his room.

"George wants to quit the play."

I stood there, not knowing if this was Mike's ultimate joke. I kept waiting for his big smile to be followed by "You schmuck. You really believed me?" Instead he was white as a ghost.

"I don't believe it. Why?"

"He just left here twenty minutes ago. He was here two hours. He says if he stays, he'll ruin the show."

"What are you talking about? He was brilliant. His reviews are brilliant. Did you hear him on the phone with Colleen? I never saw anyone so happy."

Mike nodded. "Maybe that's what triggered it. I don't know. Maybe he's afraid of success. Too much guilt; doesn't deserve it. Pick out any one of those you like. He said something was coming over him. He can always feel when it's happening. Only this one is a bad one. This one's a tornado, he said. He doesn't want to hurt Maureen or you or me."

It was still incomprehensible.

"What if we talk to him together tomorrow? With Maureen? All four of us between the matinee and evening show?"

"He's not playing tomorrow. He's leaving in the morning. He's not coming back to the play."

This time I needed something stronger than Amaretto. I called downstairs for room service and asked for a double brandy. Mike asked for a pot of coffee and chocolate ice cream.

"Ice cream? You're going to eat ice cream *now*?"

"You mean if I don't eat ice cream, maybe he'll come back to the play?"

We hardly talked until room service arrived, thinking of ways out of this blinding tunnel. I suddenly realized this was only half our troubles. "If he quits, Maureen will quit. She won't play with the understudy."

"I know."

"You *know*? You mean we close the show *tonight*? It could be the biggest hit of the year, and we're going to close it in Boston while you're eating ice cream?"

He shrugged. "Looks that way."

It was madness. No, worse. What's worse than madness? This was.

The phone rang. It was Joan. "Are you all right?"

"No. George wants to quit the show. No, George has *already* quit the show. I'll call you back later."

Mike suddenly had one of those "I have an idea" looks in his eyes. "Maureen might stay if we could find a first-rate replacement."

"Oh, come on. *George* is the only first-rate replacement."

"There are other actors in the world."

"Like who?"

"Hal Holbrook. He's a genius."

"He's way too young . . . What about Marty Balsam?"

"Yeah. Maybe . . . José Ferrer?"

"Why José Ferrer if you just said yeah, maybe to Marty Balsam?"

"Yeah, maybe isn't good enough . . . Why does he have to have a name? What about an unknown?"

"Like who?"

"I don't know. If he's an unknown, how would I know him?"

"This is nuts. Christ! . . . What about Christ?"

"All right, now don't laugh. What about Olivier?"

"*Laurence* Olivier? He's going to come to replace George C. Scott in Boston?"

"Maybe he's not working. You never know until you ask him."

"Well, why stop at Olivier? If we're going to play fantasies, how about Brando? Or Henry Fonda? Maybe I could make it funnier and we could get Jack Benny and Rochester. Does Saint know about this yet?"

"I called him first. I think he's under sedation."

The sun was starting to come up, and I went back to my room to get a few hours of staring at the wall. Joan and I appeared backstage an hour before the matinee. Maureen had already been told that George was not playing today. She said very calmly, "If you want me onstage, you'll have to go out and find a stagecoach and six horses to drag me on." Mike talked to her alone. She did the matinee. When people heard that George Scott would not appear, they asked for refunds. I went out to watch the understudy playing with Maureen. I lasted ten minutes. The disappointed audience who remained found enough to enjoy in the show, but we'd never make it in New York without George. Joan took the afternoon plane to go back and deal with real life. Mike and I went to dinner and kept pitching names at each other.

"Jeff Chandler?"

"I think he's dead."

"What if we offered him more money?"

The insanity of all this led to a strange euphoria, as if we were on some drug called In Denial.

"What about Doris Day?"

"To replace Maureen?"

"No. To replace George. I know she's wrong but she's a big name. And at the curtain call she could sing 'Que sera, sera.'"

Two and a half days passed. We began to start thinking seriously about postponing the show until next season. Only Mike had a new play to do next season, for which he'd probably get George Scott. We decided to go to the theater and see the show for what might be the last time. When we walked in the stage door, the stage manager said, "George is in his dressing room. He's putting on his makeup."

I looked at Mike. "What are you going to say now? Act one, scene one?"

Mike went in alone and stayed about twenty minutes. When he came out, he said, "He's staying. He wants to do the show. Whatever he had to go through, it's over."

I suddenly thought to myself, it all came too easy. When George Scott came down from his office at Sardi's East, threw the script on the table, and said, "I like it. Let's do it," I should have known something was wrong. When it comes that easy, somewhere along the line you're going to pay for it.

ABOUT THIS TIME, I started developing back problems. In that respect, I was joining most of the human race. I took the usual remedies and the usual advice—long, hot showers, the water directed on the back; cold packs on the back; aspirin before you play tennis; aspirin after you play tennis; don't play tennis; sit with your back straight up when eating meals (the cleaning bills trying to get wine and pasta off my pants canceled that one out); and sleep on your side. I can understand *going* to sleep on your side but no one can govern your moves while you sleep. You would need an electric spatula that would automatically turn you over every time during the night you rolled onto your back. Nothing really helped.

The trouble itself could have come from the tension of doing seven plays and three movies in seven years. It could be due to the ten hours a day I spent over a typewriter, sometimes not getting up for hours. It could also have been in what I had written. I had the theory that your mind doesn't know when you're writing. It thinks you are actually living through whatever you are putting on paper. If I had actually lived through all the weird and hectic scenes I wrote in seven years, my back would have already been removed and I'd be wearing a hanger in my shirts to keep them from falling off. Occasionally I was put out of commission for weeks at a time. I could bend down for something, forgetting to bend my knees, and a sharp pain would shoot up my back. Some moments I'd be turned into a pretzel, frozen to the spot, looking like a character in the Chinese language. With rest it would usually ease up, and the minute it did, this fool went out and played three sets of tennis. And if I did, by that night, I looked like a sailor's knot done in bronze.

My bad back followed me wherever I went and it was never far behind me. I tried everything. Acupuncture. I didn't mind the sticking of the needles all over my back, my neck, my ear lobes, and my toes. It was when they twisted them back and forth that I knew what pain God suffered upon Job.

I know many people who have benefited and swear by acupuncture. I, how-ever, would rather sleep naked on the tarmac in August in Hawaii. I tried ultra-sound. I tried meditation. Meditation is actually very good for relaxing. The problem comes when you try to get up after spending twenty minutes in that lotus position—then you would gladly try acupuncture again.

I tried chiropractors. If you trust your chiropractor, he could very well do you some good. If you don't trust him, when he grabs you in a headlock like Hulk Hogan, your body freezes up in tension, and when he cracks you, it sounds like the buckle on your belt breaking. So if you must go to a chiro-practor, go to one you trust.

I tried injections of extract of papaya, a temporary cure first practiced in Canada. The problem is, you can only use it once. What hideous things hap-pen to you if you took two injections of papaya, I can't imagine, except that apparently you soon begin to look like one. It helped me for over a year. Then the back pains returned. I was afraid to go back, because they might suggest injections of avocado, cantaloupe, watermelon, and litchi nuts.

In truth, there is no end to the indignity you will suffer for the relief of what you are already suffering. And so, you continue to search out the rem-edy that will end the pain of a back that still refuses to let you go out at night. I can't tell you how many halves of movies I've seen. Or how many plays I've stood for without seeing the second act. I have done back exercises in the aisles of airplanes, only to get run over by the dinner cart. Eventually, if you live in New York, you might end up at the office of a Park Avenue doctor, who everyone says has the absolute cure. Actually there are a number of them. They have real names, but mostly they are referred to as Miracle Max, Savior Sam, the Saint of Bleecker Street, or Gelman the God. I often wondered if any of these deities went to medical school or did they just get caught in a thun-derstorm in Lourdes, thereby rendering them God's Back Angels.

Whatever, since back pain sufferers will try anything for relief I went to the Healer of the Stars on Park Avenue in the Fifties. I called to make an appointment with his secretary, who said, "Sorry, we have no opening for the next six months, unless you want to come in today at three." I thought, What the hell. Might as well go in today at three. I walked into his ground-floor office and was immediately greeted by the eeriest sight I've ever come across. About a dozen patients, all well dressed, were sitting on soft chairs and sofas, each with twelve-inch needles protruding from their nostrils, one needle angled to the left, the other to the right, making them look like a dozen dressed-up walruses. There was one former film star sitting there, then about fifty but still one of the most beautiful women in the world. She wouldn't go out of her house with an eyelash pointing in the wrong direction. But here she was, reading a ten-year-old *Vogue* magazine, looking like a telephone operator from Mars. No one spoke to anyone else for fear that if you turned your head too quickly, your prongs might clash, causing an electrical storm or ruining the reception on a neighbor's television set. I was given a form to fill out with about a hundred questions on it and sat down next to a woman who was reading a book, and who managed somehow to turn the pages with one of her nasal antennas.

The questions on the form covered some medical history, but most of them were personal: "Where does your pain hurt most?" "How many drugs do you take for your pain?" "Are you on good terms with your spouse?" "If you have grown children, do they call you much?" The questions went on and on, and I answered until I got to one that wanted to know "if it hurts when you have sex or does it hurt your partner when you have sex?"

As I wrote, I looked at a sweet, elderly woman across from me, and wondered if she were dexterous enough, could she possibly knit a sweater with those needles in her nose?

Finally I was shown into the great doctor's office. It hadn't been painted in twenty years. The walls were covered not with diplomas, but with newspaper articles telling how an opera diva was carried into his office during a performance, unable to move her legs. After one treatment, she was back at the Met singing Brünnhilde. I saw no glistening examples of technological advances in medicine in his prewar (any war) cabinets. It was very friendly and informal in his office. As a matter of fact, two other patients, both men, were sitting on stools, prong-nosed, chatting show business with the great healer. Actually, it looked less like a doctor's office than a place where you made a bet on a horse and left by a side door, no doubt dropping your snout prongs in a receptacle on the way out. It felt more or less like a bunch of men sitting and gabbing around the hot stove in a small town general store.

The first thing the doctor did was rub my head apparently to make me feel at home. I also figured it was probably the same thing he did with any mangy dog that showed up also with a bad back. He turned a light on my face, pushed my head back, and with a medical instrument once popular in the Crimean War looked up my nose and said, "Where do you hoit?"

You heard me. He said, "Hoit."

I quickly ruled out Harvard as the source of his medical education. This was definitely a doctor by day and a cab driver by night. I told him it was my lower back. As he looked up my nose, he said, "Sure. I can see it from here." I had no idea my nostrils were so wide. "Two, three treatments, you'll be outta here." He then took a single prong out of a jar that looked like it contained hot coffee, wiped it off, put a small roll of cotton on the tip of the prong, dipped it into a medicine bottle containing what, I couldn't guess, and slowly wormed it up into my nose. When I yelled *"Agh!"* he stopped. "That's far enough," he said sagely. He did the same with another needle. I could see myself in the mirror across from me. I had become one of the walrus people. He told me to open my mouth and he popped a butterscotch candy in it.

"What's that for?" I asked ingenuously.

"You'll like it," was his medical answer. "Sit there five minutes. I'll tell you when to move."

He started to talk amiably with the other townspeople in the room. Then he looked at me and said, "What do you do, Simon?"

"Do? I'm a writer."

"What kind of writer?"

"Plays mostly."

"Like what plays?"

"Well, I wrote *Barefoot in the Park, The Odd Couple.*"

"Oh, for crissakes. Of course, I thought so when I looked up your nose." Then to the others, "Hey, boys. It's Neil Simon."

They nodded, got up, and shook my hands vigorously. One of the prongs fell out of my nose. The good doctor put it back in place. "Have you heard this one?" he starts, and I know I'm about to hear a joke. As he's telling it—one of the dumbest jokes I ever heard in my life—I begin to feel a numbness in my nose and a sense of relief in my back. He goes on with the joke. The other two are laughing. I find myself laughing as well. Although my intellect was telling me this was probably the worst joke ever told in the English language, I was now laughing hysterically. He told another one, far worse than the first. The tears started to roll down my cheeks. This doctor should be on television. He's the funniest man I've seen since Sid Caesar. Then he asked how my back was. I told him there was practically no pain. None at all.

"Good," he said. "I want to see you again."

"Shall I make an appointment with your secretary?"

"No. Come five o'clock."

"Five o'clock? Today?"

"Sure. We'll nip this thing in the bud."

I left his office walking sprightly and humming songs I never heard before. I reached home and bounced in through the front door. Joan was in the kitchen. I turned, jumped, bent over, and spun around.

"Look, Ma. No pain."

She was amazed. She knew what I had been through the last few years.

"What did he do?"

"Nothing. He just put some prongs up my nose, dipped in some medicine on cotton that affects the spinal cord and relieves the pressure on the back."

She was speechless with joy and wonder. Then I told her the joke he told me. I could barely get it out, I laughed so hard. She laughed at me laughing. I warned her to sit down because this was the funniest joke I ever heard in my life. She sat down. Somehow I managed to calm my hysterics long enough to finish the joke.

She looked at me. "That's funny?"

"Yes. Don't you get it?"

"No. Explain it to me."

I tried to but I couldn't. "You can't explain a joke like this. It's either funny or it's not funny."

She said, "No. It will never be funny. It's moronic. Are you all right?"

"All right? I never felt better in my life."

At 4:30 the pain was beginning to return in my back. I rushed over to the good doctor's office. A new family of walruses were sitting in the living room reading *Life* magazines from the late 1940s. I was told to go right in, the doctor was waiting for me. Up went the prongs, in went a butterscotch, gone was my pain, and laughter resumed as he told me a joke that was too funny to tell without being lethal.

I kept this routine up for two weeks. Each day I felt better, each night I felt worse. What was his magic potion? You must be ahead of me by now. It was cocaine. I never knew at the time, and I didn't know if his other patients knew. It was the first and last time I ever used cocaine. He was eventually found out and was at first forbidden to practice medicine again. Later on he was reinstated, but could not use cocaine as a treatment. I never went there again, but occasionally the walruses in the Central Park Zoo would remind me of him. I wish I could remember those jokes, don't you?

PLAZA SUITE OPENED at the Plymouth Theatre in the fall of 1968 and it was everything we hoped it would be. George Scott had indeed turned into a pussycat and he seemed to be a happy man at last, never missing a performance once we opened in New York. New film offers started to come his way, and one day as I walked by his dressing room, his door was open. He was not in makeup yet, but deeply engrossed in a script. I could see the title on the cover page. It was *Patton*. "Good script, George?" I asked him. Without looking up from the page, he said, "Not bad. Not half bad." It of course turned out to be the signature role in George's illustrious career.

Maureen Stapleton, on the other hand, never seemed to want to be a movie star. Oh, I'm sure she'd love the money and the acclaim, but being a major film star would probably be too much trouble to her. She dodged the public whenever she could and hated taking publicity pictures. She usually would hide behind George's back. She also never flew on planes and would take the train to California every time she did a film, which would automatically cut down the amount of movies she could make by half. Even being a star on Broadway never seemed to impress her. She still came to the theater every night on the Eighth Avenue bus carrying a shopping bag. She was not one to flaunt. She never milked a bow, and while she was glad for the applause, it seemed like it embarrassed her and that she would just as soon be in her dressing room instead. She remains to this day probably the best actress I ever worked with. With *Plaza Suite* opening at the Plymouth Theatre, *The Odd Couple* was moved to *our* theater, the Eugene O'Neill.

I soon learned that the O'Neill Theatre was a less desirable theater than others on Forty-fourth and Forty-fifth Street, where the seating capacities were much larger and the location attracted many more theatergoers. The other problem was that since it was difficult to predict or find a play that was going to be a hit, it averaged out that each theater would have a hit play about once every three years. Since the Shubert Organization, at that time, owned most of the top theaters in New York, they got first choice at the most promising plays, and because of their extremely deep pockets, could better afford to have a theater dark (unoccupied) than the owner of just a single theater. It became incumbent upon me then to try to write a play every year or so to go into the O'Neill. I stopped being a writer and was now in the play-supplying business, which was the last thing I wanted. I felt forced to write plays, whether I had a good idea for one or not (see Walter Kerr's quote), and I knew

I was caught between a rock and a kryptonite place. Even if I did not have a play in my theater, the expenses continued as though you did have one. There were taxes to pay, payrolls and maintenance bills went on and on, and you could count on slowly becoming bankrupt even as people described you as a "prominent theater owner." When I started spending more time with accountants and bank executives, I knew it was time to get out of the theater-owning business—and all business for that matter—and back to writing plays. Sometimes it costs you a lot just to learn the most basic things. Since I did not want to sell the theater at a loss, I continued putting my plays there until someone who didn't mind losing a lot of money came along.

My mother, who had worked for the last few years as a salesperson at Gimbel's, refused to leave her job even though I could now support her in style and let her live a more leisurely life. "I like to work," she'd say. "It keeps me busy and I don't like to be alone all day." I was ready to drop the subject when she said, "Although there *is* one other job I would take, if I could get it."

"What's that?"

"I want to work in the Eugene O'Neill Theatre."

"The Eugene O'Neill? What would you do there? It's mostly maintenance people, usherettes, and the box-office staff."

"I could answer the phone," she said. "I could sell tickets to my son's play on the telephone. That I would enjoy."

There were already two women working in a small room near the balcony who took phone orders all day, but if that's what my mother wanted, there could always be room for three. She was the first to arrive in the morning and the last to leave at night. If she started out the door at night and heard the phone ring, she rushed back up to answer it. You can always sell one more ticket. She reveled in her work. She often made it very clear to the customer on the phone that they were talking to the playwright's mother. She would tell me how excited the people on the other end were. My mother never got to be the professional dancer she had dreamed of as a child, but she made it into show business anyway.

For a woman who was basically victimized a good part of her life, she now had a newfound identity, a power to not only help herself but to help her son and his family. She had control of the tickets to the biggest hit on Broadway. She also visited some belated anger on my departed father for some of his errant ways. Whenever one of his old friends called for tickets, she said, "No problem," and invariably gave them the worst seats in the house. On Saturdays, when the matinees and the evenings were virtually sold out, she'd say, "I'm sorry, we're all sold out. But why don't you call the Plymouth Theatre? I hear this *Plaza Suite* is a terrific play." Now she had two shows to sell.

One night, after dinner, she called me at home. I could tell by the near sob in her voice there was a problem.

"What's wrong, Mom?"

"Nothing. I don't want you to worry about it."

"I'm already worried. You might as well tell me."

". . . They're stealing from you."

"Who is?"

"The people who work in the theater."

"You mean the men who work in the box office?"

"Not the box office. Upstairs where I work."

"You mean the other two women who answer the phone? What are they stealing?"

"Pencils. Pens. Pads. They make personal calls, God knows how many."

I restrained a laugh. "Mom, everyone takes home things like that. You expect that in business."

"I don't. I never took a pen or a pencil. I can buy my own. I'm going to start adding up what they take. You'll see at the end of the year what I save you." I suddenly thought, maybe I should make *her* my business manager.

One afternoon the phone in her office rang. She picked it up. A man with a cultured, soft voice was on the line.

"Excuse me. My name is Clifton Daniel. I would like to buy four tickets for this Wednesday night's performance. It will be for myself, my wife, and my mother- and father-in-law. But I'd like to keep the press out of this. My father-in-law just wants a quiet night out in New York."

"Who's your father-in-law?"

"Former President Truman."

"*Harry* Truman?"

"Yes."

"Harry Truman's calling me for tickets? That'll be the day."

And she hung up the phone.

"Who was that?" asked one of the ladies in the office.

"Some guy calls and wants tickets for President Truman. Like I'm going to give it to him for nothing. They can't pull that stuff on me. I know better."

Clifton Daniel called back and asked for the manager. He explained the situation to him, assuring him the tickets were indeed for the former president. The tickets were arranged for and paid by us. That night my mother and I waited in the lobby and were introduced to President Truman, Bess Truman, and Margaret and Clifton Daniel. It was a great honor for me, because I ranked Truman up there as one of our greatest presidents, along with Lincoln and Jefferson. When I drove my mother home, I said, "Wasn't that a thrill?"

She said, "Wait'll I tell my friends. They'll never believe me . . . Still, they could have been lying. I would have saved you four tickets."

THE PLAY HAD BEEN running about four months. George Scott was playing softball for our team in the Broadway Show League, a softball tournament played in Central Park from early spring to early summer. All the current shows were represented. George stood on the mound pitching for us, and if you were lucky enough to hit a single off him, he stood on the pathway to second base, an immovable object. "You may have gotten a single off me but you sure as hell ain't going to second. Go on, get back."

And back the opposing runner went.

George was in good health and good spirits. Until one day we got a call from his agent. George would be out of the play from four to six weeks. The doctors had found he had a detached retina. It was a blow to us and especially to Maureen, because you could bet she wasn't going to play four to six weeks with the understudy. We started putting out feelers for name replacements. The same ones Mike and I had talked about in the early hours of a panicky morning in Boston: José Ferrer, Martin Balsam, Fritz Weaver. And another dozen names of equal stature. They all said no. No one wanted to follow in the footsteps or reviews of George Scott.

Mike Nichols then came up with an original idea. Nicol Williamson was an English actor who had already made his name in London and in New York. He was a brilliant actor and could also do a perfect American accent. We sent the play to Nicol; he read it and agreed to do it. Three days later he was in New York rehearsing. He needed about a week or ten days to get ready.

In the meantime, Actors' Equity in America protested our choice of using an English actor in an American part. We assured them we had tried every possible American actor of appropriate stature and were unable to come up with one. Should we close the show and put other American actors out of work because of the Equity ruling? They finally agreed, but there was a large contingent of actors who were against our move. We watched Nicol Williamson in his final dress rehearsal and he was quite wonderful. That night, as he was to make his debut in the part, irate members of Actors' Equity picketed the show outside the theater, most of them carrying placards. One of the young actresses who was carrying a placard—which I didn't find out until many years later—was Marsha Mason, someone who would eventually play an important part in my life.

The curtain went up with Maureen alone on stage. She received her usual acknowledgment from the audience, then had a six-minute scene with the bellboy. Then Nicol Williamson made his entrance. As he did, a young man stood up from his aisle seat, obviously an actor from Equity who was unhappy with our choice, and began to sing "The Star Spangled Banner" at the top of his lungs. The audience was annoyed and confused and began to hiss the man to be quiet. The play onstage stopped completely. A police officer came in and ushered the young man out just as he finished. "And the home of the braaaaave." The curtain went down, then after a few moments went up again. Maureen repeated her scene with the bellboy, and Nicol made his entrance on stage. The audience gave him a standing ovation.

Nicol played out the full six weeks until George returned, then George left two months later when his six-month contract was up. George went on to win the Academy Award as Best Actor for *Patton*—which he refused to accept. He even declined to go to Hollywood to participate in the Oscar proceedings. George *does* have his strange quirks now and then, but in my eyes, he could do no wrong. And if he did, I wouldn't have the nerve to tell him.

THE CRACK IN THE CEILING

15

WHEN WE WERE first rehearsing *Plaza Suite*, Mike Nichols had a conversation with the set designer, Oliver Smith. Oliver was one of the premier set designers in the theater, with credits ranging from *My Fair Lady* to you name it. For us, he did *Barefoot in the Park, The Odd Couple*, and *Plaza Suite*. A very tall, gaunt man on the other side of fifty-five, with short-cropped white hair and a cigarette permanently lodged in his long, thin fingers, he was far from a congenial man.

When Mike first saw the set of *The Odd Couple* on the stage in Wilmington, he only had one quibble. He asked Oliver if he could tone down the color of the walls just a shade. Oliver, without even looking at Mike, said, "No." There was no discussion as far as Oliver was concerned. No was No.

"Can I tell you my reasons why?" Mike offered.

"Of course you can," said Oliver. "And when you're through, the answer will still be 'No.'"

Oliver always wore his topcoat draped over his shoulders, like the Marshall of the French Army, which I think he believed he was. Once Oliver was visiting a friend in the hospital. Another visitor came in and immediately recognized Oliver. They were old friends. The man was beside himself. "Oliver, how wonderful to see you. My God, what is it, twenty years? The work you've done, Oliver. It's magnificent. Truly incredible. I'm so proud of you. Can I call you for lunch some time?"

"Absolutely not," said Oliver, as he bid good-bye to the patient and left the room quickly.

When Mike first saw the set of *Plaza Suite* on the stage, he made sure to say the appropriate words of praise to Oliver first, how wonderful it was, how inspired. There was only one detail Mike wanted to include. He wanted a long crack in the ceiling in this otherwise perfect reproduction of an expensive suite at the Plaza.

Oliver didn't even bother saying no, so taken aback was he by such a curious suggestion. "For heaven's sake, why would you want a crack in the ceiling?"

I had the exact same thoughts.

"Because I want to show what's happened to New York. To our entire society. The crack is a metaphor for the slow coming-apart-at-the-seams of our world today. Only we're not noticing it. It's right there in front of our eyes but we're missing it."

Oliver raised his eyes in disdain and inhaled his cigarette. He never exhaled. That was beneath him.

I turned to Mike and said, "I understand what you're getting at, Mike, because I feel the same way. I think it's an important statement. But I think the audience will just look up and think it's a crack in the ceiling. Like the painters of the set did a lousy job. I don't think some man is going to turn to his wife and say, 'Look! A metaphor of how our society is coming apart at the seams!'" I went on. "I mean, unless, of course, we paint a sign next to the crack with an arrow saying 'A metaphor.'"

Mike gave me one of his "I hate you" looks.

I think we settled for a slight crack, and the only ones who knew its true meaning were Mike and all the people he told it to.

But Mike was smarter than that. His suggestions, although sometimes as wild as having the TV turned on in the poker game, always were searching for a line of truth. The more I thought of it, the more it made an impact on me. I knew what he was getting at.

New York certainly had changed since I was a boy growing up in the streets of Washington Heights. There was an innocence then that I took for granted, that things would always be like this. I knew it was a hard place for my father to make a living, but I never feared for my safety, for my life. My mother always closed our door at night, but there never was a double lock. If you had a dog, it was for pleasure, not for protection. If I came home an hour late in the summer, my mother always knew it was because I was playing ball or at the movies or in the library. Kidnapping or child molestation was never an issue. We had crime in the city, of course, but not a wave of it that brought fear and terror into our daily lives. The news was not blasted over the airwaves twenty hours a day. Before the war, I only remember one show a night dedicated to news. It was H. V. Kaltenborn, who spoke as if he were an emissary from the pope, giving us news each evening of coronations, fighting on the Manchurian border, or how the Republican party was scouring the heartland looking for a presidential candidate. No sensational stories of murders (except possibly for the horrific story of the kidnapping of the Lindbergh baby), no shootouts in grocery stores or local restaurants like the Horn and Hardart Automats, and if the word "pregnant" was too risqué for radio audiences, the word "rape" certainly would not come into our homes. There were no stories of racial discord, because as far as we knew in the North, there *was* no racial discord. Desegregation was a word hardly invented yet.

It's not to say that none of any of the above crimes, whether social or criminal, were not taking place, but there just wasn't enough access to know about them. The magazines were filled with Norman Rockwell paintings of babies and baby doctors, and stories of how Mr. and Mrs. Clark Gable decorated their den. I grew up thinking the world was like an MGM movie, and the only girl who wasn't pretty was the bad witch in *The Wizard of Oz*. My image of death was of someone in a clean hospital bed, the patient looking more tired than pained, and when the end came, his eyes closed and his head fell softly to the side on a cool pillow. They told us America was a safe haven from the rest of the world. In a sense, it was.

The closest I ever came to experiencing an actual crime took place one summer night when my parents were asleep in their bedroom. There was a fire escape just outside their window, which made entry easy since the window was never closed. If anyone or anything came in, they hoped it would be a cool breeze. Yet one night, a man crept silently into the room, looked around, and spied my father's pants draped across a chair. My father heard a noise, but only raised one eye, about a half a lid's worth. He watched as the quiet burglar went through the pants pockets, taking whatever money he could find. And he watched as the burglar slipped out the window again. My father turned over on his side and went back to sleep.

When he told my mother the story in the morning, she screamed, "We could have been killed!"

My father said, "Burglars don't kill. Burglars burgle. He took my money and left."

My mother asked, "Why didn't you close the window when he left? Suppose someone else came in?"

"Who cared?" said my father. "They already had my six dollars. What else would they take, my belt?"

For the next two nights they slept with the window closed. Then it got hot again and they kept it open every night. No one ever came back. Since it was during the Depression, the burglar probably figured he got our six dollars and wiped us out for good.

There were no murders in our neighborhood. People died of heart attacks, old age, being run over by a car, or, as my characters in *Brighton Beach Memoirs* would say softly, "from cancer." "Cancer" was always said in a whisper. The fear was that if God heard you say the forbidden word, he might strike you down with it.

There *were* neighborhood gangs in those days, only they were more like clubs, a place to hang out. We were never looking for a fight. The Jews lived two blocks away from the Irish, and the Irish lived two blocks away from the Italians. If a Jew lived on the border of the Italian neighborhood, some days he was a Jew and other days an Italian. We occasionally got into fights. One day I was punched in the jaw and I retaliated by tearing the shirt collar off an Irish boy. His only good shirt. That was about as rough as it got.

When it snowed, we went downhill sledding on 175th Street, from eight in the morning till five at night. The streets belonged to us. We could play a full half-inning of stickball on any street except Broadway, and the game would stop momentarily to wait for one lone car to pass. Traffic was not a problem. School, the rent, and getting a job were the main problems in our life.

The crack in the ceiling probably first got started when drugs, or "the weed," made its appearance in the dark alleys outside of jazz clubs where the musicians lit up between sets. It was then taken up by the few members of café society who were daring enough to use it. By the sixties, half the people I knew were experimenting with getting high. Slowly marijuana use spread, became common, even "acceptable." The next step down the ladder was cocaine.

By the early seventies, the innocence of New York had vanished. The drugs were now being used by the people who could least afford them, but who found their own ways of how to buy them. There were brazen daylight robberies of stores on chic Madison Avenue and killings that became a way of life from the West Bronx to any poorly lit neighborhood in the five boroughs.

The news of crime now dominated our lives, with five-inch headlines in the *Daily News* and the *New York Post*. We doubled and tripled our locks, and Central Park became lost to us once the sun went down. If a child was ten minutes late arriving home, parents became frantic. Yankee Stadium was not where you'd want to be twenty minutes after a night game ended. Joe Allen, the restaurateur on West Forty-sixth Street, had to enlist the aid of a group of young vigilantes to make sure that patrons came and left in safety. Cab drivers were being killed daily. It was not London during the blitz, but for an old woman walking home from the supermarket with her cart of food at 9 P.M., it might as well have been a war zone.

For me personally, the first time I was affected by it was the day I got into a taxi and found the cab had a thick, protective see-through shield that sealed the driver off from the riders in the back. I was shocked to see I had to pay him through a small slot in the shield and that my change was placed through the same tiny opening. No more friendly conversations with the drivers about sports or politics or the weather. We were cut off from each other, sitting in our solitary compartments. What was more frightening was that the cabbie locked the back doors, so that now I was his prisoner, and the doors only unlocked when I reached my destination and paid my fare.

I suddenly realized that even I could become suspect in committing a robbery or a murder. One day I was walking from the East Side of Manhattan to the West Side to see my therapist. I was on Central Park South, just inside the park where children played and old women sat on benches holding their purses protectively. Suddenly out of nowhere I was blindsided from the right and a huge fist smashed into my jaw, knocking me flat. I lay on the ground for a few seconds and saw the outline of a tall man standing above me, his finger pointing at me with the threat of more violence. "Don't you ever call me that," he said, and then quickly walked away, pushing aside anyone who was in his path. I was so dazed I didn't know what happened, and for a moment wasn't even sure I knew where I was.

Three elderly women were sitting on a bench two feet away from me, having watched this one-punch knockout. They were neither shocked nor surprised at what happened. They must see this every day, I thought.

The woman in the middle of the trio said to me in a conversational voice, "What did you say to him?"

Bewildered, I answered, "I didn't say *anything*. He just hit me."

As if it were my fault, the woman said, "You shouldn't start in with them. They're crazy."

Obviously it was just another day in the park for them.

New Yorkers were beginning to take violence in their stride. We simply accepted this as our new way of life, unless, of course, we wanted to move to the suburbs, which eventually proved to be no safer than the city.

Carefree plays like *Barefoot in the Park* and *The Odd Couple*, done just a few years before, were suddenly dated. They seemed naive. They no longer reflected a way of life that was once the New York I had grown up in. I, however, was not yet ready to give up the memories of my youth. I wanted to write a play that would bring nostalgia back to those who lived their childhood at a time comparable to mine, and to show the new generation, born twenty or thirty years after me, what it was like back then, in some naive hope that together we might find a way for the future to reflect some of the values of the past.

I thought of a time when I was thirteen years old, spending the summer of 1940 in a small bungalow in Far Rockaway, New York. Far Rockaway was a beach community on the Atlantic Ocean, about an hour from New York by elevated train, or an hour and a half if you went in a 1936 Buick on a simmeringly hot weekend with seven people crammed into the small seating space. The seats were made of a brush material, the main objective of which was to retain heat. I always sat next to my cousin-to-be, Marty Klein, the lawyer, since Marty was the only one in the family who owned a car. On the other side of me was my father. The cars were all stick shifts then, and before Marty shifted into gear, he shifted into my left leg—at least a hundred and twenty times—just to get to our destination. My leg was black and blue before we were halfway there and I was wearing short pants, making this my first physical contact with a thirty-year-old man with a mustache.

One day, I thought, it would be me driving with a pretty girl squeezed next to the stick shift, my fat friend Alvin on the other side of her, making her powerless to move away. You have to plan your sexual exploits early in life.

That summer of 1940, my mother, father, Danny, and I shared a bungalow with my mother's sister Fannie, her husband, Phil, and their two daughters, Ceil and Mimi. The bungalow was just a little larger than the Buick that we got there in. The cost to rent this bungalow from June 15 to September 4 was a hundred dollars, making that roughly twelve dollars and fourteen cents a person for the summer. One wondered what the landlord's profit was. Since there were about sixty of these bungalows, all built exactly alike, each one about four feet away from the next one, I suppose he did all right.

Even at twelve dollars and fourteen cents a person, my father had to scrimp and borrow to raise the money. My uncle Phil worked in the Post Office his entire life, and although his salary was modest, it was steadier than the money my father made as a salesman, so dependent on whether he had a good season or not. Nineteen forty wasn't a good season for him, so Uncle Phil graciously paid sixty dollars and my father paid forty. This changed the nature of the relationship somewhat. Although it was left unsaid, we were, to some degree, the renters of the bungalow and my uncle Phil was the temporary landlord. There were only two small bedrooms, but since Uncle Phil had first choice, he took the one that was six inches wider, and didn't get as much direct hot sun during the day. He was also closer to the bathroom. By about a foot. This inequity galled my father but he took it stoically, for about a week. Stoicism soon gave way to sarcasm. My brother and I slept together in the living room on a double cot, and on the other side of the dining table, four feet away, slept my cousins Ceil and Mimi in a pullout bed. Ceil was a beautiful girl, soon about to marry Marty, and Mimi was a perky, pretty thing just a few years older than I was. I stayed up half the night waiting for one of them to go to the bathroom, if only to give me a fleeting look at the silhouette of their bodies. Unfortunately I invariably dozed off before I ever got my chance. With one bathroom for the eight of us, control was the greatest lesson I learned that summer.

The war was raging in Europe, and America was beginning to mobilize in the inevitable event that we would soon be sending our boys over. The draft was on and in Washington they were pulling numbers out of a fishbowl. None of us knew that summer that Danny's number would be at the bottom of that first fishbowl.

No two men could have been more different than my uncle Phil and my father. Uncle Phil was a humorless man despite the fact that he told me jokes all day. I was only thirteen but I had heard these jokes ten years before. After each joke, Uncle Phil laughed out loud, thus filling the void of silence coming from my side of the table. I liked Uncle Phil, mostly because I knew he was dependable and would never leave his wife and family. My father, on the other hand, was still a dandy, and there was always the possibility that one day he wouldn't get off the train that came from the city and stopped at the Far Rockaway station. Most nights I would wait for him at the station, knowing that the sight of him getting off the train meant that at least the family would have one more day together. I liked to carry his box of samples back to the bungalow; it was the only time we ever spent together talking. It was times like this that I would feel really close to him. He was the best-dressed man who got off the train, his shoes polished and glaring in the late-day sun. I don't know how he could afford a shine when he could hardly afford forty dollars for a bungalow.

With eight of us sharing this tiny doll house, half as big as our small apartment in the city, it naturally led to tensions. From my cot in the living room, I could hear Uncle Phil in the middle of the night, complaining about what a show-off my father was, while I could hear my father complaining to my mother that Uncle Phil was acting like a big shot because he was paying more than my father. So staid was Uncle Phil that one night in New York when my father offered to take him to Lindy's restaurant for a piece of cheesecake, Uncle Phil refused. "I don't go to nightclubs," he said. Actually Lindy's was nothing more than a first-class deli. So in went my mother and father, Aunt Fannie, and Danny and me, while Uncle Phil stood obstinately outside on the street as we had our cheesecake.

Now, years later, I thought this constant bickering between the two families, with my mother and Aunt Fannie trying to maintain peace, could be the basis of a good play, partly because the small war that was being played out in the small bungalow was a microcosm of the harrowing great war that was then engulfing half the world.

I called the first draft *The War of the Rosens*, and as I approached page thirty-five, I hit a snag. As funny as it might be, I realized it was only about family bickering. The two men seemed to be another version of *The Odd Couple*. I saw no drama in it, and more than anything, it was drama I was searching for.

The play, as I was writing it, wasn't rich enough, deep enough, or emotional enough. There was not enough at stake. I knew that to continue on the same path I was heading was a waste of time, so I put the play in the drawer, hoping to get back to it at a later date. It was three years before I even read it again. Nothing had changed in my mind. I put it back in the drawer to simmer. I had no doubts, though, that when the time was right, I would take it out and go back to write it.

MR. BROADWAY

16

IN THE 1960s AND 1970s, David Merrick was "Mr. Broadway," the most successful producer in the theater. Mostly he imported plays and musicals from England where they were already established hits, thus minimizing his risk when he brought them to New York. He dressed and spoke the part befitting his lofty position. Although he was from the Midwest, he had acquired a cultured manner of speech, probably borrowed from the English tailor who designed his expensive and extensive wardrobe. He also wore a homburg hat, long since out of fashion, that made him look more like John Foster Dulles on a mission to Moscow than the producer of *Hello, Dolly!* He was not known for tossing his money around freely to actors or writers, but his productions were always first-class and he brought the best of the English playwrights, actors, and directors to America. He had a reputation of being a difficult and overbearing employer, and once got into such a terrible tiff with actor Nicol Williamson that Williamson knocked Merrick out cold in a Philadelphia alley.

Merrick also put on the gloves with the New York critics. One famous story that I think bears retelling originated when a Merrick play was dealt a death blow by the New York reviewers. If there was one thing that David Merrick knew how to do, it was to get his name and his play's title in the press. Two days after the fatal reviews came out, Merrick hunted through the phone book, found names exactly the same as the reviewers', rented these individuals' names for a small fee, and attributed quotes praising his play to these imposters, who, in fact, had as much right to their names as did the critics. Then in a full-page newspaper ad appeared the title of Merrick's play and quotes like:

"The Best New Play in Town"—WALTER KERR.
"A Work of Genius"—HOWARD TAUBMAN.
"I'd Pay My Own Way In to See It Again"—RICHARD WATTS.

Obviously Mr. Kerr, Mr. Taubman, and Mr. Watts vehemently objected, as did the other quoted reviewers, and the New York papers stopped printing the ad, but it did cause a sensation in town and Merrick enjoyed his joke. But it didn't save the play. You had to hand it to him, though, and if you didn't, he would take it anyway.

When I received a call from Mr. Merrick, whom I had never met, asking me to have lunch, I went more out of curiosity than of any expectations of having him produce one of my plays. He knew I would never leave Saint Subber, whom I felt had nurtured me in the beginning and served me well ever since. Merrick was furious when he couldn't get his way and could never understand my loyalty to Saint. Since Saint Subber was gay, a rumor was purportedly spread by David Merrick that I must have been gay as well. When Mr. Merrick called, I was tempted to say, "You're not calling me for a date, are you, David?" but I thought any man who wore a homburg couldn't have much of a sense of humor. To my surprise, I found him cordial, intelligent, respectful, sharp, and funny, and I rather liked him for his pragmatism and forthrightness. But I would not like to leave the restaurant before him, because turning your back to David Merrick could be lethal.

I found out the way to get David Merrick's respect was to be very independent, a trait I was quickly acquiring on my own. In the theater, and probably most other businesses as well, the ability to say no usually resulted in your adversary saying yes. I didn't say it to gain any advantage or more money or better terms or even more power. I said it because I didn't want anything so badly that I would either have to compromise my principles or get myself into a position where I'd have to give up time that I could otherwise put to better use. I'd sooner go to a ball game than go to a business meeting.

In the mid-sixties, Charles Bluhdorn, the president of Gulf and Western and the owner of Paramount Pictures—and someone I took an immediate dislike to—offered to buy the screen rights to my next seven as yet unwritten plays, sight unseen, for $250,000 each. He said, "Think about your answer. If only two of the seven are good, I'd be buying five bad plays for a quarter of a million dollars each." I didn't have to think about my answer. I said, "Thank you, but no. I have more faith in myself than you do. I don't want to sell bad plays, and I'll sell the good ones for a better price." As I walked out of his office, I was very proud of myself. And very scared. Cockiness could be just as dangerous as sincere confidence. But those two traits plus the right amount of humility seemed like a fair balance. Besides, selling seven unwritten plays seemed like I was in school with a lot of homework to do, with a teacher who looked a lot like the one who ate up Little Red Riding Hood's grandmother.

David Merrick asked me if I had any ideas for a musical and I told him I never do. I only have ideas for plays. He then approached it from another direction. "If you *did* have any ideas, are there any composers you would like to work with?" I had no trouble answering that one. Burt Bacharach and Hal David were probably the most popular writing team of the day, and I thought the new sound and unpredictable melodies of Bacharach's music would be a fresh and original addition to Broadway musicals. Merrick then said, "If they agreed, is there any book or film that you would like to adapt?" I surprised even myself as I answered immediately, "Yes. Billy Wilder's film *The Apartment*." It was a cynical love story about the infidelities of business executives who borrow the apartment of a well-meaning but ambitious minor executive for their assignations. It had won the Academy Award as Best Picture of 1960.

Merrick said, "All right, let me ask you another question. How would you like to adapt *The Apartment* with a score by Burt Bacharach and Hal David?"

I smiled at him and said, "Jesus, you are a sneaky one . . . Yes. I would."

"Fine," he said. "I'll call Bacharach today and get the stage rights of the film. Who were you thinking of to direct it?" he asked.

"You mean who was I thinking of to direct as I came here ready to tell you I didn't want to do a musical?" His smile evened the score. I knew Fosse was busy, but I had recently seen an off-Broadway play that amazed me with its frank, honest, and hilarious humor, with direction as good as anything on Broadway. "Well, I think Robert Moore, who just did *The Boys in the Band*, might be wonderful."

"I'll get right on it," Merrick said almost before I finished the sentence.

We had now put all the ingredients together for a new musical, and I hadn't even touched my fettuccine yet. There was a sharp brain up there, I could see now, since his homburg was now off and in care of the hatcheck girl. For all the horror stories I had heard about Merrick, this was an unbelievably productive meeting, and I think it went so easily because he genuinely approved of all the choices I made.

Within three weeks we had *The Apartment*, the composer and lyricist, and the director all tied up. If that lunch lasted any longer, we would have had the designer, the costumer, and a logo for the program. A few weeks later, bicoastal writing sessions started, since Bacharach lived in Los Angeles, and Hal David and I lived in New York. Since the story was about the promotions that were promised to the bachelor who was lending out his pad four nights a week to the execs for their dalliances, I thought *Promises, Promises* would be a good title. Merrick approved, and it was announced that Friday in *The New York Times* as one of next year's big musicals coming to Broadway.

The final and very important last piece in putting the project together was not suggested by me, but whoever it was, I'm grateful to him. Michael Bennett was signed on as choreographer, then just a young, over-confident kid who was on his way to brilliance. I kept wondering when Merrick was going to spring the trap that would make me his prisoner, forcing me to now obey all of his suggestions. Our first contretemps came at the beginning of April. I was in Merrick's office going over production plans when he said to me that the rehearsal date would be July 15. I looked up at him. "July fifteenth? I can't. I'm spending the summer with my family in the Hamptons. I *always* spend the summer with my family."

He said, "Not this summer. July fifteenth is the date we start."

I said, "David, there are only so many summers we have in our lives. They're not infinite. Any one you lose cannot be restored. Let's start right after Labor Day in September."

His mustache turned to steel fibers, and I saw for the first time the tiger under the homburg. "Then I call off the show. That's not an idle threat. July fifteenth or no show."

I said, "Well, I guess there's no show. I'm sorry. Good-bye, David." I walked out of his office, took the small elevator down, and started to walk up Forty-fourth Street.

Suddenly I heard this voice behind me. I turned and saw Merrick standing on the street outside his office. "All right, you son of a bitch. September 4. And I hope you have a lousy summer." He stalked back into the building.

I really didn't want to give up the show, but not as much as I didn't want to give up the summer. The truth was, I had a wonderful summer, and starting September 4, I worked my ass off for David.

Two weeks into rehearsal, I called Merrick with a tinge of panic in my voice. Jerry Orbach, the actor we had hired to play Chuck, the beset young executive with the apartment-for-hire, suddenly seemed wrong to me. He seemed sullen, dark, not really likable. Merrick, who had trusted me so far, had not seen a run-through as yet, but took my word and asked if I wanted to replace Orbach. I said I think we might have to, and asked David to track down another actor I liked and have him come in for a reading. The actor was then in Hong Kong on vacation, and it took Merrick six phone calls to reach him. The actor said he would cut a few days off his vacation if we were serious about him for the part. The next day Merrick came with his right- and left-hand men and watched the run-through. Miraculously, Jerry Orbach had changed overnight. Maybe it was Merrick's presence, but I think it was just due to the way some actors need some time before they break through a part. He went from sullen to charming, from grim to delightful, from unlikable to winning—in short, he was terrific. I suddenly couldn't imagine anyone ever playing this part but Jerry.

After the run-through, Merrick looked at me curiously. "What's wrong with him? I think he's sensational."

I said, "So do I. I don't know what gave you the impression I didn't like him."

Jerry Orbach went on to get a Best Musical Actor Tony nomination, and the show was a hit, running three years on Broadway and another two on the road. On opening night, Merrick sent me a small gift. I unwrapped it and found a framed telephone bill with a huge charge for the six phone calls to Hong Kong.

Merrick had been through a couple of marriages with expensive and hostile repercussions. When the show premiered the following year in London, the news spread that he had remarried. He walked into the theater on opening night with a lovely young woman on his arm, and I crossed to congratulate him. He said, "Neil, I'd like you to meet the future ex–Mrs. Merrick."

THERE ARE DANGERS in being out of town with a play. They don't, by a long shot, however, compare to the dangers of being out of town with a musical. After six weeks of rehearsals in New York, forty strangers have gotten to know each other, and with another seven weeks or so on the road, the strangers have become friends. Many times, more than friends. When you work with a choreographer like Bob Fosse or Michael Bennett, you can count on at least twelve or fourteen women in the show who are young, talented, beautiful, and single. With the male chorus, while not entirely so, a large number of men would be gay. That leaves a disproportionate number of women who are alone.

But not for long. Being away from home, being with each other day and night, after a hard day's work a certain amount of fraternization takes place. It is inevitable. The temptations are enormous, and it takes a man with considerable restraint and the spiritual constitution of a Tibetan monk not to test the waters. We were in a pre-AIDS world where all you had to worry about was your conscience and your discretion.

During the out-of-town tryouts of *Promises*, I had my first taste of marijuana. I was probably the last one in my age group to do it. The problem was, I never smoked anything, and it made it impossible for me to inhale anything stronger than Vicks VapoRub. Unlike President Clinton, who said he never inhaled, I tried like hell, but couldn't get the smoke as far as my tonsils without coughing loud enough to wake up the entire hotel. I was so sensitive to the chemical properties of marijuana, however, that it didn't matter. All I had to do was half-swallow two puffs, hold it in my mouth for about six seconds, then blow it out without the smoke ever invading my nostrils, and in three minutes, the effect on me was the same as if I had gone into the jungles of South America and eaten a canoe full of hallucinatory mushrooms.

The world my clouded and disoriented mind entered was not that of nubile Martian women, or seeing giant tarantulas dancing to *The Nutcracker* as played by a band from Nashville. No, where my trips of fancy took me was to my youth. I was walking in slow motion with my mother through an open-air food market in the Bronx. The aroma and smells of the fresh food in the stalls were so potent, they reached heavenly proportions. I tasted a giant chocolate cupcake—so real in my mind, so exquisite in my mouth, that I never wanted the effects of the drug to wear off. There I was, in reality sitting in someone's hotel room with six or seven members of the cast, all getting high, the girls dancing on the beds while the guys played imaginary bongos on the pillows, all looking like a rather mild version of Dante's vision of Hell. All during this, I was stoned, in a fanciful state of ecstasy from tasting imaginary pickles they used to sell in huge open barrels in the 1930s, washing it down with a humongous chocolate milk shake that never stopped coming, like the buckets of water in "The Sorcerer's Apprentice" segment from Disney's *Fantasia*.

Minutes slowed down to what seemed like hours, and the second hand on my watch seemed to move ahead whenever it felt like it. Gradually the revelers started to pair off and leave for more private parties. I vaguely remember sitting on the floor, leaning against the wall with a glass of cheap white wine in my hand, except the wine was gone. But I kept sipping from the empty glass anyway, thinking I was enjoying it. There was one girl left in the room, whose name I couldn't remember even when I was unstoned. She lay on her stomach across the bed, looking down at me while she puffed on what was left of a joint, which she held by her long fingernails. Her legs were criss-crossed, with her toes waving lazy circles in the sky. She was telling me her life story, details of which she couldn't remember whether they happened to her or her sister. I was looking off into space, still babbling like an idiot: "Most people liked Oreos but I liked the other kind. The darker kind . . . What was the name of the darker kind? . . . Who could I call now to find out what the name of the darker kind was?"

She got off the bed, sat next to me on the floor, now inhaling her finger-nails, and said, "What other kind?"

"Of cookies."

"What cookies are you talking about?"

"I don't know. What cookies are *you* talking about?"

I completely forgot the subject as her head fell into my lap. When I left her room a few centuries later, I had become a statistic. The category was, "Married men who have been unfaithful at least once in their marriage." The polls today tell us it's at least 70 percent, which doesn't take into account that not everyone owns up to it. That's a staggering number, yet I believe it was higher in the 1960s, simply because AIDS was not a deterrent. Back then, if a good man was hard to find, a monogamous one would have taken Scotland Yard, the FBI, and Interpol at least two years to track down. Especially when the man in question had just hit forty years old or thereabouts.

To say that the escapade meant nothing to me is not only a cliché but a true statement. Yet on reflection, it meant more than nothing. It meant some sort of liberation, a breaking of the rules, a way to change the pattern of my behavior. Something was offered to me and I took it. Ask Adam, he knows. I was such a conformist and if my conscience was so restrained, so were other aspects of my behavior. I was not about to make a pastime of leaving every young woman I met lying naked and exhausted on a bed, while I jumped over ten-foot fences like Mr. Hyde, escaping the law. I loved Joan and I was not about to jeopardize our relationship, but I had to at least peek at the under-belly of life to escape my own naiveté.

I suddenly had a need to explore anything that seemed dangerous to me so that I knew the fear of walking a tightrope. I needed to open myself up, within reason, otherwise I'd be writing the stories of Beatrix Potter. I just wanted to open my mind to danger, and hoped I could stop trying to please everyone, including my audience, if I could. What affected me personally also affected my work, and although I would not be so pompous as to pretend that I did this for my art, it nonetheless came into play. Tell me that Tennessee Williams' or Arthur Miller's life didn't reflect in their work. One goes with the other, whether you intend it or not. I thought I could stretch to where I wanted to go but had never yet dared. Even Jimmy Carter told us he once lusted in his heart. The question is, did he neglect to tell us there was a hotel in downtown Atlanta called "The Heart"?

AT SOME POINT in my early forties, either my chromosomes changed or the virus that infects most men at my age struck, turning the inside of my head topsy-turvy. I imagined that every woman I passed on the street turned to look at me and smile. The sexual revolution had started, and I didn't know if I should enlist or just wait to be taken prisoner. As I said, a good many of my friends' marriages were breaking up, but that was the last thing I wanted. What I wanted was a leave of absence. If I used to get two- and three-week furloughs in the Air Force, why couldn't I get them in civilian life?

Every day in the papers or on television, you saw people dancing naked at Woodstock or some such place, and heard of others making love in an open field. When did things start to change so fast? I started out my first attempts with the age-old practice of carrying a girl's books home from school and graduated to a little necking in the second balcony of the local movie house. As already described, I was twenty-one before I made my pilgrimage to the Grim Hotel in lower Manhattan. Twenty-one was middle-aged at Woodstock. I married at twenty-six, not exactly a man of the world but still an idealistic youth looking for the perfect girl. And now, when I was forty, they were dancing naked in a giant orchard in upstate New York, and I was missing it.

I was caught in between my devotion to Joan and my need to seek out what I missed. Coward that I was, I would only go with Joan's permission. This was not my rational mind speaking. It was this chemical imbalance, not unlike malaria, which makes you hallucinatory. A man will blame everything except himself. But with the parade passing by so quickly, if I didn't hurry and join the clowns, I'd get there when the sanitation workers were cleaning up afterward.

This madness was not limited just to sexual experimentation. It went so far that one of my fantasies was to meet Joan at a party and ask her to marry me. Again. Which I would have done eagerly. So what did I want? Everything, I suppose. Yet I never met anyone who ever got everything and didn't eventually pay for what he got. There was, however, the one chance that I'd be the first. I decided, out of sheer lunacy, to ask Joan for my freedom . . . for a while. All women reading this now have my permission and blessing to say, "Who does this idiot think he is?" He was about two planets away from confusion, that's who.

I decided to take Joan to a restaurant and explain my situation without hurting her. (Make that three planets away.) Maybe my recent weird behavior had already given her a sense of what was coming. I had the awful feeling I was about to commit suicide and still I pressed on.

The night of the dinner, she was getting dressed in the bedroom while I, already dressed, sat in the den watching the passing traffic from the window, wondering how to go about this. At what point during the dinner should I spring the news? Too soon and it could get ugly. Too late and I might have missed my chance. I decided to go by my instincts, knowing that I'd sense the right moment when it came, and I would pounce on it. She came out of the bedroom looking beautiful. No surprise there. She *always* came out of the bedroom looking beautiful, but this time it was hard to take.

As we drove in the cab, I was unsettled by the particularly good mood she was in. She smiled at me, put her hand on top of mine, and whatever she was wearing, she smelled beyond perfect. Things were not shaping up well for me. We sat at a quiet little table in a restaurant she'd never been to. My luck, she loved it. I wanted to order a bottle of wine, but she decided to choose it. She rarely ever did that, but this was going to be her night. I felt little beads of perspiration forming on my nervous system. She looked at the menu and said, "Mmm, everything looks so good." Not to me, it didn't. I wasn't hungry. How could she think I could eat at a time like this? As she sipped her wine, she looked at me and said, "Are you all right? You seem awfully quiet."

"No, no. I'm fine."

Then she mentioned wanting to see a new play that had just opened and could we go next week? Next week? I was planning on being in Switzerland or Paris or anywhere next week. Just me and my freedom . . . I started to drink my second glass of wine when suddenly I sensed this was the moment. A minute more and it would be too late.

"Listen . . . can we . . . can we talk about something?"

A smile came over her face. Don't ask me why, it just did. "Sure. What's up?"

How could she say "What's up?" when I was about to broach a subject that required choosing words of the most delicate nature? She didn't seem to have a care or worry in her life, while I was fighting for mine.

"How do I start this? . . . I don't know . . . something's happened . . . To me, that is."

She sipped her wine casually, bit off a piece of her breadstick, and nodded calmly. "Go on. Something's happened to you . . . Are you going to tell me?"

"That's what I'm trying to do . . . I don't know, the world has changed, hasn't it? Everything seems so different. I feel I've changed. That somehow I'm different too. Have you noticed that?"

There was not a clue that she sensed danger at all. She was cooler than the fresh wine the waiter poured in her glass. She nodded. "Well, we're both a little different. But I think that's good. I think we're growing together. Don't you?"

Every time I took a step forward, she took two steps forward. I had nothing left to do but plunge in up to my neck.

"Yes, I do . . . but I feel . . . I feel that . . . that maybe something isn't right. Not with you, with me. I'm not myself anymore. I'm all screwed up. I'm somebody else and I don't know who that person is."

Not a change of expression on her face. She was, in fact, more relaxed now than before.

"Well, do you like this change or are you having trouble with it?"

"Trouble. I'm having trouble. Big trouble. And I don't think I can figure it out . . . I don't seem to be able to help myself . . . unless maybe if I was *by* myself."

Still no change of expression. If this were a chess game, she had all her pieces left and I had one broken pawn to move around the board.

"What do you mean 'by yourself'? A trip?"

"Yes. A trip. Well, no, not a trip . . . A parting, sort of . . . A separation . . . Not permanent, of course . . . but maybe going our own way for a while . . . Maybe me leaving home, I don't know."

She hardly blinked. The waiter put down our food and there was steam coming up off her pasta. But none from her. She had this game in hand. She nodded to me as if I just said, "Would you like to go to a movie after dinner?"

Was I getting through to her? I said, "Do you understand what I'm saying to you?"

"Yes. You want to separate. You want to leave. Isn't that what you're saying?"

I couldn't even speak. I just nodded. What was she doing? What was she thinking? Didn't she care? I never expected the next line. "When were you planning on leaving?"

"I wasn't *planning* on it. I haven't been sitting up at nights *planning*. It just came up. In the last few days. I thought it would be better if I just left."

"I see . . . So how soon would you be leaving?"

Where was she coming from? Was she pleased? Was she glad I was going? Was this Joan or just someone who looked like her? But I got what I wanted. I was out. I said it to her and I was out. With a little more bravado now, I spoke up.

"Well, there's no point in dragging it out . . . Tomorrow, I guess. I could pack my things and leave tomorrow. Does that seem reasonable?"

She put a little more ground pepper on her pasta. Can you imagine? "Sure, tomorrow seems fine to me."

That was it. That was the whole conversation. I was out of the marriage. It wasn't as hard as I thought it would be. The expression on her face hadn't changed. Everything suddenly became quiet. As quiet as I ever heard the earth since the day I was born on it. I needed a reaction from her or I'd go crazy.

"So what do you think?"

"About your leaving?"

"Yes. About my leaving?"

"Well, I think if that's what it'll take to make you happy, then I think you should do it."

It was the most depressing minute of my entire life. And besides that, I'd miss her. God, would I miss her. The next words I said were barely audible.

"Never mind."

"What? I didn't hear you."

"I said 'never mind.' I don't want to leave. I don't know what the hell I was talking about. I don't want to go."

"I know."

"How did you know?"

She gave a little shrug, and looked straight into my eyes. "Because I know you."

It was over. Ended. The thought of leaving was out of my mind forever. I asked for my freedom, she gave it to me, and that was all the time experiencing freedom I needed. Five, six minutes, seven tops. My chromosomes snapped back in order. I must have been truly crazy ever to bring it up.

She was smarter than me. She was better than me. She was better than anyone. My fever broke. My pulse was normal. The crisis had passed. I was going to live to play the piano again. She never, ever mentioned the conversation after that night, and I sure as hell was never going to bring it up.

We walked home. We did the usual things like brush our teeth, wash our faces, get into our pajamas, and finally into bed. All in all, it was a very nice evening together.

THE ESSENCE OF that experience led to the next play I wrote, *Last of the Red Hot Lovers*. If I were to mention to people that this incident led to the writing of this play, they'd say, "Oh. So it's autobiographical." No, it is not autobiographical. An incident happens to you and it gives your imagination a starting point. But you turn it into someone else's experience, hoping that it touches a nerve of identification in other people so that it may connect to something in their own lives.

The play was about the owner of a fish restaurant who attempted to have brief affairs with three different women, none of them consummated because he was looking for something that he could always remember, a sweet brief encounter. The women were all distraught, angry, or neurotic. He was so frightened about being seen by someone, his would-be affairs took place in his mother's apartment while she was at the hospital all day doing charity work. Each time one of the women left, with nothing having happened, he would wash the glasses they used for drinks and puff up the cushions on the sofa. This was a man who married his high school sweetheart when he was eighteen. "Never again," he says at the end of the play. "I will never *ever* do that again."

This was the basic synopsis of the play, treated as a comedy. I was writing about a time in America, after the flower children, after the hippies, when young people all over this country were trying to find their own expression in life. They had already changed their music, their way of dressing, their politics, their language, and their hoped-for independence. The previous generation, from thirty-five to forty-five, maybe for the first time were not trying to emulate their elders, but took their signals now from their juniors. They found out that with the passage of time the style didn't fit their measurements, and while some benefited from it, more were unsuccessful and still more were ludicrous. There was no one more ludicrous than Barney Cashman, my idealistic owner of the fish restaurant. His endeavors woke him up to reality, and he realized it wasn't worth the effort.

I had seen a play called *Next*, written by Terrence McNally, in an off-Broadway theater. *Next* was both poignant and hilarious, and it starred a balding, rotund actor/comedian named James Coco. Jimmy was one of the funniest men I ever met, on- or offstage. I went backstage immediately after the curtain to introduce myself and congratulate him. The next day I sent him the script of *Last of the Red Hot Lovers* and said, "Read it. I would love you to do it on Broadway next season." He called me the next morning and said, "I'll do it. If I get paid, that'll be nice too, but it isn't necessary."

Robert Moore was my director for the second time in a row. During the previews in New Haven, the play was looking good but there were some parts that Moore felt needed fixing. He, however, was hesitant in telling me. He took Joan out for coffee and told her about his concerns, but said he didn't know how to approach me about the changes. She said, "Just tell him. He *wants* to know. He'll be the first one to want to rewrite it." Bob did talk to me about it the next day and I rewrote it that night. I was beginning to find that success breeds intimidation. It happened with most, but not all, of the directors I eventually worked with and a great many actors. They thought since I had many hits, I must know what I'm doing, and who were they to tell me they felt some things were wrong?

This phenomenon went on throughout my career. Film directors especially were afraid to work with me, for fear I would want to intrude on their territory. I never wanted to direct, especially since the time I sat behind Mike Nichols wondering what I could learn from him about directing. When I found out it was a gift that I didn't have, I stopped thinking about it. I've had many chances and many offers but never accepted any. First of all, I didn't like the hours and I didn't have the patience. Many times during rehearsals of a play, I would sometimes stop a scene that wasn't working, not because it wasn't directed or acted well, but because the words were all wrong. I was lucky to have the facility to write quickly, and I would ask the director to go on to another scene while I retreated to a little office or even to a chair outside the rehearsal room and rewrote the scene, bringing it back an hour later.

With a play, most directors would prefer to be left alone with the actors. Later in my career, when I started to work with director Jerry Zaks on *Laughter on the 23rd Floor*, he was nervous that I would be jumping up and down screaming "That's not the way I wanted it." He asked, after the first two days of reading the play, if I could leave for about ten days while he worked alone with the actors. I assumed he must have worked with a lot of playwrights who didn't do much rewriting. I told him, "Jerry, if I go away for ten days, I will never see what's wrong with what I did. What's not working with the play. In those first two weeks, I can reshape the play, rewrite what's wrong, and then turn it over to you." Reluctantly he agreed. Sure enough, in the first two weeks, I did an enormous amount of rewriting. When I felt it was right, I went back home to California for a week. On the second day I was gone, Jerry called and said, "When are you coming back? I miss you." When I did come back, I saw that Jerry had done wonderful work. Actors generally seem to get nervous when the author is around while they're rehearsing. They're afraid he's making judgments about their floundering around, not yet having discovered how to get into the part. I almost *never* watch the actors in the first few weeks. I am only listening to what I wrote.

And the more successful I became, the more people felt intimidated and nervous with me around. On the other hand, if I left because of their fears, I would feel excluded, not being able to share in the fun and the agony of putting on a play. I was made a father figure, the principal of the school. It shut me off from the camaraderie that I felt in the beginning of my career.

When we were working on the musical of *Sweet Charity*, Bob Fosse had to leave for one morning. He asked me to take over the directing of two scenes. I was scared stiff. I knew what I wanted, but I never knew how to express it to the actors. Directors have a special language they share with actors, rarely telling them exactly what to do but giving them other ways to approach the role and letting them discover it for themselves. I would be much more direct and consequently not a good director. Still, it was unsettling for both me and the actors to be there while they worked. I'd see them glancing at me from the corner of their eye, wondering what I was thinking, imagining the worst. I had to be careful not to look as though I were scowling or bored. I would try to sit out of their range of vision so they wouldn't see my expressions. That didn't work because they felt now I was spying on them. I have heard that I sometimes had the reputation of being cold and distant. My own shyness is responsible for that impression, and it bothered me. I never really wanted authority the way someone like Mike Nichols thrives on it. When I was in the Air Force, the furthest I got was corporal. When I was up for sergeant, I asked not to get it. I didn't want the responsibility of telling the other soldiers, my friends, what they should be doing.

That's why writing is so pleasurable to me. I'm alone in the room without anyone else to deal with except myself, the paper, and the typewriter. But the reputation of being a loner, an observer, which is intimidating to others just by definition, still clung to me. I was once at a party in California and Shirley MacLaine was there. After dinner, everyone wanted her to conduct one of her meditation sessions, which I heard were wonderful. She was very hesitant at first, but soon gave in. About ten of us sat in a circle on the floor, eyes closed, and Shirley talked in a soft, comforting voice about where she wanted us to go in our thoughts. She gave us images to think of, and the room became totally still except for her words and our quiet breathing. This took about an hour. I was totally transported to places and thoughts from my past, and at one time, tears came into my eyes. When it was over, Shirley asked everyone, if they so desired, to talk about where their thoughts took them. Everyone was eager to tell about his or her mystical and often soothing journey. Before she got to me, someone asked Shirley where her thoughts went. She seemed embarrassed and said she wasn't able to do it for herself, because she thought that Neil must be watching this and thinking what a crackpot she must be. I told her it was the exact opposite because I had been very affected by her meditation. But there was the intimidation thing again. I think it comes to many writers; people are fearful that we're just observers and never participants. I actually felt badly about her reaction. I felt left out of the group. I often do with people who don't know me very well.

Last of the Red Hot Lovers was a hit from the day we opened in New Haven. Linda Lavin was extraordinary, but on the first preview she did something that she may not have been conscious of, something she thought her character would do (she's that kind of an actress), but it caused Jimmy Coco to practically kill her onstage. In the first act, he has asked her to come to his apartment (actually his mother's) in his first attempt in his life at an extramarital affair. She is all business. She is a disillusioned woman, married to a drunk; all she wants is sex and she wants it now. Jimmy, however, is looking for romance. Finally he starts to tell her why he asked her to come there. It's a long, sometimes funny and sometimes poignant speech about how he never had anything happen to him—not a broken bone, not a fever over 103—that his life was a monotony of opening his fish restaurant each morning, feeling the new fish and oysters, shrimps, and clams. He wears cologne on his fingers and keeps smelling them during this long confession. Linda picked up a magazine and thumbed through the pages to show her boredom during his speech. Naturally, the audience's attention shifted to her, while Jimmy went babbling on. He suddenly screamed at her, in character but using his own words. "Put that goddamn magazine down. You pay attention to me when I'm talking because I deserve it." He threw the magazine against the wall. I don't think the audience ever thought it was not written into the play, it was all done so realistically. Linda never did it again. I was momentarily upset with her but held no grudges. I'd gladly work with her again. In fact, her performance as my mother in *Broadway Bound* was one of the most stunning pieces of acting I've ever seen. The Tony committee agreed with me when they awarded her Best Actress in a Play.

Red Hot Lovers didn't do so badly either when the Tony nominations came out. If memory serves me correctly, Jimmy got one, Linda got one, and I got one. Possibly Robert Moore as well. There was a lot of tough competition that year, but it seemed a cinch that Jimmy Coco had a Tony locked up. Everyone on Broadway was saying the same thing. On the night of the Tony Awards, as Jimmy entered the theater, everyone patted him on the back and said, "Don't even think about it. You're a cinch." Jimmy smiled modestly but it was obvious he thought so too. During the ceremonies, the nominees always sit in the aisle seats to facilitate their getting up to the stage quickly. Jimmy sat three rows in front of me, on the opposite aisle, chewing gum nervously to keep from biting his nails. As they came to his category, they mentioned the five nominees, then the host opened the envelope and said, ". . . and the winner is . . ." I looked at Jimmy, who took the gum out of his mouth and rose about an inch in his seat. "Fritz Weaver," the host announced, and without missing a beat, Jimmy put the gum back in his mouth, sat down quickly, and started chewing and applauding boisterously. It was one of the most poignant but funny things I'd ever seen.

At the party later on, Jimmy, with three drinks under his wide belt, started tearing down the Tony committee, the voters, Fritz Weaver, and the fact that he bought six seats for his family, who came from New Jersey and sat in the balcony. His rancor was hilarious and his wit was venomously funny. Eventually, I did two more plays with Jimmy, a television special, and three movies. In fact, the next play I wrote had a character who was fashioned after Jimmy. He got all the best lines in the play because I thought they were what Jimmy would have said anyway. He was diagnosed years later as having throat cancer. He threw every cigarette he had in the world in the wastebasket and swore he would never touch another one if he could beat the cancer. Soon after, he found the cancer diagnosis was wrong. He immediately went back to cigarettes and died a few weeks later from a heart attack. I miss him as much as anyone I ever met.

IT WAS A GREAT TIME in our lives. I was one of the lucky few in the world who actually liked what he did for a living, and I was able to make my own hours. From the time I was twenty and working in television, I was able to take off every summer for myself and eventually with my family. On television, in those days, we did thirty-nine shows a year and then were off for twelve weeks. When I started writing plays, Joan and I, and eventually the girls, were able to spend the summers wherever we wanted, even though I would set aside a few hours a day to work on a play. That's why I was so adamant with David Merrick about not missing a summer. This system didn't work in California, though, because it's *always* summer there; consequently I never knew when it was vacation time. That's why I wrote more during my years in California than I ever did in New York.

Growing up as a boy in New York, summers were anathema to me, since all my friends went *somewhere* between July and August. My father couldn't afford to send me anywhere, except for that forty-dollar holiday in Far Rockaway. I think that's when I began to become a loner. On a July morning, I'd have breakfast, be on the street by eight o'clock, and walk the streets of Manhattan, from top to bottom and from river to river. I began to know every street in my lonely kingdom, and the ones I didn't know, I found by playing Explorer. When I discovered a new street, I would claim it in the name of the United States of America and would christen the street by announcing its name, "Eighteenth Street and Ninth Avenue." I loved to walk the docks on the Hudson River and watch the huge, glamorous passenger liners being moored in: the *Normandy*, the *United States*, the *Queen Mary*, and the *Bremen*. I watched with envy as the large steamer trunks were unloaded at the pier with picturesque stickers plastered all over them with the names of places they had visited: Cairo, Istanbul, Tokyo, Singapore, St. Petersburg. These liners became my imaginary private fleet and the naval ships that steamed up the Hudson heading for repairs in drydock became my private armada. With a child's imagination, you can own half the world.

The summers with Joan, Ellen, and Nancy in East Hampton, however, surpassed what my imagination could provide. The girls still say to this day that it was the best time of their lives. Life was perfect for us. I used the early morning hours to write, sitting in an enclosed porch in a house we bought on Lee Avenue in East Hampton. The rest of the day was tennis or the beach, or time with the girls.

After *Red Hot Lovers* opened, our family privacy was invaded for the first time, causing some uneasiness in our lives. *Newsweek* called and said they wanted to do a cover story on me. When I told Joan of this, she made it clear she didn't want any pictures of her or the girls in the magazine. She wanted our personal life to be separate and apart from my career.

After doing the long interviews with the *Newsweek* writers, a date was set for the photographers to come to our house in the city and take the cover shot and the pictures of me at work at my desk. I advised them that my wife and children were not to be included in any of the shots. They looked puzzled but postponed dealing with that one until later. Like many people, I hate being photographed, especially sitting for a posed shot. I feel like an actor playing out a role I'm not suited for. I also hate about 90 percent of the pictures ever taken of me, posed or not. I know and recognize the man I see in the mirror, but the stranger in the photo is an imposter. Can you imagine standing in front of a mirror and smiling your best smile for almost an hour? If someone saw you doing that, they would cart you off to the Asylum for the Vain.

The cover photo was to be me with a huge smile on my face, surrounded by the masks of Comedy and Tragedy. I would sooner pose for Tragedy, although at the time Edward Albee had that photographic market cornered. Another problem was that I hated my smile. I always thought I looked like the Joker in the Batman comic books. In an effort not to smile that silly smile for photographers, I put on another affectation of biting my lower lip in a half grin. At least I was not committing myself to the phoniness of smiling because it was supposed to represent a comedy writer. As if I went around all day laughing at the things I was thinking.

This business of being photographed was even a bigger problem for Joan, even in family photos. Every time I aimed a camera at her she put a hand up in front of the lens or else scowled angrily, looking like a young novelist being photographed for the flyleaf of her new book, *The Destruction of the Human Race*. Even Nancy, as she got older, was intimidated by the camera, and during her smoking period in college I have photographs of her with Joan's angry scowl, looking like Italy's new film director on the set of her latest film, *The Volcano Within*. Ellen, although less photophobic, was hard to pin down. She usually dodged the camera, but was usually seen laughing as she hid her face. What was it we all wished to hide?

The cover photo took forever to light, and forever and a day to shoot. They must have taken a hundred head shots of me with that forced smile on my face, my cheeks looking like they were tied back around my ears, and my lips stretched to the splitting point. Unfortunately the camera doesn't lie, and my face couldn't pass the polygraph test. Finally, they had an inspiration. The photographer had his assistant pick up little Nancy, put her on his shoulders behind the camera, and made her do her best to make me laugh. I could never resist smiling at Nancy, and they got the real thing in two shots. On the cover of the magazine it said, "Last of the Red Hot Playwrights."

As the photographers were getting ready to leave, Joan walked into the house, hoping they'd be gone by then. They tried to coax a picture out of her and at first she politely demurred. They were insistent, however, and while trying to be cheerful about it they nevertheless started to aim their camera at her. She yelled at them, pushed them aside, and ran up the steps to our bedroom. The photographer couldn't understand why she didn't want to be photographed with her now-famous husband, and he tried to get me to talk her into it. I stood halfway up the staircase saying, "Look. She doesn't want to be photographed. The answer is no. I think we're finished for today." Just then Ellen walked in, and he attempted to get her picture, but I knew Joan was dead against it, so I stood there and screamed at him, pointing my hand at the door. "Come on! That's enough. I want you out of here and that's that!" In that instant he snapped my picture, my mouth wide open in anger, looking much like Senator Joseph McCarthy accusing a witness of being a communist. That was the one they used. Of the hundred or so pictures they took of me at my desk working or staring out the window, deep in thought, the picture they used in the magazine was of this maniacal playwright in his most tempestuous mood. Although the piece was complimentary, I suddenly became the Mad Playwright with the invisible family. Ahh, the press.

THE LOSERS

17

I WANTED TO write a play about losers. Not the people who were born to poverty, or to illness, or to deformities that presented obstacles they could never overcome, genetic time bombs that would one day explode no matter how much one tried to prevent it. Nor those people unfortunate enough to be sleeping in the wrong house during an earthquake, or who boarded the wrong plane when a mechanical malfunction took place. I mean the losers who have complete control over their own destiny, but who self-destruct because something moves them to make the wrong choices time and time again. Like saying yes when they should have said no, or no when they should have said yes. The ones whose instinctual compass tells them to go one way, but who choose to go the other, always the wrong way.

The Gingerbread Lady was the darkest play I had attempted so far, and I wrote about people or composites of people I knew well. It included an actress who drank too much, which kept her career and relationships from ever becoming fulfilling. A gay actor who thought his life was a failure, not because he was gay but because he chose a profession, that of an actor, for which he had too little talent and too much yearning to be acclaimed. A beautiful woman who invested her entire life in trying to remain beautiful instead of valuing the person who lived beneath the features. As frequently happens with people like that, they seek each other out, becoming close and indispensable to each other. If one stumbles, there are always the other two to pick him or her up, until inevitably the others stumble themselves.

Their own little protected world becomes the real world for them, the safe world, and they can never reach out to embrace or be embraced by others who would care for them. The specific people I chose to make up this forlorn trio started out being based on people I knew but not so well that they would be the exact prototypes for these characters. They had just enough of some of these traits for me to use as a starting point. Then they evolved into full-blown characters through my imagination and perceptions of other people I knew who fell into the same category of being dependent on those who also feed on dependency. Rembrandt sometimes used a beggar to pose for him, put a jeweled turban on his head, and painted him as a prince. The painting had a greater truth to it than if he had used a real prince to pose. The three people I chose to write about, oddly or not, were terribly funny people. Funny in the most self-deprecating way. They dished everyone else in the world but mostly took dead aim on themselves. They were the target of their own jokes and knew how to hit the bull's-eye every time out.

When I gave the finished play to Saint Subber, he called me immediately after reading it. He wouldn't say what he thought. He just asked me to walk the two blocks from where I lived to where he lived as soon as possible. He looked shaken when he opened the door. We sat down in his small study; he was still holding the script in his hand. He took his time before he spoke.

"It's hard for me to say what's on my mind, because I don't want to say the wrong thing. My hand is still shaking, if you want to know. I don't know if it's a great play or even a good play. As I read it, I never thought about what people might think of it. All I know is that it's the bravest play you've ever written. Brave because the critics might destroy you. You've gone out on a limb this time, and you have no hilarious scenes to bail you out. Not to say that it isn't funny. It's *very* funny. But it's the most painful funny I ever read. It may confuse audiences because they won't know if it's meant to be funny and maybe they just won't get the joke. I know these people like I know the back of my hand. In fact part of my own hand is right in there with them. But I'll make you a promise. I will produce this play and go all the way to the wire with it, right through the out-of-town tryout and the opening in New York. But on one condition. You must not change one word of this play. Not a comma, not a period. If you do, I'll walk away from it. Make me that promise and if we fail, we'll fail together. If it succeeds, it will be your gift to me."

I was touched and moved by his words. I believed he meant and would do everything he said. He then told me he had already called Mike Nichols, and although Mike was booked up with films for the next two years, he wanted him to read it anyway. He wanted to know if Mike felt the same way about the play that he did.

Mike called me the next night. He said it was true that he wasn't available, but he told me, "You *must* do this play." He recommended that Bob Moore might be the best one to direct it. I asked him, "Who do you think I should ask to play Evy?"

Evy Meara was the leading part, an actress who drinks to excess, so inept at controlling her own life, she gives her young daughter to her ex-husband to raise. One had to find an actress so empathetic that the audience could still care for her even though she keeps derailing her life and failing the people who need her. "There's only one actress," he said. "You must send it to Maureen."

I said, "God, I know this isn't really Maureen's life, but there's parts of Evy that she might see in herself, in her past. I don't want to hurt her. This is not really Maureen. It's ten, twenty different actresses I've met over the years who could be Evy. Some people might even think it's Judy Garland."

"Send it to Maureen," were his final words. With more than great trepidation, I sent it to Maureen by messenger and waited for the verdict. If I was guilty, I would pay the price of her friendship, which I would never want to lose because I genuinely loved her. With all the trials and tribulations in Maureen's life, she never short-changed an audience. And she always seemed to take roles that were enormously demanding, making her go to the emotional mat eight times a week. I never knew of anyone who knew her well who had an unkind word to say about her. She was beloved.

The next night my phone rang. I sensed it was she and was afraid to pick it up. I finally said "Hello," and there were a few seconds before she said anything . . . and then this: "You bastard! . . . You no-good dirty bastard! . . . When do we go into rehearsal?"

AFTER THE FINAL dress rehearsal of *The Gingerbread Lady* in New Haven, Saint Subber came up to me, obviously moved by what he had just seen. "Not a word, not a comma, not a period. You change nothing. That's our bargain," and he walked back to his hotel.

The audience filed in for our first preview the following night. There was a buzz of anticipation heard in the theater lobby like the drone of bees. I would have to brace myself not to expect too much from this audience, who were no doubt expecting another comedy. After all, the last time I did a play with Maureen Stapleton was the highly successful *Plaza Suite*. The young ushers and usherettes, all no older than high school students, trying to make an extra five or ten dollars for the night, were looking forward to watching the play themselves from the back of the house. They were standing in my territory since I was too nervous to sit anywhere. The houselights dimmed and the curtain went up on Evy Meara's seedy apartment. Already there before her was Jimmy, the actor, and her friend Toby, so beautiful, she had to keep checking herself in the mirror lest a flaw—however minor—might appear. They are there with gifts, awaiting Evy's return from a six-week stay in a Connecticut sanitarium, recovering from alcohol addiction. The door finally opens and in comes Evy with her cheap suitcase and an armful of books and magazines. Then she puts them down, opens her old mink coat, a relic from better days, to reveal her new slimmed-down body, smiles, and says, "All right, say it. I'm fucking gorgeous, right?"

You could actually hear the gasp from the audience at the words "fucking gorgeous." You could see the young high school ushers blush even in the darkened theater, and one boy almost popped open his bow tie. Remember, this was still 1970, and although the use of four-letter words was no longer news in films or in off-Broadway plays, where you could occasionally see naked bodies, the phrase—coming from Neil Simon and an expected family play—took their collective breath away. Although not far from New York, this was still staid New England, the site of Yale University, and not that far from Boston, where the words "goddamn" and "Christ" were still frowned upon, and erased on demand, by the city fathers. Having gotten through the first shock, the audience soon settled back and began to laugh, and appeared to be enjoying this new but surprising play from Mr. Comedy.

I immediately went backstage during the intermission to tell Maureen I thought the play was going very well. At the sight of me, she pointed an angry finger in my face and said, "That's the last time I say 'fucking' in this fucking theater. Did you hear the audience gasp? I almost got sucked off the stage." I laughed and said, "I know. The line is out. I'll use it in my next play when New England catches up to America."

In the subsequent performances, without the obscenity, the audience took to her character right away, and the removal of that word got us off the mark in a much better fashion. The reviews after the opening were guarded, but more on the positive side. The critics thought all three stars were excellent (Michael Lombard played Jimmy and Betsy von Furstenberg played Toby) and congratulated me on daring to go in a new direction. People came up to me in restaurants on subsequent nights and said it wasn't what they expected but they still enjoyed it very much. After their comments, if Saint was at the table with me he would still whisper, "Not a word, not a comma, not a period." Actually I didn't hold to my promise completely because I tinkered with some lines, rewrote some, cut some, but nothing that lost the essence of the play. Saint actually never noticed that I made any changes.

Boston, ten days later. We left New Haven, cheered by their approval, but we didn't fool ourselves into thinking we were coming in with an absolute hit. Respectability and a decent run were all we were hoping for. The reaction of the audience in Boston on opening night was a mystery to me. They seemed receptive and entertained, but there was no clear and obvious indication of how they truly felt. As to the reviews, we expected them to go either way; more than likely they would be mixed.

There was a very small opening-night party at a Chinese-Hawaiian restaurant, the Tiki Hut. A hut was about the size of it, and it was on the dark side with candles in glass globes providing most of the atmosphere. There couldn't have been more than twenty of us gathered there, mostly the cast, the crew, and a small contingent of friends and spouses. Joan stuck very close to me. She was very proud of the play. An hour into egg rolls, dim sum, and rum drinks with paper umbrellas floating in them, the phone rang. We knew it had to be Saint, who was down at the publicist's office getting the reviews. The stage manager answered it, then turned and said, "Neil? Saint, for you."

As I started to get up, Maureen reached across the table, grabbed me by the tie, and pulled my face to hers. "I don't care what the fucking reviews are. If you close this play, I will personally murder you in your sleep." Closing the play was the very last thing I would think of. I knew we were going into New York. I crossed to the phone booth and closed the door, but all eyes in the Tiki Hut were on me.

Solemnly, Saint said, "They're not good."

"How many aren't good?" I asked.

"All of them," he said in a weary voice.

"Really? I'm surprised. Well, I guess I've got some work to do up here."

"No," he said. "I'm going to close it in Boston."

"Close it? *Close it??*" I couldn't believe my ears. "What happened to 'Don't change a word, a comma, a period'?"

"If we bring it into New York," he said, "they'll crucify you. I don't want that to happen to you. I don't know if you'd be able to handle it."

I stood in the booth with the phone in my hand, but had nothing else to say. I think I stayed because I didn't want to go out and tell Maureen and Joan and the rest that we were closing it. I decided to say as little as possible. When I came out, I went back to my table as they all gathered around me. "The reviews weren't very good. Saint seems discouraged but he didn't read them to me. Maybe we'll be okay."

Maureen this time grabbed me by the lapel of my jacket. "Fuck the newspapers and fuck Saint Subber. You are bringing this play to New York. I put too much into it and so did you. So help me God, if you dump us, I will stab your throat at breakfast." I gave her a kiss but it wasn't one of assurance. It was one of love.

Joan and I soon left for our hotel, since she had to catch an early plane back to New York in the morning to attend a meeting at Ellen's school. In the cab she said to me, "What are you going to do?"

"I don't know. I'll have to read the papers myself. Maybe they're more encouraging than Saint realizes."

She woke up at seven in the morning and quietly got dressed, and I gave her a mid-sleep kiss good-bye. She whispered "I'll call you in the afternoon."

After she left, I knew I couldn't go back to sleep. I went down and got the papers, spread them out before me on the restaurant's breakfast table, and began to read them. They did throw a few crumbs and a few huzzahs for the acting ensemble, but all in all, this play was all but dead. I called Saint and said, "I guess you're right. I hate you for breaking your promise to me, and I know I can stand up to whatever the critics say about me. But I don't think we can beat the inevitable. Please don't tell the cast. I can't face Maureen with that news. I'll call her from New York. I'm going home today on the noon plane. I'm not hurt by this. I'm just sorry."

At eleven o'clock I was at Boston's Logan Airport waiting for the noon shuttle to New York. I looked over the newspaper racks for a magazine to get me through the hour flight, but I spied the *Christian Science Monitor*. It was the one paper I hadn't read. I bought it and took it back to my seat. Roderick Nordell, the critic, wrote a review which prompted me to quote the scriptures, "What God giveth, God taketh away." For example, his opening sentence: "Imagine a superbly acted Neil Simon comedy superimposed on a stereotype Tennessee Williams tragedy. Somewhere in the realm lies Mr. Simon's new play, *The Gingerbread Lady*, and the wonder is not that it sometimes works well but that it works at all." Then, he continues further down: "Mr. Simon has gone from intimations of mortality in the first act of *Plaza Suite* and the last act of *Last of the Red Hot Lovers* to a tragic laughter of his own. Various critics have wanted him to try something serious, as if successful comedies were not achievement enough . . . And now he shows that he can confront a darker side though he does not yet seem at home there." In the following sentence, we see how Mr. Nordell felt about the use of street language, taking into account this was 1970 and this was the *Christian Science Monitor:* "For, even though Mr. Simon is now for the first time falling more than slightly into line with the exploitation of indecencies common to today's stage, he still implies a decent point of view." In that regard, where would David Mamet and Tony Kushner stand in Mr. Nordell's favor, if he were still reviewing in the mid-1990s? His final sentence in his review was this: "Weaving the serious and the comic together remains a freshly impressive evidence of Mr. Simon's craft, but the warp is not up to the woof and the fabric falls apart."

As I read it, I pictured Mr. Nordell holding up a daisy, pulling out petals, and saying, "I love him, I love him not, I love him, I love him not." I thought this was a well-intentioned review and that Mr. Nordell was trying to tell me something, partly about playwriting and partly about weaving. He admitted that I was very funny, and he urged me to weave the serious and the comic more skillfully, but to do that, I would have to get my warp up to my woof first. This meant that I would have to do research with some folkcrafts experts to first tell me which was the warp and which was the woof. I did agree, however, that in that first draft as seen by the Boston audiences, I had not succeeded in joining the serious and the comic without the seams clearly showing. I thought it was a constructive review and an honest one, and like Elliot Norton before him, here was another Boston critic not anxious to pounce on my faults but to prod me to further examine my attributes. I was encouraged by this review and was open to Mr. Nordell's opinions, as I would be if a professor at Harvard had returned my theatrical thesis giving me the benefit of his wisdom and compassion, not for a beginning writer, but for a professional writer who was looking for a new beginning. There was an addendum to Mr. Nordell's piece, in parentheses. ("As this went to press, word came out that *The Gingerbread Lady* would be suspended for a major rewrite after the Boston engagement.")

As I reread that statement, I said to myself, why wait to do the work *after* the Boston engagement? We still had four weeks to go there and I was quite able and ready to put those four weeks to good use. It was as if I heard the battle cry and call to arms, "Man the gates and stand your guard. We shall regroup and then charge the enemy." Thank goodness I had seen enough Cecil B. DeMille and John Wayne pictures to know when to put up a fight. I would spend the next four weeks rewriting and have Bob Moore and the cast ready to go into action. If anyone deserved that opportunity, it was Maureen, and if I was to give my all it wouldn't be for king and country, it would be for a great actress who threatened to kill me if I didn't. I called Saint. He wasn't in. I called the stage manager. I told him to disregard whatever Saint said about closing after Boston. We were staying and we were going to work.

I canceled my plane reservation and booked a seat on the train back to New York for that afternoon. If I had four hours alone on a train (I always loved trains anyway), I could start to think about what the rewrites would be. I told the stage manager I would be at home in New York rewriting as much as I could, and I would send each day's pages up by Special Delivery. (Where was fax when you needed them to invent it?) I hung up exhilarated. I suddenly had a new burst of energy. I couldn't wait to start.

Though Saint Subber may have meant well, he was wrong to say, "Don't change a thing." That's why Boston was invented.

I retrieved my bags from the plane and rushed over to the train station. There was something childishly exciting about rushing from airport to train station, in a desperate effort to save a burning play. I called Joan and told her I was coming home and to put dinner on my desk upstairs. I would be writing and eating at the same time every night for the next few weeks. The four hours on the train from Boston to New York seemed to breeze by in minutes. I not only outlined what scenes I wanted to redo, but I wrote ten new pages in such swift longhand that it took me four hours at home to decipher what I wrote, given the bumpy tracks that had battled me all the way.

All in all, over the three-week period, I think I changed at least 40 percent of the play. I filled in more details in the background of the characters, giving the audience more insight into them, giving them more humor, not to lighten the play so much as to give more weight and impact in the dramatic scenes. The audiences in Boston were slowly becoming more receptive and business was picking up. We weren't fooling ourselves into thinking that I had rewritten it into a hit, but we had come a long way from "Not a word, not a comma, not a period."

Maureen Stapleton took every change that Bob Moore and I had given her. She was giving her all for a play she believed in. I was working to test myself, to see if I could meet the challenge I set forth on that day I read the review in the *Christian Science Monitor*.

On top of whatever troubles a play normally has out of town, I increased them by allowing a featured writer for *Life* magazine to cover the journey of the play, from rehearsals in New York, through New Haven, Boston, and finally to the opening night on Broadway. Our public relations people advised us of the enormous coverage we'd be getting in a national magazine, publicity you couldn't possibly buy. Sometimes it's better to pay for things. We lost all sense of privacy. It was as foolhardy as allowing a reporter to go on your honeymoon and providing him with a cot and a camera in your bedroom. In every private conversation I had with Bob Moore, I would suddenly look up and see this reporter with his head leaning in between ours, with a pencil and notebook, scribbling down all of our comments. We didn't want to be overly rude to him for fear he'd take umbrage at our behavior and tilt the piece he would eventually write as a personal vendetta against us for not fulfilling our part of the agreement. Eventually, I made a revised deal with him. He could sit in the theater and watch rehearsals, listen to all notes given to the actors in an open discussion, but he would be forbidden to listen to or be privy to any private discussions between me, the director, and the cast. In return, I agreed to walk home or to my hotel with him at the end of each day's work, and give him my immediate and personal feelings of how I thought things were going. He wasn't an unpleasant man, but by the nature of his work—a spy we hired to spy on ourselves—often the sight of him in the theater made me walk in the opposite direction. Sometimes it seemed as if I disappeared, but I was sitting alone in the balcony to watch the rehearsals in privacy. After a while we got used to him, as he knew when not to intrude, but I often put my hands over my mouth when I spoke in private to Bob Moore for fear the man from *Life* was a lip reader.

I felt it was a triumph of fortitude and devotion on the part of everyone concerned that we made it into New York. I still hated opening night because it was such a public event. Something like getting a letter of response from the girl you asked to marry you, only it's to be shown publicly on television or on the first page of the arts section of every newspaper in town. The critics, who attended opening nights at the same time in those days, took up almost two hundred seats, each one bringing a guest, then having to rush from their seats before the final curtain, into their waiting cabs, speeding through traffic to get to their respective typewriters in their respective offices, with barely an hour and a half to write their review to make the early editions. I always thought this was unfair to the playwright and just as unfair to the reviewer.

From the moment the curtain went up on that first-night performance, Maureen was mesmerizing. We laughed at her humor and felt deeply for her pain. About twenty minutes into the first act, I saw a woman get up from an aisle seat in the middle of the theater, walk to the back, and start pacing back and forth nervously and angrily. I recognized her as Elaine Stritch, no slouch as an actor herself. I walked over and asked if she was all right. She pointed to the stage and said to me, "That's my play. That play belongs to me. I should be up there right now doing this goddamn play." It was partly a compliment to the play, but even more, I presumed, there was something about the Evy Meara character that she saw in herself. She finally got her wish about a year later when she did the role in London, getting rave reviews for herself. (We were all set for a long run there, but it ended sooner than expected when an IRA bomb exploded next to the theater, and half the block was closed for the next few months to repair the damage.)

When the curtain finally fell at the end of the play, the ovation for Maureen was thrilling. We all then retired to a small restaurant on Third Avenue called Sam's, in the upstairs private room, for a party of about sixty people. One of my guests that night was Emanuel Azenberg, someone I met playing softball in Central Park's Broadway Show League. Manny put in his years working as a company manager on the road for David Merrick, then as a general manager and finally as a producer himself. He was then in partnership with a man named Gene Wolsk. From the moment I met Manny, I knew this was a man who would tell you the truth, no matter what the consequences. He was honest, sensitive, and smart as hell about the inner workings of the theater. Manny was the epitome of the expression "Tell it like it is"—a very hard commodity to find in the world of the theater. Manny came over to me at the party, took me aside, and said, "I hope you realize you've taken a huge leap tonight. You're creating a new kind of play. A play that's neither a comedy nor a drama. It's both. It's going to take some time for the audiences to accept this, but I hope you'll stick to it because eventually they'll come around." They were nice words to hear from someone who understood where I was trying to get. Saint Subber was not at the party. He never was. I never had those moments when I was able to experience the triumphs or defeats with him, when we could sit down and share the exhaustion of the marathon race we just ran, a common effort, supporting each other at the finish line and having a drink together to toast the effort and not the result. The time when you need a friend, not a producer.

At about eleven o'clock I was called to the phone. I knew it was the reviews coming in, the moment when you cross the room alone, all eyes on you waiting to see the expression on your face when you hear the verdict. As crowded as the room is, it's still a private moment and you deal with it alone. Only this time I wasn't alone. As I picked up the phone and put it to my ear, I suddenly felt another ear, a strange ear, trying to squeeze itself next to the receiver. It was the reporter from *Life* magazine. Then suddenly, like a linebacker breaking through a pro-bowl offense and hurling himself at the quarterback, there came a five-foot-three bundle of dynamite named Joan, who threw a body block on him, bouncing him halfway across the room. Joan glared at him as he tried to recover, and she said, "It's none of your business. Leave him alone." I looked at her in amazement and thought, God, am I lucky she's on my side. She was furious that Saint wasn't there to look after my interests. She walked over to Manny Azenberg and said, "*You* should be producing his plays." She played no small part in that day eventually coming.

The one review we waited for with bated breath was always that of *The New York Times*. Their critic was Clive Barnes. The following, in part, is his review:

It is one of the more ludicrous aspects of the Broadway theater that its producers care so little about it that they normally expect critics to go to first nights and produce instant opinions about works of art as if they had the easy job of opening fortune cookies. I saw the opening performance of Neil Simon's play *The Gingerbread Lady* at the Plymouth Theater last night. It is a very complex work, and frankly I would prefer to think on the notice for twenty-four hours. But the backers and producers are waiting at their little party to hear whether they are rich or not—so on with the motley. In *The Gingerbread Lady*, Mr. Simon has written his first determinedly serious play. It is not serious because of its theme or subject matter, but because of his heroine, a self-destructive nymphomaniac alcoholic. We have seen dramatic drunks before . . . drunks with loyal daughters, good friends, and compulsive needs. Modern literature is littered with hangovers, like cigarette butts from last night's party. And yet there is something special about *The Gingerbread Lady*, something that touches the skill and purpose of the playwright. Mr. Simon's humor has always been contrived. Characters talk to themselves in his plays, they even tell jokes to themselves. What mattered was the superb verbal fancy, the really incredible funny jokes that were both at the same time truthful and artificial. In *The Last of the Red Hot Lovers*, Mr. Simon started to move from his earlier pattern . . . here in *The*

Gingerbread Lady, he has broken through. The wit is self-pitying, self-destructive, and self-deprecating . . . and it has enabled him to create a larger than life and yet still credible human being. A woman with incurable honesty and incurable weakness, who hides behind jokes that would make her a fortune as a jokewriter. This is a remarkable and moving dialogue between a great actress and a playwright who has suddenly discovered the way to express the emptiness beneath the smart remark and the shy compassion that can be smothered by a wisecrack. I wonder if I would have written the same notice tomorrow? The producer and his attendant angels will never know.

It was almost a decade later that Hal Prince led the producers to allow the critics to come to previews to give them time to form their opinions. As I read this review, I kept thinking of Mike Nichols saying, "Send it to Maureen." For her performance she won the Tony Award as Best Actress in a Play. I remembered her in the Tiki Hut in Boston threatening to kill me if I closed this play. I remembered sitting at Logan Airport in Boston reading the review in the *Christian Science Monitor.* I remembered that opening-night body block by Joan, winner of the Heisman Trophy for Wives. I remembered that night as the time I finally took charge of my life as a playwright. Mistakes would still be made, but I began to trust my inner voice.

CENTER COURT

18

SOON AFTER the opening of *The Gingerbread Lady*, Joan and I went on vacation back to Round Hill, Jamaica. It was going to be tennis, sleeping late, reading books, long walks on the beach, no telephone calls except from the girls, and above all, no work. For the first time ever, I didn't bring along a single spiral notebook, in case the urge overcame me. During the time I finished the first draft of *Gingerbread Lady* and the five or six months we had to wait for the play to be cast and finally go into rehearsal, I tried diligently not to even *think* of work. Somehow I never considered it work.

As a very small child, I was taken to the movies for the first time. I was frightened by the darkness but enthralled by what I had seen up on the screen. Not even able to follow the story, I was entranced by the images, the music, the magic of it all. That night I went to sleep and had a dream, of what, I couldn't possibly remember, but there were images flying by in my mind and music flowing through the scene. When I woke up in the morning, I said to my mother excitedly, "Mommy, I saw movies for free last night." In some way, this experience followed me into adulthood. I've always wondered what composers see in their heads, but I see scenes, characters, people in conflict, whether in serious or humorous dilemmas. I never turn the picture on in my head. It just starts playing when I'm not doing something else. These little "short subjects" don't usually amount to anything, but years later they could show up as full-blown ideas. So call it work if you want.

I read that Tennessee Williams wrote practically every day of his adult life, whether at home, traveling, or vacationing. He had set up a regular schedule of hours which only illness might cause him to take a respite from, which I would wager didn't happen often. When sitting down to write, apart from my visits to the local movie house in my head—I mean the *real* work—I would put in a five-day week, no weekends and no nights. I generally worked best in the morning, although after lunch, followed by a walk around midtown and a visit to some bookstores, I would come home for the afternoon session and work almost till dinner time. I rarely made lunch dates or attended meetings of any kind.

I have always been lax in my attention to what was going on at the Dramatists Guild. In the few times I went to meetings there, I saw there were enough board members in attendance and many writers who understood and enjoyed the process of administration of the policies of the organization. I voted by proxy for all the new business that came up and paid my dues regularly from the royalties I made. During my earlier years when I was turning out a play almost every season—and altogether twenty-nine in thirty-four years—I probably paid more dues based on my royalties than any member there. Ever. I am very much for what the Dramatists Guild represents, basically, the rights and protection of the playwright from the Producers or any other Union. The irony is, there are so few plays on Broadway now, there are more members on the council than there are plays on Broadway. Yet, when I stopped going to the meetings some years ago my name disappeared from the letterhead as a member of the council. True, I was in absentia from the meetings, but my plays were appearing in theaters all over the country. Since my name was dropped, I could only gather that in their opinion it was far more important to come to the meetings than to write plays. This is a very minor complaint, but it is slightly irksome when I get a copy from my business manager of a letter from the Dramatists Guild asking for a statement of my royalties for last year's production of whatever. As long as the Dramatists Guild helps protect the new playwright's interests I will always stay on as a member and be supportive. Perhaps they might invent a new category for me, something like Council Member Busy at Work. If they're too busy to get to it, I would understand.

To be perfectly honest, I'm not a member of any club. Not the Book-of-the-Month or even the club that wouldn't have Groucho Marx as a member. I don't like to have to show up anywhere and do something I don't like to do. I once thought of starting a club with only myself as a member, but I thought I stood a very good chance of being turned down. For one thing, I couldn't get a recommendation from the Dramatists Guild, since I had no identity there except for Dues Payer in Good Standing. I did belong to the Beverly Hills Tennis Club when I played a lot, but when I began to have back problems I wrote them and resigned from the club. They wouldn't let me. So I still belong but I think I am categorized as a Resigned Member in Good Standing and have all privileges of the club, including tennis, lunch, voting for officers, and paying some sort of dues. As a matter of fact, I have all the same benefits as any other member except for the fact that I do not have the right to resign.

I am not very much of a political activist either. I have backed many candidates, given money to many candidates, and supported many propositions, but I don't much care for politics. I think we have a government that's of the people, by the people, but *for* the people who want things their own way. On Inauguration Day, the departing president shakes hands with the incoming president and asks the country, with God's help, to support this new president, for that is what makes this country great. Then the next day, the party *not* in the White House spends most of their time trying to destroy the party that's *in* the White House. The running of the government just seems like an encumbrance that gets in the way of their trying to get back into the White House.

It's beyond me that this country really cannot pass a forceful hand-gun-control bill, mostly because all the people with guns won't let us. They seem to believe it's better to have more dead people than live people with guns. Does that mean that the live people with guns could now protect themselves from the dead people who didn't have guns?

Anti-abortionists do not believe in killing an unborn child; just kill the ones who grew up and became doctors. I haven't the faintest idea of how to perform brain surgery, so I try not to get involved with it too much. I also don't know how to run a country, a state, a city, or a town, which is why I try not to meddle or peddle ideas to other people of how it should be run. It seems the ones who don't know how to run it end up running it anyway, which at least gets them out of the way from interfering with people who do know how to do what they're doing.

I grew up an idealist, a romanticist, who loved and believed in all of Frank Capra's movies. Until I read Joseph McBride's *Frank Capra*, which said Frank Capra was a cold, ruthless, manipulative bastard. I believe the book, and therefore I have vowed that after I've seen *It's a Wonderful Life* for the one thousandth time, I will not watch it anymore. I once did get involved in politics. I worked for Eugene McCarthy and wrote sketches at benefits to raise money for McCarthy. When he lost his bid for the presidency, he wasn't around anymore. I'm not privy to what he was doing, but didn't he still have an obligation to go on working and fighting for the things he would have done if he *did* become president?

While I'm in this frame of mind, I might as well state some of my other gripes. I hate people who charge by the hour. Psychoanalysts charge by the hour but my dentist doesn't. My psychoanalyst takes years to make me feel better, but in one session, my dentist gets rid of a very angry pain. I hate lawyers who charge by the hour. I'm not there when his hour goes by. He just tells me that he spent four hours on my work today. I want Polaroid pictures of him working, with a clock behind him showing me the change in time. No, better still, put it on videotape. He could always get up on a chair and change the hands on the clock himself, and then charge me for the time it took him to change the clock. I hate business managers and accountants who charge by the hour. They could be going to the dentist and their analyst during those hours, and I get to pay them for going. I believe the only worthwhile recipients of my time and money are charities and organizations who help the sick, the poor, the homeless, the elderly, the environment, and the uneducated. I'll put on my black tie twelve times a year or more for something that is beyond politics, but then again, the politicians always find a way to control the help given to all of the above. So I write plays for my own enjoyment, and I hope for the enjoyment of others, and I watch my wife of today give all her time and energy to help in matters political and charitable, and to anyone else who needs assistance. She's not as cynical as I am. That's why I write comedy.

Writing is still everything to me and it's a way for me to chart and observe my own progress as an individual and hope that my plays become a documentation of the times we lived in, at least from the perspective I had to view it all. I never wrote a political play, although I was tempted to at times but stopped, because I found you can never get a political play on the stage fast enough to be current. Events used to change from week to week, then day to day. Today we can expect them hourly. That's why we have CNN. There are many, many countries in the world just as there are religions, languages, and cultures. No one can cover them all, and be current on what is going on in all places. I think those of us who spend our lives putting our thoughts and opinions down on paper are better served to write about what interests us most and what we are self-proclaimed experts at. I don't pretend to be an expert on anything, but what interests me the most is human behavior. I know what Health Reform means to Hillary and Bill Clinton, but I'm more interested in how they deal with each other, as husband and wife, of what he thinks about in the morning and how she reacts to news she'd rather not hear.

I'm a student in Behavioral Science 101, not in an academic way, but as an investigator of how we live our daily lives and of the way we cause ourselves so much angst and pain through our unexplainable, absurd behavior. The problems we cause ourselves are not necessarily a laughing matter, but when I put it down on paper, and get it right, then put it up on the stage and make that stage a mirror of our own responses and reactions, more often than not the audiences seem to laugh at themselves. They usually say, "I know someone exactly like that," when in fact they may be talking about themselves. So I love my work. I love the feeling of a pen in my hand, the finer the nib the better, flowing smoothly across a page with narrow ruled lines, because it makes me feel like a craftsman from an earlier period.

The project I worked on as I waited for *The Gingerbread Lady* to get to the stage was a screenplay called *The Out-of-Towners*. It was partly based on the one-act play that I dropped out of *Plaza Suite* and partly on my own experiences when David Merrick asked me to fly up to Boston to help fix up a floundering musical called *How Now Dow Jones*. I did it as an exchange with Merrick. I fix up your play, you put your play into the Eugene O'Neill Theatre. Flying up there, I was caught in a major snowstorm, lost my luggage, spent three hours getting to the hotel on icy streets, a trip which normally was a ten-minute ride.

When I finished the draft of *The Out-of-Towners*, I had some business in California, and while there, I called Jack Lemmon and asked if I could have lunch with him. We met in the Polo Lounge of the Beverly Hills Hotel, then the hub of all business deals made in Hollywood. I told him about the new screenplay, but didn't bring the script with me because I didn't want to show him an unpolished work. He listened to the story, laughed as I got into a few details, and when I got to the end, I said, "That's more or less it."

Jack looked at me, smiled, and said, "Fine with me. Count me in, kid."

I said, "Don't you want to wait till I finish the second draft?"

He said, "I already like the first draft so I know the second draft will only get better. Tell me when you want to start and I'll bring my face and my makeup."

To be trusted like that, from a star of Jack's stature, was the greatest compliment I could think of. The studio okayed both our deals and we were in business. It's highly unlikely that a movie would be greenlighted with such ease in today's world. Deals today take longer than making the film.

SO THERE I WAS on the beach in Jamaica, reading a book I had totally no interest in. I panic before I go on a vacation or a long trip, because if I don't bring two or three of the right books, it's a sentence in hell. I generally don't like contemporary fiction. There's hardly a novel I care to read even though I know I'm missing out on some great talent. I always keep saying to myself as I read it, "Wait a minute. Somebody made this up. This never happened." For me, it's nonfiction every time, preferably a biography, autobiography, or the history of great events. Two wonderful books by David McCullough, for example, one on the building of the Panama Canal, the other on the building of the Brooklyn Bridge. To that you can add his biography *Truman*, one of my life-long heroes. Give me books like Henri Troyat's *Tolstoy* or *Citizen Hearst* by W. A. Swanberg. I like to read about people I admire or dislike intensely, from *Roy Cohn* to *Flaubert*. Throw in a few good books about baseball, like Keith Hernandez's description of two single baseball games in one season, or David Halberstam's *October 1964*.

But on this trip to Jamaica, I rushed my choices and brought three books, none of which held my interest. My bookshelves at home are loaded with books that are one-half or one-third read. Being on a Caribbean island without a decent bookstore leaves you with the grim option of going up to their combination drug and sunblock lotion counter, where there's a rack of paperbacks that spin around on a metal wheel, with the faint hope that as you've turned it around for the third time, something wonderful and new will show up. It doesn't, of course. Aside from paperbacks that tell you of the history of Jamaica, some Danielle Steele, Jackie Collins, or Judith Krantz novels, you are left with Agatha Christie, *The Firm*, or a James Bond book written by someone other than Ian Fleming. That's today, of course; the books in 1970 were different but comparable. I read all of Agatha Christie as a boy, but I would gladly read Dashiell Hammett, James Cain, or Raymond Chandler over again any time. So you're stuck with reading a three-day-old *New York Times* or the *Jamaican Press*, the latter telling you about a fight in Mr. Holly's bar in St. James' Parish in Montego Bay.

I played tennis for an hour and a half, then stretched out on a beach chair, staring at the sky, looking at the clouds as Chekhov once did, and playing Rorschach tests in my mind, all of it eventually leading to ideas for stories again. I started to think of an uncle of Joan's who had made a very good living with his printing business, had a lovely home on Long Island Sound, and even had his own small sailboat that Joan piloted herself.

At the age of fifty he gave up his business and bought a small-town newspaper in New Jersey. He had always dreamed of owning a newspaper and of writing his own daily editorials. He had a good many opinions on the state of the world and was extremely passionate to pass them on, even to just a small town in New Jersey. He could have been the owner of that little hand-run press machine in Tombstone, calling for law and order. Although married and with a daughter, he was a man who could gamble his security and do something he thought was his right and his duty. Unfortunately, he knew more about the printing business than he did the newspaper business. His head was in his editorials while his bank account was quickly moving into the red column. He finally went broke. As flat as can be.

He sold his house on the water, along with his sailboat, and moved into a small apartment in New York, while his wife became the breadwinner and he looked for new employment. At fifty, it's a bad time to start a new career. He eventually had a nervous breakdown.

I thought this was an idea for a play about a wonderfully interesting man who let his dreams run away from reality. As I lay on the beach, the first thing that came to me was the title, *The Prisoner of Second Avenue*. Ideas started to come to me and I had no spiral pad to jot them down, since I promised Joan this was to be a no-work vacation. I went into the hotel, got a dozen sheets of Round Hill stationery, and outlined the entire play on ten pages.

Joan looked at me and asked, "What are you writing?"

"Letters," I quickly answered. "No one writes letters anymore. I just felt like doing it again."

She smiled and went back to her book.

There are no bounds to the deceit a playwright will go to when a new idea sneaks cunningly into his head.

AT HOME ABROAD

19

THE OUTLINE I made on the sands and stationery of the Round Hill Hotel in Jamaica appeared months later as the draft of a new play, with its original title, *Prisoner of Second Avenue*, intact. Mike Nichols made himself available for this one, delaying any other projects he had in the offing. This in itself assured me that the play was on the right track.

As the beleaguered husband, the man who screamed back at his neighbors above, below, and on each side of his apartment, Peter Falk proved to be the perfect choice. He was a born New Yorker, coming originally from the area around Ossining, the home of Sing Sing Prison. Peter looked and sounded as if he had put in time there. His early performance as a small-time hood in the film *Murder, Inc.* was dazzling. As a ruthless killer with an overcoat reaching down to his shoes, wearing a hat that looked as if two heads could fit in it, Peter was electrifying, a word that was almost synonymous with Sing Sing. Yet there was humor in this mad-dog killer, the humor that sprang from the unabashed honesty of his ruthlessness. Once again, I was not looking for a comic in this fairly dark comedy I had written, but a pure actor. What George C. Scott did for *Plaza Suite*, Mike and I felt Peter could do for *Prisoner*.

To play his long-suffering wife, our first and only choice was Lee Grant. An actress out of the Actors Studio, she was equally at home with Chekhov or with Sidney Kingsley, the latter having brought her to prominence in his dramatic hit *Detective Story*. None of this prevented her from being hilariously funny as the script sometimes needed her to be. Once again the basic rule of comedy was proven. Never try to make comedy funny. Honesty will do nicely, thank you.

As with *The Odd Couple*, I again ran into third-act troubles. And as happened with *The Odd Couple*, neither Mike nor I saw it coming in the months we prepared the play. Since I don't save or remember a single word of anything I've cut from a play, I have no idea *now* what was wrong *then*. Something about the kitchen bursting into flames and smoke, which seemed hilarious on paper and embarrassing in the rehearsal room. This time, however, Mike and I pounced on the trouble early enough, and we quickly doused the fire and got back on track with a large rewrite before we ever left for the tryout in New Haven. During the final rehearsal week in New York, when the play seemed to be falling into place nicely, I saw Saint Subber pacing back and forth in the darkness at the rear of the theater as if something was terribly wrong. If it was on the stage, I couldn't see it and neither could Mike. I finally took Saint aside and asked him what the trouble was. Was it the play?

"No," he answered gloomily. "Not *this* play. *This* play is fine."

"Then what *is* wrong?"

"You haven't started *next* year's play yet."

At first I thought it was a joke, not a very good one perhaps, but a limp attempt. When I saw that Saint was serious, an outburst of anger poured loudly from me, so angry that I even surprised myself.

"What am I, a writing machine? Is my life all about turning out plays for *you*? Where is the joy in you, the excitement about putting on *this* one? Are you afraid to praise it or give it some encouragement because you might want to close this in New Haven as well? I am not your fucking Xerox machine. The plays have to be *written*. They're not punched out by pressing a goddamn button in my head."

I walked out of the theater and found myself out on the street with no place to go and nowhere to direct my anger. Later on in interviews to the press concerning me, Saint was quoted as saying, "Neil is a little crazy like most playwrights. Overly sensitive. You have to be careful if you cross him because he can be very dangerous." I suppose an outburst of anger on my part was "dangerous" to Saint. There was also no indication that Saint told the reporter about our "Where is next year's play?" argument. Ends of friendships don't just happen. The estrangement has to be fed and nurtured daily by large doses of insensitivities.

The night before our first audience preview in New Haven, an incident happened that proved to me forevermore that Mike Nichols was a director of extraordinary talent and intelligence, with the forcefulness to put those attributes to his utmost advantage. We did our final dress rehearsal in an almost empty theater, save for the understudies who were scattered throughout the house. Although no laughter was there to show the way to what we might expect the next night before a full house, the play seemed to go off flawlessly. It was midnight and we were all tired, the actors exhausted. Mike and I bid the cast good night and the two of us walked out the stage door to an empty New Haven, on our way back to our hotel about two blocks away. Mike was strangely quiet, which I attributed to the round-the-clock hours we'd been putting in the past few days, while I, even more strangely, had a calm serenity about me, feeling quite comfortable and happy about the new play we were soon going to unveil before the public.

"The end's not going to work, you know."

Mike's matter-of-fact statement shattered the stillness of the night and twisted the self-satisfied grin right off my face, though I was unaware that I even had one.

"What do you mean?" I asked, truly stupefied by this remark that you couldn't see coming even with a telescope.

He answered me with a simple declaration that still managed to point out that my question was a very feeble one: "The end of the play. Just before the curtain comes down. What the actors say. It won't work."

I countered with a childish and churlish response, the way our children very often respond to parental advice they don't want to hear.

"How do you know?"

"I just know."

"How?"

"I don't know how. I don't know why. I just know. Trust me."

Best get off the "how" question, I thought to myself. He's not looking to win an argument; he's just looking for a better ending. This was the situation in the play that led up to Mike's conclusion: Mel Edison (Peter Falk) finds out in the first act that he's been fired from his job, by the company he's worked for since he got out of college. He was a second-level executive and thought his job and his life were secure. The reason for his being let go was not for ineptitude or lack of quality in his work. It was caused by job cutbacks in a slowing economy, a deadly affliction in the corporate world of the early 1970s, and Mel was one of its first victims. He finds it almost impossible to tell his wife, and his thoughts are consumed with fear for the future and the future of his daughters who are away at college. Despondent, he prowls the darkened living room at four in the morning, dressed in his robe and slippers, and dangling a cigarette. He complains about the noise of the city, the clanging of garbage cans before dawn, the paper-thin walls of his over-priced and ill-conceived apartment, walls that make every sound and sigh of the indefatigably sexed airline stewardesses on the other side of his living room seem like the Orgy from Hell. He screams about an air conditioner that knows no moderation, only freezing or sweltering. Mel's tantrums are not received kindly by his neighbor in the apartment just above, and Mel and the Unseen Complainer have a nightly battle royal on their tiny terraces that hang precariously outside the building, spaces large enough to fit a man or a plant, but not both.

A week later Mel comes home, having no luck in finding another job, only to find instead that his apartment has been robbed. His wife, Edna, with great trepidation, tells him she went shopping and because she had lost her key, left the door open for what seemed like minutes, but was still time enough for the burglars to take everything from their new color TV to his small bottle of Valium, leaving Mel without a pill to calm his nerves.

This catastrophe leads inevitably to another screaming fight between Mel and the Unseen Neighbor on the terrace above, culminating in Mel getting doused from head to socks with a bucket full of water. Mel's anger subsides almost immediately and is sadly replaced with a loss of dignity in front of his wife and a sense of humiliation that seems unbearable to Mel. As she wipes his soaking head with a towel, Mel tearfully tells Edna that one day, when he has the strength, he will retaliate not so much against the world, but rather against the Man Upstairs, who is the very symbol of a society gone mad, a world that was once civil, where people cared for people, but has now been reduced to a dog-eat-dog battlefield.

In the second act, Mel has a nervous breakdown, and his family gathers to help with money, but one of his sisters balks when Mel's brother suggests "we give Mel X number of dollars." X is a mystery to her. She needs to know exactly what it's going to cost her. Mel realizes he can't even depend on his own kin. In his confused and angry state of mind, he goes out to a hardware store and buys a snow shovel, an unnecessary piece of aluminum and wood since any snowfall on New York's pavement would be taken care of by the janitor, handyman, or doorman in Mel's high-rise building. Mel's plan is to wait for the Enemy Upstairs to arrive home one night during a snowstorm, and Mel will shovel the snow on his terrace and drop it fourteen floors, burying his hated nemesis before he can get in the door. "They'll find him in the subway," Mel tells Edna with a maniacal chuckle.

At the end of act 2, Mel's brother, Harry, comes alone and presents a check for $25,000 to Mel to open a summer camp in New Hampshire, a dream always cherished by Mel. But he refuses the check. Through therapy and the help of Edna, Mel feels he is coming out of the tunnel of darkness that has pervaded his mind for the past months. The two brothers embrace in the first gesture of warmth between them in years. When Edna comes home from work, exhausted and spent, it is now *she* who seems to be cracking under the strain of urban life, and Mel is able to comfort her as she did for him. The play ended on an upbeat note, a promise for a healthy future for both of them. It satisfied both me and Mike—until he saw that final run-through.

"We need to see *how* Mel takes that first step toward his final rehabilitation," Mike said. "It's not enough to feel it. We have to see it dramatized."

By now Mike and I had reached the lobby of our hotel. Yawning from exhaustion, I said to him as I headed for the elevator, "Well, I guess we'll have to wait till tomorrow night to see if you're right or not."

Mike stood in the middle of the lobby, not making a move for the elevator or bed. "Why wait till tomorrow when I know it now?"

"Well, because it's too late to think of anything now. I can't even remember my room number," I pleaded.

"It's 609 . . . I'm exhausted too," said the very stubborn director. "But neither one of us will sleep until we think of it."

"All right. Whose room shall we go to?" I grumbled unhappily.

Sometimes the body and mind is so depleted, one would gladly give up a success for five hours' sleep.

"Let's sit here in the lobby," offered Mike.

"The *lobby*? Who comes up with the ending of a play at twelve-thirty at night in the lobby of a hotel?" I protested with all the petulance I could muster.

"Maybe we'll be the first," Mike said, as if we would be the first two Jews to climb Mount Everest from the south slope, or whichever slope was the hardest.

We sat in two chairs, barely facing each other, gazing silently into space while the desk clerk, a Yale pre-law undergraduate on a half-scholarship, looked up from his copy of *Torts*, prepping for his 10 A.M. law exam, wondering if the two sleepy men sitting silently in the lobby were newly hired Pinkerton men casing the hotel. Every once in a while, one of us made a suggestion. It was greeted with "No" or "Not bad but not good enough" or "I hate it" and "I hate it too."

The clock on the wall ticked louder than the one in the saloon in *High Noon*. It was now ten to one, followed by a quarter *after* one and creeping up on twenty to two. There had been dead silence for the past thirty minutes. Our eyes were closed and each thought the other one was sleeping. It was hopeless, futile, and stupid to put ourselves through this agony, knowing we'd need all our strength to get us through tomorrow's final rehearsal and preview.

Finally, in desperation I mumbled something, nervously prepared for another rejection from the man who was holding me his prisoner.

With great effort, he raised his eyelids a millimeter. "What? I didn't hear that."

"I said, what if it starts to snow? Their radio is on. The weather man says 'A major storm has descended upon New York with ten to twelve inches of snow expected.' Mel gets up, almost robotlike, gets the shovel from the closet, then sits on the sofa next to Edna, holding the shovel upright at his side like a pitchfork, both looking like the painting *American Gothic*."

Mike's reaction was extremely understated. He stood up and said, "I'll order the snow in the morning. It'll work."

We both got into the elevator, Mike getting off before me. Neither one of us had the strength to say good night. The next night, the ending worked like a charm. We envied each other's abilities. He hated me for thinking of it and I hated him for *making* me think of it. Such are the ways of a perfect collaboration.

PRISONER OF SECOND AVENUE opened at the Eugene O'Neill Theatre on November 11, 1971. The review from Clive Barnes of *The New York Times* was everything I could hope for. "Now his humor has a sad air to it; it is all the more deliciously funny for that undercurrent of discontent. It is, I think, the most honestly amusing comedy that Mr. Simon has given us so far," wrote Mr. Barnes. It was becoming clearer to me with each play that what the critics were looking for in my work was serious comedy, an oxymoron that made perfect sense to me. William Raidy of the Newhouse newspapers apparently suspected this was exactly what I had in mind. "It has laughter plus and this is what Mr. Simon has been searching for for a long time," he wrote. It was a healthy success, and Mike Nichols won his fourth Tony in the four plays of mine that he directed. Let's face it, the man was terrific in hotel lobbies.

AFTER YEARS of spending our summers in East Hampton, Joan had had enough of the same parties, the same people, and the same conversations.

We decided to sell the house on Lee Avenue and start again to live abroad as much as we could. That still meant basically the summers, since the girls were still in school, but two and a half months in Europe would do just fine. We wanted to try Spain for the first time, in some remote spot where there was no chance of our running into anyone we knew. We were looking for isolation, togetherness, and a hard place to reach by phone, since we intended to give out our number only to close family members. Saint Subber was not among them. I didn't want any calls asking about how the new play was coming, since I had no idea for a new play, which for the moment suited me comfortably.

At Home Abroad was the name of a company that finds homes and residences to rent in countries throughout the world. From them we received endless brochures through the winter months, with photos of homes from the Costa Brava to the Pyrenees to the southern coast near Barcelona. We finally selected one on the island of Majorca, between Spain and Africa. The house was on the farthest point on the northeast end of the island in a small town called Pollensa. There was little fear of meeting anyone we knew there since even the Spanish rarely dropped in. The cost of the house for three months was three thousand dollars, which in the Spain of 1971 was a great deal of money. It was a typical Spanish house, a fair-sized two-story white structure with the ever-present red Spanish tiles curving gracefully across the roof, built in the 1920s for considerably less than what we were renting it for. There were gardens, a library, and a small pool. As with all photos of houses for rent or for sale, they always put on their best face and this one looked perfect, despite the lack of color in the black-and-white photos, giving it a somewhat mysterious air which we romantically attributed to the dark, somber mood of the true Spain of Goya, Velázquez, and El Greco.

In the months before we left for Spain, I rummaged through the darkest corner of my desk for my folder titled "Beginnings of Plays." Not a separate folder for each play, carefully titled, dated, and numbered. They hadn't earned that much respect as yet. They were there as a last resort, only to be taken out on a cold, damp December afternoon, glanced through, rejected, and tossed back into the desk, hoping to come out again during another fallow period. There were about fifteen or so castoffs, looking like forgotten, exiled prisoners in *Papillon*. They were all typed on yellow paper, an early habit of mine, since forgotten, but with the passage of time, the yellow had turned brown around the edges, replicating nature in the fall, but instead of being as glorious as that autumn season, this looked more like a graveyard of stillborn ideas. None were more than twenty to twenty-five pages in length, some even less.

Three of these unfinished scripts were various versions of the same theme, but each took a different form. They were about two partners in business. The first one was about two manufacturers, partners for two decades, everything about them being almost identical, from the kinds of women they married, to the size of their families, their ages, their health, their religion, everything—with one exception. One lived the life of a rich man, the other lived within his means. It was beyond the more frugal one's understanding how his partner could live in the lap of luxury while he couldn't do so without jeopardizing his security. Surely the free-spending partner would have gone through his life's savings after twenty years, but there was no sign of that happening. The only reasonable answer was that the big spender was stealing from the firm. A Dostoyevskian paranoia overcame the suspicious partner while he pored over the account books night after night looking for a hint of dishonesty, but he could find nothing. I loved the idea as I reread it but like the crazed partner searching for a clue, I too came up with nothing, and the play stopped there, bound hand and foot and marched down to the dungeon in the bottom drawer. The second play was a rewrite of the first and again no reward. The third version of the partners play looked more promising, one that offered both the intensity of partners who spend half their daily lives together plus the added dimension that this one had the possibility of being very funny. It was about two ex-vaudeville comics, a team who had broken up their act after nearly forty years together, one amicably to go into retirement, the other with bitter anger toward his partner for depriving him of his profession and putting his life and career in mothballs long before he was ready, despite the fact he was seventy-four years old. This one was called *The Sunshine Boys.*

As Joan prepared for the Iberian summer ahead, I continued work on the rejuvenated *Sunshine Boys*. When I reached the end of act 1, I took a week off and then reread it afresh. I wasn't sure anymore. My confidence was waning. Would the story of these two ancient warhorses be of any interest to anyone? How could I like something so much each day, be happy with each line and new scene that poured effortlessly from my pen, and then suddenly, without warning, give in to doubt and despair? I was stuck on it and saw it heading for the "Dead New Play" folder, not to be heard from again for six years or more. I talked to Saint Subber about it. He was no longer willing to encourage me for fear of being wrong. He had relegated himself to the position of putting on my plays without passing judgment on them. Joan was not receptive to listening to my problem, because if anything, she wanted me to rest and concentrate on enjoying our coming adventure in Majorca.

I put the play away, forgot about it, and a week later went out to dinner with Mike Nichols, the woman in his life at the time, and Joan. Mike picked a quiet, homey little restaurant in Greenwich Village that served extraordinary food. The conversation equaled the quality of the dinner and as time quickly passed, Mike asked if I were working on anything new. I said I had been but gave up on it. Despite my reluctance to talk about it, he pressed me for some details. I think I was reluctant because I still clung to the idea that I might someday go back to it, but if I told Mike and got a negative response from him, I might reject it forever. He is a hard one to resist, though, so I told him of what I had written in the first act and where I intended to take it in the second.

He looked at me with one of his maddening stares he sometimes gives to people on the edge of insanity. "Are you crazy? It's wonderful. I love it. You must finish it."

At nine the next morning, I was back at my desk starting the second act of *The Sunshine Boys*, writing with more confidence than I can remember. On such fragile moments, our lives turn remarkable corners.

THE WEEK BEFORE we were to fly to Spain, I came down with a very mean ear infection. I am a firm believer in Freud's theory that travel causes great anxiety, which often leads to illness. "If we're sick, we don't have to go," the brain tells the body. "It's fine with me," responds the body, "but I'm not going to tell Joan. That's your job." The nose-ear-eye-and-throat doctor confirmed the gravity of the situation. "If you fly, you'll probably burst your eardrum." Not even two metal prongs dipped in cocaine could heal an ear that had blown out.

Undaunted, Joan started to check on all the sailing possibilities but found that all major ships leaving for Europe were fully booked. In early June, in the 1970s, Americans boarded anything that could float in order to buy up all of Europe's goods that were selling for ridiculous prices. We couldn't get a cabin until early July, which meant losing a full month in our house in Majorca. Again, Mike Nichols rode to the rescue. He had booked passage on the *QE2*, only to find out he had another film to start. On hearing our plight, he called his travel agent and transferred his reservations to us, which we purchased with alacrity. The only problem was they forgot to change his name on the tickets to ours, so on the voyage across the Atlantic, Joan and I became Mr. and Mrs. Mike Nichols. We got better service than Mr. and Mrs. Neil Simon would have, which proved that winning four Tonys was better than winning one.

The journey turned out to be worthy of Marco Polo. Five days across the ocean to Le Havre, then a railroad trip across France and all of Spain to Barcelona, an overnight steamship ferry to Palma, the capital city of Majorca, then the long drive to Pollensa in the tiny little SEAT we leased from the local car rental, who gave us the beaten-up auto and a map of Majorcan roads that was first drawn during the Roman occupation. We spared Ellen and Nancy this travelcade, and they followed us a week later with Maria, our new Spanish-born nanny, who would double as guardian of our children and interpreter in Pollensa.

The drive to Pollensa was scenically beautiful but the little Spanish-made SEAT took every bounce on the road personally. When we finally arrived at the house and pulled into the small driveway, we were enormously pleased with what we saw. It takes more than one look to know what a house is really like. It was anything but majestic and was smaller than it appeared in the photos, but it had a nice, quiet charm of its own, despite the fact that little items such as hot water were only, like love, a sometime thing. The two upstairs bedrooms bore the full intensity of the hot Spanish sun of July, and during the day, the bedrooms were airless and somewhere in the same range in temperature of an oven cooking for twelve. The nights cooled down to being just beastly hot. Joan and I took the master bedroom on the first floor because we were the masters. The girls would have to wait till they grew up and married before they were awarded that privilege.

The pool was small and cleaned sporadically by a gardener who never heard of chlorine or coming to work more than twice a month. The pool was guarded night and day by our Landlord's German shepherd, a crazed dog named Lobo, who literally went around in endless circles futilely chasing his own tail and barking nonstop. He never even noticed us and I think the only thing he was guarding was his tail.

There was a small wooden shed near the pool, so fragile it looked as if it were built by birds. I decided to turn it into a writing room for myself, should inspiration allow me. Inspiration was the least of my needs. The room was filthy, dusty, and foul-smelling. We eventually got rid of some of the filth and some of the dust, but the smell was here to stay. It also doubled as a sauna bath, not needing any of the knobs or mechanical equipment needed for *real* sauna baths. The humidity was so high that when I *did* finally work on my small portable typewriter, the keys stuck to the paper as I pressed down on each letter, and had to be lifted off continuously. I therefore tried to keep the script I was working on down to three-letter words.

I worked only in the mornings, amid the sound of the girls screaming as they jumped into the murky pool as Lobo did sixteen thousand barking circles a day. I considered making a fake tail and attaching it to his real tail, thus ending his lifetime search for a meaningful accomplishment. Still I managed to finish a first draft of *The Sunshine Boys* and started on the screenplay of *The Heartbreak Kid.*

Joan, as I knew she would, adored every minute of being there. The property was surrounded by the ruins of an ancient Roman aqueduct, and Joan took the girls on daily trips over the entire area searching the grounds for lost and valuable antiquities but coming home instead with beautiful flowers to adorn our mealtime table. Our landlord was an American expatriate, married about four times if the framed photos in the living room were any indication, who rented the "villa" during the summers to subsidize her expenses in Majorca for the rest of the year. Joan shared the cooking with the Majorcan housekeeper who was kept on to see that the owner's tenants did not destroy her house. The woman was an excellent cook of peasant dishes, and with Joan's flair for adventurous flavoring, mealtimes were a treat.

My one and only favorite room in the house was an old library, aging and creaking from the weight of all the volumes that occupied every inch of the dusty shelves. It did have a collection of books that would be welcomed in any library. There was also a record player that played 33 rpm albums at a 5 rpm speed, making the music unbearable to listen to but at least stretching the length of each song by a good two minutes. There was also a radio that raised static to new heights and played Castilian music coming in on its two working stations in Palma. After a week of *Ole!* music, we turned it off for good and waited for them to invent cassette players.

I decided to have a project. Before the summer was over, I would read all the philosophers whose works were crammed into the bookcases. I very nearly did. I covered Kant, Spinoza, Hegel, Plato, Descartes, Santayana, and on through the Greeks, Germans, and Italians. By early August I was spouting wisdom at every meal, making me as long-winded as the 5 rpm albums. When I took center stage, even Lobo went outside and turned on his side in the shade.

Joan was the happiest I had ever seen her that summer in Spain, having the family all to herself, fulfilling her dream of living abroad, something she had yearned for all her life. I have a photo of her shelling peas into a bowl in the garden, with the girls on the ground helping as Joan talked about her childhood with a big smile across her face and beaming into the camera lens as I snapped away. It was one of the few times that she was not fearful of being captured on film.

I would occasionally take Ellen and Nancy into the main drag in Pollensa. Two city blocks would cover it. There were a few small restaurants, usually simple and good, our favorite being Tony's Tuna (that's the name we gave it, theirs was unpronounceable). Each day at a stand on the beach, they served a tuna salad sandwich steeped in olive oil and served on bread made in God's kitchen, the high point of our midday visits. There were a few stores, many tourist shops selling mostly hand-painted seashells, a few sandal-and-beach-wear shops, one gas station, and one school room that turned into a movie theater at night.

Three nights a week they showed Spanish films; one night a week, an English-speaking film. By the third week, we were eager to see anything in English, and when we read that *My Fair Lady* was the film of the week, we drove as fast as our SEAT could take us, despite the fact that we had already seen the film *and* the show. The theater was packed and for a brief few minutes, we thought we were back at the theater on Fifty-ninth Street and Third Avenue, where we went to see all our films. The picture started off well, but after twenty minutes something felt wrong, disjointed, disconnected. The operator, no doubt a fisherman during the day, had no sense of continuity and apparently no ability to read English. Consequently he put on reel after reel completely out of order. Reel 1 was followed by reel 4, which was followed by reel 3, which was followed by reel 5, and reel 2 never showed up at all. The overall result was that after Professor Higgins discovers Liza Doolittle selling her "flowwwrs" under the columns of the Drury Lane Theater, he is suddenly taking her to a Royal Dance where Liza is mistaken for a Princess from Transylvania, then in the next reel Higgins is desperately trying to drum vowels and consonants into her lazy head to get rid of her god-awful Cockney accent. The picture made no sense at all, but the Majorcans loved it and the Simon family was grateful to at least hear that wonderful score again, despite the fact that it was like hearing the original cast album sung backward.

Much to our great surprise, in our fourth week there, walking in town with the two girls, we ran into producer/director Hal Prince and his small son, Charlie. Hal and his family were not visiting Pollensa. They were living there. Hal, in his travels, had one day come upon a beautiful house high in the hills above Pollensa. He had knocked on the door unannounced, with the faint hope that the owner might want to sell his picturesque villa. The owner listened in bewilderment to Hal's proposition, then laughed heartily, saying he did not have nor would he ever have any intention of selling his beloved home. Politely he closed the door. Hal Prince was as persuasive as he is talented, both traits he used to their fullest in his remarkable, incomparable, and lengthy list of some of the most outstanding musicals ever presented in the history of Broadway. A few days later Hal appeared again at the door of the villa he had taken such a passion for and this time made an offer that not even the Godfather could refuse. Within a month, the richer but confused owner moved out, and Hal, his wife, Judy, and their family moved in, soon to be followed by their guests such as Stephen Sondheim, composers Adolph Green and Betty Comden, performer Phyllis Newman, and on and on, many of them summer residents of East Hampton. I was, admittedly, glad to see them, and Hal and Judy were wonderful hosts to us in their dream house up in the hills, although Joan was less enthusiastic—not that she didn't like them, because she did—but she felt the sanctity of her hard-won privacy had been breached. Soon others like Tom Guinzberg, the publisher of Viking Press, and his wife appeared just outside of Pollensa, along with half a dozen more people we knew from New York. Joan suggested we go back to East Hampton since it obviously must have been empty that summer.

July turned into August and August turned into a furnace as the searing sirocco winds blew in from North Africa, making the temperature of the sea hotter than the burning sands on the beach. Our pool, having turned black as ink, was declared off-limits as a health hazard, and there was no longer any relief from taking a dip in either the nature-made or man-made watering holes.

By mid-August I'd had enough of "hot" and persuaded Joan and the girls to move on to London for the last two weeks of our vacation before our luggage completely melted. All said "Aye," and we started to pack, informing the housekeeper we would be leaving in two days. The very next afternoon two uniformed Spanish policemen appeared at our house, looking stern and very official. In a halting but bone-chilling English, they told us that we were "not permitted to leave the island." It sounded like a line from a dozen old movies I had seen, where some mad doctor who had experimented in creating zombies was now telling the hero and heroine of the B film that they were "not permitted to leave the island now that they had discovered his secret." I didn't laugh at the movie and I didn't laugh at the two policemen on our doorstep.

"Not permitted to leave the island?" I repeated with some trepidation, forgetting for the moment that we were even on an island. Manhattan is an island. Coney is an island. Majorca is a foreign country somewhere in Europe.

"Why? What did we do?" I asked, trying to make light of the situation that was growing darker by the minute.

"You have not paid the owner of this house her full rent for the summer," they proclaimed, showing us a court order from a judge, procured by the much-married owner of the house.

I did a Cary Grant double take, looking first at Joan with my head cocked to the side, then at the girls, then at the policemen, in a perfect imitation of Mr. Grant, only with the being very handsome part left out. "Of course I paid her. I sent her a check for fifteen hundred dollars before we left New York and paid the second fifteen hundred by check on July 1, as she agreed to."

They shook their head "no" in unison. "The check was sent back. Insufficient funds."

My deeply tanned face turned ashen white in a millimeter of a second. I was dumbstruck with fear. Not because of the police threat to hold me and my family hostage. What concerned me most was the thought that my accountant had absconded with my entire life's savings, left his wife and child, and flown to Rio first-class to live out a life of luxury and depravity.

"Just a minute," I said to the officer who had the thinner of the two mustaches. "Let me call my accountant in New York. I'll get this straightened out."

"The call will be added to the money you owe to Mrs. Hapsburg," they warned me. Hapsburg was one of the four last names of the owner, who used any of the four husbands' names as the occasion arose. The police eyed me carefully as I walked to the phone, watching to see if I was going to make a break for freedom out the rear door and ditch my family. It didn't occur to me. Even if I could walk to Palma, I couldn't swim to Barcelona. I knew I'd be waking my accountant at five o'clock in the morning, but better waking him in New York than in Rio. It took me ten minutes to get the call through because there were too many pigeons sitting on the telephone wires all the way to Palma. Finally I heard the phone ringing. I prayed no one on the other end was going to answer, *"Buenos dias. Hotel Copacabana."*

"Hello?" said a tired, husky, and annoyed voice. If he's annoyed now, wait'll he hears the next two minutes.

"Paul? It's Neil . . . Yes, in Majorca. The police are here . . . Yes, in my house. They're telling me I can't leave the island . . . The *island*! The check bounced . . . The check I gave them on July first . . . Insufficient funds . . . Do I have insufficient funds, Paul? I was under the impression I had sufficient funds for the next ten years . . . Paul? Are you still there?"

He waited a moment to clear his head. "No, no. It's a mistake. I changed your old account to a new account. But that check should have gone through anyway."

"Should have, could have, Paul, they're still sitting here with guns. My family and I are being held prisoners in a hundred and ten degrees."

"Tell them I'll wire a bank in Palma and transfer the money. You'll have it today."

"Paul, they don't have 'today' in Spain. They only have *now* and *this minute.*"

"It's five o'clock in the morning here. I have to wait until nine when the banks open. I promise you'll have it today."

"Paul, no more accounts. No more banks. I want all my money in cash. And money belts for me and my family. I have claustrophobia and even though I'm in a beautiful place, I have great anxiety about not being able to leave it when I want."

"Do you want me to talk to them?"

"I don't think they want to talk to you, Paul. They've got me, they've got Joan and the girls. You don't exist, Paul. We exist. I'm smiling at them now and they're not smiling back."

The money arrived at about 5 P.M. Majorcan time. The expatriate landlord was satisfied but said she would hold my five-hundred-dollar deposit for breakage and phone calls until all accounts were settled. I received the money six months later. We left the "island" the next morning and landed about noon in a 63-degree London. We checked into the Hilton and I had made sure before we arrived that Paul had sent a cashier's check to them before we arrived. I didn't want an assistant manager coming up to our room the day we were to leave for New York, accompanied by two Scotland Yard men behind him, saying in his pseudo-cultured voice, "Awfully sorry to bother you, Mr. Simon, but there seems to be some oversight in the cashier's check we received. I'm afraid you and your family will not be permitted to leave the British Isles."

COMEDIAN ALAN KING introduced me to the world of Celebrity Tennis, whereby the merit of your fame and the awards you have garnered lead to the rewards of being able to have as your doubles partner such tennis luminaries as the Wimbledon, Australian, and U.S. Open champions John Newcombe, Tony Roche, Rod Laver, Pancho Gonzales, Alex Olmeda, Roy Emerson, Ken Rosewall, a very young Jimmy Connors, and an even younger Bjorn Borg. I participated in these events in the early 1970s in places like Las Vegas, Palm Springs, Palm Beach, Forest Hills, Philadelphia, or any major city sponsoring a charity, while bolstering the ticket sales of the major professional events, which were the real attraction of that week.

The first of these celebrity tournaments I played in was in Las Vegas in 1970, with Tony Roche, then number two in the world, as my doubles partner. Joan and I became very close with many of these tennis greats, especially the Australians, and socialized with them whenever they came to New York. In the fall of 1971, after our return from Majorca, John Newcombe invited us both to his tennis camp/ranch in San Antonio, Texas, which had on its teaching staff, in addition to him, Tony Roche and Owen Davidson, a trio of the best singles and doubles players in the world.

Wanting to show up there with a sharp tennis game, Joan played doubles a few days a week in a bubble-enclosed tennis facility in New York in the East Eighties. Shy one woman in the last match she played just before our departing for Texas, Joan accepted the male club pro's offer to step in for the missing player. Since the other ladies were all fairly adept players, the pro, although far from going all out in his game, hit the ball during their match with considerable speed. Joan was playing up at the net as her partner served. During the ensuing exchange, the pro hit a blistering forehand down the line, an easy passing shot that Joan couldn't possibly reach. She tried, though, extending her body but miscalculating her steps, and instead of getting her racket on it, she was hit with full force on her left hip. The blow pushed her backward, the racket flying out of her hand as she fell to the ground. The apologetic pro jumped over the net and helped Joan to her feet, saying he never thought she would be quick enough to get that close to the ball.

Joan wanted to continue, but he told her to sit down for a few minutes while he got an ice pack and placed it on her bruised hip. She, however, was not one to give in to a simple injury, despite its sting, and minutes later was back on the court but perhaps a step slower. The Aussies were known for their endurance and for never withdrawing for an injury. "If you can stand, you can play," they often admonished us with some good humor.

Feeling better, but with some nagging pains in her back, Joan boarded the plane with me the next morning for five days of tennis at Newcombe's ranch, whose logo was Newk's well-tended military mustache. He was an extremely handsome man, with a charming Australian accent, and one wondered if his career had taken a different turn, could he have been a screen idol like fellow countryman Errol Flynn? It was a tennis hacker's dream to be on the same courts playing doubles with Roche and Davidson, or mixed doubles, with Newk playing with Joan, and me with his wife, Angie, who was a national champion in her native Germany until she met and fell in love with John while he was on a European tour.

For three days we played and learned tennis from early morning till sundown and even got in a few rounds of golf. The nights were spent around a huge open fireplace downing pints of Foster's beer, brewed to perfection in Australia, with a taste never duplicated in any other beer I ever had. Newk, Roche, and Owen filled us in on their days growing up Down Under, being sent by their parents at the age of ten or eleven to serve under the tutelage of the great Australian tennis coach Harry Hopkins. Since that final group of Aussies who dominated world tennis in the late sixties to mid-seventies has grown older and left the game, tennis has never been the same. The camaraderie and friendship they showed on and off court is unequaled in the sports world today, which is now dominated mostly by players who are millionaires by the age of twenty-four, and who, by the age of twenty-five, seem bored or disenchanted with the grueling work they have to put in to earn their fortunes, the bulk of which comes from endorsements. Pete Sampras, an ardent admirer of the Australians, and Michael Chang might be the exceptions. I once saw Roy Emerson play a fight-to-the-death finals match with fellow countryman Ken Rosewall, the winner receiving ten thousand dollars, coffee money for today's stars. The match went almost five hours under a blistering Florida sun, with Emerson finally one point away from winning the match; Rosewall fought back until a perfectly placed ball on the corner line gave him match instead. Emerson leaped over the net, a gesture usually reserved for winners, put his arm around the victorious Rosewall, and with a huge grin on his face, said "Great shot, Nails [Rosewall's nickname made in jest for his small stature], let's go have a pint." Not something you'd see today at the finals of Wimbledon, when at the end the two contestants nod politely to each other and throw their rackets into their bags with hardly a word exchanged.

On the fourth day at Newcombe's ranch, Joan started to limp, holding her hip in obvious pain. Even this didn't stop her and we played out our matches until our last day there. As Newk drove us to the airport in his pickup truck, he cautioned Joan to see a doctor. "I don't like the looks of that limp, Joanie. Have 'em take a look." We flew back home, neither one of us having much concern over an obviously minor injury.

Two days later we showed up at the offices of our family internist, Dr. Jack Bornstein of Lenox Hill Hospital. A cheerful and warm man who always rubbed the hands of his patients before examining them, he looked Joan over carefully, while I waited in his office. Whatever concerns he may have had, he reserved for fear of causing any needless alarm, but he made an appointment for us to see a radiologist the next morning. Since Dr. Bornstein didn't seem worried, neither did we. The following morning, Joan was in the X-ray room for about a half hour, then came out and sat with me in the doctor's office awaiting the results.

What happened next seemed uncommon to me and worried me more than just a little. The doctor returned to the office, smiled at Joan, and said he was still waiting for the plates to dry. Almost as an afterthought, he said, "Mr. Simon, there are some things I have to go over with you. Could you come inside for just a minute?" I shrugged to Joan, indicating something like, "must be about our medical insurance," but I could see the look of concern on her face as I left. She picked up a magazine and looked toward the window.

Instead of another office, the doctor took me into a back room where all the X-ray plates were visible on the wall. He turned on the light behind the plates and pointed to what looked like a hip bone. With a pencil, he made a circle around a small gray area about the size of a nickel. "This is her left hip bone. This dark gray area right here worries me."

I could feel my heartbeat quickening. "What do you mean, worries you? What do you think it is?"

"I don't want to say until I know for sure. It looks like a small tumor. It's very possible it's benign, but we won't know until they do a biopsy."

In 1971, medical science was certainly not in the Dark Ages, but compared to what they know now, one would have to say they were still in their infancy. Even the word "biopsy," although not foreign to me, was never brought up in any examination I ever had nor even mentioned by anyone in my family. Cancer was a word still spoken in hushed voices. I was nervous to say the very least, but there was not a chance in the world that I could believe there was anything seriously wrong with Joan. She was thirty-eight years old, looking robustly healthy and as beautiful as I had ever known her.

When the doctor and I returned to his office, Joan was sitting there, a lit cigarette in her mouth, the magazine unopened. After explaining to her in carefully chosen words what he had just told me, the doctor told her he was not positive about any diagnosis as yet, but he was setting up an appointment the next morning at Lenox Hill for a biopsy to be taken. He explained it was a fairly simple procedure, in which they'd go in, take a bone sample from her hip, and after a biopsy, they'd know better how to treat this. The words "treat this" seemed very hopeful. No one was talking about anything very drastic.

Joan looked at him with a half smile and said, "Should I be worried?"

In 1971, these questions were still handled with a great deal of optimism and a minimum of true candor. I'm sure they still are today, but things were not discussed quite so openly then. The response to that may be that in to-day's medicine, the sooner they get to the truth, the better chance they have in treating it. Too many men and women put off examinations feeling that if they don't deal with it, perhaps it will go away. The words "simple procedure" and "I don't think there's any real concern" gave us at least twenty-four hours to think perhaps there really wasn't any concern. Still, the doctors were moving on with their tests as rapidly as possible.

That night we had dinner at home with the girls and nothing was mentioned to worry them. Joan simply told them she might not be home tomorrow when they came home from school because she had to take some tests for "this pesky leg of mine." That was all. Dinner went on as usual. That night Joan brushed her hair, washed her face, brushed her teeth, put on a fresh nightgown, and got into bed next to me.

"Are you worried?" she said.

"Worried? No. Not at all."

"Would you tell me if you were?"

"Probably not. But I'm not worried."

"What did the doctor say to you when you went out of the office with him?"

"Exactly what he told you. He couldn't tell anything until they did the biopsy, but he certainly didn't seem worried."

"Then why did he have to take you out to say that?"

"I don't know. I thought it was strange too. But he wasn't concerned."

"Are you telling me the truth?"

"I am telling you the truth. I swear to God."

She turned on her side and closed her eyes. "Would you rub my back? It still hurts."

I rubbed her back as gently as I could.

"I'm not worried either," she said.

I continued to rub her back until she was asleep. Or at least until I *thought* she was asleep.

I SAT IN THE Lenox Hill waiting room with Joan's mother, Helen Baim. Joan's father, Morris Baim, or Moe, as everyone called him, had died of a heart attack at the age of fifty-five, about a year and a half after we were married. Joan adored her father, as he adored her, and I wished that he could have been with us on this day. His warm, smiling face was always a comfort to Joan.

I have no recollection of how long Joan was upstairs while the biopsy was being performed. Time goes too fast or too slow when awaiting news of such consequence. Helen sat next to me, nervously rubbing my hand. The surgeon finally appeared, still in his gown, and told us Joan would be down shortly. Helen asked if there was anything he could tell us. He said in a very polite but noncommittal voice, "I'd like to speak to Joan's husband first. Mr. Simon, could you come with me, please?"

I followed him apprehensively down the hallway, expecting to be taken to his office. Instead he took me to the worst of all possible places. Through a door, we were on a cold back stairway, a place where it was pretty certain we'd not be disturbed. He sat down on the third step and asked me to sit next to him.

"It's not good, I'm afraid."

"What do you mean? The biopsy?"

"I never did the hip biopsy. In examining her before the procedure, I found a malignant tumor in her breast. It's cancer and it's already metastasized into her hip. I didn't remove her breast. There was no need to."

The words were coming too fast for me, too much information to absorb, too many feelings and emotions bouncing around in my brain to accept the full impact of what he was saying. What exactly was he telling me? What was the treatment? What was the long-term prognosis? I heard it all in one devastating and final statement.

"She has about a year. A year and a half at most."

A hole opened up underneath me, one that I slipped into, trying to grab the sides of the wall to stop me, but the fall was far and dark and unending. I could not breathe and I could not stop sobbing, both at the same time, and he put his hand on my arm and said he was sorry. Questions were asked and answers were given, none of them making anything more acceptable.

"Are you sure? Isn't there some treatment? How can you be so sure of a year or a year and a half?" They all added up to the same thing. Joan was going to die. "Does she know?" I asked.

"I told her it was breast cancer. No, I did not tell her how long she had. That's as much a family matter as it is a medical one."

"What do I say? What do I tell her?"

"In my opinion, I would give her some hope. She'll know herself when the time comes. If I were you, I would say we caught the cancer early but that we got it all. I see this kind of thing every day. She said she had two wonderful children. If you can handle it, keep it from them for a while. That's up to you, of course. She'll be treated with some radiation. That will slow things down for a while. It'll buy you at least a year . . . I'm very sorry."

Our conversation was over. Joan was wheeled down, and the doctor went into her room and talked to her himself. I saw Helen in the hallway. She had been Joan's mother for thirty-eight years, and I didn't feel it was fair to keep the truth from her. Besides, I knew I couldn't get through it completely on my own, that I'd need an ally. I crossed to Helen. Her eyes looked at mine, waiting for an answer she already knew.

"Tell me, darling. Please tell me."

I started to but no words came out. I burst into tears and held onto her. She sobbed, saying over and over, "I knew it. I knew it all along . . . I knew it."

I finally told her everything the doctor told me and explained how he thought we should handle this.

"Of course, sweetheart. I'll do anything."

"It's just between us. I don't want anyone else to know. Not Ellen. Not Nancy. Not your family. Not until it's time. We still have plenty of time."

She nodded silently as the doctor summoned us into Joan's room. She was sitting up in bed, a hopeful smile on her face. "The doctor said they caught it early," she said. "He said they got it all. Isn't that wonderful?"

I nodded and agreed with everything the doctor said. I held her and kissed her as though we had something to celebrate. I could feel her body relax in my arms. From that moment on, I lived out a conspiracy of silence along with Joan's mother, a year of lies and hope ahead for all of us. Somehow I still firmly believed, no matter what I had just been told, that Joan would beat the odds.

A FEW DAYS LATER, Joan started radiation treatment. It was in a large office not too far from where we lived. I sat with her along with about a dozen other patients in a large waiting room. Everyone had brought someone with them. As I looked around at their faces, I couldn't tell who was there for treatment and who would be left sitting outside waiting for them. I was wrong as often as I was right. I felt guilty about playing such a macabre game in my mind.

Joan glanced at a magazine and I couldn't tell what she was thinking. Did she already know more than she was told a few days ago? The conspiracy of silence now continued between Joan and me. If I *did* know something, she didn't want to hear it. We spoke very little of her treatments and we talked very little of the future. We took one day at a time.

Gradually, as the weeks passed, her spirits seemed to rise as the pain in her hip lessened somewhat. I got so much in the habit of keeping up my own spirits, I no longer knew if I was pretending or believing. The lie became the truth. Not the real truth but one that gets you through life on a day-to-day basis. I had to live my life as before, because a change in my own behavior would be a clear signal to Joan that all was not what she had been told.

At home, I continued to work in my second-floor office every day. I picked up the script of *The Sunshine Boys* and let it swallow up all my other thoughts. Writing has always done that for me. The four or five hours a day that I sat over my typewriter was also a respite from dealing with matters too great for me to deal with on a daily, hour-to-hour basis. The work was my refuge. Because of her inability to get around much, Joan stayed in bed for most of the time writing poetry, something she had not done since she was down at Black Mountain College, studying with William Carlos Williams, almost twenty years before.

I WANTED to get something for Joan. Something that would deflect the emphasis of the shadow that hung over her to something that could engage her time and her thoughts elsewhere. Not just for herself, but for the whole family to share in. I thought of that little dream house of hers, the small farmhouse in Vermont. It was not really feasible to live there since she still had to be watched by her doctors, and it would be a difficult shift for the girls to change schools and friends so quickly. I had a few friends who lived up in the Bedford Village—Pound Ridge area of New York, about a ninety-minute drive from the city. Without giving it much thought, I rented a car and drove up by myself, telling Joan I had a lot of meetings that day about some future film projects. It would be the first time we had spent an entire day apart from each other since she was at Lenox Hill.

As I approached Bedford Village, a calm came over me. It was like driving back through time and space. The wood-shingled houses surrounded by tall trees and stone walls built along the roads gave one a sense of another era, when the world moved more slowly and less noisily, and the clear air and the bright sunshine that spread over the hills everywhere seemed to invite an aura of life and peacefulness, and God willing, of healing. I walked into a small, charming real estate office, quaint enough to live in. Mr. Bixler, a cheerful man in his thirties, asked if he could help me. I told him I wasn't sure. I just wanted to see some houses. It was questionable whether I would buy but if he had the time, I would like to see what was available. Something small, I added, a place to spend weekends with my wife and two daughters during the summer and possibly for Christmases and Thanksgivings. For someone who said he wasn't sure he wanted to buy, I certainly had the whole year planned out.

The year was just a number, a word, whose real meaning to me was beginning to be less fact and more fancy. Who knew how much time we really had? Maybe a lifetime. If Joan were happy here, who knew what miracles could occur?

Mr. Bixler and I drove around for an hour or so, seeing almost a dozen houses. Some I didn't even bother looking in at. I knew if I saw the right one, I wouldn't have to go over the kitchen and bathrooms. At about three in the afternoon, we turned into a heavily wooded area. No house was visible at first and then suddenly there was this lovely little home sitting up on a knoll. It was not an old house although it was built with the charm and simplicity of something from old New England. I was taken with it immediately. When we pulled up in front of the house, to my left about twenty yards away, I could see a small wooden footbridge with a stream running under it, and beyond that, through the trees, the sun was shimmering brightly on a lake.

"Does this house have access to the lake?" I asked.

"Oh, yes. It's Blue Heron Lake. It belongs to the Home Owners Association of all the people who live around the lakeside. It's kept private from outsiders. Come, I'll show you."

He took me across the footbridge to a small pier with a boathouse. A rowboat was tied to the rail. The lake seemed enormous to me and I could barely see the houses on the other side. It reminded me a little of the privacy we had in Pollensa but without the grueling heat, and this had water that would stay cool and clear all year round.

"My family and I go ice skating on the lake when it freezes in the winter," Mr. Bixler added. "And the fishing is good all year long."

I barely looked at the inside of the house except for the master bedroom that looked directly out on the lake and the big stone fireplace in the living room. I asked him how much it was. He gave me the price but said it was negotiable. I made a counteroffer and he said he thought that would probably satisfy the present owner. I went into his office and signed some papers. I never bothered calling my accountant, for fear he'd want to come up and see it, decide whether it was worth the price, and then negotiate some more. I didn't want to lose this place for anything. It was, for that moment, the most important thing I ever bought in my life. Money was not the object. Time was.

I drove home, not even thinking of the rashness of my decision. What would Joan think of my buying a house without her ever seeing it? And would it be a tip-off to her that I feared we didn't have much time left together? I never even considered as to whether I could get out of my commitment to buy if Joan was not happy about it. On the other hand, it was so unlike me to do something like this, maybe it was just the way she always wanted me to be. Not rash but adventurous. Plunge into life the same way she would plunge in the lake at midnight during a hot summer at Tamiment. Despite my fears, I felt strangely wonderful as I neared New York. I was no longer just standing by as Joan fought against her illness, unable to offer her anything except my support and my love. I felt like a doctor who had come up with a new discovery that may not prolong life, but could enhance the quality of those days left. I walked in the bedroom, unable to conceal the huge smile on my face.

She put her cigarette out in the ashtray and smiled back. "What are you looking so happy about?" she asked.

"I did something today. Maybe something crazy, maybe something wonderful."

"Are you going to tell me?"

"Sure, unless you want to guess."

"No. I'll stick with your telling me."

"Okay," I said, but finding myself so out of breath with fear and excitement, I thought I wouldn't be able to get the words out. How should I tell her? Slowly? In detail? . . . No. Do it quickly. All in one breath so she doesn't have time to be disappointed.

"I bought a house today. In Bedford Village. On a lake. An enormous lake called Blue Heron. I guess they have blue herons there. It has a small boathouse with a rowboat tied to the dock and we can swim and fish in the summer and skate on it in the winter and it's got eight wooded acres and deer come through the woods all year and there's a little footbridge with a stream under it and the house is so pretty and you can see the lake from your bed when you wake up in the morning and the real estate man, Mr. Bixler, has a clay tennis court and told me we can use it whenever we want and he has two little girls who can play with Ellen and Nancy and the town of Bedford Village looks like something Mark Twain used to write about . . . Do you think I'm crazy?"

The smile on her face was worth everything. "I don't believe it. Are you telling me the truth?"

"If I had a rod and a worm, I would have brought you a fish . . . I hope you're going to like it."

"Of course I will. When can I see it?"

"Maybe next week. We have to see the oncologist on Monday and he'll tell us when you can travel."

We talked all night about the house, and Nancy and Ellen were beside themselves with joy. When I turned the bed lights out about midnight, I wondered in the dark, does she know why I did it so quickly? She accepted everything so easily. But even if she did suspect, her mind was now consumed with living in the country on a place so perfectly named as Blue Heron Lake.

I BEGAN to have the reverse of nightmares. My dreams were happy dreams, of a healthy Joan, of meeting her for the first time at Tamiment, or of the laughter we shared sitting in Washington Square Park with Ellen still in a carriage, as we watched the local Villagers strolling by and guessed what they did for a living or what their names were or what they were thinking. We were writing captions for living cartoons.

I awoke feeling wonderful, until I turned and saw Joan sleeping beside me and the awakening became the nightmare. She was going to die and sleep was my only escape from facing it.

She rarely let on to her own feelings. She never asked questions and I soon learned to stop asking "How are you feeling?" She still couldn't get around without the help of a cane and I could see she didn't want me to help her. Still, when walking down the steep flight of stairs in our house, my hand was always an inch away from her arm.

We had an appointment with the oncologist and I feared that his report or handling of the situation might rob Joan of some of her hope, and the house in Bedford would become a meaningless gesture to her. After examining her, Joan and I sat alone in his office, once more waiting to hear of her progress, if any. A gray-haired man, about fifty, without much warmth in his face, but sturdy and strong, came in as he looked over the reports on his desk. What I feared most was that without consulting me alone, he might be as devastatingly frank with her as the surgeon had been with me on the hospital steps. I was definitely not prepared for what he finally did say.

"Well, Mrs. Simon, everything looks good, as far as I can see. The radiation is doing its job. The tumor is going into remission. You'll be back playing tennis by the summer."

An enormous smile of relief crossed Joan's face. I could barely believe my ears. What was happening here? Was she well? Was she cured? Was the cancer gone? Or was there an open or private conspiracy among doctors never to tell the truth to a cancer patient? So many did survive the disease. Did this apply to those whose cancer has metastasized as well?

"Remission" was the word he kept using, never "cured." We didn't press for him to go any further since what he had given us was all we were prepared to deal with. "You should always get two opinions"—that's what I've always heard about dealing with major illnesses, and it was this opinion that I chose to believe. Surely if there was any more treatment they could give her that would guarantee her recovery, the oncologist would have mentioned it. The two of us walked out of his office and I was more jubilant than I ever thought I'd feel again. "We'll be playing tennis by next summer," I kept saying to Joan in the taxi going back to our house.

It was time for me to take the next step. The following day I bought a car without telling Joan. Since we had given up the Hamptons, a car was not a necessity in New York. We had given up the little Volkswagen we first had and then the small green Triumph convertible, so tiny that we literally had to fold Ellen and Nancy into the back, and crush Chips, the dog, somewhere in their laps for the long two-hours-plus drive to East Hampton. This time I bought a Mercedes, a four-door brown automobile that was more luxurious than anything I had ever owned. You could still smell the leather seats four years later. It cost eleven thousand dollars and I thought back to my youth, knowing that in 1939, you could buy a mansion in the country for eleven thousand dollars.

I didn't tell Joan about the car. When it was time to leave for her first visit to the house in Bedford, I picked up the car early in the morning, then appeared back at our house about 10 A.M. Joan and the girls were anxiously sitting in the little room next to the front entrance. I rang the bell, opened the door, and said, "Ready?" Joan, still with her cane, walked slowly down the front steps with the girls. She looked around for the rental car. I took out my keys and opened the door of the shining new Mercedes.

"What's this?" Joan asked.

"Oh. Didn't I tell you? The car comes with the house."

She laughed but accepted it without any questions. As long as she still had the cane, I don't think she imagined she was out of the woods yet. The truth that was the lie was now muddled in my brain. I no longer knew what to believe, except that today the sun was shining and that I was going to drive Joan up to her new house in the country. Ellen, Nancy, and Chips jumped into the back seat, luxuriating in the space they never knew they had in cars, and the girls kept opening and closing the automatic windows. We arrived in Bedford ninety minutes later and I first drove through the village, pointing out the age of the stores and houses, like a local tourist guide, proud of his birthplace. Then we proceeded on to the back road that led to the house. As we approached the wooded eight acres, I stopped the car, looking as if I were lost.

"Why are you stopping here?" Joan asked.

"I think I'm lost. I think there's a house up here. I'll drive up and ask somebody."

"I love these woods," Joan said as we approached the house.

"You'd better," I added. "It's yours."

Joan was beaming with excitement. We pulled up to the front door and as I helped her out, I said, "I'll show you the house in a minute. First comes the lake."

As we walked through the woods to the lake, the girls reacted as if they were living out a fairy tale come true. Joan stood on the edge of the dock, looking at the boathouse and then out to the water. I could see by the expression on her face that it took her back to where she was her happiest. The little girl growing up in the woods of Tamiment, who took a rowboat out at night and swam in the dark, cool waters, a midnight's summer's dream.

"I'm going to get rid of this cane soon. And I'm going to swim in that lake this summer. And I'm going to catch the biggest fish in the lake and cook it for dinner."

And that summer, that's exactly what she did.

DURING THE WINTER, Chips, who was almost fourteen years old by now, could no longer climb the steps of the townhouse. We took him to the vet, who told us we would have to put him to sleep soon. Joan would not hear of it. She found a kennel in Connecticut, one that took care of and kept older dogs. Chips stayed there with other dogs for company, and slept in the house of the woman who ran the kennel. She called one day to say that Chips had passed away quietly in the night. We missed him terribly.

THE SUNSHINE BOYS was scheduled to open in the fall. I had no idea if Joan would make it till then, and Manny Azenberg, who was producing it, and I kept the plans tentative. Despite signs of her regaining her health and stamina, the ticking clock of the initial doctor's prediction reverberated in my mind constantly. By the summer, true to the oncologist's optimistic opinion, Joan seemed to be her healthy self again. We moved up to the house on Blue Heron Lake and she was soon out in a small boat fishing with Ellen and Nancy, teaching them what she learned as a girl on the lake in the Pocono Mountains. In the afternoons we borrowed the Bixlers' tennis court and spent a week just hitting balls to each other. By the second and third week, she was banging them across the net with power and speed, getting angry with me as I tried to return each ball well within her reach. "Dammit," she'd yell across the court. "Don't hit it to me like a girl. Hit the damn ball like you want to win."

It was wonderful to see her like this again. Had God granted us a reprieve of a few months, or did her inner strength and strong desire to live overcome insurmountable odds? The cane was gone. The limp was gone. The radiation treatments were over. We had our life back again. She had made me promise, from the first day she was told about her cancer, that I would never tell *any-one* except her mother about the diagnosis.

"I know I'm going to get well," she'd say, "but I don't want anyone treating me as if something was wrong. Promise me." I, of course, promised, but in those first few months of her illness, she saw no one. She never went out except for the radiation treatments and even then I had to bring the car around to the front of the house, lest anyone see her with a cane.

Now, healthy once more, she began to ask friends to come up to the lake and spend weekends with us. We had barbecues and lobsters and fried chicken, with her spending hours in the kitchen turning out the most wonderful dishes and making sure all her guests were well fed and happy. No one who came up ever had an inkling that anything was wrong with her.

To be honest, there were two people I told, but I could count on their bond of secrecy with full confidence, as something not even to be shared with their wives. One was my good friend and now producer, Manny Azenberg; the other was someone I knew I could trust with my life, or with Joan's. His name was Michael Brockman, someone I had met at East Hampton about ten years before all this happened. For the first two years of our friendship, I had no idea what Michael did for a living. Since he never brought it up, I didn't ask him. I assumed it was something in show business because he knew so much about it. In truth, he was an executive in the insurance business, but he was, in so many ways, such a private man, I knew that whatever I told him would go no further. I needed these two around me for fear, in a moment of weakness, I might suddenly burst into tears, and I could count on them to let it pass with an unspoken silence.

I am not the kind of person who goes on camping trips with the boys. Only twice in my life can I remember going off alone with a buddy. Once with Manny Azenberg to Sweden and once with Michael Brockman to Palm Beach to play tennis. Therefore, it's not hard to understand that when the crunch came, there was no one there for me and for Joan as consistently and devotedly as Manny and Michael. I had picked two pillars of strength I could lean on during the dark days and whose promise to protect Joan's privacy was never betrayed.

During those summer months in Bedford, I started to write again, playing around with a possible new project while I awaited the tentative start date for *Sunshine Boys*, still dependent on the continued progress of Joan's condition. I was reading a book of short stories and anecdotal tales by Chekhov, written when he was a young man still in medical school. He was getting paid by the word from a local newspaper but did not let his need for money take precedence over his instincts as a writer. He kept the stories short and to the point. They ranged from bitingly humorous to outrageously funny, and as I sat there reading them in the summer of 1972, I thought how contemporary these pieces still were. I thought it might be fun, just as an exercise, to dramatize these pieces and make an evening with Chekhov and me, his uninvited partner. Since Chekhov was himself a doctor and I was known as Doc—by virtue of my expertise with a toy stethoscope when I was three—might we not make an amenable partnership? Since his works were in the public domain, I voted yes for the both of us. I spent the rest of the summer writing *The Good Doctor*.

By the end of the summer, Joan was still free of all signs of the cancer, and as far as we both were concerned, she was well out of the woods. We went back to New York in the fall and I started rehearsals on *The Sunshine Boys*. I was glad now that I had never told Ellen and Nancy about Joan's recent battles and prayed the day would never come that I would have to. Once rehearsals began, I realized that I was fooling myself into thinking that life could go back to normal so easily. A change had come over Joan, not in a physical way, but the doubts for the future were apparent in her face, in her manner, and in her smile, which appeared with far less frequency. Tension had now taken up a permanent residency in my neck and no amount of exercise, deep breathing, or meditation could relax the pain, short of prescription drugs which made my head and brain unable to function the way it usually could when I needed it to rise to the occasion while doing a play. Fortunately the play was in the competent hands of actor Alan Arkin, who was now wearing the hat of director and did a terrific job with our three stars, Jack Albertson, Sam Levene, and Lewis Stadlen. We had a successful tryout in Washington and were subsequently hailed by the New York critics and audiences. Working with my new producer, Manny Azenberg, took all the weight of responsibility off my shoulders and I never felt for a minute the hounding I used to get before about "When are you going to start on your next play?" This time I not only had a producer, I had a friend to share my troubles with.

After the play had opened, Joan and I went south to warmer weather in Palm Beach, taking the girls with us. And suddenly it was there again. The limp was back. Joan was now beginning to hold on to the railing when climbing steps, breathing a little harder, moving a little more slowly. Just asking the question once, "How are you feeling?" and seeing the look on her face told me quickly that it was not a question she wanted to hear or a discussion she wanted to get into. A few days later it was evident the pain was getting sharper and she could no longer get around without the use of the cane. The only concession she made to dealing with it outwardly was to agree to cut the vacation short by a few days and return home.

The radiation treatments started again in New York. At dinner with the girls, Joan would use the word "treatments" but never mentioned radiology. She just tossed it off as that "bad leg" of hers from the time she broke it in Hawaii. The girls seemed to accept it, and I kept negotiating with myself as to when and if I should finally tell them. I expected that the signal for that moment would come from Joan. It never did. In the year since I had sat with the doctor on the metal staircase in Lenox Hill Hospital, hearing his prognosis of what to eventually expect, I had never once heard Joan complain or express her feelings. Yet finally, one weekend up in Bedford, in the middle of the night, Joan turned to me and whispered, "I'm so scared." I tried to assuage her fears but we both knew the only true comfort I could give her was to hold her tightly until she fell asleep.

She awoke in the morning and was busy in the kitchen making breakfast for the girls. I was still in bed but could see her through our bedroom window, in the kitchen just beyond the living room. I looked at her in wonder. How could I ever experience what she was going through? How could she maintain such composure in the face of what she surely must have realized was coming soon? The worst part of my thoughts was that I was consciously and selfishly thinking, what will I do without her? Was my loss going to be greater than *her* loss? There is no consolation in knowing that we will all die and that we will all lose someone we love. The only reality you can deal with is that it's happening to her and that it's happening *now*. All other major sorrows in life will come in the future, and there's plenty of time to deal with them later.

We spent Christmas in Bedford, with a warm, cozy fire and presents galore under the tree. I had outdone myself in the gift department, hoping the more presents we had to open, the less time we had to dwell on a quiet, aching sadness that even the girls couldn't help noticing. When it finally came to opening gifts and exclaiming our surprise and delights, Ellen suddenly started to complain, in the most plaintive way, "It's too much. It's too many presents." She burst into tears, not really able to explain or understand what she was crying about. I was afraid to even glance in Joan's direction for fear of seeing what I thought she believed was the cause of Ellen's pain.

Back in New York, Joan was in bed again and spent most of the winter months doing things she hadn't done for herself in years. She didn't go back to painting but she started to make collages by cutting pictures and words out of newspapers and magazines, filling them in with her own drawings and small pictures of the family. They were brighter and more cheerful than I would have expected in her frame of mind. She also started to write poetry again. The poems were a sort of Joycean gibberish, the kind that only Joyce and his academic scholars and researchers understood. Certainly not I. But Joan's choices of words and sounds that popped off the page were filled with Joanian phrases that she made up for all of us, to express her love and affection. Words like "rufus" and "puddin" and "fallow minsey" and "noodle mooning" and "cueeny fern" were all meant for us, and by some miraculous sense of communication, we knew who represented each of us in her final poem. She ended it "Write soon. Clarn."

She would probably be embarrassed to know that I've gone public with her intimate thoughts, obscure as they were, but these words bring meaningful and loving memories for me and Ellen and Nancy. In some measure, putting them down in this book is a way of preserving an unphotographed photograph of her, something I could never capture in my attempts to get her to hold still long enough for the camera to convey the way I saw her.

I wish I could say I was a bastion of strength through that cold winter of 1973. I was the first to crack under the pressure. Joan awoke at six in the morning one day and saw that I was not in the bed next to her. She crossed through the small hallway that led to my office. I was on the floor, half asleep, having crept in silently during the night to try to cap the internal explosion I thought was surely going to erupt in the twilight hours. I could feel my heart pounding and heard my pulse throbbing in my ears. What had awakened me during the night was an uncontrollable and desperate urge to throw myself off a bridge, probably the Fifty-ninth Street Bridge since it was much closer than the George Washington Bridge far uptown.

When Joan asked what was happening, I couldn't find any words to say nor any that she would want to hear. Yet she could tell by my ashen face what was going on. Her bottom lip stiffened and she looked at me and said, "I can't take care of you and take care of me at the same time." She turned and went back to the bedroom. I went downstairs and had a cup of coffee, forgetting that caffeine would only exacerbate the intensity of my panic. I threw on some clothes, waited till nine o'clock, and told Joan I was going out for a few minutes. I knew I'd better find some help for myself and find it soon. Dr. Bornstein was the first one I could think of. I ran out into the streets looking for a taxi, but a taxi was too slow for my purposes. It wouldn't get me there fast enough. So I ran. Seventeen blocks without ever stopping for a red light or on-rushing traffic. I dodged every car and bus, hoping that if I got there fast enough, I could escape the demons and fears that were chasing me.

Years later I was reminded of that feeling when I read of comedian Richard Pryor, who went running full-speed through the streets of Los Angeles in an effort to escape the flames that were consuming his body after a mishap while free-basing drugs. The effect, of course, is the opposite. You just burn more quickly. I arrived at Dr. Bornstein's office, bypassing all his waiting patients, and hurled myself into his private office, panting desperately, drenched in perspiration. There was little time for an exchange of words or feelings. I just wanted the fire out. He took my blood pressure. It was something like 250 over 170, with no indication it was about to abate soon. That was high enough to set off an emergency alarm through my nervous system, and Dr. Bornstein immediately checked me into Lenox Hill Hospital, two blocks away, where I was given a bed and an armful of injections, enough to sedate an elephant. It was the first time I ever had high blood pressure, and I've been controlling it with pills from that day to this. I fell asleep almost instantly and slept for six hours.

When I awoke, there was Michael Brockman standing by my bedside, looking down and saying both in reprimand and concern, "What kind of crap is this?" I turned and saw Joan sitting in a chair in the corner. There was a strained look on her face and yet a look of relief. Dr. Bornstein entered as if on cue. I looked at him sheepishly and told him I was fine and wanted to go home. His warm, soothing hand was feeling my pulse as he said, "Not tonight, my friend. Tonight you sleep." And I did. The first full night's sleep I'd had in almost a year. The following day I went home, my pockets bulging with pills to control whatever it was in my mind and body that thought it could be superhuman in the face of enormous stress.

The one night in the hospital, however, gave me the short but welcome break that I needed, not much different from the five minutes of freedom I had asked for and gotten from Joan in a restaurant a few years before, when she wisely averted what would have been the biggest mistake I could have made with my life. I had even written about this occasional claustrophobia some years before, in the musical *Sweet Charity*. Oscar, the romantic interest in Charity's life, was trapped with her in an elevator that stopped between floors. He started to panic and unloosened his tie and unbuttoned his shirt, crying out, "If I could just get out for two minutes. That's all I need, just two minutes. Then I'd get back in again." These symptoms followed me for years, until time and analysis opened the door and let me out.

Still, I kept looking for help. If I were to be of any help to Joan through her neediest hours, I had to shore up my own vulnerable patches. One-on-one therapy was not the answer for this emergency. Talking about my mother who tied me with a rope to my high chair was a long, long dark alley to walk through to unravel my past. I needed something that delivered quickly and came from a place much higher in the soul than something that ended after fifty minutes with, "I'll see you next week, Mr. Simon." I looked for the God I hoped existed but was too cynical to believe in. It did not, however, stop me from asking Him to point me in the right direction, as I mumbled silent prayers on the carpet of my office in the late-night hours when Joan was asleep. I haunted bookshops looking for some quick-help answers. I wanted them so fast, I even looked for the abridged editions. The closest I came to finding some answers was to read the writing of the Eastern philosophers. The teachings of Buddha and Confucius, the Bhagavad Gita, anything that was far enough removed from my own experience that seemed reasonable enough and accessible enough for me to follow. If there was a true God, I thought, surely He was wise enough to send emissaries to comfort those of us who needed to hear a different voice. My intellect followed this path. My heart, on the other hand, always kept the Almighty God as a backup.

Joan's health was not improving but the recent radiation treatments seemed to relieve the pain. In the spring, we started to go back up to Bedford. The warm sun and fresh air put color back into her cheeks. Her smile returned, yet it was not the smile that I had known for all these years. It reflected a new attitude that had come over her. It wasn't exactly acceptance but rather understanding, as if she had made a pact with someone or something that was going to get her through this, no matter what direction she would be going. I saw her walking in the woods with Nancy, who was then just ten, telling her what the names of all the flowers were and how the flowers and trees kept replenishing themselves and that even when a flower dies, it inevitably came back in a new place, with a new fragrance, always there for us to enjoy its beauty. She was telling Nancy, in her own way, what I couldn't bring myself to tell either her or Ellen.

Ellen had made plans to go on a student trip to Europe that summer, and Joan talked to her about what great and wondrous adventures she would soon experience. Nancy was enrolled in a camp in New England. How long do I wait? I kept asking myself. I kept thinking of the surgeon's advice in the hospital. "She'll know when it's time to talk about it."

The girls went back and forth from Bedford to New York while Joan and I stayed on at the lake more frequently, for greater stretches of time. She seemed happiest up there, near the lake, near the fishing, near the woods that reminded her of where she had grown up. One day I was outside the house when I heard her cry of pain. I rushed into her bedroom and found her unable to move, half standing over her bed, afraid to move for fear of making it worse. I was able to help her into the bed, and called Jack Bornstein and told him what was going on. He said to get her into Lenox Hill as soon as possible. There was no way I could get her into the car and no way could she sit up for the hour-and-a-half journey. I called for an ambulance. Joan asked me to call her mother so that she could ride back in the ambulance with her.

In the latter years of her life, before her illness, Joan did not get on all that well with her mother, but all that was quickly put aside when she needed her mother's comfort. Somehow we always seem to go back to our childhood to get the love we had then but which often gets lost or distracted in the everyday business of living our lives as adults. I remember in my father's worst hours, he would call out the word "Momma," even though she was long gone.

The doctors in the hospital told me they thought Joan would need to stay about a week, two at the very most. Joan would talk anxiously about wanting to go back to Bedford. For her it was the best time of the year and she didn't want to miss it. Two weeks came and went. Then three. A month went by. We were now in May and June was coming on fast. When I met Dr. Bornstein in the hall, I saw the glum look on his face that was so rarely there.

"I thought for sure she'd be leaving soon. She was doing so well."

"What's happening?" I asked.

"The cancer is spreading through her like wildfire. Faster than we can treat it. If she were older, it would move much more slowly. We'll do everything we can to make her comfortable . . . and let's not give up hope."

She still did not want any visitors except for the family, and I kept my vow of silence to her. There was hardly anyone who knew her who was aware that she was dying in Lenox Hill Hospital. Even I couldn't go into her room without first knocking and announcing it was me. The nurse would open the door a crack and whisper: "Joanie wants a few minutes to get ready."

"Even for me?"

"Especially for you."

When the door finally opened, I saw Joan sitting up in bed, smiling her best smile, her hair tied back in the ponytail she had worn when I first met her. She put on some makeup, a touch of lipstick, a hint of fragrance, and to me she looked years younger and healthier than anyone could imagine. She would talk to me about the girls and asked how their homework and school-work were going, about my own work, and even plans we should make when she got out of the hospital. Whether she believed it or if it was for my benefit, I couldn't tell. One day as I was sitting with her, there was a quiet knock on the door. I went to see who it was. It was Art Carney, whom I probably hadn't seen since we did *The Odd Couple*.

He whispered to me, "I was just visiting a friend and heard that Joanie was here. Just wanted to send her my love."

As he was about to walk away, Joan called from the room. "Who's that?"

"It's Art Carney. Just passing by. He sends you his love."

It surprised me when she called out, "No, no. Tell him to come in. I'd love to see him."

Art came in and stayed about fifteen minutes and it only took the first two for him to make her smile and laugh. When he left, she said, "Wasn't it nice of Art Carney to come and visit *me*?" As if she thought no one would. If she had allowed it, all of New York would have lined up to see her.

That night at home, I waited for the girls to fall asleep, then went in to Ellen's room and asked her to come with me. I needed to talk to her. We went down to the kitchen, giving me a few extra minutes to prepare myself to deal with this in the best possible way. We sat at the kitchen table, her fifteen-year-old face looking at me apprehensively.

"I should have told you this before, but I was doing what I thought, and what I was told, would be best. You know that Mom is really sick."

She nodded.

"I don't know how long she'll last. The doctors say it could be as long as August or even through the summer. I was just wondering how you'd feel about not going on that trip to Europe because—"

I didn't have to finish the sentence.

"I knew she was sick. I knew she was going to die. I just didn't know when."

Her eyes welled up with tears and as I reached across the table to touch her hand, all her sorrow and grief came pouring out. I told her I wouldn't say anything to Nancy just yet because she'd only be about two hours away and I could always bring her back before anything happened. The next day Ellen came with me to see Joan.

"Ellen's got something to tell you."

"I decided I really don't feel like going to Europe this summer. I'd rather stay here with you and Dad."

Joan smiled happily and said, "I'm so glad. Europe is so far away and I'd miss you."

Again when I spoke to the surgeon, he told me that Joan would be all right for at least another month. This was now the end of June. Nancy came up daily to see her and on the day before she was to leave for camp, she said good-bye to Joan and that she hoped she would feel better soon and come up to visit her in camp. "Of course I will," Joan said. "I wouldn't miss it for anything."

As I sat at home that night, I realized that the details of death would inevitably have to be dealt with. Where would she be buried? If Joan had still not raised the subject, I could hardly broach the question myself. Whatever it was, I would have to tend to the details myself and make the choice the way I thought Joan would want it.

In all the plays I'd ever done throughout my career, I never got ill during the rehearsals, no matter how much pressure was involved, and I saw them all through in reasonably good health that permitted me to function and think clearly right up to opening night. Shortly after the opening of *The Sunshine Boys*, however, I began to notice a sudden decline in my spirits and strength. The hits, of course, were easier to take than the misses, but after a while, it didn't matter much what the result of the finished play was, I was left drained, exhausted, and in time, depressed. The post-partum blues of a playwright. I couldn't think clearly for weeks afterward and didn't trust any of my judgments. In a sense, this is what I was faced with now in Joan's declining months. I was sure I could hold up till the very end, but how good could I be for myself afterward, and more importantly, how good could I be for Nancy and Ellen? I knew I had to prepare in advance to get the aftermath in order, because my own grief would have to be put on hold until I was able to be there for the girls. And to be quite practical, there was no one else but me to do it. For times like this, I can see the benefit of having a large family of brothers and sisters to share this burden. Those who have just lost a family member view the business of dealing with funeral arrangements as painful and agonizing. As for myself, I feel indignation and anger because, in my muddled state, I believe my wife's or mother's or father's remains will be treated by the people who run funeral homes merely as a business transaction, which, for them, it is, but they seem to overlook the deep, personal loss I am going through. There's no reasonable sense in thinking that's how they should feel, but the person they're putting to rest has been one of the most important people in your life and you don't want *anyone* treating this occasion as one might buying or selling furniture.

When my father died some years before, I was unprepared, by virtue of never having done it before, to attend to his funeral arrangements. My brother was in California and I thought perhaps he imagined I had secretaries to deal with this business. I didn't and wouldn't have used one if I did. As my father had already purchased a burial plot for himself years before, to rest alongside his family, his maternal side, it was left to me to make the funeral arrangements and choose the casket. The funeral arrangements were an easy matter because you just choose the number of cars needed and determine how many people will be coming. The cost of a funeral was pretty straightforward. The casket was another matter. The choice of a casket was, in my most cynical state of mind, where they had a chance to make extra money. The popcorn that precedes the movie, if you will allow my bitterness to be mixed with the awful truth. I was led into a large room beneath the funeral home where all the caskets were on display, looking like the showroom of a company that sells expensive single beds. No matter that this was a solemn occasion, once I walked into their showplace I knew I was leaving the world of bereavement and entering Huckster Heaven, where hushed voices and words of condolence do not in any way interfere with their business of playing on your sympathies and/or guilt to make a fast two grand. Evelyn Waugh wrote of this racket, in the blackest of black humor, in his novel *The Loved One*. As a matter of fact, the first question I was asked by Mr. Unctious was, "How are you related to the loved one?" My father was no longer Irving Simon or Mr. Simon or even "your father." He was now the "deceased" or "departed." "The loved one."

"What did you have in mind?" he asked as if I'd been thinking for years about the casket I always hoped I could find. My back was up the minute this conversation started, and I wanted desperately to walk out or ask some superior for a Human Being to help me instead of this "Used Emotions Salesman." The thing is, he has you and he knows he has you. What else are you going to do? Make a casket yourself? He whispers and looks around in a gentle hint that possibly the departed is hovering around somewhere and is watching from above, anxious to see how you're going to treat him in his afterlife. The Huckster goes through his litany of Personal Memorial Questions, to give him an understanding of what might best suit your loved one.

"What sort of man was he? Was he a quiet, simple man or one who enjoyed the arts, music, literature?" As if one precluded the other. And if the answer was the latter, was his coffin going to be lined with twenty-five of his favorite books, first editions when available?

Just when he realizes he may have pushed one button too many, he pulls out his ace in the hole.

"I can see that you're a rather private person, and I suggest you walk around and get a feeling for what you're most comfortable with. I'll leave you to wander. Take your time and when you need me, I'll be in my office just near the staircase." He leaves, goes to his office, closes his door, and proceeds to watch you from his closed-circuit video camera, hoping to find a clue as to what to offer you when you seem confused. The truth is that this ploy works far and away better than any pitch he can make. It's now between you, your father, and your conscience. You start to ask yourself questions you never dealt with before. "Who *was* my father? What kind of man was he, now that he's no longer here to intimidate me? Do I choose based on what *I* would want for my father? Or what my father would want *others* to see what his son thought of him? Or more importantly, does my father want to go out proving to the world that he was an important and much beloved man?" In the case of my father, I chose the latter. It was big, it was a touch ornate, and it was expensive. What I really hoped was that no one would judge me or my father by the casket he would soon be lying in. The bizarre thoughts we have at times like this. At any rate, I thought my father would be happy with my choice. It's not until we all get to the other side do we find the answer to that one. Commerce is a permanent part of life and death. We pay doctors and hospitals for letting us in, and morticians for letting us out. Someone will always make a buck on your welcome and on your farewell.

ONE MORNING IN JULY, I drove up to the Pound Ridge Cemetery, about a ten-minute drive from our house in Bedford. I had contacted the man in charge and he was there waiting for me when I arrived. I explained I wanted two plots together, knowing that's where I wanted to be when it was my time. He stayed beside his car as I walked around, looking at the surroundings. The cemetery was old and well taken care of, and I read the names on the headstones as if checking out who my new neighbors would be. It was a warm day, the sun was shining, and a gentle breeze rustled through the trees. I walked up a slight knoll and saw a well-trimmed patch of green grass under a large elm, giving ample shade and even a view of the quiet countryside. This time I felt Joan's presence. This was the spot I knew she would want. I pointed to it and the gentleman standing beside his car nodded to me and jotted down the location in his notebook. At last, someone who had the sensitivity to know that this was a private moment, and when to keep his distance and his silence.

THE PHONE RANG on the table next to my bed. It was ten after three in the morning. The day was July 11, 1973. A voice on the other end told me softly that Joan had passed away in her sleep. I thanked him without asking many questions. I said I would be there as soon as I could. She was forty years old. I sat up in my bed, trying to compose myself, and then after a while went upstairs, woke Ellen and told her. It came sooner than we had expected, and the finality of it all hadn't quite sunk in as yet. It was just a telephone call and the depth of the true loss comes later, when the sun rises and you realize that this new day and all the days of your life to come will be without Joan. Nancy was still up in camp, not where she would have been had I not waited so long to tell her. I made arrangements with one of the women who ran the camp to bring her home as quickly as she could. This was the day that I finally told Nancy, and it was too late. Of all the regrets I've ever had and still have till this day, it was my not telling Nancy sooner. It took her years to open up to me to tell me that she was angry and confused when she found out. Yet she never blamed me for it. She said what she regretted most was not having the five years more with her mother that Ellen had.

We drove home from the cemetery in Pound Ridge with Joan's mother in the car sitting between her grandchildren. I sat on the jump seat, looking at them, at their faces, their hands in the firm grip of their Nanny Baim. I turned and looked at the countryside passing swiftly by, pondering what kind of father would I make, knowing that the loss of a mother to two girls who still had their youth to get through was one of the most devastating traumas to endure.

The lyric of a song that Gwen Verdon sang in *Sweet Charity* suddenly came into my mind: "Where am I going and what will I find?" I hadn't a clue. At age forty-six, with two young daughters, I felt empty and frightened. The one thing we did have, however, was each other. The car turned onto the East River Drive and made its way through the heavy traffic and heat of the day toward our little house on Sixty-second Street.

THE PLAY GOES ON

Acknowledgment

My enormous gratitude to Michael Korda, for his willingness to go to bat with me again; to Charles "Chuck" Adams, Editor Extraordinaire; Gypsy da Silva, Copy Supervisor Extraordinairess; Victoria Meyer and all those supporters at Simon & Schuster, and to my invaluable assistant, Terry Oxford, and to my good friend Morton Janklow.

To Elaine Joyce—
who turned my life around.

LIFE REVISITED

1

EVERYTHING STOPPED. The sun came up, the clocks ticked on but nothing moved. I was always a morning person: the first one up in the house, the first one dressed, the first one down in the kitchen, the first one at breakfast.

But now I was still in bed, without a clue as to what time it was. I could hear the hum of the air conditioner, feel a chill in the room and yet my pajama tops were drenched through with perspiration. Were the girls upstairs in their rooms, silently waiting for me to come up to tell them what we would do with this, the first day of our lives on our own? I was fighting the act of awakening. I kept my eyes closed in hopes that sleep would overtake me once more, buying me more time before I would have to take a deep breath and then release it, acknowledging that I was alive. The future was a totally unpleasant prospect and I wasn't quite ready to deal with it. We had buried my wife, Joan, the day before at the Pound Ridge Cemetery in New York. She had just turned forty and had died of cancer, the most surprising thing she had done in a life filled with surprises.

I clung tenaciously to the darkness behind my closed lids, trying to keep the daylight at bay, much as I had as a boy when it was time to leave the local movie house, knowing that I left Humphrey Bogart or Errol Flynn still battling villains on the screen, while outside I squinted at the glaring harshness of the four o'clock sun and faced the heat of another endless summer's day.

Nancy was ten and Ellen was fifteen. It was July 12, 1973. Eight days before, on the Fourth of July, I had turned forty-six. It might as well have been sixty-six for all the lethargy and despondency I felt in my aching mind and body on that dreary morning. I pushed myself out of bed and crossed to the closet, looking for a robe that I almost never wore. Robes always made me feel either sick or old or both. Mine was a gift from Joan's mother, and I had feigned delight and pleasure when I opened it in front of her at an earlier birthday, knowing that I would never wear it, that it would only take up valuable space in my small closet. How ironic that I would be putting it on today, the day after her daughter died. But I needed a robe that morning because I did not want to face the girls in sweaty pajamas, although I had neither the strength nor inclination to get out of those pajamas, nor could I imagine myself doing so in the foreseeable future. What for? There was nothing outside that small town house on East 62nd Street that I wanted or needed to see. Nor *anyone* besides my daughters. I neither asked for nor invited friends or family to pay us a condolence call. At least not on that first day. The few really close friends I had would call later that morning, but they understood when I said, "Not yet. Give me today alone with the girls." Despite the fact that I had been aware for the past year and a half that Joan was going to die, I was unprepared for what I experienced on that first morning. It was not exactly grief, because, in a sense, I had been grieving those last few months of her life. This was a feeling of numbness, inertia and confusion, leading to a frightening inability to make a decision, trivial or otherwise. I have no memory of when I first saw the girls that morning, but Nancy told me recently that for some inexplicable reason, what she pictures in her mind today was the three of us in semi-darkness, sitting on the steps leading from the kitchen down to the basement. An implausible place to meet, and yet, for that morning, as plausible as any.

The thought uppermost in my mind was to distract the girls from dealing with the past, and to get them busy with getting on with life, making some small attempt at normalcy. I am always amazed at the resiliency of the young. They looked at me, waiting to hear what my plans were, ready and eager to comply. Neither girl had intended to be home that summer, both having made plans, not fully realizing the graveness of Joan's condition. Nancy was summoned back from camp when Joan passed away sooner than I ever imagined, and Ellen had canceled a student trip to Europe to be with her mother for her last few months. I suggested getting away from New York, as far away as possible, distancing ourselves from loss and sorrow. The summer house in Pound Ridge, New York, that I had bought expressly as a gift to Joan, where I hoped she would recover from her illness, was just a marginal choice to revisit. I offered to take them both to Europe, reasoning that traveling and being together would be, if not a fun-filled vacation, at least a chance to heal ourselves in new surroundings, in a place with fewer memories. Nancy surprised me when she opted to return to camp. It also gave me a sense of relief to know that this ten-year-old knew what was best for her. Ellen and I left together for Europe a week later.

I made the mistake of returning to all the same hotels that Joan and I had stayed in, something that proved harder for me to deal with than for Ellen. But slowly, day by day, I began to see a change in Ellen, a maturing, perhaps growing up faster than she normally would have if Joan were still alive. She started to point out things in shops in London and in Paris that might go nicely in our house. As it had been with Joan, who always brought home pretty and useful items from our trips, it was now with Ellen, who kept her eye open for unusual pieces I never thought remotely interested her before. In a sense, she was emulating Joan, perhaps not consciously, but in the normal way that a child takes on some of the traits of the parent of the same gender. By the time we returned home in late August, Ellen walked into our kitchen, opened the cabinets and said, "You know what, Dad? We need new dishes." Nancy came home a few days later, taller, tanner and a good deal happier than when she left. We were all so glad to see each other, and our conversation that night was about what we had done that summer and not about the tragedy we left behind. But it was certainly not gone from their minds; I noticed that clearly as Nancy climbed the steps that night and glanced quickly in my bedroom to see the made-up bed which Joan had occupied for so many months during her illness.

Later I heard laughter from their rooms and then the sound of tapes playing the Broadway musicals they loved so much, and their singing the lyrics to their favorite songs, loudly and slightly off-key. Eventually they switched to television and called down to me, "Dad, come on up and watch with us." I knew once I got in their room, they would bar me from leaving, forcing me to watch every fashion show, sitcom, summer rerun and old black-and-white movie. As I ascended the stairs, smelling the fresh popcorn they had just made, while scorching the bottom of the pot, I said to myself, "Thank you God for making daughters."

THE WANDERER

2

IN THE DAYS and weeks following, I walked through the streets of New York like a somnambulist, having to look up at corner signs to see where I was. Not that I was walking in any particular direction, or with any specific destination in mind. I walked through Bloomingdale's, fingering shirts or jackets without the slightest intention of buying anything. I was constantly looking at everyone who passed by, with the preposterously illogical hope that I might see Joan. There was always the possibility that the doctors had been mistaken about her death, or, just as unlikely, that I merely dreamt she died, which would explain the foggy, half-awake state in which I existed. The memory flashed in my mind how sometimes, before Joan ever got ill, I would be walking down a street and would glance up and see her looking in a store window. She would turn and see me, and we would both smile, thinking the same thing: "We just had a free one"—meaning an extra time of seeing each other, one we hadn't planned on.

I climbed the steps of the Metropolitan Museum of Art on Fifth Avenue, and wandered through the great exhibition halls, delving into Egyptian antiquity. Then I went up the stairs to the paintings of Matisse and Renoir, Van Gogh and Rembrandt; I stared at the John Sargents I loved so well, remembering when I first saw them with Joan. With her at my side, I had the added advantage of having her fill me in with minute details of the painter's art, most of which I might not have noticed on my own. For me she was like one of those tape-recorded talking guides you rent as you enter the museum, except with this one, you were allowed to hold the hand of this guide, or watch her hair bobbing up and down as she tried to peer over the crowd to see the museum's latest and most talked about acquisition.

On the day I chose to revisit the museum alone, I suddenly heard a voice directly behind me.

"Neil?"

I turned and looked.

"I'm Carol Mantz."

She said her name as though I should know it, but I didn't have a clue as to who she was. Or maybe I did know her, but like everything else in my life at that moment, I couldn't fit the pieces together.

"I think you knew my husband, Mark. He said you both grew up together in Washington Heights."

"Mark? Oh, yes. Mark. Of course." I had no idea who Mark was. Well, perhaps it sounded vaguely familiar, but if I was struggling with my own identity, I couldn't blame myself for not remembering a boy I knew thirty years before.

"I was sorry to hear about your wife. I read about it in the paper."

"Yes. Thank you." Wanting to get off the subject, I went back to hers: "So, how is Mark these days?"

"He died six months ago. Heart attack."

"Oh, God, I'm so sorry. Was he ill?"

"Never sick a day in his life. Just keeled over in his office."

"Oh, no. How terrible for you."

My words of comfort seemed as empty as the ones I had been hearing myself every day for the past three weeks. You appreciate them, but you don't quite know how to deal with them.

"When you started writing plays, Mark told me he was a friend of yours. He was so proud of you. I think we've seen all of them."

I could see the tears welling up in her eyes and I was suddenly jolted back to the past. A picture of Mark Mantz as a teenager came vividly into my mind: outgoing, funny, friendly; had to be about my age. I looked at her and this time I actually saw her. She was about thirty-six, a few years younger than Joan. She told me they had a little boy who was seven. Then, for no apparent reason, the conversation stopped. There was an awkward silence because neither one of us wanted to talk about death and losses. I wanted to walk on but didn't want to appear unsympathetic to her troubles nor self-involved by talking about mine.

"So, I guess we're sort of in the same boat, aren't we?" she said. I nodded, sensing what her next line would be.

"I don't know how you feel about it, but if you'd like to talk about—well, you know. If you'd like to have coffee or a drink or dinner, I could give you my number."

The mood changed in an instant. We had moved from tragedy to new beginnings. In a sense, whether it was coffee or a drink or whatever, it was still a date, and I was not only unprepared for a date at this time, I was also not sure I knew my way home from the museum.

"Thank you," I said. "That's very kind of you. To tell you the truth, I'm not quite—"

"Oh, I understand. I wasn't either at first."

"Then you know what I'm—"

"I do. Honestly, it was just an offer. If you change your mind, my number's in the book. Take care of yourself. Your girls are going to need you now."

She turned and walked away. Interesting that she even knew about my girls. Here was a date that was being contemplated by her, not necessarily by mutual attraction, but by mutual tragedy. By the rules of natural selection, people have been bonding that way since the beginning of man's time on earth. However, the thought of moving on with my life as yet hadn't even occurred to me.

She had six months of mourning behind her. I was hardly out of my first three weeks.

I realized I could no longer find refuge in department stores, bookstores, movies or museums. My only salvation was to get back to work. Throughout my career, whether in moods of quiet despair, painful back spasms, a high-grade flu and, amazingly, even during Joan's illness, I was able to continue working, albeit only a few hours a day. I had the ability to block everything else out of my thoughts and focus completely on the work at hand. By picking up a pen and gazing at the blank pages of the spiral notebook in front of me, I suddenly lost sight of my surroundings and circumstances, and entered the world in which the characters I created were living out their own problems or good fortune. They had no interest in *my* immediate woes, no knowledge they even existed. Which led me to think: Did they know I was there, in *their* place, *their* room, sitting in a dark corner witnessing the most personal moments of their own inner conflicts? Did these characters even care that I was committing their words, their thoughts, their actions to paper? Were they oblivious to the fact that I might one day share their lives with total strangers, who were privy to this information only by my invitation? Since they never brought it up, I didn't bother mentioning it to them.

In the year and a half of Joan's illness, I had completed the screenplay of *The Prisoner of Second Avenue*, which was to start filming in Hollywood in a matter of weeks. It was to star Jack Lemmon and Anne Bancroft. I also had completed a new play, *The Good Doctor*, based on short stories by Anton

Chekhov. Warner Brothers and director Mel Frank wanted me to attend two weeks of rehearsals in Los Angeles to do any last-minute rewrites on *Prisoner*, the kinds of changes that would inevitably be needed once the actors started digging into their roles. *The Prisoner of Second Avenue*, although a critical and commercial success on stage, worried me as film material. It was a serious comedy or a funny drama, a sort of hybrid form of play, atypical for most playwrights in the 1970s. Eugene O'Neill wrote drama/tragedies. George S. Kaufman wrote comedies. Samuel Beckett wrote poignant humor laden with a sense of anguish and loss, while Eugene Ionesco wrote abstract farces with strong social overtones. Tennessee Williams wrote poetic tragedies that managed to have a great deal of ironic humor. What they all had in common was that they did their work masterfully. These were the greats that I wanted to emulate. The problem was that I wanted to emulate them all at the same time, and often, all in the same play. What was odd about my plays was that when they were funny, they were true comedies, and when they were dramatic, they dealt with everyday people faced with serious dilemmas. What was confounding and somewhat annoying to many critics was that I was attempting to do both things in the same play. They felt I was being neither true to the comedy nor true to the drama. Since most audiences seemed to like what I was doing, however, there was the paradox of my having a great many hits that critics did not praise. It's hard to sell tickets to plays that critics frown on, yet the audiences came anyway. Since I was committing the cardinal sin of being popular without their stamp of approval, the critics (not all, but a lot) banished me to the Devil's Island of the Arts by designating me "Not Important."

In the case of *Prisoner*, I worried that the moviegoing audience wouldn't be as accommodating as a theater audience. *The Odd Couple* and *Barefoot in the Park*, both true comedies, were successes in both mediums. The darker my plays became, however, the more lackluster the results when they were transferred to the big screen.

Despite my eagerness to get back to work, I soon realized I was in no emotional shape to handle two projects at one time, no mind to do rewrites and little desire to fly to Hollywood for two weeks, leaving the girls behind. Yet I needed to occupy myself before the girls became caretakers to the one person in the world who should be taking care of them. Foolishly or not, I plunged into work, hoping somehow to keep my head above water.

As for the new play, I left that in the hands of my more than capable producer, Manny Azenberg. He started the wheels in motion, prepping *The Good Doctor* for production late in the fall. We hired a director, scenic designer and costume designer and began casting. I sat through auditions with director A. J. Antoon in a darkened theater, wondering what I was doing there, unable to concentrate on the actors, while I played mind games with myself, something in the order of "I'd give two years of my life if I could make just one phone call to Joan wherever she was in the universe that day."

Christopher Plummer accepted the starring role playing both Chekhov as narrator and as principal actor in Chekhov's creations, as interpreted by Neil Simon. Other fine actors like Barnard Hughes, Frances Sternhagen and Rene Auberjonois were soon added to the cast. What we were missing was one young, attractive, funny, touching, serious, seasoned and delightful new actress who could play five completely different roles in one evening. You could search for three years and still not find someone like that. We didn't have years; I was to leave for California in two weeks, and in that time we auditioned thirty or forty actresses. Many of them could do one, perhaps two of the roles, but not a single one could come close to doing all five roles, being convincing in each one of them.

I was worried about not being able to ever find the right actress, and being in the fragile state I was in, I wouldn't have minded if we canceled the entire production either forever or, more reasonably, until I became something more than just the shadow of my former self.

A few days before I was to leave for California, I received a call from actor's agent Phyliss Wender. She said she was representing someone very special and asked if I could see this actress in the next day or so. Phyliss was someone I respected and liked, and the fact that she called me personally and avoided going through the normal channels of calling our casting director first was a signal to me that this person was someone I should pay attention to. I told her I was about to leave for Los Angeles and asked if I could see her client when I returned in two weeks.

"She'll be gone in two weeks," Phyliss answered. "She'll be gone in two *days*. She has to be in Seattle to start a new film. Neil, I'm asking you to trust me on this one. This is someone you should really see."

"Phyliss, I trust you, but I don't trust me right now. I don't think I'm clear-headed enough to make a good judgment." I paused while I tried to force reason through the cementlike block of protection that the mind sets up while one is healing. "When is the last day I could see her?" I finally asked.

"Tomorrow. I feel terrible about pushing this, but after this movie, I may never be able to get her out of pictures."

In my silence, we could both hear my brain trying to fight through to a decision. She tried to find a way around it: "Would you leave the decision up to Manny and A. J. Antoon?"

"I would, but Manny would never sign anyone if I didn't see them first. Do I know her?"

"I'm not sure. Her name is Marsha Mason."

"No. Not familiar to me."

"She did *The Indian Wants the Bronx* off-Broadway with Al Pacino. She got great reviews. I could send them to you."

"I can't audition reviews. I can't even remember if I saw the play. Probably not." I trusted Phyliss too much to pass and I knew she wasn't just trying to get a client a job. She was too earnest and smart for that.

"All right. What about tomorrow afternoon? About four."

"Could we make it at two? Actually, she's leaving tomorrow night."

I smiled. "You really love pressure, don't you? And there's going to be a lot of it, if we all come down to audition just one girl."

She was ready for that one. "I thought of that. I'm bringing another girl as well. She's good, but this part belongs to Marsha."

"Phyliss, you should be running MGM and Paramount."

"No, thanks. I love New York, and I've got my kids in a good school. I'll see you tomorrow at two."

Tomorrow sounded like a thousand years away. I hung up and took Ellen and Nancy out to the same Chinese restaurant for the third night in a row. I had no idea it was the third night until Ellen opened up her fortune cookie and read aloud, "Hello Simon family. We were expecting you." Nancy laughed before I realized it was a joke. I was glad that someone in the family still had a sense of humor.

NIGHT VISITS

3

I BEGAN PERFORMING a ritual each night before I went to bed. I had read a good deal about meditation but found it very difficult to keep my mind and thoughts still enough to receive any benefit from it. With Joan's passing, I now had a reason to go back to meditation, not for quieting my restless mind, but to somehow find a way of keeping Joan's positive and reassuring qualities still alive within me. I was afraid if I lost contact, not with her, but what she meant to me, I would lose an important part of myself. I believed in our marriage so firmly—the give-and-take between two loving people, the bolstering of one's spirits when the other one's were flagging—I desperately needed to keep the memory of what she contributed to my life, some way, somehow, always there beside me.

Each night, after the girls were asleep, I put my favorite picture of Joan on a small table and lit a candle on each side of it. Then I sat on the carpeted floor, my back against the small sofa in the room in which I worked; with all the lights off and the shades drawn, I stared deeply at the face of Joan as I remembered her best: I was trying to burn the image of her face into my mind, burn it so deeply that it would never fade and always be there at any time of the day or night that I summoned it. After a while, I began to talk to the picture in a whisper, although low enough not to be heard by anyone (including myself) for fear I would feel foolish, embarrassed and self-conscious. Hence the drawn shades. It even occurred to me that Joan might be watching this ritual from the place in the room that she still inhabited, and that she was surprised to see a part of me she never knew existed. For that matter, neither did I. I wasn't sure if she was amused by it or simply appreciated the fact that I was making a kind of person-to-person call to her each night.

I was not looking for help to assuage my pain: I counted on the pain to assure me she was still in my thoughts. What I wanted was guidance in becoming both a father and a mother to my two daughters. I needed someone to show me the ropes, to whisper in my ear those things girls growing up needed to hear. It soon occurred to me that it wasn't Joan that I was talking to at all, but rather it was me appealing to and summoning up the best parts of me, using the image of Joan, who knew me so well, as a guide to help me to find my own answers. These sessions became such a habit that I couldn't fall asleep without them. If I had forgotten somehow, I'd get up in the middle of the night, like a fan devoted to his favorite program, cross into the "session" room and tune her in. After a while, the sessions became lighthearted and conversational chats rather than the earlier solemn, ceremonial and reverentially clandestine meetings. Sometimes they began with, "Hi, Joan, and how was your day today?"

Miraculously, it worked for me. If I had a problem at night, then sat down for a quiet midnight tête-à-tête with my deceased wife, more often than not I awoke in the morning having resolved the problem while I slept. For example, as I woke up early one morning, I answered my own question: "You can't be a mother to your daughters. Just be a better father." I never had to deal with that one again. The days were slowly getting better, but the improvement rested on the premise that I was looking forward to chatting with Joan that night—and every night. Without my realizing it, the more I held on to Joan through our talk sessions the more I was impeding my own recovery from the grief, a situation that was to remain constant for a very long time.

I ARRIVED at the theater for the audition promptly at two o'clock. I am almost never late for anything. Actors generally get there earlier than their appointed time to go over the pages they're going to read and to try and settle their nerves. As I entered the stage door, I saw one actress sitting on the steps that led up to the dressing rooms. I had no idea if this was Marsha Mason or the girl that Phyliss sent along to read as a backup if we didn't like Ms. Mason. As I passed her, the actress looked up from her pages, smiled at me and nodded. I returned the nod. Not good to get too friendly with them, I always thought. Be polite, yes, but not amiable. It makes it that much harder when and if they got rejected, which was ninety percent of the time. I was never very good at this auditioning business anyway. I was always grateful that the director or casting agent was the one to say, often before they were through reading, "Thank you very much. We appreciate your coming in." That was the standard line for, "No. Not you." The actor knows it immediately and will either look up surprised or disappointed, or will just take it in stride and leave. I always found the longest and most difficult few seconds were when he or she walked off the stage, usually having to pass the other actors who were waiting their turn. Sometimes they made casual comments to each other in passing, other times it was a quick walk out the door in silence, and if they were lucky, off to another audition. Twenty-five years ago, when the New York theater had an abundance of new plays, an actor could go to two or three auditions a day. Today they're few and far between.

Very often an actor I knew, liked and had worked with before came out to read. When it was clear that he or she was not quite right for this role, the thank-yous and goodbyes were more pleasant. There might be some funny exchange about the good times we remembered on that other play. Oftentimes, they would remark as they left, "Good luck with this. It's a great play." A generous thing to say. This despite the fact the actor *always* thinks he's right for the part. They *should* feel that, otherwise why would they be there? And if he thinks he's not right for the part, he should believe that with enough work he could *make* himself right for it. Only once in my life did I hear an actor stop himself in the middle of his reading and say, "You don't want to hear any more of this, do you? I'm stinking it up." He did eventually go on to win an Academy Award as Best Actor in a film that also won as Best Picture. It was F. Murray Abraham and the film was *Amadeus* and his award was well deserved. And in case Murray wants to know, he did not stink it up that day. I think he decided he just didn't want to do that particular play.

This auditioning business works both ways, of course. Once, an actor who had just won the Tony Award as Best Actor in a Play a few weeks before he came to audition sat in a room with us and thought carefully before he said, "Do you think the time will come when an actor who just won a major award doesn't have to audition?"

I said, "Tell me something, would you want to do my play if you hadn't had the opportunity to read it first?"

He smiled and said, "No. But you've seen my work."

"You've seen my work too," I added.

He decided to audition, but his heart wasn't in it. He took another job before we ever came to a decision about him. The truth is, yes, there comes a time when an actor doesn't have to audition. If he's Tom Hanks or Jack Nicholson or Barbra Streisand, ad infinitum. I *always* have to audition. No star will do my play until he reads it first. Jack Lemmon was the only actor *ever* who said yes to doing a film of mine after I gave him a mere five-sentence description of the story.

But back to the audition at hand. As I started for the door that led from back stage to the theater, I saw the second actress sitting on a chair, studying the pages. She looked up and smiled at me, as the first girl had, but there was something in this smile that was different. There was a warmth and intelligence and confidence in her face that left little doubt in my mind that *this* was Marsha Mason. It was also a face I had seen before—but where? In a play? A film? On television? Wait a minute. I think this is the girl in that commercial. Manufacturers Hanover Trust, I think. All she did was look straight in the camera and recite the copy the ad agency had written. About higher interest rates, more convenience, better locations. The usual boring patter that we, the viewers, dismiss out of hand. Until they show it often enough and you absorb it by repetition. But as I watched her in that commercial, the writer in me knew that the actress in her was adding a subtext to what she was saying merely by the way she looked at the camera. What was the subtext was *her* secret, and we could only guess. To me she was saying, "All else aside, if you come down to our bank, you'll have one hell of a time." Well, obviously the delivery was not that overtly sexual, but I found myself waiting for that commercial to come on again soon. And suddenly her name also seemed familiar. I had read it in a review. Now it was coming back. That movie with George Segal and Kris Kristofferson . . . Damn, what was the name of it? And as it came to me, I found myself blurting it out.

"Oh," I said in recognition. "You're that girl from *Love in Blume*, aren't you?"

"*Blume in Love*," she said, correcting me. "Yes, that was me."

Then she laughed and there was that smile again. I suddenly had an overwhelming desire to go down to a bank. Subliminal advertising had worked its powers on me again.

"Right," I said. "I thought you were terrific."

"Oh? Thank you," she said, surprised at the good review I had just given her. "I'm glad you liked it."

I had just made a mistake. I was being chatty. I was being amiable. I had told her she was terrific in the movie I had seen. Turning her down for the play after such a positive connection would be tantamount to saying, "Amazing. You were so good in that movie, but your reading for the play was lousy."

Inasmuch as she hadn't heard what I was thinking, I continued being chatty.

"Well, I'll see you again in a few minutes, won't I?"

She laughed in agreement. "Yes, I guess you will."

As I walked into the darkened theater, I remembered more clearly why I liked her performance in *Blume in Love*. She first appeared in the film coming out of an arrival gate at the L.A. airport. Coming from the opposite direction was a glum and recently separated Blume, played by George Segal. She sees him and calls out to him, an old friend she once dated. He turns, surprised and happy to see her. Strangely, so was I. What struck me most about her, aside from her being very pretty, warm and vivacious, was that she didn't seem like an actress at all. She wasn't acting. She was talking. When she started to talk to Blume, I thought to myself, "Oh, no. This woman is interrupting the movie. She must know George Segal. Maybe she's just a fan. She's not even aware there's a camera around. The director will probably shout 'Cut' and have her ushered away." But their conversation continued. Perhaps the director thought, "Say, this is good. This is like real life. I don't know who this woman is, but she's so good I'll just leave it in the picture."

Well, since I'm not a total dummy, I soon realized this *was* the movie and she was *in* the movie. And that's pretty much how I had felt when I saw Marsha Mason sitting back stage a few moments before. She's someone you connect with immediately, whether she's in a film, in a play or sitting in a chair preparing to audition. She'd even be nice to run into at a grocery store. She also had coloring I was very partial to. Reddish hair, light skin and a hint of freckles barely concealed by the small amount of makeup she was using that day. Anxiously, I took my seat next to A. J. Antoon and Manny. Manny whispered to me, "I was going to leave for the country last night. This better be good."

Good would have had a better chance if he had seen *Blume in Love*, but Manny spent less time in movie theaters than I did. And I knew I couldn't very well say, "Hey, have you seen that Manufacturers Hanover Trust commercial? She had a terrific quality in that." That quality would be fine if we were doing a play about high interest rates in a bank, but this was Chekhov, and for Chekhov, you'd do best by having a classically trained actress.

From the corner of my eye, I saw Phyliss Wender quietly take a seat about eight rows behind us, giving silent support to someone she truly believed in. The first actress, not Marsha, was introduced to us by our stage manager, who was going to read with her. We exchanged pleasantries. This young woman had the disadvantage of not being in *Blume in Love*; therefore, although she had my attention, she did not have the benefit of my anticipation. Before she began reading, she stopped for a moment to prepare. She paused, looked away and apparently moved her mental geography from 49th Street in New York to a dacha about two hundred miles north of Moscow, in the dead of winter, circa 1890. When she arrived there, she nodded to the stage manager, who spoke his first line, cueing her into her first speech. Surprisingly, it went well. She was good. Nice quality, warm and competent. Phyliss Wender was no fool. Even if this girl was just a setup for Marsha, she was in no way being sent out on stage as a human sacrifice. Phyliss did not represent anyone unless she thought they had quality. Perhaps this audition was going to turn out to be a head-to-head race to the finish line. Nevertheless, two thirds into the reading, my attention waned. She was playing one or two wonderful notes while we were looking for someone who could give us the entire concerto. I looked at Manny and A.J., who both shook their heads, "No," as did I. A.J. called out, "That's fine. Thank you very much. We appreciate your coming in." She smiled and nodded and as she turned to go, I called out, "That was very good. I really liked it." She looked pleased, even though I knew she wasn't counting on getting the part. She was seen by us and that was primarily what she wanted. Who knows? We might call her back when we were casting for understudies or possibly we'd remember her for another play we'd do in the future.

As the stage manager escorted her off, my mind momentarily went back to reality. I knew that once I left the theater after auditions, I would be back in a world that belonged to everyone else, but one that I did not feel a part of anymore. I also knew I would not be permitted back into it until I presented myself at the main gate, knocked on its door loudly and proclaimed that I was *ready* to enter again. When I got into that frame of mind, I would sometimes have to slap my thigh to remind myself to focus and attend to the business at hand. This time I didn't have to slap my thigh. I focused the minute the stage manager said from center stage, "Marsha Mason."

Almost as a reflex, I called out, "I told you we'd meet again soon."

She laughed and said, "Yes, I had a hunch we would."

I remembered that laugh from a scene in *Blume in Love*. George Segal's character had just said something to Arlene, Marsha's character, that could easily be construed as thoughtless and cruel. I expected an outburst from her, but instead, Marsha looked at him and laughed. It put him in his place more than any vitriolic words could have. It surprised me and it surprised George Segal. I wondered, Was it Marsha who made this choice or was it the director?

My hunch was that Marsha did it in rehearsal and the director loved it and told her to leave it in. She hadn't even read a word for *The Good Doctor* as yet, and already I knew more about her as an actress than I did when I entered the theater twenty minutes before. A.J. asked her a few questions to put her at ease before she tackled the first of the five shortened scenes we asked her to prepare. Very often actors will say to a director before reading, "Is there anything you want to tell me about this part?" in hopes of finding a clue to what we were looking for. I preferred it when they didn't. Marsha didn't.

Manny whispered to me before she began, "Interesting girl." "She's good," he said after she breezed through the first two scenes.

"This girl can act," he continued after the third scene. As far as I was concerned, she already had the part wrapped up and tucked in her pocket. But I let her continue through to the end of the last scene, not to make certain she could do it, but selfishly, because I got a free reading of the play so I could see what it was I wanted to rewrite later. In a sense, we were already in rehearsal. When she finished, Manny looked at us to corroborate his own feelings.

"Do we want her?" he asked.

"I want to marry her," said A.J., this coming from a man who recently left a Jesuit school where he was preparing to spend his life as a priest.

"Absolutely," I added my own vote. "She's wonderful."

"Unanimous," said Manny. He called out to Marsha and asked her if she could wait a few minutes as he walked back in the darkened theater to negotiate with Phyliss. I used the time to find out a little more about this young actress. She told me she had spent the last two seasons in San Francisco doing repertory at the American Conservatory Theater, one of the best regional theaters in America. She did everything from Ibsen's *A Doll's House*, to Rostand's *Cyrano* to Noël Coward's *Private Lives*. I breathed more easily. Besides being sexy doing a staid bank commercial, she was also a classically trained actress. Manny and Phyliss called me back to speak to them. Money and billing were not a problem, but we had a steadfast rule that all actors in featured roles had to sign on for a year's run, nine months in rare exceptions. "She'll only do six months," said Phyliss. "She has a contract with 20th Century Fox for seven pictures, and that's all the time they'd let her out for." Nine out of ten times that would be a deal breaker with us.

"Take her," I said to Manny, "I don't want to lose her." Neither did Manny nor A.J. The deal was made although I don't think Marsha knew until she left the theater. I had no idea what her reaction was. I was delighted that we finally had a cast, and I could now leave for California without having to think about the play for at least two and a half months.

As I walked home, *The Good Doctor* and Marsha Mason were no longer in my thoughts. I now had to focus on packing a bag and flying three thousand—or was it three hundred thousand or three million?—miles away from Nancy and Ellen. It would be the first time I'd been separated from the girls since Joan died, and I worried how they would be. I also wondered how I would manage on my own, and how I was going to rewrite a movie I barely had any recollection of writing in the first place.

THE STARK MAN

4

I ARRIVED in Los Angeles and took a cab to the Beverly Hills Hotel. This was a smart move on my part because if I had rented a car at Avis, I would have spent the next three days trying to find my way out of the airport. For anyone like myself, who has totally no sense of direction, getting around a city such as L.A. was unimaginable. Gertrude Stein, as I heard it, once aptly said of Los Angeles, "There is no there there." That, however, was not my problem. I knew it was there. I just couldn't find where where was. I like cities that are laid out in grids, cities like New York and Paris. They have a center which extends out to all points of the city. Los Angeles is laid out like laundry strewn about on a windy desert, which, when giving directions, makes about as much sense as saying, "Go left at the blue denim shirt, then make a right at the tan sock which turns into a gray sock and then when you get to the white pajama top, make a sharp right at the Calvin Klein undershirt, unless it's blown away."

Fortunately, the next morning Warner Brothers sent a car and driver to take me out to Burbank for the first rehearsal of *The Prisoner of Second Avenue* film. I slept badly due to jet lag and homesickness, two problems that never had bothered me before. Going up and over the hills and down the valleys, I felt queasy and had more than a touch of vertigo.

Starting a new project was usually exciting for me, but today it was the last thing in the world I wanted to do. My spirits took a turn for the better when I saw Jack Lemmon again, this being our third picture together, and I was thrilled at the prospect of working for the first time with the wonderful Anne Bancroft. Once we gathered around the table and listened to Jack and Annie read the script, I felt an enormous sense of relief and gratitude. I had two major stars who would carry the day even though I wasn't sure I could carry my weight. The vertigo and the queasiness continued and even increased as the day wore on.

Before we broke just after the reading, director Mel Frank gave me a list of cuts he thought necessary and asked if I could rewrite some speeches and add a few short scenes that would move the script further away from the play and more toward a film. I agreed to all his suggestions and intended to start doing the work that night, but as the car that drove me back to the hotel made the sharp twists, turns and coils that stretch out over Laurel Canyon, I felt I had been lowered into a lifeboat in the North Atlantic, the last male survivor of the *Titanic*.

I had no dinner that night and whatever attempts I made at rewrites were pitiful. I couldn't eat, I couldn't throw up and I couldn't stop the Matisse print over the sofa from floating around the room, barely missing the drifting Cézanne print that bobbed and weaved from the opposite direction. I had to hold on to the chairs in order to get to the telephone. I called a producer friend of mine and asked if he knew the name of a doctor I could see as soon as possible, because I didn't want to spend the night in a rolling bed, staring up at a chandelier that kept sliding around the ceiling, threatening to crash on me. He told me it would be hard finding a doctor at ten o'clock at night, but when I told him my symptoms, he said he once had the exact same thing and that one good massage cleared it up in an hour. He offered to send a masseur over to my hotel in forty minutes. I did not have the strength to say either no or yes and left my life in his hands, although as I lay there I wondered what kind of masseur comes out at twenty to eleven at night.

On the dot, forty minutes later, there was a knock on my door. So relieved was I that help was on the other side of that door that I braved getting hit by the flying Impressionist paintings that were now making sorties at my head like multicolored dive-bombers. Practically crawling along the ground, I finally made it to the door and opened it. I did not expect to see what I saw. It was a Eurasian girl, about twenty-six and beautiful. She walked into the room with a smile, a portable massage table and a face and a figure that would remain perfect even if Picasso painted three eyes on her head and gave her two extra arms. She told me her name was Yanna but that you don't pronounce the Js or the Ms. I hadn't heard any Js or Ms. She turned on her small tape player and I heard a flute and some strings playing music that was probably very popular in jungles.

As she opened her massage table, she asked in the friendliest terms if I would strip down to my shorts; then she headed for the bathroom. Two minutes later she came out with all the towels the Beverly Hills Hotel could supply, and considerably less clothes than she was wearing when she came in. She wore white denim shorts so brief and tight that I wondered if it was just an extra layer of her own skin. She wore a sheer scarf around her ample breasts and tied in the back. Taking into consideration her outfit, I soon had an inkling why she was available at twenty to eleven at night.

I sat on the sofa in my extra-long boxer shorts, shivering and clinging to two pillows from the sofa to keep me warm and my body less visible. I lay down on the massage table and for the next five minutes I was anointed with enough oil to burn a thousand lamps for a year. Yanna talked small talk as she rubbed my neck and back as gently as human hands could glide across the surface of a body. I never noticed when she had lit the incense, but as far as I was concerned, it wasn't half as pleasing as the aroma of her own skin.

I faded in and out of sleep and couldn't tell if I still had vertigo or if I was just wandering around in some benign jungle, soothed by the musical strains of its biggest hit single. About twenty minutes later, she turned me over on my back and I couldn't help notice that she was no longer wearing that sheer scarf across her breasts. As a matter of fact, her breasts were now rubbing across mine, as she was gently but rhythmically massaging my neck. It seemed pretty obvious to me by now that the massage was a prelude to sex, but what I didn't know was whether it was optional or mandatory.

I tried to make it clear without hurting her feelings that if she had planned going beyond the massage, I was neither physically nor emotionally capable of doing that; I even told her about my recent loss. She was not hurt and explained that all she cared about was giving me some relaxation, in whatever way was best for me. She then wrapped me in towels and dried me off as if I were her own baby. When she finally dressed and folded her table, I asked her how much the fee was. She said, "Oh, no. Your friend took care of all that. If you need to see me again while you're still out here, here's my card. Call me any time, night or day." And she vanished quietly somewhere into the Hollywood Hills, no doubt on to another errand of mercy. This was the kind of gift Hollywood producers often send. Had I been in New York and called a friend for help in a similar situation, he would have given me the number of a bald, sixty-two-year-old German chiropractor who loves to hear the sound of cracking necks.

I slept well that night. When I woke in the morning, I opened my eyes and looked at the ceiling. So far so good. I got to my feet and tried to stand. The room suddenly turned into a carousel. Whatever healing powers Yanna possessed, the cure for vertigo was not high on her list. I dressed slowly for fear of putting on everything backwards and getting hit by a car whose driver thought I was walking in the opposite direction.

I went out to Burbank one more time but the drive felt like sailing through a storm going around Cape Hatteras in winter. When I got out of the car, I realized I couldn't make it through the day, the rehearsal or the rewrites. I left early, making my apologies to Jack and Annie and told Mel Frank he was free to make any changes in the script as he saw fit. When I got back to the hotel and took two minutes to get my key into the trembling lock, I knew I was in trouble. I booked the first available flight out in the morning, hoping it would be a bumpy flight which might flatten out my vertigo. By seven-thirty that night I knew I couldn't even wait that long. I found another friend, more dependable than my gift-bearing producer, who gave me the number of a first-rate doctor, one who wore a white jacket instead of shortened jeans and a scarf across his breasts.

Dr. Robert Koblin met me about nine-thirty that night in the examining room of the Century City Hospital. He was a warm, friendly man, a few years younger than myself. After examining me, he said I was suffering from dehydration and gastroacidity, normally symptoms of emotional distress. Before I could get any words out, I burst into tears, giving vent and release to what I'd been holding back for almost a month. When I told him my wife had died about three weeks ago, he nodded and said with a great deal of empathy, "Well, there it is." He prescribed fluids and some pills, but suggested the best medicine for me was to go back to New York, rest and give myself time to deal with my feelings rather than filling up my days with work, which only diverted the pain that I kept bottled up.

Even as I sat on the plane the next morning, looking out on the clouds below me, knowing for the first time ever that I would have to give up control over one of my scripts, I slowly began to feel the vertigo lessening. I closed my eyes, leaned back and slept the entire way back home.

SIX MONTHS before all this happened, a man named Ray Stark had come soaring into my life like a comet. He reached down, grabbed me by the scruff of my neck and pulled me along on the wildest and most exhilarating ride I ever experienced. It lasted over twenty years. Ray Stark was an agent turned producer, whose only claim to fame, initially, was that he was married to the daughter of Fanny Brice, one of the great vaudeville and stage stars of the first half of the twentieth century. He certainly became one of the most successful and powerful producers in Hollywood, with films like *The Way We Were* and *Funny Girl* to his credit, along with dozens of others.

I received a call from him one day, without prior warning or introduction, asking if he could come over to my house to talk to me. He didn't say what it was about and I thought it was interesting that he wanted to meet me in my home rather than inviting me out to lunch in some showy restaurant. I think he did it knowing that if we met on my turf, I would not feel that he had the advantage and I would be more amenable to what he had to say. That was the day I found out how smart he was.

Minutes after he walked in the door on East 62nd Street, a big smile on his warm and very unmogul-like face, I liked him. And suddenly he had the advantage, which was probably what he had in mind all the time. He complimented me on everything in my house (all of which Joan had done) and from studying the few small paintings I had on the walls, made me feel that I had a true gift—an unfailing eye for art. As it turned out, I didn't, but he eventually taught me. He was in his late fifties but had the energy of a man in his early thirties, and his eager and avid sense of joy and good humor (if you dismissed the incessant puns) made him seem even younger than that. After five minutes with him, I could swear I had known him for years, and after ten minutes with him, I wished I *had* known him for years.

We talked for over an hour about everything except why he came there. He was too busy telling me what a genius I was and kept putting me in the same category as writers like Ben Hecht and Billy Wilder. I wasn't, of course, but I was too vain to stop him. Finally the reason for his visit. Would I be willing to write the sequel to *Funny Girl*, called *Funny Lady*, starring again, naturally, Barbra Streisand. It was an incredible opportunity—a fabulous offer to be writing for the most talented and exciting film star of the day. I surprised even myself when I said "No," without hesitation. If Fanny Brice, and that's who Barbra Streisand was portraying, never existed, I would have taken the job. What I didn't want to do was research and/or be faithful to the true story of Fanny Brice's marriage to Billy Rose. It would confine me to the facts, leaving little to my imagination, especially since Mr. Stark was the producer and the son-in-law of Ms. Brice. As fine a filmmaker as he was, I didn't want to write with his fingers on my typewriter keys.

He accepted my answer graciously and didn't push it. I think I even earned his respect by turning down something that had all the ingredients of a sure-fire hit, although that would have depended on what I did with it. (Warren

Beatty originally asked me to do the screenplay of *Heaven Can Wait*, which I turned down because I didn't want to do remakes. Elaine May took the job and wrote it brilliantly. After my daughter Nancy saw the picture and loved it, she said, "You should have done it. It was great.")

Ray Stark did not go home that day empty handed. He bought the film rights to my play *The Sunshine Boys*. I knew he would stay true to the tone and soul of the play, which was most important to me. A few months prior, I was playing tennis at a club when I received a phone call from agent Irving "Swifty" Lazar in Los Angeles. Lazar could trace you down if you were in a dungeon in Patagonia. Lazar had initially sold my first three plays, *Come Blow Your Horn*, *Barefoot in the Park* and *The Odd Couple*, all to Paramount Pictures. Irving now had another offer from Paramount to buy *The Sunshine Boys* as a vehicle for, and I gulped at this one, Bing Crosby and Bob Hope. I grew up listening to both of them on the radio and had seen all their *Road* pictures as well as Hope's other wonderful comedies. But I told a stunned Irving Lazar that I was regretfully turning it down. The essence of my play was that these two aging ex-vaudevillians were Jewish, cranky and tired. Hope and Crosby were aging, but you would never know it then. They were still quick, topical and lighthearted and flippant, and they would sure be box office, but neither of them had ever been bar mitzvahed—not that religion was important to the characters, but their culture and background was.

I knew for certain that Paramount would want me to rewrite the parts to fit the considerable talents of Hope and Crosby. I wanted to do it the other way around. I wanted to find two actors, stars hopefully, who would fit the characteristics of The Sunshine Boys. I got that promise from Ray Stark. When he left my house later that day, he had my play, and I had a mentor, a tutor and a great friend for the next two decades. The next day, a huge vase of flowers arrived, so beautiful they could have been put in a frame and hung on the wall. From that day on, whether I went to Paris or a room in Mobile, Alabama, there would always be a gift waiting there from Ray Stark, whether we had a project going or not. He didn't buy me, but he sure did woo me. And Ray Stark was the best wooer in the business.

ST. LOUIS WOMAN

5

ONCE BACK in New York, my legs and spirits grew sturdier and I began to venture out into a more sociable world. Lunches with friends, going to the theater, out to a Mets game and, finally, to dinner parties. But always alone. Which automatically makes you the extra man, for whom, inevitably, the hostess would invite "an extra woman." There is always something implied by this arrangement—a hope that the extra man and the extra woman would somehow pair off into anything from polite conversation to marriage. I preferred it when the extra woman was already married and came to "fill in" while her husband was away on business. That took the pressure off both me and her, and put it all on our hostess's *crème brûlée*.

At one of these parties, the extra woman was someone I knew and liked, equally as much as I liked her husband. Until I found out they were now divorced, hence all the eyes staring at us from the first course on. She was charming, pretty and a good conversationalist, which was fortunate because no one wanted to interrupt us. We talked neither about my deceased wife nor her ex-husband, leaving us to choose from such varied topics as movies, books, plays and health, good or bad. When you meet someone who has the same back problem as you, you're set for the night. You find yourself saying, "Right. I know that feeling," over and over again. After a while I began to feel comfortable with her, although there was definitely no sense of romance in the air from either of us. Still, I wanted to see her again, if only to go to a play or film; nothing further need be contemplated. Yet I felt guilty at the very thought of seeing or being seen with another woman so soon after Joan's death, no matter how slight my interest was in this woman. Most important, I did not want to offend Ellen or Nancy and have them think I was being thoughtless or callous to the memory of their mother. I knew a man who had lost his wife, and six months later he started to date some woman he met through a mutual friend. His sixteen-year-old daughter was furious with him. It may have partly been because she thought the woman was not right for him, and equally as important, that this woman was not the ideal stepmother for her. Or more painfully, she may have feared that if the father remarried, and possibly had more children, he might lose his need and love for her. The young girl won; the father broke off with the woman and ten years later he had still not moved on with his life.

I faced the prospect of "dating" with the same concerns. Nevertheless, I knew I had to start sometime.

I THOUGHT it important that Ellen and Nancy knew that I was occasionally dating, but made it clear that there was no romance pending. Their reaction was noncommittal, but certainly not negative. As a matter of fact, as they pored through movie and fashion magazines, they would sometimes hold up a picture of some beauty and say, "Do you think she's pretty, Dad?" One was a picture of Ali MacGraw, mostly because she resembled Joan so closely.

Finally, I decided to go to the next step. I asked the woman if she would have dinner with me and my daughters at home, the reasoning being that if the girls actually saw me in the company of another woman, it would break the ice for whatever might come later. This wasn't exactly playing fair with the woman in question, since she might think "taking her to meet the family" portended a relationship soon in the offing, but from my own observations, she gave no hint that that was what she was looking for. Nancy and Ellen, on the other hand, could not have been more enthusiastic. They felt they were playing out some important role in an exotic romance. They spent most of the afternoon trying on and changing dresses until the appropriate ones were selected. I could hear them buzzing and laughing in their rooms above me, trying out made-up English accents as if this was going to be a dinner party as written by Jane Austen.

At seven-thirty that night, my guest arrived. We had a drink together before the girls made their choreographed entrance down the stairs. They exchanged polite greetings, and from that moment on, for the rest of the evening, those were the only words they uttered. The silence was so deafening from their side of the table that I could hear the faucet dripping in my bathroom two floors above. What happened to laughing and buzzing in their rooms in the afternoon? What happened to six changes of dresses before they picked the right one? I suppose it's like public speaking: once you're introduced, you would rather be somewhere else. My guest, the former sparkling conversationalist, found fewer and fewer words forming on her lips. Aside from an occasional "Mmm" when asked if the chicken was all right, the remainder of the night was a monologue conducted by myself. The dinner took two and a half days, at least by my calculation, and when I finally exhausted all my stories, which usually got roars of laughter from the girls instead of the faint Mona Lisa smiles I was getting now, my speech was reduced to single sentences, then single words, and eventually guttural sounds that had no intelligible meaning. It was as though we were all sitting in a well-decorated Christian Science Reading Room.

I took my guest home in a cab, where we listened to the windshield wipers clearing off the light drizzle. When I said good night to her at the door of her apartment, we both knew that if we ever met at another "extra man/extra woman" dinner party, we would exchange a quick "Hi. How are you? You're looking swell," and move quickly toward the nearest hors d'oeuvre. When I returned home, I found the girls upstairs waiting for me. Since their television wasn't on, I knew they wanted to talk. I didn't even ask if they liked her or not.

"Are you going to marry her?" Nancy questioned ruefully.

"Is she going to be our stepmother?" Ellen asked in desperation.

"No," I assured them, "of course not. She's just a nice woman and I think she felt a lot of pressure. Why were you both staring at her? Why couldn't you say anything?"

"She never swallowed her food," said Nancy.

"What are you talking about? She ate her entire dinner."

"She may have eaten it, but she didn't swallow it."

Ellen added her observation. "Wrong perfume."

"Really? I didn't notice. Is that why you didn't like her?"

"I didn't say I didn't like her. But it was definitely the wrong perfume."

I decided not to push this one any further. I gave them both a kiss good night and went down to my room. As I lay in bed with my eyes still open at two in the morning, I thought, if I were ever to meet another woman who even remotely appealed to me, she would have to pass muster with the toughest board of admissions this side of the Massachusetts Institute of Technology.

Rehearsals for *The Good Doctor* began around October 5 at the Ambassador, one of the oldest theaters in New York and one of the least desirable because of its dingy location. It was used more often for rehearsals than for actual productions of plays. The stage door was located down a long, dark alleyway that made a sharp turn left to another dark alleyway. Actors generally left in pairs at the end of the day for safety's sake.

When I arrived, the cast were already assembled. I saw Marsha Mason in a conversation with Christopher Plummer and waited for her to turn away before I could catch her eye and say hello. When she did, she looked as warm and pretty as when I had seen her a few months prior at her audition. This time, however, she seemed more subdued, more tentative, which I attributed to a case of "first day rehearsal shakes." Everyone gets them, stars and playwrights included. Each time we begin a new play, we are all about to enter a world where no man or woman has ever walked before. Strangely, I did not have the shakes that day. It certainly wasn't because of overconfidence or complacency on my part, but for another more profound reason. There was still a part of me that was going through a restoring process, of getting used to talking easily to actors again. This, plus the keen awareness that at the end of the first day, I would not, as I always did before, be able to rush home and tell Joan how the reading went and filling her in on all the details.

When the actors finally gathered around the table, their freshly rewritten scripts before them, I did something that was rare for me. I sat on a stool, not *at* the table, where I always preferred to be, next to the director, but this time a few feet behind it, distancing myself from the actors and perhaps even the play itself. I was a faintly disconnected observer, hoping once again in my life to be invisible. The actors started to read the play in a soft, low key, since no one wanted to commit themselves to a performance just yet. Marsha sat on the opposite side of the table, facing me but not looking at me. Her eyes remained glued to the pages, and she made little notes on a pad. I noticed she was left-handed. I always thought there was something quirky about left-handed people and also something more graceful. Perhaps it was because they were using a different side of the brain than I was. I liked watching this difference in baseball players, and now, I discovered, I liked it in actresses.

If Marsha had been subdued and tentative in her greeting, she was nothing short of enchanting as she read the first scene. She was in heavy competition with that veteran cast, but I couldn't take my attention away from her. When I laugh at what an actor says, it is almost never at what I wrote, but rather the way the actor has injected life into the lines. Marsha was not only giving the words life, she was dressing them, feeding them and sending them off to school with a kiss and a warm lunch.

I noticed she had one hand in the air at all times as she read, the left hand, of course, with a pencil clenched in her fingers, the point protruding out about an inch. It didn't seem as though it was tension that made her hold the pencil aloft, but more as if she had a baton in her hand, conducting her own performance. The orchestra followed devotedly. She began to hear my laughter and she looked up at me, both surprised and pleased to know that I visibly and audibly approved of what she was doing. She started to look up more and more, especially when she was *not* reading. I think she was measuring me as to what this fairly well known playwright with the brooding countenance really was about.

At the end of the first act, director Antoon called for a break and I walked around to Marsha's side of the table, stood behind her and put my hand on her shoulder and said, "I love what you're doing." Her hand automatically went up and touched the back of my hand and said, "Thank you." When we finished reading the second act, the stage manager announced it was lunch. Some of the actors paired off, and not even Manny Azenberg asked what I was doing for lunch. He knew I was heading alone to the nearest deli, with script, pad and pen in hand, ready to pounce on the cuts, notes and revisions, while I juggled a turkey sandwich on rye with my free hand. As I walked up that dreary alleyway, I found Marsha walking beside me.

"You going to lunch alone?" she asked.

"Yes. I always do on the first day. I've got work to do. What about you?"

"Oh. I'm meeting a friend."

It suddenly occurred to me that a friend could be someone she was going with, living with or even married to. I knew nothing about her personal life.

Then she said rather carefully, "I didn't know about your wife until today. No one told me. I'm truly sorry."

I thanked her for her consideration. Then she smiled and said, "See you later. You are coming back, aren't you?"

"Me? Oh, yeah. This is when I do my real work. Rehearsals are for you; for me it's the rewriting." She smiled again and then practically bounced down the street knowing she got off to a flying start at the morning's reading.

At five minutes to two, having finished my revisions but not my turkey sandwich, I headed back to the theater. But first I had to maneuver my way through that dark, ominous alley. Halfway there, I heard footsteps behind me, walking at first, then running, coming closer and closer. I expected either a gun in my ribs or a knife at my throat. What happened was more terrifying: I heard a scream that sounded like "YAHHHH," then a body, a human body, hurled itself onto my back. I pulled away instantly, ready to defend my life or

willingly hand over my wallet, but not my revisions, when I saw who this at-
tacker was. It was Marsha, standing there smiling. No, not smiling. Beaming.

"Sorry. Didn't mean to scare you."

"*Scare* me? How could you not scare me? Why did you do that?"

The smile remained, then with a shrug, she said, "I don't know. Just felt
like it."

"Do you always do that?"

"Nope. First time. How was your lunch?"

And suddenly we were walking together as though nothing had happened.
She said it so innocently that I felt it was *my* fault for not enjoying it more.
After all, it's not every day that an extremely pretty girl jumps on your back
in a dark alley. I felt as if I had been given a shot of adrenaline. For the first
time in months, here was someone not treating me with kid gloves. Someone
not cautious about invading the dark world in which I had been living since
Joan had died. Someone not afraid to push the clouds away and let some sun
shine on my dour face. Her jump on my back said to me, "Smile, Neil. Life is
back. Welcome to the world."

During the afternoon's read through, our eyes made contact quite a few
times.

I FELT a strong need to keep Nancy and Ellen closer to me, more involved
with not just my life but my working life as well. For the very first time ever,
I invited them to come to the rehearsal of one of my plays. They came as
soon as school let out the following day, and sat in the fifth row, entranced,
mesmerized and stony silent as they watched the making of a play. When
they wanted to laugh, they covered their mouths with their hands, afraid to
intrude upon the serious effort that was going on up on the stage. When the
director called a ten-minute break, I briefly introduced them to all the actors,
who could not have been nicer. Once back in their seats, I asked them what
they thought of what they had seen so far.

"It's keen," said Nancy. "I never knew they worked so hard."

"It's like doing a play in school," Ellen added, "except that the director is
more patient than our teacher."

"Which part did you like best?" I inquired, meaning which scene in the
play. They had a different interpretation.

"The girl with the red hair," Nancy quickly offered.

"Marsha Mason?"

"Don't you think she's pretty?" asked Ellen.

"Pretty? Yes. Very pretty."

"Is she married?" asked Nancy.

"Married? I don't know."

"Why don't you ask her?" Ellen quickly added.

"I don't see any wedding ring on her," chimed in Nancy.

"Is that all you've been watching?" I said. "Anyway, why do you want to know?"

"We like her," Ellen announced. "Don't you?"

"Yes. I do. She's a wonderful actress."

"No. We mean like as a person. Don't you think she's neat as a person?" Nancy was being relentless for a ten-year-old.

Ellen got this impish look on her face. "Why don't you ask her out to dinner? I bet *she'd* have plenty to say."

"Hey, girls. I didn't invite you here to promote my social life."

"Just to dinner," Nancy implored. "What's one dinner?"

To placate them I said, "Fine. Swell. I'll ask her to dinner sometime."

"Not sometime," Ellen kept at it. "What about tonight? You're not doing anything."

"I am. I'm rewriting. Why are you two pushing so much?"

"You don't have to rewrite tonight," said Nancy, not letting up. "The play sounds good to us."

At this point in the inquisition, A.J. Antoon dismissed Marsha for the day while time was spent rehearsing someone else's scene. Marsha started putting on her coat, bidding good night to the other actors, then squinted out front through the lights, hand over her eyes and called out, "Good night, Neil. See you tomorrow. Nice meeting you, girls." She headed for the door.

"Now! Now!" urged Ellen. "Before she goes home."

"Hurry, Dad. You can still stop her," pleaded Nancy.

"It's too late," I said. "She's out the door."

"You can run after her down the street, can't you?" suggested Ellen.

"Hey, girls. Enough. Don't do this to me . . . come on. It's late. I'll take you home. Do you have much homework for tonight?"

"She's really neat, Dad. You should have asked her," Nancy said in one final attempt.

"Put your coats on. We're going. And enough about Marsha Mason, okay?"

"Sorry, Dad," said Nancy.

"Sorry," said Ellen.

It was quiet in the cab going home. I was staring out the window, wondering what the scene at the theater was all about. The girls murmured to each other, whispering and still plotting between themselves. Just as the cab pulled up to our house, Ellen got in her last entreaty of the day.

"You could call her tonight and ask her for tomorrow."

"I said no! . . . Geez! . . . all right. I'll see. Let me think about it. But don't ask me anymore, okay?"

"We won't," agreed Nancy. "I swear."

"Maybe, just once more at dinner," Ellen said with a devilish smile. Then they both turned and gave me an exaggerated expression of begging and pleading, contorting their faces, trying for just the right comic tone to wear me down.

I glared at them, but they couldn't possibly miss the look of amusement in my eyes.

AT EIGHT O'CLOCK that night I closed the door of my office; the girls were busy with homework on the floor above. I looked at the cast sheet that gave the addresses, phone numbers and agents for everyone connected with the production. I saw that Marsha Mason lived in the West 70s in Manhattan. I circled her phone number, then quickly dialed—and just as quickly hung up just after the first ring. What the hell was I doing? I knew if I called her it wouldn't be because of the girls' constant hammering away at me. It would be because I liked watching her on stage and being around her during the breaks. Because I was taken with her incredible audacity when she jumped screamingly on my back in a dark alleyway. It would be because I wanted to. But wanted to what? It was too soon after Joan's death to contemplate any sort of relationship with someone new. I don't think the word "relationship" even came to mind. It was an attraction, to be sure, and if I could get past the first phone call, I would take the next step, if any were required, one careful foot at a time. Dialing the phone was my first problem. "Oh, what the hell," I said to myself nervously. The girls were right. It would just be for one measly dinner. I dialed her number and hoped she would be in.

"Hello?"

There was that voice of hers, with a trace of that endearing laugh even in a simple word like "hello." Now I was stuck for a first sentence. I was reduced to feeling seventeen again.

"Hello?" she asked for the second time.

Now I was reduced to fifteen.

"Marsha?"

"Yes."

"Hi. It's Neil."

"Neil? Hello."

"Is this a bad time for you?"

"No. It's fine. Is everything all right?" There was actually a trace of nervousness in her voice, as if she were worried that something was going wrong with the play.

"No. Everything is fine . . . I just wanted to thank you for being so nice to the girls today. They were really taken with you."

"They were? Oh, I'm so glad. They're really sweet."

"Thank you . . . so, er . . . they asked me if I, er . . . well, actually *I'm* asking if you'd like to, er . . . Wait a minute. This is dumb. Can I ask you something personal?"

"Yes."

"Are you married? Are you engaged? Or with someone?"

"No."

"No" sounded too simple an answer, as if there were something not included in the word. I'd better ask.

"No what?"

"No. I'm not any of those things. I'm divorced and living with a girlfriend of mine on the West Side."

"West Seventy-Second?"

"Yes."

"I saw that looking for your number on the cast sheet." (On many occasions I have written scintillating and bright dialogue, but unfortunately this wasn't one of those times.) "So, look . . . would you like to have dinner with me and the girls one night? When you're free. When you're not busy?"

"Oh . . . Well, er . . ."

Suddenly she didn't sound sure. I hardly knew her. Why did I let the girls do this to me?

"Okay. I'd love to. That's nice of you to ask. For when?"

"Oh, I don't know. This week. Next week. Tomorrow. You busy tomorrow?"

"Well, I have something to do later on, but if you mean an early dinner, that's fine."

"Early is good for me too. You like Japanese? The girls love Japanese."

"Same here."

"Great. See you at rehearsal. Good night."

I hung up and walked slowly and quietly up the stairs and opened the door to the tiny little den that Ellen and Nancy shared.

"Okay. It's done. I called her. Early dinner in a Japanese restaurant with Marsha Mason tomorrow night. She's not married. She's not engaged. I'm very tired. Don't stay up late. Good night."

I closed the door and as I started back down the stairs I heard two young girls screaming jubilantly.

DINNER WAS AT Hime's of Japan restaurant on the East Side. I asked A.J. Antoon to let Marsha off a little early that night. I didn't tell him why. As she went out the stage door, I waited a few seconds and then followed. I didn't say good night to A.J. or the cast for fear of eyebrows being raised. Actually, I rarely say good night when I leave rehearsals. I don't want to interrupt the flow of the scene as it is being rehearsed, so usually I simply give a nod to the director and go, glad to be the writer who can leave whenever he wants. Marsha had an errand to tend to before meeting us and I was relieved. I was not quite up to sharing a cab with her and having a one-on-one conversation, since I had not been alone with someone I was attracted to, who was not my wife, in twenty years.

Things went considerably better at the restaurant than they had at the dinner at home, when my guest had found herself frozen out. This night the girls actually spoke. Full sentences and complete thoughts. Marsha was not only eating her dinner, she was also swallowing it. There was no indication that she was wearing the wrong perfume. There was laughter at our table and the two young members of the board of admissions were totally enchanted with the "girl with the laughing face," as I had one character describe her years later in The Goodbye Girl. Regretfully, she left early to fulfill her other engagement, and Nancy, Ellen and I walked home.

"She's nice," said Ellen cautiously.

"Very nice," Nancy added, looking for a hopeful sign from me.

"Yes" was all I could agree to. My mind was in a muddle, as if trying to walk up a down escalator. How can I have positive thoughts about this charming young woman while I knew that later that night I would be sitting on the floor of my room, candles lit, still trying to brand Joan's features permanently into my psyche? I had no idea if Marsha had any interest in me, so why was I, or the girls for that matter, even thinking of anything beyond a Japanese meal? And I still had a play to deal with.

"No rush," I said to myself. "All in good time." "What will be will be." "Time takes care of everything." I heard my head pouring out aphorisms by the dozens, even some that didn't apply, like, "Water seeks its own level," and "Feed a cold, starve a fever." If I kept at this, I would soon be throwing in, "A stitch in time saves nine," and "What's good for the goose is good for the gander." I find no solace or wisdom in simple homilies that were written and conceived before the Revolutionary War.

DURING THE NEXT weeks, the play and the rehearsals took second place to my attentive chats with Marsha, who at every break came down into the orchestra and sat beside me. We talked about everything except the job at hand. Those meetings led to more dinners, but now with just the two of us. The dinners led to my inviting Marsha up to the house on Blue Heron Lake, accompanied by two ten-year-old chaperones—Nancy and her best friend, Nicole Fosse, daughter of Bob, the noted director-choreographer.

Two weeks later, waiting for the elevator just outside Marsha's apartment, where I had just met her roommate, some close friends and her ex-husband, I kissed Marsha good night. The elevator door opened and I decided not to step in. Instead, I said partly in jest, partly in earnest and certainly a part in sheer madness, "So I guess we ought to get married, heh?"

She looked at me, not knowing which of the three parts this totally unexpected suggestion came from. A look of shock, bewilderment and joy appeared all at once on her startled face.

"Are you serious?" she asked.

To tell the truth, I didn't know what I was. If she had said, "Oh . . . Well, Neil, this comes as a bit of a surprise. I mean, it's only been two weeks. We hardly know each other. I think it would be rushing things, don't you?" I would have answered, "Of course, you're right. Just something that popped out, I guess." Then I would have quickly gotten on the elevator and into a cab wondering whatever possessed me to be so audacious and foolhardy. Since she didn't say that, my answer to her "Are you serious?" was "Yes. I guess so." And that was it. I can't remember if she beamed or cried or screamed or threw her arms around me or if she even accepted my proposal. She probably did one or all of the above, but the only thing I remembered, even now, was that we were back in her apartment where she announced happily to all present that I had just proposed marriage to her. Everyone was appropriately giddy with excitement and even her ex-husband offered his congratulations. "What took you so long?" he said. Not a word from anyone about "in only two weeks?" I didn't even wonder why she was so friendly with her ex-husband but if I'd just proposed to a girl after knowing her for fourteen days, I wouldn't have noticed if she had two Arabian stallions in the room.

As I drove back across Central Park alone, I thought to myself, "Did that really happen? Did I actually say that? And what will I tell the girls?"

ON THE RUN

6

THE GIRLS were not the problem. They were more than overjoyed, and even supported the idea of Marsha moving in with us immediately. "Even before we're married?" I asked, as if the roles were reversed and it was me, the worried father, asking Ellen what she was doing rushing into a marriage to someone she scarcely knew.

If I try to reason out why the girls were so in favor of this quickly conceived union, inasmuch as they both loved their mother dearly, it occurred to me that they wanted to be a complete family again, one in which Dad could be happy and life could continue as it once was. They were too young to consider the ramifications and impact on our lives that a total stranger, no matter how winning, might have. Nor did they ever stop to ask if this new person could possibly fill the void that left us all bereft a few short months ago. I do not mean to imply that it was solely because of their urging that I contemplated taking this step, one that I actually already had put into motion. Clearly, I was moving very quickly and the question was why? I knew then, but I don't know now—not that I question its wisdom. I knew that I was going to be confronted with a barrage of raised eyebrows, but at the moment I could only think about four people and their happiness: me, Marsha, Ellen and Nancy. Explanations to friends and family would have to be dealt with later.

Years later Marsha characterized me as being "a very needy" person. I won't contest that even though the implication of her remark seemed to have an air of criticism to it. I've often thought of Marsha as being an "un-needy" person, without criticism implied. She could live alone on a farm fifty miles from nowhere, while I needed to hear the footsteps of friends and family. I needed humanity at my beck and call. Is one better or worse than the other? On the other hand, I do spend the greater part of my everyday life *completely* alone, spending more hours sitting over a typewriter in a room where the phone seldom rings and visitors rarely ever appear than I do with my family. The fact is, none of these considerations needed to be dealt with when I asked Marsha to marry me. Nothing was thought out. It was done purely on instinct, a belief that this would turn out well. The consequences could certainly be that it would all blow up in my face—*all* our faces—yet no one was saying "Stop!" What was going on in Marsha's head about all this I never really knew and still don't to this day.

Two days after the proposal, I stood waiting at Park Avenue and 80th Street, outside Dr. Bornstein's office, looking for Marsha, who was to meet me in order to take the required blood tests. Dr. Jack Bornstein was the doctor who took care of Joan during her fight with cancer. It had to be early in the morning since we still had rehearsals that day. It was while I waited that I asked myself the questions again: "Why am I doing this? What's the hurry? Does this make sense at all?"

Before I could find a reasonable answer, I heard "Hi," and saw the beaming smile on Marsha's face before me. "Hi," I answered in a noncommittal manner. Her look of dismay at my lack of enthusiasm was not so much one of disappointment, but more concern for my welfare.

"Are you all right?" she asked in utter sincerity.

"Yes. Fine . . . I don't know . . . Why are we doing this? This is crazy, isn't it? . . . Look, I need time to think about this, okay?"

She nodded and said warmly, "Of course. I understand. Whatever you want."

"It's not that I don't want to."

"I know. I'm scared too."

"So do you mind if we put it off for a while? To give us both time to get to know each other better?"

"I think that's a wonderful idea."

"Thank you," I said and pulled her toward me and hugged her.

She pulled her face back, looked into my eyes and said, "It's all right, Neil. Really."

Then I looked around to see where we were. What time was it? When did we have to be at rehearsal? Where was a cab? And suddenly air came back into my lungs and I breathed easily once again, then said, without looking at her, "Well, as long as we're here, we might as well take the blood test. Don't you think?"

"Sure. If you want."

"Yeah. Why not? We'd have to do it sometime anyway."

As we started for the doctor's office a few steps away, I stopped and said, "I forgot. This is for you."

I gave her a small box which contained an engagement ring that I had bought as soon as Tiffany's opened that morning.

"Can I help you?" said the saleswoman as I perused the rings under the glass. "What kind of ring are you looking for?"

"Something for a very short engagement," I answered, not noticing the bemused look on her face.

Now Marsha was opening the box, looking at the ring and then embracing me. We then entered Jack Bornstein's office to take blood tests, two very nervous and frightened people.

A few days later we were married in the Criminal Courts Building, the same place that Joan and I had been married nineteen years earlier. It was a different judge this time and instead of our parents as witnesses, we had Ellen and Nancy, giving me all the comfort and encouragement I needed at that moment. An hour later, Ellen and Nancy were back in school and Marsha and I were back at rehearsals at the Ambassador Theatre. Before we started work, however, Manny Azenberg popped some bottles of champagne, filled the paper cups for all the cast, then held his up in a toast. "To the happy couple. May the play run longer than the engagement."

I ALWAYS HAD a soft spot in my heart for New Haven, Connecticut, because I had tried out so many of my early plays at the Shubert Theatre there. I liked walking around the Yale campus during the day while my mind worked busily trying to shore up the small and large holes that constantly appear in a play during a pre-Broadway tryout. New Haven was not, however, the best place to have a honeymoon—not while we only had two and a half days to pull the scenery, lighting, costumes and the play itself together before its first public viewing. Instead of basking in the sun on some romantic Caribbean island, we were both working harder and longer hours and had far less time for each other than we did in New York. I was now spending hours in the hotel rewriting and Marsha was at the theater rehearsing my rewrites. Marsha was still appearing as five different characters, and to add to her workload, there was a new one that I wrote especially for her that was not pure Chekhov. Because she was so gifted, I wanted to write a scene that was hers and hers alone, something that I hoped would make her shine even brighter than any Tiffany ring that she wore on her finger. The scene was called "The Audition."

In it she appeared as a poor country girl, an aspiring actress who walked all the way to Moscow from her home in Odessa, to audition for Chekhov himself. In the dead of winter.

We never see Chekhov but only hear his voice (Christopher Plummer); he was presumably sitting in the darkened theater auditioning young hopefuls. She has very little experience and Chekhov is about to thank her and quickly send her off to whence she came, when he is suddenly taken by her innocent humor, her dedication to her art and mostly by her passion for his work. He finally relents. "Oh, very well. What is it you want to read?"

"I'd like to read from *The Three Sisters*, sir."

"Really? And which sister will you be?"

"All of them, sir."

"*All* of them? Are you going to read the entire play?"

"If you wish, sir."

He is amused and doesn't take her seriously. Nevertheless, he allows her to go on. Marsha played the last scene of the play, doing all three sisters, giving each sister in turn their full weight and individuality, creating a distinct personality for each of them. When she is finished, she says humbly and quietly, "Thank you, sir," and starts to leave the stage even before she has heard his reaction.

Chekhov is so moved, so completely taken by her performance, that he can't pull himself together quickly enough to speak. She is gone when he finally calls out, "Will somebody stop that girl before she walks all the way back to Odessa."

As I watched the scene myself at that last dress rehearsal at the Shubert Theatre, I felt as I imagined Chekhov himself would have felt. Everyone in the theater was still, as if we all needed a breath before we could move on to the next scene. I realized what a tremendous talent Marsha was, and thanked Phyliss Wender silently for sending her to me.

THEN CAME the other side of the coin. I soon realized that we could only be husband and wife when the workday was over or possibly during a quick meal together. But even then the talk was about the play and not about plans for the future—the kinds of things that most honeymooners would be caught up with while sipping margaritas under a star-filled tropical sky. Our director, A. J. Antoon, was consumed with his own stars in the heaven, these literally being part of the scenery in one particular scene. He spent so much time with the production values that he was now giving less time and attention to his actors. Marsha felt unprepared and under-rehearsed and complained to Antoon, who promised he would get to it as soon as he finished his scenery problems. I had never before taken sides in differences of opinion between a director and his actors. I felt if I came to Marsha's aid, it would appear that it was because I was her husband, and that others might resent it. Marsha was quite able to take care of herself in situations like this, and eventually Manny Azenberg intervened and told A.J. to stop being "lost in the stars" and get back to the live ones in our play. I was unsettled by this incident only because I felt helpless and because I worried if this was always an ongoing dilemma when spouses work together in the theater.

AS WE APPROACHED opening night in New York, it occurred to me that no one among my family or friends had met Marsha as yet. Most probably they never laid eyes on her before unless they saw the bank commercial or *Blume in Love*. The pressure on Marsha must have been enormous. Not only was she to be reviewed by the tough New York critics, but she was also going to get reviewed by everyone I knew except Ellen and Nancy, who had already given her their own Tony Award. In her first appearance in the play, I saw heads moving together and program pages turning as she walked on stage. She was playing a very naive and nervous young wife to a petty civil servant going to the theater, where her husband humiliates himself to an important member of the government. In character and in costume, Marsha looked plain and unworldly. Audiences sometimes cannot distinguish between actors and their parts. In her next scene, she played another poor girl, a servant and governess to a wealthy aristocratic family. The young governess was overwhelmed by her mistress, and could barely find her voice when she was unfairly mistreated by the family. Despite the fact that Marsha played both parts flawlessly, I still wondered what my friends thought of this unknown actress who so captivated me in such a short time and had also won the overwhelming approval of my daughters. When at last Marsha appeared as a beautiful and elegant woman in "The Seduction," you could hear the quiet mumble of voices from one aisle to the other. She was radiant in this scene and it was clear to see that this woman was an enormously skillful actress. When she finally appeared in "The Audition," Chekhov was not the only one who was enthralled. At the opening night party afterward, I proudly introduced Marsha to all my family and friends. I thought she did as well with them as she did in the play. I never once saw Marsha have trouble winning over people and attracting them with her luminous presence. And when she laughed, you couldn't resist her.

We went home that night and both breathed a tremendous sigh of relief at having gotten through a night that caused us so much apprehension. Perhaps now we could get on with our marriage. But first we had to get to know each other.

SUNNY BOYS

7

THE GOOD DOCTOR got my usual set of mixed reviews, but for the actors they were fine-plus. The audiences, although entertained, didn't know why I was making an alliance with Chekhov. Neither did Chekhov, I imagine. Manny and I never expected this play to be a huge hit, but rather something to occupy me in the aftermath of Joan's passing. Since plays then did not cost a million six hundred thousand dollars to mount on Broadway, as they do today, it was not too expensive an indulgence. But I found that writing in a new form and with new expression helped to get me out of a style that I did not want to go on repeating in play after play. And meeting Marsha was worth whatever effort had been expended in putting on the play: Sometimes it takes years to reap the rewards, and today *The Good Doctor* lives on in theaters, colleges and schools all over the world.

Marsha's and my courtship had been a whirlwind. Then we were married. Now the play had opened, and Marsha would be appearing in it for the next six months. But what about after that? It never occurred to me to think how she was going to deal with a seven-year contract with 20th Century Fox. Or how *I* would deal with it.

As her nights and two afternoons a week were now occupied, I left for California to deal with preliminary casting for the film of *The Sunshine Boys*. They were in a sense already settled. We had picked a truly odd couple, but I thought an inspired one in Jack Benny and Red Skelton. Since the play was about two former vaudevillians, Jack was perfectly at home, since vaudeville was where he got his start. I had first seen Red Skelton in his early MGM films and thought he was hilarious—a pratfall comic who also had the ability to move you. To promote his films, he would often tour movie theaters that also presented live shows, fronted by a big band like Glenn Miller's or Benny Goodman's. The first time I saw Red Skelton live was at the Capitol Theatre in New York, where he did twenty minutes of his "drunken liquor spokesman" and a few other classics, and finished his routine by pretending to miss the wings and falling off the stage, a plunge of at least ten feet. He got up with a smile and dusted himself off before leaving more than a little wobbly. He did this every performance. Such a routine would have broken the bones in every part of the body of a normal man. Red Skelton either knew how to fall or walked around his entire life with a full set of cracked tibias.

Since neither Mr. Benny nor Mr. Skelton was any longer in his prime, MGM insisted on their doing a screen test to evaluate their chemistry together. I was not there for the screen test, but they ran it for me when I arrived in Los Angeles. The image that Jack Benny had etched in our minds in a glorious forty- or fifty-year career was indelible, and it was hard for me to fully accept him as playing someone other than himself. Yet when I saw him in the screen test, I found him enormously funny and a perfect foil for the bombastic outrages of his betrayed former partner as played by Skelton. It was just a test and not a full-out rehearsed performance, but there was little doubt in my mind that we had put a perfect match together.

It was soon apparent, however, that all would not go well. Red Skelton objected to some of the language he had to say on screen, such as calling his retired ex-partner "a crazy bastard." A mild expletive even in the films of 1975, and certainly nothing to compare to the amusing off-camera, all-out cussing that Skelton did during the rehearsals of his TV show. He also felt uneasy that Jack Benny was getting bigger laughs from the grips standing by during the rehearsals of the test. As far as I heard, that wasn't true; they were equally appreciated. But it was not to be. Skelton left, turning down the part, and everything was on hold until we found another Sunshine Boy.

To the great dismay of everyone in the industry, Jack Benny suddenly took ill. He was diagnosed with stomach cancer and died soon after. I believe he was eighty years old, but no one would ever accept that he was anything other than the beloved perennial thirty-nine-year-old tightwad that many of us were lucky enough to grow up with.

The search for the new Sunshine Boys began, and I heard that shortly before his death, Jack Benny suggested to his longtime agent, Irving Fein, that he hoped his closest friend in the world, George Burns, would be offered the part. George's great popularity was sharply diminished after the death of his co-star and wife, Gracie Allen. Lately he had been making occasional TV appearances and working the Las Vegas circuit. MGM thought we needed a bigger name. The search went on and I flew back home to New York.

AS I ARRIVED at Kennedy Airport, I was happy at the prospect of seeing Marsha and realized how much I missed her, despite the fact I'd been gone for only a few days. It never entered my mind that when I walked in the door about eight P.M., Marsha would be in the theater until eleven o'clock. Six nights a week, plus Wednesday and Saturday matinees. There would be no three-day weekends in Pound Ridge, no flying off to the Caribbean for a week of sun, sleeping late and long walks on the beach. There wouldn't be even a walk on Third Avenue at night, a movie, a dinner with friends. From a completely selfish point of view, I would rather have had Marsha at home with me than in the theater doing my play. After nineteen years of all our nights together, I realized my life with Joan had spoiled me. On the other hand, Marsha had spent almost all her adult life being in a theater every night, and for her, the adjustment was that now there was a husband and two stepdaughters waiting for her when she was done. These were things to be worked out.

Marsha and I started having lunches together, something I rarely did with Joan, and I changed my writing schedule somewhat to accommodate the shift. I started later in the afternoon, and continued to work at night, something I was unused to. But while I worked, I remained anxious for the sound of Marsha's voice coming up the stairs announcing, "Hi, everybody. I'm home."

But was it a home for her? Since Joan's death, I had not changed one piece of furniture, had not redecorated a single room, and, worst of all, kept the four-poster bed that Joan and I loved so much. Everything was on my terms, yet Marsha made hardly a sound of complaint. Of course, even if we did want to change things, Marsha would not have had much time during her busy schedule to do it. But the truth was, I was not yet inclined to give up anything that I had in my prior life. It's my feeling now that at the time Marsha thought that when the moment was right, she'd be able to make a home that was ours, and not just mine.

So it was on to the next play for me, but even that, in some sense, was written to deal with my feeling about Joan's death, albeit in an abstract way.

THE GOD PLAY

8

I THOUGHT *God's Favorite* was a funny play, but possibly the darkest one I had written up until then. I wanted answers from God, as we all do in times of great loss, but I knew I was not about to get a letter in the mail from the Almighty explaining why He had to make this decision about Joan (which was too bad, since I also wondered what kind of stationery He used and would He capitalize His name whenever He mentioned it). Spinoza in his writings clearly states (although it takes four readings before the word "clearly" can apply) that with all the planets, the galaxies, the universe and the trillions of other masses floating around out there, God does not have time to answer questions made by individual request. Still, I hoped there would be something in my mailbox.

"Dear Mr. Simon," I imagined it would begin, but then reconsidered. Who was I to command the respect of God to be called Mr. Simon? You can already see the tone and direction I would take in writing this play.

"Dear Neil?" No way. Just plain "You," perhaps. Or, if I had already bothered Him with this small question, His irritation would produce, "You dot among insignificant dots on a planet I've long given up hope for." (God was allowed to end his sentences with a preposition.) I decided He would just write a one-line sentence, dignified, powerful, deity-like and clearly not leaving it open to further correspondence.

"And thus shall it be; and thus shall it always be."

A little cryptic for me and not exactly what I was hoping for. I decided to look for my own answers in Scripture, which was not easy to find in my house since I never owned one. Bibles do not come with houses as they do in hotels. I went scurrying over to Doubleday on Fifth Avenue and asked the clerk behind the counter, "Where are the Bibles, please?" It even occurred to me they may not have one since bookstores do not generally keep old books on the shelf. They have hotter-selling products to move. Possibly he'd have to order one from the warehouse. I was in luck, however, and they indeed had Bibles in stock. "Old Testament? New Testament? King James?" the clerk asked, speaking like the computer they all use these days to hunt down exactly what it is you're looking for. "Er, gee, I don't know. Just a regular Bible. Something that has the Book of Job story," I said, as the priest standing next to me reading *Best Country Inns in New England* chuckled to himself. I felt my line was going to be quoted in a small back room after Mass that night. I purchased my Bible and was surprised when the clerk slid it into a small open-ended bag like any other book. It was this kind of disrespect that probably made God angry with the likes of us. When I hit the street, I carried the Good Book with the pages up and the binding balanced correctly in my palm. I thought this would be worth a couple of points up in heaven.

Back in my den I closed the door and immediately plunged into the Book of Job. The story of God testing the faith of a simple, common man was fascinating. Job had an unwavering belief that God was All-Powerful, All-Merciful and All-Forgiving. He stood up to a great assortment of diseases, plagues, disasters and unbearable afflictions, yet Job never relented in his belief in the Almighty. I finally found out where "he has the patience of Job" came from. Amazing how many writers plagiarize Shakespeare and the Bible since there would be no lawsuits pending. Unfortunately, I did not have the patience of Job. Nor did I have his unshakable belief. I am neither an agnostic nor an atheist. I am, as a matter of fact, a Jew, and although Jews are devoted in their belief in God, they are not above asking pesky questions sometimes. They generally find the answers they're looking for, and when they can't find them, they accept the word of the great rabbis. If the great rabbis do not have the answer, they figure the question was not all that important in the first place.

In regard to my own feelings about God, the one thing I was quite positive about was that He had a sense of humor. If He had every other trait that man has attributed to Him, why would God be without the one quality holy men and critics do not consider lofty enough to meet the standards of their own idealistic vision? In the Bible, God is not funny once, that is, unless you read between the lines, and in most Bibles, there's not much space between the lines. My version of the story of Job would not be sacrilegious, nor would it be profane or held to ridicule. My goal was to translate its message into today's world, so that the viewers would grasp the power and the majesty in the story, yet, because it's a parable, they'd see the jokes as well. My basic question would be the same as that asked by Job's family: Why did he endure the suffering and still not give up his faith? My answer, however, would just be funnier.

I recognized the danger that audiences watching the play might cringe at such irreverence, doubly irritating after paying top dollar for good seats. Still, I hoped, in our enlightened world, intelligent people would be able to accept *all* interpretations of biblical stories. If our own Constitution allows us such freedom of speech, why wouldn't a munificent being such as God do the same?

The first character I changed was the messenger who brought Job the bad news. If he was an angel, he was unlike any angel we'd met before. My messenger was named Sidney Lipton and he lived in a small apartment in Queens. He carried an umbrella and wore rubbers on his feet when it rained . . . or even if rain was just predicted. He was as susceptible to colds as all of us, and received no perks just because he worked for the Highest Judge in all the universe. To him, his is simply a nine-to-five job, and his dream in life is to retire soon and live in a condo in Florida within walking distance of the beach. He comes to warn Job (or Joe as he's called in the play) of impending disasters. And disasters they are, coming one after the other, like twisters in Kansas. Joe's house burns to the ground, then his factory burns to the ground. He is now penniless and is visited "with boils, itching, dysentery, blisters, fever and the heartbreak of psoriasis." Still he believes in the goodness of God. The messenger pleads with Joe to give up this folly and take a tiny, minuscule ad in the *New York Times* classified section, so small you'd need a magnifying glass to see it. The ad would say simply, "I, Joe Benjamin, renounce God."

JOE: Never! I will never renounce. I will endure.

MESSENGER: If I told you who renounced God today, you would be
    shocked. Do you want to know who?

JOE: I don't care who.

MESSENGER: Detroit. The entire city of Detroit renounced . . . including
    three hundred tourists just passing through.

JOE: I am what God made me.

MESSENGER: Oh, stop talking like you're Moses. Moses was a big star. He
    was a headliner. You are nobody. I told God I was coming to see you
    tonight and He said to me, "Who?"

And so on. The play starred Vincent Gardenia as Joe and the brilliantly funny Charles Nelson Reilly as Sidney Lipton, God's messenger. It was directed by Michael Bennett, the future director of *A Chorus Line* and *Dreamgirls*. I had met him when he was the young choreographer of the musical *Promises, Promises*, which I wrote with Burt Bacharach and Hal David. Michael had an enormous talent, and occasionally an enormous ego. For the most part he earned the right to be proud of what he'd accomplished in a few short years in the theater.

I will pause here for a moment to tell you a recurring nightmare I have had in all the years I've been writing plays. It may, in fact, be the same nightmare other playwrights have had. I never asked them. This is it.

I am in London or Los Angeles, New York or any other major city where I am about to have a new play open. In the dream, this play is the best one I'd written to date, the one I was most proud of. I attended rehearsals almost daily until the last week before we were to open. Then something keeps me from getting to the rehearsals. No matter how much I try, I can't get there. But I feel comfortable that my play is in the good hands of my director. I finally show up just as the house lights are dimming on the opening night and the curtain goes up. The first scene goes extremely well. I relax. This is going to be everything I hoped for. Then suddenly the leading actor starts to sing. Out of nowhere. There is no song in my play—why is he singing? Then the leading lady sings too. And then a chorus of twenty wearing garish costumes come out and dance in a number that would seem odd in *any* show. George C. Scott is doing a tap dance. Al Pacino is playing a saxophone. Robert Redford is singing like Ezio Pinza in *South Pacific*. I can't breathe. I'm suffocating. I turn to the director, scream at him and grab him by the lapels shouting, "What have you done to my play? You've turned it into a musical" . . . and the surprised director looks at me, nods and says, "I know. Don't you like it?" End of nightmare.

Now the beginning of a real-life nightmare. In the second week of rehearsals of *God's Favorite*, I was suddenly called to serve on jury duty. No matter how many excuses I made to the judge, no matter how many strings I pulled from some power lawyers I knew, the judge would not let me off. On the fourth day he relented and sent me home about noon. I rushed in a cab up to the Eugene O'Neill Theatre and as I got out of the cab, I heard the sound of drumming coming from somewhere in proximity to the theater. I wondered how long that noise would go on and if it would hinder the actors during their rehearsals. I opened the stage door and entered the theater. The drumming was coming from inside, from our stage. As I came around to the orchestra, I looked up at the stage. There was the cast, clapping their hands in rhythm, some pounding the floor with their feet. Instead of what I had written—that Joe Benjamin was praising the name of the Lord as his family and servants would murmur their "Amens" to each statement—it was now an all-out revival meeting, the actors choreographed, moving like dancers, swaying their heads and hips. I thought I was hallucinating. I went over to Michael Bennett, having to scream to be heard above the din of the actors-chorus doing what seemed to me to be something like the finale in *Show Boat*.

"Stop them!" I screamed. "Stop them!" They stopped. I shouted to Michael, "What are you doing? You've turned my play into a musical."

He looked at me, surprised, then he nodded and said, "I know. Don't you like it?" No discussion followed. Michael simply went back to the text.

I decided to find a doctor who would give me a sleeping pill which would prohibit me from ever having dreams again.

At the end of Act I of *God's Favorite*, the curtain goes down as Joe Benjamin's stately home is about to go up in smoke. As the curtain is raised on the second act, all we see are charred, smoky ruins. Gone are the library's splendid wood panels, gone are the first-edition leather-bound volumes. Gone are the antique furnishings, tapestries and paintings. They are nothing now but cinders and ashes.

The Benjamins' maid walks on in an apron and carrying a dustpan, takes one look at all this rubble and says, "Well, I'll tell you one thing. I ain't cleanin' up *this* mess." I thought it was funny. Gallows humor, I admit, but funny. The audience did not. They were too stunned. They gasped at the sight of it. They took it absolutely literally, that at every performance we built this huge, expensive set, burned it down during the intermission, and came up with charred ruins in the second act. Eight times a week. That was the second mistake I made. The first mistake was even deadlier.

I never expected the play to be a huge hit. I did not envision lines around the block with ushers giving cups of hot coffee to those who braved the frigid weather to get tickets to this, the hottest show in town. What I *did* expect was a play that most of the audience and many of the critics would enjoy. I hoped we'd have a decent run and that the backers would make a small profit on their investment and that I would have brought closure to my questions of God, Joan and death. What I did *not* expect was what eventually happened.

I repeated a blunder that cost me dearly. When we did *The Gingerbread Lady*, I permitted a journalist from *Life* magazine to accompany us on the journey from the first day of rehearsal to opening night in New York. The intrusiveness of this writer disquieted us all. To put on a play is hard enough. To do it under a public microscope, diverting our attention from the work at hand and, instead, whispering in the darkened corners of a theater lest your remarks show up in a national magazine, is theatrical suicide. Why then did I permit myself to say yes when an offer came from the most popular television show on the air, *60 Minutes*, inviting us to allow them to cover our play during the trials, tribulations or occasional joys that occur during an out-of-town tryout? The reporter was to be Mike Wallace himself, once an actor on Broadway and now the program's number one cover man. The sales pitch made by CBS and our own publicity man was all about numbers. Millions would be watching us on some Sunday night in the future. Fifteen to twenty million possibly. More people than would see *any* play, no matter how successful, if you ran on Broadway for ten years. I listened to that old bromide, "You can't buy publicity like that." It was also insane to accept it as a gift. We were going to expose ourselves even before the show was ready to be seen in New York. The list of shows that turned themselves around from failure in a tryout to a hit six weeks later is a long one. But you need the time. A honeymoon is not a marriage and we were dumb enough to not only invite the public to our honeymoon, but we were also putting a cameraman lying between a man and his wife in the marriage bed and saying, "Don't mind me. Act as if I weren't here at all."

At our very first preview performance at the Shubert Theatre in New Haven, Mike Wallace and his *60 Minutes* crew took their positions in the lobby, waiting to catch the first-night audience as they filed out, and to capture their opinions on film. As I watched the show from the back of the house, I realized this wasn't a preview at all. This wasn't the night I begin to take my notes on what to cut, what to rewrite, what to restructure, a time that I usually enjoy. Removing the deadwood and replenishing the script with new and fresher ideas, watching the play rise from its semidormant state to a blossoming flower, is for me what the fun of this process is all about. I realized suddenly that I had to forgo all that, because for all intents and purposes, this evening's performance was tantamount to an opening on Broadway.

Mike Wallace and his two cameramen were poised outside, ready to document what should not really be seen or judged by anyone except the eleven hundred people in the audience that night. They were all part of the break-in process. You try the show out, you weigh the problems, you fix it and hope for the best. What was on the stage that night was a play that you would describe as "needing work." I rarely did an opening out of town that *didn't* need work. As I documented in *Rewrites*, the first preview of *The Odd Couple* in Delaware drew notices that were anything but exuberant. We had a third act that didn't work at all. Seven weeks and fifty pages of rewrites later, we had a smash.

The audience filed out of the Shubert Theatre, and Mike Wallace was there, microphone in hand. The first couple out was the first couple interviewed.

"What did you folks think of the play?"

"It was strange. Not the usual Neil Simon."

"Give a quick review. Good or bad?"

"Well, it was okay. Not great."

The second couple snared by Mr. Wallace looked at the camera nervously.

"Tell me about the play."

"We laughed some. They still have a lot of work to do."

And on and on. Some were out-and-out positive responses, others completely negative. Most felt it was in the "not really ready yet" category. I knew we had some trouble, but what I needed was to work on it in the seclusion of a hotel room, with a typewriter and plenty of paper. Instead, I knew these negative responses were soon going to be viewed by millions of people. Tens of millions.

The verdict on the play was fatal and I was the coroner for permitting *60 Minutes* to see and report that we were bleeding. Despite the fact that we eventually got a rave review from Walter Kerr in the *New York Times*, we ran for just two months on Broadway, the shortest run I had with all of the thirty shows I've written to date. Today, if our press representative comes to me a few weeks prior to our going into rehearsal and says, "Neil, we've got a great publicity opportunity—I just got a very exciting call from—"

"No," I say, before he ever finishes the sentence. "And don't ever ask me again."

MARSHA'S DECISION

9

MARSHA HAD FINISHED her six months in *The Good Doctor* and 20th Century Fox now wanted her to fulfill her seven-year deal. It would mean her going to Hollywood or wherever they might be filming. I couldn't leave New York without Ellen and Nancy. Marsha postponed her decision as long as she could. The film she had made prior to our going into rehearsal with *The Good Doctor* was about to be released. The girls and I went with her to the first preview screening in New York.

"Cinderella Liberty" was not a girl, as most people thought, but a term used in the Navy for a short leave of duty, the requirement being you had to be back by midnight. In *Cinderella Liberty* James Caan played the sailor on leave who drops in at a pool parlor in downtown Seattle. We hear the sound of cue balls banging off each other, slamming into the pockets in rapid fire while a crowd of beer-drinking sailors cheer some unseen, phenomenal pool player. When Jimmy Caan steps through the shouting sailors and Marines, we see the focus of their rapt attention. The picture of Marsha Mason with a cue stick in her hands, bending down over the green table, the overhanging light above her casting shadows on the table and highlighting her eyes and pouty, voluptuous lips, with a look of smirking disdain at her adversary as she clips another ball into the corner pocket, was one of the greatest introductory shots of an actress I've ever seen on film. The hint of sexuality which she kept under wraps in that Manufacturers Hanover Bank commercial now came at us like a fiery red-hot bomb exploding on the screen. True, it was her second film, the first being *Blume in Love*, but this was a starring role. All I could think of as I saw her chalking up her cue stick, then knocking balls down with almost demonic confidence, was, "My God! In her first ten seconds on screen, there's not a doubt in my mind that Marsha's a star. She couldn't miss."

I was enormously pleased. Pleased for her because I knew she was going to make a huge impact on the film colony, and pleased for us as a professional couple. What would it be like if I thought that Marsha were only a competent film actress, and that if we worked on pictures together in the future, would I be doing it out of some sense of obligation? That question need never be asked now that I saw the power of her performance in this film. In fact, the reverse was true: I'd be lucky to have her star in something I wrote. I also knew there would soon be many long separations as her career took off, and since we were only married about eight months, still trying to mesh our lives together, I wondered how we would deal with this, the girls included. It also became apparent that Marsha had a lousy contract. When you're hungry for that first starring role, you unwittingly sell your body and soul for a pittance, or you allow your agent to make that decision for you. Even if *Cinderella Liberty* was a smash hit, Fox would not have paid her more than thirty thousand dollars for her next film, which was only about five thousand more than they just gave her. As it happened, she very smartly turned down the next script they sent her because it wasn't any good.

THE PICTURE, when released, was a moderate success, but Marsha's reviews were almost unanimously great. There was talk of her getting an Academy Award nomination. She, however, refused to even acknowledge the possibility. I don't think she believed it even when the phone call came from California telling her that she was nominated in the Best Actress category, in this, her second film. Our phone started ringing off the hook and Marsha was besieged with requests for newspaper interviews. "Who was this girl?" "Where did she come from?" "What's her next project?"

We sat in the kitchen one morning as she awaited her first big press interview, with the *New York Times*. She was drinking coffee, having trouble keeping her hand and the cup from shaking. She turned to me. "You've been through this before. What do I say to them?"

"Nothing. They'll ask you questions, you answer them."

"I mean, it's the *New York Times*. What if I make a fool of myself?"

"You won't. Trust me."

"Why am I so nervous?"

"Because you're empowering them with too much. Just be yourself. And don't try to please them. If they have something you want, and you let them know it, you'll never get it. Then they have you. Not just the press but anyone in this business."

"I have to remember that," she said, jotting down my elementary words of wisdom on a piece of paper, the pencil in her left hand, her head cocked to the side, as if taking notes in a college class. The interview went just fine. As I had found out a year earlier, she was hard to resist.

Marsha, myself and the two girls all flew out to California to attend the Academy Awards. I was nominated once before for the script of *The Odd Couple*, but did not attend the festivities, since I was in rehearsal with my next play. I was always in rehearsal with my next play. This trip, then, was the first for all of us. The shopping trip that ensued the following week for the three right dresses is something a man neither has to deal with nor truly understands. He puts on his four-year-old tux and he's ready. The girls had no trouble in finding the right dress for the other one ("Oh, you look great in that. Marsha, doesn't she look great in that?" which produces the inevitable answer, "If I have to wear this, I'm not going."), but finding the right one for themselves was like trying to cross the Rubicon. No one dared take the first step. The girls roamed around Bloomingdale's by themselves, searching for the perfect dress for Marsha. They came back brimming with excitement, holding something in red with little things that glittered.

"You're kidding," said Marsha. "I'd look like a prostitute."

"No," begged the girls. "You'll look hot. Don't you want to look hot?"

"I looked hot in the movie. In life I want to look lukewarm."

With all three looking absolutely fetching, we arrived early at the Dorothy Chandler Pavilion, mostly so the girls could ogle all their favorite movie stars, some of them wearing red dresses with little things that glittered. From our aisle, you could hear the excited murmurs of two young girls who were fulfilling their childhood dreams.

"Oh, my God. Jane Fonda. She is *GOR*geous."

"Ellen, Paul Newman's staring right at you, I swear."

"Dad! Dad! It's Al Pacino. Do you know him?"

"No."

"Well, make friends with him so we can meet him."

The interesting phenomenon for me was that we were all at this gala event, our hearts pounding in expectation of who would win, and for the first time it wasn't about me. For once I was rooting for someone else, and who better to cheer for than your own wife? Stars, directors and studio execs were crossing to Marsha, eager to shake her hand and to tell her how wonderful she was in that film.

The competition in her category was tough, and Marsha, being a newcomer, knew she was a long shot. She was up against Barbra Streisand in *The*

Way We Were; Ellen Burstyn for *The Exorcist*; Joanne Woodward for *Summer Wishes, Winter Dreams* and Glenda Jackson for *A Touch of Class*. My guess was either Barbra Streisand or Ellen Burstyn, because they were in the two blockbuster hits of the year, and in those days that's how the conservative bloc of voters in the Academy would go. I was wrong, it went to Glenda Jackson for her performance in a nice, light comedy. Go figure. A few years later when I wrote *California Suite*, the British actress played by Maggie Smith was, in some sense, fashioned after Glenda Jackson. She says to her husband while dressing to go to the awards, "I've done twelve Shakespeares, eight Shaws, six Ibsens and five Pinters, and I get nominated for a nauseating little comedy." *A Touch of Class* was far from nauseating, but I think they gave the brilliant Glenda Jackson the award because she surprised everyone in showing that she could also do comedy. Marsha was too pragmatic to be disappointed. The attention and respect paid to her at the awards was more than she ever expected. We flew home the next morning and Marsha's spirits were as high as the plane we were flying in.

Since a long time passes between the making of a film and the time it's actually released, the way most Hollywood stars keep their faces before the public is to start another film before the previous one hits the theaters. Marsha could not because of her commitment to the play and because we were still making an effort to get our marriage off the ground, which took work, considering the limited time we were spending with each other. Offers were now coming in to her, although none of the roles was as promising as that of *Cinderella Liberty*.

Then Marsha made a decision—a momentous decision, not based on the film offers or any contractual conflicts with the studio. She told me she would not take on another film until she felt that we had secured our marriage; that way, any separations would not endanger what we were just starting to build with each other, including her desire to be there for Ellen and Nancy in this critical time of their lives. I breathed a sigh of relief, not even realizing what an incredible gesture she ultimately would be making. Between *Cinderella Liberty* and the release of her next film, three years went by. Three years in the life of any film actress is time you can never get back, and considering that Marsha was past thirty when she made this commitment, the significance of what she gave up was inconceivable to most people. No matter what painful circumstances transpired between us many years later, I could never forget nor have my feelings diminished toward Marsha because of the sacrifice she made in giving up those years. For that alone she has my love and respect forever. It was wake-up time for me in terms of what I could give to her and to our marriage.

I knew I had to make it up to her in the only possible way I knew how, by writing a film for her considerable talents. That opportunity soon presented itself at the unlikeliest time, in the most unlikely place.

WE TOOK a belated honeymoon and flew to Italy. It was truly our first time alone and I brought no spiral notebook with me, thus avoiding the temptation of starting a new play instead of a relatively new marriage. Since we went to many of the major cities in Italy, as I had with Joan nearly twenty years before, it was hard to avoid sensing the shadow of Joan following me about. Despite the constant reminders of that first marriage and of the love and happiness that went with it, it was now Marsha's face that I was seeing each morning when I awoke, Marsha's face that was the last thing I saw each night. My imaginary clandestine meetings with Joan had now disappeared. I found my feelings toward Marsha were now deepening, even more than when I first met her. It was a sensation that I feared because just as I had lost Joan, so this one might not last either. Yet it was irresistible and I began to give myself over to it completely. I was falling in love with Marsha. This sensation, almost a year after the wedding, may sound strange, but what I initially committed to was a marriage, a partnership, and as strong as my first feelings for her were, it was also a way out of despair and hopefully into a place where I could breathe again. We were tentative with each other that first year. Now walking hand in hand with Marsha through the curved streets of Florence, I had this incredible feeling which seemed new, not familiar. New because this was Marsha and not someone else, and I was suddenly and completely in love. In *Blume in Love*, Marsha lost the leading man to his wife. In *Cinderella Liberty*, she runs away from her lover, James Caan, and even her own son, both of whom set out to find her again although no happy ending was guaranteed. Here in Florence I wanted her to get the guy. And I wanted desperately for the guy to be me.

FRIENDS HAD GIVEN us a list of Florence's better restaurants, any of which we could ride to, but we decided to walk—in a city as beautiful as Florence, a taxi ride being almost sacrilegious. We talked as we walked, and soon found that we were lost in those curved streets which seem to lead to no place very hospitable. Because we were cold and hungry, we wandered into a small, unpretentious restaurant, one that obviously generally fed local families, not tourists. We were shown the only empty table there, and we heard not a single English word from anyone, nor did we see a menu. Instead, we watched these incredible dishes pass by, and we just pointed out the most appetizing ones to the waiter. A sightless, nonspeaking person would not go wrong ordering anything in this restaurant. All that was really needed was a sense of smell.

We never got to the list of restaurants our friends had given us. We went back to the same place every one of the four nights we spent in Florence. In fact, so anxious were we to get there, we kept arriving too early and had to wait outside until they opened for business. We did not, however, find the restaurant easily, and each night we depended on getting lost and just wandering into it by chance. Indeed, those are the only directions I could give you as to finding this secret haven. Just get lost—you'll find it. Sometimes usually after vino, we weren't quite sure that this restaurant really existed except in our own minds. We were two chilled, happy lovers, ordering the exact same dishes each night for fear of breaking the magic spell. One glass of wine led to another and we began to feel free enough with each other to talk about the future, and about our future together, because we were both now confident enough to believe we actually would have one. We started to talk about working with each other, of me writing a film for Marsha to star in. "Co-star in," she added. "I don't want the responsibility of being up there alone."

There was no thought as to career or profit or even success in this joint venture we talked about. Our discussion was mostly about the joy of spending our days together on a project that was of our making, and that joy wouldn't end at the finish of each day's work. It would continue until our heads hit the pillows next to each other as sleep finally overtook us. "It's got to be a love story," Marsha said between bites of bread sticks and pasta. "A funny love story," I said, scribbling notes on the bill instead of a spiral notebook.

"Like one of those old Spencer Tracy–Katharine Hepburn movies," she said as my napkin wiped a speck of sauce from the side of her lip. I would have preferred doing it with my own lip.

"Old-fashioned but contemporary," I added. "Kind of corny but smart. These should be really bright people," I mumbled, my mouth full of osso buco.

"Jimmy Stewart and Margaret Sullavan," Marsha said with a giggle as she rubbed her shoeless toes on my cold ankles.

"Let's never go home," I said to her, now rubbing my warmed ankles on her hot toes.

"Okay," she said, smiling. "I'll get the check and you go back home and get Ellen and Nancy."

We wandered out on to the curved streets, back to the hotel, and having had two bottles of wine, I'm not positive the hotel was ours. When you're in Florence and in love, details aren't really important.

LADY ANNE AND THE
SUNSHINE BOYS

10

IT WAS TIME for me to make the film of *The Sunshine Boys* and Marsha went back to the stage in New York, accepting the role of Lady Anne to Michael Moriarty's Richard III at Lincoln Center. The pressure to return to Fox Studios to fulfill her seven-year contract was alleviated by her buying herself out of her commitment. It was costly, but the other studios were clamoring for her to come work for them.

Richard III was to have a limited run and it turned out to be more limited than Marsha anticipated. I was and am a fan of Michael Moriarty and find him to be an enormously intelligent and sensitive actor. I do not believe his Richard was conceived by Michael but rather was the choice of the director, whose name fortunately escapes me. I sat in my seat opening night, aware that Marsha had been uncomfortable all during the rehearsal period. The house lights dimmed and slowly Richard III appeared, hunched over slightly, showing a trace of his deformed hand. He spoke in a voice that was higher than I anticipated and seemed somewhat effeminate. It wasn't obviously so, but there was a trace. Moriarty spoke his first line, "Now is the winter of our discontent," and before he finished "discontent," I said to myself, "Wrong! This production is doomed." True, I hadn't given either him or the director much time before I made this rash judgment, but as the evening wore on, you could sense others in the audience coming to the same conclusion. Marsha's Lady Anne was quite good, but it was apparent that she was trying to fight through a director's concept of the role that was giving her much trouble. The newspapers at least had the courtesy of letting them finish the performance before stating their negative opinion. Unable to come to terms with the director, Marsha left the production of her own accord and sooner than she had signed on for. Little did I realize that Lady Anne and an effeminate Richard III would soon be playing a major role in that film Marsha and I had dreamed of as we sat in that wonderful little restaurant in Florence.

Most of *The Sunshine Boys* was shot on location in New York and New Jersey, and I had to spend only a few weeks in Los Angeles while they shot the interior scenes on a soundstage. Red Skelton was replaced by Walter Matthau and I couldn't have been more relieved. In all the films I've done, no one served my material better than Walter. Although he was twenty years too young for the part, he agreed to shave almost all of his rich thick head of hair, and some superior makeup made it easy to believe he was in his mid-seventies. None of that truly works, of course, unless the actor himself makes the change from within. Walter looked older when we made the picture than he does today, when he is past his mid-seventies. Director Herbert Ross and I went on auditioning other actors for the part of Al, his longtime vaudeville partner. The name George Burns came up again and this time Dan Melnick, head of the studio at the time, left the decision up to Ross and myself. George Burns, then seventy-nine years old, walked into Herb's Beverly Hills living room with his agent, Irving Fein, sat down, chewed on a cigar and started to read for us. After only three lines, I looked at Ross and tried to convey by the smile on my face that it was pointless to even go on reading—the man was perfect. Herbert knew it was as well as I did, but gave George the courtesy of at least allowing him to read a few more pages. He was signed the next day.

George Burns had the reputation as being the only man able to make Jack Benny laugh convulsively, and in only a matter of seconds. He never did it with jokes. He clearly had a wonderful acerbic comic mind and his age notwithstanding, he was as quick as anyone forty years his junior. The third part to be cast was the important role of Walter's nephew slash agent, a young man in his thirties who was Walter's/Willie's only surviving relative and more or less his caretaker. Although he cared very much for his irascible uncle, he was the constant victim of Willie's insensitive and cruel jokes.

BEN: I brought you six different kinds of soup. All low-sodium, no fat . . . are you listening?

WILLIE: I'm listening. You got six lousy-tasting soups.

BEN: You think that's funny? I don't think that's funny, Uncle Willie.

WILLIE: If you had a sense of humor, you'd think it was funny.

BEN: I have a terrific sense of humor.

WILLIE: Like your father. He laughed once in 1932.

BEN: If you're waiting for a laugh, you're not going to get one from me.

WILLIE: Who could live that long. Get me a job instead . . . you're a good
boy, Ben, but you're a lousy agent.

BEN: I'M A GOOD AGENT! Don't say that to me, Uncle Willie. I'm a God
damn good agent.

WILLIE: What are you screaming for? What is it, such a wonderful thing to
be a good agent?

One of the best young actors at the time was Harvey Keitel. Some twenty
odd years later he still is a fine actor. He gave an excellent reading for the
nephew Ben, and was hired the next day. Rehearsals began a few weeks later.
Most films never rehearse—since there is so much action and so little dialogue, what would you rehearse? However, since my films were eighty-five
percent dialogue, we rehearsed it like a play, although only for five days. It
didn't really occur to me as I was writing the play of The Sunshine Boys that
after doing a vaudeville act together for forty-five years, Willie and Al spoke
to each other in the same rhythms off stage as on, not by telling jokes, but just
the way they communicated with each other.

WILLIE: You want tea?

AL: If you got.

WILLIE: I got tea . . . you want a cracker?

AL: What kind?

WILLIE: All kinds. Chocolate, coconut, graham, whatever you want.

AL: You got a plain cracker?

WILLIE: Sure, I got a plain.

AL: Then I'll have plain.

WILLIE: They're in the kitchen. In the cabinet.

There were no pauses. The words shot out of their mouths in rapid-fire
precision. A pause was filled in with a nod or a shrug or a knock on the chair.
There was very little air between their speeches. Since Harvey Keitel read for
us without the benefit of Walter and George doing the scenes with him, we
realized we had a problem the first day. Harvey was—if not literally, then in
essence—a method actor. His speech was realistic. What he said was always
basically true and honest, but his speech rhythms were varied, according to

the emotion, sometimes rapid, sometimes halting, thinking things out. What he was doing was creating a character, but unfortunately the delivery of his dialogue did not mesh with the staccato beats of Willie and Al. Why should it? He had not been a vaudeville partner of theirs for the past forty-five years. But stylistically it didn't work; it was at odds with the music that was orchestrated on the page. It needed to mesh more. One could reason that having grown up with his Uncle Willie, he would just fall into the pattern of Willie's speech, sometimes just to make conversation between them easier.

Herbert took me aside and said he was worried. As good an actor as Harvey was, we realized we may have made a mistake. Herbert gave it two more days, then called me aside again and said that we'd have to find a new actor before we got too close to the shooting date. Herbert went with Harvey into his office and told him, regretfully, that we'd have to let him go. No actor likes to be fired, and although he would still receive his full salary, Harvey fought to stay on, convinced that he'd be able to give Herbert what he wanted. Herbert Ross was originally a choreographer, a very good one, and he had a choreographer's temperament. He was stern, professional, dogmatic, and when a decision had to be made, he wasted no time in making it. Harvey Keitel was gone from the film that day, although fortunately he went on to prove himself a fine film actor and has given us one great performance after another over the years. Herbert was stern, but he was not coldhearted, and he knew it was his place to tell George and Walter of the change, knowing that both actors had quickly grown fond of the young man. George was the most sympathetic.

"Oh, no," he said. "He was a nice kid. I liked him."

"We all did," said Herbert. "But I think it's best for the picture that we make this change."

"What if I came in early and worked with him on his lines?" offered George.

"That's very sweet, George, but you have enough to do."

"I could work with him at night. He could come over to my house, have dinner with me," George said.

"You're very thoughtful, George, but Neil and I have to find a replacement today."

Having explored all the reasonable avenues, George made a last effort to see that Harvey didn't leave completely empty-handed. "Well, then, ask him if he'd like to fuck my sister, Trixie." My mouth fell open, first in shock, then in laughter. At seventy-nine, George knew that life goes on, and there was no harm in saying so and getting a laugh at the same time. It wasn't said at Harvey's expense. It was the philosophy of a man who had been performing comedy longer than most of us had been alive. We didn't even know if he *had* a sister Trixie, and if he did, she must be about eighty-one. Plus, by using the name Trixie, he painted an image in our minds that was hilarious. In some respects, George had the youngest and fastest mind among us.

TO REPLACE Harvey Keitel, we hired Richard Benjamin, whom I had worked with before in the national companies of *Barefoot in the Park* and *The Odd Couple*. Richard fell into the speech pattern of the two men as though he were born to it.

Our troubles weren't over though. Another problem surfaced when Herbert said to me, "What am I going to do about George's hairpiece?"

"What do you mean?" I asked.

"He's worn it every day to rehearsals. He wears it to lunch. He never takes it off. I've never seen him bald. But in the scene where he's at home in New Jersey with his daughter and grandchild, the character wouldn't wear it. How do I get him to take it off?"

It was at moments like this that I was glad I wasn't a director. Two days later, Herbert was now rehearsing with the camera, lining up the shots to be filmed later that day. In the most matter-of-fact way, Herbert said, from a safe point behind the eyepiece on the lens: "George? Could you do me a favor? Take your hairpiece off a second?"

"Sure," said George, and took it off, tossing the piece into a saucer on the table. "Okay?"

"Thanks," said Herbert. "Looks swell."

"Nobody drink from that saucer," said George.

I sensed at that moment that Jack Benny was laughing himself silly somewhere in the confines of Los Angeles's Hillside Cemetery.

I WAS UNUSUALLY quiet at dinner in the little Italian restaurant on Third Avenue that Marsha and I frequented on the nights we wanted to be alone. The place was, I'm sorry to say, nothing compared to our small discovery in Florence, but the food was adequate. When I was pensive, she either assumed I was lost somewhere in the contemplation of a new play or just brooding, as I was prone to do. She was quite surprised when I finally spoke.

"I think it's time to move . . . Out of 62nd Street . . . What do you think?"

If this was the day she'd been waiting a long time for, I didn't expect to catch her quite so speechless. She looked at me for a moment, waiting to see if I was going to say anything else. I didn't; it was her turn.

"Really? Leave the house?"

I nodded. "Yes. Put it on the market. Sell it."

"Wouldn't the girls mind?" she asked carefully.

"It's not about the girls. I'll talk to them, of course, but I think they'll be happy wherever we're happy."

"I think that would be wonderful," she said. "Did you have any particular neighborhood in mind?"

"Yes . . . not in New York."

She stared at me, not really comprehending what I was saying.

"You would leave New York?"

I nodded. "The city has too many memories for me. They're getting in the way. We have to move on. I think we should be closer to where you could start making films again . . . California, I guess."

She sipped her wine. A healthy sip.

"You mean Los Angeles?"

"I don't know. L.A. scares me. I'd be so out of touch with the theater there. I need a city. A real city. A place where you could walk the streets, browse in bookstores. What about San Francisco? You worked there for a few years. You seemed to like it."

I could see the excitement building inside of her, but she was being careful not to jump at my suggestion lest it frighten me off.

"Well, yes. I love San Francisco. And there *is* a lot of good theater there. Great shops, restaurants, lots of interesting people. I don't think we should do anything though until we look it over. All of us. To be sure."

On the girls' next school break, we all flew out to San Francisco. The girls surprised me with their own exuberance at the prospect of moving. A new adventure in their lives—they were all for it.

We spent three wonderful days there. Marsha took us up to meet the actors at the American Conservatory Theater where she had worked. They were all ready to go to New York and help us pack. Everything felt so fresh, so new—and ultimately, so frightening. On the plane back to New York, I had changed my mind. As beautiful as the city by the bay was, it seemed foreign to me. Marsha had all her friends there, but I didn't know a soul. Not one. And you just didn't go out and walk the city streets there. You had to climb those hills before you found a place that was walkable. The views were great, but I knew I'd feel lonely there. My thoughts turned in a direction I never imagined I would contemplate in my lifetime: Los Angeles—Joan had hated it there, and I never liked it much. I didn't understand it. On the other hand, the work was right there for Marsha. She could do a picture and still come home every night. I had dozens upon dozens of friends there, the entire writing staff of *Your Show of Shows*, for starters—Sid Caesar and Mel Brooks and Carl Reiner and Larry Gelbart. Larry was as bright as anyone I knew and he loved it there. Then again, he grew up in L.A. But my brother, Danny, was there also; we had been separated for years, and I missed him. And Roy Gerber, the original model for Oscar in *The Odd Couple*, he was there. I could write plays just as well in California as anywhere else.

I realized, of course, that a lot of these thoughts were pure rationalizations. Los Angeles was Hollywood, and Hollywood was television and movies, not Broadway. Not by a long shot. But if, as in the past, I was able to write plays in Spain and in London and in Switzerland, surely I could write in Los Angeles, which in a sense was just as foreign to me as the cities I just mentioned. Marsha and I decided to visit there the next chance we had and investigate the possibilities.

That night I began to worry about it. I began to worry that in the end I would reject the idea, and worse, decide to stay in the same house on 62nd Street. I tried valiantly to quiet the little voice that was murmuring to me from the back of my head: "You're selling out. It's not you. You belong in New York. You'll never write a good play out there. Remember what Fred Allen said about California? 'It's a great place to live if you're an orange.'"

I turned the volume down on my thoughts as Marsha looked at me before we turned out the lights. "Are you sure about Los Angeles?" she asked.

"Yes. I'm sure." Then, as the lights went off, I said, "I'm pretty sure," leaving myself a much needed escape clause.

MARSHA DECIDED to fly to Los Angeles a few days ahead of me to scout houses on her own, mostly to avoid my having to look at dozens and dozens of homes and risk the chance that I would suffer a major attack of ennui and start asking, "Why are we leaving 62nd Street?" We talked out the kind of house we wanted, the price range, accessibility to places I could browse in and walk about and a school for Nancy, since Ellen would soon be graduating from high school and looking for a college.

When Marsha called two days later, I expected to hear her gushing with enthusiasm. Instead, I heard hesitancy, and, as good an actress as she was, she couldn't avoid the hint of what seemed to me to be a bit of a letdown.

"You okay?" I asked.

"Yes. Yes, fine," she said, sounding anything but fine.

"How'd it go? How many places have you seen? How many have you liked?"

"Well, I saw about ten. No. Nine."

"That's all? Not dozens and dozens?"

"There were very few worth seeing in our price range. Maybe three or four. It's much more expensive out here than in New York. They charge you for the sun."

"What about the ones you liked?"

"There were two, actually. But they needed work."

"How much work?"

"Almost everything."

"If it needed everything, what did you like about it?"

"Not much, really. I don't know. I'm in way over my head with this stuff. Except for this year, I've been living in two-room apartments all my life. I'm also worried you're not going to like it here. You'd better come out and look with me. I don't want the responsibility."

I flew out the next morning, and as we neared Los Angeles, I looked down and saw a desert, then the mountains, then the miles and miles of small houses bunched together and freeways circling and entwining each other endlessly like a massive nest of anacondas with millions of flies on their backs. I'd seen this sight for years now, but never through the eyes of someone who might actually be living there. It was not exactly as stimulating as the skyline of New York, whether seen in the morning or at night, or even from a steamer coming up through New York harbor as you passed the Lady with the Torch. I pondered going to the pilot and saying, "I'm really not feeling well. Could you possibly turn around, go back to New York and I'll repay the airline for the fuel a little bit each week until we're even."

Marsha looked more relaxed when I met her at the hotel, knowing that I would be lifting a large burden from her suddenly stiff shoulders. The real estate agent, who reminded me a little of Norma Desmond in *Sunset Boulevard*, with dyed black hair and makeup that looked like it was permanently scorched around her eyes, packed us into her shiny new white Cadillac. I immediately started looking around the car for a dead monkey.

"As I told Mrs. Simon," she said, enunciating as clearly as a former speech teacher who made the transition from the silents to the talkies, "I don't think there's anything you'd like in your price range. But I think I should show you what I *have* in your price range and you can judge for yourself." She kept saying "price range" as if I had a skin disease and she had no desire to get too close. Los Angeles is actually a lot prettier from the ground than from the sky above, and the orange circle of smog, which is visible at twenty thousand feet, is invisible when you inhale it into your lungs.

We drove through the Beverly Hills area and there were some very pretty houses, but the only ones that looked indigenous to the area were the Spanish-tiled ones. Most of the others looked as if they were flown in from abroad and had to show their passports before they were lowered into their two lots of land. I like my architecture old and authentic and I'd have to wait about eighty years before any of these homes became fairly old and slightly authentic. They were also out of my price range because this is where Lucille Ball lived and Gene Kelly and Alfred Hitchcock. I think Norma Desmond drove us out of our way so we could see what *she* thought we should be buying, before she made a left turn into our price range. The white Cadillac climbed up one of the canyons that stretch out above Beverly Hills and Los Angeles (they are two different cities, you know) and we were soon approaching the dirt road neighborhood.

Driving off the canyon road, we stopped at a house that looked a little better than a newly painted "tear down." The new paint did not conceal the flimsy interior, which didn't look like it could withstand a strong wind, let alone an earthquake. It did, surprisingly, have a tennis court. The court was not adjacent to the house, it was *part* of the house. As you stepped out the back door, you were *on* the court and you had to climb over the net to get out of the house. There were no sidelines to the court, unless you wanted to count the kitchen, and right on the back baseline was an iron meshed fence, giving you no room to go back for a shot. You'd have to go *outside* the fence to swing at the ball. The court was also covered with enough dead leaves to conceal a squadron of B-29 bombers, left there, no doubt, to prevent you from seeing what the last earth tremor did to the surface of the court. This house cost twice what my little town house on 62nd Street cost—the one near Bloomingdale's and twelve movie houses and great bookstores and incredible restaurants.

When we went directly back into the car, the agent said to me, "Don't you want to see the inside?"

"Why?" I asked. "I thought we *were* inside."

Two hours and ten houses later, the gloom had turned to a pall. On the few occasions that Marsha lifted her gaze from the floor of the car and her fading future, it was evident how downhearted she was. I turned to the agent and said, "Okay, let's try upscale."

Upscale houses, at least the ones she represented, all looked a little like Tara before the Civil War took its toll. Once inside, there was usually a very large vestibule with two rounded staircases coming down each side, where any minute you expected a smiling Loretta Young to descend, floating in a fluffy chiffon gown and saying, "Welcome to this week's show." These plaster and brick birthday cakes seemed less like homes than some expensive attempt to show the rest of Hollywood that they too could afford to have their bagels and Nova Scotia salmon flown in on weekends from New York, since at that time in L.A., a good deli, like a good man, was hard to find. Inside these houses hung some of the best paintings in the world, which seemed to be saying to me, "You can't judge a Matisse by its cover."

After three such houses, which fortunately for me were unaffordable, I asked the agent, "Do you have any houses where regular people live? Something that doesn't look like a fragment of a movie set, ready to be moved into storage space to make room for the next scene?"

Miss Real Estate didn't take kindly to my derisive humor, since it was clear she didn't have an inkling that it even *was* humor, which, I assume, came rarely into her life.

"I only have one last place to show you. I'm not sure you'll like it. It just came on the market. The sellers are very difficult people. It's not available to see until five o'clock, but I can drop you at your hotel and pick you up about four-thirty. It's above your price range but maybe not as high as what I've been showing you. Are you interested or shall we just forget about it?" Before I could say, "Why don't we just forget—" Marsha looked at me and said, "We might as well. We have nothing else to do at five." My feeling then was that we'd have nothing else to do out here till I died, but I nodded and said, "Sure. Why not?"

"Unless you'd like to live out at the beach. It's quite beautiful there." Ahh. Now the beach sounded promising. Since I had spent some childhood summers at Far Rockaway Beach and occasionally Brighton Beach, here was a suggestion that touched on my very roots. We took the hour-long drive out and the hour-long drive back and we were still at zero. Beaches were only for the summer, I reasoned from a mind-set that was entrenched in the past.

We had pretty much given up hope that the last house she was going to show us would be what we wanted, especially since the sellers were difficult people. As if the real estate lady wasn't.

"Should we reconsider San Francisco?" Marsha asked.

"Maybe we should just rent a house here for a year," I counteroffered, "before we decided how much I really hate this place."

At four-thirty on the dot, Norma Desmond showed up in a different outfit—a yellow tailored suit, the kind you see in Neiman's windows and are bought only by little old color-blind ladies in Texas. I guess she thought that if the house didn't cheer us up, her MGM musical costume would brighten the atmosphere. We had no expectations whatsoever as the car drove us down Sunset Boulevard, then through the gates of Bel Air. Bel Air was an anomaly in Los Angeles. It had less glitter and more taste than, say, Beverly Hills. You felt a certain serenity as you moved along the quiet and uncrowded roads. Many of the houses were not visible from the street, hidden as they were behind tall hedges or clustered trees. I looked at Marsha with my eyebrows surprisingly raised and she was obviously impressed as well, although she silently mouthed the words to me in the back seat, "Way too expensive." Norma Desmond, who apparently could hear a prospective buyer's thoughts, said, "Well, you can *try* negotiating, if you want."

What made me a little nervous was that the roads kept winding, turning and twisting, going ever upward. I knew I could never find this place again with a Sherpa guide and ten members of the Explorers Club. Norma finally turned in to a driveway and suddenly we were facing a gate. A bell had to be rung and answered before the gate opened and the price of the house went up about thirty percent. The driveway turned up a hill, and then we saw it. There was a large, flowing ficus tree, its branches spreading far and wide, and behind it—was Connecticut. Magically, we had just left Los Angeles, Beverly Hills and California behind us, and we were back East. Not an L.A. version of back East. Not a movie studio mockup. This was the real thing. A single-level house, painted white with dark green shutters. There was nothing showy, nothing ostentatious about this house. No manicured lawns, just a simple white-pebbled driveway. It was so definitively Connecticut that I was sure it was the only house in Los Angeles that had snow fall on it during the winter months. I braced myself for disappointment because this house had to be five times what I expected to pay. That figure became six times once we entered through the front door. The place was empty, devoid of furniture, not a stick, which only added to its charm. So often a house loses its advantage by the overdone or pretentious interior decorating imposed on it by someone who didn't realize what they really had. We wandered from room to spacious room, each one more spacious than you'd ever see in a large New York apartment. The views were not spectacular in the conventional sense. It was not the kind of house that wherever you looked, you saw the shining, glittering lights of Hollywood below. What you saw here were trees and more trees and, in the distance, other houses nestled quietly into the hills. The house had been built around 1930 and had lost none of that era's sense of understatement. Marsha's eyes and mouth had opened wide, each to about the same size, and they stayed open the entire time she viewed the house.

"Well, obviously I can't afford this," I said to Miss Desmond, "but how much is it?" She told me. It was a lot, but only about twice what I expected to pay and far less than the Hollywood museums I had seen earlier that day. I think because the house *was* so understated it was not as popular to more flashy-seeking minds. The money suddenly seemed less important to me, inasmuch as we were getting Connecticut with southern Italy thrown in.

"It's not negotiable," Norma said. "I've tried. They turned down ten offers. They won't come down a nickel. You pay their price or that's it. Walk around again. Look outside. I'll wait for you in the car." With that she left.

Marsha was obviously overwhelmed, but she remained cautious. "Oh, God," she said. "It's so big. I'd never be able to clean this." She wasn't joking. That's what a lifetime in two rooms will do to you.

I opened the front door and asked Miss Desmond to return. I thought that "it's not negotiable" was agent talk.

"We like it. Obviously we like it. It's beautiful. But I'm not used to figures like this." Having lost a great deal of money in previous bad investments, I was now trying to be careful about financial matters. I made a lesser offer on the house and asked the agent to put it before the owners. She shrugged skeptically and drove us back to the hotel. Marsha and I sat there without saying a word, transfixed on the picture of that utterly charming house you would never imagine existed in Hollywoodland. In the morning came the answer I pretty much expected. No deal. Not only no deal, but the owner said that for each week I didn't buy the house, the price would go up five thousand dollars. That's five thousand a week. I laughed at the insanity of it.

"Is that five thousand dollar increase limited to just a few weeks," I asked, "or does it go on for the rest of my life?"

"That's his offer, Mr. Simon. I told you they were difficult."

"No. Climbing Mount Everest is difficult. Buying this house is impossible."

We drove back to the hotel and I immediately called Ray Stark, who lived ten minutes away, outside Bel Air. I asked him to come look at the house with me the next morning.

"Do you really like the house?" he asked while we were still on the phone.

"Yes. It's beautiful. But I can't make a deal with this man. The house comes with a taxi meter that charges you while you're waiting." I told Ray what the price was.

Ray said, "If you like it, I don't have to see it. Here's what I'll do. I'll buy the house from him today myself. Then I'll sell it to you for the same price. I will also give you a note saying that whenever you wish to get rid of this house, I will give you back exactly what you paid for it. You can't lose a nickel."

"Why would you do that, Ray?" I asked.

"Because you and I will be working together for a very long time. And you won't write well if you're unhappy. Do we have a deal?"

It never came to that, but Ray's offer pushed me to make my own. I bought the house the next morning. It was ours. Well, it was ours until two more conditions arose. In the large bathroom off the bedroom, there was a mural painted on the wall. And it was a pretty ugly mural at that.

"The mural doesn't go with the house," Norma Desmond told me. "If you want it, you have to buy it. It's seventy-five hundred dollars."

"You don't understand," I said to Norma. "It's paint on a wall. What are they going to do, suck it off with sponges and take it with them on a blotter?"

"I don't know," she said. "Do you want to buy it or not?"

I was now wondering if even as smart a businessman as Ray Stark could pull off this deal.

"No. I pass on the mural. Now how much are the trees and the pebbled driveway?" Somehow the owners backed off their demand and I signed the papers before the week was over, just barely saving myself an extra five thousand dollars. But they weren't through. They then asked if I wanted to buy the complicated security system they had built in.

"No," I answered. "Tell them to rip it out of the walls. Instead I will put scarecrows all around the house." Well, they didn't pull the security system out, but I had to rebuild it anyway. They were so manic about their security that when you put the system on when you went to bed at night, every window and every door in the house had to be closed. This meant that if you wanted to go to the bathroom during the night, you'd have to turn off the system, turn it back on when you were in the bathroom, turn it off when you were through in the bathroom and back on again when you went back to sleep. I understand that when these people moved to Nevada they had the moving vans with their furniture drive very slowly because they would be in their car right behind the vans, making sure no one would steal anything from them. I believe they are now living inside a bank vault somewhere out West.

The next afternoon we were given the keys to the place, and Marsha and I walked around the empty house. It was the very first house she could call hers, or at least ours. We stood there, looking at our future together. Tears suddenly came to her eyes but they didn't seem to be about happiness.

"What's wrong?" I asked.

"I don't know," she said. "Do we deserve this?"

"Probably not," I answered, putting my arms around her. "But let's enjoy it anyway."

We went outside and looked at the trees.

"Uh oh," I said.

"What is it?"

"They forgot to charge us for the birds."

THE END OF NEW YORK

11

WE WOULDN'T make the move for another seven months so that Ellen and Nancy could finish their school terms. In the meantime, Marsha arranged to have two friends, young L.A. decorators on the rise, help to furnish and redo walls, floors and ceilings, which hadn't been repaired or painted by the two former owners since the understated 1930s. If we shipped out all the furniture we had from the small rooms on 62nd Street, it wouldn't have filled a third of the new house in California. We decided, with Marsha's blessing, to take all the best and prettiest pieces with us when we made the move to L.A. The four-poster bed that had been mine and Joan's would go into storage, simply because it was too difficult for me to give up completely. I also stored some other pieces that I thought Nancy and Ellen might want for their own homes some future day. A new bed was built for us in California and this, in a sense, was the official beginning of a new life for me and Marsha.

She was soon offered a film by Fox called *Audrey Rose*, a thriller dealing with reincarnation and co-starring Anthony Hopkins—before Anthony Hopkins became *the* Anthony Hopkins, one of the world's best actors. It was to be filmed in L.A., where Marsha could also oversee the redoing of our house and be back in plenty of time before we had to make the inevitable move. I use "inevitable" because it describes the fears that still clung to me concerning this transplantation of my soul, body and mind. I worried that after three months there I would be completely unhappy, and even worse, that I couldn't find the house driving up from Sunset Boulevard. I pictured myself calling from some stranger's home on the other side of Bel Air, pleading with Marsha to come and get me.

As for my own work, I started thinking about two projects. One was the romantic comedy film that was born in a Florence restaurant, the other was a new play I wanted to follow the disappointing *God's Favorite*. I made notes on the film to be called *Bogart Slept Here*, meaning the Chateau Marmont Hotel in the Hollywood Hills, where so many neophyte actors stayed before they became major film stars. The basic idea of the story was that Marsha, an ex-dancer, was married to a very promising but struggling off-Broadway actor who gets discovered in a small play and is whisked out to Hollywood, where he reluctantly moves with his family. He feels very out of place there (autobiography often sneaks in when you least expect it), and they have trouble adjusting, especially after his first film makes him an international star (picture Dustin Hoffman in his debut performance in *The Graduate*), and it creates chaos in their marriage. The story was coming out a little darker than I had imagined, but I envisioned the character of the wife as a very good role for Marsha.

When thinking of the new play, I was reminded of an item from a California paper sent to me by a friend. It said that playwright Neil Simon was moving to L.A., and questioned if that meant he would start to tear apart California's mode of living as he had New York's in his previous *Prisoner of Second Avenue*. Obviously that was impossible, because a man who can't find his house in Bel Air doesn't know enough about California mores to write about them. But it did occur to me to do a play about people in California who do not *live* there. In other words, it would be about people staying at a hotel—the Beverly Hills Hotel, in fact, because to the rest of the world it was L.A.'s most famous hostelry. Since I had successfully done *Plaza Suite* a few years back, why not *California Suite*?

Before any words were put to paper, Marsha and I were summoned by director-choreographer Michael Bennett to see his new show, then previewing at Joe Papp's Public Theater, called *A Chorus Line*. Michael conceived, choreographed and directed the show based on interviews he had conducted with dancers about their dreams, hopes, fears, aspirations and their personal background. He and his book writers, James Kirkwood and Nicholas Dante, then made a coherent script out of that material, and Marvin Hamlisch and Edward Kleban wrote a most wonderful score. The musical was to run close to fifteen years on Broadway and still continue to be seen today in any country that has a theater. Marsha and I were thrilled and awed by the incredible show that was so brilliantly mounted on the stage that night. At the end of the performance, Michael waited for us in the lobby, then pulled us aside and asked our opinion.

"It's a smash, Michael. You have nothing to worry about," I said exuberantly, genuinely enthused about his achievement.

"But what didn't you like?" he pushed. "Was there anything you would change?" Marsha loved the show as much as I did, but she made one important suggestion about the character development of Cassie, the lead dancer in the show. Michael loved what she said and agreed to put it into the show, which he did. He then turned to me and said, "It's not right yet. It needs more humor."

"It might, it might not, Michael," I added. "It doesn't make any difference. It's a winner just the way it is."

But he persisted with his concerns, and asked me if I could go out for a drink with him and his assistant, Bob Avian.

"When?" I asked.

"Now," he answered. "Please. It's important to me. I really need to talk to you."

Marsha urged me to go with him, and she returned home as it looked like this was going to be a long drink.

In a booth in a small, dark Greenwich Village restaurant, Michael proceeded to reiterate his fears about the show's lack of humor.

"It needs what you can give it," he said to me. "It wouldn't take you long. A few hours' work, that's all."

Everyone presumed because I was prolific that I could knock out dialogue on the spot. It never happens that way. It only starts to flow when you know the characters well, when you have a keen grasp of the story. I had only seen one performance of A Chorus Line. But Michael was in a hurry; they were nearing the end of their previews and had to open within a week. The timing, however, was the least of my concerns.

"Michael, I can't write anything without the permission of the authors. Jim Kirkwood and Nick Dante would have to agree to my coming on."

"They accept," he said quickly. "It's not a problem."

"It is to me, Michael. I'm a member of the Dramatists Guild. It's against their rules. You have to speak to them and assure me that they've agreed."

"All right," he said. "I'll talk to them. But I promise it's no problem. The only thing is, we won't be able to give you billing."

"That's fine with me," I said. I didn't ask if I would be paid for this and frankly I hadn't expected it. I again followed the old, unwritten law of the theater that states that writers go to help other writers when they're in trouble, although Michael didn't seem to be in any trouble. I soon found out, however, that that unwritten law had not been in use since the grand old playwrights like Moss Hart and Marc Connelly and George S. Kaufman had ceased working in the theater. Someone should have told me.

The next morning I received the script of *A Chorus Line* by messenger, followed by a phone call from Michael.

"It's okay with Jim and Nick. They just wouldn't want it to get around. But they would welcome your help," said Michael quickly, obviously anxious for me to get to the typewriter. I would have preferred to have heard it from Jim and Nick personally, but if they knew changes were being made in the script, and it was obvious they were, they surely would have complained to the Dramatists Guild if they were against it. Since I had not heard to the contrary from the Guild, I started to write.

I read the script through twice that morning and then picked my spots to add or change lines. Five, ten, twenty of them, maybe more, were interspersed throughout the script. I gave most of them to the character played by Kelly Bishop because Kelly could deliver a funny line better than anyone in the show. That night I sent my additions off by messenger to Michael, not knowing if he would use just a few or all of the lines I had written.

I was not witness to what happened the next day, but a friend in the cast told me that Michael sat in a chair with the pages containing my new lines sticking out from under him just enough for him to see them. He gathered the cast in front of him and said he'd been thinking of some new things for them to put in their scripts. I suppose Nick and Jim agreed that it was all right for the cast to think that Michael had rewritten them, but not for me to be given credit for the additions. Michael would look down at my pages (giving the impression that he was thinking of them on the spot), then up at an actor and say, "Honey, instead of your old line, say this." Then he gave her my line. They laughed. They laughed at the second new line, and then at the third. Someone said, "Michael, when did you get so funny?" He said, "I've just been thinking about it, that's all." I have no idea, as I said, how much actually went in, and when I went to see the show weeks later, I *never* knew what of it I wrote. I never remember what I write, even in my own plays unless someone tells me what play it's from. It's possible that Michael never told Jim Kirkwood and Nicholas Dante about the lines I wrote. Perhaps they did know. I don't recall ever meeting them later or hearing from them, or from the Dramatists Guild. I received no money from the production, but if I had insisted on even a small royalty, with a show that ran for fifteen years, I probably would have made close to half a million dollars. Another bad business judgment on my part? I don't know. I didn't do it for the money.

For years no one on Broadway ever mentioned it, and then suddenly it became part of the lore of the industry. Everyone knew I had worked on the show. Michael did send me a gift: a pair of pillowcases. Why pillowcases, you may ask, as *I* have for twenty-five years? Maybe he meant to say, "Thank you for keeping this under your pillow."

But Michael wasn't witty enough to use that double meaning. Smart, yes, but not witty. On the other hand, I was witty, but maybe not smart enough to ask to get paid for my work. The true answer, I suppose, was that helping make the show just a little better (although I still didn't think it needed to be better) was gratification enough for me. I don't think Marsha and I ever slept on those pillowcases, but if I had taken the money, Marsha and I would have slept very well in a deluxe suite in the Ritz Hotel in Paris.

IN THINKING of *California Suite*, four separate one-acters, all taking place in the same hotel suite, what I looked for first was the centerpiece. Not the funniest one, necessarily, but the most provocative, the most compelling one, so that I knew I was starting with something rock solid to build on.

I knew a number of couples in the theater and in films who had, what you might call, a marriage of convenience: the husband was bisexual, the wife heterosexual. I knew them well enough to be good friends but not intimately enough to understand exactly how their marriage worked. I suppose I wrote the way my instincts dictated. They were definitely devoted to each other, a traditional loving couple in all respects except one. She knew he had a separate life—his other lover or perhaps lovers—and she either condoned it or made a compromise with herself, realizing that if she demanded he be faithful, she would lose him. In many respects it was a poignant, if not a truly sad situation, while in other respects it was a courageous and difficult endeavor. Most of us would not tolerate such an arrangement, but those who do never let on that it's anything but bliss.

In my play, Diana Nichols, a British actress, has come to Los Angeles to attend the Academy Awards, for which she is nominated as Best Actress. She is accompanied by her husband, Sidney Nichols, an erstwhile antique dealer, a former actor and a bisexual. This one-act play was divided into two scenes. The first scene was their preparation before leaving for the awards—her complaining about how she looks and her worry that the expensive gown that producer Joe Levine bought her makes her look like Richard III because of the hump on her back that she suddenly has acquired since putting on the dress.

"Isn't that your usual hump?" Sidney says chidingly. "Or perhaps you forgot to take out the tissue paper." His quick biting humor matches hers, and although they can be cruel to each other, they adore each other's jokes. Where else would they find anyone so entertaining?

"Why didn't I dress simply?" says Diana. "Why didn't I just wear my plain black pants suit?"

"Because *I'm* wearing it," says Sidney, preening in his nifty tux. Even in their banter, their sexual differences or similarities come into play without rancor. In the second scene, they come back from the awards in the wee hours; both are fairly drunk. It's clear that Diana has not only lost the award, but she spotted Sidney paying a good deal of attention to a young, handsome actor at the Gala Ball after the proceedings. It leads to a knockdown, drag-out fight between the two when Diana realizes that she cannot bear losing the award and possibly her husband to a "young gorgeous twit" both on the same night. Sensing they are going too far this time, possibly taking that one step over the line that could destroy their marriage, they reconcile in bed, and in the darkness, Diana crawls close to Sidney, hoping for the physical affection that she gets all too infrequently.

DIANA: It's my fault, Sidney, for being a hopeless romantic. I keep believing
    all those movies I've made . . . And you do make love so sweetly.
SIDNEY: Would it help any if I made some empty promises?
DIANA: It never has . . . What's wrong with me, Sidney? We've been fighting
    this for years. Why haven't I left you for a hairier person?
SIDNEY: Because we like each other. And we are a refuge for our disap-
    pointments out there. (She lies back) Tired?
DIANA: Losing Oscars always does that to me.
SIDNEY: I'll get up first thing and order you eggs Benedict.
DIANA: You do take care of me, Sidney, I'll say that. And good help is hard
    to find these days.
SIDNEY: You scratch my back, I'll scratch yours.
DIANA: It's been an evening of ups and downs, hasn't it?
SIDNEY: Mmm.
DIANA: Care to continue the motion?
SIDNEY: Tacky. You're getting tacky, angel.
DIANA: I love you, Sidney. (He leans over and kisses her tenderly) Don't
    close your eyes, Sidney.

SIDNEY: I always close my eyes.

DIANA: Not tonight . . . Look at *me* tonight . . . Let it be *me* tonight.

(The lights dim. Curtain)

When the play successfully opened at the Ahmanson Theatre in Los Angeles, actress Lee Grant, with whom I had worked before, came to me just as the curtain went down. She looked at me in amazement.

"Where did this come from? What part of you knew who these people were?" she asked.

"I simply didn't think of him as gay," I answered. I paraphrased Tolstoy. "Any marriage in trouble is the same as all marriages in trouble."

THE SUNSHINE BOYS film came out in the latter part of 1974 and the reviews were ecstatic. The Academy Award nominations came out and we received three: Walter Matthau as Best Actor, George Burns as Best Supporting Actor (although it was far from a supporting role, but I think MGM submitted him in that category so as not to have him compete with Walter), and I received one for Best Screenplay Adapted from Another Medium, which was my own play. I was disappointed that director Herbert Ross was not nominated because I thought he did a masterful job. His big day was to come two years later.

Marsha, Nancy, Ellen and I flew out to attend the awards and to take a look at how work on our house was proceeding. Marsha and I had been married almost a year and a half at that point, and things could not have been better. In the cool, crisp winter air, the sky was practically cloud-free, although it occurred to me that the former owners might have taken them in the van back to Nevada as well. We also used this opportunity to look for a school for Nancy, and were fortunate enough to enroll her at the Westlake School for Girls. It was one of the better private schools in Los Angeles with a great reputation and the added advantage of being literally seven minutes away from our new house.

On the night of the awards, with so many things to do concerning the new house, the school and preparing to shoot *Audrey Rose*, Marsha never found time to eat a proper meal before we left for the Dorothy Chandler Pavilion. She ordered up a hamburger and a milk shake, which she soon regretted. During the ceremonies, she started to get sharp stomach pains and not even George Burns's popular win as Best Supporting Actor could assuage her discomfort, which got more severe that night back at the hotel. She finally fell asleep, however, and felt a little better in the morning, even opting to go on to San Francisco with me for a two-day vacation while the girls flew back to New York. In San Francisco she began to feel sick again, and a hurried visit to the doctor confirmed that she had a gall bladder that needed to be removed very soon. Whatever was wrong with it before had not been helped by the hamburger and milk shake on the previous night, just the kind of fatty foods that send gall bladders into an uproar.

Against the doctor's urging, she declined to have the surgery in San Francisco and instead opted to fly back home that day. The doctor told her that flying with a gall bladder problem could be risky business, but she insisted on going anyway. I called ahead to Lenox Hill Hospital in New York and they arranged to see her as soon as she arrived. Within twenty-four hours she was in the operating room, while I walked the halls of Lenox Hill, where only three years ago I learned that Joan had a cancer that had metastasized and that she only had a year and a half to live.

Marsha was brought down from the operating room and all had gone well. I walked into her room, then suddenly stopped short. This was the very same room that Joan had spent her last few months in, the very same room in which she died. The doctor walked in to tell Marsha she was fine. I took one look at the surgeon and realized he was also the one who had found the tumor in Joan's breast and in her hip, the same one who took me out to an empty stair landing to tell me that Joan's life was going to be a short one. Every horror that I had gone through three years ago, and again a year and a half later when she died, rushed into my head as if time had never passed. I ran out of the room, out of the hospital and can't even remember where I ended up.

It was the coldest and most thoughtless thing I could have done to Marsha and the hurt I caused her had to be far greater than the effects of her operation. I could say that my actions were inexcusable, but I genuinely saw no other way to control the powerful emotions that had surged inside of me. When I returned to Marsha's room, her anger and pain were apparent. It took some time for her to get over my abandoning her, and I don't know that she ever fully forgave it. Joan had popped up once again, getting in the way of our marriage. Put yourself in Marsha's place, and imagine what it felt like to have your husband run out on you just as you're wheeled into your room after an operation. It was not my finest moment.

WHEN I TOLD my mother, who was then living in Manhattan on 57th Street off Third Avenue, that we were moving to Los Angeles, she looked at me and said in no uncertain terms, "Not without me, you're not." She was in her early seventies then and had lived in New York all her life. No longer working, she still loved walking to the grocer's, to the bank, to her dentist and to the movie house just around the corner where she mostly waited for my films to appear. I couldn't picture her leaving her beloved city but the same could be said about me. To facilitate matters, I had my brother, Danny, look for a place not far from him in Sherman Oaks, about a twenty-minute drive from where I'd be living. I moved her and all her furniture out about three months before Marsha and I did, and within six weeks after arriving there, she had found a grocery she could walk to, as well as a bank, a dentist and a movie theater, and had made friends with everyone in her small apartment house. The only thing that alarmed her there was that in the morning when she awakened, instead of seeing the traffic of 57th Street, she saw snow-capped mountains in the distance. It took Danny a few days to convince her it was not an oil painting on the wall in her neighbor's apartment.

JUNE 7, 1975: The huge van stood in front of the house on 62nd Street. The first thing that was loaded on was the brown Mercedes I had bought three years earlier to drive Joan and the girls back and forth between New York and the house in Pound Ridge. That house on Blue Heron Lake, where things looked brighter and more hopeful for Joan for a year and a half and then finally turned dark and distant, was now sold, and hopefully was cheering up another family's life. The house on 62nd Street was also sold, to a family from Philadelphia. They requested we leave the four-poster bed in the bedroom, and I decided to part with it. It was too big a memory of the past for me to carry any longer.

The furniture and our clothes were loaded on carefully, and we all stood on the steps of the house as the big van moved slowly away, starting its trek across the country. It was a solemn occasion for me, Nancy and Ellen, as if we were attending one more funeral. A limousine pulled up and we all got in with our new dog, Ponti, a small white Lhasa apso, who was a gift from my former producer Saint Subber, after our first dog, Chips, passed away peacefully a few years before. As the limo pulled away, I took one last look back, allowing myself, for just an instant, a worried thought: What if, one night,

Joan came back to the house looking for us? Would she be frightened not to find me and her daughters there, without a clue of where we went?

On the flight west, Marsha seemed happy and exhilarated, as if the world she always dreamed about was finally opening itself up to her. Five and a half hours later, the jumbo jet set down on the tarmac at Los Angeles Airport, in the bright afternoon sun. As soon as the engines were cut off, we were instructed not to leave our seats and to keep our seat belts buckled. We would not be taxiing to the gate just yet. They announced on the intercom that at that very moment Los Angeles was experiencing an earthquake.

"I cannot believe this," said Marsha, admitting that this was one hell of a welcome to California.

BOGART TO GOODBYE

12

AS MARSHA was finishing *Audrey Rose*, I was completing the scripts of both *Bogart Slept Here* and *California Suite*. I worked in a room in our new house that was set up to be a replica of the room I worked in on 62nd Street. Dark wooden panels with cabinets ran along the lower part of the room. The fabric on the walls was more English than California, and I had my own desk that I had been writing on for years. The electric typewriter was at my right-hand side, and even when computers made their inroads, they got nowhere near my office. There was a pretty view from the large window, but I kept the shades down halfway in an effort to avoid anything that didn't feel familiar to me. The bookcases were filled with all my favorite books. I was very happy with these surroundings, and the writing part of my brain was neatly tricked into thinking that when I wanted to take a break I could walk around the corner to Third Avenue and have a tuna salad sandwich in a friendly luncheonette.

I sent the first draft of *Bogart* to my good friend Mike Nichols, who was now one of the most celebrated film directors in the business, with his enormous hits *Who's Afraid of Virginia Woolf?*, *The Graduate* and *Catch-22*. He read the script, loved it and agreed to direct it, making this the first film we'd do together. He set up a deal with Warner Brothers and for the lead opposite Marsha, he signed Robert De Niro to play the off-Broadway actor whose very first film becomes an international success. Though still early in his career, I thought it was a coup to land De Niro. He was clearly on his way to becoming a major star and eventually the icon that he is today. We had to postpone rehearsals of the film for a few days while De Niro was finishing *Taxi Driver* for Martin Scorsese. Travis Bickle, his character in that movie, was one of the most dangerous and complex characters De Niro ever played, and the scene where he looks at himself in a full-length mirror, armed to the teeth with weapons and challenging some unseen enemy with the threat "You talking to me? . . . Are you talking to *me*?" and then springing one of the guns out of his sleeve, taking dead aim at his own reflection, is now part of film history. It is shown on practically every film montage put together for the Academy Award shows.

De Niro finally finished *Taxi Driver* on a Friday in New York and three days later, on a Monday morning, he appeared on the set in California to start *Bogart Slept Here*. Although not nearly as big and strong as George C. Scott, to me De Niro was equally as intimidating. He didn't say very much, but what he said, you listened to. He spoke softly, nodded and shrugged a lot, and occasionally he gave you a quick smile that caused his eyes to squint. It was, however, difficult to know what he was thinking.

He looked tired on that first morning and with good reason. Having just finished one film, it's difficult for any actor to jump out of the skin of one character into the skin of another with only a weekend's rest, half of it spent on a plane. I knew instinctively that if De Niro were acting in a Scorsese film, he would have spent the last three months working in the darker shades of life usually found in Scorsese's work. How would he respond then, stepping into the light, gray areas that he would find in the more romantic-comedic areas of *Bogart Slept Here*?

De Niro was easy to deal with, however, and immediately started to immerse himself in the part. He began to think of how the character would dress, walk, carry himself, and who this man was inside, and he did all this much before he would think of how he related to the other characters in the film. He decided this young Broadway actor would wear one earring, so De Niro asked the propman to show him a few. The property man brought over a tray of earrings, followed by still another tray. He spent what seemed to be hours turning earrings over in his hand, holding them up to the light, trying them on one ear and looking at them in a mirror from every angle, as if this earring would tell us everything we wanted to know about this character. In my memory the entire day was spent with De Niro searching for the right earring. I saw that Mike was getting slightly impatient, but he was getting to know De Niro as well.

As I recall, there was very little rehearsal because I think Mike believed De Niro would be fresher before the cameras without it. I did not mind when De Niro sometimes strayed from my lines because what he paraphrased seemed just as good to me. I think Marsha was willing to go along with this sort of improvisational acting, but in the first few days of dailies, it was clear that any of the humor I had written was going to get lost. It's not that De Niro is not funny, but his humor comes mostly from his nuances, a bemused expression on his face or the way he would look at a character, smile and then look up at the ceiling.

The first scene they shot had De Niro's character coming home to tell his wife that he just got an offer to appear in his first film. Marsha's reaction was to be overjoyed, exuberant, wildly excited and happy for her talented husband's big break. De Niro, however, never told her the news as if he too was overjoyed with it. He seemed uncomfortable with happiness and good fortune. Instead, he told her the news matter-of-factly, introspectively, as though wondering if taking this job was the right thing to do. This reading, of course, made it difficult for Marsha to be overjoyed.

It was certainly not bad acting on De Niro's part because he's incapable of that. The moment did, in fact, seem very real, very honest, but if there was no joy in him, this first scene seemed confused. Why is a man who just got an offer he dreamed of all his life not excited about it? Mike said to me in confidence that he was worried. On the other hand, I was willing to compromise.

"Well, maybe it shouldn't be funny. Maybe it *should* be a more serious picture," I suggested.

Mike answered, "That's not what you wrote and it's not what I saw when I read this script. If there's no humor in the first half of the film, we're dead."

We went on this way for five days, and Marsha, try as she might to make her character and her scenes work, found it difficult to find solid footing for herself, since the picture seemed to be going in three or four different directions at one time, and none of them appeared to be right. After seven days of shooting, Mike asked two of Warner's top executives, John Calley and Frank Wells, to the screening room to view the results of the first week's filming. Calley and Wells were two of the smartest people I ever met in the film industry, and I certainly was willing to trust their opinion. Glum was their opinion, but these were two pretty cool guys. Instead of panicking, they treated the situation as a difficulty, but not as a life-and-death matter. It was a movie, and a movie, after all, is just a movie.

John smiled and said, "Well, we certainly have a problem, don't we?" No one admired Mike Nichols more than John Calley. "What do you want to do, Mike?" he said.

"Stop the picture," said Mike.

"Reshoot what we have?" asked Frank Wells calmly.

"Yes," said Mike. "But not with De Niro. He's a brilliant actor, but we've miscast it."

"Fire Robert De Niro?" John asked, knowing that this had never been done to De Niro before, nor apparently had there been any reason to before. Even when they asked my opinion, I considered it just a courtesy—my vote was not going to make any difference, and I really didn't know what my vote was.

The next day the picture was shut down and De Niro learned he was going to be replaced. He was, of course, livid, and luckily I was not in the room when he was told. It made headlines in *Variety* and in the major papers across the country, and no one could quite understand it. During the next few weeks Mike went about the business of trying to find a replacement for Robert De Niro, which in itself sounds like an oxymoron. No one was found. Eventually Mike took another film, De Niro went off to do something else that was no doubt brilliant, and Marsha and I were left with no movie and our dreams and hopes in Florence sadly dashed. The seven days on film was relegated to a small shelf in the Warner Brothers archives. I only met De Niro a few times in all the years that passed, but it was very hard to look him in the eye when I saw him again. If there's any consolation, a few years later I found two wonderful paintings in a gallery in New York, and I was so taken with them I bought them immediately and hung them in my home. The artist was Robert De Niro, Sr., Bobby's father.

Bogart Slept Here was not quite dead, however. There was always Ray Stark riding to the rescue. It was Ray's production company that was producing *Bogart*. He called and asked me to come to his office.

"Let's not give up on this," said Ray. "These two characters are wonderful and there's some really great writing in the script. We'll look and we'll find someone else." Someone else appeared a few days later. Richard Dreyfuss, fresh from *Jaws* and *Close Encounters*, expressed interest in doing the film. We decided to get together—Richard, Marsha and myself—and have them read the script aloud. As I listened to them, it was apparent they were wonderful together. Their chemistry was perfect. Marsha felt free to read the scenes the way she originally intended, and Richard's intelligence and quickness made it so easy to listen to. Although I realized they were right for each other, I thought the script was not right for them. It had to be funnier, more romantic, the way Marsha and I first imagined the picture would be. What I wanted to do was a prequel. In other words, instead of an off-Broadway actor, married with a child, why don't I start from the beginning? I'd start when they first meet. Not liking each other at first and then falling in love. I told them both to hang in while I rushed to the typewriter to write an entirely new script. As a tentative title, I put down *The Goodbye Girl.*

SETTLING IN

13

IN THE FIRST fourteen months in Los Angeles, I worked on three projects almost simultaneously: the script of the play *California Suite*, the new version of *The Goodbye Girl* movie, and another original screenplay that I had started while we were still living in New York, *Murder by Death*. I found that I now had more time to write each day than I did in New York, simply because I didn't have the stimulus and vitality of the city to otherwise occupy me. I missed the habit of walking along the New York streets, starting from my house on 62nd Street and taking a different route each day, something I did during the hour-and-a-half lunch break I took before tackling the afternoon rewrites of the pages I had completed that morning.

What I also missed were the chance meetings on the street in New York of a familiar face, very often four or five faces on the same day. With these people I'd exchange the small talk of life, the good news and the bad: the breakup of a twelve-year-old marriage you thought would last a lifetime; an affair between the most unlikely of people that made me aware of how easily shocked I could be; the sudden and serious illness of someone I hadn't seen in years and thought of calling that very day. Of course you can get all sorts of gossip in L.A. as well, but what's often discreet in New York is amazingly blatant in Los Angeles. Just walk into any Hollywood party and you will hear more than you want before you're handed a drink. By the time you start to juggle your first hot canapé, you've heard that the entire executive leadership of a major film company is about to be fired. I was always the last to hear these stories of thrones falling because I was never considered an insider in the film business—not then and not today. It was assumed I was mainly a playwright who only dabbled in films on occasion (the occasion happened about twenty-six times), and they always thought I was just visiting the Coast.

"Hi, Neil. What brings you out here?" was the standard greeting.

I never had a good answer for them because I never had one for myself. So I let the misconception linger that I was just visiting for all the years I lived here. I liked not losing my New York identity and my New York way of saying "wintuh" in February and "waituh" in restaurants. When I walked the streets of New York, cops in police cars would call out, "Hey, Neil. How you doin'?" with just enough of the sound of Little Italy or a hint of an Irish brogue passed on down through their family of patrolmen. It made New York seem like a small town to me. I knew where you could find a store on 62nd Street where they only sold buttons, or a luncheonette off 56th Street that had the best chocolate cake I ever tasted. In Los Angeles you would never just run into a friend on the street. The first year and a half I was there, walking the streets at ten in the morning in Beverly Hills for a dentist appointment, there was not a soul to be seen. I thought every day was either Sunday, the Fourth of July or one of the Jewish High Holidays.

CALIFORNIA SUITE opened on June 10, 1976, at the Ahmanson Theatre in Los Angeles, almost a year to the day of our moving there. Or out *there* as I referred to it when I was away, or out *here* when I was talking to my Angelino friends who thought it was an unnecessary description of a place we were standing in. It's not that I wasn't happy in Los Angeles or that I didn't appreciate the virtues of a city whose temperature was wonderful to bearable for most of the year. What I was most afraid of was becoming *part* of it, the part I didn't understand, the part that was as foreign to me as Tibet. In many ways, I thought eleven months of sun was almost as bad as six months *without* it. I was not a palm tree. I was more of a small unidentifiable tree planted practically in the cement on the streets of New York, fighting for its life but always hanging in there. Still, I felt an ingrate because the critics and audiences who came to the Ahmanson accepted *California Suite* with open arms. It was rare in those days to have a play originate in Los Angeles. It was still considered the lucrative prize at the end of the tour of most big hits that came out of Broadway. L.A. audiences were used to seeing finished plays and musicals. I was wary of how they'd react to a play that was being viewed by the public for the first time, wondering why there seemed to be something incomplete about it.

What was incomplete was that normally one does a play for a year or so on Broadway before it appears in L.A. The kinks, therefore, already had been taken out, and the scenes rewritten before Los Angelinos got their first viewing. Thus, when you open first in L.A., the play is shown with our kinks still showing and our rewrites still waiting their turn. It's called "opening cold," and cold is the reception you can sometimes get with a play that is not quite ready. Miraculously, *California Suite* came together almost from the first rehearsal. What they saw in L.A., even in its raw state, was pretty close to what we opened with in New York. Despite my early fears, I originated my next seven plays at the Ahmanson. The critics became a little stingier with their passing grades, but all seven of those shows were hits in New York. The only drawback for some of us was that the Ahmanson Music Center was located a fair distance from Beverly Hills, where most of my friends lived. It was built much farther east, to harness the loyal audiences who lived in Pasadena and Glendale and made up a large bulk of the yearly subscription buyers. Thanks to them, when I opened a play there, I was always guaranteed a large audience. Their attendance could be counted on, while my own friends, those who worked in films or TV, showed up less frequently. "It's too far a drive," they would say. "We'll see it when it comes to New York." As I said, it's a strange place.

AS WE BEGAN to prepare for the production of *The Goodbye Girl*, now directed by Herbert Ross, it was clear that Richard Dreyfuss was going to be the driving force in the film. Richard was highly intelligent, a true actor and not a comedian, which only made him funnier, with a rich, clear voice that strangely had a New York accent despite the fact he was raised in Southern California. He clipped off sentences as if each word were born afresh in his mind; there was virtually no hint his speech ever came out of a typewriter, especially mine. He is short, which made him empathetic, a little chubby at the time, which made him an unlikely leading romantic figure, and he had graying hair on his thirty-year-old head, and a scruffy beard which grew in any direction it chose to. He scratched it continuously throughout the shoot, making him look a little like Gabby Hayes, Roy Roger's ancient, toothless sidekick in countless Westerns. He wore mostly recycled army clothes that appeared never to have been touched by a tailor. He also wore rimless eyeglasses which had trouble clinging to the bridge of his nose and had to be pushed back incessantly with his fingers. In short, he was a mess, and consequently turned out to be one of the sexiest leading men I ever wrote for, perhaps coming in a dead heat with Robert Redford.

Herbert Ross also decided not to glamorize Marsha. Playing Paula MacFadden, a thirty-three-year-old ex-dancer with a ten-year-old daughter, left holding an empty purse when she was jilted by her lover, Marsha was to appear flat broke—she and her wardrobe achieved it to perfection. Her clothes looked like they'd been purchased in a thrift shop. Herbert had her hair cut off close to the neckline. The less hair, the less need for expensive haircuts, thought the frugal Paula. With her fairly tight weathered jeans, Marsha looked like any other struggling mother you'd see coming home lugging two heavy shopping bags to her dull, small apartment in the declassé Upper West Side of New York. With all this going against her, I defied any healthy, heterosexual man from falling in love with her at first sight. If Richard was the driving force of the film, Marsha was the backbone. Marsha's intelligence matched Richard's and she was quite able to handle this fast-talking actor from Chicago. *The Goodbye Girl* had something going for it not often found in a funny, romantic comedy in the 1970s: sheer authenticity. There wasn't a trace of Hollywood up on the screen either in the design or in the performances.

There was one last role to be cast, that of Marsha's ten-year-old daughter, Lucy. Every agent submitted every aspiring actress from eight to twelve years old, plus sneaking in an occasional sixteen-year-old who was short and who had a high-pitched voice. There are at any given time more aspiring child actresses in Hollywood than there are cars on the freeways, and more often than not, it is the parents who are more aspiring than the child. "We have an audition at MGM today," a mother would tell anyone within earshot, never leaving out the "we," since Mama often dreamed that her own failed attempts at a film career would be fulfilled vicariously if baby got the part. Sometimes the father would come to the audition as well, making you wonder what he did for a living, and hoping that it wasn't being the child's business agent and self-appointed manager.

Betting on a ten-year-old to be the family's breadwinner is more than any preadolescent girl should have to bear. At the audition, many of the children gave you all the smiles and personality their fragile little frames could muster—or that our patience could bear—and their line readings sounded very much as if the words had been driven into their heads with spikes the night before. Some of these kids, of course, were talented, and some may even have been the ones—rather than their parents—who had the overwhelming desire to "get into movies."

But then there were the kids who didn't care if they missed the audition, and cared even less if they got the part. Invariably, they were looser, more relaxed; for them, going to an audition was simply a great way of getting out of school for that day. When one of them walked in, you couldn't help but sit up and pay attention. It was someone in this category who walked into Herbert Ross's office one morning, amazingly the first face on a huge pile of photographs and résumés on Herbert's desk. Her name was Quinn Cummings, she was ten years old, she was neither pretty nor unattractive, and she didn't seem to care which way we saw her. She was neither impolite nor blasé, but she also made no effort to charm us. There was, however, an intelligence in her eyes. And she laughed loudly when we said something funny, and squirmed a little when we talked down to her, as adults have a way of doing. When Herbert finally asked her if she was now ready to read for us, she said "Sure" in a way that meant "if you've seen enough of me, that's okay too."

The reading was perfect. She was smart, slightly brash and loving toward her mother, but forthright in dealing with Mom's predilection for getting into trouble with men, mostly actors. In the script, when she learns that Paula's live-in, deadbeat lover has dumped them without a cent or a place to live, she says, "What a shitheel," and then flashes a lightning-quick look at her mother with an apology for overstepping her bounds. Herbert and I were entranced by her, since she was funny, quick and human. When Quinn left the office, I turned to Herbert and said, "That's her. That's Lucy."

Herbert nodded reluctantly, "I know, but you can't take the first one who walks in here."

"Why not?" I asked. "She's perfect."

"Because someone could walk in here who's better," he answered.

"That's not possible," I argued. "If she's perfect, how can someone be better than perfect?"

Directors usually prevail because it's in their personality and in their contracts, so we saw forty to fifty girls during the next four days. After the last one left his office, he turned to me and said, "I like the Quinn Cummings girl."

"No kidding?" I said wearily. We signed her the next day. Quinn turned out to be a highly intelligent, sweet young lady, and her mother, happily, was not a stereotypical stage mother, and was very careful of Quinn's well-being. Three weeks before shooting was to start, Quinn's father died. We felt her and her mother's loss would turn into our loss as well, but they talked it over and decided that Quinn would still do the film. Together with Richard and Marsha, I now had my first Odd Trio.

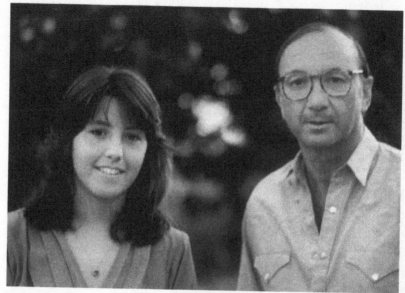

Nancy and me. Am I lucky, or what?

Ellen, my first daughter.
How pretty is that?

Nancy on the left, Ellen on the right in
New York. They're still that close today.

With Marsha and Nancy,
early days in Bel Air.

The house on Chalon Road in Bel Air. It was more Connecticut than L.A.

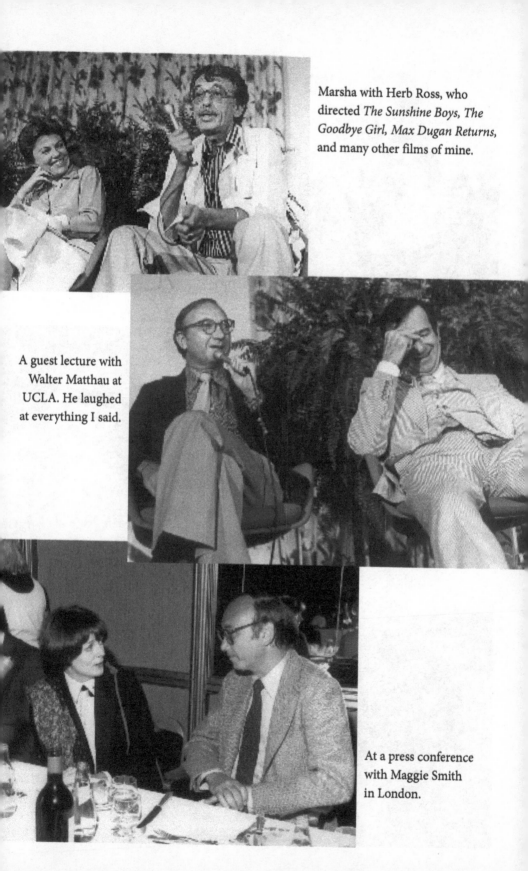

Marsha with Herb Ross, who directed *The Sunshine Boys, The Goodbye Girl, Max Dugan Returns,* and many other films of mine.

A guest lecture with Walter Matthau at UCLA. He laughed at everything I said.

At a press conference with Maggie Smith in London.

Diane and me on our wedding day in L.A., first time around.

Happier days with Diane and Bryn.

On vacation with Diane and Bryn

Bryn and me. Bryn is the beautiful one.

With Diane at the Kennedy Center honors, 1995.

A very proud father with his beautiful daughter Bryn.

Office in Chalon house.

Office in L.A.

Ellen on the left,
Nancy on the right.
Both as pretty as
their mother.

Nancy, me and Ellen *en famille*, East Hampton, NY, 1998.

GRINDING IT OUT

14

IT NEVER OCCURRED to me at the time to count up the years passing and the pages written, but by 1976 I had written fifteen plays and ten films. I had done all that in fourteen years, with no sign of slowing down. Why so much, so fast, so relentlessly? I didn't ask myself the question then, but I do now, now when I've reached my thirtieth play and twenty-fifth or twenty-sixth film. As you can see, I don't really keep score with the films. I can place where I was and what was happening in my life during each play I wrote, but the making of a film is a different experience. Very often I left the film in the hands of the director and had minimal involvement afterward, but with the play, I was there almost every day, rewriting in the rehearsal room while the actors were busy going through a scene, wondering what I was scribbling so incessantly. A play was my lifeblood; a film was my craft.

Each new play was like the beginning of a new life for me. In each new production, I met two new sets of interesting people—the actors, and the characters they played. It was possible for me to like one and not the other. If I didn't like the actor, I would have to decide if I could live with him or her. Very often, the director, producer and myself would fire an actor. I was the only one who fired a character. I would watch rehearsals and suddenly think, that character is extraneous, he doesn't push the play forward. And I would cross him out of my script. Unfortunately the actor who played him had to leave as well, even though he may have played the character faultlessly. I knew the actor was terribly disappointed, but I never knew how the character felt. Sometimes I would envision him going around to producers' offices looking for a job.

"Hi. My name is Ned Morton. I'm twenty-eight years old, and as you can see from the way I'm dressed, the year I'm living in is about 1938 or '39. Even though I'm the black sheep in the family, I'm very funny and I have these terrific lines that that Neil Simon guy isn't using anymore. If you are doing a period play, I could fit in very nicely and I think there's a lot of really good actors out there who would love to play me." So much for abstractive meditations.

Any life other than playwrighting would have been hell for me. Working in another field, spending forty years with some company, would be a lifetime jail sentence. The writing of thirty plays in thirty-six years has been liberating. I had no boss. I had no hours. There was no one place of work I would have to travel to and from, no co-workers I would have to see year after year and at the annual Christmas party, all wondering when we'd be laid off or forced to retire. I have never found it to be a lonely profession despite the fact that I speak to no one for the better part of seven hours a day. I either have a pen in my hand or a thought in my head, and both completely fill all those hours spent looking into a notebook or staring out a window, all the while never noticing that there might be something of interest out there for me to see. If anything gets my attention at all, it's the weather. I love looking at rain, pelting across the windowpane, or at snow, swirling around in the wind or falling gently on the street below. In New York especially, I'd put down the notebook and pen or hold the thought in my head, cross to the window to watch the snow pile up on the streets. As I stated earlier, I wrote more in California because I was never compelled to look out the window to see the sun. Sunlight seems so inactive, and interests me only when it comes or goes. A heavy storm, though, blowing and bending the trees, always seems to be moving, causing problems and discomfort in people's lives. Nature's conflict is as interesting to me as the conflict I give to the characters in my plays, and sunny day after sunny day is sorely lacking in excitement.

That still doesn't answer the question of what was driving me to start a new play on the day after I finished writing the previous one. One possibility was that I thought my work was a greater representation of who I was than was the person I became when I *didn't* write. Whatever I may have had on my mind, I felt more secure putting it on paper and letting that character speak for me, than in expressing it to someone as myself. In the early 1980s, I was still some years away from developing a personality that I was comfortable with. I often felt like a boxer heading toward the ring, surrounded by his coterie of bodyguards and trainers. The more success you had, the less you needed to say; others said it for you. My work served as my bodyguards and trainers, and if I surrounded myself with enough plays, I felt safe, immune from scrutiny. I knew I had matured intellectually, but something was keeping me from playing out that role in my personal life. For one thing, I truly didn't know where the plays came from, where the ability to put these thoughts on the page, shaping them and forming them with clarity and intelligence started.

Because of this insecurity, I felt I was not yet ready to sit down and handle a good conversation with Arthur Miller or Tom Stoppard without embarrassing myself. Maybe one more play would put me over the top, I thought; after one more hit, Arthur and Tom and I would become lunch buddies, with me dominating most of the conversation. Being alone in a room from nine to five was a wonderful way to keep me from being discovered as simply an average man who just happened to get lucky almost every time he picked up a pen and put it to paper. So often I thought that in choosing me the gods picked the wrong man to work in the same field as Shaw and Ibsen and Kaufman and Hart. They were giants; I was not. The irony is, I never felt inferior while in the act of writing. On the contrary, in my little room, and even while in the theater, I felt secure, strong and as capable as most of my peers. It was this living-in-the-world business that I was daunted by. I probably had at least as many commercial successes as either Truman Capote or Gore Vidal, yet I cowered at the thought of meeting them personally. But meet them I did. Gore Vidal called me Doc when he showed me and Joan around his beautiful house in Rome, and I felt fortunate that he was such a wonderful wit and conversationalist that he did almost all of the talking and I nodded and laughed in the appropriate places. I learned the art of becoming a good listener, which sometimes won me such accolades as "He's so humble for a man so witty. So quiet that I couldn't help wonder what interesting thoughts were going on inside that head of his." I met Truman Capote on a number of occasions, and even if I *did* want to state my opinions, it would be late into the night before Truman would yield the floor. And then, in one of those really odd twists, I actually *wrote* for Truman Capote. He played a part in the film *Murder by Death*, and since this was a game played on my home court, it was Truman who was nervous and ill at ease. I quickly and effortlessly wrote him a new line for one he was having trouble with. He read it, looked up and said, "Perfect. Thank you, Neil. I feel much more comfortable with this."

As time passed, I felt myself easing into the public light, looking less to hide in the shadows. Do enough TV interviews; give a few talks at Columbia University, Harvard; deliver a forty-five-minute speech at Williams College (for my daughter Nancy's commencement, with an honorary doctorate thrown in for me); participate in a three-hour informal chat at the NYU Film School; make ten appearances on the Johnny Carson show—and if you're not talking by then, check your parents to see if you were born in a foreign country, because it's possible that English is not your language.

I knew I really had gotten over my jitters when I accepted the most un-likely invitation: as guest star on a Bob Hope special for NBC. Why me? He knew I wasn't a performer and I knew for certain this was not going to be an interview. I'd never seen a writer as a guest on the Hope show (unless, of course, she was twenty-one and the current Miss America), and even though I suspected I probably would be asked to do only a walk-on line or less, I couldn't imagine why I accepted the invitation in the first place. The head writer called me and told me not to worry—he'd send me a script in a few days. To my utter surprise and shock, I discovered that the entire show was devoted to Hope and his two guests, Lucille Ball and Neil Simon. Surely they made a mistake. They probably thought I was *Paul* Simon and was coming on to sing "Me and Julio Down by the Schoolyard." Or perhaps they thought I was Neil *Diamond* coming out to sing "You Don't Bring Me Flowers."

A chauffeured limo drove me out to the Burbank Studios while I looked over the script they had written for me. I never had cared much for actors who wanted to rewrite my lines, and now I found I didn't care much for writers who wanted to write what I should be saying. I wanted out of this desperately, so much so that I was prepared to give the driver all my money to drive me to Canada. I don't mean all my money I had *on* me. I mean *all my money.* Why did I say yes to this? I thought. I'm not an actor. I'm not a comic. And I had just recently learned to talk. Maybe they thought I was Neil *Armstrong* and they were going to do a sketch where Hope and Lucille Ball were astronauts. But it said Neil Simon on the script . . . and the script wasn't all that funny. Now I suddenly was being picky. I didn't want to be on the show, but if I had to, then I wanted to be a hit. Maybe NBC would say, "Hey, he's good. Let's give him his own show."

I thought again of Hope and Lucille Ball—didn't they care that a less-than-an-amateur was on the show with them? I guess not. They could take care of themselves. They were pros. They could ad-lib their way through anything. They had timing. They had experience. They were stars. I was a playwright. Maybe I could just go out on the stage, sit at a typewriter and write something. It wouldn't be funny, but it could work if we turned it into a documentary of some kind. Like a boring kind.

The limousine arrived at the studio, and against my better judgment, I got out. I was sent to the makeup room and sat in the chair. The makeup lady asked who I was.

"Neil Simon. I'm a guest on the show," I replied.

"What show?" she asked.

"The Bob Hope show?" I answered as a question because I didn't believe it any more than she did. She just shrugged and slapped powder on my face.

They finally put me in a dressing room, which was unnecessary since I was going to be wearing my own clothes. In the room was a large gift basket with my name on it, and inside was fruit, candies and a bottle of vodka, all heavily wrapped with clear plastic. I didn't have the strength to break the plastic and get at that much needed vodka. With time on my hands before I met Hope, I did the one thing in this life I knew how to do. I rewrote. I rewrote all my lines so that it at least sounded like me, not that anyone in the audience would know what I sounded like. A writer came in and said, "Hi, Neil, Bob's ready to see you in his dressing room." We walked down the hallway together. Dead Man Walking would sum up how I felt about taking that long walk. The writer asked how I liked the script. I told him I loved it, but had just made a few small changes if he didn't mind. He didn't mind. He said Hope always changed everything he wrote. The door opened and I entered Bob Hope's dressing room where everything in *his* gift basket was opened and used. He smiled and called me kid. He called everyone kid. He even called Lucille Ball kid.

He said, "This'll be a snap. The boys really came up with some funny stuff. Why don't we just go over it a few times? When we're out there, don't get nervous if I don't look at you much. I'm reading everything off the cue cards."

I took my life in my hands and said, "Bob, if it's all right with you, I rewrote my lines a little, but they still fit yours. You don't have to change a thing." He didn't bat an eye. We read the script but with my substituted lines. He nodded, smiled and said, "Great. No problem. If I ad-lib, just go along with me." And that's what happened on the show, if I remember correctly. Actually I have no memory of doing the show and perhaps this whole thing was a dream that I told my analyst a few weeks later. But I do remember getting laughs. Big laughs. That was real. If you're in front of an audience and you get laughs, you never forget it the rest of your life. I was chauffeured home and on the way gave the driver all my money. I have never once watched the tape of the show. Some experiences are best left to not dwell on. NBC never called about my getting my own show. I thought my best move was to return to playwrighting. My only regret was that I forgot to take my gift basket home.

SO I COULD NOW TALK, but I still had not solved the mystery of where the plays come from; sometimes I had doubts that I wrote them at all. I know I didn't write *Lost in Yonkers*. It didn't come from me. I saw the play a number of times and there's no chance that I'm the author. Yet I remember each day as I sat at my desk, the words and pages flowing from my pen, the emotions of the characters taking over all my senses, so I must assume that I was the one who wrote *Lost in Yonkers*. Recently, at a tribute in my honor, I watched as scenes from various plays I had written were performed. When they got to *Lost in Yonkers*, I listened in awe at the power of the words, and silently I said to myself, "God, I wish I could write like that." No one said you had to be sane to be a playwright.

IF I HAD any regrets, it would be that I always wondered what it would have been like if I had been born ten or twelve years sooner, and been around to write films for the great stars in the Hollywood of the 1940s and 1950s: Humphrey Bogart, Cary Grant, Rosalind Russell, James Cagney, Jean Arthur, Henry Fonda and James Stewart. I never had that opportunity, but I was fortunate enough to meet James Stewart a few times, and I actually got to know Henry Fonda and Cary Grant. It wasn't hard to meet Henry Fonda, since his house was directly across the street from ours in Bel Air. He lived there with his wife, Shirlee, and Hank, as most people called him, often came over to our house to give Marsha pointers with our gardening. He had a green thumb and I thought maybe he had this avid desire to grow things because he and his family had been blown out of the dust bowl of Oklahoma in *The Grapes of Wrath*. Oddly enough, Henry and Shirlee lived directly across from us in New York as well, when a few years later Marsha and I bought an apartment on 57th Street and Park Avenue. I guess while my plants were growing in California, my roots were still in New York.

I met Cary Grant for the first time at a dinner party at the house of Robert Evans, who was then the head of production at Paramount. Bob Evans introduced us: "Cary, Neil Simon. Neil, Cary Grant."

Grant smiled his perfect smile, put out his hand, shook mine and said in that slight cockney accent, "Hello, Doc, how are you? Good to see you. Loved *The Odd Couple*. Maybe we'll do something one day," and then he was off to kiss Barbra Streisand on the cheek. I met him again, usually at other parties, but the best time of all was when I boarded a plane for London and discovered that Cary Grant was in the seat just behind me. Make that the *two* seats behind me, because whenever he flew to London, he reserved the last two seats in first class in order to stretch out and sleep during the night flight over.

It was said that the secret to his constant good looks was his ability to sleep ten to twelve hours a day and/or night. If I did that, it would be the secret to my red puffy eyes and my inability to straighten my back from sleeping that long. He was on his way to Brighton (could have been Bristol) to visit his aging "Mum," as he called her. "Where's that screenplay, Doc?" he asked me, as if all he had on his mind the past year was the screenplay I was going to write for him. But who knows? If I had written it, he might have done it. We chatted for a while; then he said good night, stretched out (if you can do that on two seats) and slept like a baby until we were a half hour out of London. He woke up looking better than when he went to sleep. I said goodbye to him as we were about to land at Heathrow Airport.

"Nonsense," he said. "Come with me. I'll get you right through customs, won't have to wait a minute." An entourage of representatives of the airline were there to greet him, and sure enough he ushered me right through customs and introduced me by saying, "This is my dear friend, Doc Simon. He's writing a screenplay for me. Take good care of him." Then he was whisked away in a Bentley limo to see Mum in Brighton or Bristol. The chief of customs turned to me and said, "Right this way, Dr. Simon. Pleasure to meet you. Don't meet many in the medical profession who write films as well." I nodded in agreement because I knew it would get me through customs much quicker.

MURDER, HE WROTE

15

THE GOODBYE GIRL was cast and ready to go, but we had to wait until Herbert Ross finished shooting *The Turning Point*, a film he was making with Shirley MacLaine and Anne Bancroft. In the interim, Ray Stark and Columbia Pictures put *Murder by Death* into production. During that time, Marsha and I began to socialize, and eventually we met, through Ray Stark and his dinner parties, most of the people who ran Hollywood and many of the stars that dazzled us almost as much as Ray's incredible art and sculpture collection. If Maillol, Giacometti and Henry Moore statues stood coolly and silently in his magnificent garden, Warren Beatty, Barbra Streisand, a young Goldie Hawn and directors like Sydney Pollack and Billy Wilder made his dining table sparkle. Years before, when I wrote *Plaza Suite*, one of the one-act plays was about a Hollywood producer who bought Humphrey Bogart's home after his death. I had no one in mind when I wrote the piece, since I never knew where Bogart's home was and what happened to it. Little did I realize as I sat in Ray Stark's luxurious house that Bogart had lived here with his wife Lauren Bacall and their children. It took on a new meaning to me since Bogart was, and is to this day, the actor I most admired—not necessarily for his skill as an actor, although he was one of the best, but because of his charismatic quality on the screen. In roles like Sam Spade in *The Maltese Falcon* or Rick Blaine in *Casablanca*, he had portrayed the quintessential loner. I admired that quality in someone, the man who couldn't be bought and who went his own way. If there was anyone else who had that quality in the years I was growing up, it would have been Joe DiMaggio and Ernest Hemingway, although Hemingway needed an entourage around him to help him stand out as a loner. One would also have to add Albert Camus to that illustrious group of brooders. Although I never thought I was charismatic, I fancied myself a loner, but only in terms of my work. As a boy, I affected that pose, fashioning myself after my heroes; later, as success came my way, it became less of a pose as the loner actually became more and more a part of my personality. Years later when

I briefly signed with the Creative Artists Agency to represent me in films, I first met its now famous ex-corporate leader Mike Ovitz. As we were introduced, he put his hand out to me and said, "Oh, sure. The man who says no to everything." I treated that remark as a compliment.

After dinner at Ray's house, I wanted to see the room where Bogart died, the little dumbwaiter in which Bogart painfully curled himself up when he needed to be lowered to the floor below, during the last months of his life in his slow death from lung cancer. The house was now completely redone and redesigned, and was the in place to be invited by Ray and his lovely wife, Fran, who reigned over these soirees. Following dinner, there was *always* a new film to be seen in the living room, even when a guest like President Reagan was present, while Secret Service men in helicopters hovered noisily above us (needless to say, the sound drowned out the dialogue of the film we were watching). A very large Picasso hung on the rear wall, and the painting was raised electrically to make room for the projectionist to show that night's film. Writer Arthur Laurents used a Picasso painting in the same position and for the same purpose in his film *The Way We Were*. In that film, the FBI planted a bug on the back of the canvas in an effort to smoke out any would-be Communists, and as the painting rose, the bug ripped a hole from top to bottom of the Picasso. A Communist was the last thing anyone would call Ray Stark.

If Ray sensed boredom with the film among the fourteen or so guests, he would simply press a button and say "Next," and the film disappeared from the screen, even if we were only fifteen or twenty minutes in. In its place would appear an entirely new film. If that film didn't win favor with those who remained, you'd hear a few whispered good nights and thank-yous as famed guests tiptoed out to their cars. Marsha and I almost always stayed because we did not consider ourselves important enough to be blasé.

Ray Stark was one of the few people in Hollywood I almost never said no to, not because of the enormous power he held in the community, but because I learned a little of everything from him. We had a symbiotic relationship, we made each other laugh, he taught me how to find the fun in life when I somehow let my moods sink low, and despite the fearsome clout he had in that town, I always saw more boy in him than man-eater. I called him for advice on everything and he had the name of a doctor for every ailment, not to mention a lawyer, a plumber, a personal trainer, a restaurant, an acupuncturist, a museum, a chiropractor and even a dog breeder.

He had about five large Labrador retrievers roaming freely through his house except during meals and Marsha and I fell in love with his dogs. Ray immediately arranged for us to buy a puppy from the breeder in Idaho. Marsha, Nancy, Ellen and I drove out to the airport one night and waited for this mid-sized cage to be removed from the plane. Out came the most beautiful whitish yellow Labrador puppy I'd ever seen. We called him Duffy and he lived out his entire life with us. Ray not only made Los Angeles bearable for me, but he taught me how to find the joys of life in places I never thought of looking. Ray had everything he could possibly want in the world but he always said to me that he envied me because I was creative and he wasn't. But creation needs to be nurtured by those who hold the creation and the creator in esteem, because I'm an authority on how quickly confidence, with no one to bolster it, can disappear on a daily basis.

MURDER BY DEATH was a spoof on every all-star murder mystery in an English mansion that I had seen and loved as a boy, the best one being the film of Agatha Christie's And Then There Were None. My story was simple and motivated by my own frustration of never being able to guess the murderer when I read a mystery novel. Figuring out who did it was much easier when the story was done as a film because inevitably the director would give away something or the actors tipped their hand by acting much too innocently. The authors of books were much more cunning and at times even cheated by withholding information you needed to be able to solve the crime until five pages from the end. "I DIDN'T KNOW THAT," I would yell after three hundred and twelve pages, and I'd fling the paperback against the wall.

My story was about a multimillionaire eccentric amateur detective who sets out to put the five greatest detectives in the world to shame. He invites them all for a weekend, with their wives or guest of choice, to his gloomy mansion in some even gloomier forest. The detectives in my movie were all famous because they were all fictional: Sam Spade, Nick and Nora Charles of The Thin Man series, Charlie Chan and his Number One Son, Hercule Poirot and Miss Marple, both Agatha Christie creations. Besides dinner, their host had arranged for an actual murder to take place, and in addition to dessert, there was to be a prize of one million dollars tax free to the sleuth who solved the crime.

On the first day of rehearsal, the actors filed in slowly at ten A.M. and I kept blinking my eyes in wonderment at the incredible cast Ray had assembled for me: Alec Guinness, David Niven, Maggie Smith, Peter Sellers, Peter Falk, Eileen Brennan, Nancy Walker, James Coco and Elsa Lanchester. Alec Guinness was to play a blind butler, and he came from England fully prepared with his own props, having already worked out his walk, his feeling the ground with his cane and making his pupils all but disappear. The comedy I wrote was broad and I feared Sir Alec might want to soften it. But he fell in quickly and he seemed to love doing the scenes although I rarely saw him smile. Perhaps he felt secure because of the next picture he was to make directly after ours—something called *Star Wars*, he said. He was quite marvelous in one scene where he is on the upper landing, leading Dick and Dora Charleston (David Niven and Maggie Smith) to their rooms. Alec had the first line.

BENSON: Not many people come to the manor these days. It's nice to hear guests again.

DORA: Oh, thank you, er . . .

BENSON: Benson, mum.

DORA: Thank you, Benson.

BENSON: No. That's Bensonmum. Jamessir Bensonmum.

DICK: Jamessir?

BENSON: Yes, sir.

DICK: Jamessir Bensonmum?

BENSON: Yes, sir.

DICK: How odd.

BENSON: My father's name, sir.

DICK: What was your father's name?

BENSON: How-ard. Howard Bensonmum.

DICK: Jamessir, are you saying your father's name was How-ard Benson-mum . . . ?

DORA: Leave it be, Dickie. I've had enough.

The only mistake Ray Stark made was casting Truman Capote as the slightly deranged host of the manor. He certainly didn't do it for Truman's acting ability, since it was nonexistent. Ray made no bones about wanting Truman in the picture for the sheer publicity value that Truman Capote attracted everywhere. I was more pragmatic. If I owned the New York Yankees, I wouldn't want Tom Cruise for my second baseman no matter how many tickets his fans bought; therefore, although I didn't own Columbia Pictures, I wouldn't want Truman Capote—who couldn't blink his eyes on cue—in a pivotal role in the film.

Actually, the man Ray and I both first wanted but couldn't get was Orson Welles. We had given it a good try, though. Weeks before the film was to start, my phone rang at home. I picked it up. On the other end I heard one of the most famous voices in the world.

"Is this Neil? Orson Welles here."

"Orson Welles?" I said in a voice that cracked just about the way it did when I reached puberty. I thought it was a gag but there was no mistaking this voice.

"I read your script, Neil. Absolutely loved it. I'd give anything to play the role but unfortunately I'm committed to do some classic for no money in Italy, which is why they treat me like a king over there."

I was astonished that he was actually calling to apologize for not being able to do my film.

"Oh, Orson," I said, pretending to be worthy of his call. "I understand completely. How wonderful of you to phone yourself. I'm honored."

"Who is playing the role anyway?" asked Mr. Welles.

"Truman Capote."

It was quiet for a moment. I thought he hung up.

"Excuse me. It's difficult drinking wine and thinking about Truman Capote acting at the same time. He's actually going to play Charlie Chan?"

"No, no," I said. "Peter Sellers is playing Chan. Truman is the host of the party."

"Oh, well, that makes sense but not much. It was the Chan role I wanted to play. Peter will be simply marvelous doing that. Truman will make a fool of himself but he does that splendidly anyway so he may just turn out fine. I wish you luck, Neil. Maybe we'll do something together one day. Goodbye."

He hung up just as Marsha walked into the room.

"I just spoke to Orson Welles. He called me. Orson Welles."

"Really?" said the impressed Marsha. "What did he want?"

"To tell me he couldn't do *Murder by Death*. But that he'd like to do something else with me one day. So far I've got Orson Welles and Cary Grant who want to do something else some day."

With those two actors I had a five million dollar check in my hand—one that I knew I could never cash. "Some day" is NO day, but I was still feeling like the most important writer in Hollywood, even though I suspected Orson Welles turned down the role to Ray Stark and Ray in turn asked Orson to call me because "Neil is your biggest fan." Ray had his way of making me feel important, and he never did it in small measures.

ALEC GUINNESS is a regal man. To me he was almost unapproachable, not because of any coolness on his part, but simply because of his bearing, his poise, his presence and the enormous respect I have for him as an actor. While Peter Sellers would clown on the set, while David Niven had wit, style, humor and a propensity to giggle on the set, telling us that he was only out-giggled by Sir Laurence Olivier, while Maggie Smith could be as droll as Noël Coward without ever using his dialogue, Alec Guinness seemed to be quietly introspective, and if he did say something amusing, you had to be on your toes to catch it. It sounded more like information than humor. We did chat between scenes, but not often, and when I asked him about the *Star Wars* script that was always protruding from the pocket of his canvas chair, he would say succinctly, "Futuristic, actually. Rather clever. We'll see."

Peter Sellers, on the other hand, usually had me in hysterics, especially when he continued to play Charlie Chan off camera either as gay, Jewish or as the Queen. One day he was late to shoot his next scene. He was soon found in his trailer reading *Variety*. When summoned by the assistant director, Peter said, "Tell them Mr. Sellers won't be filming today," and went back to his reading while reclining on a banquette.

Robert Moore, the director, who had already done two of my plays, *Promises, Promises* and *The Gingerbread Lady*, made his way quickly to Peter's trailer. "Peter, I hear you're not filming today," he said calmly.

"Ah, good. Then you got the news," said Peter, turning the pages of his paper.

"May I ask why not?" Robert asked diplomatically.

"It's this fucking article they've written about me in this paper. It's filled with fucking lies and I will not be on the set until they retract it."

Robert grabbed the paper, read it quickly just to show Peter he was interested, then said, "You're right, Peter. They should retract that. And I'll ask the publicity people to get on it right now. The thing is, even if they retract it, it couldn't be in the paper until tomorrow."

"When it's in the paper, I'll be on the set," said Peter, who was in costume and full makeup.

"What if we called them and they said on the phone they'd retract it?" Bob offered, grasping at straws.

"Well, they'd have to phone all the readers of this tripe and I'd have to listen in on all the phone calls," said Peter as if he were making sense.

"Right," said Bob, who left the trailer at this point, deciding to leave this problem to Ray Stark. He went back to the set to shoot the next scene without Peter.

Ray was outraged when he got the news, but he knew that screaming at Peter Sellers would get him nowhere. Instead he went to Peter's trailer and they had a quiet talk, the contents of which none of us ever heard. An hour later Peter was on the set, ready to shoot. Later that day, Ray sent a mock-up of *Variety*, and on the front page in large letters it said, "*Variety* Retracts Its Fucking Mistake." Peter appreciated the joke, or, as is entirely possible, thought that *Variety* actually put out an early edition to satisfy the disgruntled actor.

Whenever Peter Falk was missing from the set, everyone knew that he could be found walking around the lot learning his lines. "I can't learn my lines without walking," said Peter.

One morning Ray sent a treadmill to the set with a ribbon saying, "Here. Now we know where you're walking."

ONE NIGHT, about two weeks into the filming, I received a phone call at home that was so shocking I didn't quite know how to handle it. It was from Alec Guinness, with whom I still hadn't had more than three brief conversations.

"Hope I'm not interrupting anything, Neil. If you're busy, I could call back," he said almost timidly. I had never seen or heard this side of him, and having him call me at home surely meant something important was up.

"No, no," I said. "I'm not doing a thing. Is anything wrong?"

"Wrong? Oh, dear no. Things are going quite well, aren't they?"

"Yes," I said quickly. "I'm really happy. I think you're really amazing in the film, Alec."

"Oh, you're very kind. Good fun. Nice change of pace for me," he said, although I knew he hadn't gotten to his point as yet. "I was just thinking . . . ," he added, but then trailed off into nowhere.

"Is it the script, Alec? Because if there's anything you don't like, I'd be more than glad to rewrite it."

"The script? Oh, dear, no. Very happy with the script . . . No, no, it's er . . . well, to tell the truth, I'm all alone out here, you know."

"No, I didn't." He suddenly sounded lonely. Was that it? Did he want to socialize, have dinner with me? Since we hardly spoke before, why me? Why not his fellow Englishmen? Peter, David, Maggie? Still I pursued it. "Would you like to have dinner one night, Alec? I know my wife, Marsha, would love to meet you."

"Dinner? Oh, yes, dinner would be fine. I'd love to meet Marsha. Very nice of you to ask . . . but you see, my wife doesn't get in until next week. And as I said, I'm quite alone here . . . By myself, I mean . . . You do understand, I hope."

"Oh, yes. Yes, of course." I still didn't know what he was getting at and why it was taking so long.

He continued, practically stammering.

"The thing is, I er . . . I feel very awkward asking this."

"No, please. Tell me what I can do for you, Alec."

He blurted it out. "Would you know where I could get a tart?"

A tart? Did he mean a small dessert? The English eat tarts, don't they? And then I realized—he was asking for a woman. A tart. A hooker. A prostitute. Alec Guinness calling me asking for a hooker—I couldn't believe it. And why me, of all people? And where would I find one? Drive downtown to Santa Monica Boulevard, pull my car over to the curb and ask some six-foot-two woman in a blond wig if she'd like to spend an hour with Alec Guinness? I realized I had not answered him yet, so I started my mouth moving again.

"A tart?" I asked. "A woman, you mean . . . Well, gee. Gosh, I don't know . . . The thing is, I really haven't been living out here all that long . . . It's not exactly what I would know how to do best, Alec, you know?"

"No tart, heh?" he said rather disappointedly. "She could be an older woman, I really wouldn't mind . . ." and with that I heard a break in his voice. At first I thought he was crying, but then I realized he was giggling.

"Are you really serious?" I finally asked.

"No. I'm Peter," he answered, now fully hysterical. It was Peter Sellers doing an absolutely perfect imitation of Alec Guinness, down to the slightest inflection.

"PETER," I screamed. "You bastard . . . Why me?"

He then told me that he first did it to Ray Stark. Ray laughed so hard, he told Peter to call David Niven, Peter Falk, me and for all I know, Maggie Smith as well, but Maggie would have spotted the imitation in a second. I don't know if Alec Guinness ever heard of the prank and I was grateful to see his charming wife turn up on the set the next day. Then one day in the commissary, we were all eating lunch together and I noticed on the menu that among the desserts they listed were tarts. I was afraid to look into anyone's eyes as I put my head down and skipped dessert for that day.

THE DREAM YEAR

16

MURDER BY DEATH was a moderate success for Columbia, making a nice profit and providing a memorable experience for me. In today's world, however, the studios are not looking for moderate successes. Since so few hits come out of the studios today, they need at least one, hopefully two mega-hits that will bring in enough bucks to balance their losses on the failures and give them something to crow about in the trade papers and to the conglomerates who own the studios. The big surprise is what happened to *The Goodbye Girl*. It had only one real star, Richard Dreyfuss; one rising star, Marsha Mason; and one cute ten-year-old, Quinn Cummings, with a slight love story directed extremely well by Herbert Ross and a rather nice script by me, if I have to say so myself. Having said that, no one expected any miracles from this film and it probably wouldn't have been made were it not for Ray Stark's faith in it. Since Warner Brothers owned the underlying rights to *Bogart Slept Here*, which then became *The Goodbye Girl*, Warners had the option of staying or dropping out of the project. Since the head of Warner Brothers at the time had little faith in my script, he wanted MGM to buy him out. Others at Warners figured, however, in for a penny, in for a pound, and so decided to split the costs and profits (if any) with MGM, then run by Daniel Melnick.

The making of the film gave rise to very few problems thanks to the wonderful chemistry between Richard and Marsha, and best of all, I got to see Marsha every day on the set. A lot of free ones, you could say. We all collaborated on the film, much as if it were a play (the stars, director and writer all came from the theater), all with the blessing of Ray Stark. During the shooting, if I felt a line or even a word was needed, I'd just call it out. When Elliot (Richard) confronts Paula (Marsha) about keeping herself and her daughter out of his way in his newly acquired apartment which he has agreed to share with his two new tenants, he warns her that he likes to walk around the house at night without pajamas, which he doesn't own in the first place. I called out to Richard, "Buffo!" Richard, without blinking an eye, said the speech again and threw in "buffo" at the end of the sentence, putting, as we say, a button on it. Marsha and Richard were a perfect match and you could practically see the sparks between them lighting up the screen.

On the day I was to see the first cut of the movie, I was being interviewed by a bright young journalist who kept talking to me all the way from my office to the screening room. As he turned to say goodbye, I decided I wanted another opinion and asked him to come in and view the picture with me, with the proviso that he would not write a word about the film, which was still in its early state. He agreed, surprised and delighted with the invitation. I could have had my head removed for doing that. I'm not always very objective the first time I see a project and although I liked what I saw on the screen, it seemed so effortless to me that I wasn't sure if an audience would think it was enough. "It seems pretty good to me," I said to the writer as the lights went up. "What did you think?"

"Pretty good?" he repeated, questioning my indecision. "It's absolutely wonderful. I don't think you realize what you've got here. I'm talking major hit."

I felt I was being buttered up for another favor.

Marsha and I did a long press tour and I loved sharing the stage of a TV show with her. We bantered well together, we knew each other's timing, enjoyed each other's stories, and if I surprised her with a funny line, there was not a better laugher in the world. Magazines started to write about us as one of Hollywood's happiest couples. I thought we were too. *People* magazine ran a Valentine's Day issue in which they listed the ten most romantic couples of all time, from Napoleon and Josephine and on. Marsha and I were on the list. High on the list, I might add. Things were going so smoothly for us that the only thing that could dim our spirits was if the picture didn't make it. It opened all around the country the week before Christmas.

The reviews everywhere were mostly wonderful. They raved about all three actors. It would have been a good time to go out and celebrate except for one thing. It didn't do much business. Many of the theater owners talked about moving it out after one week and replacing it with a film with more star power than we had. Columbia and Ray Stark campaigned hard, both in newspaper ads and with the theater owners, pointing to the great reviews. The theater owners pointed to the empty seats. Sometimes you just need to allow a little time for the word of mouth to spread before a movie catches on. That's all we had, was a little time. As it turned out, that's all we needed.

Business started to pick up and the theater owners gave us another week. And then the picture exploded. At the beginning of the second week, lines started to form at the box office . . . and then down the street . . . and then down the street and around the block. It was so popular that even on *Saturday Night Live*, John Belushi and Gilda Radner, playing Richard and Marsha respectively, did a takeoff on one of the scenes when Richard starts to pull off one by one Marsha's panties hanging on the shower rod in what was now "his" bathroom. We had a gigantic hit. In 1977, we grossed around fifty million dollars. Translate that to today's dollars and it would be close to a hundred and fifty million. There was suddenly talk about Academy nominations. Marsha and I were jubilant, stunned and extremely happy that the not-yet-born movie we talked about in a small restaurant in Florence turned out to be everything we hoped for and more. We even thought about going back to Florence, finding the restaurant again, ordering the same dishes, just to see if it produced another film.

Amidst all the excitement, Marsha and I drove into Westwood, a small community just below UCLA and where we lived, to see a movie. Afterward we went to Hamburger Hamlet for a bite to eat. It was the first time in a while that we had a chance to be alone and relax. Suddenly we saw a group of people milling around. Then they multiplied.

"What's that about?" Marsha asked.

I didn't have the slightest idea. I looked up again and now there were twice as many people, so many that you couldn't see outside the windows in the elongated restaurant. I got up and went to the door to find out what was happening. Then I stepped out to look. I came back, sat down next to Marsha, playing it very cool, and said offhandedly, "It's nothing. Just a line waiting to get into *The Goodbye Girl*. It goes completely around the block until the end of the line meets the beginning of the line. They're selling tickets for shows back to back." I finally smiled because you can't carry on being cool indefinitely.

Marsha's face turned white. She suddenly didn't look well, and I couldn't imagine what was happening. I paid the check and got up to go. Marsha couldn't move.

"What's wrong?" I asked.

"I can't do it," she said.

"Can't do what?" I asked.

"Go through that line. I can't cross that line. I'm scared."

"Of what?"

"I don't know. I'm just terrified."

"Nothing will happen," I tried to assure her. "I'll put my arm around you and we'll just go through."

She held my hand as we went and I could feel her trembling. Nothing happened as we cut through the line and crossed the street, nor did I think anything *would* happen. The thing Marsha had wanted most as an actress was now happening to her. The three years she gave up for us was starting to pay her back in a bigger way than we ever dreamed, and yet she was momentarily terrified. It wasn't the last time I saw this happen to her, and whenever we had to mingle with a crowd of people, she had to get out of it as quickly as she could. Not being an analyst, I could only conjecture what was going on inside her head. Since she spent the better part of her adult life as a working actress and loving it, was stardom more than she could handle so quickly? In time, she dealt with it and the terrors seemed to disappear. Another thing that occurred to me was what she said when she moved through the large empty rooms in the house in Bel Air just prior to our buying it.

"Do we deserve this?" she said that day.

With that question comes the accompanying fear of losing it all, and thinking, "I knew it wouldn't last." Nothing does. Enjoying what's given to you, for some people, is an acquired taste.

WHEN OSCAR TIME rolled around, we hit the jackpot in nominations. Best Picture; Best Actor, Richard; Best Actress, Marsha (her second nomination in her first four films); Best Supporting Actress, Quinn Cummings; Best Screenplay, c'est moi. Herbert Ross really scored when the other film he directed that year, *The Turning Point*, also received the Best Picture nomination. I can't recall when one director had two Best Picture nominations in the same year. Our chief competition was Woody Allen's *Annie Hall*, his most commercial picture to date. It ultimately won for Best Picture, Best Actress—Diane Keaton, and Woody for Best Screenplay. We did pull off one major win, however, when Richard Dreyfuss became the youngest actor ever to win as Best Actor.

WITH ALL THIS going on, my two daughters, Ellen and Nancy, were growing up. Nancy was doing well at the Westlake School nearby and Ellen was off to Pomona College. The house seemed quiet without Ellen, whose bubbling personality was sorely missed. It was the first time in their lives that the girls were living apart. It must have been a difficult time for them, without their mother, without each other, transplanted to an environment not of their choosing. It was now just the three of us, but Marsha and Nancy grew closer now that they were spending more time with each other. Nancy's bedroom was five times the size of her tiny room back on 62nd Street, but it was also three thousand miles away from the streets and stores, her grandmother and friends she left behind. Both girls made it clear that when they were finished with their schooling, they would be moving back to New York. I projected the loss and the isolation I would feel being alone in that distant house, especially when Marsha would be off working. Because of this, it was inevitable that my thoughts would go back to Joan and perhaps that's what Marsha meant when I mentioned earlier that Marsha thought I was "needy." If she wasn't there, then I summoned up the "company" of Joan in my thoughts. I don't think this sat well with Marsha, and to tell the truth, I could see why she felt that way. I had a habit of mentioning Joan's name in conversations and when I talked of places I had visited and loved, they were obviously places that I had been to with Joan. The happiest couple in Los Angeles was showing signs of slowly surfacing trouble. The only place in the house that I kept pictures of Joan were on the walls of my office, where I spent so much time. That didn't seem to be a problem with Marsha, mostly because I chose to think it wasn't. When I embedded Joan's face deeply into my brain after she died, the aura of that imprint floated about the house, making something that was not visible into a vision that could be felt rather than seen by both Marsha and by me.

Writing, I think, is not always an act of creation. Sometimes I think it's like a poison that inhabits your being, and the only way to get rid of it is to have the pen press deeply and quickly on the empty pages, releasing your darkest secrets and your most shameful thoughts, which may be minor discretions to most, but to you are something you have to expel in order to free yourself. If you are successful, along the way it gets tempered so that your audience can see themselves in your misdemeanors, and not be so horrific that it will prohibit them from sharing your common experiences. Those writers who go to the deepest and darkest of agonies are the ones who have lived there as well: O'Neill, Chekhov, Tolstoy, Beckett. The rest of us are not so brave, or perhaps not so damaged and broken, so we do not soar. For us, to look at our own lives and to expose as much as you can allow yourself to, is to bring relief and understanding to what pains you. I wish I could go deeper, further, but then again I think I do. I make the effort if not the entire journey, but the effort exhausts me as much as the farthest journey I could take.

For all these reasons, I decided to tackle a play that would test me like no other until then.

THE DARK CHAPTER

17

BEFORE I COULD write the play *Chapter Two*—which I knew was going to be a fictionalized account that began with the way Marsha and I met, wooed and married quickly, and continued to the point that major cracks began to appear in our marriage—I felt I had to go to Marsha to get her consent to do the play. If this was too personal to go public with, despite the fact that I would try to give the characters their own personalities separate from ours, I would still have to adhere to her wishes. When I finally asked her, she said, "It's fine with me because what you'd be telling is *your* story, not mine. You'd write about what was going on in your head and could only presume what was happening to me. If I want to tell *my* story, maybe I'll put it in my own book one day." I was enormously grateful for her consent and encouragement, and although I knew I'd made no promises to her, I would have to treat the story as truthfully as I could. I already knew that in most respects the problems that occurred between us were mostly of my doing, and it was Marsha who hung in stoically until she made it clear to me that she could endure just so much before taking a very strong stand with me.

The first two acts of the play were romantic and amusing. George, the sometimes successful novelist, who sells his British style spy novels under a pseudonym that buys him a modest town house in New York, doesn't do quite as well with his more personal and serious books written under his own name. He has just returned from Europe and a dismal vacation he had undertaken alone to try to put some distance between his new life and the loss six months ago of his beloved wife. His older brother, Leo, meets him at the airport only to find George more depressed than when he left. In an attempt to move him into a new life, Leo presses George to meet a woman, any woman, just to get his mind away from the recent dark past that clings so tenaciously to him. After a catastrophic blind date that Leo arranges for George with a bombshell named Bambi ("Her name told me everything," says George the following morning), who had a platinum streak through the center of her jet black hair and wore a dress that made her look like the cover of a rock album, George decides to fend for himself, and eventually he meets the warm and likable Jenny, an actress. Since Marsha *was* an actress and my brother, Danny, *had* arranged a date for me with a Bambi-like girl, I wasn't straying as much from the truth as I had thought I would. Art not only copies life, it steals from it.

Through the rest of the act, the whirlwind romance builds to a crescendo and it's not long before George proposes marriage to Jenny. It took place not in the hallway outside her apartment as had happened with Marsha and myself, but in the play as in life, Marsha did have an ex-husband. And Danny, like Leo, tried to stop my rush into a marriage that I might not have been prepared to deal with, coming so soon after my wife's death. (Or perhaps *any* marriage, since Danny's, like Leo's, fell apart in his own life.) But the marriage takes place and George and Jenny fly off to a honeymoon in the Bahamas.

The first traces of problems arise when, on their honeymoon, George becomes moody, even sullen. It was as if his dead wife had accidentally checked into the adjoining room. When they go back to New York, Jenny starts her new life in the house and bedroom where George spent the happiest years of his life with someone else. It is a tremendous burden to Jenny, but still she tries to fight to save the marriage before it unravels completely.

In a sense, my own situation with Marsha was worse than it was for George and Jenny, because now we were living in a house three thousand miles away, with the ghost of the past in a cemetery in Pound Ridge, New York. I don't mean for it to sound as if this summoning up of a ghost was an everyday occurrence, as if it was so pervasive that we had no marriage at all. The truth is, we had a wonderful marriage, and I believe we loved each other enormously. It wasn't Joan I was missing. There were no memories lying about in the Bel Air house, no furniture, no rooms, no views that constantly brought the specter of Joan in front of me almost everywhere I turned. It was something else. Perhaps it was the newness of this house, these trees and hills, this place called Los Angeles that seemed foreign to me that caused me to lose my bearing. It almost bothered me that Marsha was comfortable here, so happy with her life while I was living in *her* world, *her* house, breathing *her* air. It was Marsha who had to make the adjustment when she first moved into Joan's house on 62nd Street. Now it was *my* turn to make the adjustment in an environment that seemed almost hostile to my way of life. Marsha gave up almost three years of her life to cement the marriage, and here I was complaining about the adjustment *I* now had to make, and we were here far less than three years. Marsha put up with my dissatisfaction as long as she could, then suddenly one day an explosion came.

After some stinging words from me, in which I threatened to leave, to get out, Marsha came to me with a torrent of words that flowed out with such anger, but such truth, that she never missed a beat, never tripped over a single syllable or consonant. Each thought was fully formed, each one following the other as if she had learned it, practiced it, rehearsed it—but I knew it was spontaneous, that it was coming from the bottom of her heart and soul, her one last chance to save something good. She always knew I was the better one with words, whether on paper or in a bedroom brawl; I was the wittier one, the quicker one. But on that day, during that speech, I sat silently, looking at her, amazed at her breathtaking demonstration of someone saying something that she knows to be so right, so honest, so truthful, that she has tossed away the possibilities of the consequences and fired away. Two things happened to me at the same time. One I was grateful for; the other I was almost ashamed of. I was grateful for her bravery, her intelligence and her love. I was ashamed because I knew that what she said was so powerful, I was going to put it in the play. It was so organic it needed to be in the play, needed to be said so that my couple could save their marriage. George had to learn from the speech, just as Neil learned from it as he listened.

There was no way I could remember exactly what she said, of course, but I paraphrased it, remembering the essential thoughts. If it sounds well written, it's not. It was a gift of words and feelings that I did not invent. I would like you to hear now what essentially Marsha said to me. In the play it happens just after George announces that he is leaving, for how long he can't say, but his bags are packed and staring up at Jenny from the floor. He expects silence, pouting, acceptance, but she surprises him. She strikes back.

JENNY: You know what you want better than me, George . . . I don't know
    what you expect to find out there except a larger audience for your two
    shows a day of suffering . . . I know I'm not as smart as you. Maybe I
    can't analyze and theorize and speculate on why we behave as we do
    and react as we do and suffer guilt and love and hate . . . You read all
    those books, not me. But there's one thing I do know. I know how I feel.
    I know I can stand here watching you try to destroy everything I've ever
    wanted in my life, wanting to smash your face with my fists because

you won't even make the slightest effort to opt for happiness—and still I know that I love you. That's always so clear to me. It's the one place I get all my strength from . . . You mean so much to me that I'm willing to take all your abuse and insults and insensitivity—because that's what you need to do to prove I'm not going to leave you. I can't promise I'm not going to die, George, that's asking too much. But if you want to test me, go ahead and test me. You want to leave me, leave! But I'm not the one who's going to walk away. I don't know if I can take it forever, but I can take it for tonight and I can take it next week. Next month I may be a little shaky . . . But I'll tell you something, George. No matter what you say about me, I feel so good about myself . . . better than I felt when I ran from Cleveland and was frightened to death of New York. Better than I felt when Gus was coming home at two o'clock in the morning just to change his clothes. Better than I felt when I thought there was no one in the world out there for me and better than I felt the night before we got married and thought that I wasn't good enough for you . . . Well, I AM *WONDERFUL!!* I'm *nuts* about me. And if you're stupid enough to throw someone sensational like me aside, then you don't deserve as good as you got. I am sick and tired of running from places and people . . . And don't tell me what I want because *I'll* tell you what I want. I want a home and I want a family and I want a career. And I want a dog and a cat and I want three goldfish. There's no harm in wanting it, George, because there's not a chance in hell we're going to get it all anyway. But if you don't want it, you've got even less chance than that . . . You want me, then you fight for me, because I'm fighting like hell for you. I think we're both worth it. I will admit, however, that I do have one major, monumental fault . . . Sometimes I don't know when to stop talking. For that I'm sorry, George, and I apologize. I am now through . . .

I sat stunned and quiet in our bedroom as she sank into a chair, breathless, exhausted, not knowing what my reaction would be, and almost not caring. I remember my reaction exactly. I looked at her, in awe of her candor. "You're right," I said. "You are absolutely right."

She looked at me in surprise, and a slight smile crossed her face. "Really?" she said, almost like a young girl whose teacher just said in class, "Marsha, I'm giving you an A-plus for intelligence, honesty and for teaching us what love is about." If I remember correctly, Marsha burst into tears of gratitude, knowing that she had broken through my sometimes obstinate nature. She might also have thought to herself, "I'm glad I got through, but why does he always make it so hard?"

Marsha decided not to do the role of Jenny on the stage but *did* decide to play it in the film, since she felt that so much time had passed before the picture was made, she could separate herself from Jenny and simply think of the role as a character she'd like to play.

Through her effort, not mine, she also got her third Academy Award nomination. But the speech she delivered that day in our house in California was not spoken by someone looking to win an award. She said it as a woman, a grown, mature woman who finally had found the strength to take charge of her own life. When she said it as the character Jenny, audiences in film theaters often applauded her when she finished, grateful that she was a spokeswoman for wives who might have had the same trouble in their own marriages.

Our lives together got considerably better after that, and I would have been a fool and a dolt not to learn from her wisdom delivered on that late afternoon in California.

THE WRITER WRITES AND HAVING
WRIT, WRITES MORE

18

CHAPTER TWO was a resounding success when it opened on Broadway, garnering five Tony nominations. After that, one would have thought I'd put my pen down for a while, rest and contemplate my future. But my future refused to wait. It was today. Not even later today, it was now, right now, this minute. I had to keep on writing, continuously, compulsively, relentlessly, and I had so many projects started in different notebooks that I had to search through the pile that was mounting on my desk each morning to see what I wanted to work on that day. The ideas flowed, not like a stream, but from atop a huge waterfall, cascading down the mountain and crashing one upon the other, flooding my brain and washing away the possibility of discovering some other outlet for my energies, leaving no room for investigations of a more subtle, potentially richer life. I played tennis with the same demonic drive, four days a week instead of two or three, and still finding time to get back to my office and put out my three to four pages a day. I often went to lunch alone, taking my pad with me and actually writing between bites.

What amazed me was that this prodigious amount of work that was pouring out of me didn't seem to amaze anyone else. Others accept what comes out as the norm for you, and my friends apparently assumed that I had some trick or device to make my brain function more rapidly than most people's. The work came out regularly, and although it probably seemed to many that I was doing it feverishly, that was not the case. I worked long and hard on each project, rewriting five times as much as I was writing, and unlike a Noël Coward, who is said on occasion to have written a play in four days during a steamer trip to Jamaica, it still took me six months to a year to complete a play. I suppose what made it noteworthy in my case was that there was never a year skipped, never a season without a new play or film and sometimes both. If the picture you get in your mind is that I was a Dr. Jekyll working through the night into the dawn to achieve the fulfillment of his scientific dreams, you may erase the image. I still worked normal hours and I was chasing neither awards nor money, nor was I looking to lighten the plight and suffering of the human race. I was having fun, and I loved hearing audiences laugh, partly because I could share something with them that would otherwise never have transpired between us. The other joy was that like a teenage boy reaching his physical maturity, I felt I could now jump ten feet in the air, hang there and drop the ball through the hoop. My energy was boundless. I felt special and unique, but in no way superior. I had a gift, albeit a simple one—but then fortunately I was not the one who God chose to lead His people out of Egypt. I might have gotten them to laugh a lot, but they wouldn't have lasted forty minutes in the desert going in my direction, much less forty years.

And still the plays and films kept parading out on the field and I was the Pied Piper leading my little band of comedies and musicals to theaters everywhere. There was *The Cheap Detective* in 1978, a film sequel in the style of *Murder by Death*. I blended the stories of *The Maltese Falcon* with *Casablanca*, getting my chance to at last work vicariously on two Humphrey Bogart classics, unfortunately without Bogart.

Then there was a new musical in 1979, *They're Playing Our Song*. It was originally to be a musical version of my earlier play *The Gingerbread Lady*, with a score by Marvin Hamlisch and Carole Bayer Sager. In real life at the time, Marvin and Carole were not only collaborators but were living together as well. Each morning Marvin would arrive at my house to begin work, but Carole rarely showed up before twelve. I truly liked Carole because she was an extremely talented lyricist with a wonderful sense of humor and irony, and as Marvin and I waited patiently for her to show up, instead of discussing the project at hand, Marvin was complaining about how difficult it was to work closely with the woman you're also romantically involved with. Carole was also writing songs on her own and had just come out with two albums on which she performed her own work. She had a small voice, not even all that melodic, but she had a wonderful style and she did her own songs better than anyone. This seemed to be another problem for Marvin. I don't want to cast aspersions on his ego, but it looked like he was afraid to be outshone by his collaborator, since he was a pretty big name in the music industry then. Carole said he wanted her to stop making albums.

I didn't take part in these confrontations and had no idea how deeply they went in the bosom of their rented house in Los Angeles, but one thing suddenly occurred to me. That the idea of a male and female composing team, fighting, scratching, loving and writing might just make a better musical than *The Gingerbread Lady*. The one thing you look for in a musical is the reason why people actually sing songs, a piece of advice that Stephen Sondheim had given me years earlier when I suggested he and I do a musical version of *The Front Page*. Stephen is a brilliant man, as anyone can tell you, and a unique voice among his generation in the musical theater. *The Front Page* is a great play, said Stephen, but why do they sing? I looked him right in the eye and said, "I haven't the slightest idea—except that you write such incredible songs." "Not without good reason," said Stephen wisely, and instead of writing with him, I decided to just enjoy listening to everything he wrote without me getting in his way.

Marvin and Carole, no doubt flattered to be the inspiration of the characters of a new musical, agreed to work on my idea. I did make a point not to ask them too many direct and private questions about their life. I was not out to write a biography but a simple, romantic comedy with characters that I invented rather than the ones who really existed. What also intrigued me was the idea to make it a very small musical. Two characters, to be exact, with an offstage character named Leon, who was the former husband of Carole's character but is never seen in the show. The shadowy ghost in Carole's former life is a much greater threat to the relationship of the two lover-composers, and his insistence on calling their house night and day or asking her to help bail him out of trouble, caused by his dependency on her, is a continuing problem.

We cast the show perfectly with the delightful Lucie Arnaz and Robert Klein, one of the funniest actor-comics I ever worked with. He had that irascible New York humor that I was so fond of, and like the two characters in *Barefoot in the Park*, they were hardly nice to each other for a moment in the play until he realizes how much he needs and misses her at the end. Robert Klein was also an excellent musician, sang well, played the harmonica and was very believable as the harassed composer. We added six dancer-voices, who played no actual parts in the show but augmented all the songs and carried out the wonderful movement staged by choreographer Pat Birch.

The show opened at the Ahmanson Theatre in L.A., received not only terrific notices, but we paid off the entire investment of the show within three months after opening in New York, where we ran for three years, followed by a two-year national company, a successful London company and world-wide engagements for another few years. So the hits kept coming. I never questioned it and never considered that it might all come to a crashing halt one day.

In California a husband and wife share community property and what I made was half Marsha's, what she made was half mine. The money was rolling in so swiftly, so regularly that neither one of us was paying all that much attention to it. Having lost all the rights to the TV version of *The Odd Couple* some years before after following some advice I shouldn't have, you'd think I would have been more wary of any future investments and advice. I wasn't, nor was Marsha. I had now moved to another business manager, a man whose name became prominent on TV since his number one client was one of television's biggest stars. The *Variety* reports kept telling us how rich the TV star was getting, due to his canny lawyer–investment advisor. He was now the owner and president of a bank in Los Angeles, he now controlled TV and radio stations in Las Vegas, Texas and other places around the country, making huge land deals and oil deals and the money kept rolling in. When you are naive and pretty foolish about such matters, there's no end to the stupidity you are capable of. Marsha and I were too busy making films and doing plays and decided to trust the money managers to manage our destiny.

Within two years we had lost millions in deals that never came through the way we thought they would. It took years more for my mentor and protector, Ray Stark, to straighten me out and to get me back on the right path.

My next financial move wasn't much wiser. I left the fancy-talking business manager and went with a staid and reliable major accounting firm and let them handle my business. Within a year, the bright young woman who handled our business for the major accounting firm decided to branch out on her own, and like lemmings toward the sea, we followed her to the edge and beyond. She was not dishonest and never cheated us, but the results of our business dealings again were not successful. It was nearly too late before Ray Stark rescued me from that imbroglio, while my money and savings were diminished once again.

But why worry about such things when you have another project coming up? I was writing shows and screenplays with such regularity that I have no memory of exactly when I wrote them, and how, because they were usually squeezed in between two other projects with which I was deeply involved.

On the heels of all this financial upset came another play, *I Ought to Be in Pictures*, presented first at the Mark Taper Forum in Los Angeles. It was the story of a young girl from New York, abandoned by her father when she was a mere child, left to be raised by her mother. The father has become a screenwriter, and although his best years—and they were few—are far behind him, his daughter believes that he can not only get her a career as an actress in films, but that it's her birthright to be helped by him, as repayment for the callous and unloving way he treated her as a child. The minute I finished the script, I had a very clear idea about who I wanted to play the failed screenwriter.

Tony Curtis was an unusual star. Certainly he was not the greatest actor in the world, but he possessed a world of charm, sex appeal, humor and on quite a few occasions had shown the ability to get deeply into a part and come up with a remarkable performance. His performance in the film *Sweet Smell of Success* may have been one of his best. To play the daughter, I hired Dinah Manoff, the daughter of actress Lee Grant; she was a perfect choice. It was to be a love story of another kind, one between a guilty but put-upon man who never achieved the success he thought was coming to him, and his angry, mistreated-but-anxious-for-approval daughter from New York. In a sense, it was another odd couple story. I called agent Irving Lazar, who represented Curtis, and told him I was interested in Tony playing the lead in the new play that I was preparing for L.A. and eventually moving on to New York. Without a beat, Irving said to me, "Neil, you're my friend, Tony is my client. My advice is not to take him." I was astounded at his quick reaction. "Why not?" I asked. "Is anything wrong? Is he ill?" "Don't ask me any questions, Neil," Irving continued. "I think Tony is a wonderful guy and a terrific actor, but I just don't think this will turn out well." "So what are we talking about here, Irving? Is it drugs? Is Tony having a substance problem?" "I never said that," Irving responded quickly. "Listen, I've said my piece," he continued. "If you really want him, if you think he'll be good for your play, then I will highly recommend Tony to do it."

Given Irving's words of advice, I knew I was headed for trouble, but I had a naive, almost unshaking belief that Tony Curtis would not only be news on Broadway, but that he would be the absolute perfect man to play the part. I knew he could charm the pants off a mannequin. "I'll send him the play. If he likes it, let's talk business," I said.

A few days later Tony Curtis, director Herbert Ross and I met, and Tony made it clear that he was excited and delighted to play the role. He saw a new career for himself—the stage, something that eluded him in his meteoric rise to Hollywood stardom. Within a few months we were into rehearsals. Tony was not used to having to learn an entire script before, since films are shot, as we all know, mostly at the rate of a page or a few lines at a time. He asked for a driver to pick him up for rehearsals each day, one who would not only drive but would coach him on his lines going to and from work. It was clear from the outset that Tony was very nervous, which we expected, but he also showed a need to be loved, to be wanted, to be the focus of our attention. He started to call me at home at night, at all hours, wondering if he was doing well, asking if we could spend more time together, becoming pals, close friends, so to speak. It was disconcerting for me, yet I felt not only a sadness for him, but a genuine fondness. He was not afraid to tell you he needed help, that he wanted to be wonderful in this part and that together we might all pull it off. He was always cooperative and hardworking, but it was obvious that the learning of the long pages of dialogue was giving him problems.

Four weeks later, after arduous rehearsals, we were ready for our first preview performance. I had no idea what to expect and had mixed feelings: I knew that if we had hired a more experienced stage actor, we would not be as worried as we were; at the same time, if we hired a more experienced stage actor, he probably wouldn't come close to the charm and warmth that Tony was showing on the stage.

We got through the first preview. On the whole, I was optimistic. Tony held up pretty well, Dinah Manoff was delightful, and the ever dependable Joyce Van Patten, whom I used in play after play in those days, was the perfect makeup girl from the studio who was having a sometimes live-in relationship with Tony's character. After the preview we quickly retired to Tony's dressing room and Herbert Ross was ready with all sorts of comments. What I was thinking above all was that the play basically worked, but still had a lot of rewriting to do, which I would undertake as I did with every play I ever mounted in my career. After Herbert's encouraging notes, Tony looked at me and said, "What do you think, Neil? You happy?" "Very," I replied. "I think we're really on the right track here. I see all the things I've done wrong and once I do the first rewrites, I think we'll begin to shape up very quickly."

Tony looked at me as if I were suddenly speaking a foreign language. He was hearing words he never heard before, not understanding the meaning of them, not getting the very concept. "What do you mean, rewrites?" he said. "I thought this was the play. I thought what I learned was the play we're going to do."

The other actors looked at me, then put their heads down, knowing that Tony was going to suddenly learn the do's and don'ts of the theater.

"Well, Tony, it's just the beginning. I can't write a play and get it all correct in one draft. There are things that don't work. Things that I have to rewrite. We could never go into New York with the play as it's written now."

His face turned white. He wiped his brow with a towel, then shook his head adamantly. "No. No way. I learned one play, that's all I can learn. Either we do this or we forget about it."

Herbert Ross tried to tactfully explain the realities of the theater, but he also knew this was not the time to bring things to a boil. "Well, let's discuss this tomorrow, Tony. You did very well for tonight."

Herbert and I went out for a drink and knew we were in trouble, that Irving Lazar's warning had finally brought home the essence of our plight. It was clear to us both that Tony Curtis was never going to make it to Broadway with this play nor would we make it with Tony Curtis. Still, we didn't want to give up. We couldn't. We still had four weeks to play out in L.A., and one never knew what miracles could happen in four weeks.

Until one day at a weekend matinee, all hell exploded. When Tony came out for his first scene on stage, all did not seem well. He was edgy, fidgety, even surly on the stage in his scenes with young Dinah Manoff. It was a play that had no four-letter words in it, since there was still a great deal of aspired love and respect between the father and his daughter. Then toward the end of the first act, Tony lashed out at Dinah with a barrage of language, a string of obscenities, of furious anger. She was stunned and didn't know how to react. He was still playing his part, but it seemed as if Mr. Hyde had emerged from his soul and Dinah was bearing the brunt of his tirade. The audience, although they had not seen the play before, sensed there was something wrong. The language that was now being flung around on stage did not seem compatible with what I had written so far. Tony stormed off the stage as the act drew to a close. Dinah ran into her dressing room, bathed in tears and frightened at what had just occurred. The stage manager waited for things to cool down, then at the appropriate moment, knocked on Tony's dressing room door and said, "Five minutes, Tony." There was no answer from the dressing room. The stage manager repeated his call. Still no answer. He knocked on the door, then opened it to see if Tony was all right. He was getting dressed, changing his clothes, but he was not putting on the clothes he was to wear in the second act. He was putting on his street clothes, his civvies, to be exact.

"What are you doing, Tony? You're putting on the wrong clothes."

"No," said Tony. "These are the right clothes. These are my going-home clothes. I've had enough acting for today. Get someone else to do the play today," and he was out of the theater in a minute. The dazed stage manager quickly ran down the hall to find the understudy, told him to get ready, and then rushed to Dinah Manoff's room, knocked, walked in and said, "Tony's not coming back for the second act. You'll have to do it with the understudy."

But Dinah was too far beyond upset to even get the meaning of what he was saying. She was crying, leaning in the arms of the protective Joyce Van Patten, mumbling she couldn't go on. She couldn't face the audience after what just happened. The befuddled stage manager walked out to the stage, never having been in this position in his entire life. He did the best he could when he announced, "Ladies and gentlemen, unfortunately Mr. Curtis and Miss Manoff have suddenly taken ill during the intermission. Their parts will be played by their understudies. Thank you," and he walked off the stage, probably wishing it could have been off the Oakland bridge. The audience began to boo, not only at their disappointment at not seeing the stars, but sensing what must have happened during the end of the first act.

In truth, I can't remember if Tony Curtis ever came back to finish the engagement. Perhaps he did, perhaps not. In a way I felt badly for him because he was coping with a lot of things in his life. In his book a few years later, he referred to Herbert Ross and myself as "those two terrible men," as if we were the cause of his troubles. Eventually Tony was replaced by actor Ron Liebman for the New York run and Ron is a first-rate, exciting and complex actor. He did extremely well for us. Dinah Manoff went on to win the Tony Award for her performance on Broadway in *I Ought to Be in Pictures*. She later repeated the role in the film opposite Walter Matthau. But the next time an agent advises me not to take his client for a role we just offered him, I would think my answer over much more carefully.

GOT TO DANCE

19

IF YOU'VE EVER SEEN a documentary of Fred Astaire's film career, you would think the man never slept a night in his life. He performed one unbelievable number after another, in every fashion, every style, every mood, with almost every beautiful actress in Hollywood as his partner; not to mention a variety of inanimate objects including drums, canes, golf clubs, gym equipment and roller skates, all of which seemed to serve him as well as his human partners. Did the man ever just walk? Did he ever sit still, read a newspaper? Did he ever see a dentist? No, he just danced. Well, that was the vision I was beginning to get of myself, dancing frantically through every day, only without the tap shoes.

Whatever I did in life, it seemed that most of it was writing. There is a drug, given in recent years, to patients who undergo surgery, and although they experience postoperative pain, the drug prohibits the *memory* of the pain. In other words, as soon as the pain appears, you forget it, although you just experienced it, so the lasting effect is as if no pain ever occurred. In terms of my writing, I was under the influence of something like that drug. A screenplay would pour out of me almost without my knowing it. Thirty pages of a new play appeared neatly typed in front of me and I never knew where it came from. I would open a drawer in my desk, take out a draft of something I wrote a week ago or a month or two years ago, and since I had no memory of doing the work, I'd look at it and wonder if someone sent it to me through the mail, asking my opinion of it. I sat in the screening room at Columbia watching the first assembled cut of a movie called *Seems Like Old Times*, and although I really liked it, I found it hard to focus because I had spent the entire morning prior to the screening working on something else. Yet there were Goldie Hawn and Chevy Chase, sitting in the screening room with me, and I remembered how much I enjoyed watching them work every day, but when did I write this screenplay, when did I find the time?

The picture was a hit and twenty-some odd years later I see it playing on a cable station and I laugh, surprised that I don't know what line or scene is coming up next. I was working, I suppose, on automatic control, and like a well-made toaster, I was popping out crusty English muffins that everyone seemed to enjoy. But I never stopped long enough to really taste them. At dinner Marsha would start a conversation and I would try to pick up the thread of what she was saying, but my mind was on something called *Actors and Actresses*, a new play that seemed to be writing itself while I watched over it like a shepherd, seeing that it didn't stray too far from the corral that I was keeping new plays in for that week.

Did I care about what I was writing? Yes, very much so. Oh, I cared about some less than others, but some meant a great deal to me. I liked *Actors and Actresses* because it was bleak and sad and yet had a kind of fragile humor (sometimes tough and biting) that I was dealing with in that period. It was about a group of over-the-hill actors coupled with a few not-ready-for-prime-time actors who traveled the highways and byways of America's small theatrical stopovers, playing one-night stands in small cities like Duluth or Peoria and sometimes the semi-big time in a place like Cincinnati. The actors traveled in a bus, the scenery went in a truck, thus it was called a bus-and-truck tour.

Where was I when I wrote this play? I don't know, but I actually tried it out some months later, either in the Hartford Theatre in Stamford, Connecticut, or the Stamford Theatre in Hartford, Connecticut—I don't remember. And how did I get there? Plane? Train? Bus? Or did I just wake up in some hotel room one morning and ask the desk clerk to direct me to the theater?

The play had its good moments and its not-so-good moments and we never brought it to New York, but I have no recollection of the struggle, the disappointment, the energy spent and the promise that went unfulfilled. The nonexistent pain remover was working its magic on me and I could write day in, day out, weekends or holidays without any strain or harm to my psyche. Or so I thought. The bill that was mounting up would have to be paid later (and pay it I did). But until then, the started plays, the half-finished musicals, the outlined films were all waiting on the assembly line, but now I felt I wasn't even pushing the buttons. At the end of each day I just picked up the finished pages, made a correction or two—or twelve or fifty—and then put them on top of the pile that the category dictated.

What was going on in Marsha's mind, I wonder now, and did she assume that I thought I was perfectly in control of a perfectly uncontrolled life? Was

I manic? Was I depressed? Was I euphoric? No, I was just writing, and as I recently read in an article by playwright David Mamet, "Writing is the thing you do so that you don't have to think about the things you'd rather not think of." That was me, or a version of that. If there were things I didn't want to think of, they must have been infinite because the writing never slowed up. I had empty notebooks strewn everywhere around my office, all fighting for a place on line to receive a portion of my daily attention. Pens of all kinds and colors were sitting on tables, in jars, on my desk so that no matter where I stepped or turned, there was always something to write on and something to write with. I was like Chaplin in the classic comedy *Modern Times*. He played a factory worker with a wrench in each hand and his sole job was to tighten any bolts that came out of a huge machine. He had been doing it so long and so repeatedly that he tightened any bolts that went by him, passed him, under him, over him or through him. Instead of bolts, I tightened scripts, and like the tireless factory worker, I never heard the five o'clock stop whistle any more than he did.

Again, to clarify the picture for you, don't suppose that if you were in my office when I worked that you would see a blur, a whirling dervish of pages flying and writing utensils brandished like knives in a duel. I sat quietly, hardly moving, very deliberate, thinking things out carefully. If you tried to watch, you'd be bored in five minutes. It was the slow, rhythmic but steady pattern of a mind at work, fingers typing and stories silently being told with no one but my imagination to hear the words. Still another play appeared, this one more of a fable. I called it *Fools*. It was based very loosely on the stories of Sholom Aleichem, wherein he wrote about a fictional village in middle Europe called, I believe, Chelm. (For those of you who don't happen to have friends of the Jewish persuasion, the "Ch" in Chelm is made with a slight coughing sound.) Chelm had one great distinction. Everyone who lived there was stupid. My Chelm was located in Russia, and I called it Kulyenchikov, a name that no one in Kulyenchikov could spell or pronounce. *Fools* was a play that I finished and loved writing, but I never thought it should go to Broadway. As a fable, and almost a children's fable at that, I thought it was more suited to off-Broadway, but in those days it was unthinkable by others that Neil Simon should appear off-Broadway.

Fools was pure vaudeville couched in the guise of a fable, the story of peasants who were so sweet, so innocent, so pure that their inability to put two coherent sentences together was as touching as they were silly. Leon, a schoolmaster from Moscow, wanders into this remote village looking for employment and instead finds love and no one to talk to who makes sense. He meets the local doctor and his wife, and their daughter, Sophia. When the doctor asks a patient to read an eye chart, the patient would read the letters aloud, "O . . . R . . . K . . . M . . . Z . . ." Then he'd say to the doctor, "Did I get them right?"

"I don't know," the doctor replies. "Sounds good to me." You get the drift. Then Leon proceeds to question Sophia:

LEON: May I call you Sophia?

SOPHIA: Why?

DOCTOR: It's your name, darling. Remember?

LEON: Would it please you if I called you Sophia?

SOPHIA: I don't know. Try it.

LEON: Tell me, Sophia, what is your favorite color?

SOPHIA: My favorite color?

DOCTOR: Oh, I used to know that one.

LEON: Once again, Sophia, what is your favorite color?

MOTHER: Why is he being so hard on her? This isn't a university.

SOPHIA: My favorite color is . . . is . . . is yellow.

LEON: Yellow! Very good, Sophia. And why is yellow your favorite color?

SOPHIA: Because it doesn't stick to your fingers as much.

DOCTOR: (To Leon) I think she's wrong. I think it's blue that doesn't stick
      to your fingers.

Well, if it was laughs, love and a two-thousand-year curse put on a village you were looking for, we had two hours of it. If it was a hit show you wanted, try *Mister Roberts*. We ran about six months in New York and the play is still performed today in theaters everywhere from Bangor, Maine, to possibly a village in Russia called Kulyenchikov.

Not all the decisions to undertake a new project started with me. For example, I received a phone call from Frank Price, then the studio head of Columbia Pictures, a bright, amiable man who came out of television with a reputation as someone who knew a good story when he read it. He invited me to breakfast at the Beverly Hills Hotel where so many other actors, agents and studio folk were making deals at the same time, you could practically order what film you wanted from the menu. Frank was not much into small talk and in his soft-spoken manner he got right to the point.

"I just wanted to know what you're up to, Neil. Is there anything you'd like to do? Any ideas kicking around?"

I was prepared. I didn't think he wanted to see me just to watch me eat French toast.

"Actually there is something, but I never brought it up to you because it's a bit offbeat."

"I like offbeat," he said. "What is it?"

"It's something I've already done as a play a few years ago, but I always thought it would make a much better movie." Perhaps the reason I never pushed it was because I thought it had a great starring role for Marsha and never wanted to put the studio in the position of having to take Marsha as part of the deal. I would hope they'd want her, of course, but I wanted it to be because they'd feel as strongly as I did that she was the best actress for it. I then told him about the play, *The Gingerbread Lady*.

For me it was a breakthrough play of sorts, one that dealt with the drama of the story even more than the comedy. It came close to failing in Boston where it previewed; it starred Maureen Stapleton. The critics were not too kind to it and said plainly that what they wanted from me was *The Odd Couple* and *Barefoot in the Park*, while I wanted to press on in other directions. When the reviews came in at the small, bleak opening party we were all attending, Maureen sensed it was over for all of us. She grabbed me by the collar and said, "If you close this play, I will personally stab you in your sleep with a fork." The next morning, buoyed by our one good review, I told the producer that I wanted the rest of the four weeks in Boston to try and save the play, then I got on the next train to New York and wrote intensely for the four-hour trip back home. The play eventually made it to Broadway, ran a year and Maureen won the Tony Award as Best Actress. I briefly outlined the story of the play to Frank Price and told him what I intended to change for the film. He nodded, more intrigued than enthusiastic, but said if I sent him the play, he'd read it by the weekend. Three days after our breakfast, Frank called me and said very simply, "I like it. Let's do it."

As simple as that. In today's world, that breakfast wouldn't have gotten past the first cup of coffee before a studio head would say, "Where's the stars? Where's the action scenes? Where's the songs? How do you get kids in to see it and who'll understand it in Europe?" In today's world, I guess I would say, "Well, we could show it on a double bill with *Twister*." I was, however, lucky enough to still be living in an era and a theatrical climate where all a studio wanted to know was, is it a good story or not? With a green light from Frank, I began writing the script, which I would produce along with director Glenn Jordan. The three leads in the film were Marsha, Joan Hackett and Jimmy Coco, and aside from a young Kristy McNichol, Marsha was the only real name that meant anything. She was going to play an alcoholic who is trying to dry out, get her acting career going again, finding herself a nonloser boyfriend and hoping to regain custody of her young daughter. In today's world, I would have been shown the door and the studio gate quickly as they ordered me off the lot forever—unless, of course, I could get Jim Carrey to play Marsha's boyfriend, and give his character this problem of having to tell the truth for twenty-four hours. But this was 1981 and we made this small picture—having changed the title from *The Gingerbread Lady* to *Only When I Laugh*—on a smaller budget. The picture probably made its money back thanks to video and cable sales, but what pleased me so much was that we were nominated for three Academy Awards: one for Marsha, her fourth Best Actress nomination in the eight films she made, possibly a record, and one each for Joan Hackett and Jimmy Coco in supporting roles. Those were still innocent times and we were all fortunate enough to be part of it before the phrase "mega-hit" was invented.

IRELAND, SANTA FE AND OBLIVION

20

SOMEHOW, BEFORE filming started, Marsha and I squeezed in a trip to Ireland with my good friend David Picker, former head of United Artists and his then wife, Nessa Hyams. We decided to rent a car and follow the Irish road maps wherever they took us, with some planned stops along the way at hotels that were recommended to us. Following the map wasn't hard. Pronouncing the names of towns and small cities was the difficulty. David, happily for all of us, elected to do all the driving and the finding of places called Broughmohal and Collygrud and Mollybulech, which after a while I began to think weren't towns at all but rather names of the local ale. David's mistake was asking strangers where he could find such and such a town, only to have a very kind and generous farmer rattle off directions sounding like a man who had his tongue tied very tightly to his tonsils. I told David to be careful because if he pronounced these places in the proper Irish brogue, he could possibly asphyxiate himself.

Ireland is as beautiful a country as you could find in the world but you'd better dress right for the weather. At one point we drove through a rainstorm for over two hours, but every time we looked behind us, there was no rain falling. I told David to drive slower so that we'd always be in the sun that was following us right at our heels, but it was not in David's makeup to drive slowly or try to make friends with the weather. We played on golf courses so thick with deep grass that to hit your ball was to lose it. If you swung and missed, you lost a stroke but saved a ball. There were, I believe, many charming small cottages in the vicinity made completely out of lost golf balls, sort of adobe huts with dimples in them.

Since we were two couples, we had to make unusual arrangements for the booking of rooms in hotels. David wisely suggested that since it was unlikely we'd each get comparable rooms, the fairest thing to do was to switch first choice at each hotel so that by the end of the trip no one would come out the loser. We tossed a coin and Marsha and I won first pick at the first hotel we stopped at. It was a very large manor house, possibly once a small castle, and although we all dream of living in a castle one day, it took an experienced traveler like Cole Porter who told us in a lyric that a castle in Ireland is the likeliest place to catch pneumonia. Nevertheless we were thrilled when we entered the large entrance hall and were greeted by a small contingent of concierges. David graciously told our host to please show the Simons to the most favorable of the rooms, and that they would be happy with the second choice. We were led into a small elevator (sorry, lift) to the third floor, then through red-carpeted hallways, past paintings of some former lord or earl who once called this mansion home, and finally into a corner suite, two extremely large rooms with an old but perfectly suitable bath. They were, however, a bit stingy with the soap. Still, it was decorated simply but tastefully, and you could picture The McGillycuddy of the Reeks, Irish chieftain of note, spending a fortnight in here, next to the warm fireplace and oversized chairs. From every large window the views were spectacular, where you could see for twenty miles all around, the loveliest green hills and pastures, looking like a Turner landscape. There were sheep in the meadows and ducks in the ponds and whatever else was in that nursery rhyme we still vaguely remembered. We were in heaven—and then our phone rang.

It was David.

"How're your rooms?" he asked pleasantly.

"David, it's incredible. I just hope yours are even half as nice as ours because this is paradise . . . How'd you make out?"

"It's interesting," he said. "You ought to come over and see."

"Sure. We'll come down before dinner."

"No," he said. "It will be dark by then and you can't get the full appreciation of this unless you see it in the light."

"Okay, I'll come now. How do I get there?"

"I'm sending a bellman up to your room. He'll show you."

"Right," I said. "Be right there."

"Take your time," he said. "It's a bit of a walk." And he hung up.

Marsha, tired from the drive, sank into the deep bed, kicked off her shoes and asked me to wake her an hour before dinner. She was asleep before the bellman knocked on the door.

Ireland is still a poor country, and real luxury is not as common there as one would find, say, in France or in America, but its simple beauty and gracious hospitality made me feel fortunate to be where we were on this cool, sunny July afternoon.

I followed the bellman across the red-carpeted hallways, down the lift to the Great Entrance Hall, then through a side door paneled in exquisite wood, then to my surprise, down a flight of stairs. Then through another door, this one not paneled, and more of a surprise, down another flight of stairs. There was no further natural light coming from anywhere. It was all wall lights, and dim ones at that. There was no doubt that when the first lords and earls inhabited the mansion, the only way through these passages would be to carry torches, which I thought would come in handy on this present trip as well.

"Is this some sort of shortcut?" I asked the bellman.

"Shortcut? No, sir. This is the only way."

I suddenly felt this man's name was Igor and I was following him through passageways from which no human was known to return.

"Where are we?" I asked the bellman with some trepidation.

"These used to be the servants' quarters in the old days," he said as the passageway now began to curve. "In recent years, when the manor became more popular, these were redone and turned into guest rooms. They're not always used, but when we're full up during the height of the season, as we are now, we open them up again. Actually, they have a certain quiet charm of their own."

"To whom?" I wanted to say. "Rabbits?"

He stopped suddenly and I had to brace myself to avoid bumping into him. He knocked on the door and called out, "Bellman."

A familiar voice, sounding more dour than usual, said, "It's open. Come in."

The bellman opened the door. Two dismal lamp lights were on either side of the bed. David and Nessa were sitting on the bed, their unopened luggage on the floor in front of them. The windows—there were two of them—were high up on the wall, making it quite clear that this room was below ground level.

The room was damp and dank, and clearly was more a part of the earth than of the hotel. When you looked up to the windows above, you could only see the shoes and ankles of people passing by. I felt a chill and wished I had worn a sweater. David and Nessa obviously wished they were on a sunny island in Greece. If Marsha and I had a Turner landscape, David and Nessa had the back of the canvas, nails and all.

"Is there anything I can get you, sir?" the bellman said to David.

"I can't possibly see what," said David. "I think everything we need to survive for two days is right here."

David gave the bellman a tip and the bellman looked for a moment as if he was going to give it back, out of respect for the situation. He left. I didn't know what to say. I felt enormously guilty and upset and miserable, coming in only second to David and Nessa's misery. David had arranged the trip, he had found the hotels, he had been driving us everywhere, telling us the history of this hotel, of its incredible food and, above all, their magnificent gardens, which at the moment were growing directly above their room. I had to restrain myself to keep from laughing, because it was an awful joke. But then those are usually the funniest kind.

"No, David," I said quickly. "This is no good. We have to do something."

He shrugged. "There's nothing to do," he said. "This is the only room they had left. We tossed, you won. We'll manage fine."

He also managed a smile and I bit my lip hard to prevent myself from falling hysterical on the floor, which proves to you that people who write comedy don't always know the parameters of decency.

"What if you stay here tonight and tomorrow night Marsha and I will exchange rooms with you?" I offered.

"No. Really. It's only for two nights . . . Does Marsha like your rooms?"

"Actually, not that much," I said with all the sensitivity I could muster. "It's really cold up there. And you can hear the people in the next room. It's okay, I guess."

David grinned. "Yeah, I'm sure," he said with more irony than was necessary.

"It'll even out," he said. "I just didn't want you to miss seeing this. We would have taken a picture of it, but there's no flash camera that's bright enough to make anything visible."

I found my way back to our room, but only before stopping every twenty steps or so to release the pangs of laughter that were building up inside of me. The worst moment came as I entered our room just as Marsha was getting up. I prayed she wouldn't ask it. I prayed she wouldn't think of it. I prayed the words wouldn't form on her lips. My prayers were not answered.

"How's their room?" she asked innocently. She must have thought I just had a stroke because I fell across the bed, laughing indecently. I never could get to describing their room. Every time I started, I was overtaken with insanity.

After dinner, David couldn't resist, and said that Marsha had to see their room. When they opened the door with their key, Marsha stepped in and her hand went to her mouth as if she had just seen the *Hindenburg* burning. Tears came to her eyes with compassion bordering on grief. She hugged Nessa like a mother would hold a child who just broke her favorite toy. Marsha was an angel. I was a fiend because I was still laughing three days later as we drove to the next hotel. That's when things evened up. David and Nessa had a sun-filled suite with a magnificent view of the sea and the Irish coastline; Marsha and I got a bleak, tiny room that looked out on the parking lot. I wondered, at two o'clock in the morning, if that was David honking the horn in his car or was it just my imagination?

IT WILL SURPRISE no one, I'm sure, to hear that somewhere between the trip to Ireland and the start of shooting *Only When I Laugh*, I wrote another screenplay. Did I write some in Ireland? Perhaps. On the plane or waiting in airport lounges? Probably. I could get a half a page in while waiting for Marsha to get dressed for dinner and sometimes the writing was done only in my head while watching a film or a play that didn't particularly interest me. I did that a lot in musicals where the number on stage held no one's attention including the person who was singing. I couldn't keep the exact dialogue of the imagined scene in my head, but the gist of it was clear enough to remember, and I emptied the contents of my memory into a typewriter the following morning.

This film turned out to be *Max Dugan Returns*, and it concerned a widowed schoolteacher, played eventually by Marsha, and her fourteen-year-old son. Her plight was to make her meager salary cover her bills when a mysterious stranger appears at her doorstep on a dark, misty night. The stranger turns out to be her estranged father who had abandoned her as a child, and now has come back with a suitcase filled with six hundred thousand dollars in cash, which he skimmed off the top as a blackjack dealer in Las Vegas. He is a man with a heart condition and about six months to live, and he wants to pay back his debt to his daughter and to the grandson he has never seen. Did it occur to me that this was the second time I had written about a child abandoned by a parent, in both cases, a father? Not consciously perhaps, but nevertheless, there it was, popping up again. It appeared in a later play as well, *Lost in Yonkers*, where a father unwillingly leaves his two sons in the charge of their grandmother, while he goes off to earn money to pay off hospital debts accrued during his wife's bout with cancer.

I always knew you could trace my life through my plays (not all, but many) and in the above paragraph there are listed three common themes that show up in various forms throughout my career: the abandoned child, a father with a failing heart (my father died of one) and a mother dying of cancer, which of course was Joan. Always abandonment in one form or another. It shows up in *Chapter Two*, in *Jake's Women*, in *Broadway Bound* (in that one, all three are present, since the mother knows her husband will leave her, the father has a heart attack, and the father still sees a woman he once had an affair with but is now dying of cancer). Even in *Proposals* the father dies of a heart attack and both he and his daughter feel abandoned by the mother who left them. And in the comedy *The Odd Couple*, the wives of both Oscar and Felix have left them. Oscar copes but Felix is almost suicidal. Abandonment, of course, doesn't always mean someone actually leaving you. They can be there *with* you, but not be there *for* you. My mother's inability to deal with my childhood illnesses made me feel just as alone as if she were the one who packed up and left instead of my father, who did it time and time again. Obviously, the ultimate abandonment in my life was Joan's death. It was a clue, even the key to why I wrote so much, always in pursuit of putting these ghosts in their place and coming to closure with my childhood fears. Apparently I didn't succeed, since the same themes keep coming up, albeit in different forms. The writer plays mind games, trying to trick himself into thinking he is moving forward in his life, but the words he puts down on paper betray him.

Knowing why you do something—in my case the enormous amount of writing—and doing something about it are not the same thing, and recognizing the "problem" doesn't necessarily mean fixing it. On the contrary, since the writing *always* makes me feel better, always improves my moods, I not only have continued to deal with my fears that way, but eventually I have become addicted to it. It's also why I rarely answer the phone in my office (since I rarely give out the number), because I'm in a safe place. No phone calls of goodbye, no messages of farewell. If it's important, they'll eventually get to me but while I'm there, in my impregnable cocoon, I am, paradoxically, free.

It's interesting, I think, that I've become extremely successful by feeding off my own insecurities and sharing them with a world of people who, in many, many cases, identify with them from their own experiences. I've also been able to find humor in my pain, and if that humor touches those who watch my work, then they find an alternate way of dealing with their own problems. I have been accused by critics of trying to sugarcoat the pain with laughter, but I never thought that was the case. I always thought the humor was the instrument I used to first reach people, and then, as an extension of the characters and stories, I would deliver the underlying issue, the pain that so many of us want to avoid at any cost.

I myself *never* wanted to avoid it. I wanted to take an audience by surprise, to be sure they never saw the pain coming, and when it came, they were pulled into dealing with it and consequently realized that none of us are really that different. This inevitably led critics into accusing me of being middle-class, of pandering to the petty problems of the middle class. Sorry, but I never knew there was a class distinction between those who were abandoned and those who weren't, or between those who were abused or alone or discarded.

By that criterion, then, Shakespeare's kings, queens and princes were no less middle-class. Who felt abandonment worse than Hamlet? Who felt discarded more than Ophelia? And what delights us more than Shakespeare's comedies, the aim of which is not only to make us laugh, but to show us what asses we mortals are?

The final abandonment for the writer, I'm certain, is when he feels he has lost his power to convey himself through words, or even worse, has lost his enthusiasm even to try. And the final humiliation, of course, comes when backs are turned and ears are covered so that people can even avoid listening.

IT BECAME APPARENT, despite the fun we had in Ireland, despite the two new projects that would enable us to work together again, that a change was taking place between Marsha and me. It was not so bad, I thought, that it threatened our relationship, but something had shifted; it wasn't tangible, though, and since it had no name and there were no words to describe it, I let it pass. But something in the shift must have left enough of an impression on me to suggest we might consider finding a place where we could go for weekends and holidays and vacations—a retreat for just the two of us, far from the maddening pressures of our life in Los Angeles.

THE NAME Santa Fe came up. The city was only an hour and thirty minutes by plane from Los Angeles, and its natural and exotic beauty appeared almost monthly in full color in every chic magazine in the country. I had to fly back to New York to meet Manny Azenberg to discuss a proposed revival of the musical *Little Me*, and I told Marsha I would stop off in New Mexico first, and if I wasn't carried off by a pack of coyotes, I would see if I felt comfortable living where the buffalo used to roam.

When I arrived there, I realized why the buffalo disappeared. Santa Fe was just too expensive for them. Someone forgot to tell me that the hour-and-a-half flight only got you to Albuquerque. It was an additional hour-and-a-half drive from there to Santa Fe. I rented a car and as I moved through the prairie and then into the red-clay hills, I was seeing some of the most beautiful country in America. Santa Fe tried desperately to hold on to its simple and historic past, and although it had too many tourist shops, the city had charm, a warm ambience, clean air and the pleasing aroma of mesquite wood burning in fireplaces almost everywhere. It's situated a little over seven thousand feet above sea level, and it took my lungs by surprise.

Since no one was expecting me, I wandered into one of the many adobe real estate offices in town. The man in the bolo tie looked up from his desk and said, "Can I help you, sir?" The four other estate agents suddenly looked up as well when I said, "Yes. I'm looking for a house. Something with a great view." The man in the bolo tie smiled, knowing his work was already half done; I had done the other half by indicating I was in a shopping mood.

As we drove around the city of Santa Fe, I said, "I love the town, but what I am looking for is a retreat, a place for my wife and myself to be alone."

"Privacy," he said as though he had just invented the word. "Know just what you're looking for," and he shifted his four-wheel-drive into high and we headed not only further away from Santa Fe but higher as well. The air got thinner and even clearer, if possible, and I began to feel giddy. "It takes a day or two to get used to the altitude," he said, no doubt noticing that I was taking four breaths to his one.

We soon ran out of asphalt and were now driving on terrain so rough, bumpy and dusty that I was sure even the deer and rabbits looked for alternate routes. We were seeing fewer and fewer houses, and the ones we saw became further apart from one another, until they seemed to disappear entirely, in part because the houses were built to blend in with what nature had built eons ago. We kept climbing until he pointed to the highest point we could see and said, "There's one I think is just what you're talking about."

I could barely see it; I could make out the few geometrical lines of the roof but nothing else. I saw no visible roads leading to the place, and wondered if you just drove up there by instinct or had to attack it with a plan like scaling something in Nepal. "Is there an actual road that goes up to this place?" I asked.

"Oh, yes. Folks who owned it cleared this out when they built it two years ago. You'll get the hang of it."

We were now moving out of the realm of "privacy" and into what would be better described as "isolation." I was now questioning my judgment; did I really want to live in a place you couldn't find or breathe in? And suddenly the house appeared before me, as if rising behind a hill and revealing itself. I stepped out of the car and even if we had been at sea level, my breath would have been taken away. I had never seen views like this in my life.

All around me were three hundred and sixty degrees of the most magnificent vistas, from distant snow-capped mountains to prairies a hundred miles away, to rolling hills and rivers that moved like an endless snake glistening in the sun. Above us the sky was so blue you felt you could see the end of the universe. No matter in what direction you looked, the mood was different. Ahead of me the dark clouds seemed cold and threatening, behind me the sun looked as if it would shine there forever. To my left the trees were green and young, and to my right, the leaves were changing. If you just turned your head slowly, you could see all four seasons at the same time. The wind that blew through the canyons below whistled softly as the leaves on the trees and the tall grass swayed gently in a rhythmic pattern that lulled and quieted your thoughts as you realized you were experiencing, for the very first time, a true glance at tranquility.

Eventually I walked through the house, merely glancing at the rooms. As charming and inviting as they were, I couldn't wait to go back outside and sit on the old bench that looked out on the horizon, knowing I could get lost forever in the kinds of sights and sounds I had never experienced in all my urban life.

As we drove back into Santa Fe, I realized neither one of us was talking. The realty agent knew he didn't have to. He could never be as good a salesman as nature was. I kept hearing the wind as I heard it from where the house was perched on top of the world, saying, "If you turn your back on this house, on this place, on this day, you'd be the biggest fool alive."

I sat in a small room in the realtor's office, talking on the phone to Marsha back in Los Angeles. I rambled on and on, trying to capture in words what my eyes and ears and all my senses had experienced twenty minutes before. Her enthusiasm and excitement were fired by my energy and she was as anxious to see it as I was to describe it. If our relationship had shifted off center by a few degrees, her voice was telling me that maybe we were back on line. I told her I was going to make an offer on the house, contingent on her seeing it and wanting it as much as I did.

Now another common thread was winding itself through my life. It was almost ten years since I drove myself up to Bedford Village, New York, to look for a summer house that might cheer up and possibly heal Joan in her fight against cancer. I bought that house on my own since Joan was in no condition to be driving through the countryside looking at houses. Now, years later, I was looking at another summer house alone, hoping that by my taking the initiative toward something positive, it would heal an ailment of another kind. It was a matter of days before Marsha and I stood together atop that perfect spot a few miles outside Santa Fe. The winding, bumpy, dusty roads never bothered Marsha for a moment. In fact, I think she preferred it that way, just as she never thought it was an "isolated" spot. I watched her face as she stepped out of the car and saw what was waiting. One hand went over her mouth and I could see the tears of pure joy filling up her eyes.

"You mean we could really have this?" she said to me, a variation on her question, "Do we deserve this?" when she first saw the house in Los Angeles.

After filling out the appropriate papers regarding the house, we checked into a nearby hotel. Marsha was animated, discussing how she wanted to furnish the place, and how she wanted to leave the land untouched, preserving its natural state. From the small balcony outside our room, we could see the huge bolts of lightning miles away, turning night into day every few seconds.

On that night in Santa Fe, was I conscious of the identical scenario of those two events, that "common thread," the search for a house on my own, first in an effort to save the loss of a wife and now to save the loss of a marriage? No, I was not. The first time it occurred to me was this very minute, as I write these words on these pages. I find that the writing of a memoir has two functions. One is to pass on, as much as you're willing to tell, the facts and deeds of your life to those who might be at all interested. The other function is to discover a truth about yourself that you never had either the time or the courage to face before. You will never investigate yourself as vehemently as you do when you put one word after another, one thought after another, one revelation after another, in the pages that make up your memoirs, and you will suddenly realize the person you are instead of the person you *thought* you were. To force memory is to open yourself up to that which you have chosen to forget. It's your own Rashomon. You begin to see all the different sides of your own story.

TO PUT THINGS in perspective, I have to back up a little and bring my daughters, Ellen and Nancy, into the picture again. In 1980 Nancy was graduating from the Westlake School. I was asked to give the commencement address for her class. I had long since given up my fear of public speaking, but it returned with a vengeance on that day. The last thing I wanted to do was embarrass Nancy and I worked as hard writing that speech as I would on the first act of a new play. In the fall, she was off to Williams College in Massachusetts and as all parents who put their child on a plane that will carry them away from their childhood, we think to ourselves, "Where did the time go and what will replace those incredible years for me?"

To go back even further with Ellen, she had already given two schools a chance in California, searching for a clue to her future. She moved back to New York on her own, found an apartment, reunited with her former girlfriends from the Dalton School, then attended New York University for a while. She soon found a job in the Holly Solomon Art Gallery in SoHo, but still worked out regularly in dance classes. One of her aspirations was to become a choreographer. Her inspiration was Bob Fosse and eventually she presented an evening of her work at New York's prestigious Lotus Club on Park Avenue.

But there was something pulling Ellen in a completely different direction. As many young people were doing then, she soon found herself looking to fulfill the spiritual side of her life, possibly influenced by Marsha's own interest in Eastern religion and philosophy. I was surprised how deeply Ellen's interest ran when she decided to fly to Bombay, India, to study under the tutelage of a master guru, Swami Muktananda. Neither Ellen nor Nancy had much religious training, and this trip to India must have come from a very deep need to search for something she was missing. When she finally arrived back in California, Ellen seemed more centered than I ever remembered her, and she seemed ready to take the next step in her life. When Muktananda made one of his few pilgrimages to America, he set up an ashram in Santa Monica, just a fifteen-minute drive from our house. She and Marsha went down there quite often and Nancy and I were invited to come to one of Muktananda's sessions. I was amazed to see how many devotees he had. It seemed to me there were almost two thousand happy people squeezed together on the floor, made possible, I suppose, because they all left their shoes outside the main hall.

Nancy and I were respectfully quiet as we listened to Muktananda speak through his interpreter, and what he said was quite inspiring; I could see why he had so many followers throughout the world. Nancy and I, however, did not become converts. It was not because of any lack of faith in his sincerity and his wisdom, but like so many good things that are offered to you in this life, it either has something for you or it doesn't. Through this guru, Ellen not only found the answer to some questions that needed clarifying for her, but she also found a tall, lanky devotee with a warm smile named John Leland. It eventually led to marriage and in December of 1980, she gave birth to a son, Andrew Leland, my first grandchild. Nothing could please a father more or make him feel older than becoming a grandfather.

When one looked at both Ellen's and Nancy's faces, you couldn't help seeing the face of Joan, the same color hair, the same smile, the same special aura that was part of Joan's nature. There was no doubt in my mind that Joan found a way to attend the graduation, the wedding and the birth of her first grandson.

ELLEN DECIDED after living almost a year in Los Angeles that she wanted her son to grow up in the same environment as she had. She and John found a house near Nyack, New York, and from her back porch she could see the Tappan Zee Bridge and the Hudson River. Downriver a few miles was the George Washington Bridge, the same bridge that I passed every day as a boy on my way to school. With my family all now living back East—since Nancy also made it clear that after she graduated from Williams she wanted to find a place of her own in New York—I was wondering what I was doing in California, and now in New Mexico as well. I never seemed or felt comfortable in any other environment than the one I was conceived in, and I'm sure I must have been born with an umbilical cord so ferociously tied to New York that I thought someone in the delivery room never took the time to sever it. This was especially so on the nights I had to drive myself from Santa Fe to our hidden house in the hills without the benefit of a full moon. I never did get the hang of it as the bolo-tied salesman had told me I would, and I wondered if Marsha would mind my installing eight miles of ground lamps that, while they might have bothered the local naturalists, sure as hell would have helped me find home before dawn.

WHEN WORK ON the house in Santa Fe was finished, when Marsha had planted her last tree and hung her last picture, when the last towel rack was in place, hung with the appropriate towels, I stood by in awe. In the early morning she loved sitting on the bench outside, wearing a robe and holding a large mug of coffee, her legs crossed, contemplating the beauty that surrounded her. Perhaps her studying a different way to view life on her trips to Muktananda's ashram in India had prepared her to look within herself and to connect with nature. She found something to do there that I found almost impossible to achieve: she relaxed. I could read a book, I could watch a basketball game, I could play tennis, but I could not sit for two hours or even twenty minutes and just let my mind wander. It had nothing to do with achievement. I was not looking for ideas—they came on their own, and when they did, I sifted through them, tossing out the worthless ones and holding aside those that had a sparkle. Do artists look at a mountain or a sunflower without thinking of how it would look on canvas? I don't know. I must ask one.

I never became disenchanted with the house, but after a while I found that a beautiful view is always just a beautiful view, and my restless mind was suddenly searching for new ways to achieve satisfaction. The day I told Marsha I was going to Connecticut to try out *Actors and Actresses*, the look on her face went from surprise to anger as quickly and as threateningly as the lightning bolts that were almost a nightly occurrence.

"You said you weren't going to do a play for a while," she said with a look of irritation and disbelief I can still remember.

"I'm not doing a play," I answered defensively. "I'm just going to try it out. See how it goes."

"We've just done the house and you're going off to try out a play you may never even do?" she said, her tone incredulous.

"I can't tell unless I try it out. I'm getting restless. I can't paint or plant or just hang out all the time. The fun was doing the house; now it's finished, isn't it?"

She looked at me with a coldness that was chilling.

"Yes. You're right," she said almost calmly. "It is definitely finished."

The word "finished" resonated through the hills and the canyons, making an impact that was all too clear to me. I should have stayed. I should have called off the tryout. But the show was cast, the theater was booked, the director was waiting for me. Whatever compelled me to be in a theater again obviously was more powerful than watching the clouds roll by or staring at a billion stars at night. The stars didn't need my help, but a play about to be born did. My newfound passion for the great outdoors was short-lived. I was an indoor person who thrived in a world where I never got lost trying to find my way home. I was hoping that once I got back from Connecticut, Marsha and I would be able to work things out. I was as wrong as I could be.

I MET MARSHA at the appointed time in the office of her therapist. He was an attractive man in his late forties, extremely bright, but without a trace of warmth or compassion, which I was hoping to find. He was there as an arbiter to help reconcile us. He was, in fact, not a therapist for individual cases any longer, but was now doing something called corporate counseling. I could only picture sixty-seven executives in suits, lying on sofas in a huge gym, where he counseled them from atop a lifeguard's stand, bellowing cheerful clues to more productive gross output through a bullhorn. Marsha was one of his last remaining individual patients. He sat behind a large desk, Marsha and I opposite him but not close to each other. The look on her face, as I recall it, was pained but determined. Her therapist opened the proceedings by explaining to me the state of Marsha's emotional stress, her pain, her dilemma, her sorrow, her regrets and her determination to do what she thought was the only solution to our situation. I was hoping for a reprieve, a last-minute stay of execution. It seemed unlikely. He summed it up in one sentence.

"Marsha would like a separation of six months."

I thought he said six years but six months sounded just as long to me. I nodded that I understood but not that I necessarily was in agreement.

"And how do we accomplish that?" I asked, not knowing what it's like to be separated for six months.

"Marsha will leave. She would like to do this as soon as possible."

I looked at her. She glanced at me to see my reaction, then put her head down. I had screwed up and I knew it, but I was still in love with her and naively thought that a dinner alone with her that night would straighten out everything, clearly another example of the overconfident playwright who thinks he can rewrite anything. I turned back to the therapist, facing reality for the first time.

"Six months?" I repeated as if it had just sunk in. "And how do we live our lives? Does Marsha see other men? Do I see other women? Because I think that six months would be disastrous. It's the same as saying it's all over."

"Not necessarily," he said. "I did it myself," he continued, revealing his own life, which I always thought was anathema to therapists and analysts. "My wife and I separated for months. It can be done."

"And how did it work out?" I asked.

"Not well, we eventually divorced."

I was stunned by his answer. Then I laughed because what else could I do? "Gee, that really worked out swell, didn't it?" I said with needless sarcasm. It was quiet for a moment. No one chose to speak, so I guessed it was my turn again.

"Is this your recommendation?" I asked him.

"It is," he said. "But more importantly, it's Marsha's wish. The situation is regrettable, but it's not negotiable. Still, you never know how these things work out."

I knew how they worked out if he was any example. I looked at Marsha again. I could see the tears about to surface and she turned away again; the look of determination, though, was still there. The meeting was over. I was instructed that Marsha would need the next two afternoons to get her clothes and belongings out. The house would remain the way it was, at least for the time being.

I left the office first. Only in movies would the two of us go down the elevator together. When I got outside, the sun was beating down on me like everything else was, only it didn't warm me. Inside I was as cold as a dead man. Marsha packed up during the next two afternoons and I stayed away in my office. I came back to the house after calling to make sure she had left. I walked around in a daze and wondered what Marsha was feeling at that same moment. I went into her dressing room and opened the closets. Some of her things were still there, but enough was gone to make the emptiness more vivid than even I anticipated. Nine years before I had opened Joan's closet on the day after she died. Everything was still there exactly as she left it, which made her absence even more acute. In both instances, I felt guilty about opening their closets, knowing then that Joan was never coming back, and now that Marsha might never return as well. I felt I was invading their privacy, because in some sense the space was still theirs, even after death or separation. I closed Marsha's closet door, walked into my office, sat at my desk, picked up a pen, looked at it and realized that for the first time in years, I had no desire to write a single word.

Marsha's request was fulfilled. We didn't see each other again for well over six months, and by then, as anticipated, it was too late for both of us. The awful thing about losing a spouse is that, unlike any other bad day you've had at the office, when you come home, there's no one there with whom to share it.

THE SHOT HEARD 'ROUND BEL AIR

21

AFTER FOUR MONTHS of separation, I filed for divorce. There was no word, no sign from Marsha that she wanted it any other way. In California, you have six months after filing to change your mind; during that time, if both parties are willing, you could call off the divorce and return to your marital status. This never happened. As I look back on it, I don't believe my going to Connecticut to try out a play was the only reason for the breakup. It's my belief that some marriages end because they have run out their time. If there are genetic faults in our systems that determine the length of our lives, I believe to some extent that holds true for marriages as well.

From my point of view, Marsha and I had seven incredible years together, but in the eighth year, something terminal infected our marriage, and there was nothing either one of us could do to save it. This is not to say that there weren't other specifics that led to the breakup, but I think even those were inevitable. We simply could not fulfill each other's needs past eight years. In the heat of any marriage that is heading for destruction, it's amazing how many things remain unsaid, unspoken, and it's probably those silent issues that are the ones that do you in. In time, at least in my case, you may even forget what they were. I put no blame on Marsha nor do I accept full responsibility. It takes two to untangle.

Now, almost two decades later, Marsha and I remain friends. We still have the Nancy and Ellen connection, and I have often gone to see plays or films that Marsha is in, always happy to see that she's doing well. This benign state, however, did not exist at the time of our breakup. I was bitterly and ferociously angry at her for leaving. Once obsessed by an abandonment complex, as I was, there was nothing that could defuse the bomb within me to keep it from exploding. Perhaps it was that the split came so soon after Nancy went off to college and Ellen moved back to New York with her new family that triggered my anxiety. I was now living alone in a house that was too big for two people, let alone one. I at least had our dog, Duffy, the sweetest friend a man alone could have. He was, legally, community property, but fortunately I had him for a few years, until Marsha bought her own home and then he spent the rest of his days with her. It's amazing, when you're alone, angry, dismal and fairly neurotic, how much you will talk to your dog. I told him things I wouldn't even reveal to my analyst. He always listened attentively, never interrupted and, above all, never disagreed with me. I let him listen to all my phone calls. I had nothing to hide from him. He occasionally heard some foul language from me, but I always assured him it was never directed at him. And every night he slept with me in my bed. In the early days of bachelorhood, his licking my face could be very comforting.

If Marsha thought I was needy, I don't think she had any idea how deep the bottom of the well was. Abandonment, in my case, only applied to women. When my father died, I accepted it as the natural fate of man. Joan's death probably set the stage for the intensity of my rage at Marsha's going, because, in a way, it was not much different than a death. I knew intellectually that time heals everything, but the bitter weeks and months that followed brought no relief, and suddenly I had no time to allow time to pass.

Marsha was gone from the house; now I wanted her out of my mind. She refused to move, though; in fact, she took over every foot of the house, and even sat staring at me as I ate my meals. She invaded my office as well, sat on my typewriter, made disapproving looks at whatever I had typed on the page, and finally she became the first person ever to find out how to stop me from writing.

Finally, one night, I felt I had to do something so outrageous, so unlike me, so close to madness, that I might be able to stem the tide. I remembered that I had a .38-caliber pistol in the house and a small box of bullets. I had bought the gun right after we had moved into the house, and, for the first and only time it ever happened, someone tried to break in through a back window while Nancy, Marsha and I were at home. The alarm went off and so did the would-be intruder, but the vigilante in me, the protector of his family and his goods, decided to arm himself against any more attempts to harm his loved ones. A while later, I was told by a police officer that a .38-caliber gun was the worst protection I could have had.

"It's a good way to get yourself killed," he said. "Chances are any burglar with a gun knows how to use it better than you. If you feel you really need a weapon, get yourself a double-barreled shotgun. That usually stops them."

This conversation was getting too Wild West for me, so I tossed my small gun far back on the top shelf of a closet, deciding against arming myself for an outbreak of war. But now, years later, I had the gun in my hand, and I loaded two bullets into the chamber. I wasn't quite sure what I was going to do, but there was no chance I was going to empty those bullets into my head. I was angry, but I wasn't crazy. I left Duffy in the house and heard him whimpering as I walked down the steps that led to the pool. I turned the pool lights on. It was about eleven at night and the darkened windows in the large house next door above my hill indicated my neighbors must all be asleep. I sat on the cold brick steps that led down to the pool and just stared into the water. How long I sat there like that, I can't remember, but finally I took one bullet out of the chamber, put it in my pocket and then clicked the other bullet into its firing position. Then I slowly raised my arm, gun in hand, feeling the heavy weight of the barrel; I aimed it carefully, squeezed the trigger ever so slowly . . . and shot the pool. I got it dead center, about where the four-foot part drops off to the deep end. The blast was deafening. I was sure it reverberated all through Bel Air and over into Westwood. I looked up to see if the neighbors' lights had come on, but they hadn't. I waited for two or three patrol cars to suddenly pull up, but they didn't. Actually nothing happened. No one called; no one came. The only thing I heard was my own voice saying in astonishment, "Holy shit! You are nuts!"

Perhaps I was, but sudden calm came over me, a release of all the pent-up anger that I had been storing inside ever since Marsha had left. Firing the gun had set off a noise infinitely louder and more powerful than I could ever have made myself, and I felt like some gorilla in the wild, pounding his chest at what a fearsome creature he was. Then I started to laugh at the idiocy of it, thinking of what would have happened if the police had shown up.

"We heard a gunshot, sir. What happened?"

"It was me, Officer, I fired the gun."

"Someone try to break in?"

"No. Someone broke out."

"Broke *out*? Who was that, sir?"

"My wife. But it's all right. I shot the pool."

"You shot the *pool*? Why would you do that?"

"Well, for one thing, I knew I could hit it . . . I had another bullet but I didn't need it. It was dead."

"The pool?"

"No. The pain."

And it was. I went back into the house, tossed the gun into the back of the closet, got into bed with Duffy at my feet and had the best sleep I'd had in months.

THE PAIN was gone but the complaining lingered on. I no longer made Duffy the sole, dutiful listener of my residual anger. I now turned to my friends, who would nod politely at my daily harangues about the pitfalls of marriage while they tried to eat their Caesar salads and listen at the same time. I was extremely boring for about three and a half months, and then I eased off to being just plain annoying. I had only reached the point of being better than somewhat bearable when the most unlikely person put an end to all of my complaining with one devastating sentence.

I first met Sean Connery and his wonderful wife, Micheline, at a party when Marsha and I were still together and happy. My friendship with Sean developed more fully on a Sunday afternoon at Barbra Streisand's home in Malibu Canyon. It was a fun, games and sports party, and somehow I ended up playing tennis singles with Sean. He was new to the game and I had been playing for about twenty years. As we rallied before the game started, I thought I was the superior player. I decided I was not going to use my A game against him because that would have been poor form, and also because I didn't *have* an A game. At best, I had a B-minus game, although on occasion, I had an A version of a B-minus game, which meant I could sometimes beat B-minus players but was helpless against genuine A players. What I didn't take into account was Sean's competitiveness, his skill as an all-around athlete (he was, I heard, a first-rate soccer player), and that he had learned to play golf to make the *Goldfinger* film and turned into a low handicap player. He also had twice the stamina I did. Still, I was able to keep up with him, and if I won the match that day, it was by the narrowest of margins. I knew that if there was going to be a next time, he already would have taken lessons, and by then would have been a B-plus player, and my fight would be uphill.

After that we began to see each other socially—although only occasionally because he spent most of his time living in Spain—and we had dinners out or dinners at our house. One night we got into a private conversation and I began to tell him what it was like growing up in New York during the Depression with two parents whose behavior with each other was anything but normal. I told him how my mother was playing gin rummy in the kitchen with her lady friends one night, and my angry father, who had not been speaking to her, walked into the kitchen in his pajamas, drank a glass of water over the sink, and then, having said nothing, left and turned off the lights, leaving them all in the dark. Or how he left his suit, shoes and a hat laid out on the floor near the front door looking like someone who just died, just to give my mother the fright of her life as she came home from her sister's one night. Sean laughed uproariously. He loved those stories and wanted more.

He then told me what his dad and brother were like, all growing up in Scotland and how his mother dealt with them. Amazingly, his stories of family life weren't that much different from mine, and we realized how much we had in common in our youth. I was about three years older than Sean. I enjoyed his company enormously and told him it always had been my hope to write a film for him in which he could co-star with Michael Caine, with whom I had already worked in *California Suite*. Sean was eager to do a comedy, although I think audiences preferred him in his action films or in the darker dramas he sometimes undertook.

One day I called Sean in his L.A. apartment that he used as a pied-à-terre, to tell him I thought I had an idea for the film. He asked me to come over and tell him the story, but he warned me that he didn't have too much time since he had a golf date at the Bel Air Country Club. Sean got his golfing clothes ready as I talked and he listened, smiling his broad smile at the parts he liked. When I was halfway through my story, he realized he was going to be late for his match, so he asked me to finish it as we went down to get his car. He closed his apartment door, which was high up on the seventeenth floor or thereabouts, and crossed to the elevator. Suddenly he realized he had left his clubs back in the apartment and didn't have his keys with him. I suggested going down to the concierge and getting an extra key.

"It will take *tew* long," he said in that inimitable Scottish brogue. "I'll get them. I'll be right back."

I watched as he walked down to the end of the hall and opened the window. When I saw him climb out, I rushed down to see where he was going. There he was, climbing along the ledge, seventeen stories above the earth; he eventually found a window open in his apartment and disappeared inside. *Tew* minutes later, he came out of the apartment, his golf clubs slung over his shoulder, and without any comment on what he had just done, said to me, "Go on. Tell me the rest of the shtory." The SH sound was his trademark. He didn't just act James Bond. He *was* James Bond.

Months after the split with Marsha, I was up in Sean's apartment waiting to go out to dinner while Micheline fixed us both a drink. As I had been doing for some time, I continued my harangue about the breakup of the marriage. Sean obviously had had enough of it, and the expression on his face turned as stern as that of a sergeant major in the British Special Forces. He fixed his eyes directly on mine, practically piercing my pupils. He then said to me, making it clear he was going to say it once and *only* once, "Get *off* it, Neil." Then he looked away and finished his drink.

I was shaken but not stirred. I understood immediately that what he was saying was not only that he didn't want to hear it again, but that it was time for me to give it up. The only thing he spared me was not saying, "Be a man, fer Crise sakes." His remark was spoken in a low, almost threatening voice that packed so much power it came at me a thousand times louder than the gunshot that killed the pool.

I finally moved on with my new life, looking to a brighter future, when I suddenly realized that while I had been busy brooding away my time, something awful had been happening to my career.

FROM THE BOTTOM UP

22

ACTORS AND ACTRESSES never made it out of Connecticut. *Fools* ran a few months and closed. The revival of *Little Me* was short-lived. Suddenly the rumor around Broadway was that Neil Simon was through. He had lost his touch. The long consistent ride to the top was over.

If I looked closely for clues as to what went wrong, the answers could be found just in reading the titles of the three failed plays. I had gotten away from my roots, away from the kind of plays that audiences so closely identified with, plays like *Barefoot in the Park, The Odd Couple, Plaza Suite, Chapter Two, California Suite,* and *The Sunshine Boys.* Those plays expressed my own feelings about people and experiences that I knew well, and since writing those plays I had gotten far off the track. Recognizing it was one thing. Getting back on wasn't so easy. I now knew what direction to take, but I wasn't sure what vehicle would be the one to carry me there. There were no ideas flowing freely from my mind as they had done in the past. I felt shaky, and loss of confidence can rob you of the ability to tell a good idea from a bad one. You find yourself staring at a blank wall, one that had never been blank before.

I sat for days and weeks wondering what would happen to me if my playwrighting career truly was over. I was not trained for or experienced in any other kind of work, and like Job, I was wondering if God was testing me or just bored with me. I started to think about the classic, older plays and movies, trying to take them apart, scene by scene, so I could see what made them work, only to reach the conclusion that what made them work was an inspiration on the part of the author. There isn't a writer alive who hasn't gone through this experience. It was especially frightening to me, though, because this was my first time. Was I drying up or had the gunshot explosion clogged my ears, blocking all thoughts from getting through to my brain?

One afternoon, out of sheer desperation, I started to rummage through the drawers of my desk, looking for some idea that I had discarded, but now might spark me if I saw it in a better and fresher light. There was nothing there that was any good, though, and I couldn't think why I even saved them in the first place. I looked in my files where I kept my original first drafts of plays. *Barefoot in the Park* was there, typed originally on cheap yellow paper that was now drying up and beginning to disintegrate, looking something like the Dead Sea Scrolls. (I eventually put it in airtight plastic bags.) I found *The Odd Couple*, drafts one through twelve. I didn't remember doing it over so many times. I was about to close the file when I noticed that in a faded manila envelope, unmarked, was another script. I took it out and read the title: *Brighton Beach Memoirs.* I looked at the date on the lower right corner. I had written it nine years before and had never even looked at it since then. There were thirty-five pages, held together by a small paper clip. I remembered how much Ellen and Nancy had loved those pages at the time, and how they prodded me to finish it. I was unresponsive; I had hit a wall with the play, so I just filed the pages away.

I sat back and read it slowly, surprised by how much I was smiling, even laughing at it. When I finished, I looked up at the blank wall and said to myself, "Wait a minute. I think this is good. *Really* good." I read it once again, and whatever block that stopped me from going on nine years ago had mysteriously disappeared. I knew at that instant in what direction the play should go, and the years that had passed seemed as if they never happened at all. I put a fresh sheet of paper into the typewriter, and seven weeks later I was finished with the first full draft of *Brighton Beach Memoirs.* The mistakes I had made in planning the play the first time became clear. The play took place in 1937, just as the clouds of war were gathering over Europe. I wanted some depth to the characters, to show their anguish and fears in the face of hard times in America during the Depression, and their worries about their relatives in Poland, who might never get out in time. I had tried to write the first version with some humor, but it felt strained and forced. This time I decided there would be only one character in the play with humor, and that would be fourteen-year-old Eugene Morris Jerome, no doubt my own alter ego. The Depression didn't really affect him, and the impending war was a million miles away. He was going through puberty and all he had on his mind was sex, baseball and his annoyance at always having to go to the store for his mother. Fourteen-year-olds have no idea that anything in the world is important except their own immediate needs. To get his own thoughts across to the audience, I had him quote to them from his diary, which he called

"The Unbelievable, Fantastic and Completely Private Thoughts of I, Eugene Morris Jerome, in this, the fourteenth year of his life, in the year 1937, in the Community of Brighton Beach, Borough of Brooklyn, Kings County, City of New York, Empire State of the American Nation." I think I may have borrowed a little of Thornton Wilder's *Our Town* in that description, but if you borrow, borrow from the best.

I sent the play to Manny Azenberg and waited anxiously for his reaction. Manny was ecstatic but also guarded, and even though I thought this play was one of the best I had written, I was extremely tentative about investing my own money in it, as I had done with every play since *The Odd Couple*. Our faith in it dropped still more when the Shubert Organization, who owned most of the theaters in New York, turned the play down. They read it and said it was too episodic. This news invariably would get around Broadway, making our task only more difficult. We then sent the play to James Nederlander, who, with his brothers, were the second largest theater owners in America. I'm not sure if they were crazy about the play, but they took it on, in part, I think, because they were happy to get me away from the Shuberts, whose theaters were the ones I used for almost all my early successes. The offers from investors to put money into the play didn't come quite as freely as they did when I was riding high, but we did have our supporters. One was Bernard Gersten, now one of the guiding lights of the Lincoln Center complex of theaters, but then he was working for Radio City Music Hall Productions. On Bernie's recommendation, they put in a hundred thousand dollars and became co-producers with Manny, along with actor Wayne Rogers, who had his own group of investors.

The pressure on me to succeed was now even greater than it had been with my first play, *Come Blow Your Horn*. One more flop and I would be worse off than a newcomer. I would be a has-been, and a has-been is nothing more than a newcomer whose promise has eroded. On the upside was our choice of director, Gene Saks, who last did the hit *California Suite* for me. For *Brighton Beach* we gathered a wonderful ensemble cast featuring a young teenage boy who was soon to become a major star named Matthew Broderick. Matthew was everything I hoped Eugene Morris would be—shy, intelligent and funny without ever trying to be. Our tryout was to be at the Ahmanson Theatre in Los Angeles and then, barring disastrous notices, it would be on to San Francisco and then the Alvin Theatre in New York.

The set of the small Brooklyn house was perfectly done by designer David

Mitchell. It was small enough to be claustrophobic, especially since it had to house seven people. The walls were paper thin and there were no secrets in the Jerome household. I created the family by doing the exact opposite to what happened to me in my own life. My father left my mother when I was Eugene's age and she and I were taken in by my cousins, Ceil and Martin Klein, who then lived in a small apartment in the East 60s. They later moved to their first home, a little house in Forest Hills, and my mother and I were given a tiny room together, sleeping in the same bed. For a fourteen-year-old boy to be sleeping in the same bed with his mother gave me more emotional scars than I like to think of. I literally slept in the small crack between the bed and the wall, for fear of touching her during the night. That episode was worth at least a year of analysis. My brother, Danny, was taken in by my mother's brother and his wife, Sol and Marie Levy. He did not have the same trouble, since they did not invite him into their bed. With all this happening in two separate houses, I had to rearrange our lives to fit us all into the same house for the sake of the play. What happened in the play was that my mother and father (actually Eugene's) lived with their two sons, Eugene and Stanley, and took in the mother's sister Kate and her two daughters, Nora and Laurie, since Kate's husband died from cancer. When I was a boy, the word "cancer" was never uttered unless spoken in a whisper. This is how Eugene explained it to the audience:

EUGENE: . . . Aunt Blanche's husband, Dave, died—from this thing. It was . . . *(he whispers)* . . . cancer. I think they were afraid if you said it out loud, God would say, "I HEARD THAT! YOU SAID THE DREADED DISEASE! JUST FOR THAT I SMITE YOU DOWN WITH IT" . . . There are some things that grown-ups just won't discuss. For example, my grandfather died from . . . *(He whispers)* . . . diphtheria. Anyway, after Uncle Dave died, he left Aunt Blanche with no money. Not even insurance. And she couldn't support herself because she had . . . *(He whispers)* . . . asthma . . . My father thought it would just be temporary, but it's been three and a half years so far and I think because of Aunt Blanche's situation, my father is developing . . . *(He whispers)* . . . high blood pressure.

Since I was raised in Manhattan, why was this semiautobiographical play taking place in such a distant place as Brighton Beach? The answer: because it was such a distant place. I wanted my father to be beleaguered with problems like a) having to hold down two jobs to support seven people, b) after a hard day's work, having to hear the problems of everyone else in the family, and c) being expected to give advice as sage as that of King Solomon. That responsibility and pressure was enough to give him (whisper) a nervous breakdown. To travel by subway from Brighton Beach to the garment center in New York in the freezing winter or in the brutal heat of summer was more than one man could handle. But Jack did his duty without complaining, and his lack of complaining is what leads to his heart attack in the second act. Troubles beget troubles and to me, this was the stuff that good plays are made of.

During the rehearsals of the play in Los Angeles, a situation arose with our cast of actors that I had never seen before. It was an ensemble company, meaning there were no prominent stars in the cast and no one role more important than anyone else's. There was one exception, however, a very good actress, who was once pretty well known in films. To her credit I'd say she asked for no special favors, no higher salary or more prominent billing. She worked as hard as any other member of the company. But as we got to the beginning of the third week, meaning we had less than two weeks to go before we started previews in front of an audience, the woman in question seemed to get nervous. During rehearsals she would stop the flow of a scene to ask Gene Saks for an interpretation or a different move on stage. Or she might ask, "Wouldn't it be better if I did this or that?" All actors do this kind of thing, but there must come a time when they start to act as a group, and I could see the rest of the cast losing their patience. They were now at the stage where they wanted to rehearse the play without stopping, waiting to hear Gene's comments after they finished the scene. We never could get that far. The actress continued to interrupt, stopping the flow of the other actors' performance, always to ask about *her* part, *her* motivation, *her* position on the stage.

Finally, during a break one day, I talked to Gene about this problem and he agreed that he foresaw trouble ahead, but he is a patient man, and directors always feel they can correct the situation through their own efforts. Another day went by and things did not get any better. That night I left the rehearsal hall shortly after all the actors were gone. It was quite dark, and I started to look for my car parked on a side street in a fairly questionable neighborhood. Suddenly, from across the street, I heard a hissing sound, like four tires going flat one after the other as the air escaped in fits and stars. I turned and looked. From behind a car, I saw shadowy figures beckoning to me with their hands, all hissing to get my attention. I couldn't make out who they were, and was understandably hesitant to respond to hissing and shadowy figures, especially in an area that required cautious people to walk quickly to their cars and drive off with the doors locked. Curiosity, not prudence, got the better of me, however, and I crossed over. Behind the car were six members of the company minus the actress who was causing us so much worry. Their spokesman said to me that it pained them to say what they had to say, that they felt guilty talking about one of their own, and he made it clear that none of them had ever done this kind of thing before in their careers, ever.

Their spokesman continued: "Neil, none of us here wants to hurt a member of our profession, but we also want to protect this play. We all feel this actress is hurting us, hurting Gene and ultimately why we all wanted this job. We've been as patient as we could, but things are not getting any better, and if a move is not made soon, everybody will suffer for it. We're saying this not only as actors, but as the characters you created, the Jerome family, because that's who we feel we are. Obviously the decision is yours and Gene's, and we'll abide by whatever you decide. We love this play and it's the only reason we're standing here whispering in the dark behind a parked car."

With that, they all dispersed into the darkness and went their separate ways. That night I called Gene Saks and he agreed that something had to be done. Our only worry was who could we get to replace her on such short notice. A favorite actress of mine and Gene's was Joyce Van Patten. I had already used her in *I Ought to Be in Pictures*, in which she was superb. We called her, found she was available, and she showed up early the next morning, read the part for us and we signed her on the spot. We did more good work with her in the next ten days than we did in the previous three weeks with the other actress. It may sound cruel to talk so frivolously about dismissing (aka firing) another actress, but the move was made for the betterment of all concerned. It wasn't only Shakespeare who said, "The play's the thing."

When an actor or actress is replaced, the actor who leaves is entitled to their full pay for as long as their contract has stipulated. I've always thought this was grossly unfair to the other actors. One actor who doesn't work out leaves and gets full pay for nine months, while the actor who is a major plus for the play has to perform eight shows a week for nine months to get the same salary. I never thought the producers should benefit for their error in judgment in casting the wrong person, but I did feel a fairer arrangement would be that the fired actor receives full salary for half the term of their contract while the other half of the money should go to the Actors Fund or to Equity, the actors union, for those actors who are in need. I doubt that this change will ever happen but I'm just throwing it out on the table for someone else to examine.

THE PLAY received excellent reviews in Los Angeles and then again in San Francisco. This was still no reason to feel optimistic, however. Success in the New York theater is almost wholly dependent on receiving praise and support from two sources: a good review in the *New York Times*, and a healthy advance sale from the agents who book theater parties, the latter being those large groups of people who buy out half a house or more for a specific night in the future, usually to raise funds for charitable organizations. The largest advance sale in history was the twenty million dollars booked for *The Lion King*. A play, any play by any author in today's world, is lucky to get a million dollar advance sale. In the early 1980s, when I had a play coming in that was preceded by three hits in a row, we often had as much as a two million dollar advance sale. But after two failures in a row, the agents had backed off, and waited to see if the *New York Times* would be favorable to our play. Many people often say to me, "Oh, you don't have to worry about the reviews. You're Neil Simon. People will come to your plays no matter what." Unfortunately, that's not true, and to be perfectly frank, why should it be? The two failures that preceded *Brighton Beach Memoirs* were proof enough of that. We arrived in New York with nowhere near the advance we had had in the past, and the negative review we got from the *New York Times* on the opening of *Memoirs* was certainly no help.

If I can stop the action here for just a moment, I'd like to make a point about the relationship between critics and playwrights, or, more to the point, *this* playwright. Of the thirty plays I've done to date, I can barely remember what the critics in New York wrote about them, with the possible exception of five or six of the plays. I imagine most playwrights would best remember what they said about his or her *first few* plays; the ones that would make the most impact on his or her career. Three strikes and you're out. Your first play, of course, would be the most important. An out-and-out pan could send you scurrying to the nearest community college in hopes of finding a career that would pay you a decent salary and keep your name out of the papers forever. An overwhelming rave review will, of course, keep you temporarily euphoric. After the hoopla recedes, after the parties you're invited to dwindle down to a precious few, after you've heard the question "What are you writing now?" for the thousandth time, the paralyzing fear of having not only to repeat your success, but to surpass it, causes you to lose the strength and confidence to pick up a pen again and aim it at a blank piece of paper. I was lucky. My first play was a moderate success. It bought me time and courage to go back to work immediately because no one out there knew I was out there in the first place.

By the time I had done my tenth play and even the twentieth play, I literally scanned through the opening night reviews, looking for the phrase or two that would predict the future of my latest work. It was a pass-fail business and you took the news stoically or happily. The reviews were obviously important, but only on *that* night, for *that* play, for *that* moment in time. Ask me today what *Times* critic Frank Rich had to say about *Brighton Beach Memoirs*, I'd have to think hard and probably come up with, "I think he didn't like it but he said some pretty nice things about it. I'm really not sure." The point is that time throws all your reviews into a blender and you get no special joy or disappointment in drinking the concoction that pours out because by now your doctor told you you are lactose intolerant. The past is past and you get on with your life because a review that was written ten years ago is only important to some theater student who looks it up on a Web site for an article he is writing about you. We have all of Shakespeare's plays but only a smattering of his reviews.

Now then, back to 1983. With two flops behind me, a weak advance sale and a not-so-good review from the *Times*, it seems implausible now that *Brighton Beach Memoirs* would go on to become the highest-profit-making play in the history of the New York theater, at least up until that time. The audiences simply adored it, and from the day after opening night, they came in droves. What *did* help, of course, was excellent word of mouth and a strong contingent of critics that *did* support the play, so much so that there was almost an out-and-out war among the critics themselves when it came to voting for the New York Critics Circle Award for Best Play. Led by Clive Barnes of the *New York Post*, formerly of the *New York Times*, he and his associates championed our cause, and our play won in a close contest. It was my first New York Critics Award ever. I have this award hanging on the wall of my office and as I was writing these pages, I looked closely at the award and at all the signatures of the critics. I am not a handwriting expert, but it's obvious that one hand signed the names of all twenty-two critics. Was that done not to embarrass those who did not wish to sign the award just because it was given to me? Or is that the way it's usually done? I have a similar award on my wall from the Dramatists Guild and it is clearly signed by each individual playwright—Arthur Laurents, Stephen Sondheim, Peter Stone, Wendy Wasserstein and so on. Is that because writers write and critics don't have the time? It's just another one of life's little puzzles to ponder. I do not take exception to critics or their reviews and I admire a great many of them and have often been helped by them. I cannot in good conscience defend all my plays. Some deserve what they got, and some got better than I thought they would. I guess I'm just wondering who signed all twenty-two signatures for them.

It was the grandest opening night party we ever had, and thanks to our investor, it was held in the lobby of the Radio City Music Hall. That imposing staircase alone is so enormous, we never worried that there weren't enough places for people to sit. I not only felt I was back on track, but that I was starting on a new journey, writing in a style I had been searching years to find. I never had any intention of making *Brighton Beach Memoirs* the first play of a trilogy dealing with the life and adventures of Eugene Morris Jerome, because if *Brighton Beach* failed, who would want to see a sequel to a flop? I will say one thing positive for Frank Rich, since that one thing is all I can count at the moment: despite a negative review, he admitted that there was something to admire in the play, and he wrote at the end of his review, "One hopes there will be a Chapter Two to *Brighton Beach Memoirs*." I did consider that a constructive idea, so one might suggest that these two unlikely people actually collaborated in a way. Talk about Odd Couples.

The play ran for four years on Broadway, a very long time for any play in the post-1950s era; by then I knew where I wanted to get to in my career. My personal life was another matter. I was alone, single and somewhat lost, yet I knew I never wanted to marry again. After one death and one failed marriage, for all the good days it afforded me, another loss was a higher price than I ever wanted to pay again.

SHALL WE DANCE

23

OUR MEMORIES do not always move forward in linear fashion. Our thoughts often jump from real to imaginary, from the present to the past, to better times and to unhappier times, independent of our will. Since I have not planned ahead about what I'm going to write in this book, for some reason, probably a very obvious one, my thoughts suddenly just went back to my mother, now deceased. I miss her today. Not that she was very affectionate, but I always knew I had her full approval—which is what I probably need for an hour or two at this particular moment in my life. I am going through a bad patch as I write this, and the reason why might very well appear in the later pages of this memoir.

I'm not trying to be coy, but merely honest. Just as I never plan what play or film I might write next, I don't plan on what I will write next in these memoirs. As I write these lines at this moment, the "bad patch" I am going through feels as though it might linger, and it might be worth writing about. If it turns out to be a "fleeting pain," it might disappear and not even be worth thinking about. A memoir is in a sense akin to a day-to-day diary, and since I don't know what will happen with my life, I also can't tell as yet what I am willing or not willing to divulge on these pages.

When I think of my mother, I think of two particular days that were unforgettable. This is the first one.

Sometime after the opening of *The Sunshine Boys* film and George Burns's winning of the Oscar, Marsha threw a fiftieth birthday party for me, upstairs at the Bistro Restaurant in Beverly Hills. There were about a hundred guests and my mother sat at our table, a seat away from Jack Nicholson. She looked her best, as she always tried to do, and was basking in the glory of her son's success. The irrepressible Jack Nicholson, wearing his usual dark glasses, even at night, seemed to be starting his sentences somewhere in the middle of a thought, which did not encourage my mother to attempt to enter into conversation with him. Instead, she was looking down at the far end of the room where George Burns was sitting with Walter Matthau and his wife, Carol.

In a play I had not yet written nor even thought about at that time, there is a scene where the mother (based on my own) talks to her son about the night she danced with actor George Raft when she was a young girl. The scene was based on a story my mother had told me over and over, ever since I was a boy. When she was sixteen years old, living in the Bronx, Mamie Levy (my mom) was known as one of the best ballroom dancers in the neighborhood. A young man would have to be pretty light-footed on the dance floor to have the nerve to ask my mother for a spin around the room. One night, a young George Burns, who was better known then for his fox-trots and his tangos than he was for his comedy, dropped in to look over the new crop of up-and-coming young dancers. In the play I used the name of George Raft instead of George Burns, since a Latin Lover made the story more provocative. But it was George Burns who spied her on the floor that night, and chose her as his dancing partner for the better part of the evening. The next day, Mamie Levy was the talk of the East Bronx. Overnight she had become, at least in that small corner of the world, a star.

My mother played and replayed that glorious night in her life, telling it to me over and over again from the time I was seven, through my entire childhood. I'd nod each time she told it to me and say, "Gee, that's great, Mom." And each time she'd say to me, "You don't believe me." No matter how much I protested that I did, she would still insist that I didn't believe her. Especially when George became a great comic star with his wife, Gracie Allen, my mother was positive that I would never believe her.

Now it was fifty-five or sixty years later, and she was finally in the same room with George again. I knew this was an opportunity not to be missed and I said, "Mom, come with me. I want to introduce you to George." To my surprise, she declined. "No, I'd be embarrassed. He'd never remember me."

"Well, you could remind him," I said.

"No, it's all right. Besides, you never believed that story."

I felt frustrated but I didn't push it. Twenty minutes later, George started to make his way around the room to take a few bows for his Academy Award. With the ever-present cigar in hand, he stopped to say hello to everyone, and never left a table before he got his big laugh, which was always well earned. The six-piece orchestra was playing and people started to get up to dance. I watched my mother's eyes as she watched George getting closer to where we were sitting, never giving an indication of how she would handle it if they were to meet. When he finally came over, he put his arm around my shoulder and said to me, "Keep up the good work, kid. Someday you'll make it." I laughed, my mother smiled politely. Then he looked at my mother and said to me, "And who is this attractive lady, Neil?"

I said, "George, this is my mother, May Simon."

She nodded, smiled and said nothing more than "How do you do."

I assumed George would turn and move away to work the next table, but instead he said, "Mrs. Simon, would you give me the honor of this dance?"

She didn't miss a beat. "I would love to," she said as she got up and was led by George onto the dance floor. She danced gloriously with him, and he moved her gracefully across the hardwood as if time had never passed, although he was now eighty and she was just a few years younger. As I watched them, they didn't seem to exchange a word, their feet being more compatible than their conversation. Everyone was watching them as they glided to the far side of the room, sensing something special was happening, but not having a clue as to what. They made their way now toward our side of the room and I was praying the music would never stop. As she neared our table, George gave her a little spin as his back was to our table and she was facing me. She caught my eye, looked at me and said softly so that not even George could hear, "Now do you believe me?"

The tears welled up in my eyes. It is an indescribable moment when a son sees his mother getting the greatest thrill in her life. She handled it with grace and dignity, but I could see she was overflowing with joy. She never once said anything to George about that night sixty years before in a Bronx ballroom, and she never repeated the story to me ever again. There was no need to.

THE OTHER OCCASION was a much sadder one. As my mother reached her late seventies, for the first time in her life she began to show her age. She always had youthful-looking skin, right up to her mid-seventies, but now the ravages of time were taking their toll. It was also evident in her walk and in her lack of energy; by this time, she would not have had the strength to dance around the room with George Burns, even to prove to me that she had been telling me the truth.

I found her a very nice hotel for elderly citizens called Westwood Horizons, just a short drive from my house. I managed to get her an extra large suite, despite her protests that I should save my money, but she eventually luxuriated in it. I spoke to her on the phone every day, and if I missed a single day, she would call saying, "When I didn't hear from you, I thought, God forbid, you were in a terrible accident." I picked her up on as many Sunday afternoons as I could to take her out to dinner along with Marsha. She loved lobster tails, but only once in a great while could I coax her to order them, since she feared it would send me to the poorhouse.

Her eightieth birthday was coming up, and although she frowned on birthday parties, I persuaded her to come to my house to celebrate this very special occasion. She couldn't refuse when she heard that her two sons and her four grandchildren all would be there. On the day, I picked her up at the Westwood Horizons; she was looking particularly frail. Still, when I entered the lobby, she was sitting erect in a straight-backed armchair, looking as regal and as well dressed as she could, a message to the other mothers who were sitting there for *their* children to pick them up that she was doing just fine. It was, in some respects, a poignant sight to see these aging parents waiting for and depending on their offspring to bring some much-needed joy into their lives. The silk and lace competitions that were waged by these women, wearing their Sunday best, continued every weekend. On some weekends their children couldn't come, but they'd sit there as if waiting anyway, not to allow anyone to think that their children didn't care. Since the men rarely lived as long as the women, they were seen less often in the lobby, choosing either to wait for their family on the street outside the hotel, or to stay in their rooms and play cards rather than face the "indignity" of being cared for.

My mother nodded and smiled when she saw me and always made a point to introduce me as her son, Neil Simon, to all the women I had already met over a dozen times. Her hand was cold and bony as I helped her up and out of the lobby to my car parked out front. She was quiet as I drove, and she seemed not to want her thoughts exposed to me for fear of ruining the party we had prepared. Arriving at my house, she was extremely slow in getting out of the car, even with my help. It was difficult for her to maneuver the few steps to my front door, and she stopped a second to catch her breath.

"Are you all right, Mom?" I asked her.

Before she took the next step, she said to me without resignation or self-pity, "I think I've had enough."

She was telling me that she knew she was going soon and it was the first time she ever admitted something like that to me. In times of sickness or crisis in her life, she would always say to me, "Don't worry. You know me.

I'm a fighter." She had suffered in many ways during her life, but she always weathered the storms. I think it was the dancer that still danced within her that kept her going.

The dinner went well, but as she opened the many presents set before her, you could see the anguish on her face. She wouldn't say it, but I knew she was thinking, "Why buy me all these beautiful gifts when I know I won't be around to enjoy them?" When she eventually died, I found her bankbooks. All the money I gave her, all the weekly checks were intact in her account, and all of it was left to her grandchildren.

In the last four or five months at Westwood Horizons, I hired a nurse to keep her company from breakfast till dinnertime. The nurse was an African-American woman in her fifties, whose name I regret not remembering now, but she was very close to my mother. The nurse owned a very small apartment in Palm Springs. The very mention of Palm Springs conjured up images of large, expensive homes of the rich and famous, with a pool for every house and a golf course for every resident. This was obviously not what my mother's nurse owned. My mother was not one to ask for favors, but surprisingly, one day she said to the nurse, "Why don't you take me to your fancy apartment in Palm Springs one weekend?"

"It's not fancy, May," she said. "It's just a studio apartment, but if you'd like to go, I'll take you this weekend."

That Sunday morning I got a call from my mother. "You'll never guess where I am," she said with more vigor than I had heard from her for months.

"Where?" I asked.

"I'm in Palm Springs with all the swells."

It pleased me and amused me. With all the major celebrities she met at the openings of my plays and films, somehow she seemed more impressed at spending a weekend with "the swells in Palm Springs," albeit not in very fancy digs. She called me again later that afternoon sounding even healthier and happier than she had in the morning.

"You'll never guess what I did this morning," she said, sounding more like my daughter than my mother.

"Well, I know you didn't play eighteen holes of golf, so tell me."

"I went to church. The nurse was going to leave to go to her church and I said I didn't want to be left alone. So, I said, good, I'll come with you . . . Well, you know I'm Jewish and I've never been in a church in my life, but it was beautiful and the priest, or whatever he was, made a wonderful speech.

When we started to leave, he stood at the door shaking everyone's hand. He blessed them and thanked them for coming. When he took my hand, I said, I have to tell you the truth. I'm Jewish . . . He smiled and said, 'I'm delighted. We welcome all faiths here. Thank you for coming' . . . Can you imagine?" she finished.

She had just had the time of her life, and told the nurse she wanted to go again soon. They planned to drive back to L.A. in the morning. Two hours later my phone rang again.

"Oh, Mr. Simon. I'm so sorry . . . Your mother just passed away. She was taking a shower. I was two feet away from her, holding her robe. But she went so quickly. I'm so sorry, Mr. Simon," she said through her tears.

I was stunned but not grief-stricken. I was happy that my mother died painlessly and quickly, and that her last day of life was such a happy one.

She was buried at Hillside Cemetery, in a plot not too far from where all the stars of her youth were now resting: Al Jolson, Jack Benny, and Eddie Cantor. George Burns would join them later. I knew she'd be pleased, and I pictured her telling all the friends in her building where she was buried.

It wasn't until the day of the funeral that I allowed all my tears to flow. It was not the same enormous pain I felt when Joan died, but more of a remembrance of how much love I always felt and received from my mother.

Two days after she died, I did the strangest thing. Unwittingly, I picked up the phone, called the Westwood Horizons, and asked to speak to my mother. I hung up before the operator could even answer me.

Some habits are just hard to break.

THERE IS one more story about my mother that I think is worth telling, since it's always been on my mind.

When I was about seven years old, I had warts on many fingers of my hand. Conventional wisdom would tell you to see a doctor, who would painlessly remove them with an acid solution. My mother thought that doctors were only good to marry but not to go to. Like many mothers of that generation, she had her own cure for the removal of warts.

"First," she said to me, "you go to an empty lot." Already I began to worry. "You take a raw potato with you," she said. I was now almost willing to live with my warts into old age. She continued. "You rub the potato on the warts, then drop the potato over your left shoulder. Then you walk away . . . but remember," she said emphatically, "don't look back at the potato."

Some of it sounded, to my seven-year-old mind, almost practical. Perhaps there was a chemical compound in raw potatoes that was able to remove a wart, which, I later found out, is actually a virus. Where she lost me was when she said, "Don't look back at the potato." This was obviously Jewish voodoo. I was surprised she didn't also add that at the same time I must have a dead owl on my shoulder . . . and burnt plucked chicken feathers in my pocket.

I wondered if this remedy was based on old folk lore. Since my mother came from Lithuania, I didn't believe the part about "go to an empty lot," because *all of Lithuania* was an empty lot, and since all of the Jewish peasants were penniless, no one would leave a perfectly good potato on the ground.

What was more amazing than my mother's frighteningly illogical instructions was that the next day I found myself actually standing in an empty lot with a raw potato in my hand. All alone. I even wore my only tie because I thought this might be a sacred ritual.

The other problem was that there was an apartment house on either side of the empty lot. This meant that if someone in those buildings was looking out the window, they would call their entire family together to watch—and laugh hysterically—while this seven-year-old kid rubbed a potato on his hands and then dropped it over his left shoulder. However, they wouldn't think it odd that I didn't look back at the potato, because who could think someone would tell you not to look back at a potato?

I braved it anyway. I stood there in the middle of the empty lot, looked up and nonchalantly whistled a happy tune as if I were waiting for a bus that drove into empty lots to pick up any children who were holding potatoes.

Then I held the hand with the potato *over* the hand with the warts, and I looked up at the sky, hoping that my audience in the windows would look up at the sky as well, while I quickly rubbed the potato over the warts. Then I yawned, stretched my arm up behind me, and quietly dropped the potato over my left shoulder. I was only seven years old, but I *knew* I was doing something unbelievably stupid. I then slowly walked away from the lot. The temptation to look back at the potato was enormous, and resisting it taught me more about discipline than two years in the Army. I thought if I brought a hand mirror, I could hold it up and look at the potato, without turning my head, thus avoiding the curse that would have followed me all my life. Lot's wife knew what I was talking about. But I resisted, and it wasn't so much that I was afraid of being turned into salt. I just wanted to get rid of warts.

For the next three days I not only looked to see if the warts were gone, but

I watched them *all day long*. I wanted to see them actually disappear, proving that my mother had more medical knowledge than Louis Pasteur and Albert Schweitzer together. On the fourth day the warts were still there. On the fifth day, they looked like they were getting bigger. I was afraid I had angered the Jewish Voodoo God by being a disbeliever, and he was now going to turn my entire body into one giant wart. I would be headlined in circuses as Waldo, the living wart. I'd be shown all around the world. I would meet presidents, kings and queens and P. T. Barnum. They all would want to meet me, but they wouldn't want to shake my hand—which I wouldn't have anymore anyway.

Finally I couldn't take it, and I went to my mother and showed her my hand. "Look, Ma. The warts didn't go away." She looked at my hand carefully, then said to me, "You must have looked back at the potato."

The next day my father took me to a doctor who dabbed an ointment on the infamous warts, and they soon started to disappear. I said to him, "Doctor, is it possible to make warts disappear by rubbing a potato on them in an empty lot?"

"My mother told me the same story," he said to me. "That's why I went to medical school."

AFRICA HOT

24

IT WAS TIME to follow up on Frank Rich's suggestion that I write a Chapter Two to *Brighton Beach Memoirs*. I was told by a feature writer at the *New York Times* that Mr. Rich hoped I would write about my days as a young writer on the hit television program *Your Show of Shows* starring Sid Caesar. It was a good idea, but it wasn't time for that play yet. Since I was now planning to do a series of semiautobiographical plays, I wanted to do them in sequence, as they happened in my life. Following the years covered in *Brighton Beach*, the next major event in my life came when I entered the Army Air Force and took my basic training in Biloxi, Mississippi.

In 1943, I was sixteen years old and months away from graduating from DeWitt Clinton High School in the Bronx. Sixteen is young to finish your high school education today, but back then I went through the "rapids" where you could do four years in two, if your grades were good enough. The war was still raging in Europe as well as in the Pacific. I am not brave, not by a long shot. Yet at sixteen, I found myself downtown at the Naval Recruiting Station trying to enlist to be a part of our fighting forces. The petty officer in charge looked over my application, then looked me over from head to toe.

"How old are you, son?" he asked.

"Seventeen, sir," I lied.

"Do you have a letter of consent from your parents to join the Navy?"

That stopped me for a moment, but *just* a moment. "Yes, sir, I do. I forgot to bring it with me. I can have it here tomorrow," knowing I would go home that night and forge a letter from my parents. I would also have to forge some weight on my body because I was skinny as a pencil.

"You look a little thin," he said. "I'll tell you what. You go home, put on about fourteen pounds, then wait till you're eighteen and come see me again in two years. I'll remember you, I promise . . . Next!"

So much for the Navy. When I graduated school that spring the war was still going on, but I thought that in two years it would be over and I'd miss it.

My desire to join was not predicated on my patriotism or my desire to fight our country's enemies. It was based solely in what I was seeing in the movies in those war years, films like *Flying Tigers* with John Wayne, *Air Force* with John Garfield and *Destination Tokyo* with Cary Grant. I never thought about dying overseas because every few months John Wayne, John Garfield and Cary Grant were always in a new movie. What I was really looking forward to, though, was walking into a USO dance in my Air Force uniform and meeting starlet Susan Hayward, who was willing to give up her film career to spend the rest of her life with me. I was also looking forward to being wounded (not in a life-threatening place, of course) and cared for by nurse Lana Turner, who spent more time with me than any other patient, including top-ranking officers. It was the medals on my uniform as I walked through Times Square, meeting Judy Garland under the clock at the Biltmore Hotel on my last night's leave and deciding to get married right then, or maybe we'd just take a bus ride down Fifth Avenue, so much in love she thought she would die. For a high school graduate, I was the Most Adolescent in My Class.

Waiting impatiently to grow older and heavier, I spent the next year working in an advertising agency as a messenger boy, writing comedy sketches in my few spare minutes and showing them to copywriters and asking them for opinions and suggestions. They didn't have any. They were too busy trying to come up with a catchy phrase to sell their Black and White Scotch, with the ever-present black and white Scottie dogs in the ad. In the years before television, you could get away with running the same ad in the paper for three or four years. That was why the copywriters were taking three-hour lunches. It was also possible they were imbibing the product they were advertising. I got my best results by showing my sketches to the secretaries, one in particular. I had an incurable crush on a girl there who was both the prettiest and the smartest because she laughed at every line I had put down on paper. Unfortunately I lost her to a Marine who was twenty-eight and covered with battle ribbons from the epaulet on his left shoulder to the one on his right shoulder.

At seventeen, I found I could enlist in the Army's Specialized Training Reserve Program, which meant that you would be sent to a university, where you could train for active duty and get a year's worth of college education at government expense. I enlisted, was accepted and waited for my shipping orders. I was crazy about the term "shipping orders." I had never been out of New York City until then and I was hoping I'd be sent to the University of Arizona or Georgia Tech or Texas A&M. This could be my only chance to travel and see America before the war ended, and I would have to go back to being a messenger boy for Black and White Scotch. I was thrown a goodbye party by my parents and friends and the best gift I got was an ID bracelet. I wore it proudly and wisely, since it was possible I could get killed in the crowd following the football game between the University of Texas and Texas A&M. I envisioned being sent home in a slow-moving train, taking the same route that President Lincoln's body took shortly after his assassination. I would be buried in Arlington Cemetery with full honors. Maybe Susan Hayward would be there in a veil to cover her tears.

A few weeks after I turned seventeen, I received my shipping orders. With trembling, excited fingers, I tore open the official-looking document. It was not the University of Arizona or Georgia Tech or Texas A&M. I was being sent to New York University, which had an additional campus up in the Bronx. I went there on a trolley car, but I could have just as easily walked. Life is much more shattering than we could ever imagine.

AT NYU, we mostly marched and did gym exercises. The most difficult for me was climbing the thick hemp rope that hung from the ceiling twenty feet above the floor. I could get about five feet off the ground and that was about it. I would hang from there for about four or five minutes, making them think I was having a gall bladder attack but still bravely trying to make my way up to the top. It didn't work after a while because no one could have that many gall bladder attacks. Most of the other soldiers could get up there as fast as those Pacific natives who climb up palm trees to get coconuts. I asked the sergeant why this exercise was necessary. I assumed you would use it only if you were taken prisoner of war and wanted to escape by climbing over the wall. But what were the chances of there being a rope exactly where you wanted to escape? He failed to see my logic.

I didn't do well in the classroom either. We were taught only three subjects: trigonometry, physics and advanced science. All three were my very worst subjects. My luck was running bad. I was at the bottom of my class in studies and at the bottom of the rope in gym. I was, however, quite good at marching. As a matter of fact, since I was doing so badly in the first two, very often they would send me out to march alone. All around the campus. In snow or sleet.

There was another problem that soon came up. I had enlisted to go into officer candidate school once I was in the actual Air Force, and there I would be trained to be either a fighter pilot or the pilot of a bomber. No one asked if I could drive a car, which I couldn't, but I assumed someone would drive me out to the field and help get me into my plane. I was also found to be color-blind, unable to distinguish some colors from others, particularly blue and brown. This left a very good chance that I could easily bomb London instead of Berlin. I could sense that the Air Force would have to rethink their plans for me.

On July 4, 1945, I turned eighteen, and a week later I received my orders from the Air Force. I was to report to Grand Central Station on the morning of August 8, where I would be met, along with a hundred or so other young men, all from New York State, by three noncommissioned officers, and then taken by train to Fort Dix, New Jersey. There we were to receive our shots, uniforms and indoctrination into a life that I was completely unfit for. My parents, much to my embarrassment, accompanied me to Grand Central to say goodbye.

The war in Europe was already over, and Japan was just about to capitulate after the bombings of Hiroshima and Nagasaki. Nevertheless, our company sergeant shouted as we were about to board the train, "Say goodbye to Momma, we're off to Yokohama."

In a lot of ways, the Army was like a bad musical comedy.

ON MY SECOND DAY at Fort Dix, our arms were pounding with pain from the myriad of shots we had received from the medics, whose ineptitude at giving shots was so great that we could only assume they arrived as recruits just the day before we did. On that morning, we received our first day's duty. Wearing our fatigues, sort of a dark khaki jumpsuit that was issued already prestained to show you how it should be done, our job was to pick up every cigarette butt in the area, the area being most of New Jersey. We had to split them open with our fingers, roll up the paper and release the left-over tobacco to the winds, which eventually blew into Pennsylvania, making its way across country to Idaho. In Idaho, the tobacco was served to pigs that produced bacon that was already smoked. It was menial and embarrassing work and I was glad Lana Turner didn't drive by that day. The lowest point of the day was when a truckful of soldiers rode by, laughing their heads off at us. What made it so humiliating was that the truckful of soldiers were German prisoners of war. German laughter, a rare sound indeed, is infuriating when you're the recipient.

After a five-day railway trip from Fort Dix, New Jersey, to Biloxi, Mississippi, where we tried to sleep on hard-back seats, the floor, the baggage rack above or on the john after a two-hour wait to get in, we looked like seasoned veterans. For fuel, the engine of the train was fed a combination of coal, wood, paper, Army shoes and used tires from jeeps. The soot that emanated from the funnels covered the once beautiful green hills of Delaware, North Carolina, Georgia and the Gulf Coast with ten inches of black residue that didn't come off until the Korean War some five years later. It got into our hair, our eyes, ears, nostrils and mostly on our food. Everything looked like it was made by the cook who created blackened catfish. You kept chewing long after you finished your food. Our blackened faces made us look like camouflaged commandos just back from blowing up munition dumps. At every whistle-stop along the thousand or more mile trip, people appeared from nowhere, waving flags at us and throwing doughnuts, kisses and, in some cases, telephone numbers, to the brave young men who were giving their all for their country. And we hadn't even arrived at Biloxi yet.

It's not true that the equator is the hottest spot in the world. Biloxi, Mississippi, in August easily topped it by twenty degrees, all humidity. As I marched and crawled from the train to the camp two miles away, I also carried a duffel bag that was not only sweating, but which also seemed weighted with unused cannonballs from the Revolutionary War. I thought to myself, "I can't take this. I'll be dead in three days. I must talk to our sergeant and tell him that the Army would be better served if they sent me to Nantucket or to Maine in the early fall when the leaves were just turning. I would definitely not be able to do my best soldiering in this oven."

In the play *Biloxi Blues*, Eugene Morris Jerome, né Marvin Neil Simon, complained weakly as he trudged the dusty road with his buddies.

"Boy, it's hot . . . This is really hot . . . This is like Africa hot . . . Even Tarzan couldn't take this kind of hot."

For years afterward, these words were quoted by cab drivers in New York, football announcers in Southern Florida and gamblers who just stepped out of a casino in Las Vegas. It caught on everywhere. When traffic cops recognized me as they stood in the middle of traffic at 57th and Broadway, they'd smile and call out, "Hey, Neil, it's like Africa hot today, right?"

Once in San Diego, I was driving to the airport, deep in thought on the new play I was trying out at the Old Globe Theatre, and I missed a stop sign. I was pulled over by a policeman.

"You know you just went through a stop sign there?"

"Did I? I'm sorry, I wasn't thinking. I guess I did."

"Let me see your driver's license." He looked it over carefully, then squinted at me. "Neil Simon? Are you Neil Simon?"

"Yes, officer."

"Africa hot? That Neil Simon?"

"That's right."

"Wait a minute," he said, then turned and called to another cop. "Charley! You know who this is? It's Africa hot."

Charley came over, smiled and shook my hand. "Not even Tarzan could take this kind of hot, heh?" he said, laughing. After two autographs signed "Africa Hot . . . Neil Simon," I was set free with a polite warning to watch out for stop signs.

I've always worried about the translation of my plays into foreign languages. I write idiomatically. Also very New York. There is some humor that is almost impossible to explain to someone who just doesn't get it. I cannot explain why "Africa Hot" is funny, but it just is. The audience laughed at every performance of the play that I attended and every time I saw it on the screen. What Eugene means, obviously, is that "this is as hot as Africa." Not funny. Just a statement. "Even Tarzan couldn't take this kind of heat" is mildly amusing, but not as funny as "this kind of hot." What I was trying to convey was the state Eugene was in when he arrived in Biloxi on that steaming day, dragging two tons of duffel bag—that was how he was going to spend the next two months.

During times of great stress, your mind plays cruel tricks on you, and you realize that you don't have the mental capacity or physical strength to say things correctly. A man who's lost in the desert for a week and suddenly sees a caravan come along might drop to his knees, hold out his arms and ask pitifully through his cracked, parched lips, "Water . . . water." If he were in a restaurant, he would say, "Oh, waiter. May I have a glass of water, please?" Biloxi in August was not a restaurant. Saying fewer words, mangling the syntax and not giving a damn about the grammar would be the only way you could communicate. Thus, "this is like Africa hot" not only makes sense to Eugene, it is understood perfectly by the other dehydrated soldiers whose brains have turned to dry rot. So far I think I've been able to explain this to you in understandable English. But to put these expressions into Spanish, Swedish, Russian or French, there probably is no equivalent expression as "this is like Africa hot." They would inevitably go to the nearest translation, which would be, of course, "this is as hot as Africa." No laughs. No applause. No good reviews. No royalties.

I guess one would have the same concerns for Shakespeare. How did they translate all his magnificent plays and still have them rhyme in couplets? Their rhyme would have to be different from Shakespeare's English, and I doubt that he ever saw a penny in foreign royalties. Still, many of my plays have enjoyed great success in Europe although sometimes for different reasons. They lose the humor so they go more for the character and the story. I once saw *Plaza Suite* performed in Holland. Some of *Plaza Suite* consists of meaty, gritty dramatic scenes, but more than two thirds of it is meant to be funny. In the Dutch production that I sat through painfully, there was hardly a laugh all evening. Not even a hint of one. But as the final curtain fell, the audience rose to their feet and gave it a standing ovation. They didn't see the play I meant but saw it as being more serious, which Europeans generally prefer. Charlie Chaplin solved the international problem by never speaking a word. Unfortunately, I didn't know how to write silence.

HAVING GROWN UP in the safe confines of Washington Heights in upper Manhattan, I never noticed the word "bigotry" used nor even the act of bigotry, certainly not in the ugly way we've come to know it in the last few decades. There were neighborhood fights, to be sure, but mostly it was because you lived below 170th Street or on the wrong side of St. Nicholas Avenue. We fought for our territorial rights, not our color or creed. Even at that, there wasn't much fighting. There was a lot of wrestling to the ground and once in a while there was a punch thrown. None of us knew or even suspected that in a few more years, six million Jews and others would go to their deaths in gas chambers in Germany, or that blacks were being lynched in the South. By the time I joined the service, I knew there was mass murder going on, but I still hadn't seen much bigotry. At least until I came face-to-face with it when I was thrown together with a kind of people I never knew existed before I hit the Army. On my second day in Biloxi, I was passing the post exchange where the beer was sold, and I was tripped up by a couple of tipsy noncoms, who laughed and said, "Don't they teach you how to walk in New York, Jew boy?" Another flipped a lit cigarette at me and said, "Pick that up, Hymie. Don't think you Jews can come down here and mess up the beautiful state of Mississippi." These two men were our cooks and weighed about two hundred and sixty pounds each, most of it beer sweat, so I didn't need a lot of experience to know I'd better keep my mouth shut, continue walking and not look back.

The "colored boys" were segregated and the word "nigger" was still quite popular in this region. At eighteen, some boys hardly shaved, and the smoother your skin was, the more likely you'd be called "faggot" with an invitation to come into the latrine and "have some of this." I was so naive that the more my eyes were opened to a world I barely knew existed, the more my mouth was closed for fear of getting my teeth knocked out behind the barracks by an angry cook who hated anyone who could spell a word with more than five letters in it.

It was this story I wanted to tell in *Biloxi Blues*, not to open the minds of audiences in the 1980s, who knew it only too well, but to make the generation of eighteen-year-olds aware that we must always be on guard. I also wanted to tell of Eugene's rite of passage, of losing his virginity and then meeting the first girl he ever fell in love with at a dance in a Catholic girls school in Gulfport, Mississippi. This, plus the fear and poignancy of young men being thrust into a life much more harshly and speedily than they would have had they never left the comfort and safety of family and home, were to be the themes of my play.

FEAR AND LOATHING aside, I made a pretty poor soldier. At five A.M. we were thrust out of our semibearable cots, onto the dusty ground in front of our barracks. We were going on a ten-mile forced march. I never knew what that expression meant except that we were forced to do it. We were given ten brief minutes of instruction of how to pack our backpacks correctly and how to fold our mosquito netting, which would be the most important piece of equipment we'd be taking. This was followed by the phrase "swamp land," which put terror into my New York heart. I am not always a very good listener, especially to directions. In the external world, I am an explorer without a map. I was never taught how to write a play. I found my way through years of experimenting, making mistakes and painstakingly fixing them. I did not, however, have years to learn how to pack my gear or fold my netting before leaving for our forced march into Swamp City; I had only moments.

A mile into the march, under a blazing hot sun, my backpack simply fell apart, falling piece by piece onto the dusty road. There was no one willing or anxious to help me since they were all busy enough laughing their heads off.

They made the German prisoners seem like my best friends. It was right out of an Abbott and Costello movie. Every time I bent down to pick up my small shovel, I would drop my canteen. When I picked up my canteen, my helmet fell off. It felt as if I were carrying three cartons of milk without the cartons. As we approached the end of the ten miles, I was not only exhausted, I was also missing half the equipment the Army gave me. Needless to say, I had to pay them for the loss. For what it cost me, I would have been better off taking a forced cab ride.

But there was good news ahead. I saw cabins in the distance. I would not need my shovel to dig a foxhole. Why the cabins were hotter than the blazing sun, I'll never know. There were bunks with wooden slats but no mattresses. That was no problem because we were told to double-fold our blankets across the slats and use our backpack as a pillow. Mine would be a very flat pillow, since my pack was almost empty and my blanket was five miles back, just off the dusty road, now probably the home of squirrels and field mice. I watched how my buddies carefully unfolded their mosquito netting and stretched it over the bunk, and then tucked in the sides. Even if I was smart enough to remember their instructions on how to put your mosquito netting into place, I was too tired to care. I collapsed onto my slats and threw the damn netting over my head, arms, body and feet. I soon fell asleep, being serenaded by the buzzing of a billion insects now gathering at the edge of the swamp, synchronizing their watches for the exact time they would attack.

I awoke in the morning to find soldiers looking at my face and saying, "Holy shit, what happened to you?" I was told that my face looked like a field of fresh strawberries. What it felt like was tiny little bubbles of hot lava. I also now had earlobes the size of a Ubangi tribesman. The mosquitoes went home that day with enough of my blood to start up their own blood bank in the woods.

Since the mosquito netting episode was noted on my record, the Air Force nixed the fighter pilot idea. Six weeks later, I was shipped off to Lowry Field in Denver, Colorado, just about the same time the swollen strawberries were shrinking. The war was now over and we young recruits had to fill the shoes of the departing veterans. Since they still had an Air Force and planes to go with it, I was sent to gunnery school. I was put in a small darkened room, barely making out a screen set up just ahead of me. There were buttons to push, located on a stand just at my fingertips.

"An enemy plane will appear on the screen at any time. The moment you see him, you start to fire. Wait a second too long, and you and your crew are dead men . . . Are you ready?"

"Ready, sir."

I squinted at all four corners of the screen, waiting for the enemy plane to show up. My fingers were a millimeter away from the buttons.

"Here we go," said the officer. Before I could see anything and fire, the officer said, "You're dead, son," just as a tiny speck on the screen grew slightly larger and then promptly went out of sight. I prepared for the next one, squinting even harder.

"You're dead, son," he said without emotion, as the dot came out of another direction.

After five "you're dead, sons," the lights went up. "Let's forget about gunnery school, son. Maybe they can find some office work for you." I could imagine an entire battery of German prisoners writing home about this humiliation.

One morning I saw a notice on the bulletin board: "All personnel interested in Journalism, report to Capt. Burke at 0900 hours." What could this be? Was the Army looking to turn us into journalists to cover the war? And what war? That was over. Did they want us to cover the peace? Since I was inquisitive by nature, I showed up. I was also the only one to show up. Captain Burke waited until a quarter after nine and since there were no other comers, he called me into his office and said, "Well, Simon. Since no one else wants it, you are now the editor-in-chief of the *Rev-Meter*, the official Army Air Force newspaper. Good luck and good day."

I stepped out into the hallway and looked left and then right. I didn't know where the official Army Air Force newspaper was. I was finally given a small office and a typewriter and since I had no journalists working under me, I had to write my own stories and then edit them. I was a tough editor. I kept correcting my mistakes and cutting out the parts that bored me. I wanted to fire me but that didn't seem practical. Eventually, I started to cull items and stories from magazines and newspapers about anything aeronautical. After three months of this, I was so bored, I was hoping they would put me back on cigarette duty, where at least I could see tobacco flying off to more interesting places than my tiny office.

Finally, I was reprieved. I was told that almost all the draftees were now out of the armed forces and the government wanted to build up a new and more permanent regular army. Now there was another phrase that confused me. Wasn't the Army that fought the war a "regular army"? Or were they just like regular guys but nothing special? I was much too literal-minded for Army terminology. At any rate, my job was now shifted to recruitment to help build up this "regular" army. They wanted me to write a short radio program, heard only in the Denver area, to entice young men away from their homes, their girlfriends, dates, sex and good food, to join the "regular army." Can you just picture young men rushing home from basketball practice to hear this incredible new radio show that was on from 4:00 to 4:10 P.M., their ears pressed against the speaker since our program came out of a small station with just enough wattage to light a firefly for one glowlette? After a month, we were getting neither recruits nor an audience. I threw caution to the wind and suggested a revolutionary idea to Captain Burke.

"What if you gave us more time? Say fifteen minutes. And what if I made it funny? And in between the funny news items or Army humor, we could put in a plug for the benefits of joining the regular army, where you could end up with a college education given under the G.I. Bill of Rights and perhaps learn a new trade that would steer you into a new career."

To my enormous surprise, he said, "Fine. Let's try it."

Together with an announcer, a singer and a couple of G.I.'s who could get my humor across, we put on a show. Eventually the show was stretched to a half hour, but we were still heard only in the Denver area. Then we were sent out on the road, to Colorado Springs and to other Western towns with Marlboro Country type names. I was actually enjoying myself and people had started to listen to our little amateur show with down-home humor. Were we a success? Well, just look at the size of our armed forces today; count our nuclear submarines and Stealth bombers. However, before I could get into building our space program and float my idea of putting a man on the moon, I was discharged, after a year and a half of dedicated service to my country. When I arrived home in New York, I had no clothes that fit me, since I had grown taller and more muscular, but I did know what I wanted to do for the rest of my life. I wanted to write for the stage, for films, for television and I still wanted to find out what the "regular army" was and why did they call it a "forced march"?

BILOXI BLUES opened on March 28, 1985. I finally got my first rave from Frank Rich of the New York Times. And my last. The play also won the Tony Award. Brighton Beach had opened two years before at the Alvin Theatre. Biloxi Blues opened at the same theater, but the name had now been changed.

A few months before, Jimmy Nederlander, the owner of the Alvin Theatre and the second largest theater owner in America, called and asked if he could come to my New York apartment to talk to me. He wants me to do a musical or fix up a play that was coming into his theater was all I could think of. When I heard what he had to say, I was completely bowled over.

"I've been thinking for a long time," he started, "and this is what I'd like to do with your permission. I want to change the name of the Alvin Theatre to the Neil Simon Theatre."

I looked at him blankly. Was he serious?

"Look, it's good business for me," he continued, since I wasn't able to form words just yet. He went on: "The Alvin Theatre is a great theater but I never liked the name. It was named after two men who owned it before me. Alex somebody and Vinton Freedley. They put their two names together, Al and Vin, and they got Alvin and to me that sounds like one of the Chipmunks. To call it the Neil Simon Theatre gives it a built-in atmosphere. It doesn't mean just comedy. It means the kind of entertainment that you've been bringing to New York for years. And with your permission, I would like to do it for your next play, *Biloxi Blues*."

I started to think of all the plays and musicals I had seen at the Alvin since I was a boy: Moss Hart's *Lady in the Dark*, *The Great White Hope*, *A Tree Grows in Brooklyn* and *Mister Roberts*—the list went on and on.

This honor had come so suddenly, so out of the blue, that I grew suspicious. "Does this mean that I have to do all my plays in a Nederlander theater? Not that I mind because you have great theaters, but if this is a payoff, I would feel very uncomfortable accepting it. It would be a business deal rather than an honor."

"No strings attached," said Jimmy. "I just want to see your name on one of my theaters. What do you say, Neil? Can I do it?"

"I'll have to sleep on it, Jimmy," I said. "Wait right here. I'll go inside, take a ten-minute nap and come out with my answer . . . Are you kidding? OF COURSE YOU CAN."

The name of the theater was officially changed from the Alvin to the Neil Simon. On the day that the official ceremony was going to take place, with so many of my friends, actors, directors, etc., in attendance, I got into a cab, my heart beating like a Bob Fosse number.

I did not want the cabbie to stop in front of the theater at 52nd Street off Eighth Avenue. I told him I wanted to get off at 51st Street and Eighth Avenue. I wanted to walk up the block, then turn the corner onto 52nd Street, so I would see the sign for the first time. I was going to milk every drop of ego out of this. I turned the corner and saw it. You couldn't miss it if you tried. It wasn't big, it was enormous. It was at least twenty feet high, and at night, when it was lit up, you could probably see it from New Jersey. Maybe even from Fort Dix. I thought to myself, from tearing up cigarette butts to this is a long way. For a long time I actually had trouble saying it. If someone asked me where *Biloxi Blues* was playing, I thought I exceeded the bounds of humility by saying aloud, "It's at the Neil Simon Theatre." Being proud was one thing, but self-aggrandizement is another.

But even today, as I drive in a cab down Broadway to see a play, as we pass 52nd Street, I turn my head to the right, just to see if it's still there.

THE ODD COUPLETTES

25

FOR YEARS I had received dozens upon dozens of letters from all over the country asking me to allow an all-woman production of the play of *The Odd Couple.* Those making this request included numerous stars based in both Los Angeles and New York, who wanted to tour the production and then bring it to Broadway. None of the letters, however, made any mention of how they would do it. Did they intend to simply change the names of Oscar and Felix to Olive and Florence, and have them drink Diet Cokes instead of beer? It *could* be done, I thought, but not that way; I would have to rewrite it completely. I'd keep the exact same structure as the original, but make the characters women—real women, not women behaving as men as played by women.

Rather than take the risk and head straight for Broadway, I had a reading of the new version of the play in the game room at my brother Danny's apartment, where he often taught comedy to his always packed classes. Danny was considered to be the best teacher of comedy writing on the West and East Coasts, and eventually he traveled all over America and Europe giving his classes. His classes have spawned countless numbers of young men and women who are first-rate comedy writers, and who eventually filled the staffs of some of the best television comedies on the air. Heads of studios and networks even took his classes, predicated on the sensible theory that if they wanted their writers to write well, they'd be better off knowing what they're talking about themselves. There was only one person he did not allow to take his class: me.

He said he would feel self-conscious with me in the room, despite the fact that he was the only mentor I ever had. Actually there was one other to whom the embargo applied. Woody Allen was also not allowed in Danny's class, and for the same reason I wasn't. Danny had written with Woody Allen, and Woody was quoted as saying, "I learned more about comedy from Danny Simon than anyone else I know." So the moral is, if you made it big in this business because of Danny, you couldn't take his class.

Danny directed the read-through of *The Female Odd Couple*, doing an incredible job. It erased my misgivings about the project, and the new version finally ended up on Broadway starring Rita Moreno and Sally Struthers. *The Female Odd Couple* is now performed almost as frequently as the original. One of the scenes that benefited from the transformation was turning the English Pigeon Sisters into the Spanish Costazuela Brothers, formerly of Barcelona, where they worked for Iberian Airlines. The Brothers, Jesús and Manolo, are invited to dinner at Olive and Florence's apartment. The boys, a little shaky with their English but long on charm and manners, arrive with flowers and candy.

OLIVE: Well, come in, amigos.

MANOLO: Amigos. Very good. Jesús, you have something to say?

JESÚS: Sí. With our deep felicitations, we have brought you fresh flowers and fresh candy.

OLIVE: Oh, how sweet.

JESÚS: I hope you like the candies. They are no good.

OLIVE: They're no good?

JESÚS: Sí. The candy is no good.

MANOLO: Sí. Is very chewy.

OLIVE: You mean nougat?

MANOLO: Ah, yes. Nou-gat. Not no good. Nou-gat.

JESÚS: I'm sorry. We're still new at English.

OLIVE: But very thoughtful. I'll put these in water.

MANOLO: Just the flowers. Candy in water is no good.

JESÚS: I thought it was nou-gat.

OLIVE: (Holding the flowers) Well, the flowers are certainly beautiful. I feel like Miss America.

JESÚS: I feel the same. I miss Spain sometimes.

Comedy is not always profound, but laughter often makes it feel as if it is.

THE GIRL FROM NEIMAN MARCUS

I HAD BEEN a bachelor for almost three and a half years, and I can't deny that the many attractive women I met during those years were more than a single man could ask for. Surprisingly, it also got tiresome. Each first date was like a first session with a new analyst. It was mostly about giving information about your past. I also found out that sex without love was not very satisfying. (Then again, love without sex can be a drag as well, as can love without love, which is when you're just saying "love" in order to get sex.)

The best years of my life had been the nineteen years with Joan, and then the eight and a half years with Marsha. After that I had to learn step by step how to be a bachelor. It had its benefits, to be sure, but freedom doesn't always bring happiness. On the other hand, the opposite of freedom (we're talking marriage here) implies obligations, responsibilities, accountabilities and burdens. But without a partner, what you miss most is sharing, giving, connection, kinship and commonality. What I missed the most was caring for someone so much that I couldn't wait until morning to see her serene, placid face, half asleep just inches away from mine, giving me a warm, quiet "Hi" to start the day. My problem was that I wanted all of the latter without again going through the excruciating pain of death or divorce, not to mention that endless feeling of anger, despair, loneliness and desolation. I know that I either had to take a chance one more time or be lucky enough to find a woman who would want all the things I desire in life, without the commitment of marriage. Since I had not met that woman in three and a half years, having to make that choice was not an issue. What I also feared greatly was that I would meet that woman, but shy away because of fear that I was not then, and possibly never would be again, able to enter into a relationship that didn't end disastrously.

It was with this new sense of cautiousness that I wandered into the Neiman Marcus department store in Beverly Hills on November 22, 1985. I was there to look for a Christmas gift for the young daughter of Ann Bell, who was no longer my companion, but had become my friend. I always made a point of shopping early to beat the holiday rush. I found the gift I wanted, had it wrapped and sent. I walked down the three flights of stairs without a clue of what I was going to do next. On the ground floor was the large, imposing perfume and cosmetic section. Why I was wandering through there was another mystery because there was no one I knew for whom I wanted to buy perfume or cosmetics. The gifts I bought for Ellen and Nancy were always more personal, and something I would search for with care. I turned to leave and suddenly, behind the Anne Klein counter, I caught sight of a woman, a girl, a presence, an aura, a quality and an existence you couldn't help but see.

I always remembered what Mildred Newman, a doctor friend I knew and admired, once said to me. When you see someone for the very first time, you know more about them than you think you do. It doesn't mean you know specifics, but you do have a sense of what kind of person this is. It pleases you or it doesn't. You admire that person or you don't. That person gets your respect or doesn't. And all this happens in a flash of an eye, mind you.

The woman I saw in my eye in Neiman Marcus, just before my lid closed for the first time, was tall and fair, dressed conservatively, and she did nothing to present herself as beautiful because there was no need to. She was blessed with beauty. And while the appeal of her looks was enough to attract me, looking at her I realized I wanted something more: I wanted to know her. For now, though, I would settle for just speaking to her. She had that fresh clean look that made you think she'd be as lovely sitting atop a tractor as she would behind a counter in one of the most expensive stores in the world. I was simply drawn to her, as though someone had slipped roller skates on me unnoticed, I found myself moving closer and closer to her. She looked up and smiled, not necessarily at me, but it didn't matter. Her smile was warm as well as breathtaking. I had the feeling we had met before, but that was unlikely. You don't quickly forget a woman who makes you feel you're wearing roller skates in a department store.

"Can I help you?" she asked, not as a salesperson, because she really wasn't selling anything. As I later found out, she was doing inventory. She offered help because I looked lost.

I murmured something about "just looking" even though I never once glanced down at the counter.

She peered at me for a moment before she said, "You look familiar. Do I know you?"

"I don't know," I said. "My name is Neil Simon. I'm a writer." I knew it was a shameless plug I gave myself, but I hoped it might give me a slight advantage.

"Oh, God. I'm sorry. I should have known."

"Why should you have known?"

"Because I'm an actress. I just work here part-time. Yes, I've seen you on television a few times."

Later on she confessed I looked like an English professor at UCLA, although at the time I was wearing a beaten-up old Air Force jacket and an old scarf, not my idea of what professors at UCLA wore.

I suddenly ran out of conversation and thought that anything else I said would be brazen and pushy. I said, "Well, nice meeting you," turned and left the store with my valet parking ticket in my hand.

The parking attendant started walking toward me. In the brief few seconds it took him, this is what I thought to myself: "If I drive away now, I will never see her again . . . Ever . . . Go back in. Say something . . . Maybe she's not married but small chance of that . . . Find out. You haven't met anyone like her in years even though you don't know a thing about her. Trust your instincts. You said that last time about Marsha, twelve years ago, but can't you be forward and cautious at the same time?" All this while the parking attendant was still walking toward me. I waved him aside and walked back into Neiman Marcus.

"Hi again," I said as I approached the counter. "I'm back."

"Did you forget anything?" she asked.

"Yes. I know this is crazy, but could I look at your fingers?"

"My fingers?"

"Please."

She seemed as much puzzled as amused by my request, but she put her ten fingers down on the counter. I looked at them.

"Not a wedding ring on them, I see," not believing I had that much nerve. I held up my hands. "Same here."

Where this surge of audaciousness, boldness and courage was coming from, I couldn't say. I was just tap-dancing as fast as I could, possibly even with roller skates on.

"Look, this is the first time I've ever done this in my life," I said. "I do not wander around department stores trying to meet someone . . . But I knew if I drove away just now, I'd never see you again. So I'll just plunge in . . . Do you have a lunch hour because I do and maybe we could have a bite together."

"I'm sorry. I don't have a lunch hour. And we're not supposed to see customers on the outside."

"What about if we ate here, in the chocolate department? That's not outside." Was that a mistake? I wondered. I was afraid she might think I was "on" all the time, and that's not how I was. "Does that mean you can't *ever* have dinner out sometime with someone you meet?"

She smiled and said, "Right."

I was dead. Stone dead. A tall man in a dark suit was walking the aisles, and he glanced over at us a few times. If he was a company man, which he was, was he angry with her or with me? Still, I made one last entreaty.

"Tomorrow night. Coffee, a drink, a Perrier. I'd settle for anything."

"I'm going to a Republican convention tomorrow with a friend," she said. Ah, there was hope. She didn't say no. She just said she had other plans.

She looked nervously at the man walking the aisles and she got busy doing her inventory. I pretended I was looking at merchandise. I whispered, "If I had your phone number, I could call you and you could turn me down then."

She tried to hold back the smile just beginning at the corners of her mouth and quickly wrote something on a Neiman card and handed it to me.

I picked it up as preciously as I would a diamond and slid it into my pocket. This time I walked out of the store, got into my car, drove off and wondered if tonight was too soon to call.

I waited a day to call her. Perhaps two. After all, if she was a Republican and I was a Democrat, there'd be trouble ahead.

I dialed her number as carefully as if I were opening a safe.

"Hello. It's me. The guy in the Army jacket from Neiman Marcus."

"Oh, hi. I wasn't expecting you to call so soon."

"You want to hang up? I could call back in ten minutes." I thought humor was safe by now.

"No, it's fine. I just walked in the door actually."

"Look, I hope you didn't get into any trouble the other day. Talking to me so long, I mean."

"I got fired."

"WHAT?" I was shocked. Devastated. Did I ruin her life? "Oh, my God, I'm so sorry. What can I do? Can I make it up to you? What if I called them? I can explain it was all my fault, which it was."

"No, it's okay, really. I was going to leave there soon anyway. I just took the job for a few days to make some extra money. Mostly I go out on auditions for commercials. That's what I just came back from."

"I have to make it up to you. Dinner isn't enough. I have to buy you a small restaurant. A diner or something."

She laughed. If I could have recorded it, I would have played it for a week.

"So is tomorrow okay or am I rushing it?"

"Tomorrow? Sure, tomorrow's fine."

"Morton's, seven o'clock? Do you know where it is?"

"Yes, I know. By the way, my name is Diane Lander . . . and I just wanted to say that I've never done this either. I'll see you tomorrow, okay?"

"Very okay," I said and we both hung up.

We sometimes remember moments like this with the dialogue a little more perfect than it actually was. To me, it was close enough to what I've recorded. If Diane remembers it otherwise, that's fine, but this is my memoir and I've put it down the way I would like to remember it.

I'M NEVER LATE. At seven o'clock I was sitting at a table in Morton's, sipping my vodka on the rocks. It was raining outside and I assumed the traffic would be heavy. I could see her through the window as she approached the restaurant, but she couldn't see me. Her hair was a little wet and windblown. I couldn't have asked for it to look any better. She came in and instead of asking for me, she made a beeline for the ladies' room. I was halfway through my vodka so I slowed it down. One was always enough for me. She came out of the ladies' room and her hair was brushed back and the smattering of raindrops on her face had vanished. She was shown to my table and sat breathlessly. She had, no doubt, put in a full day, but we greeted each other not as strangers, but as two people who had more than just a five-minute clandestine conversation over a counter in Neiman's. After all, we'd been through a lot together. I had managed to muster more nerve and aggressiveness than I ever had shown before, and she had gotten fired. We had a history and something to talk about beside the rain. I have very little memory of our conversation that poured out that night because there was so much of it to remember. We virtually closed up Morton's some four hours later. All I did remember was her telling me that she had a child, a year-and-a-half-old girl named Bryn, and that the father and Diane had already gone their separate ways. I accepted everything as good news. I don't know if it happened that night or some time later, but had I known what she was thinking as I approached her in Neiman's, I would have been far less nervous. She said that when she saw me, the first thing she said to herself was, "Oh, God, I'm in trouble." It meant two things: one was, she was attracted to me; the other was "Oh, no. A celebrity. They're all slightly crazy."

I assume we ate dinner during that evening while we talked about everything. She finally looked at her watch and said she had to rush home. Baby-sitters cost money. I said something like, "When do I see you again?" It was just a few short days till Thanksgiving. She said, "Well, you could come to my house tomorrow for dinner if you don't mind watching me bake pies and amusing my daughter now and then." I accepted, conditions and all.

She lived in the Valley and she wrote out the address and the directions very explicitly. It didn't help. I drove past her house three times and circled back three times. She lived in an apartment in a two-story house, and when I saw outside a few unopened boxes still tied with cord, I knew she lived a somewhat transitory life. I rang the bell, waited, knocked on the door, waited and rang the bell again. When I saw how she was dressed for our second date, I knew *I* was the one who was in trouble. She was wearing an oversized sweatshirt covered with flour, baggy pants also covered with flour, and if I could see them, possibly sneakers. There wasn't an ounce of pretense in her, and baking Thanksgiving pies seemed to be just as important to her as our second date together. If the pies were as delicious as she looked to me, someone was in for a great holiday dinner. Everything about her was natural and easy and in the previous three and a half years I hadn't come close to meeting anyone like her.

Bryn had not yet made her appearance, busily absorbed in whatever it is that year-and-a-half-old children dream about in bed. In the kitchen, I marveled how Diane was handling both the dinner she was preparing for us plus the pumpkin pies, among others, that she was baking. She asked me to come into the kitchen to sit and keep her company. It was my first glimpse of the woman who would ultimately juggle being a single mom, a magazine writer, chairperson for every charitable function who clamored for her vitality and dedication and one of the hardest campaigners for the presidential election. It turned out she was a Democrat after all, and it was the date she had the night after we met at Neiman's who was the Republican. We crossed that river safely, I'm glad to say.

She asked me to read the baking instructions for one of the pies she was making, beginning to get flour on her face, making her already perfect nose all the more appealing. I read everything exactly as written until I said, "Two eggs beaten or thoroughly scolded."

She looked up puzzled and asked, "Does it really say that?"

"No," I answered, "just trying to lighten up the recipe."

She laughed and said, "But you didn't say it funny. You said it real."

I said, "The essential ingredient in humor. If the words are funny, you don't have to say them funny."

"You should be an actor," she said.

"No, thanks. I'm doing fine where I am."

Later on I made another comment on something, a pass at humor or a stab at irony, but it was clearly just a joke. It went by her, so I said, "I just did it again." After a while, she was finally able to separate fact from fun, and my dry humor began getting through to her. She was not used to anyone talking like that, especially in Jeffersonville, Indiana, where she was raised, a stone's throw from Louisville, across the Ohio River. She had no Southern accent except when she was on the phone with one of her three sisters and a brother, and she would suddenly turn into a country girl, which is why I think the tractor image of her became clear to me. When it came time to eat, she wouldn't let me help with the dinner dishes, but I was allowed to put the chairs at the table. I put one on each side. She said, "And the high chair goes in the middle."

It never occurred to me that Bryn would be eating with us. When a woman invites you to her home for dinner, you expect the atmosphere to lean at least a little toward the romantic. This one was purely domestic. Diane went into the bedroom and brought out a sleepy-eyed, blond-haired beauty who rubbed her eyes and stared at me. She had Diane's face all right, and weren't they both lucky. Now with Bryn at the table, I expected dinner to be directed toward childhood behavior. "Don't throw your spoon, Bryn," or "Bryn, don't drink the water with your fingers." I was wrong. Bryn sat quietly, never making a sound, just watching me and Diane talk as if she understood what we were saying. She never once cried and never once made a demand. This experience was probably new to her and she was taking it in like a new television cartoon she didn't quite understand.

When we were through, Diane brought the dishes into the kitchen, again rejecting my offer to help.

She left Bryn in my care. I tried my year-and-a-half children's conversation. "Hi, Bryn. My name is Neil. Do you have a doll? Can I see your doll? Would you like me to tell you a story?" As I was floundering, Bryn just stood staring at me, holding her bottle, and once in a while offering me a sip. Diane was in the kitchen fielding a couple of telephone calls, one from a friend and another from her agent about two auditions for commercials coming up the next day, and while doing all this, she probably also painted the kitchen an eggshell white just to keep her hands busy.

I put a cartoon on television for Bryn, but she'd have none of it. She was still standing there, staring me down, giving no indication if she approved or otherwise. Finally, she made her move. She crossed the room, handed me her bottle, then proceeded to climb up my legs and into my lap, where she took her bottle again and seemingly settled in for the night. It was all so perfect, the suspicious paranoid in me thought that Diane had been rehearsing Bryn to do this all day.

Diane came out of the kitchen, shocked to see Bryn in my lap, and laughed loudly. "She almost never does that," she said. "I think I have competition." I didn't mind hearing that at all.

Bryn was finally put to bed, the pies were put out to cool, the dishes were put out to dry and Diane put on a new face in the bathroom, washing off the flour that I had enjoyed looking at.

"God! Why didn't you tell me I looked like that?" she said.

We were finally alone, talking and finding out who we both were, when a little figure appeared around the corner of the room, just wanting to listen.

"Go to bed, Bryn," Diane said sternly. "Neil and Mommie are talking."

Bryn ran quickly back to her bed, but not willingly. Four times during our conversation Bryn appeared, each time just enough of her visible around that corner for us to know she was there. Each time she learned more about how to be discreet and yet be part of the activities. The last time, however, Bryn looked at me, pulling the zipper on her pajamas up and down slowly.

Diane laughed hysterically, although she was shocked. "It's not what you think," she said. "She's not a vamp. She just likes her zippers." Bryn finally retired from show business and went to sleep for the night.

All in all, it was a great evening, and I learned more about who Diane was than I would have learned on fifty dates with someone else.

Although I had plans to spend Thanksgiving with friends, Diane's invitation to spend it with her at her friend's house instead was not a difficult choice to make.

"I'm not making a pass at you," she said. "I just need someone to help me carry the pies." Which I ended up doing with pleasure. Her Indiana humor did not take second place to mine.

A BICOASTAL ROMANCE

27

OUR DATING continued, and our relationship grew steadily, despite the fact I was making that long, nightly trip out to the Valley, still driving past her house two or three times before I found it. In the ensuing weeks, we spoke to each other almost every day and I saw her as many nights as we both could manage. She was also not baking as many pies at this point. I was so glad she got fired from Neiman's because it was their loss and my gain. Each night I came to her house, Bryn crawled up my legs, nestled in and almost got me to drink from her bottle.

One day a call came from Diane to tell me she was moving again. The owner of the building where she was staying decided he was going to give the apartment to his mother, possibly because his mother would pay more rent than Diane could afford. Since Diane had neither a lease nor the money to get a lawyer to fight this outrage, she let it go and found herself another apartment. Perhaps that's why she rarely unpacked everything. The new apartment was in a nearby neighborhood, but I couldn't find that one either. Every place in California has names of things that grow, like Sycamore or Oak or Maple, all the way down to Creepy Vines and Crab Grass.

Diane was exceptionally self-sufficient, and had packed everything by the time I arrived to help. I did, however, help her unpack and move her worldly goods up the new, long flight of stairs. Diane was always surprised when someone did something nice for her, and I think what cemented our relationship was the sight of me carrying a number of heavy objects, including Bryn's tricycle, up the stairs. Diane is also a compulsive furniture mover, but she wouldn't let me help her. I watched as chairs crisscrossed the room, and the sofa was tried in fifteen different positions. Bryn and I helped with the more portable items, like Bryn's storybooks, which were unpacked one at a time. Within two hours it looked like a home, and Diane still found time to hang all her pictures (mostly family), albeit in temporary positions. She was capable of getting up in the middle of the night and rehanging them.

I almost always called her when I got home because that's when we had our most personal conversations. I might add that by now, our relationship had grown more intimate, and it had become increasingly difficult for me to leave at night and drive back to Bel Air. Being the good mother she was, Diane didn't want Bryn to wake up in the morning and see a man in the house, although by now Bryn had seen me so often, she must have thought I was a piece of furniture.

CHRISTMAS WAS approaching, and on that day Nancy would celebrate her seventeenth birthday. Long before I met Diane, I had promised Nancy I would take her someplace in Europe where we'd never been. We chose Gstaad in Switzerland, and were scheduled to arrive a day or two before Christmas and stay through New Year's Eve. I invited Diane and Bryn to come with us. She declined because she and Bryn always spent the Christmas holidays with her family in Indiana, and they especially wanted to be with Diane's mother, Valerie, or Gingee, as she was affectionately called by her grandchildren. When it was time for Nancy and me to leave for Switzerland, I asked Diane one more time to come with us. With some hesitation, she finally relented. She flew to Gstaad a few days after Christmas and stayed with me while Nancy had a room down the hall. It was a perfect holiday. We then decided to fly to London for a few days before going home. While we were in London, I was forced to deal with a subject I dreaded. Diane began to talk of marriage. Not pushing, not aggressively, but she made it clear it was something to think about in the future. I explained to her, for the very first time, my experiences after the death of Joan and the divorce from Marsha. As much as I cared for Diane, and I was clearly falling in love with her by now, I said that marriage wasn't a possibility for me. Couldn't we just go on living as we did?

"Not with a young baby, I can't," she said. "I have her future to think about, and a long affair leading nowhere is not what I want for either of us."

We returned to New York and Diane flew off to Indiana to pick up Bryn and then went back to California. I returned to my new apartment in New York on 70th Street and Park Avenue. I hadn't been so foolish as to think the subject of marriage would never come up, but I was steadfast in my resolve that marriage would end badly for us. I spoke to Diane a few nights later and it ended badly sooner than I thought. Diane broke off with me. I tried hard not to think of her and once more returned to the one place that was always a safe haven for me—the typewriter.

THE THIRD B.B. PLAY

28

SINCE I HAD no idea I would write a trilogy, I also had no idea that all these titles would be "B.B." plays. *Brighton Beach Memoirs* was chosen because it was more alliterative than "Far Rockaway Memoirs," a low-rent beach community close by to Brighton Beach, where most of the original story took place. I used *Biloxi Blues* because that's where I took my basic training that hot summer in 1945. The third play was to be about the final breakup of my family, the ultimate parting of my parents, with Danny and me moving to Manhattan to pursue our writing careers. I liked *Broadway Bound* because it was also part of the lexicon of the theater, meaning that a play that had passed its tryout stage somewhere in the hinterlands was now bound for Broadway. The symmetry of the titles happened by accident and coincidence; if I had only done one play instead of three, it still would have ended up with the same title.

Since the first two plays were extremely successful, the burden of making *Broadway Bound* equally successful lay heavily on my shoulders. Like any other chain, if one of the links were weak, the strength of the trilogy would be broken. Since I had a very clear picture in my mind of who the characters were and how they behaved, I became more confident and secure each day I worked on it.

It all started with one image in my mind: my mother waxing her dining room table. It was a metaphor of all she would be left in a life that still needed her love and attention. A scratch left on the table by any of us would be like a stab in the back. Her life was falling apart and she realized she couldn't live out her days without taking care of someone, but instead she decided to take care of some *thing*. I knew that basically I was writing a tragedy, and that the laughs that came often during the evening were all bittersweet. I created her aging Socialist father because he was needed as the go-between in an effort to save his daughter's marriage. He had the wisdom of experience, and although he knew his son-in-law had been unfaithful to his wife, he understood and accepted it by admitting he had done the same thing to his own wife in younger days. He also knew that throwing away a thirty-two-year-old marriage for an indiscretion was a foolish thing. He knew too that his daughter was stubborn and obstinate, and so he tried to get her to bend a little, to forgive and forget.

As for the mother (his daughter), she could have looked the other way, but her jealousy, anger and humiliation wouldn't permit it, so her husband leaves. Her father, now ailing, reluctantly moves to Florida to be with his wife—an unfortunate circumstance since neither one has any love left for the other. (Although his wife, unlike his daughter, would rather be with him no matter how cold the relationship than not have him at all.) For him, it was against his Socialist beliefs to move where the rich and idle live—not exactly an honest statement, but like so many of us, we all have to rationalize the truth to fit our moods.

At the end of the play, the two young brothers leave to fulfill their hopes under the bright lights of Broadway. They take with them a blessing from their mother, and a batch of freshly baked cookies to "see them through their first lonely week in New York." As the curtain falls, the mother is seen waxing her beloved table, given to her years ago by her own grandmother. Eugene, the younger son (my alter ego), who is also the narrator of the evening, says to the audience:

EUGENE: Contrary to popular belief, everything in life doesn't come to a
    clear-cut conclusion. Mom didn't do anything very exciting with the
    rest of her life except wax her grandmother's table and bask in the glory
    of her sons' success. But I never got the feeling that Mom felt she sacri-
    ficed herself for us. Whatever she gave, she found her own quiet plea-
    sure in. I guess she was never comfortable with words like "I love you."
    A hard life can sometimes knock the sentiment out of you . . . But all in
    all, she considers herself a pretty lucky woman . . . After all, she did once
    dance with George Raft.

At the first reading of the play I discovered two flaws, not recognizable to anyone, except possibly Manny Azenberg, our producer. When people ask me, "How do you know there's a flaw in the play after only one reading?" the only answer I have is that I am following my instincts. I not only see and hear the play in that rehearsal room, but I can also visualize it on the stage on opening night in New York. What sounds bad in one place is sure to follow suit in the other. The first flaw was that I created an unnecessary character in the second act, a young girl who was in love with Eugene. In her one scene, Eugene is sick in bed with the flu and she comes to visit him at night in Brighton Beach. The two of them shared a similar problem; her parents were breaking up as well. It was an attempt on my part to say that in life, we are all, at some period, losers. The young actress, a very adept one, was reading her scene intelligently and honestly. The other actors sat in rapt attention—all except me, and then I soon noticed that Manny Azenberg was distracted as well. Usually he reads the script silently to himself as the play moves along. This time, however, he was turning the pages of this scene fairly quickly, looking to see where it ended. In a sense, he was saying quietly to himself, "How long does this thing go on?" I had reached that conclusion before he did. I took my pad, wrote something on it and passed it to Manny, who was sitting next to me. It said, "Don't worry. I can fix it." He smiled at me and nodded, then put his arm around my shoulder in appreciation. That note is now framed and sits in Manny's office just above his desk.

After the first reading that day, Manny, director Gene Saks and I walked slowly to the Chinese restaurant we usually frequented on the first day's reading.

Gene said, "What do you think about the scene with the girl? I think it needs something, don't you?"

Manny offered a suggestion how the scene might be more potent, more relevant to the play. My mind was elsewhere as they spoke, thinking ahead to what I would do. Then I turned to them and said, "Oh, don't worry. The girl is out of the play."

Gene said, "You mean the actress? I thought she was pretty good."

"No, not the actress. The part. We don't need that scene at all. It doesn't push the play forward. I have another idea of what should be there."

This was the second flaw, and cutting the play wouldn't do it. As I listened to the play in its entirety, I realized that the mother did not have a truly happy moment of her own. She had nothing to celebrate, nothing to look forward to, and we never got to see the joyful side of her. Was she always like this? I wondered, thinking of the audience's reaction to her. If they thought her a drab, self-pitying misanthrope, they would miss who she truly was. If indeed she was a cheerless woman, the audience would understand the husband's reason for leaving her. Did she ever love him? Did he ever love her? I had to find a scene in the play that revealed the mother *and* the father completely devoted to each other and aware of each other's special qualities. The problem was that I could not stop the play or break the continuity to show this scene, nor could I go to a flashback, thus breaking the tone and style of the play. It all came to me when I thought of the story that the mother constantly told and retold about the night she danced with George Raft. I would have to go to the past through the mother's memory, prodded on by her sympathetic son, Eugene.

When all seemed bleakest, Eugene encourages the mother to tell the story once again. As she does, she reminisces about her early life, about the gift her grandmother gave her, the dining room table. She tells about how her parents didn't like the idea of her going to a dance hall. She tells about how she met her husband, how she respected him and ultimately came to love him. She remembers him as he was and not as he is in the present. As she continues to tell the story, Eugene gets up, turns on the radio and we hear the soft clarinet sound of Benny Goodman and his band. He tries to coax the mother up to dance with him. At first she is reticent, embarrassed, afraid to go back to that place which was once so perfect. Eugene is persistent, and finally he takes her hand, leads her to the center of the room, and says, "Show me. Show me how you danced with George Raft." She slowly takes a step, holding Eugene tentatively. Then another step . . . and then they are dancing, her leading, teaching Eugene how to hold her, to turn her, and as we watch, we see her when she was sixteen, the dancing pride of the East Bronx. She is as graceful as she was then, as perfectly controlled in her movements as a young girl, and as happy in her reverie as she probably was on that night she became the talk of the neighborhood. We see the mother as a wonderful, hopeful and lovely young thing, some thirty-five years ago. As acted and danced by actress Linda Lavin, she was as brilliant as any actress I've ever worked with. When the dance stopped, the applause from the audience was thunderous. It seemed as if I must have had that scene in my mind from the outset and had built a play around it. You never know how the mind works. Perhaps that scene was always embedded in my subconscious . . . and it took its sweet time before it revealed itself to me. *Broadway Bound* became a huge hit, and with my picture on the cover of *Time* magazine, it was called "The Best Play of the Decade."

As I wrote the play, I connected into my own life—the one I was going through while I wrote—and projected it to the future, thirty-five or forty years later. Would I be alone, throwing away my own happiness as my mother did? I called Diane in California. I told her how much I missed her and missed Bryn. She admitted she felt the same way but that nothing had really changed between us. I asked her to give it more time, to let the relationship grow instead of ending it without giving it the chance for me to feel secure in taking that major step she needed for herself. She decided to come to Washington, D.C., where we were still previewing *Broadway Bound*. When she arrived, and we embraced, I thought that all was well again, that we'd go on, as before, knowing in the future I would have to make that commitment. We didn't discuss it much, but shared (she for the first time) the nerve-wracking business of going through another opening. As the curtain went up on that first night, I knew that nothing was really settled between Diane and me, but with the fate of the play and my life both hanging in limbo, at least for the next two and a half hours, I just hung in there. I felt jittery and nervous, more than I had since my first play some twelve years before. I could hardly breathe and wanted to run out of the theater. I stayed pulled together long enough for the final curtain to come down. If enthusiastic audiences were any sign, we were a hit. More experienced by then, I knew nothing was a hit until the reviews came in. We all waited anxiously at a small party and I suddenly felt I had to sit down alone, away from the mingling guests. I began to get chest pains, which I attributed to nerves, but the pains persisted. Surely they would disappear once the reviews were read. Good or bad, nerves usually abate and either joy or anger takes over.

As the first review was read aloud, written by David Richards, the critic from the *Washington Post*, the most important paper in town, it became clear very quickly that he was enchanted by *Broadway Bound*. The review was so glowing with praise and affection that I felt overwhelmed. Still, I had fears. Did I write a good play and did I treat my parents fairly? I knew I'd been honest, but had I been fair? Since both were now gone, I didn't want to be haunted from the grave, thinking that I betrayed my parents, invading the privacy of their own inner turmoil. But by doing so, I think I made the play accessible to all. The audience could identify with their own parents, and in some cases, their very own experiences. Some could applaud, but you never knew what went on inside their own private thoughts. They might completely miss the fact that the people on stage reflected their own experiences, and instead, they would assume they were just watching the problems of other people.

Despite the fact that David Richards's review was probably the best I ever got from anyone, the pains in my chest did not abate. By now I had begun to worry. Diane came over and sat next to me, asking what's wrong, and I could hardly get the breath to tell her. She called Manny Azenberg aside and said, "I think we'd better get Neil to a hospital quickly." Senator Alan Simpson of Wyoming and his wife were there and instantly rushed all five of us to his car, then sped through Washington to the nearest hospital.

We reached the hospital and I got out of the car, helped carefully by Manny and Senator Simpson. As we reached the front door a nurse asked what we wanted. Alan said, "I think our friend here may be having a heart attack."

"I'm sorry," the nurse said. "This is a woman's hospital only. We can't take any male patients."

Manny didn't want to say the word "death" in front of me, but stated that I could be in real trouble. The nurse wouldn't budge. It was so ludicrous, that through my pain, I started to laugh. We piled into the car and headed for the next hospital, hoping they wouldn't say, "Sorry. Catholics only."

A Wyoming native, Alan Simpson could drive a car as well as he probably rode a horse. Whatever hospital it was we got to next, I was taken in immediately, with IVs stuck in my arm, and every other gadget we're used to seeing on TV's *ER*. In the meantime, Diane, always cool and clear-thinking in times of trouble, called and woke up Ben Bradlee, then still the managing editor of the *Post*, whom we had met in East Hampton. Almost as quickly as he broke the Watergate story in his paper, he called his cardiologist, who arrived at the hospital within ten minutes. And this was about one in the morning.

Did I die? No, but it felt like it. It turned out it wasn't a heart attack, but a combination of not eating all day, nerves about the play and probably hoping Diane and I could stay together and that the word "marriage" would be outlawed in America. I was told by the doctor to go back to L.A., to rest and do nothing for a few weeks. I had to leave *Broadway Bound* just the way it was, and I never saw another performance of it in Washington. The play remained unchanged thereafter although, once I saw it at the first New York preview, I didn't think it needed changing. The further good news was that Diane and I were seeing each other again in Los Angeles.

I was back in New York for the opening and Diane and Bryn flew in a few days before, but they stayed in a hotel instead of with me. At the party following the opening, Diane assumed the role of hostess, which was perfectly fine with me because if there was one thing Diane could do, it was give a great party. She made all the arrangements for the food, a four-piece orchestra (who easily could have played a dirge if we were a flop) and the seating for all my friends and family. The party was held in an Italian restaurant in the East 60s. Diane greeted everyone with a smile, found them a place to sit and something to drink. I watched her only peripherally as I sat with Bob Fosse, Paddy Chayefsky and my brother, Danny, while waiting for just one review. That, of course, would be from Frank Rich. Paddy and Fosse were great supporters and told me not to worry. Danny was also enormously reassuring, but Danny always had a problem with his height, which never stopped him from winning the favors of more women than I thought possible. Danny's only complaint about the play had to do with Jason Alexander. Not that Jason wasn't fantastic in the play, portraying the role of my brother more than brilliantly, but he was upset because Jason was even shorter than Danny. As if we first looked for a short actor and then hoped he could act. It took a few minutes to convince Danny that we first look for a great actor and never pay attention to his height.

Diane seemed at home and left the worrying about the play to me while she got the orchestra to play a lively tune and picked out the first guest she could find to get up and dance with her, hoping that others would soon follow. I didn't want to discourage her from her gaiety even though I thought that this was the last thing that should be going on that night. *Broadway Bound* was an important play to me, and one so personal to write that even if the reviews were good, I didn't think a celebration was in order. Not to make any comparisons, but I couldn't imagine Eugene O'Neill sitting in a restaurant on the night that *Long Day's Journey into Night* opened, a play so searing he asked that it not be performed until twenty-five years after his death. In it he revealed that his mother was a morphine addict, his brother an incurable drunk and his father a tyrant and a deeply selfish man. When the reviews would come in, would O'Neill jump up and scream happily, "A hit! I've got a hit. I'll make millions from this."? I think not. That's why he preferred to be dead instead of at a party. Eventually, the *New York Times* review came in. There were a few respectful quotes from Mr. Rich, but again, as usual, there was a lecture on how a play should be written. He is a fine writer, I'll give him that, but fine writers don't always make good critics. Perhaps he was even a good critic, but since he received so little joy from and had so little respect for my work, I really don't have the inclination to give him the benefit of the doubt. My doubt, not his. Still, his review was important, and despite those reviews that soon filed into the restaurant that night, extolling the play's virtues, it was Mr. Rich's review that pained me most. Time heals all that. As I write this many years later, it all means nothing to me. The good *or* the bad.

As we left the party later in the evening, not knowing I'd be on the cover of *Time* the following week, I was simply drained, and glad that Diane was with me. She was encouraging and warm as we drove back to my apartment. I was exhausted and started to undress slowly, exhausted from the experience. Taking off a shoe was an enormous effort. I looked at Diane, assuming she would soon climb into bed next to me and we would both sleep off the joy and the fears of that memorable night. But her coat was still on as she was saying good night.

Surprised, I said, "Where are you going?"

"Back to the hotel," she answered.

"*Tonight*? You won't even stay with me tonight?"

"I don't think it would be right," she said. "Nothing has changed."

If God tested Job's patience, He was now giving me my college entrance exams, and I hadn't even cracked open a book in preparation.

ONE GREAT STEP FOR
MARRIAGE-KIND

29

I KEEP NO JOURNALS, no diaries, no date books. Since I write so much in my plays and films, it would be as pointless as me taking a picture of me taking a picture of me. Consequently, although this is a memoir—meaning what I remember of my life—the chronological order of events may not be in the exact order of when the events actually happened. What I do remember correctly is what happened, where it happened and most importantly, why it happened. This distinction runs counter to what every person of my age was taught as a schoolkid, especially in early history lessons. Dates, dates and more dates: Columbus, 1492. Lindbergh's flight, 1927. The U.S. entry into the First World War, 1917 to 1918, and the easiest one to remember, the War of 1812. If you got those correct, you were two thirds of the way toward a good grade. Of course, you had to wait until adulthood before you found out *why* any of these things happened or were important, but at least you knew *when* they happened. Well, I'm not like that. I am not a scorekeeper. To a writer, it's the story that counts.

Diane and I finally got married quickly and quietly one morning at the City Hall in Los Angeles. Not a soul knew about it—not my daughters, not my brother, not Diane's family, no one. Except Bryn, and Bryn thought a wedding was a party and why were we going to a party at nine-thirty in the morning? she asked. I drove downtown, nervously and silently, barely sharing a word with Diane. We moved down the empty streets without a sound. Sort of like a romantic commando raid. Suddenly on Melrose Avenue, I pulled the car over to the curb, stopped, opened the door and disappeared out of Diane's sight. It didn't occur to me that Diane thought I was taking a quick powder, abandoning her with the motor still running. When I returned moments later, her face had gone completely white, almost to the point that it erased her makeup as well. I slid into my seat and put a bouquet of flowers in her hands, kissed her cheek and drove on. She was still so completely flustered that she looked at the flowers on her lap as if to say, "What are these for?" I soon learned that Diane is not someone you should sneak up on. If she opened her bathroom door at the same moment you were about to knock on it, her bathrobe went into cardiac arrest.

We arrived at City Hall about ten A.M. and took our seats on the benches in the old marble hall waiting room, along with dozens of other nervous and much younger couples, some of them holding hands, some laughing and some drinking coffee from a paper cup and sharing an Egg McMuffin. Most of them looked like the price of a one-day honeymoon trip would be a hardship.

When the official in charge boomed over the blaring speaker system, "Diane Lander and Neil Simon," not a head turned. No one there ever heard of me or even cared, which is partly why we chose City Hall. The marriage ceremony was brief and businesslike, and our witnesses were two female court employees. As soon as the "Judge"—if that's what he was, wearing a purple shirt and a green striped tie—said, "I now pronounce you man and wife," our unmoved witnesses offered their hurried congratulations, no doubt wondering how many more times they would have to do this before their lunch break.

Our wedding breakfast was actually a brunch. About three hundred people attended, but none of them knew us, looked at us or were even aware we were just married. We were in a huge Chinese restaurant just a few blocks from City Hall, and for this meal only dim sum was served. These wonderful, tasty Chinese dumplings came with about fifty different kinds of fillings and there wasn't a loser in their vast ovens. We were, as I recall, the only Caucasians in the building, and we felt as if we were in Shanghai without having to take the sixteen-hour flight. We each had about six or seven dumplings, which had enough calories and protein in them to get you halfway up Mount Everest. That, plus the four glasses each of Chinese wine, made it seem possible that with one more sip, I would get up and toast my bride in fluent Cantonese. We would have thrown rice at each other but this was the kind of rice that would stick to your face and eyelids. I may have been a reluctant groom but there was no doubt that I was in love with my two-hour-new wife.

Diane was wearing a brown linen suit and a silk scarf around her neck, which was mine, an art deco relic I found one day in SoHo in New York. I wore a sports jacket, a sleeveless sweater and a shirt with no tie, which for Los Angeles in the morning was very dressy. Now that I think of it, I realize I was making some sort of statement that I didn't want to make a big deal out of this ceremony. The truth is, I married Joan, Marsha and now Diane, all in municipal buildings. Still, I'm sure you'll agree that Diane was a knockout when you see the wedding picture as you drift through the pages of this book. The photo was taken hurriedly outside City Hall by a fast-talking photographer, who I'm sure sometimes used a pony in his work.

We drove home, told our housekeeper the good news; she smiled happily and kissed us both. The rest of the morning was spent on the phone calling family, friends and anyone who was in our separate phone books.

"Yes. We're very happy . . . Yes, we're surprised too . . . You'll never guess . . . Chinese dumplings . . . I swear . . . In a Chinese restaurant . . . Wait! Talk to Neil . . . Hello, who's this? . . . Oh, hi . . . Yeah. We did it . . . This morning . . . What's wrong with City Hall? . . . Wait! Talk to Diane . . . Mom! Your daughter's married . . . Oh, God, my mother's crying . . . Her dog is crying too . . . Who? . . . Who's this? . . . No, miss. We already subscribe to the *L.A. Times.* Will you please get off the phone?"

Bryn smiled and kissed us both when she returned from preschool. She was mostly overjoyed at the big, creamy cake that was being lifted out of the freezer . . . I never thought I'd be married three times . . . I was in a slight daze . . . No matter what you plan in life, it's the unexpected that always takes over . . . After all the phone calls ceased, the house became quiet . . . I looked at the ceiling . . . It was only about one-thirty in the afternoon . . . I wondered if I should go inside to my office and write for a few hours?

SEND IN THE FARCE

30

WHEN PEOPLE ASK where the idea for a play comes from, very often my answer is "It depends on what state of mind I'm in." Having just finished a dark examination of my parents, of their broken promises and lost love, I wanted to erase those bitter thoughts from my mind and spend a year enjoying myself. A trip around the world would have been a good solution, but I had a different yearning. I wanted to laugh and to make audiences laugh. I chose to write a farce, not realizing that technically speaking, writing a good farce may be the hardest undertaking in a writer's career.

Oddly enough, in the 1930s and 1940s, the New York theaters were filled with good farces—plays like *Once in a Lifetime, Room Service, Three Men on a Horse* and *Arsenic and Old Lace*. They're still good enough to be revived in regional theaters all over the country, but perhaps a little naive for today's world. The irony is that, though these once classic farces are now considered old-fashioned, if you attempt a *new* farce for Broadway, you will inevitably be asked to measure up to the old farces I've just mentioned. "Catch-22," Joseph Heller calls it. Worse still, you will also be compared to the classic farces of Molière and Feydeau, which are always considered in style, and if you're really looking for trouble, don't try anything that is brittle, wise and witty because they'll say "a cheap ripoff of Oscar Wilde's *The Importance of Being Earnest.*" Lesson One, don't mess with masterpieces.

I did not know a thing about the mechanics of farce until I got caught up in the endlessly intricate details of its machinery. For those foolhardy enough to test these white-water rapids, I'll pass on a few hints I learned along the way and also give you the names of a few doctors who attended me after the battle was over:

1. The play must move like greased lightning. Any kind of grease will do.

2. The story starts with a minor problem, complicated very soon by a slightly more complicated problem, and inevitably never ceases being caught

up in ever increasing minor problems, which soon become catastrophic problems. In the end, all the problems are solved in one hilarious sentence. If you can do that, you should have been the one who invented the computer.

3. It must be funny. Then funnier. Then funniest. Only two people have gone beyond funniest, but they didn't live to tell the story.

4. The stakes must be high. Since almost all the characters are hiding something, if caught, it could be calamitous. Calamity always hovers two feet above everyone in a farce.

5. You cannot do a farce without swinging doors (which go in and out), closets to hide in and beds to crawl under. Very often someone hiding in a closet is joined by someone else hiding in the same closet. They may or may not see each other depending on how many fur coats separate them. A sure laugh is when the adulterer's wife in the play says, "I feel chilly. I think I'll get my fur coat." If the audience doesn't laugh at that, give them their money back. They don't belong in the theater.

6. This is not a steadfast rule, but farces, historically speaking, are about rich people and never about poor people. Poor people have enough trouble without getting caught in a farce. Rich people, on the other hand, deserve what's coming to them. Watching them squirm gets howls from the audience. If they don't laugh, send them home with the people who didn't laugh at the fur coat joke.

7. In many farces, characters often have infirmities or various disorders. These include people who lisp, stutter, are almost blind, have the gout, a tic, a whining nasal problem, are allergic to mattresses, which causes them to sneeze while hiding under beds, or—a device Shakespeare often used—two sets of twins, male and female, who cannot be told apart even by each other.

If you got all that, you may now write your farce. Good luck. You may never be heard from again.

EVEN AWARE of all these difficulties, I still undertook the writing of *Rumors*. We rehearsed and tried it out at the Old Globe Theatre in San Diego. At the first reading, we knew we were funny. But not funny enough. We thought we had enough complications in the play until you realize that in a farce enough is never enough. At the final curtain, the audience must be as spent as the actors, who by now are on oxygen support. If the audience is only wheezing with laughter, you need rewrites or actors with stronger lungs.

I WAS PRETTY MUCH spent myself because in the year and a half that Diane and I were married, I also did the film of *Brighton Beach Memoirs* and wrote the screenplay of *Biloxi Blues*. Diane was kept busy redoing the house on Chalon Road, the house I bought with Marsha, although it took some re-adjusting Diane, moving from a tiny apartment in the Valley to a more im-posing home in the green hills of Bel Air. She was still unsure if she should unpack everything. In some way, I think Diane was inundated by my busy schedule, even though I was totally unaware that I had such a busy schedule.

There were constant parties and events to attend—film premieres, charity dinners, private parties and as much socializing as your clothes closet could keep up with. Diane had no trouble fitting in with any crowd, although pri-vately, it may have taken a toll on her. Since I had been through all this for the past couple of decades, I was used to it even though I didn't necessarily enjoy it. Someone once said to me, "It must be very difficult for someone to be married to a celebrity," but in truth, I never considered myself one. I was neither flattered nor annoyed by giving autographs, and if possible, would try to walk away from a crowd rather than go through it. It didn't occur to me whether Diane thought she was just "tagging along with someone famous," or if she enjoyed the limelight herself. I thought we were together, no matter how many photographers were shouting on an opening night, "Hey, Neil! Neil! Look this way!" I was not with them. I was with her. But, if I put the shoe on the other foot, I suppose it would be a touchy situation.

Before I met Diane, I went out on a date with a very pretty and well-known TV newswoman from CNN. We walked into a restaurant, through the crowded tables until we were seated. My date seemed a little miffed. She said, "That's the first time I walked into a restaurant where everyone was looking at the man I was with instead of me." She didn't like the competition. It was our first and last date. It truly wouldn't have bothered me if she were the one they were all looking at. I am not insecure about my personal popu-larity. Unlike an actor or a famous athlete, whose physical presence is always right there in front of the public, it's my work that I'm known for and I never write in front of a crowd.

Meanwhile, back in San Diego, I was still rewriting *Rumors*. It was like a huge animal that needed constant feeding and there were times, many times, that I simply ran out of food.

There were so many plot points that needed clarifying, so many scenes that needed a new concept, so many lines that weren't as sharp as they could be and so many actors who had to be made happy for fear that someone else was getting bigger laughs than they were. "Neil, couldn't I get a better exit line here?" "Sure," I would say to myself. "Get on a plane, say good-bye and fly back to New York." I really needed help and the best person to turn to is almost always the director.

Gene Saks is a truly funny man and a wonderful director, and like many others in that job, was unable to tell me *how* to fix it. I depended on him to tell me *where* it needed fixing. Sometimes a director can just redirect a scene into working, but his and the actors' jobs would all be easier if I could get the script right all through the play.

Each night after the show, Gene and I would go to the restaurant in the hotel where we were staying and I'd have Gene quiz me. I was so busy with my own rewriting that Gene was more objective about the play as a whole and would point out where he thought our ship was sprouting holes and listing a few degrees into the water. I needed him to ask me questions. *Any* questions. I didn't need answers. I would eventually supply those myself. But I needed him to be the diagnostician, indicating to me where he saw symptoms in need of my doctoring, all this despite the fact the audience was howling with laughter through the play every night. It's why the theater is such a hard place to succeed in.

Perhaps we were more demanding than the audience, but we knew the critics in New York were more demanding than any audience alive. Our twelve-character cast were simply wonderful and too numerous to list all their names here, but I thought Christine Baranski was our standout and she went on to win the Best Supporting Actress Tony Award in New York. As for the play, the critics carped, praised, cheered, smeared, loved, loathed, liked and disliked it enormously. That's about all you could ask for. All in all, I was happy with what I did. I juggled twelve balls in the air at the same time and dropped only two or three along the way. We ran well over a year and the play runs on today almost everywhere, especially in schools where the teachers wisely take out all the F words.

Diane and I were now married a year and a half, and without my really noticing it, the marriage was quickly collapsing in front of my eyes. They say you never see the bullet that kills you.

ALONE AGAIN . . . AGAIN

31

IT ALWAYS amused me, in a grim sort of way, when a couple breaks up after some years of marriage, someone, anyone, even your closest friend, will inevitably say, "My God! What happened?" . . . As if it could be answered that easily, or even answered at all. To me, the answer probably lies in some ancient Chinese lesson for children about where the ocean comes from.

"A bird sits in a tree waiting for the rain to stop. The sun comes out and he flies off, as a single drop of water falls from his wing onto a shiny rock. The droplet slides from the rock into a tiny puddle and the puddle soon finds its way into a quiet pool, which flows into a lake that runs into a river, which eventually gathers force from the wind and finally blows into the great ocean which was born when a tiny droplet of water fell from a bird's wing." Go around that one a few hundred times and you'll know what it feels like to try to remember when your marriage first started to fall apart. Why does "I love you more than I thought it was possible to love" slide slowly but progressively into "It's over"?

In retrospect, it's fairly amazing, given our disparate backgrounds, histories, families, temperaments, attitudes and outlooks on life that Diane and I would fall in love. Yet fall in love we did, despite both the thousand things right between us, and the thousand things wrong. What does it take to throw the balance one way or the other? Nine hundred ninety-nine things right and one thousand and one things wrong? And what was the one thing wrong that started the slide? "Are you drinking from my coffee mug?" Could it be that fragile? The petty squabbles that most people endure during their first year of marriage are pretty universal, and as was the case with Diane and me, once a bond of trust is established, the squabbles disappear rather quickly.

As far as I was concerned, I was finally in a marriage that would last a lifetime. Yet, one day, Diane sat me down on our bedroom sofa and said to me, with tears in her eyes, that she had to go, to leave the marriage and to leave as soon as possible. Where did this come from, and why didn't I see it coming? There are some things in a marriage that one partner would never divulge to the other, or some things they will just touch on but make it clear it's nothing they need to share since it's well under control, while there are other things they are quite willing to discuss.

I thought we were pretty frank with each other, and I quite honestly saw nothing so dire that it would interfere with our happiness. With that in mind, there we were, with our marriage not only in trouble, it was virtually over. Before we were married, Diane asked me to promise that I would never write about her, whether fictionalized or in truth. She wanted her life, Bryn's life and our life together to be private and never public, whether good or bad, wanting and needing something so valuable as our marriage to be simply that: our marriage was not for public consumption. Given my history with using my family in many of my plays, I had no trouble in agreeing. In the first place, no one I ever wrote about, no one, ever came to me and said they were hurt by what I said. In many cases, I've taken the truth and fictionalized it to the point that if I did write about someone, they would never guess I was writing about them. In most cases, I write about the essence of someone, not the facts. No one has accused me of stealing their essence.

To even write about Diane in this book, I had to get her written permission. Somewhere in that wish for privacy is a thread that may or may not have led to the dissolution of our marriage. I don't think Diane left easily or without pain. I didn't want her to leave at all. Diane moved out to our beach house where she was staying for a while with her family, and I asked her to come back to meet me and talk, to discuss the possibilities of avoiding this breakup. Less was said than I thought there would be.

"Can we work this out?" I asked Diane, without really and truly knowing what it was we had to work out. Diane was cryptic about it and I knew that pushing her would get us nowhere. She looked up at the ceiling, seemingly for minutes on end, as if looking for an answer somewhere in the minuscule cracks that were forming in the paint overhead and in some similar crack in our relationship. She looked calm, not puzzled. By the look on her face, I was positive she was going to say, "Yes. I would like that very much." She didn't. She said, quite simply, "No. I can't. I have to leave."

There was nothing left to say. I shrugged my shoulders and said, "I'm sorry." There was no argument, no shouting, no anger, no tears. Just a simple, quiet loss. She got up, went to the door, got into her car and drove away. I sat there stunned, but quietly stunned. I said to myself, "I've been through a death and a divorce before, I guess I can get through this." We were only married a year and a half, and I think the lack of longevity in the marriage made it at least bearable to deal with. I was still sitting in the same chair a half hour later when the phone rang. It was Diane, calling from somewhere on the road to the beach. There was a plaintive sound in her voice when she said to me, "I just want you to know that I love you more today than I ever have before." End of phone call. End of marriage. It sounded like the title of some off-Broadway comedy. *I Love You More Than I Ever Have Before So Goodbye.* If I couldn't truly understand why she was leaving, how could I understand why, today of all days, could she love me more than she ever did before? What do you do when something like that happens and you still have the rest of the day to get through? Watch a ball game? Call someone for a game of tennis? I already shot the pool once and I was not angry enough to toss in a hand grenade on a beautiful afternoon.

I knew what she just said on the phone was sincere, which only made the question of why she was leaving more unanswerable. Maybe for Diane it was "not yet time for happiness." This was my third loss of a wife and what I hoped would never happen again, happened again. I fought against getting married for a third time, instinctively knowing it would end disastrously. At least my instincts were intact, but being right about something like this offers very little consolation. I walked into the den, turned on the television and watched a baseball game. There is nothing worse than watching a ball game when your wife just left. I turned it off and walked into my office and sat down behind my desk and answered some mail.

I NEVER THOUGHT I was one to philosophize about life, but today, a good deal older and perhaps a little wiser, but certainly more experienced in life, I think about this: If you can go through life without ever experiencing pain you probably haven't been born yet. And if you've gone through pain and think you know exactly why, you haven't examined all the options. And if you think you can avoid that pain the next time it confronts you, you haven't looked over your shoulder. And if you give up living and loving to avoid the pain, you don't appreciate the good things you once had.

Time went by without my seeing Diane, and no phone calls were exchanged between us. I knew she had moved back to the Valley, to a small house, rather than to one of the transitory apartments she used to hop to and from before I met her. We made a financial settlement and she was on her own. You always think you won't get over something, but you do. Life has made room for that to happen. I never got over Joan, but yearning for someone who is dead is a pointless exercise. I always think of her and I could still talk to her occasionally by candlelight in my darkened room, wondering if she hears me or not, and yet, as before, when I awoke the next morning, things seemed clearer for me. Eventually Diane would bring Bryn over to my house so that she and I could spend some time with each other. I truly missed Bryn, as much for her joyfulness and sweet personality as for her youthful wisdom. I looked forward to those Saturday afternoons and pizza lunches, which eventually grew into Disney movies and the Disney movies grew into a trip to the zoo, even though Dad got lost, flustered and bewildered until Bryn said, almost patronizingly, "Dad, why don't you drive up to that gas station and ask for directions?" She got me again.

I noticed at the zoo or at those Disney movies how many single fathers were escorting their son or daughter or both through the Saturday afternoons that were allotted to them. I was now one of them and that's one of the pains I never saw coming. There were days, when she was still small, that Bryn wanted to stay with me a little longer. When time is limited, it is so much more precious.

The house on Chalon was actually too big for one person to live in and I rarely went down the long hall to see the empty bedroom Bryn used to sleep in. Gradually, I let the house put its arms around me and comfort me. I loved the paintings on the walls that I had started buying with Joan, and then continued with Marsha; a few had been bought with Diane. I went to Paris alone once and a few times with Ann Bell, the girl I always seemed to turn to. I enjoyed buying these paintings in obscure shops around Paris and finding, through the eyes of Ray Stark, who taught me about art in our various trips to museums and galleries all over the country, that I did indeed have an eye for quality. I didn't buy masters because they were simply too expensive and I thought, even if I could afford a Renoir or a Matisse or a Picasso, I wasn't interested in owning them. The discovery of someone new and young, or even old and overlooked, was a much pleasanter experience for me.

The days were never a problem for me. Writing and some tennis allowed me to avoid loneliness. What I had to get through were the hours of the night, and the sound of nothingness that echoed silently throughout the house.

I was back to dating again and those timeworn expressions from friends who were always pitching new prospects. "Very attractive . . . lots of fun . . .

extremely intelligent . . . loves the theater . . . a former model . . . her father owns the left side of Wall Street . . ." Followed by, "Just have a drink with her, what can you lose?"

I was hesitant. I already had my three strikes and you're out. I didn't think there were any more home runs for me. Maybe I'd had enough times at bat. No one ever introduced me to the three women in my life. I met Joan, Marsha and Diane on my own, and I knew if there was ever anyone again, that's how it would have to happen.

During this time, I found no one I wanted to risk my future for, nor anyone who had measured up to the women I loved most.

Instead what I found was the play I was waiting all my life to write.

LOUIE THE GANGSTER

32

MY FATHER had a sister who was married to an accountant, as the story was told to me when I was about ten or twelve years old. Perhaps I was eleven but everything that far back is sketchily remembered. Actually, the story wasn't told to me personally, because grown-ups don't usually tell eleven-year-old boys the innermost secrets of their lives. This is what I overheard as the family talked in hushed tones in the living room while I pretended to read a comic book in the adjoining room. My aunt's husband, the accountant, worked for a firm in the garment district on Seventh Avenue in New York. It seems the firm also had some connections with the underworld, gangsters, the Mafia or whatever nefarious group one wants to label the organization my unsuspecting uncle worked for. Whether he knew of the underworld connections, or naively thought he was just keeping the books of an upstanding dress manufacturing company, no one knows. What ultimately happened was that my uncle mysteriously disappeared. He left home, went to work one morning and was never seen or heard from again. The consensus was that he was done in by the mob for probably knowing a little too much about their finances. Since I don't remember ever meeting him, he became sort of a romantic figure in the mind of this imaginative adolescent. From a small neighborhood where the biggest crime I could remember was the boy who stole two books from the library, a real-life murder in my very own family was chilling stuff. For my aunt and her children, my cousins, it was a terrible tragedy and a great loss.

Now we fast-forward to 1989 and I am sitting in my office in Los Angeles, searching the blank ceiling or the trees outside my window for an idea for a play. Remembering parts of this story loaded with color and mystery, I began to jot these notes down on my pad.

I envisioned my father (my fictional father) having to go somewhere down South to earn some money to repay what he borrowed from the not-so-friendly loan sharks to pay for my mother's hospital expenses as she lay dying from cancer. Having no place to leave me, a boy of thirteen, he goes to his mother, a tyrannical aging German Jewish woman of eighty, who walks with a cane, a limp and a permanent scowl. He pleads with her to take on his only son for about eight months. The father has to beg and shed tears before this selfish tyrant will do any one of her children a favor. She finally relents, but assures my father that if I am noisy, dirty or break anything, I will be out on the street. Occasionally living with her is her other son, a small-time crook who often comes by to lay low in Mom's apartment above the candy store she owns in Yonkers, New York.

All this takes place in the early 1940s, during the Second World War. Louie, the name I gave this petty hood, befriends me and teachers me how to cheat at cards, how to steal something from the five-and-ten-cent store and how to smoke my first cigarette. Uncle Louie was my fictional hero, a much safer and less dangerous version of a Mafia warlord. Those were the first characters and sketchy outline for a story that I put down in my spiral notebook on that first day. I called it "Louis the Gangster." Was it a comedy? A farce? A drama or a tragedy? I hadn't gotten that far yet. Let it rattle around in your brain for a few days first, I wisely advised myself.

RARELY WHEN A PLAY comes to me do I know how I will develop it. I never know who all the characters are nor how many there will be. It comes out drop by drop, as I let them sink into my thoughts, picking out what I can use and discarding anything and anyone who is less than of major importance. On the first day I start to write, I will put down almost anything, just trying to get the first introductory scene on paper, whether it's good or not. I am introducing myself to the characters and them to me. Amenities over, they begin to speak. I envision the father sitting in his mother's bedroom, the door closed behind him, talking in a quiet, plaintive way, pleading with her to take in his son. I also know we will never hear this scene because in the stage plan I have in my mind, the interior of her bedroom is not visible. This leaves the young boy, Jay, sitting by himself in the living room, not even knowing his life is being discussed a few feet away from him. But how do we know what his thoughts are? What fears he has? No problem. I give Jay a younger brother, Arty. Now they can discuss at length how much they fear the grandmother and hope that Pop will come out soon so they can all leave. We've not only established the brothers and their plight, we know a great deal about Grandma Kurnitz long before she makes an appearance.

Would Eddie, the boys' father, be Grandma Kurnitz's only child? Hardly. She was brought up in the era of large families. I arbitrarily pick the number of her children as six. Is her husband alive? I pictured him as a hardworking German immigrant, who might have tempered Grandma's cold and unemotional dispositions. Still I couldn't see him in the play. I decided that he died shortly after the family arrived in America and moved to Yonkers, where they opened the candy store. It was a job that needed no skills. If they migrated in the 1920s or 1930s, the rate of death among newborns and small children would be high. I killed off a son and a daughter, Aaron and Rose. These enormous losses are the bedrock of the grandmother's anger toward the world, and shape her philosophy for raising children. Survival is everything. Joy, happiness, love, charity—these are only for the rich. Survive at all costs.

If Eddie is successful in convincing his mother to take his sons in, it would be a disaster for all of them. The boys needed a confidant, someone who would be a buffer between them and their grandmother. I invented Aunt Bella. About thirty-six or thirty-seven, and still living with her mother, working in the candy store from early morning till closing time; even giving the mother back rubs and leg rubs to ease her pain. There would have to be something wrong with Bella, frightened as a child. In the first draft, I wrote Bella as a sweet, shy and nervous woman, but loving to her two nephews. It wasn't enough. With a mother whose only concern is that her children survive, without love, without warmth, without affection, they would have to become a dysfunctional family. In the next draft, Aunt Bella changed. She was almost retarded, but not in a clinical way. Her growth as a human being was stunted. She became a fifteen-year-old child in the body of a thirty-eight-year-old woman, with all the desires and needs of a mature woman, but with the inability to understand these desires. With Arty and Jay now moving in, we see Bella happier than she's ever been before, even though Jay, fourteen, and Arty, about twelve, seem more grown-up than she is.

Who then are the other surviving, dysfunctional children? There is Eddie, of course—weak, still frightened of his mother, and seemingly unable to get over the death of his wife. Then there is Gert, Bella's sister, who is married and lives with her husband, but scarred like her siblings. When Gert cried as a child, the mother pounded her cane onto the floor and shouted, "STOP DOT CRYING! BE HAPPY YOU'RE ALIVE!" Gert stopped her crying immediately, but only by stifling her own breath, thereby being unable to speak a full sentence without gasping for air. It's not a surprise when Gert later tells

Arty and Jay that she doesn't do that all the time. It's mostly when she comes to visit her mother.

Louis the gangster, or Uncle Louie to the boys, began in my mind as the uncle who disappeared gangland style, but soon gave way to being just a petty crook, the only one strong enough to stand up to his mother. He may stand up to her, but he can never win a battle, whether with her or with life. He's a survivor, but he's also a loser.

With my characters all now in place, I began to write the play, going back to the first page. As the story began to reveal itself, I found myself identifying most with Aunt Bella. She is the one I loved, the heroine of what became *Lost in Yonkers*. Late in the play, she fights a pitched battle with her mother, wanting permission from her to marry a boy—a boy of forty—because like Bella, he too cannot function in a normal world. Perhaps the two of them together can make a go of it. Bella pleads with her mother to say yes, to let her marry this boy, to let her be his wife and eventually a mother to her own babies—babies she will love and cherish and not let them grow up to be weak and twisted like her own brothers and sisters. The mother, of course, denies her this right by saying nothing and leaving the room without a word, and Bella cries out to her family, "Help me. Someone put their arms around me . . . please."

Bella never quite wins her freedom, but when she says to her mother in a later scene, referring to her dead brother and sister, "Maybe Aaron and Rose were the lucky ones," she has finally wounded her mother. Bella leaves the room while the mother, alone in her chair, wants to scream in anguish, and has to put a handkerchief in her mouth to keep the world from hearing her final punishment.

GENE SAKS again was picked to direct the play. Gene did such a brilliant job with the Brighton Beach Trilogy, and then again with *Lost in Yonkers*, because he knew the very fiber of these people. He grew up with all of them and probably understood the characters in these plays as well as I did. Maybe better.

The first time I saw Kevin Spacey was in a revival of Eugene O'Neill's greatest play, *Long Day's Journey into Night*. It starred Jack Lemmon, and Kevin played the role of the older, wayward son, an incurable alcoholic, played in the original production by Jason Robards, Jr. Kevin took my breath away, as he still does in everything he touches. He was my first and only choice for Uncle Louie. I breathed a sigh of gratitude and relief when Kevin said yes to us.

Casting the role of Aunt Bella, I imagined, would be the hardest. Since I was living in California again, it was decided by Jay Binder, our casting agent, and probably the most important casting agent on Broadway today, that I see some preliminary people in Los Angeles by myself, and if I found anyone I thought was a possible contender, to send her into New York to be seen by Gene and Manny Azenberg. The first actress to walk through the door of my office (and the first time I would hear spoken any of the words I had written) was Mercedes Reuhl. I had seen her in smaller roles in a few films and knew she was talented. But could she be Bella?

With a young man seated on the sofa next to her to read the lines of the other characters, Mercedes took a few moments to look through the first scene again, then looked up at me and said, "May I ask a question? Just how far-out is Bella?"

I said, "She's not retarded, if that's what you mean. I think the mother kept her as a child through the force of her will."

I was about to say more, when Mercedes nodded her head and said, "Okay. I get it. Let's see what happens." And she began to read.

Within a few minutes I felt so moved that there were tears coming into my eyes. I knew in an instant that she was perfect. There was no point in seeing anyone else, even though I did have to go through the motions. I remembered Herbert Ross not wanting to take Quinn Cummings until he had seen forty other young girls, but of course we ended up with Quinn Cummings. We quickly flew Mercedes into New York to read for Gene and Manny. She was signed immediately. As Marsha Mason so wisely said to me years before, "You don't pick them. They pick themselves."

The grandmother would be the most difficult role to perform. She could easily come off as a hateful character, and the part called for an actress of great depth who could show us why this woman behaved as she did, without ever being sentimental about it. Any number of actresses were submitted, but the one name that came up the most was Irene Worth, pronounced Irenee. She was born in the States but appeared so often in London, acquiring an English accent along the way, she was thought of as British. We sent her the script. She read it and accepted. No problem. Except for us. Gene wondered if she could do a convincing German accent. The only way to find out was for Gene, Manny and myself to fly to London and meet with the Great Lady herself.

We met her for lunch at the Inn on the Park Hotel in London. In her perfect English, she said she thought it was a very fine play and was looking forward to doing it. Since she already accepted the part, she thought it very extravagant of us to fly all the way over just to have lunch with her. None of us knew how to bring up the issue of the German accent without insulting her.

Gene jumped in first. "Are you comfortable playing a German Jew?" Gene asked.

"Yes, darling. I'm an actress. May I have some more Chablis, please?"

We all looked at each other. We'd better be more direct.

"Have you ever played a German before?" Manny asked.

"I've played everything, darling. Am I the only one having dessert?"

Finally, Gene made the big push. He laughed first, to soften her up, and then said, "Is there any special dialect you would do? That you could show us so we'd know which one to pick?"

She looked at us with a cold, chilling stare.

"If you're asking me to audition for you, you've come a long way for nothing. I haven't auditioned in forty-two years."

"No, of course not," Gene rushed in trying to save the day. "I wasn't thinking of an audition," he begged off.

"Then let's drop the subject . . . Waiter, may I see the dessert cart, please?"

We had lost. We were never going to hear the accent. The waiter wheeled over the large dessert cart and placed it before her to peruse. She looked from one dessert to the other and then said, in a perfect German accent, "Should I haff ze strudel, or perhaps ze apple tart? Nein. I sink ze chocolate tart looks best, yah? Danke schoen."

She never looked at us or smiled. She was smarter than all of us. We had our Grandma Kurnitz.

ON THE NIGHT of the Tony Awards, I thought our biggest competition was John Guare's *Six Degrees of Separation*, a wonderful play that Frank Rich called "his masterpiece." He had given us only a middling review. The Tony Awards show began, and pretty soon the awards began to mount up.

"Best Supporting Actor in a Play . . . Kevin Spacey."

"Best Supporting Actress in a Play . . . Mercedes Reuhl."

"Best Actress in a Play . . . Irene Worth."

"Best Play . . . Neil Simon's *Lost in Yonkers*."

Almost a clean sweep except for Gene Saks, who I thought was a shoo-in. Perhaps he didn't get it that year because he had already won for two plays in the Brighton Beach Trilogy.

ON APRIL 9, 1991, I received a telegram from Michael Sovern of Columbia University. It was a short, understated, single sentence.

"You were awarded Pulitzer Prize for Drama today. Congratulations."

I won something I never dreamed would come to me. I called my brother and said, "Danny, I just won the Pulitzer Prize."

"Wait a second," he said. "I have to stop the water in my tub." A few seconds later he was back. "So what happened today?"

The little things of everyday life sometimes temper the magical things. And that's how it should be.

JEFF

33

I thought perhaps what eventually happened in writing *Lost in Yonkers* found its seed in the dark and calamitous years that preceded it. Not just to me, but to my family, to my eldest daughter, Ellen, in particular.

In 1984, Ellen, divorced from John Leland and living with her son, Andrew, in Nyack, New York, went to her best friend's wedding. Sitting at the same table as Ellen was a young man with a vibrant personality, attractive and intelligent, with a maturity beyond his twenty-six years. Jeff Bishop could not take his eyes off Ellen, who was sitting across from him at the large round table filled with guests. He soon rearranged the seating, which put him in the chair next to Ellen. Ellen has a smile and a personality that light up a room, and Jeff was now sitting in the glow of that light.

He had graduated from Princeton University and was now going for his Ph.D. in astrophysics at the University of Chicago. I can readily say that no one in my family had ever majored in astrophysics, nor, I'm sure, even knew exactly what it was. Ellen, in those days, was far more reticent to talk to me about her personal life, since she was so determined to become her own person. As time went on, Ellen relaxed her concerns and as she became surer of herself, began to include me in most matters that concerned her. The cycle of the child clinging to her parents, then moving away as she took on her own life and personality, eventually came full circle to a point where she can now include me in most of the important events that happen to her. I like it better this way.

She appeared one day at my new apartment on 70th Street and Park Avenue (that was a move made somewhere in this story that has no date nor time that I can recall) with Jeff Bishop, following a whirlwind romance that blossomed as Ellen was making almost weekly visits to Chicago. I was living alone at the time and enjoying the first apartment I ever owned with a terrace; it was on the twentieth floor, and had a view from New Jersey to the

East River. There were, once again, women in my life, but not *a* woman and certainly not *the* woman.

I was, however, delighted to see that Ellen had found *the* man in her life. Jeff never flaunted his intelligence or his academic success. All he ever talked about was Ellen. All he ever looked at was Ellen. No matter how much he lived his intellectual life in the mysteries of the universe, nothing shined and glittered more to him than the dark-haired girl he was sitting next to on the sofa, both beaming at me, anxious to tell me their secret. The inept Inspector Clouseau could have figured this one out. They had come to tell me they were getting married. I feigned surprise, but Ellen didn't want a feign from me. She wanted a YIPPEE AYE YAY OKAY from me, which I did in my own quiet, subdued sort of way. I hugged them both, delighted and overjoyed with their happiness.

They married, Jeff graduated, Andrew was growing up and I was ecstatic, except for the news that they would soon be moving to Toronto, Canada, where Jeff received a postdoctoral fellowship at the Canadian Institute for Theoretical Astrophysics. I now had the comfort of knowing that if ever I had a problem with theoretical astrophysics, I knew exactly to whom I should turn. By 1987, they missed being home and Jeff applied for and received an associate professorship at Columbia University in the heart of New York City. They moved back to the house in Nyack and I kept wondering if Joan had a bird's-eye view from the same heavens that Jeff explored, and could see how happy her daughter and grandson, Andrew, were.

Jeff began to cough quite a bit and since he didn't smoke, the symptoms were worrisome. After examination, the diagnostic results came back. Jeff had cystic fibrosis. The news was staggering and devastating. I called a doctor friend and asked what the prognosis was. He said, in a very solemn tone, that if you had the disease as a child, you wouldn't live much past twenty. Since Jeff was an adult, the news was somewhat reassuring. There was no telling how long a life he would have. With proper care and exercise, his life expectancy could be anything. He could live to forty, fifty, even sixty and possibly longer.

Much has been learned about the disease since that time, and great progress has been made in fighting cystic fibrosis, but all that knowledge was not available then as it is today. Each morning Jeff would run a few miles on the roads of Nyack to help open his lungs to ensure better breathing and better health. Ellen always prepared breakfast for him while he was gone, waiting for his return. One morning he seemed later than usual, and Jeff was very prompt about everything. When he was a half hour late, a worried Ellen decided to get in her car and look for him, in the event he was having some difficulty. Eventually she saw a few cars parked at the rim of a hill along with two police cars. She stopped and asked if anyone had seen her husband, describing the running outfit he was wearing. The officer eyed her slowly and said, "Yes. He was in an accident. They took him to the hospital." Ellen's reaction was, "Just like Jeff. He's probably lying there with a broken leg." Since the policeman didn't show too much concern, Ellen didn't either. She drove to the hospital and asked a nurse standing near the desk where she could find her husband, Jeff Bishop. The nurse took Ellen aside, sat her down on a bench, then got a paper bag and told Ellen to start breathing into the bag.

"Tell me what happened," Ellen asked.

"First breathe into the bag," the nurse repeated.

As Ellen took a few breaths, the nurse said, "He didn't make it. He was hit by a car. He died instantly."

The room began to spin for Ellen, and she couldn't quite grasp what the nurse was telling her. Dead? No, that's not possible.

I was three thousand miles away and there was nothing I could do for her. I heard the news about five-thirty in the morning. Ellen's friend and next-door neighbor, Claudette, called to tell me what happened. In one short, somber, declarative sentence, she said to me, "Jeff was killed a half hour ago." I never heard what else she said because a sound emanated out of my body that never occurred before. It was a long, plaintive cry of "Nooooooo." It seemed to go on forever. The only time in my life I experienced grief so deep and so quickly was when the doctor in New York told me on a back staircase that Joan only had about a year and a half to live. But Ellen didn't have another year and a half with Jeff. Ellen was never going to say goodbye to Jeff. It was over in an instant, and the blow she felt must have been as sudden and as devastating as the one that killed Jeff in a single moment. I got on a plane as quickly as I could. All I could think of was that she was too young to lose her mother and then her husband, too young to go through such losses just as she was experiencing the happiest days of her life. The only comfort I had was to know that by now her son, Andrew, and her sister, Nancy, would be by her side, holding her hands. I realized then that we not only grieve for our own losses, but we grieve for the loss that our loved ones have to endure themselves.

MAYBE THIS TIME WE'LL GET IT RIGHT
34

THE NEW YORK winters were getting harder for me to take, so I was back in California, living in the house on Chalon Road. The work poured out, day after day, while I filled out the other hours with tennis and dates, generally unsatisfying. Not the tennis. The dates. If there were a prize for the Worst Bachelor of the Year, I would win it.

But why did I pursue another marriage at all? I wondered why I thought that marriage was preferable to staying single. God knows my parents weren't very good at marriage, nor was my brother, Danny, whose marriage ended years before. The truth was, it wasn't the idea of marriage that really appealed to me; it was simply the idea of meeting the right person. That was what I hoped for. But I knew I couldn't have met anyone righter than Joan, and perhaps there was my problem. I talked to her again one night in my meditative position. "Joan," I said softly. "I think dying was a big mistake. Got any ideas?"

I felt I had been born on the day I met her, and while I hadn't died on the day she did, I definitely had been crippled, and have hobbled my way through the rest of life. Of course, that's not an accurate statement; it's a very dramatic and theatrical statement. I get that way sometimes. I had a wonderful marriage to Marsha, if you leave out the divorce part, and a wonderful marriage to Diane, if you leave out the "No, I have to go" part. Was I an ideal husband? I doubt it. But I was a first-rate father because neither Ellen nor Nancy ever said to me, "I want out. I'm getting a lawyer." If I was blessed with anything in my life, it was my daughters, and now their children and their husbands.

If you can follow my time lapses, we have reached 1990 and Diane and I were apart for almost a year and a half. I no longer thought of her very much, but since that statement is not definitive, it must have meant that I thought of her occasionally. Dating became more meaningless to me and I hated it when I found myself repeating phrases to another new face in another new restaurant. Why was it so important to me to be with one woman and why was I so caught up in the past, thinking I could never find someone to compare with

Joan? Comparisons such as these are hazardous and should never be made. They cause you to miss the "Someone New" person's virtues. You can't see the forest for the memories. For example, after Marsha and I broke up, I couldn't find anyone who had *her* virtues. Still I kept on dating, often blind dating, a form of social behavior that has, for the most part, absolutely *no* virtues.

Each new date was a repetition of the previous date. I'd ring the bell and a surly twelve-year-old girl would open the door. I'd say, "Hi. I'm—" and she'd say quickly, "I know, she's upstairs getting dressed," then walk back to her television set, leaving me in the doorway. To be generous, one has to consider how many times the twelve-year-old girl would open the door to another loser. As I entered the house, certain telltale signs warned me this would be a one-time-only date. The sight of two cats prowling around the living room was enough to give me my walking papers. Cats, birds, fishbowls and hamsters not in their cage were indications for me that the small talk I made at dinner would be so small it would be inaudible. Dogs, on the other hand, can win me over handily. If I found the right dog, I wouldn't care if my date ever descended the stairs. Many times, in fact, I wished I had taken the dog for a walk instead of my date to a restaurant. If I sound misogynistic, I don't mean to be. I knew how many times the woman opened the door, saw me there, and recognized two hours of her life being thrown down the drain. She most certainly must have hated blind dates as much as most of us do. And she must have thought to herself as she sat across the table from me, "My God, is he going to talk about his dead wife all night long?" She had a point.

PBS HAD (and possibly still may have) a series of one-hour profiles of people in the arts who had achieved, in their estimation, a singular reputation in their own field. The program was the *American Masters* series, and I was fortunate to be chosen as the subject of a one-hour documentary on my work. It took them from three to four months to put the program together, because the details of one's career and life were carefully documented in the course of that one hour. Producer Mannya Starr and her husband, producer-director Amram Starr, did an impeccable job, my favorite footage being a visit they arranged for and filmed of me in Far Rockaway, now a tumbledown beach resort. When I was young, my family and I spent a few summers there, in a boxlike cottage that housed my family and my aunt's family, eight people in all, none comfortably. It was the memory of those summers at this place that turned out to be the origin for the three plays in the Brighton Beach

Trilogy. When the documentary was completed, there was a screening for a few hundred people in Los Angeles, to which I invited my friends and family and ex-family. Marsha showed up and I was very pleased to see her. When it was over, there was a cocktail party in the lobby of the theater, in an area that extended out onto a patio. I made the rounds, chatting with almost all the guests, and then I stepped out on to the patio to get some relief from the smoke. L.A. had not yet cracked down on smoking in certain areas. I was talking to a few of my friends when I spotted a woman who looked vaguely familiar coming up the stairs. I was about to turn away when the woman called out to me: "Hi, Neil."

I looked at her again. She was portly, and had a very pretty face, and I still did not recognize her. Politely, I said hello, ready to walk on, when she smiled. It was a smile I definitely had seen before, and I stood there trying to make out who she was.

"It's Diane," she said.

"Diane?" I asked, taken aback for a moment. "Diane, hi. I didn't know you would be here." I also didn't know she had put on at least thirty pounds. It became immediately apparent that in the year and a half since we had been divorced, she had gone through some major personal changes. I could see the struggle reflected clearly in her eyes. Still, extra weight and all, I was glad to see her, recognizing immediately that whatever spell she cast on me that first day at Neiman Marcus was still working its magic on me. Some people have it, some don't. Despite the fact her face was now puffy, Diane was still beautiful to me.

She told me she hadn't been invited, but had heard about the screening and just wanted to come by and say hello. We talked a little about Bryn and about what Diane had been doing for the past eighteen months. She had been going to a school—a college, if you will—that both taught and had its students participate in their own psychotherapy, one playing the analyst to the patient and then reversing the roles. It's clear as I talked to Diane that the effort had taken its toll. This was a different Diane than the one I had known. She was far more subdued than when I first met and fell in love with her, yet whatever attracted me a year and a half before was still there—the embers miraculously were still glowing. It was a dimmer light to be sure, but nevertheless, the glow was unmistakable. All the twelve-year-old girls who scowled at me as they opened the door, all the dates that descended their stairs, all the dinners in all the restaurants, and all the meaningless small talk I engaged in, had vanished in this one moment of seeing her again, and I realized I was not quite through with Diane just yet. Still, I did not see myself getting married again.

It was with some caution that I later visited her in her small rented house in the Valley. I knocked on the door, which was opened by Bryn, who stood looking up at me with a smiling face. Then suddenly a tiny red-haired poodle started to bark at me, first running whirlwind circles around me and then excitedly running from one end of the house to the other, surely breaking every existing record for covering that distance. Her name was Annabelle, and she'd been given to Bryn by Diane on the previous Christmas. Mabel Zeno, Bryn's nanny, was still with them, only her duties had probably tripled by then. Mabel Zeno is one of the good people in this world, and Bryn benefited enormously by having this loving woman watch over her.

If you've ever been through it, walking into the house of someone you once loved, lived with and was married to is a humbling experience. No matter how sophisticated you might be, you don't know where to sit, what to say or how to say it. There is also a peculiar feeling of familiarity, yet of not knowing which rooms you are allowed to enter. I realized immediately that all the closeness I had felt during our marriage no longer applied here, and I wondered if Diane felt as uneasy as I did.

Bryn had grown in the year and a half and, if possible, was even more beautiful than I remembered her. It is not only easy to love Bryn, it's impossible not to. She was certainly not yet twelve, but of all the girls who opened the door for me in her mother's house, she was the only one who greeted me with a smile and a kiss. Diane may have gone through some dark days, but she was blessed in having the best child, the best nanny and the cutest dog in the neighborhood. She also seemed comfortable where she was living, away from the glitz and brashness of Hollywood.

We got into my car and drove to an Italian restaurant not far from where Diane lived. When you're nervous, you tend to read the menu eight times before you realize these are the names of food that they have to serve you. You also tend to push your food around the plate a lot, even making designs in your spaghetti before you understand that you're supposed to eat it as opposed to making art out of it. The closeness between us was gone, glowing embers or not, and we were virtually starting from the beginning again. Still, one had to make conversation, and I wasn't afforded the chance to ask or answer questions like "And what is it you do?" A vodka for me and a glass of wine for her thankfully lowered the pressure we both must have felt, and suddenly Diane laughed her winning laugh, almost always getting the mumbled nuances of my humor, which I was aware of using as a device for avoiding the hurts of the past.

The evening went okay—not great, not bad. Actually, maybe it even went better than okay. We were polite when I got her back to the house, and a kiss on her cheek was all I could offer or all she was ready to accept. I told her I would call her again and I made the thirty-five-minute drive over the hills to my house in Bel Air, thinking to myself, "Slowly. Go slowly with this, Neil." Still, over the next few dates, I did notice that she was beginning to lose some weight and was laughing more easily and readily as we tried all the restaurants in her neighborhood. I think what I was hoping for was for Diane to greet me at the door, dressed in her bulky pie-making outfit, and ask me to help her read the recipe while she baked. The embers were glowing more brightly now with each new visit.

AS THE MEMORY bank in my mind occasionally breaks down, it's hard for me to remember exactly how long it was before the time came when I drove to Diane's house with something burning in my pocket. I do know I was more nervous than I could ever remember being before. Was I about to walk into another situation, one which would lead into another mangled marriage? There was nothing to indicate that history would *not* repeat itself. Yet there I was, about to put myself in harm's way again. And was Diane worried about the same future for herself? I rang the doorbell and in my nervous mind, the bell sounded as loud as all the bells that rang throughout the country on the day World War II ended. Diane did not seem a bit nervous, however, but rather cheerful. She and I kissed Bryn good night and Mabel Zeno smiled from the kitchen and called out, "You two have a good time tonight," as if the past year and a half had never happened. We got in the car, shut the doors but I didn't start the engine.

Diane looked at me, concerned for the first time. "What's wrong?" she asked.

"I don't know when to do it," I said.

"Do what?"

I reached into my pocket and took out a small box. "Do this," I said, as I handed her the box with the familiar name of Tiffany on the top. She kept looking at the box. "It's better when you open it," I advised her.

She did, and her eyes opened wide, and the music I thought I heard was coming from inside her head. She took out the diamond ring and put it on her finger.

"Oh, God. It's incredible. Don't start the car. I have to show Bryn and Zeno." She ran inside, with me trailing behind.

"Is it real?" Bryn said.

"Yes," I answered. "But I just rented it for the evening."

"Do I smell another wedding?" Zeno asked with a laugh.

"Well, either that or my brain is on fire," I thought nervously. All I can remember as we walked around the area after dinner was that we held hands and we kissed a lot. Another Chapter Two to my life.

THE WEDDING took place in the large foyer—or gallery, if you prefer—in the Chalon house. It was also the largest room in the house. It was the first time that Diane's family and mine were all under the same roof together, although each group tended to stay on their own side—not out of animosity, but simply because they didn't know each other. If anyone felt the difference, it was me. We had such disparate backgrounds. Diane's family was Catholic, mine was Jewish. Diane's family were Midwest, mine strictly East Coast.

It's not the differences that cause problems in a marriage, because when they come up, with a little understanding, you can ride out the storm. It's the lack of common responses and attitudes that sometimes can make people feel like total strangers to each other. It's when he or she feels so right, and so sure that the other is dead wrong. I once said something to Diane that hurt her feelings, although that wasn't intended. I hadn't realized she would be so sensitive to my remark, so I apologized and hoped we could move on.

"No," she said. "Once something is said, it can never be taken back."

I looked at her, bewildered. I didn't know what culture or religion or tribe that rule came from, but it was so unforgiving, it made me feel that I was damned for life. And I also didn't know that twenty years later I still would be begging her to forgive what I once said in a casual conversation.

"Isn't there such a thing as forgiveness?" I asked her.

"Of course. I forgive you. But what you said can never be taken back."

I said, "What if I went to a doctor and had a laser beam remove it from my tongue?" Sarcastic humor doesn't always work.

I didn't know if she heard this unforgiving dictum in a sermon at church, or from some girlfriend she grew up with who heard her parents say it. I do know that when the chance came to retaliate, I jumped at it.

"Diane, what time is it?" I asked.

She looked at her watch. "It's five after six . . . No. I'm sorry. It's five after seven."

"No," I said. "It's too late. It's five after six. You said it, and it can never be taken back."

Marriage is not always for adults. It sometimes brings out the child in us. Geography also plays an important role in marriage. We fall victims to our own folklore, imprisoned by our separate cultures. Stray too far, and problems arise. Sometimes the wise decision is to marry "the girl next door." The problem is, it's not always the girl next door that we fall in love with.

A PLAY FOR NANCY

35

I WROTE THE PLAY *Jake's Women* to do the impossible. Years after Joan's death, my daughter Nancy expressed to me a wish she had for a long time. Nancy was ten when Joan died, her sister Ellen was fifteen. Nancy told me she always wished she could have had the five extra years that Ellen had with her mother. As time passed, Nancy was willing to settle for just one day with Joan. She wanted Joan to meet the man she had fallen in love with and married, David Florimbi, knowing that Joan would have overwhelmingly approved of her choice. Most especially, Nancy wanted Joan to see her granddaughter, Sofia, who in so many ways resembled Joan's dark-haired, olive-skinned beauty. Of course, no one was able to grant Nancy's wish, but I wanted to give it a try.

Jake's Women is not, in a true sense, an autobiographical play, because almost seventy percent of the play takes place in Jake's mind, in his ever active imagination. Are your thoughts autobiography? Webster says, a little skimpily, it's the biography of a person narrated by himself. Biography, they go on to say, is the written history of a person's life. Are thoughts part of your life or does it become actual life only when those thoughts are put into words or deeds? Webster says, "I'm not in that business. Try a philosopher." I decided to make up my own definition. *Jake's Women* is a thoughtographical play. It's "auto" because it's my thoughts. It's also a fictional nonfiction play, since Jake is fiction and I am Jake, I being nonfictional. Look how complicated it gets, and I haven't even put down a word of the play. Actually the audience doesn't care much about these scholarly excursions. Only critics do. That aside, I decided to write about Jake/Neil, surrounded by the most important women in "his" life, since it's women from whom I've drawn my greatest strength.

The magic that writing plays gives you is the ability to make anyone you want to appear on a stage for all to see—and then to disappear just as quickly. You can see your daughter at twelve, and in a flash, she reappears at twenty-one. You can make your analyst say anything you want to hear, and you can summon your wife from the dead, so that you can relive all the joys you both shared when you were young. When Jake needs advice from his sister, he can pull her out of a movie theater and make her appear in his living room. Even though his thoughts are in his imagination, he still gives them a life of their own. When his sister is summoned, she looks in the mirror and is furious with Jake for dressing her so gaudily. She thinks she looks like Bette Midler in mid-concert. He apologizes: "I'm sorry. I didn't have time to go shopping for you." He can and does talk to his second wife in the present (not in his imagination), and in the past (as he remembered it), or in his mind (as he wished she would behave). He is a controlling human being, this Jake, but that's why he became a writer. Writers are given this privilege. Bad writers abuse it.

But Jake plays the "summoning game" too often, ultimately making it difficult for him to know when he's functioning in reality or operating in an imagining mode. As the play and Jake's life move on, the imagined women start to appear even when Jake hasn't summoned them, just as Mr. Hyde begins to appear long after Dr. Jekyll regrets ever giving him a life. These women start to take over Jake's life, and in the process reprimand him for the bad choices he sometimes makes. It's only Jake's daughter, Molly, and Julie, his deceased wife, whose appearances always please Jake.

In the play, I reversed Nancy's wish. It's his dead wife, Julie, who appears and asks Jake to let her see Molly, to talk to her, to be filled in on Molly's life that Julie never lived long enough to see. Under duress, Jake agrees, and Julie returns to Jake's room on her birthday. The gift she asked for is to see Molly the way she is today, all grown up, a college senior. Julie waits in the shadows of the room as Jake conjures Molly to appear at the door. Molly is slightly worried (playing out the game that Jake is inventing) because she was just taking a college exam and if her dad pulled her out of class to be in his room, it must be something important.

"Are you all right, Dad? Are you sick?" she asks.

He shakes his head no, glancing back into the shadows, wondering how to effect this reunion without Molly backing away fearfully, maybe even running out of the room. But of course, she can't run because Jake controls the situation, although in his mind he is turning this reunion over to the mother and her daughter. Before Molly appears, Julie asks Jake to please leave when Molly arrives. She wants to be alone with her daughter.

Jake says, "I can't leave the room. You can't talk to each other without my thinking of it."

"Sure you can," says Julie. "You're smart. You'll figure a way how to do it."

Jake knows he can't think of something, then walk out of the room and leave his thoughts behind to continue a life without him. But this is not time for logic. Imagination can move mountains. He plunges ahead.

"Molly," says Jake. "There's someone here to see you."

Julie steps out of the shadows and Molly sees her. She is confused at first, even a little frightened. She takes a step back.

JULIE: Jake, she's having trouble with it. She doesn't understand. Help her to accept it, Jake.

JAKE: I'm sorry. I didn't think it out. Let me start over . . .

MOLLY: O! . . . It's all right . . . Now I understand. Now it's fine . . . Hello, Mom.

JULIE: Would you like to sit down with me? Would that be all right?

MOLLY: Yes. Of course . . . I have a million things to ask you.

And Jake steps back into the shadows as he watches the impossible come true. He sees Molly getting her wish. He sees Julie getting her wish. And I saw Nancy getting her wish. Mother and daughter talk, filling in the days they never shared. They talk about school, about the boy that Molly is seeing. They talk about the past, the trips they took together when Molly was small and Julie was there for her. They talk about the best day they ever had together and soon they're laughing and reminiscing as if nothing ever happened.

Jake watches all this but never interferes. He lets them play the moment out on their own, but he turns to the audience, to include them:

JAKE: (To audience) Am I the only one who's ever done this? I don't think so. There's not one of you who hasn't thought, at three o'clock in the morning staring up at a ceiling, of what it would be like to talk to your father who died five or twenty years ago. Would he look the same? Would you still be his little girl? . . . Or the boy you loved in college who married someone else. What would your life be if he proposed to you instead . . . You've played that scene out. We all do it . . . My problem is I never stop doing it.

We all know Andy Warhol's prediction that eventually we'll all have our fifteen minutes of fame. Would you trade that for fifteen minutes with someone who's passed on, someone that you loved dearly? I would. Well, that's not exactly fair—I've had my forty years of fame. And about seeing someone you loved who is now gone? I still do it all the time. With enough imagination, everything is within our grasp.

As the scene in the play between Julie and Molly progresses, Molly starts to talk about the mother leaving one day and never coming back. She tells how lonely she was, how much she missed her mother as she grew up. Sensing that this conversation is going too far, going to places Jake hoped would never come up, he tries to stop it. But Molly gets angry with him.

MOLLY: *(To Jake)* I didn't ask to play this game. You brought me here. You
    brought Mom here. You bring us together after eleven years and you
    give us ten lousy minutes together. What is that? Why do you do it? It's
    so cruel. What is it you wanted to see?
JAKE: I wanted to see you both happy again.
MOLLY: By doing the impossible?
JAKE: Not so impossible. I saw you both laughing again, together again. It
    made me happy to see that.

But soon he realizes you can't live life only in your imagination; he realizes that writing is only a part of his life, and that it's time for him to get back into the world he so often avoids. He created this reunion between mother and daughter, but Jake is the one who has benefited most.

Thanks to Alan Alda's brilliant and demanding performance of Jake, the play had a successful run on Broadway and then again in Los Angeles. What mattered most to me was Nancy's reaction to it, especially to the reunion scene. It was only a play, and what went on in Nancy's mind when she saw it, I couldn't exactly say. But I treasured the night she first saw the play and came to me afterward with tears in her eyes, and I embraced her, knowing I couldn't really do the impossible, but only Nancy knows how possible the impossible can sometimes be.

BRYN LANDER SIMON

36

SINCE THERE WERE no obstacles in the way, I decided to adopt Bryn. I adored her and my only fear was that if this marriage to Diane were as short-lived as our first one, it would not be fair to either Bryn or myself. I wanted to be a permanent father in a permanent marriage. There was every indication that Diane and I were here to stay as a couple, so we applied for the proper papers. Having done that, we were all interviewed in our house by a warm and friendly gentleman from the California state adoption system, whose job it was to see that this was something that all three of us wanted.

There are some professions that must be more satisfying than others, and I would think that the person responsible for bringing families together would be happier than someone whose job it is to separate them. Does a divorce lawyer like what he does? I don't know. I've known one or two who seem to be extremely decent people, but I've also seen some who are like sharks who smell blood in the water. They are out to get the best judgment for their clients, but in doing so, they sometimes push a husband or a wife to such extreme measures, advising their clients to make enormous demands on the other, that what could have been a friendly divorce—the mother of all oxymorons—instead turns into a wound so deep, painful and everlasting that they become enemies forevermore. It's in that instance, and only in that instance, that I agree with Diane's earlier statement about how once something is said, it can never be taken back. Divorce, and the act of breaking up what once was a relationship, is painful enough in itself, so one would hope that two people who once loved each other enough to take marriage vows might try to be fair and reasonable in the dispensation of money and property. Or am I being too naive? Yet I've seen lawyers for both parties reach into their bag of expertise and come up with demands that neither the wife nor the husband had ever dreamed of. For some lawyers, it's just a way of drawing the process out as long as they can, earning themselves bigger fees; for others, it's all about triumphing over their opponent, thereby inheriting a reputation of being a dangerous gunslinger, and thus increasing the demand for them as a divorce lawyer—and thus increasing their fees as well. As I said, there are some lawyers like that, but certainly not all.

Adoption, however, unlike divorce, is a joyous occasion. Diane tried to explain to young Bryn that I was soon going to adopt her and she would forevermore be my daughter, and I her father. Bryn nodded and smiled in agreement, although it's hard to know if someone seven or eight years old really understands the rules and legal interpretations conceived by adults.

Once again Diane and I drove down the familiar road to the County Courthouse, but this time it was for a marriage of another kind. This time I wore a tie and this time Diane was not nervous about me jumping out of a car on Melrose Avenue. Bryn sat silently in the back seat, lost in her thoughts, showing no emotion one way or the other. We were now about ten minutes away from the courthouse when Bryn broke her silence. Out of nowhere she said, "Will I still be able to see you both?"

Diane and I looked at each other, puzzled, not quite understanding the question.

"What do you mean, Bryn?" Diane asked.

"After I'm adopted, will I still be able to see you both?"

Diane and I were about to break into tears. Bryn thought she was being put *up* for adoption, that she would have new parents, and she was wondering if she would still be able to see us. The innocence and poignancy of her question was so overwhelming, so heartbreaking and touching, that it haunts me to this day. If that's what she thought, why wasn't she sitting in that back seat screaming and wailing? Was she so terrified or so confused about how life was dictated by adults, that if something like that could really happen to her, she would just have to accept it?

Diane almost broke down when she explained to Bryn that she was going to be my legal daughter, even though I wasn't her biological father. I think that went over Bryn's head too, but by this time she was so relieved, even euphoric, that she wasn't leaving us or that we were not abandoning her, she simply smiled and said, "Oh. I get it. That's a lot better."

The courtroom was filled with anxious men, women and children. Some in the same position as we were, while others were childless couples who were ecstatic that they were now able to adopt a child, fulfilling all of their dreams. The judge was a warm, gentle man who obviously loved his position as one who makes families instead of breaking them. He spoke slowly to Bryn, as he did to the children who went before us, informing her that becoming the daughter of her new parent was not a temporary thing. He explained that a mother or father could get a divorce, but a child or parent could *never* divorce each other. Bryn would be my daughter for life; I would be her father for life.

Every parent and child who walked out of the courtroom that day was either crying tears of happiness or smiling joyfully. Bryn Lander became Bryn Lander Simon, and I just had my third daughter. This time we did not go to Chinatown for dim sum. Instead we went to Bryn's favorite restaurant where she ate sparingly until she got the huge dessert that she obviously had been thinking of all the way from the County Courthouse.

GOODBYE, GOODBYE GIRL

37

ALTHOUGH I WAS enormously pleased with the film of *The Goodbye Girl*, I had great doubts it would make a good Broadway musical. The idea originated with David Zippel, the lyricist of the very funny musical *City of Angels* (not to be confused with the Nicholas Cage movie). I thought the story was too small in scope to be opened up for the kind of outsize musicals that seem to work today, basically because it was a story of just three people. True, there had been successful small musicals, some that had only *two* characters, among them *I Do, I Do* and even *They're Playing Our Song*, which I wrote with Marvin Hamlisch and Carole Bayer Sager. Strangely, a two-character musical makes sense, but adding just one more character makes it seem unwieldy. Four wheels on a car is fine, five wheels and you might go off in all directions. But David Zippel and Marvin Hamlisch doggedly pursued the idea, and finally convinced me they could write a full score for a cast of about twenty-four people. I didn't know where the twenty-four people would come from, unless they planned on using the audience in the first two rows. Still, Manny Azenberg was very keen on the idea, as was director Gene Saks. Manny tested the waters with the theater party people and they were enormously optimistic. I decided to take a stab at writing the book, expanding the scope by adding other characters, some of whom already appeared in the film, but in smaller parts. I now made them *bigger* parts.

I already had learned that other people's enthusiasm should never affect what is doubtful in your own mind. Making larger parts out of smaller parts does not automatically make them *better* parts. Still, I wrote what I thought was a funny script, and once people read a funny script for a musical, they see the magical but usually elusive words in the sky, "LONG RUN."

The script enticed actors Martin Short and Bernadette Peters, and once their names were released to the press, the show suddenly became the hottest item coming to Broadway in the fall. Marvin and David Zippel wrote the first seven or eight songs for the show, and those who heard them suddenly were taking money out of the bank to invest in the show. Manny, who could budget a show down to its final twenty-five cents, told us the show should come in for close to five million dollars. For the very first time in my career, we did a backers' audition, complemented by two or three first-rate singers (who were not necessarily going to be in the show), and it was decided that I should read scenes from the show, assuring them that Martin Short had nothing to worry about.

A backers' audition is very often a *Reader's Digest* version of the final work. You hear only the best work, and what eventually will run two hours and fourteen minutes on the stage runs only about fifty minutes at the reading. Would you buy a house if you only saw the living room and the kitchen? If you would, then you'd probably put money into our musical. Nevertheless, the audition was a resounding success. Everything seemed to work. They loved the songs, howled at the book, and by the time the theater party people and other independent ticket agents jammed Manny's phone lines, we had a nine million dollar advance sale. Nine million dollars is a very, very large sum to have as an advance. I was now beginning to assume I was initially wrong, that my fears about the show being too small were unfounded, even though I was aware that I knew a lot more about a play's chances than I did of a musical's. When you read the script of a play and you're knowledgeable, you get a pretty accurate feeling as to whether it will work or not. Knowing if it works does not necessarily mean it will be a hit, of course. It just means that it works, that it has something to say and that it says it well, that it might have a life for years to come, but not necessarily on Broadway. I haven't a clue if a musical is going to work *and* be successful until I see it, and then I have to see it with an audience. And then I have to see it with the critics. And then I have to read the reviews. And then I have to see how much money they took in on the first week. And after all that, I still don't know.

But things were looking good. We signed Graciela Daniele as our choreographer and Santo Loquasto as our scenic designer. And suddenly we were into rehearsals. In the rehearsals you get more misinformation. If there are twenty or twenty-four dancers, singers and actors watching scenes, they tend to laugh. Big laughs. Dancers are notorious optimists about the shows they are in, simply because they want the shows to be a hit. Laughter at rehearsals is about as reliable as a fortune-teller with a cracked crystal ball.

I will say this, however: Martin Short was wonderful from the first reading of the script straight through our out-of-town tryout to opening night.

He was, many said, less acerbic than Richard Dreyfuss in the film, warmer and more likeable. Richard Dreyfuss, however, won the Academy Award as Best Actor playing the same part, the youngest actor ever to win that award. Should that have told us something? If it did, we weren't listening. Bernadette Peters was the darling of Broadway audiences as well as the critics, but Marsha was a better actress and was nominated for the Academy's Best Actress Award in the same part. Did that mean anything to us? Not yet. The young girl in our musical who played Lucy, the third most important role in the show, was simply darling; she was also pretty and could sing rings around anyone her own age. Quinn Cummings had none of those attributes, but she almost stole the movie from Richard and Marsha. Was anyone listening? No, because we were too busy rehearsing. And we had a nine million dollar advance sale, which was more than the movie ever had, although the film brought in about 50 million dollars, which, in today's equivalent money, would be more like a hundred and fifty million. We kept on rehearsing.

As well as rehearsals went, something still didn't seem quite right, but I couldn't put a finger on it, which usually means that the trouble is so big that a finger wouldn't cover it.

The set, by Santo Loquasto, who did a brilliant job for us with his design for *Lost in Yonkers*, came in a little late, but we could look at drawings and blueprints. I can't read a road map, much less blueprints. Director Gene Saks nodded to Santo that he thought it was good, but Gene did not display the exuberance that he usually does. When we finally saw the set, it was up on the stage of the Shubert Theatre in Chicago, where we were to have the world premiere. When I saw the set, I was confused. I knew I didn't like it, but I was still confused, because I respected Santo's work so much, and if *he* liked it, I was probably wrong.

I'm not sure Santo actually did like it. It was a difficult challenge. He had to put five rooms on the stage, all at the same time, and our three principals had to walk from room to room without ever leaving the stage. What he came up with was something that looked like a merry-go-round, and in fact, worked like a merry-go-round. All the rooms were on a circular set and could turn in either direction. It could turn clockwise or counterclockwise. It was ingenious. Ingenious and bizarre. If you were in the kitchen and wanted to walk into the living room, the set would turn and you would walk in place as the living room would turn to meet you. Sometimes, however, if you had a character in the living room who you wanted to talk to someone in the kitchen, yet have both be seen at the same time, the set would turn clockwise, then quickly counterclockwise, stopping somewhere in the middle while the actors held on to something stable to keep them from flying out into the audience. No one saw the set at the backers' audition.

But the set was only one of our problems. We had a huge opening number where Lucy took two of her girlfriends to an ice cream parlor, where sixteen other people were either eating ice cream or playing waiters and waitresses. This number had totally nothing to do with the rest of the show. This was also not seen at the backers' audition. It was, however, seen by the critics in Chicago, who promptly said, "What is that god-awful number doing at the top of the show? Or the bottom of the show, for that matter?" It took weeks to rehearse and stage, and it went out as fast as a candle in a hurricane. And so the show suddenly opened with Bernadette and Lucy coming home to their cozy little merry-go-round, which not only confused the audience, it caused some of them to feel the effects of vertigo.

Despite the lackluster reviews in Chicago, the audiences responded enthusiastically, to which authors generally go into denial and say, "What the hell do critics know?" But Richard Christianson is a first-rate critic, one who went all-out in his wonderful review of *Lost in Yonkers*. Am I now going to say "What does he know?" I did not. I knew we were in trouble, despite the fact that Martin Short was getting every laugh that was possible to get. Bernadette, however, accustomed to getting laughs as well, suddenly realized that her role was not a comic role. Marsha didn't get very many laughs in the film, but she was the backbone, the spine of the movie. Being the most empathetic character in the film, we rooted for her and Richard to get together at the end, since Paula, Marsha's character, got nothing from any other man in her life. Giving her jokes would have turned the piece into a sitcom. But there were rumblings of Bernadette being unhappy, and even more rumblings from her agents that she might want to quit the show. I liked Bernadette a lot and it was fun to work with her. If we lost her, we might as well have taken a huge ad in the *New York Times* saying, "Bernadette leaving show. Goodbye, *Goodbye Girl*." I gave in and started writing funny lines for her. She got the laughs, but we paid the price. The show was losing its heart. We didn't feel for the characters, we just laughed at what they said. I use the editorial "we" because I wasn't laughing at anything. I felt we were sailing on a ship designed by the architect of the *Titanic*. We didn't have enough lifeboats either.

Still, other problems arose. As I've said before, when I do a musical, if I have any problems, it's usually with the lyricist, and it's happened twice. If a song isn't working, the composer is usually facile enough to come up with a lively tune. Lyric writing is an arduous task, as even Stephen Sondheim will tell you, and it's hard to find anyone better than he. Stephen will work forever until he gets what he is looking for. Other lyricists, with the best of intentions, might look to put the blame on someone like the singer, the orchestration, the acoustics in the theater or the audience. I've already mentioned that I think David Zippel is a talented writer, but we hit an impasse with two lines he wrote in a song for Martin Short. They were comedy lines, and comedy lines usually have one obligation—they have to get a laugh. They don't have to bring the house down or get their own mention in the critic's review, but *some* people simply have to laugh. These two lines never got the laugh. David's answer to me was that the orchestra was playing it a tad too slow. I gave him the benefit of the doubt. That night the orchestra played it a tad faster. Still no laugh. David said, "No. Now it's a tad too fast." The next night the orchestra tadded it down. The audience was not amused. I said, "David, you could time it with twelve stopwatches, this line is never going to get a laugh. It needs to be a better line." David and I were still patient with each other, but Martin Short was the one who had to go out on stage at night and sing the laughless line. "Maybe I could just mouth the words and bring the sound of the trumpets up," Martin suggested to me one night. I said, "No. Because if there's a lip reader out there, it still wouldn't get a laugh."

To make matters worse, Marvin Hamlisch, always a hard worker, had to fulfill contracts he made before accepting the show, and so he left every now and then to do a concert. Suddenly the nows were coming up more often than the thens. Tempers were beginning to flare and egos were slamming doors everywhere. Late one afternoon there was a meeting in Marvin's hotel room to discuss all our problems. I didn't think the room was large enough to house all our problems. Once again I begged David to change the lines in his lyric. I was changing mine every day because there were a lot of mine that weren't working any better than his. But I never said, "It was because the audience was a tad too dumb."

I finally said to David, and quite sincerely, "David, you're too good a lyricist not to be able to fix it. Just write another line."

David said, "Don't patronize me."

The room got silent but I pushed on. "Jesus, David, why fight it? You write truly funny lyrics. Just give us another line."

David said, "Don't stroke me."

The silence in the room was deafening. Everyone else just looked down at the floor. I then said, as a matter of practicality, "Well then, why don't you go fuck yourself because I've run out of suggestions."

Manny covered his smile with his hand, while Marvin Hamlisch packed a bag to do a concert in Pittsburgh. Gene said we were getting nowhere, which most of us already noticed. Later that day, Manny called a meeting in the theater for the entire creative staff. We all met in the empty theater.

"We're falling apart here, guys. We're not fixing the show. We don't have a captain. We need a captain to steer the ship. So who's the captain?"

Silence until Gene said, "Neil is. Neil is the captain."

I said, "Whoa! Wait a minute. In a musical, at most I'm a second lieutenant. Maybe a chief petty officer, but never the captain. I've been in this business my whole life and I still don't know how they make the curtain go up and down. You need words, I'll give you words. You need a story, I'll give you a story. But I'm never the captain. That's a tad too much responsibility for me."

David Zippel laughed and I said, "If you just thought of something funny, David, we could use it in the place where we're not getting the laugh." I smiled and shrugged, hoping to diffuse the tension. I didn't. The meeting was over and Marvin was off to Cincinnati for another concert. Steven Spielberg, a good friend of Martin Short's, was in Chicago and came in to see the show with his wife. Spielberg loved it, but it's hard to tell friendship from sincere compliments. At least he was very convincing in his praise, and if I'm not mistaken, Spielberg came back to New York to see our opening. Still, we knew we had major fixing to do. Graciela Daniele left the show of her own accord and I was sorry to see her go.

If one of the creative staff was supposed to be the captain, Manny Azenberg, as the producer, was definitely the general. It was up to him to make a very difficult decision. If a musical is in trouble, more times than not it's the director who takes the brunt of the blame. I didn't think Gene knew how to fix it any more than I did, but neither did Zippel or Hamlisch. But we all couldn't get replaced. Manny decided to bring in Michael Kidd (*Guys and Dolls, Seven Brides for Seven Brothers*, etc.), but Gene stayed with the show, so now we had a captain, but the rest of us were common seamen. Gene got very angry with me for not standing up for him. I got angry with him for assuming I should be the captain. David Zippel offered to take over the direction, but he was a tad too late since Michael Kidd was there. Marvin did another concert and I kept writing jokes for Bernadette. Michael Kidd did his best in the little time we had, but no one's best was doing us any good at this point. My only solace was that my instincts were right from the beginning. *The Goodbye Girl* did not make suitable material for a big Broadway musical.

We opened in New York to thunderous applause from the audience, while the critics went home and wrote, "No, thank you. We'll find our entertainment elsewhere."

Gene and I eventually started talking to each other again, and later I was happy to see his terrific direction of Christopher Plummer in the wonderful *Barrymore*. Gene was in his milieu again. *The Goodbye Girl* did good business for a while, but once Bernadette left, and then Martin, who could have kept the show running if he stayed, that was that. We ran six months and the nine million dollar advance turned into a five million dollar loss. David Zippel is now writing animated films for Disney and I hear they like his work enormously. Marvin will always do concerts and I will always be fond of Marvin. Martin Short came back to Broadway for one week to do an encore production of *Promises, Promises.* He was spectacular. He also did a revival of *Little Me* at the Roundabout Theatre. He was brilliant once more.

From this experience and other experiences I either took part in or observed, I conclude that the fate of a show is not decided by who stars in it or by who's directing or who's writing it. More often than not, a show that is questionable is destined to fail on the day that someone who has the power to make it happen says, "Hey! I think this would make a great show. Let's do it."

MRS. SIMON GOES
TO WASHINGTON
38

BRYN WAS GROWING another quarter inch every night or so it seemed to those of us who stopped growing years ago. Ellen and Nancy each gave birth to a girl, about a year apart. Sofia for Nancy and David, Nikki for Ellen and Michael, Ellen's third husband. I didn't get to see my grandson, Andrew, much because he was either in school, reinventing the computer or riding his bike across and over the foot of the Rocky Mountains.

Diane was on the board of almost every charity in town and with good reason. She could raise more money than anyone else. Diane could charm a worm out of the beak of the first bird up in the morning, and was usually designated the one to go after studio heads for a donation, or perhaps to go even higher up—like to the wives of studio heads.

One morning the phone at Chalon Road rang. Diane answered it and suddenly her excitement decibels went up a few points. She called out, "Neil, for you."

"Who is it?" I asked, annoyed to be pulled away from the sports pages of the *New York Times*. It's a sure bet that if you read the batting averages of baseball players every morning when you're ten years old, you'll still be doing it when you're sixty-five.

"Bill Clinton."

"Who's Bill Clinton?" I asked. He sounded familiar, but my concentration was still on how the Yankees were doing.

"The governor of Arkansas," she said. "He's running for president, dummy."

I hoped he didn't hear her say "dummy" to me, because I knew it would probably hurt my chances to be picked as his running mate. Diane once said to me, in all seriousness I think, that I would make a great president. "I could never run," I said to her. "I always have a play in rehearsal in November."

I went to the phone.

"Ha, Neil. Bill Clinton here. Just callin' to say hello and get acquainted 'cause Hillary and I are comin' out to Los Angeles to get you and your friends behind our campaign."

I assumed Hillary was his wife because I think the Hillary who climbed Mount Everest was either dead or probably had already climbed enough mountains in his time. Clinton sounded very friendly, very down-home, but his "down-home" wasn't the "down-home" that I was from. No one ever called New York City "down-home." Still, he was very sincere, and I pictured Hillary standing next to him with a fistful of quarters to keep our phone conversation going. I worked on a few presidential campaigns in my time, but accomplished nothing you'd notice that much. I got Joan to vote for Kennedy, but I think she was ahead of me on that one. I suddenly remembered reading a speech that Clinton made at Georgetown University and I thought it was a first-rate talk and told him so.

"Well, I'm glad you liked it, Neil. I think I have some other interesting new ideas you ought to hear that could move this country in a whole new direction."

I also remembered that in an interview on television he was using the phrase "A New Covenant," and I wanted to tell him, "I'd think twice about that New Covenant pitch, Bill. People on the East Coast think a covenant is an old Pilgrim expression used in Salem during that witch hullabaloo a few hundred years back." I chose not to say it, although his speechwriters eventually chose to cut it.

I did eventually become an avid Clinton backer, but he was calling the wrong Simon. If Diane could raise money for Big Sisters, the Neil Bogart Memorial Labs that do cancer research and most of the hospitals in L.A., wait till he sees what she could do for a presidential candidate who spoke with the same accent as her brother and three sisters. Within a few weeks of our meeting, the Clintons were on a first-name basis with Diane, while I stood on the line, eating my hot buttered corn, waiting to have my picture taken with the affable candidate. It may have been my name and my contributions they wanted, but they got ten times more work from Diane in all the time she put in for him and the Democratic party. And this from a girl who came from Indiana, a state with a Republican governor.

Diane was in Little Rock, Arkansas, on election night, whooping it up as the results came in declaring that we had a new president and a new first lady. Diane had caught political fever, and in gratitude for her efforts, we were invited to the inauguration in Washington. Being invited to the inauguration by the president is a great honor, but don't picture yourself sitting on a podium, three rows behind the Supreme Court, with your feet warmed by heavy blankets to keep out the freezing January winds. No, sir. You'll be standing for five hours among thousands of other honored guests, stamping your feet and blowing on each other's hands, a crowd of people getting frostbite, a group of disciples who would eventually lose the tips of their collected noses. I voted for him but I wasn't going to get hypothermia over it. Every president I ever watched getting inaugurated on the bittercold podium didn't wear a hat while he was being sworn in, and that's another reason I decided not to run for office. What I did was wander over to the Folger Library, a beautiful and stately building that housed manuscripts of Shakespeare, and from where you can watch the inauguration in a lovely paneled room that was fashioned after the original Globe Theatre in Shakespeare's time, while drinking brisk tea or brisker vodka, and eating a small plate of smoked salmon sandwiches. As I said, I voted for him, but I still have the tip of my nose.

That night, we went to the President's Ball, and I heard more yahooing and country music than I'd ever like to hear in one night again. But when the president and the first lady entered and the gigantic room went wild, I knew I was experiencing a piece of history firsthand. The chill up my spine that I didn't get in the frosty crowds that afternoon was tingling now in the excitement of that incredible moment. Diane was like a little girl, and the tears ran down her cheeks as the Clintons held hands and raised them above the crowd. The explosion of victory, cheers, tears and utter joy was an experience I'll never forget. With all the problems the president ran into in his second term in office, for which I lost a lot of respect for him, I will always think of him as one hell of a president.

A few years later at Christmastime, the Clintons invited us to Washington for the lighting of the tree ceremony on the lawn. In addition, we were to be their overnight guests, sleeping in the Lincoln Bedroom. Okay, now this was big-time. Even Lincoln would be thrilled to sleep in the Lincoln Bedroom. We were told that most dignitaries preferred the room right opposite, which I believe was considered the Churchill Bedroom. I would have said yes to the Churchill Bedroom at 10 Downing Street, but this was Washington and it was the Lincoln Bedroom for me. On the lawn and in the White House I felt like a mere outsider because Diane knew the names of everyone on the staff, and they greeted her as one of their own. I wanted to wear a small pin saying "I wrote *The Odd Couple*," so I wouldn't get lost in the shuffle.

I was interviewed by the National Press Club a few days later and they asked me my impressions of being on the lawn for the tree lighting.

I said, "Well, I saw a very interesting thing. Just before President Clinton was going to light the tree, Newt Gingrich asked the president, in a show of solidarity, if he would let Mr. Gingrich light the tree. Graciously, the president agreed. I was standing right near him and as the speaker of the House was about to do the honors, I said, 'Excuse me, Mr. Gingrich, but I don't think you're supposed to light the tree with a match.'" That was my contribution to the Democratic campaign.

A few days later, we were picked up by a Secret Service man in his Secret Service car in front of the Willard Hotel. Lincoln also once slept at the Willard Hotel, but he was not president as yet, so they changed the sheets the next day and the room lost its historic importance. When you know you're going to sleep in the White House, you spend days deciding which pair of pajamas to wear, worried that you might possibly wander around on the second floor about midnight and suddenly run into the president, who is wearing the exact same pajamas. I believe that would be a breach of etiquette on my part and I would be asked to sleep in the Herbert Hoover Bedroom instead, a tiny, garreted room which now houses documents about Prohibition. True, pajamas are a dumb thing to think about, but at a time such as this you think about a lot of dumb things. For example, I knew we were invited to sleep in the Lincoln Bedroom, but I don't think they meant that you should actually sleep in his bed. There was a nice rocking chair in there and I thought of curling up in that with a bathrobe over me and try to get in a few catnaps. If a Secret Service man were to suddenly walk in to check things out, I could sit up and say, "I'm up, I'm up. I wasn't sleeping on the bed."

You're told that if there's anything you'd like to eat during the night, to just press the button next to your bed, tell them what you want and it will be brought up. You can't avoid the fear of pressing a button in the White House because of the odd chance that you may have just wiped Russia off the map. Can you imagine calling downstairs at two in the morning, waking up a Marine captain by mistake and telling him you'd like a corned beef sandwich on rye and to please trim the fat? What do you do if the bulb in your lamp starts to flicker? Is this a signal to go immediately to the underground safe zone in Montana? You just can't help thinking things like that.

What actually happened was a lot more prosaic. I fell asleep about eleven P.M., while Diane paced in her expensive new robe out in the hall for the *entire* night, too nervous to sleep. She walked gingerly down the corridor and there in his office, sitting at his desk was the president, working into the wee hours. He stopped and chatted with Diane and eventually Hillary came out and they all talked together for a while. I could hear them but what could I do? Stick my head out the door and yell, "Hey, knock it off down there. Some people have to work in the morning, you know."

We were served breakfast in Lincoln's office right next to his bedroom. They brought juice and eggs and toast and coffee, but once again, I wasn't sure we were supposed to eat it. Maybe it was the ritual breakfast that Lincoln had every morning and we were just supposed to look at it. Then they would take it away and bring us something that came in a little brown bag that said "White House," something to eat in the Secret Service car as we drove away. We left early in the morning, and I thought the president would consider me rude if we didn't say goodbye and thank him for putting us up for the night. But the president was in an emergency cabinet meeting and Diane stopped me from slipping a thank-you note under the door of the Cabinet Room.

As we drove away, we were exhausted from the strain, especially Diane, who hadn't slept a wink. Then I thought, should we have made up the bed before leaving although it was only slightly wrinkled? I decided not to ask Diane because she would have gone back and made up the bed. All in all, it was a hectic night.

ANDREW MEETS DAVID MAMET

39

MY GRANDSON, Andrew, lived with his mother, Ellen, in Santa Fe, New Mexico, and spent most of his school holidays with his dad, John Leland, who lived in San Francisco. As a result, I didn't have the opportunity to see my only grandson as much as I'd like. Andrew had just turned thirteen, and at a family Thanksgiving dinner I suddenly had an overwhelming desire to go off on a vacation, just me and Andrew, a couple of guys on the loose. I asked Ellen if I could take him to London for a week as soon as his summer vacation started. By the time I finished my question, Andrew was already half packed, and in late June we both flew to London on the Concorde. If you're going to give your grandson a thrill, go all the way. He sat in the cabin flying at supersonic speed, not talking very much because he was busy flying the plane.

He was a little shy with me at first because we had never actually spent much prime time together. I got a lot of "Yeah"s and "No"s to most of my questions about school and his life. However, once we unpacked at the Four Seasons Hotel facing Hyde Park, he began to take over the trip. Ellen warned me how sloppy he could be, and despite the long talk she gave him about how "Papa likes things neat," Andrew's clothes started to pop up in the strangest places, but rarely in the drawers. He did make an effort, and his winning smile was hard to argue with. After all, we were just "a couple of guys on the loose."

Even at thirteen, Andrew had a wonderful sense of ironic humor, amazingly sophisticated for someone so young, but the normal pesky thirteen-year-old part of him decided to see how far it could push me. He started to taunt me, annoy me, bother me and pester me. Because he was my grandson, the more he did it, the more I enjoyed it, and as long as he saw me laughing, he knew he was safe. There was no way, even if I really felt it, I could let myself get really angry at him. A jar of jelly beans in the mini-bar was about fifteen dollars. He started to tear off the wrapper and I said, "Andrew, that costs fifteen dollars. If you really want it, fine. But if you're only going to eat a few of them, no deal. This is not 'Let's Spoil Andrew Week.'" He opened the jelly beans, of course, and soon grew tired of them, but each morning I'd put them in front of him and say, "Here's your breakfast." He'd laugh, and now he knew the rules—which didn't mean it stopped him from breaking them.

At night, when he was ready for bed, which was two minutes after BBC Television went off the air, I'd say, "Andrew, I like to have breakfast in the dining room about eight o'clock in the morning. If you want to sleep in, tell me now and I'll tiptoe out so I don't wake you." He elected for sleeping in. At a quarter to eight in the morning, I dressed quietly and started to tiptoe past the Sleeping Giant. His eyes opened for a moment. I whispered, "I'm going down. If you want to go, I'll wait for you." He mumbled, "No," and turned over on his side. I walked across the room, and had opened the door as quietly as I could when Andrew called out, "Wait, Papa. I'm coming with you." He dressed in three minutes, wearing almost everything he did the day before, and started after me, his hair standing straight up. Needless to say, he ate very little breakfast: two sips of juice, half a bagel, and a small piece of fruit, pulling out the stem like the wings off a fly. He looked at me and smiled, knowing I didn't approve. And still I laughed. This ritual was repeated every day for the seven days we were there. He announced he was sleeping in, and just as he heard the doorknob turn, I'd hear, "Wait, Papa. I'm coming." He finally changed his clothes more regularly, but his hair was still standing at attention. His breakfast choices didn't vary much. If he ordered bacon, they would put down four strips on his plate. He ate only one strip and made cholesterol designs with the rest.

We were up and out early every morning. I got tickets in advance to visit the House of Lords at Parliament. Andrew sat in rapt attention, involved with everything going on. We went to the Old Bailey, the picturesque courthouses of London, and he sat enthralled with the various trials we attended, where the judges and barristers still wear their periwigs and black cloaks. We went to Madame Tussaud's Wax Museum, to Hatchard's, my favorite English bookstore, to Fortnum and Mason for lunch, to the Tower of London, and on and on, every day.

As the days went on, Andrew began to feel his oats and started taking over, picking out a restaurant where he wanted to have lunch.

I said, "Andrew, I know this place. It's the pits."

"No, no, Papa," he said. "I've got a feeling about this. It's going to be great."

We went in and sat down to an inedible meal. All I did was glare at him as I pushed my food away. He found this funny. Not funny—hysterical. Once outside, I rubbed my stomach and said, "God, what was that soup? I think they dipped a ladle into the Thames River." Andrew doubled up with laughter. "If I die of food poisoning," I said, "you walk home across the Atlantic." Tears of laughter ran down his face.

When I finally stopped talking about the bad meal, he said, "Papa, can we go back there for lunch tomorrow?"

I took a swipe at him and missed. He found that excruciatingly funny. For some reason, I fell in with it. Making him laugh was as joyous to me as hearing an opening night audience screaming with laughter. "Andrew," I said, "we're staying in tonight. I'm calling that restaurant and having them send over dinner." He rolled his eyes, rubbed his stomach and said, "Mmmm, yummy. I'd love that."

I took another swipe at him and he ducked, laughed and said, "Ooh, beating your grandson in public. I may have to press charges against you."

He never knew when to stop and I never wanted him to stop. There we were, two thirteen-year-old kids on the street, and I wondered if anyone could guess which one was the grandfather.

On and on we trekked, from the War Museum to the Tate Gallery. "That was great, wasn't it?" I said as we left the Tate.

He looked at me and said, "Yeah, but not as good as that restaurant." This time he ducked without my even swinging at him.

Finally, I said, "Andrew, truce, please. No more. Try to get something out of this trip."

He nodded in compliance. "You're right. That was a great gallery. I really loved that gallery. Let's go back tonight because I want to remember that gallery all my life," and then I got the big smile. Ellen told me he did the same thing at home, the same thing with his friends, the same thing in school in Santa Fe. I guess it explained why his grades went up and down, but also why he was the most popular boy in school and girls a foot taller and two years older wanted to be his girlfriend. I thought, "The only thing better than having Andrew as a grandson was if I could have been a little more like him when I was thirteen." Actually, I wasn't all that different but I'd never have the nerve to behave so brazenly with my grandfather, who never would have gotten the jokes anyway.

If your grandfather was a playwright, chances are you'd go to the theater every night, which was exactly what we did. Andrew adored Tom Stoppard's *Arcadia*, a brilliant play that challenged an audience's imagination and intelligence. Andrew was deeply engrossed in it, and at the intermission it was clear that he observed some nuances in the play that even I missed. It was the serious side of Andrew, the one that seemed more like a college student than a teenager, and I loved that side of him as well.

We saw *The Woman in Black*, the perfect mystery for someone with Andrew's imagination, and he never moved in his seat. When something interested him, his concentration was enormous.

Another play sounded like a good change of pace, and I thought it might be fun. From the title, I assumed it was a nice British farce, but it turned out to be a *not* so nice British SEX farce, with very little clothes, very little wit and very little reason for a thirteen-year-old to be seeing this with his grandfather. Andrew didn't hear much of it, because I kept apologizing all during the performance and bribed him not to tell his mother what I had done. He was amused that I was in trouble.

The next night I made sure we saw something much weightier, and during the intermission I met a friend who was doing the color commentary for HBO's televising of the Wimbledon matches. He set us up the next day with terrific seats on Court One. The match went five sets, a first-class thriller that lasted almost four hours. It turned out to be one of the best matches of that year's tournament. There wasn't a day in that week that didn't present a high spot for us.

The following afternoon we went to St. Paul's Cathedral, and suddenly the Huckleberry Finn side of Andrew showed itself. He climbed to the very top of the great dome, while Papa sat in a pew, grateful for the twenty-minute respite. Andrew called out to me from the top of the dome, but you didn't have to shout to be heard. The acoustics made it possible for Andrew to call in a modulated voice, "Papa," but the voice echoed and bounced around the cathedral, repeating itself all the way down to my seat. "PAPA . . . PAPA . . . PAPA . . . papa . . . papa . . ." When he came down, he wanted to go up again. "Not today," I said. "Come back one day with your own grandson."

On our final night in London, we went to see *Cryptogram*, a play by David Mamet. Andrew had never seen a David Mamet play, while I had seen pretty much all of them. Mamet is clearly one of America's top playwrights, and he has his own style. When you see his work for the first time, you have to adjust to the unique cadences of his speeches, which he uses in most of his plays.

They are always intelligent, unique and powerful. He writes short, staccato sentences, some of which are never finished before the other character interrupts or finishes the other's thought. It's a rapid-fire chess game with the chess pieces coming at you fast and furiously from any point on the board. When it is done correctly, as in the brilliant *Glengarry Glen Ross*, the effect is magical. It becomes seamless, and although you think you are missing words or speeches, in effect, you miss nothing. He glues you to your seat, daring you to move or to take a breath.

Whatever attributes *Cryptogram* had, I think the English actors had trouble dancing to Mamet's music, and in a Mamet play, when the actors miss the beat, it sounds like they are forgetting their lines. (The same play was done much better the following season in New York.) But Andrew never heard actors read Mamet's dialogue before, and he was so taken with the style that once outside the theater, he turned into a character in a David Mamet play, written by Andrew, even before I suspected what he was doing.

I said to him, "Did you like the—"

"Yes," he answered. "I found it very—"

"Unusual," I said, falling in with him. "But what did you think of the—"

"Exactly," he answered. "What did *anyone* think of it? And what does thinking of it mean?"

I found a taxi and we headed back to the hotel for our last night in London. By now my mind was on other things besides the Mamet play, but once Andrew takes hold, he does not let go easily.

"We have to get up very early in the—" I started to say.

"What?" he asked me. "We have to what?"

"I was saying we have an early plane to—"

"To catch? Is that what you're saying? To catch a plane?"

"Yes, David. Can we put the play aside for a moment?"

"A moment? Why a moment? Why not an hour? Why not eternity?" he went on.

By now the cab driver was glancing at us through the rearview mirror.

I tried to continue. "I had a great time with you, Andrew. I thought the—"

"The cathedral? Is that what you're thinking? Don't think of the cathedral. Hear me out—"

I heard him out in the elevator, in our room in our beds and while I turned the lights out. I was soon asleep as Andrew continued speaking broken and interrupted sentences. In the morning we had our last breakfast and drove out to the airport. Andrew was silent, probably thinking of all he had seen and done during the last week. They announced our flight to New York and we got on the end of the line waiting to board with the other passengers. A tall, elegant woman stood in front of us, immersed in her morning London newspaper. I turned to Andrew and said, "It was really great fun, wasn't it?"

"What? Wasn't what? Fun, is that what you said?"

He was back in a Mamet play, so I indulged him. "The trip. The trip to London. I thought it was—"

"Fun. Oh, I see what you mean. Yes. But why did we—?"

"Did we what?" I answered.

"I don't know. Does anyone know?"

"Does anyone know what?"

The woman in front of us turned, listening to us, a very slight trace of a smile on her face. Andrew continued.

"Does anyone know what they mean? What does 'mean' mean?"

"Exactly my—"

"Point? No. I never mentioned points."

The elegant woman surprised us when she said, "I assume you've just seen the David Mamet play?"

Andrew looked as if he got caught with his hand in the cookie jar.

"Yes," I said. "Last night. Have you seen it?"

"Many times," she said, smilingly. "I produced it."

Andrew suddenly looked up at the ceiling and I jumped in to save the day. "Oh. Congratulations. We loved it. We loved the play. This is my grandson. Didn't we love the play, Andrew?"

All he did was nod. Where was he when I needed him?

She thanked me, then moved on as we began to board the plane. Andrew was uncommonly quiet for quite some time.

We were both tired and slept for a good deal of the trip. Once in New York, I took him to another airline that he was going to take to Santa Fe, to be met there by Ellen.

I put my arms around him and gave him a hug. "I just want to thank you for one of the best weeks in my life, Andrew."

He nodded, shyly. "Thanks, Papa. It was great."

As he started for the plane, I called out, "Andrew. Don't eat the food on the plane. I ordered you something special from that restaurant in London you loved so much."

He nodded, smiled and then flew back home. I remember someone once saying to me, "If you have an instinct to do something good, don't dwell on it. Just do it." I always think of that when I remember asking Ellen if I could take Andrew for a week to London. And thirteen was just the right age to get him. I lived vicariously through him all that week, and I was grateful that by taking him on a journey, he took me on a journey into his world. I loved every minute of it.

THE DAY I WAS PICKETED

40

MANNY AZENBERG and I had been mulling over the possibility of doing my next play off-Broadway. The financial figures no longer made doing a play *on* Broadway a viable option. It cost a million six hundred thousand dollars to mount a play on Broadway a few short years ago, while that same play could be done *off*-Broadway for less than a third of that sum, somewhere under five hundred thousand. True, if we were a hit off-Broadway, the profits would be infinitely smaller, but the chances of having a long run with a play *on* Broadway seemed near to impossible. Musicals were fast taking over all the available theaters, and even getting a play *on* took a major star or a successful run in London prior to New York. We opted for going off-Broadway.

Like *Plaza Suite* and *California Suite*, both highly successful as plays and then films, *London Suite* was comprised of four one-act plays, all taking place in the same hotel, this time, obviously, in London. In doing *London Suite*, I think I was prompted in wanting to complete another trilogy. We had a good start by reprising the best play from *California Suite*, the story of Sidney and Diana Nichols, a bisexual antique dealer married to a major British actress. Maggie Smith had won the Oscar for playing Diana in the film version.

In the new play, it is sixteen years later. The couple have parted, divorced, Diana has moved to California, and is now starring in a hit TV series, while Sidney has moved to the Greek island of Mykonos, this time following his true instincts by living with a younger man, a painter-sculptor from Switzerland. Sidney and Diana have a reunion in a posh hotel in London, where he has come, hat in hand, to borrow money in order to care for his sick and dying lover in Greece. Diana eventually discovers the lie, that it is Sidney who is dying and the money he wants is to leave his cherished companion with some security for the future. Diana, who still yearns for Sidney, no matter what his sexual preference, gets him back by promising to take care of Sidney through to the end, if he comes back to California with her. He agrees on the condition that his penniless Swiss mate can come with them. Diana, who has just been shocked to learn that her own secretary, Grace, is gay as well, accedes to Sidney's wish.

DIANA: Of course. We'll all be together. You, me, Max and Grace. Can't you see *that* story in *People* magazine? "TV star takes in dying gay ex-husband, his male Swiss sculptor lover and her devoted female secretary who turns out to be a cowboy."

SIDNEY: And we'll go on those daytime talk shows. And people will call in from Omaha and Memphis and ask questions like, "I know you people are all disgusting but your life seems so interesting, doesn't it?"

Sidney seems to relax as he knows that Max, his Swiss friend, will be taken care of, and that Diana will be there for Sidney during his last days. He says, with his typical black humor, referring to his cancer:

SIDNEY: . . . Aren't we lucky that something like this came along?

We first tried out the play at the Seattle Repertory Theatre, run by the gifted director Dan Sullivan. *London Suite* was a huge hit in Seattle, garnering excellent reviews and breaking a few attendance records at the same time. We were all ecstatic and wondered if we were making a mistake by bypassing Broadway. But we stuck to our guns and moved east to the Union Square Theatre on 17th Street.

It was an odd building for a theater, principally because it was never built for that purpose. It was originally Tammany Hall, a wonderful place for political rallies or meetings of various trade unions. It had a high domed ceiling which was lovely to look at, but unfortunately sent most of the actors' words aloft, where they stayed, suspended in air next to a few pigeons who had flown in on a pass. This caused pockets of silence in many areas of the auditorium, principally where the audience was sitting. Still, it had a nice ambience and I was glad to be there, despite an unsettling feeling that somehow in the middle of the night, truckers had moved me, my family and all our furniture to a dark corner in Pittsburgh. Where were the milling crowds gathering in front of all the theaters on 44th and 45th Streets? Neil Simon was off-Broadway but the Neil Simon Theatre was *on* Broadway. I found myself going to the Union Square Theatre at night and dressing *down*. An expensive Ralph Lauren camel's hair coat looked out of place here.

On the night of our first preview, the crowds began to gather, waiting for the theater to open its doors to the public to view Neil Simon's first off-Broadway play. There was electricity in the air, but the wattage couldn't compete with what was so bright on the Great White Way. Suddenly reporters and photographers turned their attention to two men walking with placards. As I got closer, I saw they were pickets from the Stage Hands Union. Their signs read, NEIL SIMON UNFAIR TO STAGE HANDS UNION. HE BELONGS ON BROADWAY. At first I thought they were strikers picketing on behalf of the young writers who were trying to get *into* an off-Broadway theater. It was quite the opposite. They were strikers for the Broadway Stage Hands Union, protesting that I was hurting their income by doing my play off-Broadway.

Imitation is not the highest form of flattery. Protestors from the Broadway Stage Hands Union complaining that I was depriving them of my talent by working for *less* money off-Broadway was more than flattery. It was downright reverence, shown in the most absurd way. The crowd outside mildly booed the strikers, who, I must admit, smiled and shrugged. I crossed to them and said, in my most amiable manner, "Are you seriously picketing me because you think it's wrong for me to abandon Broadway?" They shrugged and said, "Sorry, Neil. It's our job. We're told to do it. You know?" "Sure," I said. "No problem. Good publicity for my play." Two nights later they were gone.

The off-Broadway audience who came to our previews didn't look much different than a Broadway audience, but these days very few people dress for the theater. The reaction to the plays was unclear. The audience laughed, but not as much as in Seattle. They applauded, but not as much as in Seattle. They stood at the end of the play, but not as high as in Seattle. In sports, we have what is called "home court advantage," that is to say, the Mets should win more ball games at Shea Stadium than they will at their opponent's stadium. In the Union Square Theatre, I somehow felt I had lost my home court advantage. No boos, no cheering for other authors, but something was missing. The reviews, as usual, were mixed, and Vincent Canby of the *New York Times* said the play "was somewhere in the middle of my oeuvre."

If we had done the play on Broadway, we would have lost about a million dollars. Having done it downtown, running five or six months, we paid off a good deal of our investment, and today with *London Suite* released to playhouses around the country and abroad, we are now in profit. Our risks had been diminished but so had the excitement. Still, I knew I'd better get used to it. As far as I was concerned, a play on Broadway is something an audience goes to on the night the musicians forgot to show up.

AS DIANE and I were moving into the seventh year of our second marriage, the ebb and flow of our relationship was beginning to ebb more than flow. This is the sort of private information that Diane wanted to avoid making public by virtue of her wishes in our prenuptial agreement. I agree with her. The difficulty in adhering to that restriction while being honest in one's memoirs creates a thorny issue for the writer. Having taken you so far down the road with my life, I now have to put up a detour sign and skirt the cracks and crevices that were confronting Diane and me more and more. It is neither my wish nor intention to relate my side of the issues at hand and only conjecture what was going on in Diane's mind. I will say this, however: in a marriage that is beginning to stumble, the difficult part to go through is not just the disagreements and disappointments. What causes the real pain is the matter of residual love that still exists. The good times were so very, very good—but where did they go to, when did they leave and why did they disappear? The hurt is so much sharper when a cry of deep anger comes *at* you and *from* you, and the person on the receiving end is someone you once deeply loved. I couldn't bear another item in a gossip column that said I was divorcing again. I had never left anyone before. Joan died, Marsha left for reasons of her own and Diane left the first time to confront major issues in her own life that didn't seem related to our marriage, as odd as that may sound. I still remember the day she left seven years prior, when she said, "I love you more today than I ever have before." Aside from Joan, I asked myself, "Is it me? Is it because I'm a writer? Is it because I'm a *successful* writer? Is it my own fame that diminished *them*?" There were no answers left on my desk that morning.

I decided to stick this one out, even if I slipped into oblivion in the soft armchair I sat in each night after dinner, while the arms of the chair warmly engulfed me and finally swallowed me whole until I disappeared, thus avoiding the shame of still another divorce.

PROPOSALS was my thirtieth play. A magic number for me, not that it held any real personal significance. Somehow I just didn't want my obituary to read, "Neil Simon, writer of twenty-nine plays, etc., etc., . . ." As I look for the right rhythm and music in my dialogue, twenty-nine seemed to lack both rhythm *and* music. It was flat. The image in my mind was that my fingers were reaching for the tip of the high wall that surrounds the playwrights' Valhalla, and if I weakened and could climb no higher than twenty-nine, the rest of the obituary would read, "... who fell short by one play of attaining the heights that all playwrights dream of." Nowhere did I ever read that thirty was the number that all playwrights dream of. It's something you make up in your mind, as I did when I was ten or eleven years old, sick with the flu and fever, wrapped in my father's heavy bathrobe, looking out my bedroom window and counting cars: "If I see ten trucks by the time I count to one hundred, I will have a wonderful life." When I had counted eight trucks and was coming up fast on "ninety-one, ninety-two, ninety-three . . . ," I stretched those last remaining numbers by speaking as if my tongue were paralyzed. No matter how long it took, you just didn't say one hundred until you had seen that tenth truck, then you'd let out a whoop and a holler and cry, "Yes! I made it. I'm going to have a wonderful life." I may have cheated a little, but the truth is, yes, I did have a wonderful life.

I had worked on and off for almost five years to complete *Proposals*. Every time I got stuck, I'd move on to something else, and when finished, I'd return to *Proposals*. It was a play I would simply never let get away from me. I knew it would be the last play I'd ever write about Joan as I remembered her, as she was when I first met her, when I knew immediately that this was the girl I wanted to spend the rest of my life with. This, however, was not strictly a play about Joan, or about me, either—it was more than that. It was about a time and a world that no longer exists, that was not necessarily better than this time and world, but it did have values, principles and qualities that seemed to have gotten lost today, and that should not be forgotten.

I cannot be objective as to whether *Proposals* was as good as I wanted it to be. But as we moved from city to city, audiences in Los Angeles, then Phoenix, then New Haven received the play progressively better and better. By the time we reached the Kennedy Center in Washington, D.C., the play exploded with our best reviews and immediately became the biggest hit I ever had in that city. In our four-week run there, there was not an empty seat. Not even for me.

The play then moved on to New York, and once again I was on Broadway, where I thought *Proposals* belonged. It was, if not in structure, but in intent, a sort of *Midsummer Night's Dream*. Ten characters, all in various states of love—new love, old love, unrequited love, lost love and the love that lasts beyond the grave. It is all seen through the eyes of Clemma, Josie's black nanny, as Clemma steps out of the past, having died long ago, only to come back to revisit the summer house where she worked and helped raise Josie when she was a child. The bond between Josie and Clemma dominates the play. The part of Clemma was played by L. Scott Caldwell, a former Tony winner in August Wilson's *Joe Turner's Come and Gone*, and she was consistently praised in our play as being "humorous, loving and touching, whose presence commands our complete attention and respect."

In the review by Ben Brantley of the *New York Times*, the heading above the review in large, bold type read, "A Black Woman Walking Down a Country Road? This is Neil Simon?" I know that in most cases the reviewer does not necessarily write the headline, although I never knew why. In any case, what the headline was saying to me was, "Why is Neil Simon veering into new territory? He's never written about blacks before. Shouldn't that be left in the hands of more qualified ethnic writers like August Wilson?" The quotes are mine. I was confused, to say the least.

We opened in November, and as we neared the Christmas holidays, most theaters drop in attendance, since most people are out shopping. Musicals, however, succeed in the face of hurricanes, fires and earthquakes. *The Lion King* and *Ragtime* were selling out, as was *Chicago* and all the old standbys like *Phantom*, *Les Misérables*, and *Cats*, whose nine lives will exist past nine thousand performances. A mixed review or even a bad review from the *Times* has not always stopped one of my plays from going on to a successful run. But now I was up against something much bigger. Without all the critics' approval (and we did have the cheers from many), the audiences would now walk right past our theater to the nearest musical, if they could get in. *Scarlet Pimpernel*, which did not receive much better reviews than we did, still did business. *Proposals* lasted two short months on Broadway. Since we had no star names to help us woo the audiences in, we didn't stand a chance.

It was a bleak season all around for Manny Azenberg and myself. He produced *Side Show*, a wonderful and courageous new musical—courageous because the story was about Siamese twin sisters. The reviews for that show from the *Times* critics, both Mr. Brantley and Vincent Canby, were glorious. They praised the show for all the right reasons, and even Frank Rich, the former reviewer of the *Times* and now a writer of editorials, was seen at the play on many nights and it was no secret that he championed the musical.

But the audiences never came. The reason, or one of the reasons being, to quote someone on the street, "I don't want to see two women stuck together, no matter how brilliant it is." Ten, or even five years ago, the physical close-ness of two sisters would not be an issue. Good is good and *Side Show* was good—and more. The audiences today are not necessarily tougher. Quite the opposite: they are easier for a more accessible theater. They say, "Don't test me. I just want to be entertained." There's nothing wrong with that, but it certainly limits the parameters of good theater. *Side Show* closed soon after *Proposals*. It was the worst beating Manny and I ever took in one season, and a great personal and financial loss to us both. I was saddened by the closing of *Proposals*, but not despondent. I have had too much success to cry foul. But I was confused. I do believe there will be an afterlife for both my play and Manny's musical.

I was uplifted, to say the least, almost three weeks after the closing of *Proposals* when Jack Klugman and Tony Randall revived my play *The Sunshine Boys* for Tony's National Actors' Theatre. The reviews were unanimously joy-ous. Vincent Canby went so far as to say, "It's his [Simon's] *War and Peace*, his *Long Day's Journey into Night*." Amazing quotes that made me read them a dozen times before I allowed myself to believe them. So I was a flop on Broadway and a smash on Broadway within a period of less than a month. I thought to myself, "Ah, I see what they want. From now on I will only write twenty-five-year-old revivals."

IN MAY of 1998 I filed for divorce.

I knew I had been unhappy and depressed for over a year. I had stopped playing tennis, I had less and less desire to see friends in California, and work was no longer the joy or escape that it once was. During the pre-Broadway tour of *Proposals*, I was beginning to get agonizing pains in my stomach, bouts of diarrhea, sleepless nights and days that dragged on pointlessly. My daily routine was so confining, I thought I was living in the only prison cell in Bel Air. I had no outlets, no places to go that seemed inviting to me, and no one in particular that I wanted to see. I was making fewer and fewer visits to Santa Barbara to see my daughters and their families, I only called my brother, Danny, occasionally and saw him even less, and my trips to New York, always a safe haven for me, now grew tiresome, and after just three days, I wanted to return to my cell on Chalon Road.

I was looking and feeling older, and on my seventieth birthday, Diane had thrown a huge party for me at the house; it looked like anyone and everyone in the Los Angeles telephone book had been invited. More is not always better. I saw a few close friends and my family, of course, but they were in the minority. I was so spiritless that I hardly recognized many of the faces that smiled at me and wished me the best, all the while I was feeling my worst, and the two vodkas I had made it almost impossible for me to remember a name. "Hey, how are you?" was the best I could do at putting names and faces together. If it were up to me, I would have gone into my room, closed the door, gotten into bed and pulled a few yards of grass over me and put up a headstone that said, "SHH. He's Dying."

My doctor, Rob Huizinga, knew I was depressed for some time, and though he was one of the busiest doctors in L.A., he asked me to come by his office late one day. I sat with him and we talked for over an hour. An hour for him was equal to about fifteen normal patient visits, but he knew unless I could break through my depression, it could easily lead to illness. What he eventually suggested was that I break my routine, look for other outlets, change my life in whatever way I could. He had been treating me for many years and keeping me in very good shape and he knew me better than I knew myself. I trusted him and I knew his advice was sound, but once I got home, try as I might, I couldn't break the habits of a lifetime. I went to my office at the same time each day, but now I had little desire to write. I'd fall asleep after a few hours, and when I awoke, I was too tired to think clearly. I had little appetite for food and little desire to phone a friend. I was trapped inside my own loneliness and despair, and there wasn't a soul I knew who had a key to unlock my chains.

I knew my marriage to Diane had fallen apart, despite the fact we still managed to go out to a movie or a Lakers game or see some friends. Diane was working as a feature writer for *Live* magazine and more times than not came home late so that Bryn ate dinner first, since she had her homework to do, I ate next because Diane would say, "Don't wait for me," and when she got home she ate in the den as I sat four feet away watching a basketball game without any investment of interest in who won or lost.

There was only one dependable ray of hope: our dog, Annabelle. She greeted me warmly when I came home each night (as she did both Bryn and Diane), and she ran for her ball. Dogs are not interested in your depression. They love you and assume you love them (which you do, of course), and she'd look at me, wagging her tail as if to say, "If you'll throw the ball to me, I'll run and chase it, catch it in my mouth, bring it back and drop it at your feet and then we'll do it again. And then you won't be depressed, I promise you." Dogs are the best doctors in the world and you don't need an appointment. Just open your front door and she'll drop everything for you. After a while, though, even Annabelle couldn't help. She could run down a ball, but she couldn't chase away my blues. The sad fact is, if you *don't* play with your dog, they can easily get depressed as well. Solving her problem was easy—you throw the ball. I couldn't even find mine.

The stomach pains persisted and I was urged to see Dr. Gary Gitnick, head of Digestive Diseases at UCLA Hospital, one of the best in the country. After a brief examination and a long heart-to-heart talk (Dr. Gitnick calls you at home or in your office every few months just to ask you how you're doing), he prescribed a number of procedures which we started almost immediately. First there was a colonoscopy, which came up negative. Then an upper GI examination, which also came up negative. Next an examination by a cardiologist—no problem there. Finally, he ordered a test for lactose intolerance, the inability to digest foods which contained lactose, or dairy products, e.g., milk, cheese, chocolate. Bingo! We nailed that one. I had a moderate case of it, but moderate or not, it doesn't go away unless you adhere strictly to the rules. No problem for me because discipline is a competitive game I play with myself and I almost always win. It comes with forty-five years of writing and meeting deadlines. Slowly the pains in the pit of my stomach receded, but it gave me a low punch in case my mouth ever got too close to a cookie.

Still the depression persisted. I couldn't read more than three pages of a book before I had to read them again, and still I didn't understand what I'd read. I couldn't sit through an entire movie alone, or watch a ball game on TV without changing the station every three minutes, hoping to find a better game. I wouldn't know a better game if it hit me in the groin. Plus, since my diet had been cut by more than half, the food I ate was as bland as my life.

I was referred to a therapist, a doctor who dealt primarily with patients suffering from moods and depression. If I had my choice, I would have taken moods because moods sounded as if you got breaks once in a while. Depression is your day and night job. One of the first questions he asked was did I ever feel suicidal. I said, yes, many times, but that didn't seem like much fun either. There was humor in my answer but despair in my subtext. I was not ready to die yet, but I also was not ready to live. Oscar Hammerstein beat me to that thought in the lyric for "Ol' Man River": "I'm tired of livin' but fear'd a dyin'." That may have been true, but at least that guy was singing.

After a few sessions, the doctor explained that obviously I was depressed, but not in such an acute way that drastic measures needed to be taken immediately. Still, it's not something you want lingering around as you drive your car on the freeway at night. He told me that basically there were three ways of dealing with the state of depression I was in, which has since been called "Simon's Syndrome," meaning, "Sad enough to be sad, but not happy enough to be happy." Number one, he said, would be analysis. Well, since we figured out that I had more analysis than Freud's first patient, we could skip that. The second was medication. I am not keen on mood manipulators because I would rather be in the mood I'm in than the mood he's going to *put* me in. Mine was miserable, but at least it was mine. Still, I decided to give it a try. He gave me a low dose of Wellbutrin, which sounded like a name Disney gave it, like a chummy old German bear with glasses who chuckles while he eats honey, and his name is Dr. Wellbutrin. But it was a better name I suppose than something called "Uplift" or "Stop Whining." Americans seem to like for their drugs to have names similar to their illness, like Halcion, to prevent you from taking the wrong pill. For example, you would *never* take something called "The Big Sleep" by mistake.

To be honest, the Wellbutrin helped. It does not give you a high, otherwise it would outsell Viagra, but it does level your feelings off but with very little pleasure attached. For example, it's a little like kissing an absolutely gorgeous girl but you both have gauze on your lips. I thought perhaps a better name for the drug would be "Standoff," because that's what it was. No one won, no one lost. I now started to call my depression "Submarine" because you couldn't see it but you knew it was there lurking just underneath the surface.

The third alternative to my coming back to a meaningful existence was to change my environment. "You mean move?" I asked. "Why? I love my house."

"No," he said. "Not your house. Your life."

Pretty much the same thing that Dr. Huizinga had said. But how do I change my life? Stop writing? No. Bad idea, he said. Work you love, and being productive is always healthy. But there are other things to life. I looked at him, honestly without a clue as to what that other thing could be. Take a year off and go to some South Sea island? A year in Bora Bora? I would sooner rethink that suicide thing. He smiled at what I said. I still had the ability to make someone laugh, but totally none to do the same for myself.

After seven weeks, he took me off the antidepressant. "You don't really need it anymore."

I said, "So can we upgrade me from depressed to just merely totally miserable?" In another seven weeks I could look forward to going from being bored to death with my life to watching reruns of *I Love Lucy* for a year.

I could actually be amusing in the doctor's office, but once out on the street, I felt hopeless. What a state to be in. Is this what the Catholics call "limbo"? Diane and I continued to live our lives as if nothing had changed, mainly because nothing had changed. But we were both unhappy with each other, and somebody had to make a first move. What I had to wrestle with was my inability to leave someone, to be the first to say goodbye, since I was on the receiving end of goodbye so often in my life. I saw my father leave my mother time and time again, and I saw the deep anguish it caused her. From that time in my childhood, I never wanted to be the cause of someone else's unhappiness by leaving them. But the problem was, by staying, I wasn't able to make them happy either. Again, a standoff. Joan left when she died, but there was no betrayal there—just tragedy. Everyone lost by Joan's dying, but I think that by never breaking up in our marriage, it's possible that my two daughters, Ellen and Nancy, are stronger for it. Marriage was something they believed in, even if it failed once for Ellen.

So there I was, in a stalemate with myself. My life was not getting any better, our marriage was drifting toward the rapids, and yet the chess pieces stood motionless on the chessboard, waiting for someone to make a move. I went into the guest room to sleep one night, knowing that the battle that was raging inside of me would surely wake Diane and another nocturnal husband-and-wife fight would do no one any good—not that there was any guarantee that Diane was sleeping that night either.

It had been a long time since I had turned to Joan for an answer, not that I ever truly believed that she would hear my plea and send down a message giving me clearance to take off. I was in a half sleep and suddenly sat up and looked at the clock. It was just after two in the morning. The message—no matter where it came from, most likely from the year of unfulfillment that had been building up like a stockpile of nuclear fission—came in a voice that was clear and unequivocal. I had to leave. I had to change my life, to find myself or get hopelessly lost in the entanglement of my own neurosis. The words were short and simple: "Get out, Neil." If I didn't, I would only make myself and Diane unhappier than we already were.

Telling Diane early the next morning as she went to wake Bryn up for school may not have been timely, but I was afraid if I did not say the words, I might back off. It was the hardest thing I ever did in my life, yet I knew, difficult as it was, it was the right thing. I could see the pain in Diane's face, and she turned and walked away without saying a word, which was a lot more devastating to me than if she stood there and argued with me. But how different was it when Marsha did it or Diane did it the first time? Of course the circumstances are always different, and either of them could argue, "Yes, but you don't know what I was going through." Granted. Nobody knows at a time like that. There is, of course, always much, much more to the story of why two people break up, and even if we could find the words or the answers, it is certainly nothing that either one of us would want to share with anyone but ourselves.

I moved out of the house and into a hotel, and found that I had just traded one lonely place for another. Room service doesn't make it less lonely. I knew it was important for me to keep contact with Bryn, because the child in me identified with the child in her. Except that Bryn was smarter and more grown-up than I could even imagine. I called her and faxed her. We met and had lunch. She was cold at first, perhaps even angry, and certainly she was confused. But she was always polite and respectful. At fourteen, girls or boys do not usually communicate their inner feelings to their parents all that much, maybe even in something so dire as a divorce. It was not the first time she had seen it, since it is as much a topic of conversation at school with friends as grades, boys and Leonardo DiCaprio, not that I mean to denigrate her feelings. They had to be powerful, even though they were not always articulated. I knew she loved her mother. I could only hope she loved me. I love her very much and I am so proud to see the headway she is making during these difficult years, divorce or not. She is a beautiful, sweet and highly intelligent girl with a unique sense of humor, and I know from experience that humor is the ability to see the world from a very objective viewpoint. I found that she was unwilling to talk about the breakup, so I learned to steer clear of that issue.

Eventually, the ghastly business of divorce dominates your life. If you're lucky, you find a lawyer who is sensitive to the issues and feelings of both parties, thereby facilitating an early settlement. No matter what, both parties feel they found the right lawyer. Why not? They're on your side. I don't believe it's possible to go through a divorce without experiencing various degrees of pain, anger, relief, sadness and in some odd moment during the hostilities, something that strikes you funny simply because in one brief second, you find it all so ludicrous.

You'll notice that ministers, priests and rabbis rarely perform divorces. Since they are emissaries of God, they are interested in joining couples in the sacred business of matrimony, and one expression you'll never hear in a divorce court is "You may now kiss your ex-wife."

Our divorce turned out to be contentious and a battle royal ensued. No matter how much each party trusts his or her lawyer, that lawyer very often has to bring news to his client that makes the client want to punch in every wall in the Chrysler Building.

Of course friends of each party invariably side with the one to whom they feel closer, offering advice like, "Go for everything you can get from him," or, "I wouldn't give her a nickel." Bad advice. This is like throwing ten redwood trees on a blazing fire. Mind you, in many cases, you never hear things directly from your adversary. Once I got a note from a woman lawyer from the opposite camp saying, "We can keep you in court for the rest of your life." I don't care if you're the greatest brain surgeon in the world, that threat scares the life out of you. There is also no saying that Diane had anything to do with that statement. Some lawyers just take charge and send these nuclear bombs on their own.

Our battle went on for six months and then suddenly, almost without warning, the two lawyers spoke to each other on the phone (for the jillionth time) and then called their respective clients to say, "It's all over. We have a settlement." Suddenly all becomes quiet. All is still. What do battlefields sound like on the day *after* the war stops? There *is* no sound. You get the picture in your mind of troops silently dragging themselves back through the deep, noiseless snow, headed home, to family and a warm meal. It's as though the fight never took place, as if the hurtful words, uttered with such anger, were never spoken at all. A few days after the dust had settled, Diane and I spoke to each other on the phone to arrange a lunch between me and Bryn. Diane said, "Hi, honey." I asked, "How are you?" The exchange felt warm and friendly although our lives were now changed forever.

Eventually, you begin to lick your wounds. In my case, during the angry faxes that flew into each other's camp like deadly missiles, a boxed painting I had bought arrived at my apartment in New York where I was staying, far from the field of battle. In anger, I fought to get the painting out of its box. I gave it one terrific yank and suddenly heard something tear. It was my rotator cuff. It took six months to fully heal. The same amount of time it took to complete the settlement. The inner hurt and sadness, the deeper wounds, however, will take much, much longer to heal.

TAKE IT FROM THE TOP

AS I WRITE THIS, a year has passed since Diane and I separated and eventually divorced. My torn rotator cuff has healed, but the end of an eight-year marriage still gives you aches and pains, whether it's rainy weather or not. If there was true love in the marriage, and there would have to be for two people to stick it out so long—at least a trace of it will linger, continually finding a way, somehow or somewhere, to remind you. For both of us, I hope there eventually will be friendship. I have achieved that with Marsha, and recently we worked together again, when she went to London, reunited with Richard Dreyfuss (since *The Goodbye Girl*) in a play I wrote thirty years ago, *The Prisoner of Second Avenue*. It was great fun watching Marsha saying my words on a stage, and saying them brilliantly. Time does not necessarily heal everything, but it does give you a chance to forget the anger and make you remember why you loved in the first place.

For Diane, I hope for a life that will make her happy. She always did find a way for herself. For Bryn, I hope she still has faith that a good relationship and/or marriage is always possible for her, if that's what she wants. Although it's not possible for me to see Bryn as much as we did when we lived under the same roof, as her father and someone who cherishes her, I hope we will always be close. For myself, I've already found the stirrings of a new way of living. At the age of seventy-one and in relatively good health, I'm still vigorous and excited about life. I'm not all that keen about plunging into old age, but I feel if I keep on working and being with exciting people, I may never notice that it came knocking on my door.

And I am writing again. I recently finished a new play called *The Dinner Party*. What is the subject? Divorce. No surprise there. It's not anything about Diane and myself, or even about Marsha and me. What I've tried to do was to follow three couples who were divorced two or three years ago, and I attempted to see what would happen if they were all to meet unexpectedly in very unusual circumstances. There's also another play I've started, one that takes place in South America. I can't explain it yet since it's making up its mind in its own good time to reveal itself to me. I said in my previous book, *Rewrites*, that I didn't know how to *stop* writing. I think now I actually *do* know how to stop, but the thing is, I don't choose to. It's an old friend, and it continues to travel with me wherever I go.

I still love the mechanics of it. I still feel an intense desire to put pen to paper, to put words to use, to put ideas into stories and to wed new stories into even newer forms. At this point I have no need or concern as to where my plays appear. Broadway would be fine, but so would a small regional theater in Louisville or San Diego. To paraphrase someone else's line, if you write them, they will come. That is, if you write them well. There will always be an audience somewhere who yearn for the excitement of discovering a new play or a new play playwright. That I might even be that new playwright.

For me, I hope there will be additional satisfactions besides my work. I hope to finally find more time for my family, for my friends, old and new, to enjoy a world of places I planned on seeing but put off because I had a play opening in a place not nearly so attractive. I need to become aware of ideas to which I've paid no heed before; to see for the first time that which I have so often turned my back; to pay attention to what someone asks of me instead of using "I'm working" as an excuse to explain that I don't have the time. I hope for all this and more. I feel now that while I have fewer years to live, I have more time in which to live them. I don't necessarily think of marriage again, but as for love and companionship, the door remains open. I've learned that you can't have everything but I've also learned that the simple truth is, you don't *need* everything.

In closing, I would just repeat a philosophy that the woman analyst in *Jake's Women* leaves with Jake as she slowly fades out of his imagination.

"Remember, Jake," she says. "You always have options . . . options . . . . . . options. . . . . options."

Afterword

I will always treasure what Neil wrote on the dedication page of *The Play Goes On*: "To Elaine Joyce—who turned my life around." But please don't get the idea I was on some kind of rescue mission. Far from it. What happened between us was a glorious, exciting, head-over-heels love affair.

Our paths almost crossed in 1971. I was at the Kennedy Center in pre-Broadway tryouts, playing the title role in *Sugar*, a new musical based on the Billy Wilder film *Some Like It Hot*. Our producer, David Merrick, decided we had book problems. He called Neil, who by that time was known as a reliable show doctor. "Doc," which was a family nickname from his youth, took on a different meaning with his colleagues in the theatre. For his friends, Neil was willing to take a look and share his thoughts. But he would never touch a script without the consent of the book writer, in this case Peter Stone. Peter greeted Neil warmly and said if Neil changed one word he would bring him up on charges at the Dramatists Guild. Neil took the next train back to New York.

About a year later, when I was on Broadway in *Sugar*, my then-husband, Bobby Van, was two blocks north at the Forty-Sixth Street Theatre (now the Richard Rodgers), starring in a hit a revival of *No, No, Nanette* with Ruby Keeler. One night after our shows, we went to an opening night party where we ran into Neil. Bobby had known him for years. I was introduced, and for the rest of the evening the three of us were inseparable. I learned that Bobby and Neil had grown up in the same neighborhood in the Bronx. During the conversation, Neil talked to us about the recent passing of his wife, Joan, a terrible loss for him and their young daughters, Ellen and Nancy.

After the party, we shared a taxi home, dropping Neil at his house on 62nd Street. Still in the cab, Bobby said, "Don't take this the wrong way, but if anything ever happens to me—that's the guy for you."

In the late seventies and early eighties, Bobby and I were both doing film and television work. During hiatuses, I loved getting back to the theatre, touring in summer stock productions on the straw-hat circuit. My true awakening to the brilliance of Neil Simon, the playwright, came through performing in *Barefoot in the Park*, *Chapter Two*, and *Sweet Charity*. His writing is so skillful, his characterization so deep, his understanding of human foibles so poignant, that an actor has everything he needs to take the part and run with it.

My life was going well, professionally and personally. Bobby and I were blessed with a baby girl we named Taylor. Then, all of a sudden, our world was shattered. Doctors discovered that Bobby had a malignant brain tumor. Four months later, he was gone. I was devastated, confused, angry and broken. Eight months went by before I felt ready to go back to work.

I got a call to audition for a new Neil Simon play, *Jake's Women*. When I arrived at the audition, Neil immediately came over to give me a hug and say how sorry he was about Bobby. I crumbled. It was too soon. Neil understood.

We didn't meet again until 1998, when fate took charge. Neil and I spotted each other across the room at Benihana in Los Angeles. Yes, Benihana. We smiled, waved, and held each other's gaze for a few long moments. I knew we were making a connection, and so did he. Years later, Neil told me our brief encounter that night gave him hope he would again find happiness.

Neil was on his way to London for discussions about a West End production of *The Gingerbread Lady*. Upon arrival at the Savoy, he called me. We talked for almost two hours. My kids kept coming in and out asking who I was talking to. I said, "The guy I waved to at Benihana." My daughter said, "He's cute." My son Mick said, "I don't like him."

Neil called me again the next night, and the night after that. "I'm coming to LA. Do you want to go out on a date? How do I get to your house?"

I replied, "Make a left on Sunset and a right on Roxbury."

He knocked on my door. I opened it.

He said, "Hi." I said, "Hi," and that was it.

On our first date, we went to an intimate Hollywood dinner party for 120 people at the home of industry mogul Marvin Davis, and his wife, Barbara. The house was filled with mutual friends, but Neil and I only had eyes for each other. Our hostess was famous for strict seating assignments at her very long table, but Neil persuaded her to allow us to sit together. Throughout dinner we behaved like smitten teenagers, lost in our own world. Sitting next to Neil was Sidney Poitier, who said, "I've known you for a long time, Neil, and this is definitely more than a first date." We knew, we knew.

Six weeks later, Neil proposed. We were married in September, 1999. I entered his world and he entered mine. We naturally fell into loving, laughing, and sharing our days. If I knew you better, right now I would share some of the personal notes Neil would leave around the house—oh, boy! We were happy, even when he realized I'm as stubborn as he is. We revealed secrets and dreams. Soon, our two worlds became one. We spent lovely afternoons snuggling on a bench in Central Park as Neil made observations only he can make. He invented relationships and backstories for people, canines, even pigeons passing by. No detail escapes him. Everything Neil writes springs from a lifetime of these unique observations. From thousands of bits and pieces, he draws well defined characters, invents a world where they live, then shapes the story he wants them to tell.

This is the point where I give up trying to explain Neil's genius. Even he doesn't know where it comes from. He disappears into a private, solitary space, alone with his imagination. I remember him telling me, "My work and I have a thing together. No matter how upset I get, I go to work. It asks me 'Where were you?' and I start writing."

A regular part of living with Neil is listening to an ongoing report of his recurring aches and pains. There are news bulletins announcing the onset of a new ailment. The bad back. Tennis elbow. One day he turned to me and whispered, "I've got arthritis in my big toe." These episodes were passing. But that changed when he began facing serious health problems in 2003.

Neil's kidneys were failing. Life became a series of round trips to the dialysis clinic, four times a week for five hours. It was awful. He felt sick all the time. The only possible solution was a kidney transplant, rarely performed on someone Neil's age. In our darker moments, we began to lose hope. But doctors at New York's Rogosin Institute assessed the situation and concluded Neil was a good candidate for a kidney transplant.

One of the people closest to Neil is his publicist, Bill Evans. What began as a professional relationship in 1976 grew into a true friendship. Neil calls him "my consigliere." There are no words to express how we felt when Bill offered to become Neil's kidney donor.

Two weeks later, we arrived early one morning at the hospital. I sat close to Bill's partner (now husband) Chuck Fischer, as we watched Bill roll out of the room on his gurney, followed by Neil on his. The short version of this triumphant story is, it worked. Neil's health was restored. Before the transplant, Bill privately asked the doctors what a good result would mean for Neil. "You could add ten years to his life." We have recently passed the twelve-year mark.

Since the publication of *The Play Goes On* in 1999, Neil returned to Broadway with *45 Seconds from Broadway*, a love letter to the now-closed Café Edison ("the Polish Tea Room"), a legendary gathering place for everyone who worked in the theatre. Neil's play *Rose and Walsh* was successful in Los Angeles, but not in New York. He wrote screenplays for Showtime's movie version of *Laughter on the 23rd Floor* and TNT's new take on *The Goodbye Girl*. He updated his scripts for the hit Broadway revivals of *Sweet Charity* and *Promises, Promises*. Nathan Lane and Matthew Broderick, as Oscar and Felix in *The Odd Couple*, sold out the entire Broadway engagement.

Today, Neil and I are full-time New Yorkers. His lifelong obsession with the Yankees is stronger than ever. We love walking around the city, dining at favorite restaurants, seeing Broadway shows and ballet at Lincoln Center. People on the street recognize Neil and say hello. In the theatre district, everyone knows him. Theatregoers stop to say wonderful things about how much they love his work. However, on one occasion, a woman walked right up to him and barked, "Say something funny!" We moved on.

He is, maybe, the quintessential New Yorker—urbane, witty, a poor son of the Bronx who conquered Broadway, a man with more sensitivity than perhaps anybody else to what constituted the character of New York and New Yorkers.

—The New York Times

I have no sweeping, profound insights to offer regarding the life and work of my husband. I'll leave that to others. But here's what I believe. If you're looking for the heart and soul of Neil Simon, you'll find everything you need to know in *Brighton Beach Memoirs*.

—*Elaine Joyce Simon, New York City, 2016*

Index

About the Author

Neil Simon has written more than 40 Broadway plays, including Barefoot in the Park, The Odd Couple, and Lost in Yonkers, along with movies such as The Goodbye Girl, The Heartbreak Kid, and The Out-of-Towners. He has won three Tony Awards, a Pulitzer Prize for Drama, and the Mark Twain Prize for American Humor. He lives in New York with his wife, the actress Elaine Joyce.

More Than you know
I only have eyes for you
Too beautiful for words
Ill take manhattan
If I Didn't care
Beas Crosby Rado Theme Song
That Rainy Day is Here
Harbor LIGHTS
I fall in love too easily
Kiss of fire
I concentrate on you
KCTS9. org
WISHING WILL MAKE IT SO